Consumer Power

Also by Margaret Ambry

1990-1991 Almanac of Consumer Markets: A Guide to Today's More Complex and Harder-to-Find Customers

Coming soon from New Strategist

RealTrends: Negotiating the 1990s
Consumer Power: How Americans Spend Their Money, 2nd edition

Consulting services

Market Power Reports, New Strategist's customized analyses of the consumer trends that drive demand for products and services.

For details on how you can save on updates of *Consumer Power* and other books about Americans' spending habits and demographics, see the back of this book for a handy order form. You will also receive information about how a customized *Market Power Report* can help you target your markets more efficiently.

Consumer Power

How Americans Spend Their Money

by Margaret K. Ambry

New Strategist Publications

Ithaca, New York

New Strategist Publications
P.O. Box 242, Ithaca, NY 14851
607 / 273-0913

Ambry, Margaret, 1947–
Consumer Power.

ISBN 0-9628092-0-9

Printed in the United States of America.

#223369237

Designed by Rebecca Wilson

For my parents, who are lavish consumers of experiences.

Acknowledgements

Three people helped to produce this book and I would like to thank them. Penelope Wickham, the publisher of New Stategist, assisted with all stages of its production. Cheryl Russell, former editor-in-chief of *American Demographics* and the vice president for special projects at New Strategist, edited the text and gave advice along the way. Rebecca Wilson designed the book and provided very useful software education.

A thank-you is also extended to those who endured the war stories, especially Kells, Grady, Jack, Barbara, Ed, Marge, Aldor, and Marjorie.

Table of Contents

4 Housing: Household Operations and Utilities

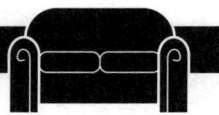

5 Apparel and Apparel Services

6 Transportation

7 Health Care

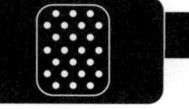

8 Entertainment

9 Personal Care, Reading, Education, Tobacco Products

10 Financial Products and Services, Cash Contributions, Gifts, Other Items

11 Summary Tables for All Products and Services

APPENDIX

1

Putting Consumer Power to Work

Consumers with dollars in hand are the real power behind every market. How consumers spend those dollars is a key to understanding the markets you serve. Spending patterns tell you who buys more or less of a product or service, how much they spend, the size of each market, and which markets are growing or shrinking. *Consumer Power* reveals these patterns, directing you to the important markets of the 1990s.

Consumer Power is based on data from the Consumer Expenditure Survey, a nation-wide, on-going study of household spending. The Survey collects more than 35,000 spending records from some 25,000 U.S. households.* The Survey covers only household spending and does not include expenditures made by government, industry, or institutions. It is conducted annually by the Bureau of the Census and analyzed and published by the Bureau of Labor Statistics. There is about a two-year lag-time between data collection and publication.

The Survey is an exhaustive compilation of household expenditures, including everything from big-ticket items such as homes and cars to small purchases like laundry detergent and hair accessories. Users of the Consumer Expenditure Survey include government agencies, private research groups, data companies, and other business people like you.

Consumer Power is organized by product and service categories—food, housing, transportation, etc.—and includes all typical household expenditures. Chapters two through ten are each devoted to a household spending category.

Because age, income, and household type are the best predictors of spending,

---

**The Consumer Expenditure Survey uses consumer units instead of households as its sampling unit. A consumer unit is defined by the Bureau of Labor Statistics as "a single person or group of persons in a sample household related by blood, marriage, adoption or other legal arrangement, or who share responsibility for at least two out of the three major types of expenses—food, housing, and other expenses." For more information about the Consumer Expenditure Survey and about consumer units see Appendix A.*

expenditures for each category are analyzed by those three variables. The age tables give you the big picture, such as how much spending is concentrated in middle-aged markets. But they also tell you the details—such as how much householders aged 75 or older spend on cheese. Spending on transportation rises rapidly with income, while spending on health care does not. The income tables tell you which product and service markets are flat, which are upscale, and which income groups are your best customers. The spending power of married couples is clearly revealed in the tables detailing spending by household type.

Because the Consumer Expenditure Survey is ongoing, it is a valuable tool for looking at both current spending patterns and spending trends. You can see at a glance which product and service categories are gaining or losing budget shares. Between 1984 and 1988, for example, the share of food and alcohol expenditures devoted to restaurant, carry-out, and other food prepared away from home increased from 37 to 40 percent. Households devoted less to food prepared at home and to alcohol.

Since the spending data are linked with the demographic characteristics of consumers, it is possible to forecast the effect of changing demographics on expenditures. *Consumer Power* projects expenditures by age of householder in 1995 and 2000. These projections estimate how spending will be affected by a shifting age structure. Middle-aged households, for example, will boost the food-away-from-home market from $153 billion in 1988 to $171 billion in 2000 (in 1988 dollars).

Chapter 11 consists of expenditure data for all household products and services, summarizing spending by age, income, and household type. It also contains summary tables reporting expenditures by household size, number of earners, race, homeownership status, and region of residence. A table for each age group, segmented by income, also appears in this chapter.

Consumer Power focuses on national-level spending data to give you the overall picture of consumer spending. Consumer Expenditure Survey data have been adapted by data companies such as National Planning Data Corporation in Ithaca, New York, to examine smaller geographic areas. National Planning Data Corporation's geography-specific products, for example, identify market sizes and consumer spending patterns in areas ranging from states to census tracts to customized sales regions.

How to use the tables in this book

Spending data can show you how the average American household or specific households in a single age group, income group, or of a particular type allocate their spending dollars. Average annual expenditures are the starting point for all calculations in *Consumer Power*. Spending share indicates the importance of a product or service in overall household spending. Indexed expenditures tell you whether spending by households in a given segment is above or below the average for all households (or for all households in that segment), and by how much. Aggregates, the dollar value of a total market, can be used to determine the market share of any single group; i.e., to gauge its market potential. If you combine those aggregates with household projections you can see how market potential will change during the 1990s.

Each set of tables is prefaced by a brief analysis and has a set of explanatory notes. The glossary in Appendix C gives definitions of expenditure items and terms used in the Consumer Expenditure Survey.

Average annual expenditures for apparel and apparel services, by type of consumer unit.

	all cu's	married couples	single parents	single persons and other cu's
GIRLS' APPAREL	**$94.86**	**$124.93**	**$291.02**	**$22.26**
Coats and jackets	7.88	10.23	20.75	2.61
Dresses and suits	12.12	16.66	23.55	3.99
Shirts, blouses, and sweaters	27.34	33.37	121.44	4.33
Skirts, pants, shorts and short sets	22.49	30.33	58.04	6.02
Active sportswear	8.58	11.91	23.25	1.52
Underwear and sleepwear	5.69	7.68	13.94	1.64
Hosiery	4.40	6.03	14.82	-
Accessories	4.30	5.70	9.83	1.45
BOYS' APPAREL	**$77.02**	**$105.80**	**$163.84**	**$22.42**
Coats and jackets	8.12	11.60	10.25	2.78
Sweaters	3.86	5.31	9.97	0.88
Shirts	19.64	26.50	51.73	4.86
Underwear	1.59	2.34	3.33	-
Nightwear	2.68	3.55	2.63	1.44
Hosiery	3.74	5.39	8.75	0.60
Accessories	2.64	4.02	4.68	-
Suits, sportcoats, and vests	2.92	4.79	0.76	0.55
Pants, shorts, and shorts sets	26.34	28.59	60.22	8.53
Uniforms and active sportswear	5.22	7.74	8.38	1.21

Excerpt from an Average Spending table

Average Spending tables

These tables report the average annual expenditure per consumer unit on each item or category of items in 1988. In the Consumer Expenditure Survey average annual expenditures are based on the total number of consumer units in a segment; i.e., those with incomes of $30,000 to $40,000, not just those that purchase the item. Including both purchasers and non-purchasers in the calculation of the average dilutes the average, especially for infrequently purchased items. Married couples, for example, spent an average of $115 on motor boats in 1988. Since the number of married couples that actually purchased a motor boat is considerably smaller than the number of married couples, the average expenditure underestimates the amount spent by purchasers.

Average annual expenditures are good for comparing spending levels by consumer segment. They can also be used to determine market potential for any item in a sales area. By multiplying the average amount married couples spend on children's clothing by the number of married couples in your sales area, for example, you can start to estimate the potential market for children's clothing in that area.* Add in how much single parents and other types of households spend

*Area demographics are available from local planning departments or from your local library if it receives census volumes. If it does not receive census data, ask your librarian to help you locate the information. Private data vendors provide household demographics for standard areas such as states, counties, ZIP Codes, metropolitan areas, census tracts, etc., or for custom geographic areas. For more information about sources of demographic data, call New Strategist in Ithaca, New York, at 607-273-0913.

Percent of total average annual expenditures spent on food and alcoholic beverages, by age of reference person.

	all cu's	under 25	25 to 34	35 to 44	45 to 54	55 to 64	65 to 74	75+
ALCOHOLIC BEVERAGES	1.04%	1.91%	1.38%	0.85%	0.92%	0.93%	0.80%	0.67%
At home	**0.54**	**0.94**	**0.67**	**0.44**	**0.46**	**0.54**	**0.43**	**0.44**
Beer and ale	0.32	0.74	0.47	0.26	0.24	0.28	0.19	0.18
Whiskey	0.04	0.03	0.03	0.03	0.05	0.06	0.08	0.03
Wine	0.11	0.11	0.13	0.12	0.11	0.12	0.10	0.10
Other alcoholic beverages	0.06	0.06	0.04	0.04	0.06	0.08	0.06	0.13
Away from home	**0.50**	**1.96**	**0.71**	**0.41**	**0.46**	**0.39**	**0.38**	**0.23**
Beer and ale	0.14	0.33	0.21	0.11	0.12	0.09	0.08	0.05
Wine	0.07	0.14	0.09	0.06	0.07	0.05	0.07	0.04
Other alcoholic beverages	0.22	0.36	0.31	0.17	0.20	0.17	0.17	0.12
Alcoholic beverages purchased on trips	0.07	0.13	0.08	0.07	0.07	0.07	0.06	0.03

Excerpt from a Share of Spending table

on children's clothing, and you've calculated the total potential market. If you publish a newspaper, you now have figures on market potential you can use to show the spending power of parents in your area.

Share of Spending tables

The share of average household expenditures (also called budget share) devoted to each category and item is presented in these tables. Share of spending figures give you a good feel for the relative importance of each product and service to the average household. Spending shares tell a beer distributor that the average householder under age 25 allocates almost 1 percent of his annual budget to beer for home consumption. This is three times the spending share that the average householder aged 45 to 54 devotes to beer consumed at home.

Spending shares also track changes in spending priorities over time. Chapters two through ten each begin with an analysis of spending trends based on spending shares. You can see, for example, that the average household allocated a larger share of its expenditures to housing, a smaller share to alcohol, and the same share to transportation in 1988 as it did in 1984.

Indexed average annual expenditures for apparel and apparel services, by type of consumer unit.

	all cu's	married couples	single parents	single persons and other cu's
GIRLS' APPAREL	100	132	307	23
Coats and jackets	100	130	263	33
Dresses and suits	100	137	194	33
Shirts, blouses, and sweaters	100	122	444	16
Skirts, pants, shorts and short sets	100	135	258	27
Active sportswear	100	139	271	18
Underwear and sleepwear	100	135	245	29
Hosiery	100	137	337	-
Accessories	100	133	229	34

Excerpt from an Indexed Expenditures table

Aggregate expenditures, in millions, for food and alcoholic beverages in 1988 and 2000, by age of reference person (in 1988 dollars).								
	all households	under 25	25 to 34	35 to 44	45 to 54	55 to 64	65 to 74	75+
FOOD AWAY FROM HOME (1988)	$152,766	$9,627	$35,576	$40,554	$30,052	$20,034	$12,234	$4,689
FOOD AWAY FROM HOME (2000)	$175,348	$5,926	$29,134	$51,609	$47,733	$22,201	$12,447	$6,297

Excerpt from an Aggregate Expenditures table

Indexed Expenditures tables

In these tables the expenditures of each household segment are compared with the national average (or the average for all households in that segment; i.e., householders aged 35 to 44), which is represented by 100. Indexed expenditures immediately identify the best customers for a product or service. Households with an above-average index for outdoor furniture, for example, are the strongest markets for this product. Those with an index below average are either weaker or underserved markets.

A glance at the indexed expenditure tables by age group show you that the middle-aged are the big spenders for most products and services. Indexed income tables show you how rapidly spending increases with income. The indexed expenditures by household type document the importance of the married-couple market. The indexes also highlight surprising markets. Single-parent families tend to spend less than the average household on most products and services. But they outspend other households, including married couples, on children's clothing.

Aggregate Expenditures tables

Here the expenditures of all households in each age, income, or household-type segment are summed. The aggregates show you how much households with incomes of $40,000 to $50,000 spent on new cars in 1988, or how much all households spent on pets. When comparing these figures to total spending estimates from the Bureau of Economic Analysis or other agencies, you must remember that the Consumer Expenditure Survey includes only household spending, not spending by businesses or institutions.

Aggregates are useful for looking at market shares. They show, for example, that householders aged 35 to 54 accounted for 46 percent of the market for food prepared away from home in 1988. Aggregate expenditures in 2000 can be projected for 35-to-54-year-olds by multiplying expenditures in 1988 by projections of householders by age in 2000. According to those projections, householders aged 35 to 54 will account for 57 percent of the market for food prepared away from home in 2000. The share of the market accounted for by householders under age 35 will drop from 30 percent in 1988 to 20 percent in 2000.

CHAPTER

2

Food and Alcoholic Beverages

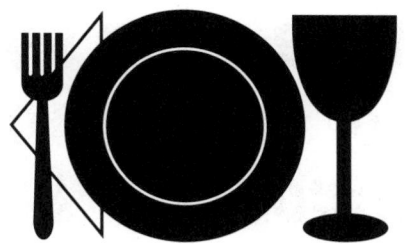

An average American household spent nearly 16 percent of its expenditures on food and alcohol in 1988. Between 1984 and 1988, the share of household spending devoted to food increased, while the share going to alcohol decreased.

In 1988, households devoted 40 percent of their food and alcohol expenditures to food prepared away from home, an increase of 3 percentage points since 1984. Eating out, buying school lunches, and picking up carry-out dinners are easy ways to simplify food preparation in busy households. The budget share devoted to food consumed at home dropped, with meats, poultry, fish, and eggs leading the decline. During these five years, the share of the food and alcohol budget devoted to alcohol dropped a full percentage point, due to both an aging population and growing health concerns.

A slightly larger share of the food and alcohol dollar went to cereals and cereal products; fresh fruits and vegetables; dairy products other than milk and cream such as cheese and ice cream; and miscellaneous foods such as canned and prepared food and soups, snacks, and condiments, in 1988 than in 1984.

Five-year spending trends for food and alcoholic beverages

	1984	1985	1986	1987	1988	change 1984 to 1988
Share of household expenditures devoted to food and alcoholic beverages, share of food and alcoholic beverages expenditures devoted to food items and alcoholic beverages, and change in share, 1984 to 1988.						
Food, share of household expenditures	15.0%	14.8%	14.5%	15.0%	14.5%	-0.5%
Alcoholic beverages, share of household expenditures	1.3%	1.3%	1.1%	1.2%	1.0%	-0.3%
Food and alcoholic beverages, expenditures	100.0%	100.0%	100.0%	100.0%	100.0%	0.0%
FOOD AT HOME	55.3%	53.8%	53.6%	53.1%	53.2%	-2.1%
Cereals and bakery products	7.3	7.5	7.4	7.6	7.8	0.5
Cereals and cereal products	2.4	2.4	2.5	2.6	2.7	0.3
Bakery products	5.0	5.1	4.9	4.9	5.1	0.1
Meats, poultry, fish, and eggs	16.4	15.3	15.1	14.5	13.7	-2.7
Beef	5.6	5.1	5.1	4.8	4.5	-1.1
Pork	3.3	3.2	3.1	2.9	2.7	-0.6
Other meats	2.3	2.3	2.1	2.1	2.0	-0.3
Poultry	2.4	2.2	2.3	2.2	2.1	-0.3
Fish and seafood	1.9	1.7	1.7	1.7	1.6	-0.3
Eggs	1.0	0.8	0.8	0.7	0.7	-0.3
Dairy products	7.1	7.0	6.7	6.9	6.8	-0.3
Fresh milk and cream	3.6	3.5	3.3	3.3	3.3	-0.3
Other dairy products	3.5	3.6	3.4	3.6	3.5	0.0
Fruits and vegetables	8.8	8.5	8.6	9.0	9.3	0.5
Fresh fruits	2.6	2.5	2.7	2.8	3.0	0.4
Fresh vegetables	2.6	2.5	2.5	2.8	2.7	0.1
Processed fruits	2.0	2.1	1.9	2.0	2.1	0.1
Processed vegetables	1.6	1.4	1.5	1.4	1.4	-0.2
Other food at home	14.8	14.7	14.9	14.4	15.6	0.8
Sugar and other sweets	2.1	2.0	2.0	1.9	1.9	-0.2
Fats and oils	1.6	1.5	1.4	1.3	1.4	-0.2
Miscellaneous foods	6.1	6.2	6.3	6.3	6.6	0.5
Nonalcoholic beverages	5.0	4.9	5.2	4.9	5.0	0.0
Food prepared by cu on out-of-town trips	0.8	0.8	0.8	0.8	0.7	-0.1
FOOD AWAY FROM HOME	37.0%	38.1%	39.1%	39.6%	40.1%	3.1%
ALCOHOLIC BEVERAGES	7.7%	8.1%	7.3%	7.3%	6.7%	-1.0%

Note: Numbers may not add to total due to rounding.

PART I
Spending by age for food and alcoholic beverages

The 1990s look good for most businesses, according to the Consumer Expenditure Survey, but few industries will benefit more than food. The average American household spent $4,017 on food and alcoholic beverages in 1988, or 16 percent of the total household budget. But spending on food varies dramatically by age, and the biggest spenders are aged 35 to 54.

In the grocery store, middle-aged householders spend 22 percent more than the average household. They also spend more than average in restaurants, school cafeterias, and other eating places. Out-of-home food spending peaks among 45-to-54-year-olds, at 37 percent above average.

At the other extreme are the youngest and oldest householders. Those under age 25 spend 34 percent less than the average household on food, while householders aged 65 or older also spend well below the household average on food. On selected items, however, the youngest and oldest householders have expenses that are well above average. Because so many householders under age 25 are college students or work in restaurants, they spend 25 percent more than average on board, and they're much more likely than the average household to receive meals-as-pay. Younger householders also spend more than average on alcohol.

Among householders aged 65 to 74, spending on food is 20 percent below average. But these households spend more than average on flour, fruit, vegetables, poultry, seafood, and coffee. Although they spend 40 percent less than average on alcohol in general, these retirement-aged households spend 40 percent more than average on whiskey.

Rapid growth in the number of middle-aged households during the 1990s should boost the annual food expenditures of households headed by 45-to-54-year-olds by 58 percent, to $111 billion Householders aged 35 to 44 will still be the biggest market for food, however. They will spend $125 billion in 2000, or 27 percent more than in 1988.

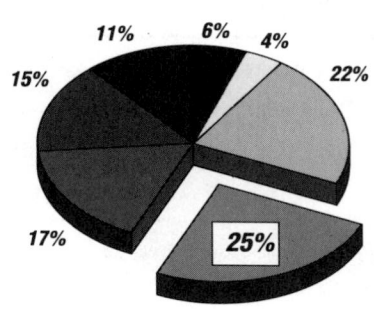

Householders aged 35 to 44 are the largest share of the market for food at home...

11% 6% 4%
15% 22%
17% 25%

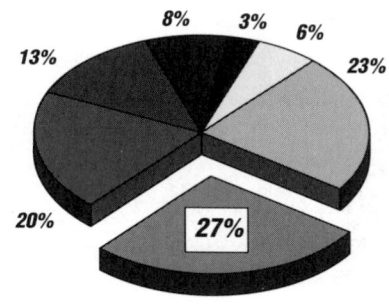

...and for food away from home...

8% 3% 6%
13% 23%
20% 27%

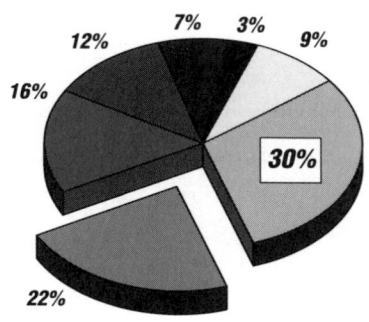

...although 25-to-34-year-olds are the largest market for alcohol.

7% 3% 9%
12%
16% 30%
22%

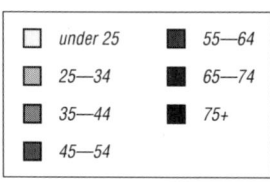

☐ under 25	■ 55—64
■ 25—34	■ 65—74
■ 35—44	■ 75+
■ 45—54	

Average expenditures

	all cu's	under 25	25 to 34	35 to 44	45 to 54	55 to 64	65 to 74	75+
Number of consumer units (in thousands)	94,862	7,216	21,985	19,911	13,601	12,546	11,319	8,284
Average number of persons per cu	2.6	1.8	2.8	3.3	2.9	2.2	2	1.5
Average total before-tax income	$28,540.00	$14,827.00	$28,318.00	$36,428.00	$39,934.00	$29,979.00	$20,704.00	$13,707.00
TOTAL AVERAGE ANNUAL EXPENDITURES	$25,891.85	$16,373.17	$25,770.27	$33,077.72	$33,204.87	$25,765.35	$20,119.90	$13,339.49
FOOD, AVERAGE ANNUAL EXPENDITURES	$3,748.01	$2,455.07	$3,664.02	$4,636.19	$4,814.60	$3,951.78	$3,013.40	$1,938.54
ALCOHOLIC BEV., AVER. ANNUAL EXPEN.	$268.69	$311.92	$354.56	$281.13	$306.57	$239.04	$161.90	$89.24
FOOD AT HOME	$2,135.87	$1,121.02	$2,045.83	$2,599.42	$2,605.04	$2,354.91	$1,932.54	$1,372.54
Cereals and bakery products	312.14	165.78	291.28	387.40	387.47	333.59	277.31	215.05
Cereals and cereal products	109.34	65.52	108.93	137.01	132.68	109.58	90.99	71.63
Flour	4.65	2.03	3.95	4.79	5.49	5.63	6.04	3.78
Prepared flour mixes	9.46	6.02	10.46	10.07	11.22	10.25	7.91	6.50
Ready-to-eat and cooked cereal	72.95	42.45	70.75	93.35	89.63	72.53	60.04	49.66
Rice	7.77	3.43	9.56	10.25	9.43	6.97	4.29	4.58
Pasta, cornmeal, and other cereal products	14.50	11.58	14.19	18.54	16.91	14.20	12.72	7.11
Bakery products	202.80	100.26	182.36	250.39	254.79	224.02	186.32	143.42
Bread	64.48	31.75	56.91	74.92	83.65	70.97	63.34	50.05
Crackers and cookies	51.25	24.80	48.56	65.35	60.72	55.56	45.45	35.40
Frozen and refrigerated bakery products	13.67	6.97	12.23	17.25	16.51	15.99	12.45	8.54
Meats, poultry, fish, and eggs	551.07	249.13	505.84	660.83	675.49	647.80	533.46	357.26
Beef	182.18	90.83	166.21	228.17	217.65	221.42	152.20	122.14
Pork	109.90	40.22	97.53	123.39	138.15	124.10	129.67	79.17
Other meats	82.22	39.36	77.26	105.44	95.10	95.36	72.31	52.15
Poultry	84.17	35.73	77.35	99.31	108.32	95.81	86.40	49.31
Fish and seafood	64.98	26.33	62.07	74.54	79.98	80.27	66.39	34.49
Eggs	27.63	16.66	25.43	29.99	36.30	30.84	26.49	19.99
Dairy products	274.28	151.50	275.68	332.65	329.25	295.29	235.62	174.79
Fresh milk and cream	133.78	82.37	135.62	159.83	162.08	135.27	112.57	94.82
Other dairy products	140.50	69.13	140.06	172.82	167.18	160.03	123.05	79.97
Butter	8.63	3.97	9.01	10.11	8.69	10.47	8.64	5.48
Cheese	77.44	40.62	80.65	91.66	93.75	88.72	63.31	43.66
Ice cream and related products	40.82	18.75	37.16	53.13	50.70	45.77	38.18	21.03
Fruits and vegetables	373.08	175.84	327.72	433.55	450.15	433.34	389.77	290.10
Fresh fruits	120.63	52.47	97.93	140.53	145.39	144.06	135.13	100.44
Fresh vegetables	110.31	45.93	93.88	129.01	133.24	132.64	119.00	85.14
Processed fruits	84.87	45.81	80.67	96.99	101.13	92.13	83.55	67.44
Processed vegetables	57.27	31.63	55.24	67.02	70.39	64.51	52.10	37.08
Other food at home	625.30	378.76	645.30	784.99	762.68	644.88	496.38	335.33
Sugar and other sweets	78.16	39.83	74.81	96.61	93.86	85.41	73.84	47.17
Candy and chewing gum	44.20	22.22	42.11	56.91	54.88	48.02	38.20	24.39
Sugar	16.63	9.72	16.35	19.55	19.83	17.85	15.53	11.14

Average annual expenditures for food and alcoholic beverages, by age of reference person.

(continued from previous page)	all cu's	under 25	25 to 34	35 to 44	45 to 54	55 to 64	65 to 74	75+
Fats and oils	54.52	23.50	49.89	63.01	67.61	62.68	56.92	37.67
Miscellaneous foods	263.88	184.26	302.03	331.54	301.84	250.76	190.44	131.76
Frozen prepared foods	44.18	33.46	43.53	57.29	51.22	40.62	34.50	32.15
Canned and packaged soups	21.11	13.71	20.72	25.24	23.65	22.25	18.68	16.73
Potato chips, nuts, and other snacks	58.43	34.61	62.18	78.00	69.34	61.03	41.86	24.24
Condiments and seasonings	59.67	39.40	62.36	74.23	74.45	61.71	46.68	25.80
Other canned/packaged prepared foods	80.48	63.08	113.25	96.78	83.17	65.16	48.72	32.83
Baby food	15.17	21.62	41.75	10.67	5.87	3.79	1.42	0.65
Nonalcoholic beverages	198.54	117.10	192.67	250.92	261.45	205.98	154.26	108.44
Cola	89.62	64.86	92.35	123.51	117.00	85.18	53.67	34.27
Other carbonated drinks	31.94	20.97	31.86	41.41	45.17	29.64	20.70	16.62
Coffee	40.17	10.40	26.51	42.59	52.05	58.85	52.75	32.17
Food prepared by cu on out-of-town trips	30.21	14.08	25.90	42.91	37.92	40.05	20.91	10.30
FOOD AWAY FROM HOME	**$1,612.13**	**$1,334.05**	**$1,618.19**	**$2,036.76**	**$2,209.56**	**$1,596.86**	**$1,080.86**	**$566.01**
Meals at restaurants, carry-outs, and other	**1,254.03**	**1,075.07**	**1,350.10**	**1,560.26**	**1,663.39**	**1,177.75**	**801.43**	**460.95**
Lunch	493.21	418.19	530.24	652.63	665.67	418.32	290.59	182.55
Dinner	549.19	440.86	577.00	634.70	725.76	578.07	401.64	219.52
Snacks and nonalcoholic beverages	131.70	147.74	162.66	186.33	158.68	98.42	46.70	23.91
Breakfast and brunch	79.93	68.28	80.19	86.60	113.28	82.94	62.50	34.96
Board(including at school)	**46.42**	**57.80**	**7.27**	**51.10**	**121.93**	**80.66**	**11.10**	**1.61**
Catered affairs	**41.03**	**14.69**	**19.74**	**29.41**	**92.38**	**61.31**	**57.90**	**10.37**
Food on out-of-town trips	**200.51**	**110.58**	**160.65**	**255.89**	**259.54**	**246.12**	**196.55**	**90.93**
School lunches	**42.97**	**2.96**	**36.56**	**113.59**	**57.14**	**11.49**	**5.54**	**0.65**
Meals as pay	**27.17**	**72.95**	**43.88**	**26.52**	**15.18**	**19.53**	**8.34**	**1.50**
ALCOHOLIC BEVERAGES	**$268.69**	**$311.92**	**$354.56**	**$281.13**	**$306.57**	**$239.04**	**$161.90**	**$89.24**
At home	**138.83**	**153.99**	**172.64**	**146.90**	**152.80**	**139.50**	**86.27**	**58.38**
Beer and ale	83.24	121.23	120.48	84.45	80.31	73.10	38.60	23.41
Whiskey	11.61	5.36	8.18	11.20	17.16	16.07	16.34	4.15
Wine	29.62	18.33	32.66	38.54	35.34	29.83	20.22	13.75
Other alcoholic beverages	14.37	9.08	11.31	12.71	19.99	20.50	11.12	17.06
Away from home	**129.86**	**157.93**	**181.92**	**134.23**	**153.77**	**99.53**	**75.63**	**30.86**
Beer and ale	36.23	54.46	55.07	36.03	41.46	23.17	16.43	6.14
Wine	18.51	22.58	24.22	19.06	22.45	13.98	13.31	4.82
Other alcoholic beverages	55.85	59.60	80.80	55.29	66.49	43.91	33.70	16.13
Alcoholic beverages purchased on trips	19.26	21.28	21.83	23.85	23.38	18.47	12.20	3.76

Note: Expenditures listed for items in a given category may not add to the total for that category because the listing is incomplete. "Other dairy products," for example, includes "butter, cheese, ice cream and related products" and "miscellaneous"—"miscellaneous" is omitted here. Numbers may not add to total due to rounding.

Share of spending

	all cu's	under 25	25 to 34	35 to 44	45 to 54	55 to 64	65 to 74	75+
Number of consumer units (in thousands)	94,862	7,216	21,985	19,911	13,601	12,546	11,319	8,284
Average number of persons per cu	2.6	1.8	2.8	3.3	2.9	2.2	2	1.5
Average total before-tax income	$28,540	$14,827	$28,318	$36,428	$39,934	$29,979	$20,704	$13,707
TOTAL AVERAGE ANNUAL EXPENDITURES	100.00%	100.00%	100.00%	100.00%	100.00%	100.00%	100.00%	100.00%
FOOD, AVERAGE ANNUAL EXPENDITURES	14.48%	14.99%	14.22%	14.02%	14.50%	15.34%	14.98%	14.53%
ALCOHOLIC BEV., AVER. ANNUAL EXPEND.	1.04%	1.91%	1.38%	0.85%	0.92%	0.93%	0.80%	0.67%
FOOD AT HOME	8.25%	6.85%	7.94%	7.86%	7.85%	9.14%	9.61%	10.29%
Cereals and bakery products	1.21	1.01	1.13	1.17	1.17	1.29	1.38	1.61
Cereals and cereal products	0.42	0.40	0.42	0.41	0.40	0.43	0.45	0.54
Flour	0.02	0.01	0.02	0.01	0.02	0.02	0.03	0.03
Prepared flour mixes	0.04	0.04	0.04	0.03	0.03	0.04	0.04	0.05
Ready-to-eat and cooked cereal	0.28	0.26	0.27	0.28	0.27	0.28	0.30	0.37
Rice	0.03	0.02	0.04	0.03	0.03	0.03	0.02	0.03
Pasta, cornmeal, and other cereal products	0.06	0.07	0.06	0.06	0.05	0.06	0.06	0.05
Bakery products	0.78	0.61	0.71	0.76	0.77	0.87	0.93	1.08
Bread	0.25	0.19	0.22	0.23	0.25	0.28	0.31	0.38
Crackers and cookies	0.20	0.15	0.19	0.20	0.18	0.22	0.23	0.27
Frozen and refrigerated bakery products	0.05	0.04	0.05	0.05	0.05	0.06	0.06	0.06
Meats, poultry, fish, and eggs	2.13	1.52	1.96	2.00	2.03	2.51	2.65	2.68
Beef	0.70	0.55	0.64	0.69	0.66	0.86	0.76	0.92
Pork	0.42	0.25	0.38	0.37	0.42	0.48	0.64	0.59
Other meats	0.32	0.24	0.30	0.32	0.29	0.37	0.36	0.39
Poultry	0.33	0.22	0.30	0.30	0.33	0.37	0.43	0.37
Fish and seafood	0.25	0.16	0.24	0.23	0.24	0.31	0.33	0.26
Eggs	0.11	0.10	0.10	0.09	0.11	0.12	0.13	0.15
Dairy products	1.06	0.93	1.07	1.01	0.99	1.15	1.17	1.31
Fresh milk and cream	0.52	0.50	0.53	0.48	0.49	0.53	0.56	0.71
Other dairy products	0.54	0.42	0.54	0.52	0.50	0.62	0.61	0.60
Butter	0.03	0.02	0.03	0.03	0.03	0.04	0.04	0.04
Cheese	0.30	0.25	0.31	0.28	0.28	0.34	0.31	0.33
Ice cream and related products	0.16	0.11	0.14	0.16	0.15	0.18	0.19	0.16
Fruits and vegetables	1.44	1.07	1.27	1.31	1.36	1.68	1.94	2.17
Fresh fruits	0.47	0.32	0.38	0.42	0.44	0.56	0.67	0.75
Fresh vegetables	0.43	0.28	0.36	0.39	0.40	0.51	0.59	0.64
Processed fruits	0.33	0.28	0.31	0.29	0.30	0.36	0.42	0.51
Processed vegetables	0.22	0.19	0.21	0.20	0.21	0.25	0.26	0.28
Other food at home	2.42	2.31	2.50	2.37	2.30	2.50	2.47	2.51
Sugar and other sweets	0.30	0.24	0.29	0.29	0.28	0.33	0.37	0.35
Candy and chewing gum	0.17	0.14	0.16	0.17	0.17	0.19	0.19	0.18
Sugar	0.06	0.06	0.06	0.06	0.06	0.07	0.08	0.08

Percent of total average annual expenditures spent on food and alcoholic beverages, by age of reference person

(continued from previous page)	all cu's	under 25	25 to 34	35 to 44	45 to 54	55 to 64	65 to 74	75+
Fats and oils	0.21	0.14	0.19	0.19	0.20	0.24	0.28	0.28
Miscellaneous foods	1.02	1.13	1.17	1.00	0.91	0.97	0.95	0.99
Frozen prepared foods	0.17	0.20	0.17	0.17	0.15	0.16	0.17	0.24
Canned and packaged soups	0.08	0.08	0.08	0.08	0.07	0.09	0.09	0.13
Potato chips, nuts, and other snacks	0.23	0.21	0.24	0.24	0.21	0.24	0.21	0.18
Condiments and seasonings	0.23	0.24	0.24	0.22	0.22	0.24	0.23	0.19
Other canned/packaged prepared foods	0.31	0.39	0.44	0.29	0.25	0.25	0.24	0.25
Baby food	0.06	0.13	0.16	0.03	0.02	0.01	0.01	0.00
Nonalcoholic beverages	0.77	0.72	0.75	0.76	0.79	0.80	0.77	0.81
Cola	0.35	0.40	0.36	0.37	0.35	0.33	0.27	0.26
Other carbonated drinks	0.12	0.13	0.12	0.13	0.14	0.12	0.10	0.12
Coffee	0.16	0.06	0.10	0.13	0.16	0.23	0.26	0.24
Food prepared by cu on out-of-town trips	0.12	0.09	0.10	0.13	0.11	0.16	0.10	0.08
FOOD AWAY FROM HOME	**6.23%**	**8.15%**	**6.28%**	**6.16%**	**6.65%**	**6.20%**	**5.37%**	**4.24%**
Meals at restaurants, carry-outs, and other	**4.84**	**6.57**	**5.24**	**4.72**	**5.01**	**4.57**	**3.98**	**3.46**
Lunch	1.90	2.55	2.06	1.97	2.00	1.62	1.44	1.37
Dinner	2.12	2.69	2.24	1.92	2.19	2.24	2.00	1.65
Snacks and nonalcoholic beverages	0.51	0.90	0.63	0.56	0.48	0.38	0.23	0.18
Breakfast and brunch	0.31	0.42	0.31	0.26	0.34	0.32	0.31	0.26
Board(including at school)	**0.18**	**0.35**	**0.03**	**0.15**	**0.37**	**0.31**	**0.06**	**0.01**
Catered affairs	**0.16**	**0.09**	**0.08**	**0.09**	**0.28**	**0.24**	**0.29**	**0.08**
Food on out-of-town trips	**0.77**	**0.68**	**0.62**	**0.77**	**0.78**	**0.96**	**0.98**	**0.68**
School lunches	**0.17**	**0.02**	**0.14**	**0.34**	**0.17**	**0.04**	**0.03**	**0.00**
Meals as pay	**0.10**	**0.45**	**0.17**	**0.08**	**0.05**	**0.08**	**0.04**	**0.01**
ALCOHOLIC BEVERAGES	**1.04%**	**1.91%**	**1.38%**	**0.85%**	**0.92%**	**0.93%**	**0.80%**	**0.67%**
At home	**0.54**	**0.94**	**0.67**	**0.44**	**0.46**	**0.54**	**0.43**	**0.44**
Beer and ale	0.32	0.74	0.47	0.26	0.24	0.28	0.19	0.18
Whiskey	0.04	0.03	0.03	0.03	0.05	0.06	0.08	0.03
Wine	0.11	0.11	0.13	0.12	0.11	0.12	0.10	0.10
Other alcoholic beverages	0.06	0.06	0.04	0.04	0.06	0.08	0.06	0.13
Away from home	**0.50**	**0.96**	**0.71**	**0.41**	**0.46**	**0.39**	**0.38**	**0.23**
Beer and ale	0.14	0.33	0.21	0.11	0.12	0.09	0.08	0.05
Wine	0.07	0.14	0.09	0.06	0.07	0.05	0.07	0.04
Other alcoholic beverages	0.22	0.36	0.31	0.17	0.20	0.17	0.17	0.12
Alcoholic beverages purchased on trips	0.07	0.13	0.08	0.07	0.07	0.07	0.06	0.03

Note: Expenditures listed for items in a given category may not add to the total for that category because the listing is incomplete. "Other dairy products," for example, includes "butter, cheese, ice cream and related products" and "miscellaneous"—"miscellaneous" is omitted here. Numbers may not add to total due to rounding.

Indexed expenditures

	all cu's	under 25	25 to 34	35 to 44	45 to 54	55 to 64	65 to 74	75+
Number of consumer units (in thousands)	94,862	7,216	21,985	19,911	13,601	12,546	11,319	8,284
Average number of persons per cu	2.6	1.8	2.8	3.3	2.9	2.2	2	1.5
Average total before-tax income	$28,540	$14,827	$28,318	$36,428	$39,934	$29,979	$20,704	$13,707
TOTAL AVERAGE ANNUAL EXPENDITURES	100	63	100	128	128	100	178	52
FOOD, AVERAGE ANNUAL EXPENDITURES	100	66	98	124	128	105	80	52
ALCOHOLIC BEV., AVER. ANNUAL EXPEND.	100	116	132	105	114	89	60	33
FOOD AT HOME	100	52	96	122	122	110	90	64
Cereals and bakery products	100	53	93	124	124	107	89	69
Cereals and cereal products	100	60	100	125	121	100	83	66
Flour	100	44	85	103	118	121	130	81
Prepared flour mixes	100	64	111	106	119	108	84	69
Ready-to-eat and cooked cereal	100	58	97	128	123	99	82	68
Rice	100	44	123	132	121	90	55	59
Pasta, cornmeal, and other cereal products	100	80	98	128	117	98	88	49
Bakery products	100	49	90	123	126	110	92	71
Bread	100	49	88	116	130	110	98	78
Crackers and cookies	100	48	95	128	118	108	89	69
Frozen and refrigerated bakery products	100	51	89	126	121	117	91	62
Meats, poultry, fish, and eggs	100	45	92	120	123	118	97	65
Beef	100	50	91	125	119	122	84	67
Pork	100	37	89	112	126	113	118	72
Other meats	100	48	94	128	116	116	88	63
Poultry	100	42	92	118	129	114	103	59
Fish and seafood	100	41	96	115	123	124	102	53
Eggs	100	60	92	109	131	112	96	72
Dairy products	100	55	101	121	120	108	86	64
Fresh milk and cream	100	62	101	119	121	101	84	71
Other dairy products	100	49	100	123	119	114	88	57
Butter	100	46	104	117	101	121	100	63
Cheese	100	52	104	118	121	115	82	56
Ice cream and related products	100	46	91	130	124	112	94	52
Fruits and vegetables	100	47	88	116	121	116	104	78
Fresh fruits	100	43	81	116	121	119	112	83
Fresh vegetables	100	42	85	117	121	120	108	77
Processed fruits	100	54	95	114	119	109	98	79
Processed vegetables	100	55	96	117	123	113	91	65
Other food at home	100	61	103	126	122	103	79	54
Sugar and other sweets	100	51	96	124	120	109	94	6
Candy and chewing gum	100	50	95	129	124	109	86	55
Sugar	100	58	98	118	119	107	93	67

Indexed average annual expenditures for food and alcoholic beverages, by age of reference person.

(continued from previous page)

	all cu's	under 25	25 to 34	35 to 44	45 to 54	55 to 64	65 to 74	75+
Fats and oils	100	43	92	116	124	115	104	69
Miscellaneous foods	100	70	114	126	114	95	72	50
Frozen prepared foods	100	76	99	130	116	92	78	73
Canned and packaged soups	100	65	98	120	112	105	88	79
Potato chips, nuts, and other snacks	100	59	106	133	119	104	72	41
Condiments and seasonings	100	66	105	124	125	103	78	43
Other canned/packaged prepared foods	100	78	141	120	103	81	61	41
Baby food	100	143	275	70	39	25	9	4
Nonalcoholic beverages	100	59	97	126	132	104	78	55
Cola	100	72	103	138	131	95	60	38
Other carbonated drinks	100	66	100	130	141	93	65	52
Coffee	100	26	66	106	130	147	131	80
Food prepared by cu on out-of-town trips	100	47	86	142	126	133	69	34
FOOD AWAY FROM HOME	**100**	**83**	**100**	**126**	**137**	**99**	**67**	**35**
Meals at restaurants, carry-outs, and other	**100**	**86**	**108**	**124**	**133**	**94**	**64**	**37**
Lunch	100	85	108	132	135	85	59	37
Dinner	100	80	105	116	132	105	73	40
Snacks and nonalcoholic beverages	100	112	124	141	120	75	35	18
Breakfast and brunch	100	85	100	108	142	104	78	44
Board(including at school)	**100**	**125**	**16**	**110**	**263**	**174**	**24**	**3**
Catered affairs	**100**	**36**	**48**	**72**	**225**	**149**	**141**	**25**
Food on out-of-town trips	**100**	**55**	**80**	**128**	**129**	**123**	**98**	**45**
School lunches	**100**	**7**	**85**	**264**	**133**	**27**	**13**	**2**
Meals as pay	**100**	**268**	**162**	**98**	**56**	**72**	**31**	**6**
ALCOHOLIC BEVERAGES	**100**	**116**	**132**	**105**	**114**	**89**	**60**	**33**
At home	**100**	**111**	**124**	**106**	**110**	**100**	**62**	**42**
Beer and ale	100	146	145	101	96	88	46	28
Whiskey	100	46	70	96	148	138	141	36
Wine	100	62	110	130	119	101	68	46
Other alcoholic beverages	100	63	79	88	139	143	77	119
Away from home	**100**	**122**	**140**	**103**	**118**	**77**	**58**	**24**
Beer and ale	100	150	152	99	114	64	45	17
Wine	100	122	131	103	121	76	72	26
Other alcoholic beverages	100	107	145	99	119	79	60	29
Alcoholic beverages purchased on trips	100	110	113	124	121	96	63	20

Note: An index of 100 represents the average for all consumer units. An index of 132 means that the average for the subgroup is 32 percent above the average for all consumer units. An index of 68 indicates spending that is 32 percent below the overall average.

Aggregate expenditures, 1988

Aggregate expenditures in 1988 for food and alcoholic beverages, by age of reference person.

	all cu's	under 25	25 to 34	35 to 44	45 to 54	55 to 64	65 to 74	75+
Number of consumer units (in thousands)	*94,862*	*7,216*	*21,985*	*19,911*	*13,601*	*12,546*	*11,319*	*8,284*
Average number of persons per cu	*2.6*	*1.8*	*2.8*	*3.3*	*2.9*	*2.2*	*2*	*1.5*
Aggregate before-tax income (in millions)	*$2,722,037*	*$106,992*	*$622,571*	*$725,318*	*$543,142*	*$376,117*	*$234,349*	*$113,549*
TOTAL AGGREGATE EXPENDITURES (in millions)	*$2,456,432*	*$118,149*	*$566,559*	*$658,610*	*$451,619*	*$323,252*	*$227,737*	*$110,504*
FOOD, AGGREGATE EXPENDITURES (in millions)	*$355,810*	*$17,716*	*$80,553*	*$92,311*	*$65,483*	*$49,579*	*$34,109*	*$16,059*
ALCOHOLIC BEV., AGG. EXPEND. (in millions)	*$25,384*	*$2,251*	*$7,795*	*$5,598*	*$4,170*	*$2,999*	*$1,833*	*$739*
FOOD AT HOME	**$203,044**	**$8,089**	**$44,978**	**$51,757**	**$35,431**	**$29,545**	**$21,874**	**$11,370**
Cereals and bakery products	**29,689**	**1,196**	**6,404**	**7,714**	**5,270**	**4,185**	**3,139**	**1,781**
Cereals and cereal products	10,398	473	2,395	2,728	1,805	1,375	1,030	593
Flour	442	15	87	95	75	71	68	31
Prepared flour mixes	898	43	230	201	153	129	90	54
Ready-to-eat and cooked cereal	6,940	306	1,555	1,859	1,219	910	680	411
Rice	741	25	210	204	128	87	49	38
Pasta, cornmeal, and other cereal products	1,376	84	312	369	230	178	144	59
Bakery products	19,291	723	4,009	4,986	3,465	2,811	2,109	1,188
Bread	6,132	229	1,251	1,492	1,138	890	717	415
Crackers and cookies	4,878	179	1,068	1,301	826	697	514	293
Frozen and refrigerated bakery products	1,299	50	269	343	225	201	141	71
Meats, poultry, fish, and eggs	**52,389**	**1,798**	**11,121**	**13,158**	**9,187**	**8,127**	**6,038**	**2,960**
Beef	17,325	655	3,654	4,543	2,960	2,778	1,723	1,012
Pork	10,451	290	2,144	2,457	1,879	1,557	1,468	656
Other meats	7,822	284	1,699	2,099	1,293	1,196	818	432
Poultry	7,997	258	1,701	1,977	1,473	1,202	978	408
Fish and seafood	6,171	190	1,365	1,484	1,088	1,007	751	286
Eggs	2,623	120	559	597	494	387	300	166
Dairy products	**26,075**	**1,093**	**6,061**	**6,623**	**4,478**	**3,705**	**2,667**	**1,448**
Fresh milk and cream	12,720	594	2,982	3,182	2,204	1,697	1,274	785
Other dairy products	13,356	499	3,079	3,441	2,274	2,008	1,393	662
Butter	821	29	198	201	118	131	98	45
Cheese	7,358	293	1,773	1,825	1,275	1,113	717	362
Ice cream and related products	3,880	135	817	1,058	690	574	432	174
Fruits and vegetables	**35,480**	**1,269**	**7,205**	**8,632**	**6,122**	**5,437**	**4,412**	**2,403**
Fresh fruits	11,476	379	2,153	2,798	1,977	1,807	1,530	832
Fresh vegetables	10,493	331	2,064	2,569	1,812	1,664	1,347	705
Processed fruits	8,071	331	1,774	1,931	1,375	1,156	946	559
Processed vegetables	5,441	228	1,214	1,334	957	809	590	307
Other food at home	**59,410**	**2,733**	**14,187**	**15,630**	**10,373**	**8,091**	**5,619**	**2,778**
Sugar and other sweets	7,430	287	1,645	1,924	1,277	1,072	836	391
Candy and chewing gum	4,203	160	926	1,133	746	602	432	202
Sugar	1,581	70	359	389	270	224	176	92

Aggregate expenditures for food and alcoholic beverages in 1988, by age of reference person.

(continued from previous page)	all cu's	under 25	25 to 34	35 to 44	45 to 54	55 to 64	65 to 74	75+
Fats and oils	5,183	170	1,097	1,255	920	786	644	312
Miscellaneous foods	25,069	1,330	6,640	6,601	4,105	3,146	2,156	1,091
Frozen prepared foods	4,202	241	957	1,141	697	510	391	266
Canned and packaged soups	2,008	99	456	503	322	279	211	139
Potato chips, nuts, and other snacks	5,553	250	1,367	1,553	943	766	474	201
Condiments and seasonings	5,662	284	1,371	1,478	1,013	774	528	214
Other canned/packaged prepared foods	7,644	455	2,490	1,927	1,131	817	551	272
Baby food	1,435	156	918	212	80	48	16	5
Nonalcoholic beverages	18,862	845	4,236	4,996	3,556	2,584	1,746	898
Cola	8,509	468	2,030	2,459	1,591	1,069	607	284
Other carbonated drinks	3,034	151	700	825	614	372	234	138
Coffee	3,816	75	583	848	708	738	597	266
Food prepared by cu on out-of-town trips	2,866	102	569	854	516	502	237	85
FOOD AWAY FROM HOME	**$152,766**	**$9,627**	**$35,576**	**$40,554**	**$30,052**	**$20,034**	**$12,234**	**$4,689**
Meals at restaurants, carry-outs, and other	**118,796**	**7,758**	**29,682**	**31,066**	**22,624**	**14,776**	**9,071**	**3,819**
Lunch	46,773	3,018	11,657	12,995	9,054	5,248	3,289	1,512
Dinner	51,992	3,181	12,685	12,638	9,871	7,252	4,546	1,819
Snacks and nonalcoholic beverages	12,472	1,066	3,576	3,710	2,158	1,235	529	198
Breakfast and brunch	7,558	493	1,763	1,724	1,541	1,041	707	290
Board(including at school)	**4,404**	**417**	**160**	**1,017**	**1,658**	**1,012**	**126**	**13**
Catered affairs	**3,893**	**106**	**434**	**586**	**1,256**	**769**	**655**	**86**
Food on out-of-town trips	**19,021**	**798**	**3,532**	**5,095**	**3,530**	**3,088**	**2,225**	**753**
School lunches	**4,076**	**21**	**804**	**2,262**	**777**	**144**	**63**	**5**
Meals as pay	**2,577**	**526**	**965**	**528**	**206**	**245**	**94**	**12**
ALCOHOLIC BEVERAGES	**$25,384**	**$2,251**	**$7,795**	**$5,598**	**$4,170**	**$2,999**	**$1,833**	**$739**
At home	**13,120**	**1,111**	**3,795**	**2,925**	**2,078**	**1,750**	**976**	**484**
Beer and ale	7,845	875	2,649	1,681	1,092	917	437	194
Whiskey	1,096	39	180	223	233	202	185	34
Wine	2,815	132	718	767	481	374	229	114
Other alcoholic beverages	1,364	66	249	253	272	257	126	141
Away from home	**12,264**	**1,140**	**4,000**	**2,673**	**2,091**	**1,249**	**856**	**256**
Beer and ale	3,413	393	1,211	717	564	291	186	51
Wine	1,746	163	532	380	305	175	151	40
Other alcoholic beverages	5,278	430	1,776	1,101	904	551	381	134
Alcoholic beverages purchased on trips	1,827	154	480	475	318	232	138	31

Note: Expenditures listed for items in a given category may not add to the total for that category because the listing is incomplete. "Other dairy products," for example, includes "butter, cheese, ice cream and related products" and "miscellaneous"—"miscellaneous" is omitted here. Numbers may not add to total due to rounding. The "all cu's" aggregates will differ slightly from table to table because they are the sums of the aggregates in each row.

Aggregate expenditures, 1995

Aggregate expenditures for food and alcoholic beverages, by age of householder in 1995 (in 1988 dollars).

	all households	under 25	25 to 34	35 to 44	45 to 54	55 to 64	65 to 74	75+
Number of households (in thousands)	100,308	4,316	19,927	23,916	18,035	12,233	12,006	9,876
FOOD, AGGREGATE EXPENDITURES IN 1995 (in millions)	$375,955	$10,596	$73,013	$110,879	$86,831	$48,342	$36,179	$19,145
ALCOHOLIC BEVERAGES, ANNUAL AGGREGATE EXPENDITURES (in millions)	$26,952	$1,346	$7,065	$6,724	$5,529	$2,924	$1,944	$881
FOOD AT HOME	$214,245	$4,838	$40,767	$62,168	$46,982	$28,808	$23,202	$13,555
Cereals and bakery products	31,310	716	5,804	9,265	6,988	4,081	3,329	2,124
Cereals and cereal products	10,968	283	2,171	3,277	2,393	1,340	1,092	707
Flour	466	9	79	115	99	69	73	37
Prepared flour mixes	949	26	208	241	202	125	95	64
Ready-to-eat and cooked cereal	7,317	183	1,410	2,233	1,616	887	721	490
Rice	779	15	191	245	170	85	52	45
Pasta, cornmeal, and other cereal products	1,454	50	283	443	305	174	153	70
Bakery products	20,342	433	3,634	5,988	4,595	2,740	2,237	1,41
Bread	6,468	137	1,134	1,792	1,509	868	760	494
Crackers and cookies	5,141	107	968	1,563	1,095	680	546	350
Frozen and refrigerated bakery products	1,371	30	244	413	298	196	149	84
Meats, poultry, fish, and eggs	55,277	1,075	10,080	15,804	12,182	7,925	6,405	3,528
Beef	18,274	392	3,312	5,457	3,925	2,709	1,827	1,206
Pork	11,024	174	1,943	2,951	2,492	1,518	1,557	782
Other meats	8,247	170	1,540	2,522	1,715	1,167	868	515
Poultry	8,443	154	1,541	2,375	1,954	1,172	1,037	487
Fish and seafood	6,518	114	1,237	1,783	1,442	982	797	341
Eggs	2,772	72	507	717	655	377	318	197
Dairy products	27,512	654	5,493	7,956	5,938	3,612	2,829	1,726
Fresh milk and cream	13,419	356	2,702	3,822	2,923	1,655	1,352	936
Other dairy products	14,093	298	2,791	4,133	3,015	1,958	1,477	790
Butter	866	17	180	242	157	128	104	54
Cheese	7,768	175	1,607	2,192	1,691	1,085	760	431
Ice cream and related products	4,095	81	740	1,271	914	560	458	208
Fruits and vegetables	37,423	759	6,530	10,369	8,118	5,301	4,680	2,865
Fresh fruits	12,100	226	1,951	3,361	2,622	1,762	1,622	992
Fresh vegetables	11,065	198	1,871	3,085	2,403	1,623	1,429	841
Processed fruits	8,513	198	1,608	2,320	1,824	1,127	1,003	666
Processed vegetables	5,745	137	1,101	1,603	1,269	789	626	366
Other food at home	62,723	1,635	12,859	18,774	13,755	7,889	5,960	3,312
Sugar and other sweets	7,840	172	1,491	2,311	1,693	1,045	887	466
Candy and chewing gum	4,434	96	839	1,361	990	587	459	241
Sugar	1,668	42	326	468	358	218	186	110

Aggregate expenditures for food and alcoholic beverages, by age of householder in 1995 (in 1988 dollars).

(continued from previous page)	all households	under 25	25 to 34	35 to 44	45 to 54	55 to 64	65 to 74	75+
Fats and oils	5,469	101	994	1,507	1,219	767	683	372
Miscellaneous foods	26,469	795	6,019	7,929	5,444	3,068	2,286	1,301
Frozen prepared foods	4,432	144	867	1,370	924	497	414	318
Canned and packaged soups	2,118	59	413	604	427	272	224	165
Potato chips, nuts, and other snacks	5,861	149	1,239	1,865	1,251	747	503	239
Condiments and seasonings	5,985	170	1,243	1,775	1,343	755	560	255
Other canned/packaged prepared foods	8,073	272	2,257	2,315	1,500	797	585	324
Baby food	1,522	93	832	255	106	46	17	6
Nonalcoholic beverages	19,915	505	3,839	6,001	4,715	2,520	1,852	1,071
Cola	8,990	280	1,840	2,954	2,110	1,042	644	338
Other carbonated drinks	3,204	91	635	990	815	363	249	164
Coffee	4,029	45	528	1,019	939	720	633	318
Food prepared by cu on out-of-town trips	3,030	61	516	1,026	684	490	251	102
FOOD AWAY FROM HOME	**$161,710**	**$5,758**	**$32,246**	**$48,711**	**$39,849**	**$19,534**	**$12,977**	**$5,590**
Meals at restaurants, carry-outs, and other	**125,789**	**4,640**	**26,903**	**37,315**	**29,999**	**14,407**	**9,622**	**4,552**
Lunch	49,473	1,805	10,566	15,608	12,005	5,117	3,489	1,803
Dinner	55,088	1,903	11,498	15,179	13,089	7,072	4,822	2,168
Snacks and nonalcoholic beverages	13,211	638	3,241	4,456	2,862	1,204	561	236
Breakfast and brunch	8,018	295	1,598	2,071	2,043	1,015	750	345
Board(including at school)	**4,656**	**249**	**145**	**1,222**	**2,199**	**987**	**133**	**16**
Catered affairs	**4,116**	**63**	**393**	**703**	**1,666**	**750**	**695**	**102**
Food on out-of-town trips	**20,113**	**477**	**3,201**	**6,120**	**4,681**	**3,011**	**2,360**	**898**
School lunches	**4,310**	**13**	**729**	**2,717**	**1,031**	**141**	**67**	**6**
Meals as pay	**2,725**	**315**	**874**	**634**	**274**	**239**	**100**	**15**
ALCOHOLIC BEVERAGES	**$26,952**	**$1,346**	**$7,065**	**$6,724**	**$5,529**	**$2,924**	**$1,944**	**$881**
At home	**13,926**	**665**	**3,440**	**3,513**	**2,756**	**1,707**	**1,036**	**577**
Beer and ale	8,350	523	2,401	2,020	1,448	894	463	231
Whiskey	1,165	23	163	268	309	197	196	41
Wine	2,971	79	651	922	637	365	243	136
Other alcoholic beverages	1,441	39	225	304	361	251	134	168
Away from home	**13,026**	**682**	**3,625**	**3,210**	**2,773**	**1,218**	**908**	**305**
Beer and ale	3,634	235	1,097	862	748	283	197	61
Wine	1,857	97	483	456	405	171	160	48
Other alcoholic beverages	5,602	257	1,610	1,322	1,199	537	405	159
Alcoholic beverages purchased on trips	1,932	92	435	570	422	226	146	37

Note: Households are used here because projections of the number of consumer units in 1995 and 2000 are not available. Projections show how annual aggregate expenditures will change as the number of households in the age groups changes in 1995 and 2000. Household projections are from the Census Bureau. Projections are based on the average annual expenditures in 1988 and have not been adjusted for price increases or for changes in expenditure patterns. Expenditures listed for items in a given category may not add to the total for that category because the listing is incomplete. "Other dairy products," for example, includes "butter, cheese, ice cream and related products" and "miscellaneous"—"miscellaneous" is omitted here. Numbers may not add to total due to rounding.

Aggregate expenditures, 2000

Aggregate expenditures for food and alcoholic beverages, by age of householder in 2000 (in 1988 dollars).

	all households	under 25	25 to 34	35 to 44	45 to 54	55 to 64	65 to 74	75+
Number of households (in thousands)	105,933	4,442	18,004	25,339	21,603	13,903	11,516	11,126
FOOD, AGGREGATE EXPENDITURES IN 2000 (in millions)	$409,571	$10,905	$65,967	$117,476	$104,010	$54,942	$34,702	$21,568
ALCOHOLIC BEVERAGES, AGGREGATE EXPENDITURES IN 2000 (in millions)	$27,696	$1,386	$6,383	$7,124	$6,623	$3,323	$1,864	$993
FOOD AT HOME	$234,222	$4,980	$36,833	$65,867	$56,277	$32,740	$22,255	$15,271
Cereals and bakery products	**34,391**	**736**	**5,244**	**9,816**	**8,371**	**4,638**	**3,194**	**2,393**
Cereals and cereal products	11,958	291	1,961	3,472	2,866	1,523	1,048	797
Flour	510	9	71	121	119	78	70	42
Prepared flour mixes	1,019	27	188	255	242	143	91	72
Ready-to-eat and cooked cereal	8,016	189	1,274	2,365	1,936	1,008	691	553
Rice	848	15	172	260	204	97	49	51
Pasta, cornmeal, and other cereal products	1,565	51	255	470	365	197	146	79
Bakery products	22,433	445	3,283	6,345	5,504	3,115	2,146	1,596
Bread	7,144	141	1,025	1,898	1,807	987	729	557
Crackers and cookies	5,642	110	874	1,656	1,312	772	523	394
Frozen and refrigerated bakery products	1,506	31	220	437	357	222	143	95
Meats, poultry, fish, and eggs	**60,676**	**1,107**	**9,107**	**16,745**	**14,593**	**9,006**	**6,143**	**3,975**
Beef	20,069	403	2,992	5,782	4,702	3,078	1,753	1,359
Pork	12,145	179	1,756	3,127	2,984	1,725	1,493	881
Other meats	9,031	175	1,391	2,672	2,054	1,326	833	580
Poultry	9,283	159	1,393	2,516	2,340	1,332	995	549
Fish and seafood	7,115	117	1,118	1,889	1,728	1,116	765	384
Eggs	3,032	74	458	760	784	429	305	222
Dairy products	**29,942**	**673**	**4,963**	**8,429**	**7,113**	**4,105**	**2,713**	**1,945**
Fresh milk and cream	14,591	366	2,442	4,050	3,501	1,881	1,296	1,055
Other dairy products	15,351	307	2,522	4,379	3,612	2,225	1,417	890
Butter	930	18	162	256	188	146	99	61
Cheese	8,429	180	1,452	2,323	2,025	1,233	729	486
Ice cream and related products	4,504	83	669	1,346	1,095	636	440	234
Fruits and vegetables	**41,133**	**781**	**5,900**	**10,986**	**9,725**	**6,025**	**4,489**	**3,228**
Fresh fruits	13,374	233	1,763	3,561	3,141	2,003	1,556	1,117
Fresh vegetables	12,203	204	1,690	3,269	2,878	1,844	1,370	947
Processed fruits	9,292	203	1,452	2,458	2,185	1,281	962	750
Processed vegetables	6,263	141	995	1,698	1,521	897	600	413
Other food at home	**68,080**	**1,682**	**11,618**	**19,891**	**16,476**	**8,966**	**5,716**	**3,731**
Sugar and other sweets	8,562	177	1,347	2,448	2,028	1,187	850	525
Candy and chewing gum	4,863	99	758	1,442	1,186	668	440	271
Sugar	1,812	43	294	495	428	248	179	124

Aggregate expenditures for food and alcoholic beverages, by age of householder in 2000 (in 1988 dollars).

(continued from previous page)	all households	under 25	25 to 34	35 to 44	45 to 54	55 to 64	65 to 74	75+
Fats and oils	6,006	104	898	1,597	1,461	871	655	419
Miscellaneous foods	28,323	818	5,438	8,401	6,521	3,486	2,193	1,466
Frozen prepared foods	4,810	149	784	1,452	1,107	565	397	358
Canned and packaged soups	2,295	61	373	640	511	309	215	186
Potato chips, nuts, and other snacks	6,348	154	1,119	1,976	1,498	849	482	270
Condiments and seasonings	6,470	175	1,123	1,881	1,608	858	538	287
Other canned/packaged prepared foods	8,400	280	2,039	2,452	1,797	906	561	365
Baby food	1,321	96	752	270	127	53	16	7
Nonalcoholic beverages	21,842	520	3,469	6,358	5,648	2,864	1,776	1,207
Cola	9,792	288	1,663	3,130	2,528	1,184	618	381
Other carbonated drinks	3,527	93	574	1,049	976	412	238	185
Coffee	4,511	46	477	1,079	1,124	818	607	358
Food prepared by cu on out-of-town trips	3,348	63	466	1,087	819	557	241	115
FOOD AWAY FROM HOME	**$175,348**	**$5,926**	**$29,134**	**$51,609**	**$47,733**	**$22,201**	**$12,447**	**$6,297**
Meals at restaurants, carry-outs, and other	**135,284**	**4,775**	**24,307**	**39,535**	**35,934**	**16,374**	**9,229**	**5,129**
Lunch	53,515	1,858	9,546	16,537	14,380	5,816	3,346	2,031
Dinner	59,212	1,958	10,388	16,083	15,679	8,037	4,625	2,442
Snacks and nonalcoholic beverages	13,906	656	2,929	4,721	3,428	1,368	538	266
Breakfast and brunch	8,650	303	1,444	2,194	2,447	1,153	720	389
Board(including at school)	**5,584**	**257**	**131**	**1,295**	**2,634**	**1,121**	**128**	**18**
Catered affairs	**4,796**	**65**	**355**	**745**	**1,996**	**852**	**667**	**115**
Food on out-of-town trips	**22,171**	**491**	**2,892**	**6,484**	**5,607**	**3,422**	**2,263**	**1,012**
School lunches	**5,015**	**13**	**658**	**2,878**	**1,234**	**160**	**64**	**7**
Meals as pay	**2,498**	**324**	**790**	**672**	**328**	**272**	**96**	**17**
ALCOHOLIC BEVERAGES	**$27,696**	**$1,386**	**$6,383**	**$7,124**	**$6,623**	**$3,323**	**$1,864**	**$993**
At home	**14,398**	**684**	**3,108**	**3,722**	**3,301**	**1,939**	**993**	**650**
Beer and ale	8,304	539	2,169	2,140	1,735	1,016	445	260
Whiskey	1,283	24	147	284	371	223	188	46
Wine	3,210	81	588	977	763	415	233	153
Other alcoholic beverages	1,601	40	204	322	432	285	128	190
Away from home	**13,298**	**702**	**3,275**	**3,401**	**3,322**	**1,384**	**871**	**343**
Beer and ale	3,622	242	991	913	896	322	189	68
Wine	1,906	100	436	483	485	194	153	54
Other alcoholic beverages	5,735	265	1,455	1,401	1,436	610	388	179
Alcoholic beverages purchased on trips	2,036	95	393	604	505	257	140	42

Note: Households are used here because projections of the number of consumer units in 1995 and 2000 are not available. Projections show how annual aggregate expenditures will change as the number of households in the age groups changes in 1995 and 2000. Household projections are from the Census Bureau. Projections are based on the average annual expenditures in 1988 and have not been adjusted for price increases or for changes in expenditure patterns. Expenditures listed for items in a given category may not add to the total for that category because the listing is incomplete. "Other dairy products," for example, includes "butter, cheese, ice cream and related products" and "miscellaneous"—"miscellaneous" is omitted here. Numbers may not add to total due to rounding.

PART II
Spending by income for food and alcoholic beverages

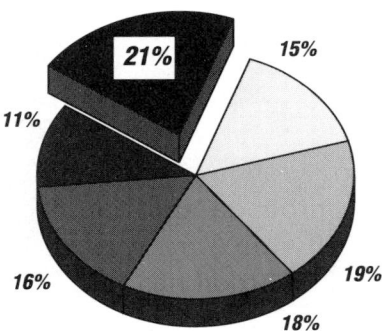

High-income households are the largest market for food at home...

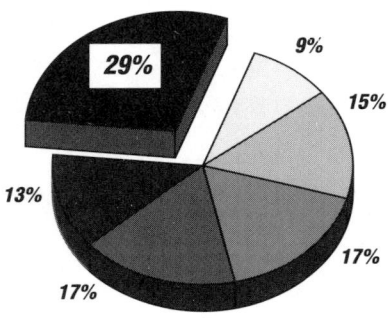

...and for food away from home...

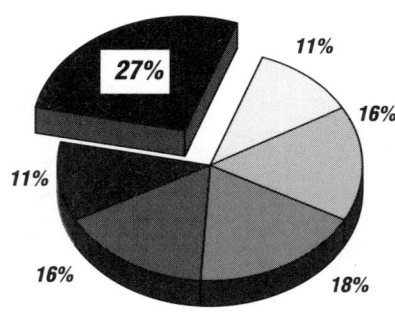

...and for alcohol.

☐ under $10,000	◼ $30,000–39,999
◻ $10,000–19,999	◼ $40,000–49,999
◼ $20,000–29,999	◼ $50,000 and over

From the lowest to the highest income households, spending on food increases by 212 percent and spending on alcoholic beverages by 260 percent. Items most affected by income are frozen and refrigerated bakery products, foods prepared away from home, and all alcohol except beer, ale, and whiskey.

Spending on food rises from a low of $2,019 for households with annual incomes below $10,000 to fully $6,296 for those with incomes of $50,000 or more. Households with the lowest incomes spent an average of $141 on alcohol, those with the highest incomes spent $506.

Although they spend more, food takes a smaller bite out of the budgets of high-income households. Households with incomes under $10,000 devote 18 percent of their budgets to food. That figure drops to just 12 percent for households with incomes of $50,000 or more.

American households, on average, spend 53 percent of their food and beverage budget on food prepared at home, another 40 percent on food prepared away from home, and about 7 percent on alcohol. But households with incomes of $50,000 or more spend more than half of their food dollars at restaurants or on carry-out meals.

The 12 million households with incomes of $50,000 or more spent $83 billion on food and alcohol in 1988. They are the biggest market for these products. The 18 million households with incomes between $30,000 and $50,000 spent a total of $94 billion. Those with incomes below $30,000 numbered 51 million and spent a total of $156 billion. With the number of both low- and high-income households projected to grow the fastest during the 1990s, market expansion will occur at both ends of the income scale.

The low-end market

Although households with annual incomes of $30,000 or less cannot be considered affluent, they do spend more than average amounts on certain foods. Households with incomes under $20,000 spend above-average amounts on flour, eggs, sugar, and meals as pay, for example. These households on average have only two people and one earner—two factors that strongly affect food consumption. Food and beverage spending in households with incomes under $10,000 is only about half the amount spent by the average household. Among those with incomes of $10,000 to $20,000, grocery bills are 22 percent below the norm.

Households with incomes between $20,000 and $30,000 spend an average amount on food at home and they spend just 2 percent less than average on food away from home. They spend more than the average, however, on ice cream, snack foods, colas, cheese, and beer and ale.

The high-end market

The highest income groups also have the largest households and the most earners. They average three people and two earners per household which boosts their spending on food.

Households with incomes of $30,000 to $40,000 spend 17 percent more than the average household on food at home; 25 percent more on food at restaurants and carry-outs; and 22 percent more on alcohol. Their spending for cheese, ice cream, condiments and seasonings, noncola carbonated drinks, food eaten on out-of-town trips, restaurant meals and take-outs, school lunches, snacks and drinks consumed away from home, and alcohol bought for at-home use is at least 25 percent above average.

Spending by those with incomes between $40,000 and $50,000 is 34 percent above average for food at home, 46 percent above average for food away from home, and 25 percent above average for alcohol. They spend an exceptional amount relative to other households on candy, canned and packaged soups, snacks, baby food, and school lunches.

With the exception of flour, fats and oils, baby food, and meals as pay, households with incomes of $50,000 or more spend well above average on foods and beverages. These households spend 96 more than the average household on food eaten away from home. They spend 80 percent more than average on alcohol and their at-home wine expenditures are 118 percent above average.

High-end households spend above average for every category, especially for eating out...

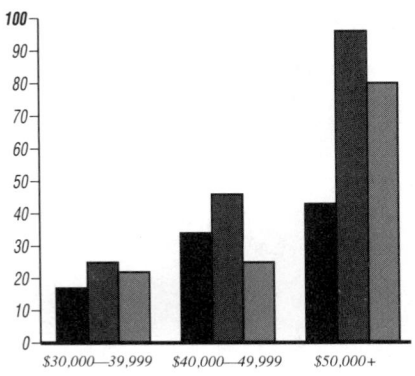

...while lower-income households spend less than the average household on everything but alcohol.

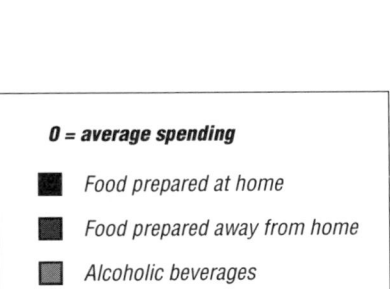

0 = average spending

- ■ Food prepared at home
- ■ Food prepared away from home
- ■ Alcoholic beverages

Average expenditures

(consumer units include complete income reporters only)	all cu's	under $10,000	$10,000 to $19,999	$20,000 to $29,999	$30,000 to $39,999	$40,000 to $49,999	$50,000 and over
Number of consumer units (in thousands)	81,354	18,809	17,652	14,586	10,901	7,198	12,209
Average number of persons per cu	2.6	1.8	2.3	2.7	2.9	3.2	3.1
Average number of earners per cu	1.4	0.7	1.0	1.5	1.8	2.0	2.1
TOTAL AVERAGE ANNUAL EXPENDITURES	$26,389.07	$11,269.43	$18,078.25	$24,896.36	$31,659.60	$37,562.00	$52,320.19
FOOD, AVERAGE ANNUAL EXPENDITURES	$3,804.39	$2,019.46	$2,971.58	$3,765.02	$4,587.49	$5,281.61	$6,296.11
ALCOHOLIC BEV., AVER. ANNUAL EXPENDITURES	$281.70	$140.56	$207.24	$290.56	$343.77	$352.96	$506.47
FOOD AT HOME	$2,176.94	$1,371.16	$1,876.86	$2,174.01	$2,556.74	$2,906.55	$3,109.86
Cereals and bakery products	317.03	202.40	270.12	320.55	375.38	417.06	450.19
Cereals and cereal products	111.15	76.63	100.99	111.31	134.59	145.71	138.66
Flour	4.83	4.56	5.57	4.99	5.06	4.15	4.17
Prepared flour mixes	9.88	5.69	9.26	10.32	11.92	14.72	12.18
Ready-to-eat and cooked cereal	73.49	50.79	65.35	72.80	89.56	98.06	92.85
Rice	7.98	5.97	7.10	7.95	9.66	9.48	10.14
Pasta, cornmeal, and other cereal products	14.97	9.63	13.71	15.24	18.39	19.30	19.34
Bakery products	205.88	125.78	169.13	209.23	240.80	271.35	311.53
Bread	65.72	47.66	59.77	68.58	72.19	78.50	86.03
Crackers and cookies	51.76	29.20	42.12	53.39	60.40	75.75	77.18
Frozen and refrigerated bakery products	13.55	7.16	10.30	13.12	15.29	17.64	24.89
Meats, poultry, fish, and eggs	560.01	360.39	513.55	541.91	635.94	699.55	812.35
Beef	183.66	103.79	176.66	185.96	215.42	225.57	263.75
Pork	114.19	81.84	106.21	108.24	132.60	131.31	157.61
Other meats	83.61	53.47	73.45	79.96	98.98	113.62	118.21
Poultry	85.49	57.06	75.05	82.16	85.67	111.40	133.20
Fish and seafood	65.24	41.06	53.76	56.89	74.24	86.03	109.89
Eggs	27.83	23.18	28.43	28.69	29.02	31.61	29.68
Dairy products	277.91	171.12	241.63	287.05	337.97	365.06	383.11
Fresh milk and cream	134.41	93.42	128.99	135.91	160.12	158.15	168.53
Other dairy products	143.50	77.71	112.65	151.15	177.85	206.92	214.57
Butter	8.89	5.54	8.23	8.63	9.20	12.22	13.04
Cheese	79.01	43.40	61.28	83.03	98.98	111.72	119.08
Ice cream and related products	41.68	20.35	32.38	46.55	53.10	60.05	61.85
Fruits and vegetables	376.38	251.79	331.11	366.35	441.76	487.04	526.17
Fresh fruits	120.98	79.00	103.73	116.33	148.47	156.62	172.21
Fresh vegetables	110.67	79.73	101.42	106.30	124.19	123.40	158.76
Processed fruits	86.81	55.20	77.65	82.22	98.04	126.19	121.27
Processed vegetables	57.92	37.87	48.31	61.49	71.05	80.82	73.92
Other food at home	645.61	385.44	520.45	658.15	765.69	937.83	938.05
Sugar and other sweets	80.66	48.36	65.02	82.49	97.73	122.23	111.61
Candy and chewing gum	45.41	23.49	31.64	46.37	55.74	75.32	71.53
Sugar	17.07	15.44	18.12	17.61	18.27	17.57	16.01

Average annual expenditures for food and alcoholic beverages, by total before-tax income of consumer unit.

(continued from previous page)	all cu's	under $10,000	$10,000 to $19,999	$20,000 to $29,999	$30,000 to $39,999	$40,000 to $49,999	$50,000 and over
Fats and oils	56.65	39.79	47.17	59.62	69.18	76.24	70.54
Miscellaneous foods	272.98	159.43	218.97	278.73	325.17	410.76	393.38
Frozen prepared foods	46.13	24.34	38.98	47.46	54.87	69.97	66.80
Canned and packaged soups	21.41	13.82	17.33	21.06	24.10	35.62	28.50
Potato chips, nuts, and other snacks	59.78	29.14	39.45	64.36	71.49	95.82	100.20
Condiments and seasonings	61.52	35.65	52.42	58.41	77.90	82.89	92.16
Other canned/packaged prepared foods	84.14	56.47	70.79	87.44	96.82	126.46	105.73
Baby food	16.25	15.13	12.55	16.91	19.52	26.99	12.93
Nonalcoholic beverages	204.37	128.51	174.74	210.29	233.06	283.11	287.11
Cola	92.19	56.36	76.62	99.91	101.86	140.51	123.90
Other carbonated drinks	32.62	19.16	26.16	28.70	40.86	43.90	53.99
Coffee	40.93	32.36	38.67	38.15	43.16	47.73	54.95
Food prepared by cu on out-of-town trips	30.94	9.36	14.55	27.01	40.55	45.49	75.42
FOOD AWAY FROM HOME	**$1,627.45**	**$648.30**	**$1,094.71**	**$1,591.02**	**$2,030.75**	**$2,375.06**	**$3,186.24**
Meals at restaurants, carry-outs, and other	**1,275.77**	**519.39**	**911.02**	**1,294.24**	**1,591.66**	**1,870.30**	**2,351.22**
Lunch	499.88	205.04	337.67	514.76	619.15	709.45	956.78
Dinner	549.30	211.51	386.37	550.06	662.77	822.65	1,057.00
Snacks and nonalcoholic beverages	142.56	68.14	113.10	145.83	190.00	225.33	207.78
Breakfast and brunch	84.04	34.69	73.88	83.59	119.74	112.87	129.66
Board(including at school)	**43.62**	**24.90**	**7.28**	**27.65**	**36.46**	**39.33**	**153.00**
Catered affairs	**41.27**	**5.07**	**6.64**	**34.97**	**50.79**	**47.01**	**142.76**
Food on out-of-town trips	**195.31**	**64.33**	**103.47**	**165.61**	**254.20**	**300.02**	**451.05**
School lunches	**42.24**	**11.48**	**23.16**	**41.51**	**67.39**	**84.77**	**70.55**
Meals as pay	**29.24**	**23.13**	**43.15**	**27.04**	**30.27**	**33.64**	**17.65**
ALCOHOLIC BEVERAGES	**$281.70**	**$140.56**	**$207.24**	**$290.56**	**$343.77**	**$352.96**	**$506.47**
At home	**148.36**	**79.33**	**116.31**	**152.37**	**189.69**	**178.29**	**246.36**
Beer and ale	89.05	57.34	74.87	95.86	108.21	102.60	126.68
Whiskey	12.73	7.32	9.65	13.17	16.76	13.43	21.68
Wine	32.15	9.88	14.84	31.70	40.94	46.88	70.20
Other alcoholic beverages	14.43	4.79	12.29	11.65	23.78	15.38	27.80
Away from home	**133.34**	**61.23**	**90.94**	**138.19**	**154.08**	**174.67**	**260.11**
Beer and ale	37.50	22.97	26.06	39.59	40.20	53.06	62.61
Wine	18.54	7.51	13.76	19.17	18.68	24.52	38.32
Other alcoholic beverages	58.12	24.25	43.14	60.89	71.66	67.59	113.53
Alcoholic beverages purchased on trips	19.17	6.49	7.99	18.54	23.54	29.50	45.66

Note: Expenditures listed for items in a given category may not add to the total for that category because the listing is incomplete. "Other dairy products," for example, includes "butter, cheese, ice cream and related products" and "miscellaneous"—"miscellaneous" is omitted here. Total expenditure exceeds total income in some income categories due to a number of factors including the underreporting of income, borrowing, and the use of savings. Numbers may not add to total due to rounding.

Share of spending

(consumer units include complete income reporters only)	all cu's	under $10,000	$10,000 to $19,999	$20,000 to $29,999	$30,000 to $39,999	$40,000 to $49,999	$50,000 and over
Number of consumer units (in thousands)	81,354	18,809	17,652	14,586	10,901	7,198	12,209
Average number of persons per cu	2.6	1.8	2.3	2.7	2.9	3.2	3.1
Average number of earners per cu	1.4	0.7	1.0	1.5	1.8	2.0	2.1
TOTAL AVERAGE ANNUAL EXPENDITURES	100.00%	100.00%	100.00%	100.00%	100.00%	100.00%	100.00%
FOOD, AVERAGE ANNUAL EXPENDITURES	14.42%	17.92%	16.44%	15.12%	14.49%	14.06%	12.03%
ALCOHOLIC BEV., AVER. ANNUAL EXPENDITURES	1.07%	1.25%	1.15%	1.17%	1.09%	0.94%	0.97%
FOOD AT HOME	8.25%	12.17%	10.38%	8.73%	8.08%	7.74%	5.94%
Cereals and bakery products	1.20	1.80	1.49	1.29	1.19	1.11	0.86
Cereals and cereal products	0.42	0.68	0.56	0.45	0.43	0.39	0.27
Flour	0.02	0.04	0.03	0.02	0.02	0.01	0.01
Prepared flour mixes	0.04	0.05	0.05	0.04	0.04	0.04	0.02
Ready-to-eat and cooked cereal	0.28	0.45	0.36	0.29	0.28	0.26	0.18
Rice	0.03	0.05	0.04	0.03	0.03	0.03	0.02
Pasta, cornmeal, and other cereal products	0.06	0.09	0.08	0.06	0.06	0.05	0.04
Bakery products	0.78	1.12	0.94	0.84	0.76	0.72	0.60
Bread	0.25	0.42	0.33	0.28	0.23	0.21	0.16
Crackers and cookies	0.20	0.26	0.23	0.21	0.19	0.20	0.15
Frozen and refrigerated bakery products	0.05	0.06	0.06	0.05	0.05	0.05	0.05
Meats, poultry, fish, and eggs	2.12	3.20	2.84	2.18	2.01	1.86	1.55
Beef	0.70	0.92	0.98	0.75	0.68	0.60	0.50
Pork	0.43	0.73	0.59	0.43	0.42	0.35	0.30
Other meats	0.32	0.47	0.41	0.32	0.31	0.30	0.23
Poultry	0.32	0.51	0.42	0.33	0.27	0.30	0.25
Fish and seafood	0.25	0.36	0.30	0.23	0.23	0.23	0.21
Eggs	0.11	0.21	0.16	0.12	0.09	0.08	0.06
Dairy products	1.05	1.52	1.34	1.15	1.07	0.97	0.73
Fresh milk and cream	0.51	0.83	0.71	0.55	0.51	0.42	0.32
Other dairy products	0.54	0.69	0.62	0.61	0.56	0.55	0.41
Butter	0.03	0.05	0.05	0.03	0.03	0.03	0.02
Cheese	0.30	0.39	0.34	0.33	0.31	0.30	0.23
Ice cream and related products	0.16	0.18	0.18	0.19	0.17	0.16	0.12
Fruits and vegetables	1.43	2.23	1.83	1.47	1.40	1.30	1.01
Fresh fruits	0.46	0.70	0.57	0.47	0.47	0.42	0.33
Fresh vegetables	0.42	0.71	0.56	0.43	0.39	0.33	0.30
Processed fruits	0.33	0.49	0.43	0.33	0.31	0.34	0.23
Processed vegetables	0.22	0.34	0.27	0.25	0.22	0.22	0.14
Other food at home	2.45	3.42	2.88	2.64	2.42	2.50	1.79
Sugar and other sweets	0.31	0.43	0.36	0.33	0.31	0.33	0.21
Candy and chewing gum	0.17	0.21	0.18	0.19	0.18	0.20	0.14
Sugar	0.06	0.14	0.10	0.07	0.06	0.05	0.03

Percent of total average annual expenditures spent on food and alcoholic beverages, by total before-tax income of consumer unit.

(continued from previous page)	all cu's	under $10,000	$10,000 to $19,999	$20,000 to $29,999	$30,000 to $39,999	$40,000 to $49,999	$50,000 and over
Fats and oils	0.21	0.35	0.26	0.24	0.22	0.20	0.13
Miscellaneous foods	1.03	1.41	1.21	1.12	1.03	1.09	0.75
Frozen prepared foods	0.17	0.22	0.22	0.19	0.17	0.19	0.13
Canned and packaged soups	0.08	0.12	0.10	0.08	0.08	0.09	0.05
Potato chips, nuts, and other snacks	0.23	0.26	0.22	0.26	0.23	0.26	0.19
Condiments and seasonings	0.23	0.32	0.29	0.23	0.25	0.22	0.18
Other canned/packaged prepared foods	0.32	0.50	0.39	0.35	0.31	0.34	0.20
Baby food	0.06	0.13	0.07	0.07	0.06	0.07	0.02
Nonalcoholic beverages	0.77	1.14	0.97	0.84	0.74	0.75	0.55
Cola	0.35	0.50	0.42	0.40	0.32	0.37	0.24
Other carbonated drinks	0.12	0.17	0.14	0.12	0.13	0.12	0.10
Coffee	0.16	0.29	0.21	0.15	0.14	0.13	0.11
Food prepared by cu on out-of-town trips	0.12	0.08	0.08	0.11	0.13	0.12	0.14
FOOD AWAY FROM HOME	**6.17%**	**5.75%**	**6.06%**	**6.39%**	**6.41%**	**6.32%**	**6.09%**
Meals at restaurants, carry-outs, and other	**4.83**	**4.61**	**5.04**	**5.20**	**5.03**	**4.98**	**4.49**
Lunch	1.89	1.82	1.87	2.07	1.96	1.89	1.83
Dinner	2.08	1.88	2.14	2.21	2.09	2.19	2.02
Snacks and nonalcoholic beverages	0.54	0.60	0.63	0.59	0.60	0.60	0.40
Breakfast and brunch	0.32	0.31	0.41	0.34	0.38	0.30	0.25
Board(including at school)	**0.17**	**0.22**	**0.04**	**0.11**	**0.12**	**0.10**	**0.29**
Catered affairs	**0.16**	**0.04**	**0.04**	**0.14**	**0.16**	**0.13**	**0.27**
Food on out-of-town trips	**0.74**	**0.57**	**0.57**	**0.67**	**0.80**	**0.80**	**0.86**
School lunches	**0.16**	**0.10**	**0.13**	**0.17**	**0.21**	**0.23**	**0.13**
Meals as pay	**0.11**	**0.21**	**0.24**	**0.11**	**0.10**	**0.09**	**0.03**
ALCOHOLIC BEVERAGES	**1.07%**	**1.25%**	**1.15%**	**1.17%**	**1.09%**	**0.94%**	**0.97%**
At home	**0.56**	**0.70**	**0.64**	**0.61**	**0.60**	**0.47**	**0.47**
Beer and ale	0.34	0.51	0.41	0.39	0.34	0.27	0.24
Whiskey	0.05	0.06	0.05	0.05	0.05	0.04	0.04
Wine	0.12	0.09	0.08	0.13	0.13	0.12	0.13
Other alcoholic beverages	0.05	0.04	0.07	0.05	0.08	0.04	0.05
Away from home	**0.51**	**0.54**	**0.50**	**0.56**	**0.49**	**0.47**	**0.50**
Beer and ale	0.14	0.20	0.14	0.16	0.13	0.14	0.12
Wine	0.07	0.07	0.08	0.08	0.06	0.07	0.07
Other alcoholic beverages	0.22	0.22	0.24	0.24	0.23	0.18	0.22
Alcoholic beverages purchased on trips	0.07	0.06	0.04	0.07	0.07	0.08	0.09

Note: Expenditures listed for items in a given category may not add to the total for that category because the listing is incomplete. "Other dairy products," for example, includes "butter, cheese, ice cream and related products" and "miscellaneous"—"miscellaneous" is omitted here. Numbers may not add to total due to rounding.

Indexed expenditures

(consumer units include complete income reporters only)	all cu's	under $10,000	$10,000 to $19,999	$20,000 to $29,999	$30,000 to $39,999	$40,000 to $49,999	$50,000 and over
Number of consumer units (in thousands)	81,354	18,809	17,652	14,586	10,901	7,198	12,209
Average number of persons per cu	2.6	1.8	2.3	2.7	2.9	3.2	3.1
Average number of earners per cu	1.4	0.7	1.0	1.5	1.8	2.0	2.1
TOTAL AVERAGE ANNUAL EXPENDITURES	100	43	69	94	120	142	198
FOOD, AVERAGE ANNUAL EXPENDITURES	100	53	78	99	121	139	165
ALCOHOLIC BEV., AVER. ANNUAL EXPENDITURES	100	50	74	103	122	125	180
FOOD AT HOME	**100**	**63**	**86**	**100**	**117**	**134**	**143**
Cereals and bakery products	**100**	**64**	**85**	**101**	**118**	**132**	**142**
Cereals and cereal products	100	69	91	100	121	131	125
Flour	100	94	115	103	105	86	86
Prepared flour mixes	100	58	94	104	121	149	123
Ready-to-eat and cooked cereal	100	69	89	99	122	133	126
Rice	100	75	89	100	121	119	127
Pasta, cornmeal, and other cereal products	100	64	92	102	123	129	129
Bakery products	100	61	82	102	117	132	151
Bread	100	73	91	104	110	119	131
Crackers and cookies	100	56	81	103	117	146	149
Frozen and refrigerated bakery products	100	53	76	97	113	130	184
Meats, poultry, fish, and eggs	**100**	**64**	**92**	**97**	**114**	**125**	**145**
Beef	100	57	96	101	117	123	144
Pork	100	72	93	95	116	115	138
Other meats	100	64	88	96	118	136	141
Poultry	100	67	88	96	100	130	156
Fish and seafood	100	63	82	87	114	132	168
Eggs	100	83	102	103	104	114	107
Dairy products	**100**	**62**	**87**	**103**	**122**	**131**	**138**
Fresh milk and cream	100	70	96	101	119	118	125
Other dairy products	100	54	78	105	124	144	150
Butter	100	62	93	97	103	137	147
Cheese	100	55	78	105	125	141	151
Ice cream and related products	100	49	78	112	127	144	148
Fruits and vegetables	**100**	**67**	**88**	**97**	**117**	**129**	**140**
Fresh fruits	100	65	86	96	123	129	142
Fresh vegetables	100	72	92	96	112	112	143
Processed fruits	100	64	89	95	113	145	140
Processed vegetables	100	65	83	106	123	140	128
Other food at home	**100**	**60**	**81**	**102**	**119**	**145**	**145**
Sugar and other sweets	100	60	81	102	121	152	138
Candy and chewing gum	100	52	70	102	123	166	158
Sugar	100	90	106	103	107	103	94

Indexed average annual expenditures for food and alcoholic beverages, by total before-tax income of consumer unit.

(continued from previous page)	all cu's	under $10,000	$10,000 to $19,999	$20,000 to $29,999	$30,000 to $39,999	$40,000 to $49,999	$50,000 and over
Fats and oils	100	70	83	105	122	135	125
Miscellaneous foods	100	58	80	102	119	150	144
Frozen prepared foods	100	53	85	103	119	152	145
Canned and packaged soups	100	65	81	98	113	166	133
Potato chips, nuts, and other snacks	100	49	66	108	120	160	168
Condiments and seasonings	100	58	85	95	127	135	150
Other canned/packaged prepared foods	100	67	84	104	115	150	126
Baby food	100	93	77	104	120	166	80
Nonalcoholic beverages	100	63	86	103	114	139	140
Cola	100	61	83	108	110	152	134
Other carbonated drinks	100	59	80	88	125	135	166
Coffee	100	79	94	93	105	117	134
Food prepared by cu on out-of-town trips	100	30	47	87	131	147	244
FOOD AWAY FROM HOME	**100**	**40**	**67**	**98**	**125**	**146**	**196**
Meals at restaurants, carry-outs, and other	**100**	**41**	**71**	**101**	**125**	**147**	**184**
Lunch	100	41	68	103	124	142	191
Dinner	100	39	70	100	121	150	192
Snacks and nonalcoholic beverages	100	48	79	102	133	158	146
Breakfast and brunch	100	41	88	99	142	134	154
Board(including at school)	**100**	**57**	**17**	**63**	**84**	**90**	**351**
Catered affairs	**100**	**12**	**16**	**85**	**123**	**114**	**346**
Food on out-of-town trips	**100**	**33**	**53**	**85**	**130**	**154**	**231**
School lunches	**100**	**27**	**55**	**98**	**160**	**201**	**167**
Meals as pay	**100**	**79**	**148**	**92**	**104**	**115**	**60**
ALCOHOLIC BEVERAGES	**100**	**50**	**74**	**103**	**122**	**125**	**180**
At home	**100**	**53**	**78**	**103**	**128**	**120**	**166**
Beer and ale	100	64	84	108	122	115	142
Whiskey	100	57	76	103	132	105	170
Wine	100	31	46	99	127	146	218
Other alcoholic beverages	100	33	85	81	165	107	193
Away from home	**100**	**46**	**68**	**104**	**116**	**131**	**195**
Beer and ale	100	61	69	106	107	141	167
Wine	100	41	74	103	101	132	207
Other alcoholic beverages	100	42	74	105	123	116	195
Alcoholic beverages purchased on trips	100	34	42	97	123	154	238

Note: An index of 100 represents the average for all consumer units. An index of 132 means that the average for the subgroup is 32 percent above the average for all consumer units. An index of 68 indicates spending that is 32 percent below the overall average.

Aggregate expenditures, 1988

Aggregate expenditures in 1988 for food and alcoholic beverages, by total before-tax income of consumer unit.

(consumer units include complete income reporters only)	all cu's	under $10,000	$10,000 to $19,999	$20,000 to $29,999	$30,000 to $39,999	$40,000 to $49,999	$50,000 and over
Number of consumer units (in thousands)	81,354	18,809	17,652	14,586	10,901	7,198	12,209
Average number of persons per cu	2.6	1.8	2.3	2.7	2.9	3.2	3.1
Average number of earners per cu	1.4	0.7	1.0	1.5	1.8	2.0	2.1
TOTAL AGGREGATE EXPENDITURES (in millions)	$2,148,492	$211,967	$319,117	$363,138	$345,121	$270,371	$638,777
FOOD, AGGREGATE EXPENDITURES (in millions)	$310,249	$37,984	$52,454	$54,917	$50,008	$38,017	$76,869
ALCOHOLIC BEV., AGG. EXPENDITURES (in millions)	$23,012	$2,644	$3,658	$4,238	$3,747	$2,541	$6,183
FOOD AT HOME	$177,391	$25,790	$33,130	$31,710	$27,871	$20,921	$37,968
Cereals and bakery products	25,841	3,807	4,768	4,676	4,092	3,002	5,496
Cereals and cereal products	9,056	1,441	1,783	1,624	1,467	1,049	1,693
Flour	393	86	98	73	55	30	51
Prepared flour mixes	805	107	163	151	130	106	149
Ready-to-eat and cooked cereal	5,986	955	1,154	1,062	976	706	1,134
Rice	651	112	125	116	105	68	124
Pasta, cornmeal, and other cereal products	1,221	181	242	222	200	139	236
Bakery products	16,785	2,366	2,986	3,052	2,625	1,953	3,803
Bread	5,354	896	1,055	1,000	787	565	1,050
Crackers and cookies	4,218	549	744	779	658	545	942
Frozen and refrigerated bakery products	1,106	135	182	191	167	127	304
Meats, poultry, fish, and eggs	45,634	6,779	9,065	7,904	6,932	5,035	9,918
Beef	14,975	1,952	3,118	2,712	2,348	1,624	3,220
Pork	9,308	1,539	1,875	1,579	1,445	945	1,924
Other meats	6,809	1,006	1,297	1,166	1,079	818	1,443
Poultry	6,958	1,073	1,325	1,198	934	802	1,626
Fish and seafood	5,321	772	949	830	809	619	1,342
Eggs	2,262	436	502	418	316	228	362
Dairy products	22,660	3,219	4,265	4,187	3,684	2,628	4,677
Fresh milk and cream	10,958	1,757	2,277	1,982	1,745	1,138	2,058
Other dairy products	11,703	1,462	1,988	2,205	1,939	1,489	2,620
Butter	723	104	145	126	100	88	159
Cheese	6,446	816	1,082	1,211	1,079	804	1,454
Ice cream and related products	3,400	383	572	679	579	432	755
Fruits and vegetables	30,670	4,736	5,845	5,344	4,816	3,506	6,424
Fresh fruits	9,862	1,486	1,831	1,697	1,618	1,127	2,103
Fresh vegetables	9,021	1,500	1,790	1,550	1,354	888	1,938
Processed fruits	7,066	1,038	1,371	1,199	1,069	908	1,481
Processed vegetables	4,721	712	853	897	775	582	902
Other food at home	52,586	7,250	9,187	9,600	8,347	6,751	11,453
Sugar and other sweets	6,568	910	1,148	1,203	1,065	880	1,363
Candy and chewing gum	3,700	442	559	676	608	542	873
Sugar	1,388	290	320	257	199	126	195

Aggregate expenditures in 1988 for food and alcoholic beverages, by total before-tax income of consumer unit.

(continued from previous page)	all cu's	under $10,000	$10,000 to $19,999	$20,000 to $29,999	$30,000 to $39,999	$40,000 to $49,999	$50,000 and over
Fats and oils	4,615	748	833	870	754	549	861
Miscellaneous foods	22,234	2,999	3,865	4,066	3,545	2,957	4,803
Frozen prepared foods	3,756	458	688	692	598	504	816
Canned and packaged soups	1,740	260	306	307	263	256	348
Potato chips, nuts, and other snacks	4,876	548	696	939	779	690	1,223
Condiments and seasonings	5,019	671	925	852	849	597	1,125
Other canned/packaged prepared foods	6,844	1,062	1,250	1,275	1,055	910	1,291
Baby food	1,318	285	221	247	213	194	158
Nonalcoholic beverages	16,653	2,417	3,085	3,067	2,541	2,038	3,505
Cola	7,504	1,060	1,352	1,457	1,110	1,011	1,513
Other carbonated drinks	2,661	360	462	419	445	316	659
Coffee	3,333	609	683	556	470	344	671
Food prepared by cu on out-of-town trips	2,517	176	257	394	442	327	921
FOOD AWAY FROM HOME	**$132,858**	**$12,194**	**$19,324**	**$23,207**	**$22,137**	**$17,096**	**$38,901**
Meals at restaurants, carry-outs, and other	**104,247**	**9,769**	**16,081**	**18,878**	**17,351**	**13,462**	**28,706**
Lunch	40,863	3,857	5,961	7,508	6,749	5,107	11,681
Dinner...	44,873	3,978	6,820	8,023	7,225	5,921	12,905
Snacks and nonalcoholic beverages	11,635	1,282	1,996	2,127	2,071	1,622	2,537
Breakfast and brunch	6,877	653	1,304	1,219	1,305	812	1,583
Board(including at school)	**3,549**	**468**	**128**	**403**	**397**	**283**	**1,868**
Catered affairs	**3,358**	**95**	**117**	**510**	**554**	**338**	**1,743**
Food on out-of-town trips	**15,889**	**1,210**	**1,826**	**2,416**	**2,771**	**2,160**	**5,507**
School lunches	**3,436**	**216**	**409**	**605**	**735**	**610**	**861**
Meals as pay	**2,379**	**435**	**762**	**394**	**330**	**242**	**215**
ALCOHOLIC BEVERAGES	**$23,012**	**$2,644**	**$3,658**	**$4,238**	**$3,747**	**$2,541**	**$6,183**
At home	**12,127**	**1,492**	**2,053**	**2,222**	**2,068**	**1,283**	**3,008**
Beer and ale	7,263	1,079	1,322	1,398	1,180	739	1,547
Whiskey	1,044	138	170	192	183	97	265
Wine	2,551	186	262	462	446	337	857
Other alcoholic beverages	1,186	90	217	170	259	111	339
Away from home	**10,885**	**1,152**	**1,605**	**2,016**	**1,680**	**1,257**	**3,176**
Beer and ale	3,054	432	460	577	438	382	764
Wine	1,512	141	243	280	204	176	468
Other alcoholic beverages	4,759	456	761	888	781	487	1,386
Alcoholic beverages purchased on trips.....................	1,560	122	141	270	257	212	557

Note: Expenditures listed for items in a given category may not add to the total for that category because the listing is incomplete. "Other dairy products," for example, includes "butter, cheese, ice cream and related products" and "miscellaneous"—"miscellaneous" is omitted here. Numbers may not add to total due to rounding. The "all cu's" aggregates will differ slightly from table to table because they are the sums of the aggregates in each row.

PART III
Spending by type of household for food and alcoholic beverages

Married couples dominate the market for food at home...

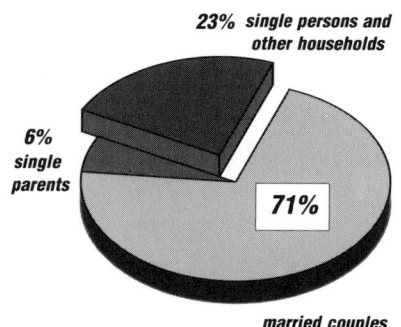

23% single persons and other households

6% single parents

71%

married couples

...and for food away from home...

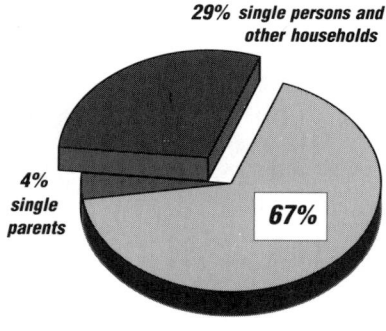

29% single persons and other households

4% single parents

67%

married couples

...and for alcohol.

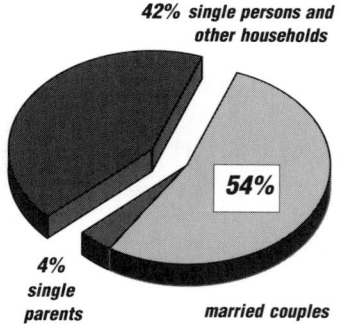

42% single persons and other households

54%

4% single parents

married couples

The food and alcohol market easily falls into two segments—married couples and everyone else. Couples spend more than average on nearly every food and beverage item. Single parents, single-person households, and "other" households* spend less than average on most foods. People who live alone and those living in "other" types of households, however, spend more than average on alcohol.

Although married couples are just 55 percent of all households, they account for fully 69 percent of the food market. This disproportionate spending is due in part to their size—an average of 3.3 people per household. Couples with children at home account for 61 percent of all food spending by married couples. Those with no children at home account for 31 percent of the market; married couples who share their home with extended family members or unrelated people are 8 percent of the market. Married couples account for a smaller share of the alcohol market—just 54 percent.

Single person and "other" households average 1.5 people and are 39 percent of all households. They account for just 26 percent of the food market but 42 percent of the alcohol market. Single-parent households have 2.9 people on average and are only 5 percent of the food market and 4 percent of the alcohol market.

Married-couple market

Married-couple households spent an average of $4,991 on food and alcohol in 1988—15 percent of their household budget. Married couples with children outspend those without children at home, $5,554 to $4,074, and this gap grows steadily with the age of the children. Food and alcohol spending peaks at $6,265 among married couples with children aged 18 or older at home.

Couples without children at home devote 44 percent of their food dollar to restaurants, take-outs, and other food prepared away from home. Married couples with children trail behind, with 41 percent of their food budget going to meals at restaurants and carry-outs.

Married couples with children spend 41 percent more than the average household on food, but they are slightly below-average spenders on alcohol. They spend at least 50 percent more than average on cereals, pastas, crackers and cookies, beef, sugar and sweets, snacks, condiments and seasonings, baby food, and colas.

On food prepared away from home, couples with children outspend the average by 36 percent. It is no surprise that they spend more than double the

*In this analysis, single-person households are grouped with "other" households. "Other" households are unrelated people living together and families that are not married-couple or single-parent families, such as siblings. Single-person households account for 72 percent of the households in this category.

average on school lunches and board. Although they are below-average spenders on alcohol consumed away from home, they spend 18 percent more than the average household on wine for at-home use, and 11 more on beer for the home.

Spending on food rises from just 9 percent above average for married couples with preschoolers, to 59 percent above average for those with children aged 18 or older at home. Households with children aged 18 or older are the biggest spenders on restaurant meals and carry-outs, with spending 65 percent above average. Couples with preschoolers or children aged 18 or older spend more than average on alcohol.

Other married couples, those with extended family members or unrelated people in the home, spend well above average on all foods except butter. They spend 21 percent more than the average household on restaurant and take-out food.

The age of the children in married-couple households helps to determine purchasing patterns. Spending on pasta, crackers, cookies, and ice cream peaks among households with school age children, for example. Spending on bread; meat, poultry, fish, and eggs; and catered affairs is highest in households with older children or with extended family members.

Other household markets

Among all household types, people who live alone and "other" households spend the smallest budget share, 14 percent, on food. They spend the largest share, 2 percent, on alcohol. The only item for which their food spending is above average is meals as pay. But these householders spend 19 percent more than average on alcohol consumed away from home, and they spend slightly more than average amounts on beer, wine, and other alcohol consumed at home.

Single parents spent $1,722 less on food in 1988 than married couples although the average size of their households was not much smaller—3.3 people in married-couple households versus 2.9 in single-parent households. Food takes the biggest bite, 16 percent, out of the budgets of single-parent households.

Single parents spend 20 percent less than the average household on food. Their spending is 10 percent below average for food prepared at home and 33 percent below average for restaurant and other food prepared away from home. They spend 38 percent less than the average household on alcohol. These households spend more than average, however, on cereal, rice, pastas, pork, milk and cream, sugar, baby food, and school lunches.

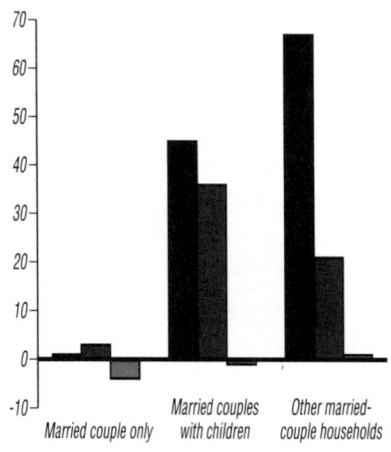

Married couples living with children or other people spend above average for food at home...

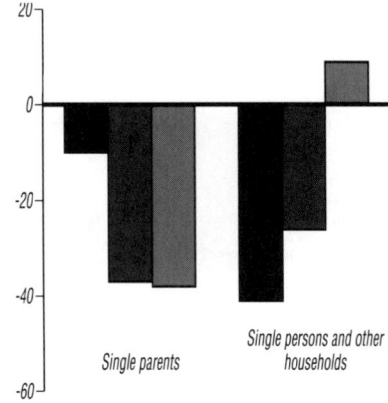

...while single persons and other households spend well below average.

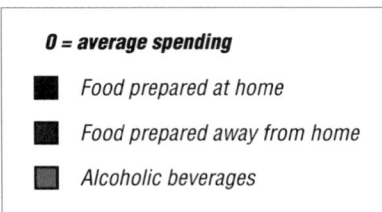

0 = average spending

■ Food prepared at home

■ Food prepared away from home

■ Alcoholic beverages

Average expenditures

	all cu's	married couples	single parents	single persons and other cu's
Number of consumer units (in thousands)	94,862	52,010	5,716	37,136
Average number of persons per cu	2.6	3.3	2.9	1.5
Average number of earners per cu	1.4	1.7	1.0	0.9
Average total before-tax income	$28,540.00	$37,299.00	$16,276.00	$18,509.00
TOTAL AVERAGE ANNUAL EXPENDITURES	$25,891.85	$32,314.50	$18,615.80	$17,950.80
FOOD, AVERAGE ANNUAL EXPENDITURES	$3,748.01	$4,727.28	$3,005.19	$2,452.28
ALCOHOLIC BEVERAGES, AVERAGE ANNUAL EXPENDITURES	$268.69	$263.31	$166.82	$292.02
FOOD AT HOME	$2,135.87	$2,760.76	$1,931.38	$1,264.95
Cereals and bakery products	312.14	406.89	290.69	178.56
Cereals and cereal products	109.34	142.35	119.64	60.10
Flour	4.65	6.14	4.02	2.60
Prepared flour mixes	9.46	12.75	8.42	4.88
Ready-to-eat and cooked cereal	72.95	94.65	81.95	40.24
Rice	7.77	10.12	8.67	4.25
Pasta, cornmeal, and other cereal products	14.50	18.71	16.57	8.12
Bakery products	202.80	264.53	171.06	118.46
Bread	64.48	81.23	57.05	41.42
Crackers and cookies	51.25	68.01	45.96	27.84
Frozen and refrigerated bakery products	13.67	18.76	11.80	6.60
Meats, poultry, fish, and eggs	551.07	710.02	511.14	327.55
Beef	182.18	241.14	169.74	98.91
Pork	109.90	141.96	113.09	63.10
Other meats	82.22	104.60	71.14	51.56
Poultry	84.17	106.81	78.29	52.35
Fish and seafood	64.98	81.84	52.38	42.54
Eggs	27.63	33.67	26.50	19.08
Dairy products	274.28	353.26	256.16	162.95
Fresh milk and cream	133.78	169.94	141.47	80.37
Other dairy products	140.50	183.32	114.68	82.58
Butter	8.63	10.74	8.32	5.63
Cheese	77.44	100.78	66.19	45.45
Ice cream and related products	40.82	54.61	29.64	22.58
Fruits and vegetables	373.08	474.86	314.02	235.03
Fresh fruits	120.63	154.55	91.44	76.08
Fresh vegetables	110.31	139.21	98.11	70.42
Processed fruits	84.87	106.91	70.22	55.26
Processed vegetables	57.27	74.19	54.25	33.28
Other food at home	625.30	815.73	559.37	360.86
Sugar and other sweets	78.16	104.06	67.66	42.34
Candy and chewing gum	44.20	60.08	33.94	22.82
Sugar	16.63	20.79	20.98	9.97

Average annual expenditures for food and alcoholic beverages, by type of consumer unit.

(continued from previous page)

	all cu's	married couples	single parents	single persons and other cu's
Fats and oils	54.52	71.88	48.17	30.41
Miscellaneous foods	263.88	345.20	255.77	147.65
Frozen prepared foods	44.18	53.37	34.26	32.42
Canned and packaged soups	21.11	26.61	20.12	13.32
Potato chips, nuts, and other snacks	58.43	78.83	50.85	30.13
Condiments and seasonings	59.67	80.08	50.47	31.60
Other canned/packaged prepared foods	80.48	106.32	100.06	40.18
Baby food	15.17	21.75	26.30	3.98
Nonalcoholic beverages	198.54	251.67	175.48	125.30
Cola	89.62	114.67	83.50	54.37
Other carbonated drinks	31.94	39.93	28.40	20.94
Coffee	40.17	49.54	28.12	28.47
Food prepared by cu on out-of-town trips	30.21	42.92	12.29	15.16
FOOD AWAY FROM HOME	**$1,612.13**	**$1,966.52**	**$1,073.81**	**$1,187.34**
Meals at restaurants, carry-outs, and other	**1,254.03**	**1,493.05**	**844.78**	**970.94**
Lunch	493.21	590.41	364.65	372.34
Dinner	549.19	656.19	336.96	426.88
Snacks and nonalcoholic beverages	131.70	159.20	106.57	95.78
Breakfast and brunch	79.93	87.24	36.60	75.94
Board(including at school)	**46.42**	**64.11**	**29.60**	**24.24**
Catered affairs	**41.03**	**60.05**	**12.06**	**18.86**
Food on out-of-town trips	**200.51**	**263.26**	**75.59**	**131.85**
School lunches	**42.97**	**64.29**	**92.40**	**5.51**
Meals as pay	**27.17**	**21.77**	**19.39**	**35.94**
ALCOHOLIC BEVERAGES	**$268.69**	**$263.31**	**$166.82**	**$292.02**
At home	**138.83**	**146.31**	**72.89**	**138.04**
Beer and ale	83.24	85.23	40.27	86.88
Whiskey	11.61	12.23	2.92	12.02
Wine	29.62	33.89	21.96	24.62
Other alcoholic beverages	**14.37**	**14.95**	**7.74**	**14.53**
Away from home	129.86	117.00	93.93	153.97
Beer and ale	36.23	31.67	24.04	44.68
Wine	18.51	16.44	15.28	21.98
Other alcoholic beverages	55.85	48.12	49.02	68.06
Alcoholic beverages purchased on trips	19.26	20.77	5.60	19.26

Note: Expenditures listed for items in a given category may not add to the total for that category because the listing is incomplete. "Other dairy products," for example, includes "butter, cheese, ice cream and related products" and "miscellaneous"—"miscellaneous" is omitted here. "Single parents" is one-parent consumer units with a child or children under age 18 living at home. "Other cu's" includes persons living with unrelated persons and families other than married-couple and single-parent families. Numbers may not add to total due to rounding.

Share of spending

	all cu's	married couples	single parents	single persons and other cu's
Number of consumer units (in thousands)	94,862	52,010	5,716	37,136
Average number of persons per cu	2.6	3.3	2.9	1.5
Average number of earners per cu	1.4	1.7	1.0	0.9
Average total before-tax income	$28,540	$37,299	$16,276	$18,509
TOTAL AVERAGE ANNUAL EXPENDITURES	100.00%	100.00%	100.00%	100.00%
FOOD, AVERAGE ANNUAL EXPENDITURES	14.48%	14.63%	16.14%	13.66%
ALCOHOLIC BEVERAGES, AVERAGE ANNUAL EXPENDITURES	1.04%	0.81%	0.90%	1.63%
FOOD AT HOME	**8.25%**	**8.54%**	**10.37%**	**7.05%**
Cereals and bakery products	**1.21**	**1.26**	**1.56**	**0.99**
Cereals and cereal products	0.42	0.44	0.64	0.33
Flour	0.02	0.02	0.02	0.01
Prepared flour mixes	0.04	0.04	0.05	0.03
Ready-to-eat and cooked cereal	0.28	0.29	0.44	0.22
Rice	0.03	0.03	0.05	0.02
Pasta, cornmeal, and other cereal products	0.06	0.06	0.09	0.05
Bakery products	0.78	0.82	0.92	0.66
Bread	0.25	0.25	0.31	0.23
Crackers and cookies	0.20	0.21	0.25	0.16
Frozen and refrigerated bakery products	0.05	0.06	0.06	0.04
Meats, poultry, fish, and eggs	**2.13**	**2.20**	**2.75**	**1.82**
Beef	0.70	0.75	0.91	0.55
Pork	0.42	0.44	0.61	0.35
Other meats	0.32	0.32	0.38	0.29
Poultry	0.33	0.33	0.42	0.29
Fish and seafood	0.25	0.25	0.28	0.24
Eggs	0.11	0.10	0.14	0.11
Dairy products	**1.06**	**1.09**	**1.38**	**0.91**
Fresh milk and cream	0.52	0.53	0.76	0.45
Other dairy products	0.54	0.57	0.62	0.46
Butter	0.03	0.03	0.04	0.03
Cheese	0.30	0.31	0.36	0.25
Ice cream and related products	0.16	0.17	0.16	0.13
Fruits and vegetables	**1.44**	**1.47**	**1.69**	**1.31**
Fresh fruits	0.47	0.48	0.49	0.42
Fresh vegetables	0.43	0.43	0.53	0.39
Processed fruits	0.33	0.33	0.38	0.31
Processed vegetables	0.22	0.23	0.29	0.19
Other food at home	**2.42**	**2.52**	**3.00**	**2.01**
Sugar and other sweets	0.30	0.32	0.36	0.24
Candy and chewing gum	0.17	0.19	0.18	0.13
Sugar	0.06	0.06	0.11	0.06

Percent of total average annual expenditures spent on food and alcoholic beverages, by type of consumer unit.

(continued from previous page)

	all cu's	married couples	single parents	single persons and other cu's
Fats and oils	0.21	0.22	0.26	0.17
Miscellaneous foods	1.02	1.07	1.37	0.82
Frozen prepared foods	0.17	0.17	0.18	0.18
Canned and packaged soups	0.08	0.08	0.11	0.07
Potato chips, nuts, and other snacks	0.23	0.24	0.27	0.17
Condiments and seasonings	0.23	0.25	0.27	0.18
Other canned/packaged prepared foods	0.31	0.33	0.54	0.22
Baby food	0.06	0.07	0.14	0.02
Nonalcoholic beverages	0.77	0.78	0.94	0.70
Cola	0.35	0.35	0.45	0.30
Other carbonated drinks	0.12	0.12	0.15	0.12
Coffee	0.16	0.15	0.15	0.16
Food prepared by cu on out-of-town trips	0.12	0.13	0.07	0.08
FOOD AWAY FROM HOME	**6.23%**	**6.09%**	**5.77%**	**6.61%**
Meals at restaurants, carry-outs, and other	**4.84**	**4.62**	**4.54**	**5.41**
Lunch	1.90	1.83	1.96	2.07
Dinner	2.12	2.03	1.81	2.38
Snacks and nonalcoholic beverages	0.51	0.49	0.57	0.53
Breakfast and brunch	0.31	0.27	0.20	0.42
Board(including at school)	**0.18**	**0.20**	**0.16**	**0.14**
Catered affairs	**0.16**	**0.19**	**0.06**	**0.11**
Food on out-of-town trips	**0.77**	**0.81**	**0.41**	**0.73**
School lunches	**0.17**	**0.20**	**0.50**	**0.03**
Meals as pay	**0.10**	**0.07**	**0.10**	**0.20**
ALCOHOLIC BEVERAGES	**1.04%**	**0.81%**	**0.90%**	**1.63%**
At home	**0.54**	**0.45**	**0.39**	**0.77**
Beer and ale	0.32	0.26	0.22	0.48
Whiskey	0.04	0.04	0.02	0.07
Wine	0.11	0.10	0.12	0.14
Other alcoholic beverages	0.06	0.05	0.04	0.08
Away from home	**0.50**	**0.36**	**0.50**	**0.86**
Beer and ale	0.14	0.10	0.13	0.25
Wine	0.07	0.05	0.08	0.12
Other alcoholic beverages	0.22	0.15	0.26	0.38
Alcoholic beverages purchased on trips	0.07	0.06	0.03	0.11

Note: Expenditures listed for items in a given category may not add to the total for that category because the listing is incomplete. "Other dairy products," for example, includes "butter, cheese, ice cream and related products" and "miscellaneous"—"miscellaneous" is omitted here. "Single parents" is one-parent consumer units with a child or children under age 18 living at home. "Other cu's" includes persons living with unrelated persons and families other than married-couple and single-parent families. Numbers may not add to total due to rounding.

Indexed expenditures

	all cu's	married couples	single parents	single persons and other cu's
Number of consumer units (in thousands)	94,862	52,010	5,716	37,136
Average number of persons per cu	2.6	3.3	2.9	1.5
Average number of earners per cu	1.4	1.7	1.0	0.9
Average total before-tax income	$28,540	$37,299	$16,276	$18,509
TOTAL AVERAGE ANNUAL EXPENDITURES	100	125	72	69
FOOD, AVERAGE ANNUAL EXPENDITURES	100	126	80	65
ALCOHOLIC BEV., AVER. ANNUAL EXPENDITURES	100	98	62	109
FOOD AT HOME	100	129	90	59
Cereals and bakery products	100	130	93	57
Cereals and cereal products	100	130	109	55
Flour	100	132	86	56
Prepared flour mixes	100	135	89	52
Ready-to-eat and cooked cereal	100	130	112	55
Rice	100	130	112	55
Pasta, cornmeal, and other cereal products	100	129	114	56
Bakery products	100	130	84	58
Bread	100	126	88	64
Crackers and cookies	100	133	90	54
Frozen and refrigerated bakery products	100	137	86	48
Meats, poultry, fish, and eggs	100	129	93	59
Beef	100	132	93	54
Pork	100	129	103	57
Other meats	100	127	87	63
Poultry	100	127	93	62
Fish and seafood	100	126	81	65
Eggs	100	122	96	69
Dairy products	100	129	93	59
Fresh milk and cream	100	127	106	60
Other dairy products	100	130	82	59
Butter	100	124	96	65
Cheese	100	130	85	59
Ice cream and related products	100	134	73	55
Fruits and vegetables	100	127	84	63
Fresh fruits	100	128	76	63
Fresh vegetables	100	126	89	64
Processed fruits	100	126	83	65
Processed vegetables	100	130	95	58
Other food at home	100	130	89	58
Sugar and other sweets	100	133	87	54
Candy and chewing gum	100	136	77	52
Sugar	100	125	126	60

Indexed average annual expenditures for food and alcoholic beverages, by type of consumer unit.

(continued from previous page)

	all cu's	married couples	single parents	single persons and other cu's
Fats and oils	100	132	88	56
Miscellaneous foods	100	131	97	56
Frozen prepared foods	100	121	78	73
Canned and packaged soups	100	126	95	63
Potato chips, nuts, and other snacks	100	135	87	52
Condiments and seasonings	100	134	85	53
Other canned/packaged prepared foods	100	132	124	50
Baby food	100	143	173	26
Nonalcoholic beverages	100	127	88	63
Cola	100	128	93	61
Other carbonated drinks	100	125	89	66
Coffee	100	123	70	71
Food prepared by cu on out-of-town trips	100	142	41	50
FOOD AWAY FROM HOME	**100**	**122**	**67**	**74**
Meals at restaurants, carry-outs, and other	**100**	**119**	**67**	**77**
Lunch	100	120	74	75
Dinner	100	119	61	78
Snacks and nonalcoholic beverages	100	121	81	73
Breakfast and brunch	100	109	46	95
Board(including at school)	**100**	**138**	**64**	**52**
Catered affairs	**100**	**146**	**29**	**46**
Food on out-of-town trips	**100**	**131**	**38**	**66**
School lunches	**100**	**150**	**215**	**13**
Meals as pay	**100**	**80**	**71**	**132**
ALCOHOLIC BEVERAGES	**100**	**98**	**62**	**109**
At home	**100**	**105**	**53**	**99**
Beer and ale	100	102	48	104
Whiskey	100	105	25	104
Wine	100	114	74	83
Other alcoholic beverages	100	104	54	101
Away from home	**100**	**90**	**72**	**119**
Beer and ale	100	87	66	123
Wine	100	89	83	119
Other alcoholic beverages	100	86	88	122
Alcoholic beverages purchased on trips	100	108	29	100

Note: An index of 100 represents the average for all consumer units. An index of 132 means that the average for the subgroup is 32 percent above the average for all consumer units. An index of 68 indicates spending that is 32 percent below the overall average. "Single parents" are one-parent consumer units with a child or children under age 18 living at home. "Other cu's" include persons living with unrelated persons and families other than married-couple and single-parent families. Numbers may not add to total due to rounding.

Aggregate expenditures, 1988

Aggregate expenditures in 1988 for food and alcoholic beverages, by type of consumer unit.

	all cu's	married couples	single parents	single persons and other cu's
Number of consumer units (in thousands)	94,862	52,010	5,716	37,136
Average number of persons per cu	2.6	3.3	2.9	1.5
Average number of earners per cu	1.4	1.7	1.0	0.9
Aggregate before-tax income (in millions)	$2,720,305	$1,939,921	$93,034	$687,350
TOTAL AGGREGATE EXPENDITURES (in millions)	$2,453,706	$1,680,677	$106,408	$666,621
FOOD, AGGREGATE EXPENDITURES (in millions)	$354,111	$245,866	$17,178	$91,068
ALCOHOLIC BEV., AGG. EXPENDITURES (in millions)	$25,493	$13,695	$954	$10,844
FOOD AT HOME	**$201,602**	**$143,587**	**$11,040**	**$46,975**
Cereals and bakery products	29,455	21,162	1,662	6,631
Cereals and cereal products	10,319	7,404	684	2,232
Flour	439	319	23	97
Prepared flour mixes	892	663	48	181
Ready-to-eat and cooked cereal	6,886	4,923	468	1,494
Rice	734	526	50	158
Pasta, cornmeal, and other cereal products	1,369	973	95	302
Bakery products	19,135	13,758	978	4,399
Bread	6,089	4,225	326	1,538
Crackers and cookies	4,834	3,537	263	1,034
Frozen and refrigerated bakery products	1,288	976	67	245
Meats, poultry, fish, and eggs	52,014	36,928	2,922	12,164
Beef	17,185	12,542	970	3,673
Pork	10,373	7,383	646	2,343
Other meats	7,762	5,440	407	1,915
Poultry	7,947	5,555	448	1,944
Fish and seafood	6,136	4,256	299	1,580
Eggs	2,611	1,751	151	709
Dairy products	25,889	18,373	1,464	6,051
Fresh milk and cream	12,632	8,839	809	2,985
Other dairy products	13,257	9,534	656	3,067
Butter	815	559	48	209
Cheese	7,308	5,242	378	1,688
Ice cream and related products	3,848	2,840	169	839
Fruits and vegetables	35,220	24,697	1,795	8,728
Fresh fruits	11,386	8,038	523	2,825
Fresh vegetables	10,416	7,240	561	2,615
Processed fruits	8,014	5,560	401	2,052
Processed vegetables	5,405	3,859	310	1,236
Other food at home	59,024	42,426	3,197	13,401
Sugar and other sweets	7,371	5,412	387	1,572
Candy and chewing gum	4,166	3,125	194	847
Sugar	1,571	1,081	120	370

Aggregate expenditures in 1988 for food and alcoholic beverages, by type of consumer unit.

(continued from previous page)

	all cu's	married couples	single parents	single persons and other cu's
Fats and oils	5,143	3,738	275	1,129
Miscellaneous foods	24,899	17,954	1,462	5,483
Frozen prepared foods	4,176	2,776	196	1,204
Canned and packaged soups	1,994	1,384	115	495
Potato chips, nuts, and other snacks	5,510	4,100	291	1,119
Condiments and seasonings	5,627	4,165	288	1,173
Other canned/packaged prepared foods	7,594	5,530	572	1,492
Baby food	1,429	1,131	150	148
Nonalcoholic beverages	18,746	13,089	1,003	4,653
Cola	8,460	5,964	477	2,019
Other carbonated drinks	3,017	2,077	162	778
Coffee	3,795	2,577	161	1,057
Food prepared by cu on out-of-town trips	2,866	2,232	70	563
FOOD AWAY FROM HOME	**$152,510**	**$102,279**	**$6,138**	**$44,093**
Meals at restaurants, carry-outs, and other	**118,539**	**77,654**	**4,829**	**36,057**
Lunch	46,619	30,707	2,084	13,827
Dinner	51,907	34,128	1,926	15,853
Snacks and nonalcoholic beverages	12,446	8,280	609	3,557
Breakfast and brunch	7,567	4,537	209	2,820
Board(including at school)	**4,404**	**3,334**	**169**	**900**
Catered affairs	**3,893**	**3,123**	**69**	**700**
Food on out-of-town trips	**19,021**	**13,692**	**432**	**4,896**
School lunches	**4,077**	**3,344**	**528**	**205**
Meals as pay	**2,578**	**1,132**	**111**	**1,335**
ALCOHOLIC BEVERAGES	**$25,493**	**$13,695**	**$954**	**$10,844**
At home	**13,152**	**7,610**	**417**	**5,126**
Beer and ale	7,889	4,433	230	3,226
Whiskey	1,099	636	17	446
Wine	2,802	1,763	126	914
Other alcoholic beverages	1,361	778	44	540
Away from home	**12,340**	**6,085**	**537**	**5,718**
Beer and ale	3,444	1,647	137	1,659
Wine	1,759	855	87	816
Other alcoholic beverages	5,310	2,503	280	2,527
Alcoholic beverages purchased on trips	1,827	1,080	32	715

Note: Expenditures listed for items in a given category may not add to the total for that category because the listing is incomplete. "Other dairy products," for example, includes "butter, cheese, ice cream and related products" and "miscellaneous"—"miscellaneous" is omitted here. "Single parents" are one-parent consumer units with a child or children under age 18 living at home. "Other cu's" include persons living with unrelated persons and families other than married-couple and single-parent families. The "all cu's" aggregates will differ slightly from table to table because they are the sums of the aggregates in each row. Numbers may not add to total due to rounding.

Average expenditures

	all cu's	all married couples	married couple only	all married couples with children	AGE OF OLDEST CHILD			other married couples
					under 6	6 to 17	18 or older	
Number of consumer units (in thousands)	94,862	52,010	20,227	28,100	5,858	14,194	8,047	3,684
Average number of persons per cu	2.6	3.3	2.0	3.9	3.5	4.1	3.9	5.1
Average number of earners per cu	1.4	1.7	1.2	2.1	1.7	1.9	2.7	2.4
Average total before-tax income	$28,540.00	$37,299.00	$33,825.00	$39,354.00	$34,318.00	$38,039.00	$45,596.00	$40,846.00
TOTAL AVERAGE ANNUAL EXPENDITURES	$25,891.85	$32,314.50	$27,954.50	$35,015.30	$30,942.80	$35,248.40	$37,763.90	$35,739.60
FOOD, AVERAGE ANNUAL EXPENDITURES	$3,748.01	$4,727.28	$3,814.69	$5,288.83	$4,077.07	$5,473.27	$5,965.93	$5,512.90
ALCOHOLIC BEV., AVER. ANNUAL EXPEND.	$268.69	$263.31	$259.12	$265.27	$292.97	$244.08	$299.10	$271.84
FOOD AT HOME	$2,135.87	$2,760.76	$2,147.95	$3,104.15	$2,515.72	$3,268.02	$3,313.10	$3,563.55
Cereals and bakery products	312.14	406.89	302.24	467.42	346.45	514.69	483.96	528.88
Cereals and cereal products	109.34	142.35	99.57	164.29	125.72	186.20	155.98	214.74
Flour	4.65	6.14	5.15	5.76	4.97	4.91	8.16	14.94
Prepared flour mixes	9.46	12.75	10.57	13.77	11.85	15.81	11.48	17.16
Ready-to-eat and cooked cereal	72.95	94.65	64.67	111.13	82.14	126.19	107.65	136.48
Rice	7.77	10.12	6.27	11.35	10.92	13.32	7.82	22.58
Pasta, cornmeal, and other cereal products	14.50	18.71	12.92	22.29	15.84	25.96	20.87	23.59
Bakery products	202.80	264.53	202.67	303.13	220.73	328.49	327.98	314.13
Bread	64.48	81.23	64.01	90.91	65.36	94.93	106.27	103.47
Crackers and cookies	51.25	68.01	52.04	78.09	59.14	86.61	78.46	79.85
Frozen and refrigerated bakery products	13.67	18.76	15.09	20.67	17.04	22.03	21.26	24.72
Meats, poultry, fish, and eggs	551.07	710.02	558.31	792.09	595.45	813.45	929.23	932.50
Beef	182.18	241.14	180.84	277.54	216.83	275.77	336.49	299.20
Pork	109.90	141.96	121.18	151.58	97.13	163.18	178.26	185.41
Other meats	82.22	104.60	76.77	122.19	85.89	133.43	133.01	125.08
Poultry	84.17	106.81	84.20	117.63	94.31	118.16	137.87	151.39
Fish and seafood	64.98	81.84	71.23	85.34	72.28	83.13	101.64	115.37
Eggs	27.63	33.67	24.09	37.82	29.02	39.78	41.96	56.05
Dairy products	274.28	353.26	265.51	403.88	340.46	431.14	407.62	456.63
Fresh milk and cream	133.78	169.94	119.59	196.79	169.02	208.76	198.36	246.93
Other dairy products	140.50	183.32	145.93	207.09	171.44	222.37	209.26	209.70
Butter	8.63	10.74	9.17	12.25	10.39	13.53	11.42	7.72
Cheese	77.44	100.78	77.42	115.49	101.54	121.76	115.79	118.40
Ice cream and related products	40.82	54.61	45.28	60.90	42.25	67.18	65.45	58.33
Fruits and vegetables	373.08	474.86	413.37	499.60	427.42	509.29	546.26	633.34
Fresh fruits	120.63	154.55	142.65	159.55	128.85	162.22	182.28	183.51
Fresh vegetables	110.31	139.21	125.76	144.09	120.08	145.36	163.50	178.12
Processed fruits	84.87	106.91	84.99	115.39	104.83	118.74	118.38	166.09
Processed vegetables	57.27	74.19	59.98	80.57	73.66	82.97	82.10	105.63
Other food at home	625.30	815.73	608.52	941.16	805.94	999.46	946.02	1,012.20
Sugar and other sweets	78.16	104.06	74.10	121.29	90.95	136.06	119.64	139.84
Candy and chewing gum	44.20	60.08	39.73	73.30	54.12	82.74	72.04	72.21
Sugar	16.63	20.79	15.36	22.95	17.22	26.19	21.74	35.00

Average annual expenditures for food and alcoholic beverages, by married couples with and without children.

(continued from previous page)

	all cu's	all married couples	married couple only	all married couples with children	AGE OF OLDEST CHILD			other married couples
					under 6	6 to 17	18 or older	
Fats and oils	54.52	71.88	59.78	77.40	58.04	82.53	84.87	97.84
Miscellaneous foods	263.88	345.20	246.53	407.61	414.17	427.84	361.41	417.42
Frozen prepared foods	44.18	53.37	43.60	59.87	49.06	67.61	54.36	57.90
Canned and packaged soups	21.11	26.61	20.45	29.57	24.58	32.22	28.86	38.65
Potato chips, nuts, and other snacks	58.43	78.83	57.48	93.77	69.03	108.44	87.19	82.96
Condiments and seasonings	59.67	80.08	62.10	91.53	73.44	100.18	90.87	92.58
Other canned/packaged prepared foods	80.48	106.32	62.91	132.87	198.05	119.39	100.13	145.34
Baby food	15.17	21.75	2.29	36.26	114.18	14.42	8.51	18.31
Nonalcoholic beverages	198.54	251.67	187.81	290.70	211.03	311.07	322.99	309.30
Cola	89.62	114.67	74.14	141.06	108.05	146.91	159.57	138.25
Other carbonated drinks	31.94	39.93	28.80	47.40	35.58	49.11	54.81	44.62
Coffee	40.17	49.54	52.00	46.87	28.05	49.17	59.49	56.61
Food prepared by cu on out-of-town trips	30.21	42.92	40.30	44.16	31.75	41.95	57.11	47.80
FOOD AWAY FROM HOME	**$1,612.13**	**$1,966.52**	**$1,666.74**	**$2,184.68**	**$1,561.35**	**$2,205.25**	**$2,652.83**	**$1,949.35**
Meals at restaurants, carry-outs, and other	**1,254.03**	**1,493.05**	**1,288.13**	**1,654.25**	**1,343.23**	**1,685.47**	**1,876.27**	**1,389.55**
Lunch	493.21	590.41	462.89	680.57	534.64	708.52	758.29	607.56
Dinner	549.19	656.19	632.81	689.75	568.77	668.96	841.58	522.65
Snacks and nonalcoholic beverages	131.70	159.20	107.25	196.07	167.56	218.67	177.20	165.08
Breakfast and brunch	79.93	87.24	85.18	87.86	72.27	89.33	99.19	94.27
Board(including at school)	**46.42**	**64.11**	**23.44**	**97.12**	**4.62**	**51.62**	**244.69**	**35.62**
Catered affairs	**41.03**	**60.05**	**60.79**	**49.24**	**10.72**	**9.52**	**147.34**	**138.43**
Food on out-of-town trips	**200.51**	**263.26**	**280.66**	**245.41**	**143.67**	**256.55**	**299.81**	**303.82**
School lunches	**42.97**	**64.29**	**-**	**110.45**	**7.00**	**179.58**	**63.74**	**64.86**
Meals as pay	**27.17**	**21.77**	**13.64**	**28.23**	**52.10**	**22.50**	**20.98**	**17.06**
ALCOHOLIC BEVERAGES	**$268.69**	**$263.31**	**$259.12**	**$265.27**	**$292.97**	**$244.08**	**$299.10**	**$271.84**
At home	**138.83**	**146.31**	**140.33**	**149.54**	**163.65**	**140.71**	**154.20**	**155.14**
Beer and ale	83.24	85.23	72.48	92.21	101.80	82.87	102.01	103.25
Whiskey	11.61	12.23	15.83	9.90	5.11	12.84	8.45	10.05
Wine	29.62	33.89	33.61	34.94	44.74	33.81	28.24	27.15
Other alcoholic beverages	14.37	14.95	18.41	12.48	11.99	11.18	15.50	14.68
Away from home	**129.86**	**117.00**	**118.79**	**115.73**	**109.32**	**103.37**	**144.90**	**116.70**
Beer and ale	36.23	31.67	29.02	33.86	42.29	27.68	38.42	29.52
Wine	18.51	16.44	16.77	16.04	15.41	14.56	19.55	17.81
Other alcoholic beverages	55.85	48.12	49.06	47.93	39.50	44.01	63.40	44.23
Alcoholic beverages purchased on trips	19.26	20.77	23.94	17.91	12.12	17.11	23.53	25.15

Note: Expenditures listed for items in a given category may not add to the total for that category because the listing is incomplete. "Other dairy products," for example, includes "butter, cheese, ice cream and related products" and "miscellaneous"—"miscellaneous" is omitted here. Expenditures are not given (-) when the amount is too small to be reliable. Numbers may not add to total due to rounding. Other married couples include extended family members or unrelated persons in addition to the married couple.

Share of spending

Percent of total average annual expenditures spent on food and alcoholic beverages, by married couples with and without children.

	all cu's	all married couples	married couple only	all married couples with children	AGE OF OLDEST CHILD			other married couples
					under 6	6 to 17	18 or older	
Number of consumer units (in thousands)	94,862	52,010	20,227	28,100	5,858	14,194	8,047	3,684
Average number of persons per cu	2.6	3.3	2.0	3.9	3.5	4.1	3.9	5.1
Average number of earners per cu	1.4	1.7	1.2	2.1	1.7	1.9	2.7	2.4
Average total before-tax income	$28,540	$37,299	$33,825	$39,354	$34,318	$38,039	$45,596	$40,846
TOTAL AVERAGE ANNUAL EXPENDITURES	100.00%	100.00%	100.00%	100.00%	100.00%	100.00%	100.00%	100.00%
FOOD, AVERAGE ANNUAL EXPENDITURES	14.48%	14.63%	13.65%	15.10%	13.18%	15.53%	15.80%	15.43%
ALCOHOLIC BEV., AVER. ANNUAL EXPEND.	1.04%	0.81%	0.93%	0.76%	0.95%	0.69%	0.79%	0.76%
FOOD AT HOME	8.25%	8.54%	7.68%	8.87%	8.13%	9.27%	8.77%	9.97%
Cereals and bakery products	1.21	1.26	1.08	1.33	1.12	1.46	1.28	1.48
Cereals and cereal products	0.42	0.44	0.36	0.47	0.41	0.53	0.41	0.60
Flour	0.02	0.02	0.02	0.02	0.02	0.01	0.02	0.04
Prepared flour mixes	0.04	0.04	0.04	0.04	0.04	0.04	0.03	0.05
Ready-to-eat and cooked cereal	0.28	0.29	0.23	0.32	0.27	0.36	0.29	0.38
Rice	0.03	0.03	0.02	0.03	0.04	0.04	0.02	0.06
Pasta, cornmeal, and other cereal products	0.06	0.06	0.05	0.06	0.05	0.07	0.06	0.07
Bakery products	0.78	0.82	0.72	0.87	0.71	0.93	0.87	0.88
Bread	0.25	0.25	0.23	0.26	0.21	0.27	0.28	0.29
Crackers and cookies	0.20	0.21	0.19	0.22	0.19	0.25	0.21	0.22
Frozen and refrigerated bakery products	0.05	0.06	0.05	0.06	0.06	0.06	0.06	0.07
Meats, poultry, fish, and eggs	2.13	2.20	2.00	2.26	1.92	2.31	2.46	2.61
Beef	0.70	0.75	0.65	0.79	0.70	0.78	0.89	0.84
Pork	0.42	0.44	0.43	0.43	0.31	0.46	0.47	0.52
Other meats	0.32	0.32	0.27	0.35	0.28	0.38	0.35	0.35
Poultry	0.33	0.33	0.30	0.34	0.30	0.34	0.37	0.42
Fish and seafood	0.25	0.25	0.25	0.24	0.23	0.24	0.27	0.32
Eggs	0.11	0.10	0.09	0.11	0.09	0.11	0.11	0.16
Dairy products	1.06	1.09	0.95	1.15	1.10	1.22	1.08	1.28
Fresh milk and cream	0.52	0.53	0.43	0.56	0.55	0.59	0.53	0.69
Other dairy products	0.54	0.57	0.52	0.59	0.55	0.63	0.55	0.59
Butter	0.03	0.03	0.03	0.03	0.03	0.04	0.03	0.02
Cheese	0.30	0.31	0.28	0.33	0.33	0.35	0.31	0.33
Ice cream and related products	0.16	0.17	0.16	0.17	0.14	0.19	0.17	0.16
Fruits and vegetables	1.44	1.47	1.48	1.43	1.38	1.44	1.45	1.77
Fresh fruits	0.47	0.48	0.51	0.46	0.42	0.46	0.48	0.51
Fresh vegetables	0.43	0.43	0.45	0.41	0.39	0.41	0.43	0.50
Processed fruits	0.33	0.33	0.30	0.33	0.34	0.34	0.31	0.46
Processed vegetables	0.22	0.23	0.21	0.23	0.24	0.24	0.22	0.30
Other food at home	2.42	2.52	2.18	2.69	2.60	2.84	2.51	2.83
Sugar and other sweets	0.30	0.32	0.27	0.35	0.29	0.39	0.32	0.39
Candy and chewing gum	0.17	0.19	0.14	0.21	0.17	0.23	0.19	0.20
Sugar	0.06	0.06	0.05	0.07	0.06	0.07	0.06	0.10

Percent of total average annual expenditures spent on food and alcoholic beverages, by married couples with and without children.

(continued from previous page)	all cu's	all married couples	married couple only	all married couples with children	AGE OF OLDEST CHILD			other married couples
					under 6	6 to 17	18 or older	
Fats and oils	0.21	0.22	0.21	0.22	0.19	0.23	0.22	0.27
Miscellaneous foods	1.02	1.07	0.88	1.16	1.34	1.21	0.96	1.17
Frozen prepared foods	0.17	0.17	0.16	0.17	0.16	0.19	0.14	0.16
Canned and packaged soups	0.08	0.08	0.07	0.08	0.08	0.09	0.08	0.11
Potato chips, nuts, and other snacks	0.23	0.24	0.21	0.27	0.22	0.31	0.23	0.23
Condiments and seasonings	0.23	0.25	0.22	0.26	0.24	0.28	0.24	0.26
Other canned/packaged prepared foods	0.31	0.33	0.23	0.38	0.64	0.34	0.27	0.41
Baby food	0.06	0.07	0.01	0.10	0.37	0.04	0.02	0.05
Nonalcoholic beverages	0.77	0.78	0.67	0.83	0.68	0.88	0.86	0.87
Cola	0.35	0.35	0.27	0.40	0.35	0.42	0.42	0.39
Other carbonated drinks	0.12	0.12	0.10	0.14	0.11	0.14	0.15	0.12
Coffee	0.16	0.15	0.19	0.13	0.09	0.14	0.16	0.16
Food prepared by cu on out-of-town trips	0.12	0.13	0.14	0.13	0.10	0.12	0.15	0.13
FOOD AWAY FROM HOME	**6.23%**	**6.09%**	**5.96%**	**6.24%**	**5.05%**	**6.26%**	**7.02%**	**5.45%**
Meals at restaurants, carry-outs, and other	**4.84**	**4.62**	**4.61**	**4.72**	**4.34**	**4.78**	**4.97**	**3.89**
Lunch	1.90	1.83	1.66	1.94	1.73	2.01	2.01	1.70
Dinner	2.12	2.03	2.26	1.97	1.84	1.90	2.23	1.46
Snacks and nonalcoholic beverages	0.51	0.49	0.38	0.56	0.54	0.62	0.47	0.46
Breakfast and brunch	0.31	0.27	0.30	0.25	0.23	0.25	0.26	0.26
Board(including at school)	**0.18**	**0.20**	**0.08**	**0.28**	**0.01**	**0.15**	**0.65**	**0.10**
Catered affairs	**0.16**	**0.19**	**0.22**	**0.14**	**0.03**	**0.03**	**0.39**	**0.39**
Food on out-of-town trips	**0.77**	**0.81**	**1.00**	**0.70**	**0.46**	**0.73**	**0.79**	**0.85**
School lunches	**0.17**	**0.20**	**-**	**0.32**	**0.02**	**0.51**	**0.17**	**0.18**
Meals as pay	**0.10**	**0.07**	**0.05**	**0.08**	**0.17**	**0.06**	**0.06**	**0.05**
ALCOHOLIC BEVERAGES	**1.04%**	**0.81%**	**0.93%**	**0.76%**	**0.95%**	**0.69%**	**0.79%**	**0.76%**
At home	**0.54**	**0.45**	**0.50**	**0.43**	**0.53**	**0.40**	**0.41**	**0.43**
Beer and ale	0.32	0.26	0.26	0.26	0.33	0.24	0.27	0.29
Whiskey	0.04	0.04	0.06	0.03	0.02	0.04	0.02	0.03
Wine	0.11	0.10	0.12	0.10	0.14	0.10	0.07	0.08
Other alcoholic beverages	0.06	0.05	0.07	0.04	0.04	0.03	0.04	0.04
Away from home	**0.50**	**0.36**	**0.42**	**0.33**	**0.35**	**0.29**	**0.38**	**0.33**
Beer and ale	0.14	0.10	0.10	0.10	0.14	0.08	0.10	0.08
Wine	0.07	0.05	0.06	0.05	0.05	0.04	0.05	0.05
Other alcoholic beverages	0.22	0.15	0.18	0.14	0.13	0.12	0.17	0.12
Alcoholic beverages purchased on trips	0.07	0.06	0.09	0.05	0.04	0.05	0.06	0.07

Note: Expenditures listed for items in a given category may not add to the total for that category because the listing is incomplete. "Other dairy products," for example, includes "butter, cheese, ice cream and related products" and "miscellaneous"—"miscellaneous" is omitted here. Other married couples include extended family members or unrelated persons in addition to the married couple. Numbers may not add to total due to rounding.

Indexed expenditures

Indexed average annual expenditures for food and alcoholic beverages, by married couples with and without children.								
	all cu's	all married couples	married couple only	all married couples with children	AGE OF OLDEST CHILD			other married couples
					under 6	6 to 17	18 or older	
Number of consumer units (in thousands)	94,862	52,010	20,227	28,100	5,858	14,194	8,047	3,684
Average number of persons per cu	2.6	3.3	2.0	3.9	3.5	4.1	3.9	5.1
Average number of earners per cu	1.4	1.7	1.2	2.1	1.7	1.9	2.7	2.4
Average total before-tax income	$28,540	$37,299	$33,825	$39,354	$34,318	$38,039	$45,596	$40,846
TOTAL AVERAGE ANNUAL EXPENDITURES	100	125	108	135	120	136	146	138
FOOD, AVERAGE ANNUAL EXPENDITURES	100	126	102	141	109	146	159	147
ALCOHOLIC BEV., AVER. ANNUAL EXPEND.	100	98	96	99	109	91	111	101
FOOD AT HOME	100	129	101	145	118	153	155	167
Cereals and bakery products	100	130	97	150	111	165	155	169
Cereals and cereal products	100	130	91	150	115	170	143	196
Flour	100	132	111	124	107	106	175	321
Prepared flour mixes	100	135	112	146	125	167	121	181
Ready-to-eat and cooked cereal	100	130	89	152	113	173	148	187
Rice	100	130	81	146	141	171	101	291
Pasta, cornmeal, and other cereal products	100	129	89	154	109	179	144	163
Bakery products	100	130	100	149	109	162	162	155
Bread	100	126	99	141	101	147	165	160
Crackers and cookies	100	133	102	152	115	169	153	156
Frozen and refrigerated bakery products	100	137	110	151	125	161	156	181
Meats, poultry, fish, and eggs	100	129	101	144	108	148	169	169
Beef	100	132	99	152	119	151	185	164
Pork	100	129	110	138	88	148	162	169
Other meats	100	127	93	149	104	162	162	152
Poultry	100	127	100	140	112	140	164	180
Fish and seafood	100	126	110	131	111	128	156	178
Eggs	100	122	87	137	105	144	152	203
Dairy products	100	129	97	147	124	157	149	166
Fresh milk and cream	100	127	89	147	126	156	148	185
Other dairy products	100	130	104	147	122	158	149	149
Butter	100	124	106	142	120	157	132	89
Cheese	100	130	100	149	131	157	150	153
Ice cream and related products	100	134	111	149	104	165	160	143
Fruits and vegetables	100	127	111	134	115	137	146	170
Fresh fruits	100	128	118	132	107	134	151	152
Fresh vegetables	100	126	114	131	109	132	148	161
Processed fruits	100	126	100	136	124	140	139	196
Processed vegetables	100	130	105	141	129	145	143	184
Other food at home	100	130	97	151	129	160	151	162
Sugar and other sweets	100	133	95	155	116	174	153	179
Candy and chewing gum	100	136	90	166	122	187	163	163
Sugar	100	125	92	138	104	157	131	210

Indexed average annual expenditures for food and alcoholic beverages, by married couples with and without children.

(continued from previous page)

	all cu's	all married couples	married couple only	all married couples with children	AGE OF OLDEST CHILD			other married couples
					under 6	6 to 17	18 or older	
Fats and oils	100	132	110	142	106	151	156	179
Miscellaneous foods	100	131	93	154	157	162	137	158
Frozen prepared foods	100	121	99	136	111	153	123	131
Canned and packaged soups	100	126	97	140	116	153	137	183
Potato chips, nuts, and other snacks	100	135	98	160	118	186	149	142
Condiments and seasonings	100	134	104	153	123	168	152	155
Other canned/packaged prepared foods	100	132	78	165	246	148	124	181
Baby food	100	143	15	239	753	95	56	121
Nonalcoholic beverages	100	127	95	146	106	157	163	156
Cola	100	128	83	157	121	164	178	154
Other carbonated drinks	100	125	90	148	111	154	172	140
Coffee	100	123	129	117	70	122	148	141
Food prepared by cu on out-of-town trips	100	142	133	146	105	139	189	158
FOOD AWAY FROM HOME	**100**	**122**	**103**	**136**	**97**	**137**	**165**	**121**
Meals at restaurants, carry-outs, and other	**100**	**119**	**103**	**132**	**107**	**134**	**150**	**111**
Lunch	100	120	94	138	108	144	154	123
Dinner	100	119	115	126	104	122	153	95
Snacks and nonalcoholic beverages	100	121	81	149	127	166	135	125
Breakfast and brunch	100	109	107	110	90	112	124	118
Board(including at school)	**100**	**138**	**50**	**209**	**10**	**111**	**527**	**77**
Catered affairs	**100**	**146**	**148**	**120**	**26**	**23**	**359**	**337**
Food on out-of-town trips	**100**	**131**	**140**	**122**	**72**	**128**	**150**	**152**
School lunches	**100**	**150**	**-**	**257**	**16**	**418**	**148**	**151**
Meals as pay	**100**	**80**	**50**	**104**	**192**	**83**	**77**	**63**
ALCOHOLIC BEVERAGES	**100**	**98**	**96**	**99**	**109**	**91**	**111**	**101**
At home	**100**	**105**	**101**	**108**	**118**	**101**	**111**	**112**
Beer and ale	100	102	87	111	122	100	123	124
Whiskey	100	105	136	85	44	111	73	87
Wine	100	114	113	118	151	114	95	92
Other alcoholic beverages	100	104	128	87	83	78	108	102
Away from home	**100**	**90**	**91**	**89**	**84**	**80**	**112**	**90**
Beer and ale	100	87	80	93	117	76	106	81
Wine	100	89	91	87	83	79	106	96
Other alcoholic beverages	100	86	88	86	71	79	114	79
Alcoholic beverages purchased on trips...........	100	108	124	93	63	89	122	131

Note: An index of 100 represents the average for all consumer units. An index of 132 means that the average for the subgroup is 32 percent above the average for all consumer units. An index of 68 indicates spending that is 32 percent below the overall average. Expenditures are not given (-) when the amount is too small to be reliable. Other married couples include extended family members or unrelated persons in addition to the married couple.

Aggregate expenditures, 1988

	all cu's	all married couples	married couple only	all married couples with children	AGE OF OLDEST CHILD			other married couples
					under 6	6 to 17	18 or older	
Number of consumer units (in thousands)	94,862	52,010	20,227	28,100	5,858	14,194	8,047	3,684
Average number of persons per cu	2.6	3.3	2.0	3.9	3.5	4.1	3.9	5.1
Average number of earners per cu	1.4	1.7	1.2	2.1	1.7	1.9	2.7	2.4
Aggregate before-tax income (in millions)	$2,722,910	$1,942,526	$684,178	$1,107,871	$201,035	$539,926	$366,911	$150,477
TOTAL AGG. EXPENDITURES (in millions)	$2,455,594	$1,682,565	$565,436	$985,465	$181,263	$500,316	$303,886	$131,665
FOOD, AGG. EXPENDITURES (in millions)	$355,294	$247,048	$77,160	$149,579	$23,883	$77,688	$48,008	$20,310
ALCOHOLIC BEV., AGG. EXPEND. (in millions)	$25,628	$13,830	$5,241	$7,588	$1,716	$3,464	$2,407	$1,001
FOOD AT HOME	$202,374	$144,359	$43,447	$87,784	$14,737	$46,386	$26,661	$13,128
Cereals and bakery products	29,584	21,291	6,113	13,229	2,030	7,306	3,894	1,948
Cereals and cereal products	10,355	7,440	2,014	4,635	736	2,643	1,255	791
Flour	443	324	104	164	29	70	66	55
Prepared flour mixes	893	663	214	386	69	224	92	63
Ready-to-eat and cooked cereal	6,912	4,949	1,308	3,139	481	1,791	866	503
Rice	733	526	127	316	64	189	63	83
Pasta, cornmeal, and other cereal products	1,374	977	261	629	93	368	168	87
Bakery products	19,228	13,852	4,099	8,595	1,293	4,663	2,639	1,157
Bread	6,126	4,261	1,295	2,585	383	1,347	855	381
Crackers and cookies	4,851	3,554	1,053	2,207	346	1,229	631	294
Frozen and refrigerated bakery products	1,292	980	305	584	100	313	171	91
Meats, poultry, fish, and eggs	52,326	37,240	11,293	22,512	3,488	11,546	7,478	3,435
Beef	17,296	12,652	3,658	7,892	1,270	3,914	2,708	1,102
Pork	10,443	7,454	2,451	4,320	569	2,316	1,434	683
Other meats	7,802	5,481	1,553	3,467	503	1,894	1,070	461
Poultry	7,991	5,600	1,703	3,339	552	1,677	1,109	558
Fish and seafood	6,166	4,287	1,441	2,421	423	1,180	818	425
Eggs	2,626	1,766	487	1,072	170	565	338	206
Dairy products	25,962	18,447	5,370	11,394	1,994	6,120	3,280	1,682
Fresh milk and cream	12,671	8,878	2,419	5,549	990	2,963	1,596	910
Other dairy products	13,291	9,569	2,952	5,845	1,004	3,156	1,684	773
Butter	815	559	185	345	61	192	92	28
Cheese	7,323	5,257	1,566	3,255	595	1,728	932	436
Ice cream and related products	3,866	2,858	916	1,728	248	954	527	215
Fruits and vegetables	35,346	24,823	8,361	14,128	2,504	7,229	4,396	2,333
Fresh fruits	11,434	8,086	2,885	4,524	755	2,303	1,467	676
Fresh vegetables	10,458	7,282	2,544	4,082	703	2,063	1,316	656
Processed fruits	8,037	5,583	1,719	3,252	614	1,685	953	612
Processed vegetables	5,418	3,872	1,213	2,270	432	1,178	661	389
Other food at home	59,156	42,558	12,309	26,520	4,721	14,186	7,613	3,729
Sugar and other sweets	7,400	5,441	1,499	3,427	533	1,931	963	515
Candy and chewing gum	4,182	3,141	804	2,071	317	1,174	580	266
Sugar	1,577	1,087	311	648	101	372	175	129

Aggregate expenditures in 1988 for food and alcoholic beverages, by married couples with and without children.

(continued from previous page)

	all cu's	all married couples	married couple only	all married couples with children	AGE OF OLDEST CHILD			other married couples
					under 6	6 to 17	18 or older	
Fats and oils	5,169	3,764	1,209	2,194	340	1,171	683	360
Miscellaneous foods	24,877	17,932	4,987	11,407	2,426	6,073	2,908	1,538
Frozen prepared foods	4,179	2,780	882	1,684	287	960	437	213
Canned and packaged soups	1,999	1,390	414	834	144	457	232	142
Potato chips, nuts, and other snacks	5,523	4,113	1,163	2,645	404	1,539	702	306
Condiments and seasonings	5,643	4,181	1,256	2,583	430	1,422	731	341
Other canned/packaged prepared foods	7,533	5,468	1,272	3,661	1,160	1,695	806	535
Baby food	1,354	1,056	46	942	669	205	68	67
Nonalcoholic beverages	18,845	13,189	3,799	8,251	1,236	4,415	2,599	1,139
Cola	8,508	6,011	1,500	4,002	633	2,085	1,284	509
Other carbonated drinks	3,033	2,093	583	1,347	208	697	441	164
Coffee	3,819	2,601	1,052	1,341	164	698	479	209
Food prepared by cu on out-of-town trips	2,865	2,232	815	1,241	186	595	460	176
FOOD AWAY FROM HOME	**$152,921**	**$102,690**	**$33,713**	**$61,795**	**$9,146**	**$31,301**	**$21,347**	**$7,181**
Meals at restaurants, carry-outs, and other	**118,950**	**78,065**	**26,055**	**46,891**	**7,869**	**23,924**	**15,098**	**5,119**
Lunch	46,803	30,892	9,363	19,291	3,132	10,057	6,102	2,238
Dinner	52,103	34,325	12,800	19,599	3,332	9,495	6,772	1,925
Snacks and nonalcoholic beverages	12,455	8,289	2,169	5,511	982	3,104	1,426	608
Breakfast and brunch	7,589	4,560	1,723	2,489	423	1,268	798	347
Board(including at school)	**4,403**	**3,334**	**474**	**2,729**	**27**	**733**	**1,969**	**131**
Catered affairs	**3,892**	**3,123**	**1,230**	**1,384**	**63**	**135**	**1,186**	**510**
Food on out-of-town trips	**19,020**	**13,692**	**5,677**	**6,896**	**842**	**3,641**	**2,413**	**1,119**
School lunches	**7,417**	**6,684**	**3,342**	**3,103**	**41**	**2,549**	**513**	**239**
Meals as pay	**2,578**	**1,132**	**276**	**793**	**305**	**319**	**169**	**63**
ALCOHOLIC BEVERAGES	**$25,628**	**$13,830**	**$5,241**	**$7,588**	**$1,716**	**$3,464**	**$2,407**	**$1,001**
At home	**13,150**	**7,607**	**2,838**	**4,197**	**959**	**1,997**	**1,241**	**572**
Beer and ale	7,896	4,440	1,466	2,593	596	1,176	821	380
Whiskey	1,100	637	320	280	30	182	68	37
Wine	2,789	1,749	680	969	262	480	227	100
Other alcoholic beverages	1,364	780	372	354	70	159	125	54
Away from home	**12,361**	**6,106**	**2,403**	**3,274**	**640**	**1,467**	**1,166**	**430**
Beer and ale	3,442	1,646	587	950	248	393	309	109
Wine	1,763	859	339	454	90	207	157	66
Other alcoholic beverages	5,329	2,522	992	1,366	231	625	510	163
Alcoholic beverages purchased on trips	1,827	1,080	484	503	71	243	189	93

Note: Expenditures listed for items in a given category may not add to the total for that category because the listing is incomplete. "Other dairy products," for example, includes "butter, cheese, ice cream and related products" and "miscellaneous"—"miscellaneous" is omitted here. Expenditures are not given (-) when the amount is too small to be reliable. Numbers may not add to total due to rounding. Other married couples include extended family members or unrelated persons in addition to the married couple. The "all cu's" aggregates will differ slightly from table to table because they are the sums of the aggregates in each row. In this table they include aggregates for single parents, single persons, and other types of consumer units, in addition to all married couples. Aggregates for "all married couples" and "all married couples with children" are sums of the appropriate aggregates in each row.

CHAPTER

3

Shelter and Utilities

Housing took the biggest chunk, 31 percent, out of the average household's expenditures in 1988. Between 1984 and 1988 the share of expenditures allocated to housing increased 1 percentage point. More than three-quarters of the average housing budget is devoted to dwellings, utilities, and public services, with the rest going to household services, household supplies, and furnishings and equipment.

Between 1984 and 1988, the share of housing expenditures devoted to owned and rented dwellings rose 3 full percentage points. Rental expenses accounted for about two-thirds of that increase. The budget share allotted to utilities and public services declined during this time period.

Five-year spending trends for shelter and utilities

Share of household expenditures devoted to housing, share of housing expenditures devoted to housing items, and change in share, 1984 to 1988.						
	1984	1985	1986	1987	1988	change 1984 to 1988
Housing, share of household expenditures	*30.4%*	*30.2%*	*30.6%*	*31.0%*	*31.2%*	*0.8%*
*Housing, expenditures**	*100.0%*	*100.0%*	*100.0%*	*100.0%*	*100.0%*	*0.0%*
SHELTER	52.3%	54.1%	54.6%	54.9%	55.6%	3.3%
Owned dwellings	30.9	31.9	31.6	31.4	31.8	0.9
Mortgage interest	18.7	19.5	19.6	19.3	19.4	0.7
Property taxes	6.3	6.2	5.7	6.1	6.2	-0.1
Maintenance, repairs, insurance, other	5.8	6.2	6.3	5.9	6.1	0.3
Rented dwellings	16.0	16.7	17.3	17.8	18.2	2.2
Other lodging	5.3	5.5	5.7	5.7	5.6	0.3
UTILITIES, FUELS, AND PUBLIC SERVICES	24.5%	23.3%	22.6%	22.1%	21.6%	-2.9%
Natural gas	4.5	3.9	3.4	3.1	2.9	-1.6
Electricity	9.4	9.1	9.2	9.1	8.8	-0.6
Fuel oil and other fuels	2.1	1.8	1.5	1.2	1.2	-0.9
Telephone	6.5	6.4	6.5	6.6	6.6	0.1
Water and other public services	2.1	2.0	2.0	2.0	2.1	0.0

* Housing expenditures also include those for household operations and furnishings (see page 96). Note: Numbers may not add to total due to rounding.

PART I
Spending by age for shelter and utilities

The average American household devotes 31 percent of its budget to housing. On average, this amounted to $8,080 in 1988, with 56 percent of that going to the mortgage, rent, repairs, and maintenance, 22 percent to utilities and public services, 13 percent to furnishings and equipment, and about 5 percent each to household services and supplies.

Householders aged 35 to 44 spend the most on housing, with total expenditures of over $208 billion in 1988. This age group will continue to be the biggest spender in 2000, devoting $265 billion to housing by then. The second largest segment of the housing market today is 25-to-34-year-olds, but the total housing expenditures of this group are projected to shrink. By 2000, 45-to-54-year-olds will move into second place, spending some $209 billion on housing.

Householders under age 25 spend 83 percent less than the average household on mortgages and other costs of homeownership. But they spend well above average on rent and housing at school. Among householders in the next age group, 25 to 34, rental expenses are still high, but the costs of homeownership are only 7 percent below the average.

Households headed by 35-to-44-year-olds spend 30 percent more than the average household on housing. Their mortgage interest and related charges alone are 82 percent above average, and they spend about double the average on vacation homes, hard surface flooring, and heating and cooling equipment. The utility expenditures of this group are above average.

Spending on housing is also well above average for 45-to-54-year-olds. They spend 30 percent more than the average on owned homes and outspend the others on out-of-town lodging, utilities, fuels, and public services.

Housing expenditures fall off rapidly among older households, from 6 percent below average for 55-to-64-year-olds to 42 percent below in the oldest age group. But even the oldest householders spend more than average on some items. Spending on home maintenance, repairs, and insurance is above average among householders aged 55 or older.

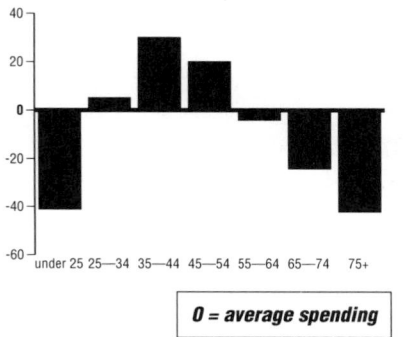

Householders aged 35 to 44 spend much more than the average household on housing...

0 = average spending

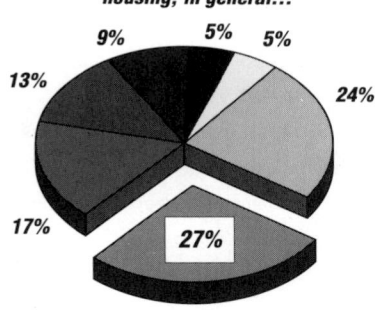

...they're the biggest market for housing, in general...

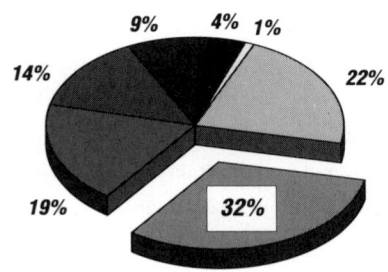

...and for owned dwellings.

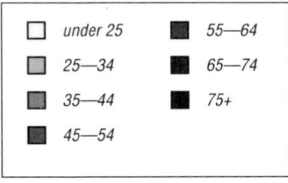

	under 25		55—64
	25—34		65—74
	35—44		75+
	45—54		

Average expenditures

Average annual expenditures for shelter and utilities, by age of reference person.

	all cu's	under 25	25 to 34	35 to 44	45 to 54	55 to 64	65 to 74	75+
Number of consumer units (in thousands)	94,862	7,216	21,985	19,911	13,601	12,546	11,319	8,284
Average number of persons per cu	2.6	1.8	2.8	3.3	2.9	2.2	2.0	1.5
Average total before-tax income	$28,540.00	$14,827.00	$28,318.00	$36,428.00	$39,934.00	$29,979.00	$20,704.00	$13,707.00
TOTAL AVERAGE ANNUAL EXPENDITURES	$25,891.85	$16,373.17	$25,770.27	$33,077.72	$33,204.87	$25,765.35	$20,119.90	$13,339.49
HOUSING, AVERAGE ANNUAL EXPENDITURES	$8,078.63	$4,746.39	$8,469.29	$10,466.69	$9,672.11	$7,756.96	$6,177.84	$4,681.58
SHELTER	$4,492.75	$3,003.76	$4,942.22	$6,147.15	$5,231.57	$3,928.82	$3,018.20	$2,276.38
Owned dwellings*	2,568.69	440.37	2,384.16	3,946.15	3,344.99	2,630.09	1,888.76	1,163.18
Mortgage interest and charges	1,569.02	321.32	1,833.92	2,855.91	2,098.73	1,153.56	460.51	133.98
Property taxes	503.66	46.83	281.29	546.23	679.54	751.90	692.16	467.17
Maintenance, repairs, insurance, and other expenses	496.01	72.23	268.95	544.01	566.71	724.63	736.08	562.02
Homeowners and related insurance	149.84	29.20	101.07	166.33	182.51	187.02	203.00	162.16
Ground rent	25.45	21.94	19.86	14.26	26.98	29.90	40.05	41.10
Maintenance and repair services	257.99	12.74	93.28	278.78	284.85	407.83	435.70	344.94
Painting and papering	54.05	4.84	12.19	63.32	33.58	86.33	118.61	82.17
Plumbing and water heating	23.46	1.41	7.67	28.47	27.53	40.51	29.23	32.15
Heat, air conditioning, electrical work	42.06	1.02	20.45	35.76	50.56	61.01	85.14	48.75
Roofing and gutters	42.59	2.38	8.38	52.60	33.67	70.22	78.00	68.80
Hard surface flooring	8.91	0.72	3.79	17.30	12.95	10.92	3.24	7.54
Maintenance and repair commodities	61.98	8.13	53.87	83.92	71.46	99.16	56.54	13.23
Paint, wallpaper, equipment, and supplies	19.16	3.89	19.00	27.34	23.39	23.99	13.96	6.05
Plumbing supplies and equipment	5.21	1.40	3.73	8.00	7.41	5.91	4.70	1.80
Electrical supplies, heating/cooling equipment	3.65	0.00	2.42	7.35	5.02	3.61	2.70	-
Roofing and gutters	4.84	0.00	1.75	1.85	6.66	16.85	6.27	1.30
Insulation, remodeling, and finishing room or basement	13.10	1.00	14.25	22.44	11.72	15.77	9.75	0.94
Miscellaneous supplies and equipment	16.02	1.82	12.71	16.94	17.25	33.03	19.13	2.91
Rented dwellings	1,467.79	2,395.72	2,252.69	1,518.83	1,178.66	769.69	771.69	936.80
Rent	1,426.08	2,354.67	2,189.21	1,479.70	1,139.70	744.98	734.09	910.22
Rent as pay	17.19	23.16	27.84	10.53	15.14	7.68	21.34	11.85
Maintenance, repairs, and insurance	24.52	17.89	35.64	28.60	23.82	17.02	16.25	14.73
Tenant's insurance	7.90	5.87	10.36	8.86	8.98	4.52	5.89	6.89
Maintenance and repair services	10.55	7.21	13.57	14.41	8.13	10.65	5.73	6.56
Maintenance and repair commodities	6.07	4.81	11.70	5.33	6.71	1.86	4.64	1.28
Other lodging	456.27	167.67	305.37	682.17	707.92	529.05	357.76	176.40
Owned vacation homes	76.61	0.00	14.19	151.67	134.39	108.52	51.84	19.29
Expenses for other properties	160.42	3.50	146.28	245.65	224.06	175.47	117.40	61.25

Average annual expenditures for shelter and utilities, by age of reference person.

(continued from previous page)	all cu's	under 25	25 to 34	35 to 44	45 to 54	55 to 64	65 to 74	75+
Housing while attending school	36.27	68.99	3.60	48.38	97.73	39.22	7.02	0.00
Lodging while out-of-town	182.97	95.18	141.31	236.47	251.74	205.84	181.50	95.86
UTILITIES, FUELS, AND PUBLIC SERVICES	**$1,747.42**	**$896.96**	**$1,544.84**	**$2,022.94**	**$2,172.87**	**$1,935.10**	**$1,738.55**	**$1,393.04**
Natural gas	**233.75**	**88.26**	**186.38**	**262.88**	**284.93**	**272.34**	**265.32**	**230.61**
Electricity	**708.82**	**326.24**	**634.22**	**837.72**	**887.35**	**780.21**	**697.17**	**544.99**
Fuel oil and other fuels	**97.76**	**18.03**	**56.30**	**93.95**	**115.86**	**143.58**	**142.32**	**126.36**
Fuel oil	60.10	6.91	27.61	56.49	66.84	100.47	90.25	87.97
Coal	3.57	0.00	3.45	3.31	2.40	5.78	5.51	3.53
Bottled gas	24.05	8.56	16.60	22.19	30.01	30.59	33.11	29.74
Wood and other fuels	10.03	2.56	8.65	11.96	16.61	6.74	13.46	5.13
Telephone	**537.04**	**416.55**	**534.00**	**617.49**	**669.27**	**542.86**	**458.32**	**338.36**
Water and other public services	**170.05**	**47.88**	**133.93**	**210.92**	**215.45**	**196.11**	**175.42**	**152.71**
Water and sewerage maintenance	130.31	35.90	103.61	162.16	162.64	150.40	133.16	119.44
Trash and garbage collection	38.19	11.40	29.16	46.97	50.50	43.59	40.39	32.93
Septic tank cleaning	1.55	0.57	1.16	1.78	2.31	2.12	1.86	-

*Note: Expenditures listed for items in a given category may not add to the total for that category because the listing is incomplete. "Maintenance and repair services," for example, includes "other maintenance and repair services," which is omitted here. Expenditures are not given (-) when the amount is too small to be reliable. Numbers may not add to total due to rounding. *See Appendix B for information on mortgage principle reduction.*

Share of spending

	all cu's	under 25	25 to 34	35 to 44	45 to 54	55 to 64	65 to 74	75+
Number of consumer units (in thousands)	94,862	7,216	21,985	19,911	13,601	12,546	11,319	8,284
Average number of persons per cu	2.6	1.8	2.8	3.3	2.9	2.2	2.0	1.5
Average total before-tax income	$28,540	$14,827	$28,318	$36,428	$39,934	$29,979	$20,704	$13,707
TOTAL AVERAGE ANNUAL EXPENDITURES	100.00%	100.00%	100.00%	100.00%	100.00%	100.00%	100.00%	100.00%
HOUSING, AVERAGE ANNUAL EXPENDITURES	31.20%	28.99%	32.86%	31.64%	29.13%	30.11%	30.71%	35.10%
SHELTER	17.35%	18.35%	19.18%	18.58%	15.76%	15.25%	15.00%	17.06%
Owned dwellings*	9.92	2.69	9.25	11.93	10.07	10.21	9.39	8.72
Mortgage interest and charges	6.06	1.96	7.12	8.63	6.32	4.48	2.29	1.00
Property taxes	1.95	0.29	1.09	1.65	2.05	2.92	3.44	3.50
Maintenance, repairs, insurance, and other expenses	1.92	0.44	1.04	1.64	1.71	2.81	3.66	4.21
Homeowners and related insurance	0.58	0.18	0.39	0.50	0.55	0.73	1.01	1.22
Ground rent	0.10	0.13	0.08	0.04	0.08	0.12	0.20	0.31
Maintenance and repair services	1.00	0.08	0.36	0.84	0.86	1.58	2.17	2.59
Painting and papering	0.21	0.03	0.05	0.19	0.10	0.34	0.59	0.62
Plumbing and water heating	0.09	0.01	0.03	0.09	0.08	0.16	0.15	0.24
Heat, air conditioning, electrical work	0.16	0.01	0.08	0.11	0.15	0.24	0.42	0.37
Roofing and gutters	0.16	0.01	0.03	0.16	0.10	0.27	0.39	0.52
Hard surface flooring	0.03	0.00	0.01	0.05	0.04	0.04	0.02	0.06
Maintenance and repair commodities	0.24	0.05	0.21	0.25	0.22	0.38	0.28	0.10
Paint, wallpaper, equipment, and supplies	0.07	0.02	0.07	0.08	0.07	0.09	0.07	0.05
Plumbing supplies and equipment	0.02	0.01	0.01	0.02	0.02	0.02	0.02	0.01
Electrical supplies, heating/cooling equipment	0.01	0.00	0.01	0.02	0.02	0.01	0.01	-
Roofing and gutters	0.02	0.00	0.01	0.01	0.02	0.07	0.03	0.01
Insulation, remodeling, and finishing room or basement	0.05	0.01	0.06	0.07	0.04	0.06	0.05	0.01
Miscellaneous supplies and equipment	0.06	0.01	0.05	0.05	0.05	0.13	0.10	0.02
Rented dwellings	5.67	14.63	8.74	4.59	3.55	2.99	3.84	7.02
Rent	5.51	14.38	8.50	4.47	3.43	2.89	3.65	6.82
Rent as pay	0.07	0.14	0.11	0.03	0.05	0.03	0.11	0.09
Maintenance, repairs, and insurance	0.09	0.11	0.14	0.09	0.07	0.07	0.08	0.11
Tenant's insurance	0.03	0.04	0.04	0.03	0.03	0.02	0.03	0.05
Maintenance and repair services	0.04	0.04	0.05	0.04	0.02	0.04	0.03	0.05
Maintenance and repair commodities	0.02	0.03	0.05	0.02	0.02	0.01	0.02	0.01
Other lodging	1.76	1.02	1.18	2.06	2.13	2.05	1.78	1.32
Owned vacation homes	0.30	0.00	0.06	0.46	0.40	0.42	0.26	0.14
Expenses for other properties	0.62	0.02	0.57	0.74	0.67	0.68	0.58	0.46

Percent of total average annual expenditures spent on shelter and utilities, by age of reference person.

(continued from previous page)	all cu's	under 25	25 to 34	35 to 44	45 to 54	55 to 64	65 to 74	75+
Housing while attending school	0.14	0.42	0.01	0.15	0.29	0.15	0.03	0.00
Lodging while out-of-town	0.71	0.58	0.55	0.71	0.76	0.80	0.90	0.72
UTILITIES, FUELS, AND PUBLIC SERVICES	**6.75%**	**5.48%**	**5.99%**	**6.12%**	**6.54%**	**7.51%**	**8.64%**	**10.44%**
Natural gas	**0.90**	**0.54**	**0.72**	**0.79**	**0.86**	**1.06**	**1.32**	**1.73**
Electricity	**2.74**	**1.99**	**2.46**	**2.53**	**2.67**	**3.03**	**3.47**	**4.09**
Fuel oil and other fuels	**0.38**	**0.11**	**0.22**	**0.28**	**0.35**	**0.56**	**0.71**	**0.95**
Fuel oil	0.23	0.04	0.11	0.17	0.20	0.39	0.45	0.66
Coal	0.01	0.00	0.01	0.01	0.01	0.02	0.03	0.03
Bottled gas	0.09	0.05	0.06	0.07	0.09	0.12	0.16	0.22
Wood and other fuels	0.04	0.02	0.03	0.04	0.05	0.03	0.07	0.04
Telephone	**2.07**	**2.54**	**2.07**	**1.87**	**2.02**	**2.11**	**2.28**	**2.54**
Water and other public services	**0.66**	**0.29**	**0.52**	**0.64**	**0.65**	**0.76**	**0.87**	**1.14**
Water and sewerage maintenance	0.50	0.22	0.40	0.49	0.49	0.58	0.66	0.90
Trash and garbage collection	0.15	0.07	0.11	0.14	0.15	0.17	0.20	0.25
Septic tank cleaning	0.01	0.00	0.00	0.01	0.01	0.01	0.01	-

Note: Expenditures listed for items in a given category may not add to the total for that category because the listing is incomplete. "Maintenance and repair services," for example, includes "other maintenance and repair services," which is omitted here. Expenditures are not given (-) when the amount is too small to be reliable. Numbers may not add to total due to rounding. *See Appendix B for information on mortgage principle reduction.

Indexed expenditures

	all cu's	under 25	25 to 34	35 to 44	45 to 54	55 to 64	65 to 74	75+
Number of consumer units (in thousands)	94,862	7,216	21,985	19,911	13,601	12,546	11,319	8,284
Average number of persons per cu	2.6	1.8	2.8	3.3	2.9	2.2	2.0	1.5
Average total before-tax income	$28,540	$14,827	$28,318	$36,428	$39,934	$29,979	$20,704	$13,707
TOTAL AVERAGE ANNUAL EXPENDITURES	100	63	100	128	128	100	78	52
HOUSING, AVERAGE ANNUAL EXPENDITURES	100	59	105	130	120	96	76	58
SHELTER	**100**	**67**	**110**	**137**	**116**	**87**	**67**	**51**
Owned dwellings*	**100**	**17**	**93**	**154**	**130**	**102**	**74**	**45**
Mortgage interest and charges	100	20	117	182	134	74	29	9
Property taxes	100	9	56	108	135	149	137	93
Maintenance, repairs, insurance, and other expenses	100	15	54	110	114	146	148	113
Homeowners and related insurance	100	19	67	111	122	125	135	108
Ground rent	100	86	78	56	106	117	157	161
Maintenance and repair services	100	5	36	108	110	158	169	134
Painting and papering	100	9	23	117	62	160	219	152
Plumbing and water heating	100	6	33	121	117	173	125	137
Heat, air conditioning, electrical work	100	2	49	85	120	145	202	116
Roofing and gutters	100	6	20	124	79	165	183	162
Hard surface flooring	100	8	43	194	145	123	36	85
Maintenance and repair commodities	100	13	87	135	115	160	91	21
Paint, wallpaper, equipment, and supplies	100	20	99	143	122	125	73	32
Plumbing supplies and equipment	100	27	72	154	142	113	90	35
Electrical supplies, heating/cooling equipment	100	0	66	201	138	99	74	-
Roofing and gutters	100	0	36	38	138	348	130	27
Insulation, remodeling, and finishing room or basement	100	8	109	171	89	120	74	7
Miscellaneous supplies and equipment	100	11	79	106	108	206	119	18
Rented dwellings	**100**	**163**	**153**	**103**	**80**	**52**	**53**	**64**
Rent	100	165	154	104	80	52	51	64
Rent as pay	100	135	162	61	88	45	124	69
Maintenance, repairs, and insurance	100	73	145	117	97	69	66	60
Tenant's insurance	100	74	131	112	114	57	75	87
Maintenance and repair services	100	68	129	137	77	101	54	62
Maintenance and repair commodities	100	79	193	88	111	31	76	21
Other lodging	**100**	**37**	**67**	**150**	**155**	**116**	**78**	**39**
Owned vacation homes	100	0	19	198	175	142	68	25
Expenses for other properties	100	2	91	153	140	109	73	38

Indexed average annual expenditures for shelter and utilities, by age of reference person.

(continued from previous page)	all cu's	under 25	25 to 34	35 to 44	45 to 54	55 to 64	65 to 74	75+
Housing while attending school	100	190	10	133	269	108	19	0
Lodging while out-of-town	100	52	77	129	138	112	99	52
UTILITIES, FUELS, AND PUBLIC SERVICES	**100**	**51**	**88**	**116**	**124**	**111**	**99**	**80**
Natural gas	**100**	**38**	**80**	**112**	**122**	**117**	**114**	**99**
Electricity	**100**	**46**	**89**	**118**	**125**	**110**	**98**	**77**
Fuel oil and other fuels	**100**	**18**	**58**	**96**	**119**	**147**	**146**	**129**
Fuel oil	100	11	46	94	111	167	150	146
Coal	100	0	97	93	67	162	154	99
Bottled gas	100	36	69	92	125	127	138	124
Wood and other fuels	100	26	86	119	166	67	134	51
Telephone	**100**	**78**	**99**	**115**	**125**	**101**	**85**	**63**
Water and other public services	**100**	**28**	**79**	**124**	**127**	**115**	**103**	**90**
Water and sewerage maintenance	100	28	80	124	125	115	102	92
Trash and garbage collection	100	30	76	123	132	114	106	86
Septic tank cleaning	100	37	75	115	149	137	120	-

*Note: Expenditures are not given (-) when the amount is too small to be reliable. An index of 100 represents the average for all consumer units. An index of 132 means that the average for the subgroup is 32 percent above the average for all consumer units. An index of 68 indicates spending that is 32 percent below the overall average. *See Appendix B for information on mortgage principle reduction.*

Aggregate expenditures, 1988

Aggregate expenditures in 1988 for shelter and utilities, by age of reference person.

	all cu's	under 25	25 to 34	35 to 44	45 to 54	55 to 64	65 to 74	75+
Number of consumer units (in thousands)	94,862	7,216	21,985	19,911	13,601	12,546	11,319	8,284
Average number of persons per cu	2.6	1.8	2.8	3.3	2.9	2.2	2.0	1.5
Aggregate before-tax income (in millions)	$2,722,037	$106,992	$622,571	$725,318	$543,142	$376,117	$234,349	$113,549
TOTAL AGGREGATE EXPENDITURES (in millions)	$2,456,432	$118,149	$566,559	$658,610	$451,619	$323,252	$227,737	$110,504
HOUSING, AGGREGATE EXPENDITURES (in millions)	$766,428	$34,250	$186,197	$208,402	$131,550	$97,319	$69,927	$38,782
SHELTER	$426,192	$21,675	$108,655	$122,396	$71,155	$49,291	$34,163	$18,858
Owned dwellings*	243,672	3,178	52,416	78,572	45,495	32,997	21,379	9,636
Mortgage interest and charges	148,841	2,319	40,319	56,864	28,545	14,473	5,213	1,110
Property taxes	47,778	338	6,184	10,876	9,242	9,433	7,835	3,870
Maintenance, repairs, insurance, and other expenses	47,052	521	5,913	10,832	7,708	9,091	8,332	4,656
Homeowners and related insurance	14,214	211	2,222	3,312	2,482	2,346	2,298	1,343
Ground rent	2,415	158	437	284	367	375	453	340
Maintenance and repair services	24,474	92	2,051	5,551	3,874	5,117	4,932	2,857
Painting and papering	5,127	35	268	1,261	457	1,083	1,343	681
Plumbing and water heating	2,226	10	169	567	374	508	331	266
Heat, air conditioning, electrical work	3,990	7	450	712	688	765	964	404
Roofing and gutters	4,040	17	184	1,047	458	881	883	570
Hard surface flooring	845	5	83	344	176	137	37	62
Maintenance and repair commodities	5,879	59	1,184	1,671	972	1,244	640	110
Paint, wallpaper, equipment, and supplies	1,817	28	418	544	318	301	158	50
Plumbing supplies and equipment	494	10	82	159	101	74	53	15
Electrical supplies, heating/cooling equipment	344	0	53	146	68	45	31	-
Roofing and gutters	459	0	38	37	91	211	71	11
Insulation, remodeling, and finishing room or basement	1,243	7	313	447	159	198	110	8
Miscellaneous supplies and equipment	1,520	13	279	337	235	414	217	24
Rented dwellings	139,237	17,288	49,525	30,241	16,031	9,657	8,735	7,760
Rent	135,280	16,991	48,130	29,462	15,501	9,347	8,309	7,540
Rent as pay	1,631	167	612	210	206	96	242	98
Maintenance, repairs, and insurance	2,326	129	784	569	324	214	184	122
Tenant's insurance	749	42	228	176	122	57	67	57
Maintenance and repair services	1,001	52	298	287	111	134	65	54
Maintenance and repair commodities	576	35	257	106	91	23	53	11
Other lodging	43,283	1,210	6,714	13,583	9,628	6,637	4,049	1,461
Owned vacation homes	7,268	0	312	3,020	1,828	1,361	587	160
Expenses for other properties	15,217	25	3,216	4,891	3,047	2,201	1,329	507

Aggregate expenditures for shelter and utilities in 1988, by age of reference person.

(continued from previous page)	all cu's	under 25	25 to 34	35 to 44	45 to 54	55 to 64	65 to 74	75+
Housing while attending school	3,441	498	79	963	1,329	492	79	0
Lodging while out-of-town	17,357	687	3,107	4,708	3,424	2,582	2,054	794
UTILITIES, FUELS, AND PUBLIC SERVICES	**$165,764**	**$6,472**	**$33,963**	**$40,279**	**$29,553**	**$24,278**	**$19,679**	**$11,540**
Natural gas	**22,174**	**637**	**4,098**	**5,234**	**3,875**	**3,417**	**3,003**	**1,910**
Electricity	**67,241**	**2,354**	**13,943**	**16,680**	**12,069**	**9,789**	**7,891**	**4,515**
Fuel oil and other fuels	**9,273**	**130**	**1,238**	**1,871**	**1,576**	**1,801**	**1,611**	**1,047**
Fuel oil	5,702	50	607	1,125	909	1,260	1,022	729
Coal	339	0	76	66	33	73	62	29
Bottled gas	2,282	62	365	442	408	384	375	246
Wood and other fuels	952	18	190	238	226	85	152	42
Telephone	**50,945**	**3,006**	**11,740**	**12,295**	**9,103**	**6,811**	**5,188**	**2,803**
Water and other public services	**16,131**	**346**	**2,944**	**4,200**	**2,930**	**2,460**	**1,986**	**1,265**
Water and sewerage maintenance	12,361	259	2,278	3,229	2,212	1,887	1,507	989
Trash and garbage collection	3,622	82	641	935	687	547	457	273
Septic tank cleaning	144	4	26	35	31	27	21	-

Note: Expenditures listed for items in a given category may not add to the total for that category because the listing is incomplete. "Maintenance and repair services," for example, includes "other maintenance and repair services," which is omitted here. Expenditures are not given (-) when the amount is too small to be reliable. Numbers may not add to total due to rounding. The "all cu's" aggregates will differ slightly from table to table because they are the sums of the aggregates in each row. *See Appendix B for information on mortgage principle reduction.

Aggregate expenditures, 1995

Aggregate expenditures for shelter and utilities, by age of householder in 1995 (in 1988 dollars).

	all households	under 25	25 to 34	35 to 44	45 to 54	55 to 64	65 to 74	75+
Number of households (in thousands)	100,308	4,316	19,927	23,916	18,035	12,223	12,006	9,876
HOUSING, AGGREGATE EXPENDITURES IN 1995 (in millions)	$829,231	$20,485	$168,768	$250,321	$174,437	$94,813	$74,171	$46,235
SHELTER	$459,554	$12,964	$98,484	$147,015	$94,351	$48,022	$36,237	$22,482
Owned dwellings*	270,424	1,901	47,509	94,376	60,327	32,148	22,676	11,488
Mortgage interest and charges	165,036	1,387	36,545	68,302	37,851	14,100	5,529	1,323
Property taxes	53,241	202	5,605	13,064	12,256	9,190	8,310	4,614
Maintenance, repairs, insurance, and other expenses	52,147	312	5,359	13,011	10,221	8,857	8,837	5,551
Homeowners and related insurance	15,734	126	2,014	3,978	3,292	2,286	2,437	1,601
Ground rent	2,570	95	396	341	487	365	481	406
Maintenance and repair services	27,341	55	1,859	6,667	5,137	4,985	5,231	3,407
Painting and papering	5,675	21	243	1,514	606	1,055	1,424	812
Plumbing and water heating	2,500	6	153	681	497	495	351	318
Heat, air conditioning, electrical work	4,428	4	408	855	912	746	1,022	481
Roofing and gutters	4,517	10	167	1,258	607	858	936	679
Hard surface flooring	973	3	76	414	234	133	39	74
Maintenance and repair commodities	6,426	35	1,073	2,007	1,289	1,212	679	131
Paint, wallpaper, equipment, and supplies	1,992	17	379	654	422	293	168	60
Plumbing supplies and equipment	552	6	74	191	134	72	56	18
Electrical supplies, heating/cooling equipment	391	0	48	176	91	44	32	-
Roofing and gutters	493	0	35	44	120	206	75	13
Insulation, remodeling, and finishing room or basement	1,355	4	284	537	211	193	117	9
Miscellaneous supplies and equipment	1,640	8	253	405	311	404	230	29
Rented dwellings	140,735	10,340	44,889	36,324	21,257	9,408	9,265	9,252
Rent	136,639	10,163	43,624	35,389	20,554	9,106	8,813	8,989
Rent as pay	1,647	100	555	252	273	94	256	117
Maintenance, repairs, and insurance	2,450	77	710	684	430	208	195	145
Tenant's insurance	800	25	206	212	162	55	71	68
Maintenance and repair services	1,057	31	270	345	147	130	69	65
Maintenance and repair commodities	593	21	233	127	121	23	56	13
Other lodging	48,395	724	6,085	16,315	12,767	6,467	4,295	1,742
Owned vacation homes	8,473	0	283	3,627	2,424	1,326	622	191
Expenses for other properties	17,005	15	2,915	5,875	4,041	2,145	1,410	605

Aggregate expenditures for shelter and utilities, by age of householder in 1995 (in 1988 dollars).

(continued from previous page)	all households	under 25	25 to 34	35 to 44	45 to 54	55 to 64	65 to 74	75+
Housing while attending school	3,853	298	72	1,157	1,763	479	84	0
Lodging while out-of-town	19,064	411	2,816	5,655	4,540	2,516	2,179	947
UTILITIES, FUELS, AND PUBLIC SERVICES	**$180,507**	**$3,871**	**$30,784**	**$48,381**	**$39,188**	**$23,653**	**$20,873**	**$13,758**
Natural gas	**24,312**	**381**	**3,714**	**6,287**	**5,139**	**3,329**	**3,185**	**2,278**
Electricity	**73,373**	**1,408**	**12,638**	**20,035**	**16,003**	**9,537**	**8,370**	**5,382**
Fuel oil and other fuels	**10,248**	**78**	**1,122**	**2,247**	**2,090**	**1,755**	**1,709**	**1,248**
Fuel oil	6,317	30	550	1,351	1,205	1,228	1,084	869
Coal	363	0	69	79	43	71	66	35
Bottled gas	2,505	37	331	531	541	374	398	294
Wood and other fuels	1,064	11	172	286	300	82	162	51
Telephone	**54,757**	**1,798**	**10,641**	**14,768**	**12,070**	**6,635**	**5,503**	**3,342**
Water and other public services	**17,817**	**207**	**2,669**	**5,044**	**3,886**	**2,397**	**2,106**	**1,508**
Water and sewerage maintenance	13,648	155	2,065	3,878	2,933	1,838	1,599	1,180
Trash and garbage collection	4,007	49	581	1,123	911	533	485	325
Septic tank cleaning	158	2	23	43	42	26	22	-

*Note: Expenditures listed for items in a given category may not add to the total for that category because the listing is incomplete. "Maintenance and repair services," for example, includes "other maintenance and repair services," which is omitted here. Expenditures are not given (-) when the amount is too small to be reliable. Numbers may not add to total due to rounding. Households are used here because the number of consumer units in 1995 and 2000 is not available. Household projections are from the Census Bureau. Projections show how annual aggregate expenditures will change as the number of households in the age groups changes in 1995 and 2000. Projections are based on the average annual expenditures in 1988 and have not been adjusted for price increases or for changes in expenditure patterns. *See Appendix B for information on mortgage principle reduction.*

Aggregate expenditures, 2000

Annual aggregate expenditures for shelter and utilities, by age of householder in 2000 (in 1988 dollars).

	all households	under 25	25 to 34	35 to 44	45 to 54	55 to 64	65 to 74	75+
Number of households (in thousands)	105,933	4,442	18,004	25,339	21,603	13,903	11,516	11,126
HOUSING, AGGREGATE EXPENDITURES IN 2000 (in millions)	$878,803	$21,083	$152,481	$265,215	$208,947	$107,845	$71,144	$52,087
SHELTER	$485,810	$13,343	$88,980	$155,763	$113,018	$54,622	$34,758	$25,327
Owned dwellings*	288,392	1,956	42,924	99,991	72,262	36,566	21,751	12,942
Mortgage interest and charges	174,982	1,427	33,018	72,366	45,339	16,038	5,303	1,491
Property taxes	57,416	208	5,064	13,841	14,680	10,454	7,971	5,198
Maintenance, repairs, insurance, and other expenses	55,995	321	4,842	13,785	12,243	10,075	8,477	6,253
Homeowners and related insurance	16,849	130	1,820	4,215	3,943	2,600	2,338	1,804
Ground rent	2,733	97	358	361	583	416	461	457
Maintenance and repair services	29,479	57	1,679	7,064	6,154	5,670	5,018	3,838
Painting and papering	6,051	21	219	1,604	725	1,200	1,366	914
Plumbing and water heating	2,718	6	138	721	595	563	337	358
Heat, air conditioning, electrical work	4,742	5	368	906	1,092	848	980	542
Roofing and gutters	4,862	11	151	1,333	727	976	898	765
Hard surface flooring	1,063	3	68	438	280	152	37	84
Maintenance and repair commodities	6,853	36	970	2,126	1,544	1,379	651	147
Paint, wallpaper, equipment, and supplies	2,119	17	342	693	505	334	161	67
Plumbing supplies and equipment	592	6	67	203	160	82	54	20
Electrical supplies, heating/cooling equipment	420	0	44	186	108	50	31	-
Roofing and gutters	543	0	32	47	144	234	72	14
Insulation, remodeling, and finishing room or basement	1,425	4	257	569	253	219	112	10
Miscellaneous supplies and equipment	1,751	8	229	429	373	459	220	32
Rented dwellings	145,158	10,642	40,557	38,486	25,463	10,701	8,887	10,423
Rent	140,927	10,459	39,415	37,494	24,621	10,357	8,454	10,127
Rent as pay	1,682	103	501	267	327	107	246	132
Maintenance, repairs, and insurance	2,548	79	642	725	515	237	187	164
Tenant's insurance	838	26	187	225	194	63	68	77
Maintenance and repair services	1,104	32	244	365	176	148	66	73
Maintenance and repair commodities	606	21	211	135	145	26	53	14
Other lodging	52,259	745	5,498	17,286	15,293	7,355	4,120	1,963
Owned vacation homes	9,322	0	255	3,843	2,903	1,509	597	215
Expenses for other properties	18,187	16	2,634	6,225	4,840	2,440	1,352	681

Aggregate expenditures for shelter and utilities, by age of householder in 2000 (in 1988 dollars).

(continued from previous page)	all households	under 25	25 to 34	35 to 44	45 to 54	55 to 64	65 to 74	75+
Housing while attending school	4,335	306	65	1,226	2,111	545	81	0
Lodging while out-of-town	20,416	423	2,544	5,992	5,438	2,862	2,090	1,067
UTILITIES, FUELS, AND PUBLIC SERVICES	**$192,421**	**$3,984**	**$27,813**	**$51,259**	**$46,941**	**$26,904**	**$20,021**	**$15,499**
Natural gas	**25,972**	**392**	**3,356**	**6,661**	**6,155**	**3,786**	**3,055**	**2,566**
Electricity	**78,203**	**1,449**	**11,418**	**21,227**	**19,169**	**10,847**	**8,029**	**6,064**
Fuel oil and other fuels	**11,018**	**80**	**1,014**	**2,381**	**2,503**	**1,996**	**1,639**	**1,406**
Fuel oil	6,818	31	497	1,431	1,444	1,397	1,039	979
Coal	381	0	62	84	52	80	63	39
Bottled gas	2,685	38	299	562	648	425	381	331
Wood and other fuels	1,135	11	156	303	359	94	155	57
Telephone	**58,159**	**1,850**	**9,614**	**15,647**	**14,458**	**7,547**	**5,278**	**3,765**
Water and other public services	**19,069**	**213**	**2,411**	**5,345**	**4,654**	**2,727**	**2,020**	**1,699**
Water and sewerage maintenance	14,601	159	1,865	4,109	3,514	2,091	1,533	1,329
Trash and garbage collection	4,294	51	525	1,190	1,091	606	465	366
Septic tank cleaning	169	3	21	45	50	29	21	-

*Note: Expenditures listed for items in a given category may not add to the total for that category because the listing is incomplete. "Maintenance and repair services," for example, includes "other maintenance and repair services," which is omitted here. Expenditures are not given (-) when the amount is too small to be reliable. Numbers may not add to total due to rounding. Households are used here because the number of consumer units in 1995 and 2000 is not available. Household projections are from the Census Bureau. Projections show how annual aggregate expenditures will change as the number of households in the age groups changes in 1995 and 2000. Projections are based on the average annual expenditures in 1988 and have not been adjusted for price increases or for changes in expenditure patterns. *See Appendix B for information on mortgage principle reduction.*

PART II
Spending by income for shelter and utilities

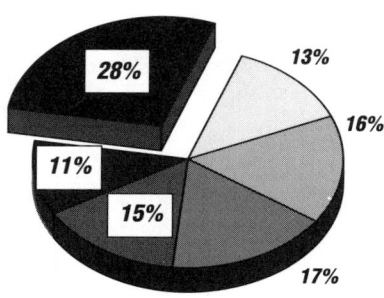

More than half of the shelter and utilities market is accounted for by households bringing in $30,000 or more.

28%   13%

16%

11%

15%

17%

☐ under $10,000	■ $30,000–39,999
■ $10,000–19,999	■ $40,000–49,999
■ $20,000–29,999	■ $50,000 and over

The higher their household income the more people spend on housing. The average housing expenditure of the highest income group is four times greater than that of the lowest. Spending on owned dwellings, vacation homes, other properties, and out-of-town lodging climbs rapidly with increases in household income. But the amount people spend on rental housing declines with income.

Homeownership and rental expenses absorb 16 to 17 percent of the budgets of households with incomes of $10,000 or more. The lowest income households devote over 20 percent of their expenditures to this category. Utilities gobble up 10 percent of the lowest income group's spending dollar but just 5 percent of the highest income group's.

Households with incomes of $50,000 or more spent $140 billion on shelter and utilities in 1988—accounting for 28 percent of the total market. Households with incomes between $30,000 and $50,000 spent $134 billion, another 26 percent of the market, while all those with incomes below $30,000 accounted for 46 percent of the market.

The low-end market

Households with annual incomes under $30,000 spend less than average on housing. Homeownership expenses are 23 percent below average for households with incomes of $20,000 to $30,000. But these households spend more than average amounts on home maintenance services and products, especially plumbing and roofing supplies. They spend 23 percent more than the average household on rent and rental maintenance. And they are a big market for coal with spending for that fuel that is 77 percent above average.

Those households with incomes below $20,000 spend at least 30 percent less than the average for their dwellings. Their spending on mortgage interest, property taxes and other homeownership expenses are well below the norm. But the rental expenses of households with incomes of less than $10,000 are just 6 percent below average. Households in the $10,000 to $20,000 income range spend fully 20 percent more than the average household on rent, and nearly 30 percent more on rental maintenance and repairs. All the utility expenditures of low-income households are below the average except for bottled gas and coal.

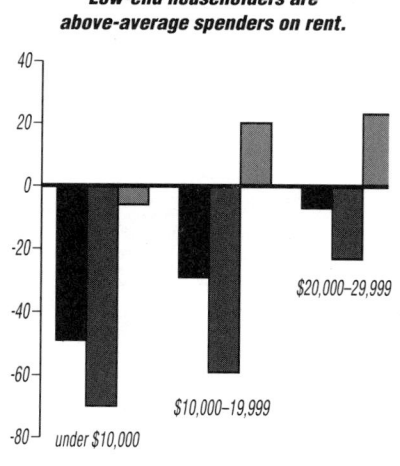

Low-end householders are above-average spenders on rent.

40

20

0

-20

-40

$20,000–29,999

-60

$10,000–19,999

-80

under $10,000

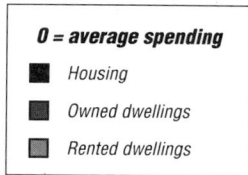

| **0 = average spending** |
| ■ Housing |
| ■ Owned dwellings |
| ■ Rented dwellings |

The high-end market

In the $30,000 to $40,000 income bracket, people spend more on mortgages and property taxes and their spending on owned homes climbs to 16 percent above average. Home maintenance and repair service bills are lower than average, while those for maintenance and repair products are higher. This is a do-it-yourself group, spending over 30 percent more than the average household on electrical supplies, heating and cooling equipment, insulation and remodeling/refinishing equipment and supplies. These households spend 19 percent more than average on wood and kerosene.

Households with incomes of $40,000 to $50,000 spend 59 percent more than the average household on owned homes. Along with those in the highest income group, their spending on rented dwellings is relatively low. Unlike the highest income households, they spend less than average on painting, papering, and hard surface flooring services as well as roofing supplies.

The spending of households with incomes of $50,000 or more is well above average for owned homes, utilities and public services. Their spending drops below average only for rent, coal, and bottled gas.

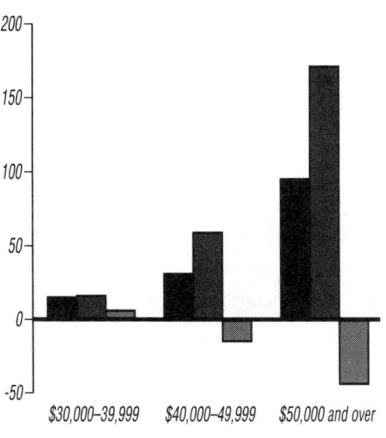

High-end householders spend more than average on everything but rent.

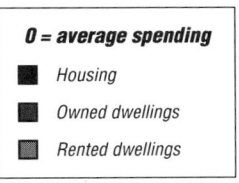

0 = average spending

- Housing
- Owned dwellings
- Rented dwellings

Average expenditures

(consumer units include complete income reporters only)	all cu's	under $10,000	$10,000 to $19,999	$20,000 to $29,999	$30,000 to $39,999	$40,000 to $49,999	$50,000 and over
Number of consumer units (in thousands)	81,354	18,809	17,652	14,586	10,901	7,198	12,209
Average number of persons per cu	2.6	1.8	2.3	2.7	2.9	3.2	3.1
Average number of earners per cu	1.4	0.7	1.0	1.5	1.8	2.0	2.1
TOTAL AVERAGE ANNUAL EXPENDITURES	$26,389.07	$11,269.43	$18,078.25	$24,896.36	$31,659.60	$37,562.00	$52,320.19
HOUSING, AVERAGE ANNUAL EXPENDITURES	$8,069.13	$4,108.61	$5,705.41	$7,511.85	$9,260.85	$10,608.79	$15,719.12
SHELTER	$4,470.25	$2,270.26	$3,087.99	$4,124.86	$5,049.86	$5,901.40	$8,909.44
Owned dwellings*	2,554.04	758.01	1,049.56	1,976.74	2,970.57	4,060.42	6,925.93
Mortgage interest and charges	1,560.38	298.92	412.35	1,051.78	1,925.39	2,783.87	4,724.01
Property taxes	496.08	207.22	309.60	417.03	599.30	643.81	1,125.91
Maintenance, repairs, insurance, and other expenses	497.48	251.87	327.61	507.92	445.87	632.74	1,075.35
Homeowners and related insurance	151.74	76.11	103.83	139.48	163.01	200.84	313.16
Ground rent	26.88	31.54	31.86	35.13	23.98	14.38	12.57
Maintenance and repair services	252.68	122.12	163.47	260.79	187.82	293.13	607.16
Painting and papering	52.01	33.80	24.41	55.29	21.09	49.82	144.99
Plumbing and water heating	23.06	10.12	14.34	22.72	17.23	32.94	55.39
Heat, air conditioning, electrical work	42.03	22.60	31.16	28.44	44.68	61.59	90.02
Roofing and gutters	46.96	14.05	35.79	49.75	40.70	55.18	111.23
Hard surface flooring	8.14	0.44	3.86	2.46	7.98	6.77	33.94
Maintenance and repair commodities	65.41	22.02	27.12	71.76	70.93	122.37	141.50
Paint, wallpaper, and supplies	19.35	6.28	7.07	16.21	20.21	36.73	49.91
Plumbing supplies and equipment	5.65	1.19	2.82	6.92	6.24	11.04	11.40
Electrical supplies, heating/cooling equipment	3.76	1.21	2.26	3.32	4.94	2.21	10.24
Roofing and gutters	5.18	-	3.48	8.46	4.25	3.31	5.16
Insulation, remodeling, and finishing room or basement	13.89	4.58	3.27	8.52	18.98	43.49	28.02
Miscellaneous supplies and equipment	17.57	3.22	8.22	28.33	16.32	25.59	36.76
Rented dwellings	1,469.41	1,380.04	1,764.45	1,804.99	1,563.71	1,248.94	825.42
Rent	1,428.30	1,346.41	1,713.00	1,762.19	1,521.88	1,216.05	785.55
Rent as pay	17.34	20.97	28.73	15.87	14.30	0.70	9.59
Maintenance, repairs, and insurance	23.76	12.65	22.72	26.92	27.53	32.19	30.29
Tenant's insurance	8.68	6.12	6.61	9.27	12.89	10.61	10.03
Maintenance and repair services	9.01	2.75	11.65	11.46	9.64	6.78	12.67
Maintenance and repair commodities	6.07	3.79	4.46	6.19	5.00	14.80	7.59
Other lodging	446.79	132.21	273.97	343.13	515.57	592.04	1,158.09
Owned vacation homes	78.26	13.26	91.43	48.70	89.46	52.59	199.82
Expenses for other properties	154.47	40.73	89.27	137.28	169.04	223.95	390.55

Average annual expenditures for shelter and utilities, by total before-tax income of consumer unit.

(continued from previous page)	all cu's	under $10,000	$10,000 to $19,999	$20,000 to $29,999	$30,000 to $39,999	$40,000 to $49,999	$50,000 and over
Housing while attending school	35.48	28.52	3.57	17.58	30.76	35.15	118.12
Lodging while out-of-town	178.58	49.70	89.70	139.57	226.31	280.35	449.60
UTILITIES, FUELS, AND PUBLIC SERVICES	**$1,726.29**	**$1,159.08**	**$1,473.19**	**$1,711.07**	**$1,924.68**	**$2,089.68**	**$2,593.22**
Natural gas	**232.22**	**157.84**	**213.75**	**215.34**	**246.68**	**276.67**	**354.61**
Electricity	**700.08**	**459.00**	**592.14**	**695.11**	**801.49**	**859.67**	**1,048.84**
Fuel oil and other fuels	**94.02**	**74.65**	**79.06**	**99.42**	**92.78**	**114.59**	**128.02**
Fuel oil	55.60	37.42	43.06	54.62	53.00	82.53	89.36
Coal	3.50	2.33	3.93	6.20	3.64	5.23	-
Bottled gas	24.48	26.52	22.97	28.34	23.75	17.90	23.47
Wood and other fuels	10.43	8.37	9.09	10.26	12.38	8.93	14.87
Telephone	**528.79**	**362.00**	**463.89**	**539.06**	**590.21**	**601.80**	**769.38**
Water and other public services	**171.19**	**105.60**	**124.35**	**162.14**	**193.53**	**236.49**	**292.34**
Water and sewerage maintenance	131.02	81.02	95.31	124.06	150.67	178.26	222.63
Trash and garbage collection	38.67	24.33	28.29	37.16	40.93	55.27	65.76
Septic tank cleaning	1.50	0.25	0.73	0.92	1.94	2.96	3.95

*Note: Expenditures listed for items in a given category may not add to the total for that category because the listing is incomplete. "Maintenance and repair services," for example, includes "other maintenance and repair services," which is omitted here. Expenditures are not given (-) when the amount is too small to be reliable. Total expenditure exceeds total income in some income categories due to a number of factors including the underreporting of income, borrowing, and the use of savings. Numbers may not add to total due to rounding. *See Appendix B for information on mortgage principle reduction.*

Share of spending

(consumer units include complete income reporters only)	all cu's	under $10,000	$10,000 to $19,999	$20,000 to $29,999	$30,000 to $39,999	$40,000 to $49,999	$50,000 and over
Number of consumer units (in thousands)	81,354	18,809	17,652	14,586	10,901	7,198	12,209
Average number of persons per cu	2.6	1.8	2.3	2.7	2.9	3.2	3.1
Average number of earners per cu	1.4	0.7	1.0	1.5	1.8	2.0	2.1
TOTAL AVERAGE ANNUAL EXPENDITURES	100.00%	100.00%	100.00%	100.00%	100.00%	100.00%	100.00%
HOUSING, AVERAGE ANNUAL EXPENDITURES	30.58%	36.46%	31.56%	30.17%	29.25%	28.24%	30.04%
SHELTER	16.94%	20.15%	17.08%	16.57%	15.95%	15.71%	17.03%
Owned dwellings*	9.68	6.73	5.81	7.94	9.38	10.81	13.24
Mortgage interest and charges	5.91	2.65	2.28	4.22	6.08	7.41	9.03
Property taxes	1.88	1.84	1.71	1.68	1.89	1.71	2.15
Maintenance, repairs, insurance, and other expenses	1.89	2.23	1.81	2.04	1.41	1.68	2.06
Homeowners and related insurance	0.58	0.68	0.57	0.56	0.51	0.53	0.60
Ground rent	0.10	0.28	0.18	0.14	0.08	0.04	0.02
Maintenance and repair services	0.96	1.08	0.90	1.05	0.59	0.78	1.16
Painting and papering	0.20	0.30	0.14	0.22	0.07	0.13	0.28
Plumbing and water heating	0.09	0.09	0.08	0.09	0.05	0.09	0.11
Heat, air conditioning, electrical work	0.16	0.20	0.17	0.11	0.14	0.16	0.17
Roofing and gutters	0.18	0.12	0.20	0.20	0.13	0.15	0.21
Hard surface flooring	0.03	0.00	0.02	0.01	0.03	0.02	0.06
Maintenance and repair commodities	0.25	0.20	0.15	0.29	0.22	0.33	0.27
Paint, wallpaper, equipment, and supplies	0.07	0.06	0.04	0.07	0.06	0.10	0.10
Plumbing supplies and equipment	0.02	0.01	0.02	0.03	0.02	0.03	0.02
Electrical supplies, heating/cooling equipment	0.01	0.01	0.01	0.01	0.02	0.01	0.02
Roofing and gutters	0.02	-	0.02	0.03	0.01	0.01	0.01
Insulation, remodeling, and finishing room or basement	0.05	0.04	0.02	0.03	0.06	0.12	0.05
Miscellaneous supplies and equipment	0.07	0.03	0.05	0.11	0.05	0.07	0.07
Rented dwellings	5.57	12.25	9.76	7.25	4.94	3.33	1.58
Rent	5.41	11.95	9.48	7.08	4.81	3.24	1.50
Rent as pay	0.07	0.19	0.16	0.06	0.05	0.00	0.00
Maintenance, repairs, and insurance	0.09	0.11	0.13	0.11	0.09	0.09	0.06
Tenant's insurance	0.03	0.05	0.04	0.04	0.04	0.03	0.02
Maintenance and repair services	0.03	0.02	0.06	0.05	0.03	0.02	0.02
Maintenance and repair commodities	0.02	0.03	0.02	0.02	0.02	0.04	0.01
Other lodging	1.69	1.17	1.52	1.38	1.63	1.58	2.21
Owned vacation homes	0.30	0.12	0.51	0.20	0.28	0.14	0.38
Expenses for other properties	0.59	0.36	0.49	0.55	0.53	0.60	0.75

Percent of total average annual expenditures spent on shelter and utilities, by total before-tax income of consumer unit.

(continued from previous page)	all cu's	under $10,000	$10,000 to $19,999	$20,000 to $29,999	$30,000 to $39,999	$40,000 to $49,999	$50,000 and over
Housing while attending school	0.13	0.25	0.02	0.07	0.10	0.09	0.23
Lodging while out-of-town	0.68	0.44	0.50	0.56	0.71	0.75	0.86
UTILITIES, FUELS, AND PUBLIC SERVICES	**6.54%**	**10.29%**	**8.15%**	**6.87%**	**6.08%**	**5.56%**	**4.96%**
Natural gas	**0.88**	**1.40**	**1.18**	**0.86**	**0.78**	**0.74**	**0.68**
Electricity	**2.65**	**4.07**	**3.28**	**2.79**	**2.53**	**2.29**	**2.00**
Fuel oil and other fuels	**0.36**	**0.66**	**0.44**	**0.40**	**0.29**	**0.31**	**0.24**
Fuel oil	0.21	0.33	0.24	0.22	0.17	0.22	0.17
Coal	0.01	0.02	0.02	0.02	0.01	0.01	-
Bottled gas	0.09	0.24	0.13	0.11	0.08	0.05	0.04
Wood and other fuels	0.04	0.07	0.05	0.04	0.04	0.02	0.03
Telephone	**2.00**	**3.21**	**2.57**	**2.17**	**1.86**	**1.60**	**1.47**
Water and other public services	**0.65**	**0.94**	**0.69**	**0.65**	**0.61**	**0.63**	**0.56**
Water and sewerage maintenance	0.50	0.72	0.53	0.50	0.48	0.47	0.43
Trash and garbage collection	0.15	0.22	0.16	0.15	0.13	0.15	0.13
Septic tank cleaning	0.01	0.00	0.00	0.00	0.01	0.01	0.01

*Note: Expenditures listed for items in a given category may not add to the total for that category because the listing is incomplete. "Maintenance and repair services," for example, includes "other maintenance and repair services," which is omitted here. Expenditures are not given (-) when the amount is too small to be reliable. Numbers may not add to total due to rounding.*See Appendix B for information on mortgage principle reduction.*

Indexed expenditures

Indexed average annual expenditures for shelter and utilities, by total before-tax income of consumer unit.

(consumer units include complete income reporters only)	all cu's	under $10,000	$10,000 to $19,999	$20,000 to $29,999	$30,000 to $39,999	$40,000 to $49,999	$50,000 and over
Number of consumer units (in thousands)	81,354	18,809	17,652	14,586	10,901	7,198	12,209
Average number of persons per cu	2.6	1.8	2.3	2.7	2.9	3.2	3.1
Average number of earners per cu	1.4	0.7	1.0	1.5	1.8	2.0	2.1
TOTAL AVERAGE ANNUAL EXPENDITURES	100	43	69	94	120	142	198
HOUSING, AVERAGE ANNUAL EXPENDITURES	100	51	71	93	115	131	195
SHELTER	100	51	69	92	113	132	199
Owned dwellings*	100	30	41	77	116	159	271
Mortgage interest and charges	100	19	26	67	123	178	303
Property taxes	100	42	62	84	121	130	227
Maintenance, repairs, insurance, and other expenses	100	51	66	102	90	127	216
Homeowners and related insurance	100	50	68	92	107	132	206
Ground rent	100	117	119	131	89	53	47
Maintenance and repair services	100	48	65	103	74	116	240
Painting and papering	100	65	47	106	41	96	279
Plumbing and water heating	100	44	62	99	75	143	240
Heat, air conditioning, electrical work	100	54	74	68	106	147	214
Roofing and gutters	100	30	76	106	87	118	237
Hard surface flooring	100	5	47	30	98	83	417
Maintenance and repair commodities	100	34	41	110	108	187	216
Paint, wallpaper, and supplies	100	32	37	84	104	190	258
Plumbing supplies and equipment	100	21	50	122	110	195	202
Electrical supplies, heating/cooling equipment	100	32	60	88	131	59	272
Roofing and gutters	100	-	67	163	82	64	100
Insulation, remodeling, and finishing room or basement	100	33	24	61	137	313	202
Miscellaneous supplies and equipment	100	18	47	161	93	146	209
Rented dwellings	100	94	120	123	106	85	56
Rent	100	94	120	123	107	85	55
Rent as pay	100	121	166	92	82	4	55
Maintenance, repairs, and insurance	100	53	96	113	116	135	127
Tenant's insurance	100	70	76	107	149	122	116
Maintenance and repair services	100	31	129	127	107	75	141
Maintenance and repair commodities	100	62	73	102	82	244	125
Other lodging	100	30	61	77	115	133	259
Owned vacation homes	100	17	117	62	114	67	255
Expenses for other properties	100	26	58	89	109	145	253

Indexed average annual expenditures for shelter and utilities, by total before-tax income of consumer unit.

(continued from previous page)	all cu's	under $10,000	$10,000 to $19,999	$20,000 to $29,999	$30,000 to $39,999	$40,000 to $49,999	$50,000 and over
Housing while attending school	100	80	10	50	87	99	333
Lodging while out-of-town	100	28	50	78	127	157	252
UTILITIES, FUELS, AND PUBLIC SERVICES	**100**	**67**	**85**	**99**	**111**	**121**	**150**
Natural gas	**100**	**68**	**92**	**93**	**106**	**119**	**153**
Electricity	**100**	**66**	**85**	**99**	**114**	**123**	**150**
Fuel oil and other fuels	**100**	**79**	**84**	**106**	**99**	**122**	**136**
Fuel oil	100	67	77	98	95	148	161
Coal	100	67	112	177	104	149	-
Bottled gas	100	108	94	116	97	73	96
Wood and other fuels	100	80	87	98	119	86	143
Telephone	**100**	**68**	**88**	**102**	**112**	**114**	**145**
Water and other public services	**100**	**62**	**73**	**95**	**113**	**138**	**171**
Water and sewerage maintenance	100	62	73	95	115	136	170
Trash and garbage collection	100	63	73	96	106	143	170
Septic tank cleaning	100	17	49	61	129	197	263

Note: Expenditures are not given (-) when the amount is too small to be reliable. An index of 100 represents the average for all consumer units. An index of 132 means that the average for the subgroup is 32 percent above the average for all consumer units. An index of 68 indicates spending that is 32 percent below the overall average.*See Appendix B for information on mortgage principle reduction.

Aggregate expenditures, 1988

Aggregate expenditures in 1988 for shelter and utilities, by total before-tax income of consumer unit.

(consumer units include complete income reporters only)	all cu's	under $10,000	$10,000 to $19,999	$20,000 to $29,999	$30,000 to $39,999	$40,000 to $49,999	$50,000 and over
Number of consumer units (in thousands)	81,354	18,809	17,652	14,586	10,901	7,198	12,209
Average number of persons per cu	2.6	1.8	2.3	2.7	2.9	3.2	3.1
Average number of earners per cu	1.4	0.7	1.0	1.5	1.8	2.0	2.1
TOTAL AGGREGATE EXPENDITURES (in millions)	$2,148,492	$211,967	$319,117	$363,138	$345,121	$270,371	$638,777
HOUSING, AGGREGATE EXPENDITURES (in millions)	$656,788	$77,279	$100,712	$109,568	$100,953	$76,362	$191,915
SHELTER	$363,678	$42,701	$54,509	$60,165	$55,049	$42,478	$108,775
Owned dwellings*	$207,785	$14,257	$18,527	$28,833	$32,382	$29,227	$84,559
Mortgage interest and charges	126,945	5,622	7,279	15,341	20,989	20,038	57,675
Property taxes	40,359	3,898	5,465	6,083	6,533	4,634	13,746
Maintenance, repairs, insurance, and other expenses	40,473	4,737	5,783	7,409	4,860	4,554	13,129
Homeowners and related insurance	12,345	1,432	1,833	2,034	1,777	1,446	3,823
Ground rent	2,186	593	562	512	261	104	153
Maintenance and repair services	20,557	2,297	2,886	3,804	2,047	2,110	7,413
Painting and papering	4,232	636	431	806	230	359	1,770
Plumbing and water heating	1,876	190	253	331	188	237	676
Heat, air conditioning, electrical work	3,419	425	550	415	487	443	1,099
Roofing and gutters	3,821	264	632	726	444	397	1,358
Hard surface flooring	662	8	68	36	87	49	414
Maintenance and repair commodities	5,321	414	479	1,047	773	881	1,728
Paint, wallpaper, and supplies	1,573	118	125	236	220	264	609
Plumbing supplies and equipment	460	22	50	101	68	79	139
Electrical supplies, heating/cooling equipment	306	23	40	48	54	16	125
Roofing and gutters	318	-	61	123	46	24	63
Insulation, remodeling, and finishing room or basement	1,130	86	58	124	207	313	342
Miscellaneous supplies and equipment	1,430	61	145	413	178	184	449
Rented dwellings	119,544	25,957	31,146	26,328	17,046	8,990	10,078
Rent	116,200	25,325	30,238	25,703	16,590	8,753	9,591
Rent as pay	1,411	395	507	231	156	5	117
Maintenance, repairs, and insurance	1,933	238	401	393	300	232	370
Tenant's insurance	706	115	117	135	141	76	122
Maintenance and repair services	733	52	206	167	105	49	155
Maintenance and repair commodities	494	71	79	90	55	107	93
Other lodging	36,349	2,487	4,836	5,005	5,620	4,262	14,139
Owned vacation homes	6,367	249	1,614	710	975	379	2,440
Expenses for other properties	12,567	766	1,576	2,002	1,843	1,612	4,768

Aggregate expenditures in 1988 for shelter and utilities, by total before-tax income of consumer unit.

(continued from previous page)	all cu's	under $10,000	$10,000 to $19,999	$20,000 to $29,999	$30,000 to $39,999	$40,000 to $49,999	$50,000 and over
Housing while attending school	2,886	536	63	256	335	253	1,442
Lodging while out-of-town	14,528	935	1,583	2,036	2,467	2,018	5,489
UTILITIES, FUELS, AND PUBLIC SERVICES	**$140,447**	**$21,801**	**$26,005**	**$24,958**	**$20,981**	**$15,042**	**$31,661**
Natural gas	**18,893**	**2,969**	**3,773**	**3,141**	**2,689**	**1,991**	**4,329**
Electricity	**56,955**	**8,633**	**10,453**	**10,139**	**8,737**	**6,188**	**12,805**
Fuel oil and other fuels	**7,649**	**1,404**	**1,395**	**1,450**	**1,011**	**825**	**1,563**
Fuel oil	4,524	704	760	797	578	594	1,091
Coal	281	44	69	90	40	38	-
Bottled gas	1,992	499	405	413	259	129	287
Wood and other fuels	848	157	160	150	135	64	182
Telephone	**43,019**	**6,809**	**8,189**	**7,863**	**6,434**	**4,332**	**9,393**
Water and other public services	**13,927**	**1,986**	**2,195**	**2,365**	**2,110**	**1,702**	**3,569**
Water and sewerage maintenance	10,659	1,524	1,682	1,810	1,642	1,283	2,718
Trash and garbage collection	3,146	458	499	542	446	398	803
Septic tank cleaning	122	5	13	13	21	21	48

Note: Expenditures listed for items in a given category may not add to the total for that category because the listing is incomplete. "Maintenance and repair services," for example, includes "other maintenance and repair services," which is omitted here. Expenditures are not given (-) when the amount is too small to be reliable. Numbers may not add to total due to rounding. The "all cu's" aggregates will differ slightly from table to table because they are the sums of the aggregates in each row. *See Appendix B for information on mortgage principle reduction.

PART III
Spending by type of household for shelter and utilities

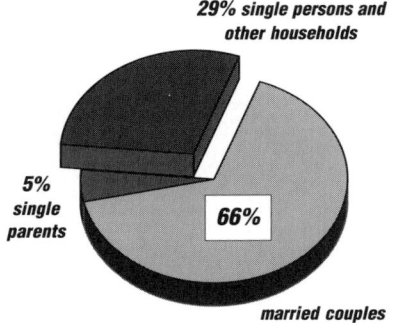

Married couples account for at least two-thirds of the housing market...

29% single persons and other households

5% single parents

66%

married couples

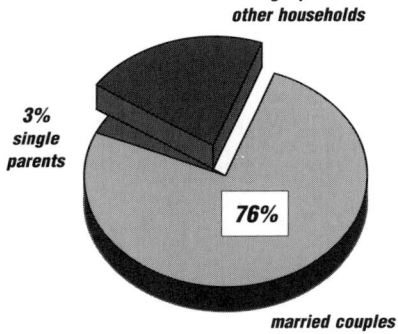

...and the market for owned dwellings...

21% single persons and other households

3% single parents

76%

married couples

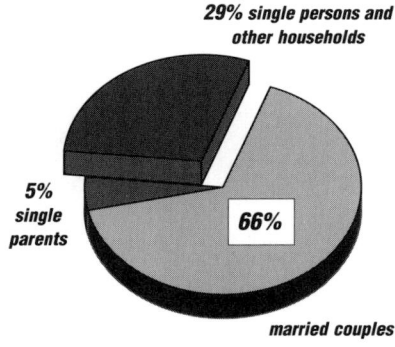

...and for rented dwellings.

29% single persons and other households

5% single parents

66%

married couples

When it comes to putting a roof over their heads, married couples again are the big spenders. They spend more than average on all housing items except rent. Rent is one of the few housing items for which other types of households spend more than average.

Married couples spent $9,731 on housing in 1988— 30 percent of their household budget. Single- person and "other" households* devote one-third of their budget to housing although they spend 40 percent less than married couples. Housing takes the biggest bite out of the budgets of single parents— fully 38 percent or $7,113 in 1988.

Married couples account for two-thirds of the housing market, and for over 75 percent of the homeowners market. They spent $506 billion on housing in 1988, $269 billion on dwellings and more than $109 billion on utilities, fuels, and public services. Single-person and "other" households spent $219 billion on housing, accounting for 29 percent of the market. They are 21 percent of the market for owned homes, spending $133 billion on their homes in 1988. Single parents are just 5 percent of the housing market and 3 percent of the homeowners market.

Married-couple market

Married couples with children spend 30 percent more than the average household on housing. Couples without children at home spend just 5 percent more than average on housing. Spending on owned homes peaks at 70 percent above average among married couples with school-aged children. These are larger households, averaging 4.1 people.

Couples with children under age 6 are the only married couples who spend more than average on rent. Couples with preschoolers spend 29 percent more than average on rent and 40 percent more on owned homes. Married couples with children aged 18 or older at home spend more than any other household type on property taxes; maintenance and repair services and commodities; other lodging; and utilities, fuels, and public services.

Although married couples without children at home spend slightly less than average on dwellings, their spending on homeownership-related items and on other lodging is well above average. They are also above-average spenders on utilities, fuels, and public services.

---

*In this analysis, single-person households are grouped with "other" households. "Other" households are unrelated people living together and families that are not married-couple or single-parent families, such as siblings. Single-person households account for 72 percent of the households in this category.

Other household markets

Single-person and "other" households spend 27 percent less than the average household on housing—20 percent less on dwellings, and 26 percent less on utilities. But their spending on rental housing is 31 percent above average. They spend 13 percent more than average on rental maintenance, repairs, and insurance; and they spend 39 percent more than average on ground rent (mobile home lots). These households also spend above average amounts on roofing and gutter materials.

Spending by single parents on housing is 12 percent below average. They spend 5 percent less than average on dwellings and 15 percent less on utilities. Spending on rent peaks among single parents at 60 percent above average. These households also spend above-average amounts on hard surface flooring and lodging other than their dwelling. Like single-person and "other" households, single parents spend 45 percent less than the average household on owned homes.

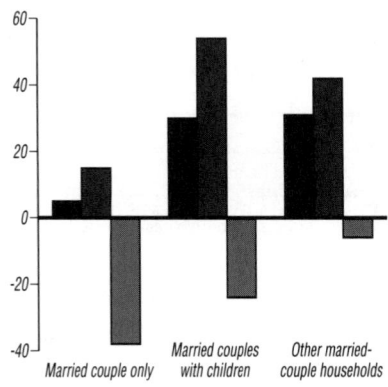

Married couples spend more than average on owned dwellings...

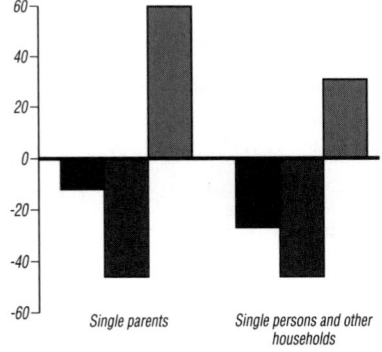

...while these households are strong rental markets.

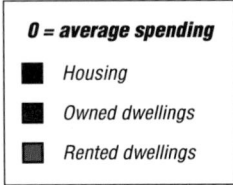

0 = average spending
- ■ Housing
- ■ Owned dwellings
- ■ Rented dwellings

Average expenditures

	all cu's	married couples	single parents	single persons and other cu's
Number of consumer units (in thousands)	94,862	52,010	5,716	37,136
Average number of persons per cu	2.6	3.3	2.9	1.5
Average number of earners per cu	1.4	1.7	1.0	0.9
Average total before-tax income	$28,540.00	$37,299.00	$16,276.00	$18,509.00
TOTAL AVERAGE ANNUAL EXPENDITURES	$25,891.85	$32,314.50	$18,615.80	$17,950.80
HOUSING, AVERAGE ANNUAL EXPENDITURES	$8,078.63	$9,731.21	$7,112.65	$5,902.84
SHELTER	$4,492.75	$5,174.18	$4,248.71	$3,575.93
Owned dwellings*	2,568.69	3,537.64	1,396.64	1,392.05
Mortgage interest and charges	1,569.02	2,242.24	950.73	721.10
Property taxes	503.66	665.20	227.42	319.94
Maintenance, repairs, insurance, and other expenses	496.01	630.04	218.48	351.01
Homeowners and related insurance	149.84	200.09	70.23	91.72
Ground rent	25.45	19.62	13.89	35.40
Maintenance and repair services	257.99	322.29	104.57	191.55
Painting and papering	54.05	63.82	29.62	44.12
Plumbing and water heating	23.46	29.50	6.42	17.63
Heat, air conditioning, electrical work	42.06	52.07	13.71	32.40
Roofing and gutters	42.59	50.82	22.24	34.20
Hard surface flooring	8.91	12.48	10.36	3.69
Maintenance and repair commodities	61.98	87.34	29.55	31.44
Paint, wallpaper, and supplies	19.16	27.69	10.42	8.55
Plumbing supplies and equipment	5.21	7.62	1.61	2.40
Electrical supplies, heating/cooling equipment	3.65	4.82	3.15	2.08
Roofing and gutters	4.84	4.99	-	5.30
Insulation, remodeling, and finishing room or basement	13.10	19.35	7.71	5.18
Miscellaneous supplies and equipment	16.02	22.89	6.23	7.91
Rented dwellings	1,467.79	1,049.62	2,343.88	1,918.58
Rent	1,426.08	1,009.44	2,309.28	1,873.64
Rent as pay	17.19	17.18	16.60	17.30
Maintenance, repairs, and insurance	24.52	23.00	18.00	27.64
Tenant's insurance	7.90	6.86	5.41	9.74
Maintenance and repair services	10.55	9.33	9.52	12.42
Maintenance and repair commodities	6.07	6.81	3.07	5.49
Other lodging	456.27	586.92	508.19	265.29
Owned vacation homes	76.61	94.16	273.85	21.67
Expenses for other properties	160.42	202.93	152.34	102.11

Average annual expenditures for shelter and utilities, by type of consumer unit.

(continued from previous page)	all cu's	married couples	single parents	single persons and other cu's
Housing while attending school	36.27	45.33	27.76	24.91
Lodging while out-of-town	182.97	244.50	54.25	116.60
UTILITIES, FUELS, AND PUBLIC SERVICES	**$1,747.42**	**$2,099.88**	**$1,481.57**	**$1,294.71**
Natural gas	**233.75**	**276.56**	**206.48**	**178.00**
Electricity	**708.82**	**875.58**	**626.82**	**487.90**
Fuel oil and other fuels	**97.76**	**126.78**	**31.07**	**67.37**
Fuel oil	60.10	75.98	16.14	44.64
Coal	3.57	5.20	1.53	1.59
Bottled gas	24.05	32.18	7.27	15.25
Wood and other fuels	10.03	13.42	6.13	5.89
Telephone	**537.04**	**597.64**	**493.82**	**458.83**
Water and other public services	**170.05**	**223.32**	**123.38**	**102.61**
Water and sewerage maintenance	130.31	170.41	97.69	79.16
Trash and garbage collection	38.19	50.46	25.24	22.99
Septic tank cleaning	1.55	2.45	-	-

Note: Expenditures listed for items in a given category may not add to the total for that category because the listing is incomplete. "Maintenance and repair services," for example, includes "other maintenance and repair services," which is omitted here. Expenditures are not given (-) when the amount is too small to be reliable. Numbers may not add to total due to rounding. "Single parents" is one-parent consumer units with a child or children under age 18 living at home. "Other cu's" includes persons living with unrelated persons and families other than married-couple and single-parent families. *See Appendix B for information on mortgage principle reduction.

Share of spending

	all cu's	married couples	single parents	single persons and other cu's
Number of consumer units (in thousands)	94,862	52,010	5,716	37,136
Average number of persons per cu	2.6	3.3	2.9	1.5
Average number of earners per cu	1.4	1.7	1.0	0.9
Average total before-tax income	$28,540	$37,299	$16,276	$18,509
TOTAL AVERAGE ANNUAL EXPENDITURES	100.00%	100.00%	100.00%	100.00%
HOUSING, AVERAGE ANNUAL EXPENDITURES	31.20%	30.11%	38.21%	32.88%
SHELTER	**17.35%**	**16.01%**	**22.82%**	**19.92%**
Owned dwellings*	**9.92**	**10.95**	**7.50**	**7.75**
Mortgage interest and charges	6.06	6.94	5.11	4.02
Property taxes	1.95	2.06	1.22	1.78
Maintenance, repairs, insurance, and other expenses	1.92	1.95	1.17	1.96
Homeowners and related insurance	0.58	0.62	0.38	0.51
Ground rent	0.10	0.06	0.07	0.20
Maintenance and repair services	1.00	1.00	0.56	1.07
Painting and papering	0.21	0.20	0.16	0.25
Plumbing and water heating	0.09	0.09	0.03	0.10
Heat, air conditioning, electrical work	0.16	0.16	0.07	0.18
Roofing and gutters	0.16	0.16	0.12	0.19
Hard surface flooring	0.03	0.04	0.06	0.02
Maintenance and repair commodities	0.24	0.27	0.16	0.18
Paint, wallpaper, equipment, and supplies	0.07	0.09	0.06	0.05
Plumbing supplies and equipment	0.02	0.02	0.01	0.01
Electrical supplies, heating/cooling equipment	0.01	0.01	0.02	0.01
Roofing and gutters	0.02	0.02	-	0.03
Insulation, remodeling, and finishing room or basement	0.05	0.06	0.04	0.03
Miscellaneous supplies and equipment	0.06	0.07	0.03	0.04
Rented dwellings	**5.67**	**3.25**	**12.59**	**10.69**
Rent	5.51	3.12	12.40	10.44
Rent as pay	0.07	0.05	0.09	0.10
Maintenance, repairs, and insurance	0.09	0.07	0.10	0.15
Tenant's insurance	0.03	0.02	0.03	0.05
Maintenance and repair services	0.04	0.03	0.05	0.07
Maintenance and repair commodities	0.02	0.02	0.02	0.03
Other lodging	**1.76**	**1.82**	**2.73**	**1.48**
Owned vacation homes	0.30	0.29	1.47	0.12
Expenses for other properties	0.62	0.63	0.82	0.57

Percent of total average annual expenditures spent on shelter and utilities, by type of consumer unit.

(continued from previous page)	all cu's	married couples	single parents	single persons and other cu's
Housing while attending school	0.14	0.14	0.15	0.14
Lodging while out-of-town	0.71	0.76	0.29	0.65
UTILITIES, FUELS, AND PUBLIC SERVICES	**6.75%**	**6.50%**	**7.96%**	**7.21%**
Natural gas	**0.90**	**0.86**	**1.11**	**0.99**
Electricity	**2.74**	**2.71**	**3.37**	**2.72**
Fuel oil and other fuels	0.38	0.39	0.17	0.38
Fuel oil	0.23	0.24	0.09	0.25
Coal	0.01	0.02	0.01	0.01
Bottled gas	0.09	0.10	0.04	0.08
Wood and other fuels	0.04	0.04	0.03	0.03
Telephone	**2.07**	**1.85**	**2.65**	**2.56**
Water and other public services	**0.66**	**0.69**	**0.66**	**0.57**
Water and sewerage maintenance	0.50	0.53	0.52	0.44
Trash and garbage collection	0.15	0.16	0.14	0.13
Septic tank cleaning	0.01	0.01	-	-

*Note: Expenditures listed for items in a given category may not add to the total for that category because the listing is incomplete. "Maintenance and repair services," for example, includes "other maintenance and repair services," which is omitted here. Expenditures are not given (-) when the amount is too small to be reliable. Numbers may not add to total due to rounding. "Single parents" is one-parent consumer units with a child or children under age 18 living at home. "Other cu's" includes persons living with unrelated persons and families other than married-couple and single-parent families. *See Appendix B for information on mortgage principle reduction.*

Indexed expenditures

	all cu's	married couples	single parents	single persons and other cu's
Number of consumer units (in thousands)	94,862	52,010	5,716	37,136
Average number of persons per cu	2.6	3.3	2.9	1.5
Average number of earners per cu	1.4	1.7	1.0	0.9
Average total before-tax income	$28,540	$37,299	$16,276	$18,509
TOTAL AVERAGE ANNUAL EXPENDITURES	100	125	72	69
HOUSING, AVERAGE ANNUAL EXPENDITURES	100	120	88	73
SHELTER	100	115	95	80
Owned dwellings*	100	138	54	54
Mortgage interest and charges	100	143	61	46
Property taxes	100	132	45	64
Maintenance, repairs, insurance, and other expenses	100	127	44	71
Homeowners and related insurance	100	134	47	61
Ground rent	100	77	55	139
Maintenance and repair services	100	125	41	74
Painting and papering	100	118	55	82
Plumbing and water heating	100	126	27	75
Heat, air conditioning, electrical work	100	124	33	77
Roofing and gutters	100	119	52	80
Hard surface flooring	100	140	116	41
Maintenance and repair commodities	100	141	48	51
Paint, wallpaper, and supplies	100	145	54	45
Plumbing supplies and equipment	100	146	31	46
Electrical supplies, heating/cooling equipment	100	132	86	57
Roofing and gutters	100	103	-	110
Insulation, remodeling, and finishing room or basement	100	148	59	40
Miscellaneous supplies and equipment	100	143	39	49
Rented dwellings	100	72	160	131
Rent	100	71	162	131
Rent as pay	100	100	97	101
Maintenance, repairs, and insurance	100	94	73	113
Tenant's insurance	100	87	68	123
Maintenance and repair services	100	88	90	118
Maintenance and repair commodities	100	112	51	90
Other lodging	100	129	111	58
Owned vacation homes	100	123	357	28
Expenses for other properties	100	126	95	64

Indexed average annual expenditures for shelter and utilities, by type of consumer unit.

(continued from previous page)

	all cu's	married couples	single parents	single persons and other cu's
Housing while attending school	100	125	77	69
Lodging while out-of-town	100	134	30	64
UTILITIES, FUELS, AND PUBLIC SERVICES	**100**	**120**	**85**	**74**
Natural gas	**100**	**118**	**88**	**76**
Electricity	**100**	**124**	**88**	**69**
Fuel oil and other fuels	**100**	**130**	**32**	**69**
Fuel oil	100	126	27	74
Coal	100	146	43	45
Bottled gas	100	134	30	63
Wood and other fuels	100	134	61	59
Telephone	**100**	**111**	**92**	**85**
Water and other public services	**100**	**131**	**73**	**60**
Water and sewerage maintenance	100	131	75	61
Trash and garbage collection	100	132	66	60
Septic tank cleaning	100	158	-	-

*Note: An index of 100 represents the average for all consumer units. An index of 132 means that the average for the subgroup is 32 percent above the average for all consumer units. An index of 68 indicates spending that is 32 percent below the overall average. Expenditures are not given (-) when the amount is too small to be reliable. Numbers may not add to total due to rounding. "Single parents" is one-parent consumer units with a child or children under age 18 living at home. "Other cu's" includes persons living with unrelated persons and families other than married-couple and single-parent families. *See Appendix B for information on mortgage principle reduction.*

Aggregate expenditures, 1988

Aggregate expenditures in 1988 for shelter and utilities, by type of consumer unit.

	all cu's	married couples	single parents	single persons and other cu's
Number of consumer units (in thousands)	94,862	52,010	5,716	37,136
Average number of persons per cu	2.6	3.3	2.9	1.5
Average number of earners per cu	1.4	1.7	1.0	0.9
Aggregate before-tax income (in millions)	$2,720,305	$1,939,921	$93,034	$687,350
TOTAL AGGREGATE EXPENDITURES (in millions)	$2,453,706	$1,680,677	$106,408	$666,621
HOUSING, AGGREGATE EXPENDITURES (in millions)	$765,984	$506,120	$40,656	$219,208
SHELTER	$426,190	$269,109	$24,286	$132,796
Owned dwellings*	243,671	183,993	7,983	51,695
Mortgage interest and charges	148,832	116,619	5,434	26,779
Property taxes	47,778	34,597	1,300	11,881
Maintenance, repairs, insurance, and other expenses	47,052	32,768	1,249	13,035
Homeowners and related insurance	14,214	10,407	401	3,406
Ground rent	2,414	1,020	79	1,315
Maintenance and repair services	24,473	16,762	598	7,113
Painting and papering	5,127	3,319	169	1,638
Plumbing and water heating	2,226	1,534	37	655
Heat, air conditioning, electrical work	3,990	2,708	78	1,203
Roofing and gutters	4,040	2,643	127	1,270
Hard surface flooring	845	649	59	137
Maintenance and repair commodities	5,879	4,543	169	1,168
Paint, wallpaper, and supplies	1,817	1,440	60	318
Plumbing supplies and equipment	495	396	9	89
Electrical supplies, heating/cooling equipment	346	251	18	77
Roofing and gutters	457	260	-	197
Insulation, remodeling, and finishing room or basement	1,243	1,006	44	192
Miscellaneous supplies and equipment	1,520	1,191	36	294
Rented dwellings	139,237	54,591	13,398	71,248
Rent	135,280	52,501	13,200	69,579
Rent as pay	1,631	894	95	642
Maintenance, repairs, and insurance	2,326	1,196	103	1,026
Tenant's insurance	749	357	31	362
Maintenance and repair services	1,001	485	54	461
Maintenance and repair commodities	576	354	18	204
Other lodging	43,282	30,526	2,905	9,852
Owned vacation homes	7,267	4,897	1,565	805
Expenses for other properties	15,217	10,554	871	3,792

Aggregate expenditures in 1988 for shelter and utilities, by type of consumer unit.

(continued from previous page)

	all cu's	married couples	single parents	single persons and other cu's
Housing while attending school	3,441	2,358	159	925
Lodging while out-of-town	17,357	12,716	310	4,330
UTILITIES, FUELS, AND PUBLIC SERVICES	**$165,764**	**$109,215**	**$8,469**	**$48,080**
Natural gas	**22,174**	**14,384**	**1,180**	**6,610**
Electricity	**67,240**	**45,539**	**3,583**	**18,119**
Fuel oil and other fuels	**9,273**	**6,594**	**178**	**2,502**
Fuel oil	5,702	3,952	92	1,658
Coal	338	270	9	59
Bottled gas	2,282	1,674	42	566
Wood and other fuels	952	698	35	219
Telephone	**50,945**	**31,083**	**2,823**	**17,039**
Water and other public services	**16,131**	**11,615**	**705**	**3,811**
Water and sewerage maintenance	12,361	8,863	558	2,940
Trash and garbage collection	3,622	2,624	144	854
Septic tank cleaning	127	127	-	-

Note: Expenditures listed for items in a given category may not add to the total for that category because the listing is incomplete. "Maintenance and repair services," for example, includes "other maintenance and repair services," which is omitted here. Expenditures are not given (-) when the amount is too small to be reliable. Numbers may not add to total due to rounding. The "all cu's" aggregates will differ slightly from table to table because they are the sums of the aggregates in each row. "Single parents" is one-parent consumer units with a child or children under age 18 living at home. "Other cu's" includes persons living with unrelated persons and families other than married-couple and single-parent families. *See Appendix B for information on mortgage principle reduction.

Average expenditures

	all cu's	all married couples	married couple only	all married couples with children	AGE OF OLDEST CHILD			other married couples
					under 6	6 to 17	18 or older	
Number of consumer units (in thousands)	94,862	52,010	20,227	28,100	5,858	14,194	8,047	3,684
Average number of persons per cu	2.6	3.3	2.0	3.9	3.5	4.1	3.9	5.1
Average number of earners per cu	1.4	1.7	1.2	2.1	1.7	1.9	2.7	2.4
Average total before-tax income	$28,540.00	$37,299.00	$33,825.00	$39,354.00	$34,318.00	$38,039.00	$45,596.00	$40,846.00
TOTAL AVERAGE ANNUAL EXPENDITURES	$25,891.85	$32,314.50	$27,954.50	$35,015.30	$30,942.80	$35,248.40	$37,763.90	$35,739.60
HOUSING, AVERAGE ANNUAL EXPENDITURES	$8,078.63	$9,731.21	$8,452.92	$10,541.90	$10,807.80	$10,850.20	$9,819.12	$10,567.30
SHELTER	$4,492.75	$5,174.18	$4,432.59	$5,639.26	$5,772.26	$6,002.68	$4,901.41	$5,698.47
Owned dwellings*	2,568.69	3,537.64	2,951.86	3,946.24	3,587.62	4,356.64	3,483.43	3,637.17
Mortgage interest and charges	1,569.02	2,242.24	1,496.65	2,757.94	2,764.59	3,215.91	1,945.27	2,402.37
Property taxes	503.66	665.20	731.78	622.19	390.07	623.14	789.51	627.63
Maintenance, repairs, insurance, and other expenses	496.01	630.04	723.02	566.11	432.95	517.58	748.65	607.17
Homeowners and related insurance	149.84	200.09	214.22	190.31	149.19	192.78	215.88	197.15
Ground rent	25.45	19.62	27.59	16.07	31.10	11.69	12.87	2.91
Maintenance and repair services	257.99	322.29	395.72	270.93	182.78	226.66	413.17	310.93
Painting and papering	54.05	63.82	92.21	45.42	25.98	45.97	58.60	48.29
Plumbing and water heating	23.46	29.50	33.85	26.07	30.27	19.85	33.98	31.80
Heat, air conditioning, electrical work	42.06	52.07	63.85	38.56	26.37	33.17	56.93	90.46
Roofing and gutters	42.59	50.82	65.34	44.80	8.06	31.85	94.39	17.04
Hard surface flooring	8.91	12.48	7.83	16.19	6.92	10.79	32.45	9.69
Maintenance and repair commodities	61.98	87.34	84.29	88.39	69.46	85.88	106.59	96.18
Paint, wallpaper, and supplies	19.16	27.69	20.43	31.54	28.98	32.64	31.46	38.17
Plumbing supplies and equipment	5.21	7.62	7.33	7.37	4.17	8.05	8.50	11.14
Electrical supplies, heating/cooling equipment	3.65	4.82	5.59	4.51	1.49	3.67	8.18	2.92
Roofing and gutters	4.84	4.99	5.63	4.65	4.40	1.73	9.96	4.10
Insulation, remodeling, and finishing room or basement	13.10	19.35	12.85	23.53	17.83	28.10	19.62	23.16
Miscellaneous supplies and equipment	16.02	22.89	32.45	16.80	12.59	11.69	28.87	16.69
Rented dwellings	1,467.79	1,049.62	903.78	1,110.41	1,890.71	1,104.32	553.12	1,386.71
Rent	1,426.08	1,009.44	873.87	1,061.70	1,781.84	1,069.76	523.23	1,355.17
Rent as pay	17.19	17.18	11.10	21.85	49.06	14.35	15.28	15.00
Maintenance, repairs, and insurance	24.52	23.00	18.81	26.86	59.81	20.21	14.60	16.53
Tenant's insurance	7.90	6.86	7.48	6.65	12.81	5.80	3.69	4.95
Maintenance and repair services	10.55	9.33	6.79	11.34	26.88	6.90	7.84	7.93
Maintenance and repair commodities	6.07	6.81	4.53	8.87	20.13	7.51	3.07	3.66
Other lodging	456.27	586.92	576.95	582.61	293.94	541.72	864.86	674.59
Owned vacation homes	76.61	94.16	112.13	79.02	33.04	72.07	124.75	111.02
Expenses for other properties	160.42	202.93	175.47	207.79	108.86	199.15	295.05	316.67

Average annual expenditures for shelter and utilities, by married couples with and without children.

(continued from previous page)	all cu's	all married couples	married couple only	all married couples with children	AGE OF OLDEST CHILD			other married couples
					under 6	6 to 17	18 or older	
Housing while attending school	36.27	45.33	15.21	70.77	3.04	38.87	176.33	16.63
Lodging while out-of-town	182.97	244.50	274.14	225.03	148.99	231.63	268.73	230.27
UTILITIES, FUELS, AND PUBLIC SERVICES	**$1,747.42**	**$2,099.88**	**$1,872.64**	**$2,218.99**	**$1,840.55**	**$2,197.20**	**$2,532.93**	**$2,438.94**
Natural gas	**233.75**	**276.56**	**248.70**	**287.80**	**244.91**	**270.89**	**348.85**	**343.77**
Electricity	**708.82**	**875.58**	**769.13**	**941.07**	**747.69**	**975.28**	**1,021.52**	**960.44**
Fuel oil and other fuels	**97.76**	**126.78**	**133.49**	**123.53**	**96.96**	**109.76**	**167.15**	**114.71**
Fuel oil	60.10	75.98	76.66	74.35	58.58	62.03	107.57	84.64
Coal	3.57	5.20	5.58	5.44	5.29	4.50	7.20	1.30
Bottled gas	24.05	32.18	36.18	30.32	23.69	29.59	36.43	24.46
Wood and other fuels	10.03	13.42	15.07	13.42	9.40	13.63	15.96	4.31
Telephone	**537.04**	**597.64**	**526.60**	**627.79**	**575.98**	**592.01**	**728.64**	**757.66**
Water and other public services	**170.05**	**223.32**	**194.72**	**238.80**	**175.01**	**249.26**	**266.77**	**262.35**
Water and sewerage maintenance	130.31	170.41	149.75	180.55	129.63	192.00	197.41	206.51
Trash and garbage collection	38.19	50.46	43.21	55.57	44.22	53.80	66.96	51.29
Septic tank cleaning	1.55	2.45	1.76	2.68	1.16	3.46	2.41	4.55

*Note: Expenditures listed for items in a given category may not add to the total for that category because the listing is incomplete. "Maintenance and repair services," for example, includes "other maintenance and repair services," which is omitted here. Numbers may not add to total due to rounding. Other married couples include extended family members or unrelated persons in addition to the married couple. *See Appendix B for information on mortgage principle reduction.*

Share of spending

	all cu's	all married couples	married couple only	all married couples with children	AGE OF OLDEST CHILD under 6	AGE OF OLDEST CHILD 6 to 17	AGE OF OLDEST CHILD 18 or older	other married couples
Number of consumer units (in thousands)	94,862	52,010	20,227	28,100	5,858	14,194	8,047	3,684
Average number of persons per cu	2.6	3.3	2.0	3.9	3.5	4.1	3.9	5.1
Average number of earners per cu	1.4	1.7	1.2	2.1	1.7	1.9	2.7	2.4
Average total before-tax income	$28,540	$37,299	$33,825	$39,354	$34,318	$38,039	$45,596	$40,846
TOTAL AVERAGE ANNUAL EXPENDITURES	100.00%	100.00%	100.00%	100.00%	100.00%	100.00%	100.00%	100.00%
HOUSING, AVERAGE ANNUAL EXPENDITURES	31.20%	30.11%	30.24%	30.11%	34.93%	30.78%	26.00%	29.57%
SHELTER	**17.35%**	**16.01%**	**15.86%**	**16.11%**	**18.65%**	**17.03%**	**12.98%**	**15.94%**
Owned dwellings*	**9.92**	**10.95**	**10.56**	**11.27**	**11.59**	**12.36**	**9.22**	**10.18**
Mortgage interest and charges	6.06	6.94	5.35	7.88	8.93	9.12	5.15	6.72
Property taxes	1.95	2.06	2.62	1.78	1.26	1.77	2.09	1.76
Maintenance, repairs, insurance, and other expenses	1.92	1.95	2.59	1.62	1.40	1.47	1.98	1.70
Homeowners and related insurance	0.58	0.62	0.77	0.54	0.48	0.55	0.57	0.55
Ground rent	0.10	0.06	0.10	0.05	0.10	0.03	0.03	0.01
Maintenance and repair services	1.00	1.00	1.42	0.77	0.59	0.64	1.09	0.87
Painting and papering	0.21	0.20	0.33	0.13	0.08	0.13	0.16	0.14
Plumbing and water heating	0.09	0.09	0.12	0.07	0.10	0.06	0.09	0.09
Heat, air conditioning, electrical work	0.16	0.16	0.23	0.11	0.09	0.09	0.15	0.25
Roofing and gutters	0.16	0.16	0.23	0.13	0.03	0.09	0.25	0.05
Hard surface flooring	0.03	0.04	0.03	0.05	0.02	0.03	0.09	0.03
Maintenance and repair commodities	0.24	0.27	0.30	0.25	0.22	0.24	0.28	0.27
Paint, wallpaper, equipment, and supplies	0.07	0.09	0.07	0.09	0.09	0.09	0.08	0.11
Plumbing supplies and equipment	0.02	0.02	0.03	0.02	0.01	0.02	0.02	0.03
Electrical supplies, heating/cooling equipment	0.01	0.01	0.02	0.01	0.00	0.01	0.02	0.01
Roofing and gutters	0.02	0.02	0.02	0.01	0.01	0.00	0.03	0.01
Insulation, remodeling, and finishing room or basement	0.05	0.06	0.05	0.07	0.06	0.08	0.05	0.06
Miscellaneous supplies and equipment	0.06	0.07	0.12	0.05	0.04	0.03	0.08	0.05
Rented dwellings	**5.67**	**3.25**	**3.23**	**3.17**	**6.11**	**3.13**	**1.46**	**3.88**
Rent	5.51	3.12	3.13	3.03	5.76	3.03	1.39	3.79
Rent as pay	0.07	0.05	0.04	0.06	0.16	0.04	0.04	0.04
Maintenance, repairs, and insurance	0.09	0.07	0.07	0.08	0.19	0.06	0.04	0.05
Tenant's insurance	0.03	0.02	0.03	0.02	0.04	0.02	0.01	0.01
Maintenance and repair services	0.04	0.03	0.02	0.03	0.09	0.02	0.02	0.02
Maintenance and repair commodities	0.02	0.02	0.02	0.03	0.07	0.02	0.01	0.01
Other lodging	**1.76**	**1.82**	**2.06**	**1.66**	**0.95**	**1.54**	**2.29**	**1.89**
Owned vacation homes	0.30	0.29	0.40	0.23	0.11	0.20	0.33	0.31
Expenses for other properties	0.62	0.63	0.63	0.59	0.35	0.56	0.78	0.89

Percent of total average annual expenditures spent on shelter and utilities, by married couples with and without children.

(continued from previous page)

	all cu's	all married couples	married couple only	all married couples with children	AGE OF OLDEST CHILD			other married couples
					under 6	6 to 17	18 or older	
Housing while attending school	0.14	0.14	0.05	0.20	0.01	0.11	0.47	0.05
Lodging while out-of-town	0.71	0.76	0.98	0.64	0.48	0.66	0.71	0.64
UTILITIES, FUELS, AND PUBLIC SERVICES	**6.75%**	**6.50%**	**6.70%**	**6.34%**	**5.95%**	**6.23%**	**6.71%**	**6.82%**
Natural gas	**0.90**	**0.86**	**0.89**	**0.82**	**0.79**	**0.77**	**0.92**	**0.96**
Electricity	**2.74**	**2.71**	**2.75**	**2.69**	**2.42**	**2.77**	**2.71**	**2.69**
Fuel oil and other fuels	**0.38**	**0.39**	**0.48**	**0.35**	**0.31**	**0.31**	**0.44**	**0.32**
Fuel oil	0.23	0.24	0.27	0.21	0.19	0.18	0.28	0.24
Coal	0.01	0.02	0.02	0.02	0.02	0.01	0.02	0.00
Bottled gas	0.09	0.10	0.13	0.09	0.08	0.08	0.10	0.07
Wood and other fuels	0.04	0.04	0.05	0.04	0.03	0.04	0.04	0.01
Telephone	**2.07**	**1.85**	**1.88**	**1.79**	**1.86**	**1.68**	**1.93**	**2.12**
Water and other public services	**0.66**	**0.69**	**0.70**	**0.68**	**0.57**	**0.71**	**0.71**	**0.73**
Water and sewerage maintenance	0.50	0.53	0.54	0.52	0.42	0.54	0.52	0.58
Trash and garbage collection	0.15	0.16	0.15	0.16	0.14	0.15	0.18	0.14
Septic tank cleaning	0.01	0.01	0.01	0.01	0.00	0.01	0.01	0.01

Note: Expenditures listed for items in a given category may not add to the total for that category because the listing is incomplete. "Maintenance and repair services," for example, includes "other maintenance and repair services," which is omitted here. Numbers may not add to total due to rounding. Other married couples include extended family members or unrelated persons in addition to the married couple. *See Appendix B for information on mortgage principle reduction.

Indexed expenditures

	all cu's	all married couples	married couple only	all married couples with children	AGE OF OLDEST CHILD			other married couples
					under 6	6 to 17	18 or older	
Number of consumer units (in thousands)	94,862	52,010	20,227	28,100	5,858	14,194	8,047	3,684
Average number of persons per cu	2.6	3.3	2.0	3.9	3.5	4.1	3.9	5.1
Average number of earners per cu	1.4	1.7	1.2	2.1	1.7	1.9	2.7	2.4
Average total before-tax income	$28,540	$37,299	$33,825	$39,354	$34,318	$38,039	$45,596	$40,846
TOTAL AVERAGE ANNUAL EXPENDITURES	100	125	108	135	120	136	146	138
HOUSING, AVERAGE ANNUAL EXPENDITURES	100	120	105	130	134	134	122	131
SHELTER	**100**	**115**	**99**	**126**	**128**	**134**	**109**	**127**
Owned dwellings*	**100**	**138**	**115**	**154**	**140**	**170**	**136**	**142**
Mortgage interest and charges	100	143	95	176	176	205	124	153
Property taxes	100	132	145	124	77	124	157	125
Maintenance, repairs, insurance, and other expenses	100	127	146	114	87	104	151	122
Homeowners and related insurance	100	134	143	127	100	129	144	132
Ground rent	100	77	108	63	122	46	51	11
Maintenance and repair services	100	125	153	105	71	88	160	121
Painting and papering	100	118	171	84	48	85	108	89
Plumbing and water heating	100	126	144	111	129	85	145	136
Heat, air conditioning, electrical work	100	124	152	92	63	79	135	215
Roofing and gutters	100	119	153	105	19	75	222	40
Hard surface flooring	100	140	88	182	78	121	364	109
Maintenance and repair commodities	100	141	136	143	112	139	172	155
Paint, wallpaper, and supplies	100	145	107	165	151	170	164	199
Plumbing supplies and equipment	100	146	141	141	80	155	163	214
Electrical supplies, heating/cooling equipment	100	132	153	124	41	101	224	80
Roofing and gutters	100	103	116	96	91	36	206	85
Insulation, remodeling, and finishing room or basement	100	148	98	180	136	215	150	177
Miscellaneous supplies and equipment	100	143	203	105	79	73	180	104
Rented dwellings	**100**	**72**	**62**	**76**	**129**	**75**	**38**	**94**
Rent	100	71	61	74	125	75	37	95
Rent as pay	100	100	65	127	285	83	89	87
Maintenance, repairs, and insurance	100	94	77	110	244	82	60	67
Tenant's insurance	100	87	95	84	162	73	47	63
Maintenance and repair services	100	88	64	107	255	65	74	75
Maintenance and repair commodities	100	112	75	146	332	124	51	60
Other lodging	**100**	**129**	**126**	**128**	**64**	**119**	**190**	**148**
Owned vacation homes	100	123	146	103	43	94	163	145
Expenses for other properties	100	126	109	130	68	124	184	197

Indexed average annual expenditures for shelter and utilities, by married couples with and without children.

(continued from previous page)	all cu's	all married couples	married couple only	all married couples with children	AGE OF OLDEST CHILD			other married couples
					under 6	6 to 17	18 or older	
Housing while attending school	100	125	42	195	8	107	486	46
Lodging while out-of-town	100	134	150	123	81	127	147	126
UTILITIES, FUELS, AND PUBLIC SERVICES	**100**	**120**	**107**	**127**	**105**	**126**	**145**	**140**
Natural gas	**100**	**118**	**106**	**123**	**105**	**116**	**149**	**147**
Electricity	**100**	**124**	**109**	**133**	**105**	**138**	**144**	**135**
Fuel oil and other fuels	**100**	**130**	**137**	**126**	**99**	**112**	**171**	**117**
Fuel oil	100	126	128	124	97	103	179	141
Coal	100	146	156	152	148	126	202	36
Bottled gas	100	134	150	126	99	123	151	102
Wood and other fuels	100	134	150	134	94	136	159	43
Telephone	**100**	**111**	**98**	**117**	**107**	**110**	**136**	**141**
Water and other public services	**100**	**131**	**115**	**140**	**103**	**147**	**157**	**154**
Water and sewerage maintenance	100	131	115	139	99	147	151	158
Trash and garbage collection	100	132	113	146	116	141	175	134
Septic tank cleaning	100	158	114	173	75	223	155	294

*Note: An index of 100 represents the average for all consumer units. An index of 132 means that the average for the subgroup is 32 percent above the average for all consumer units. An index of 68 indicates spending that is 32 percent below the overall average. Other married couples include extended family members or unrelated persons in addition to the married couple. *See Appendix B for information on mortgage principle reduction.*

Aggregate expenditures, 1988

Aggregate expenditures in 1988 for shelter and utilities, by married couples with and without children.

	all cu's	all married couples	married couple only	all married couples with children	AGE OF OLDEST CHILD under 6	6 to 17	18 or older	other married couples
Number of consumer units (in thousands)	94,862	52,010	20,227	28,100	5,858	14,194	8,047	3,684
Average number of persons per cu	2.6	3.3	2.0	3.9	3.5	4.1	3.9	5.1
Average number of earners per cu	1.4	1.7	1.2	2.1	1.7	1.9	2.7	2.4
Aggregate before-tax income (in millions)	$2,722,910	$1,942,526	$684,178	$1,107,871	$201,035	$539,926	$366,911	$150,477
TOTAL AGGREG. EXPENDITURES (in millions)	$2,455,594	1,682,565	565,436	985,465	181,263	500,316	303,886	131,665
HOUSING, AGGREGATE EXPENDITURES (in millions)	$766,105	$506,241	$170,977	$296,334	$63,312	$154,008	$79,014	$38,930
SHELTER	$426,190	$269,109	$89,658	$158,458	$33,814	$85,202	$39,442	$20,993
Owned dwellings*	243,671	183,992	59,707	110,886	21,016	61,838	28,031	13,399
Mortgage interest and charges	148,831	116,618	30,273	77,495	16,195	45,647	15,654	8,850
Property taxes	47,778	34,597	14,802	17,483	2,285	8,845	6,353	2,312
Maintenance, repairs, insurance, and other expenses	47,052	32,768	14,625	15,907	2,536	7,347	6,024	2,237
Homeowners and related insurance	14,214	10,407	4,333	5,347	874	2,736	1,737	726
Ground rent	2,414	1,020	558	452	182	166	104	11
Maintenance and repair services	24,474	16,762	8,004	7,613	1,071	3,217	3,325	1,145
Painting and papering	5,127	3,319	1,865	1,276	152	652	472	178
Plumbing and water heating	2,226	1,534	685	733	177	282	273	117
Heat, air conditioning, electrical work	3,990	2,708	1,291	1,083	154	471	458	333
Roofing and gutters	4,040	2,643	1,322	1,259	47	452	760	63
Hard surface flooring	845	649	158	455	41	153	261	36
Maintenance and repair commodities	5,879	4,543	1,705	2,484	407	1,219	858	354
Paint, wallpaper, and supplies	1,817	1,440	413	886	170	463	253	141
Plumbing supplies and equipment	495	396	148	207	24	114	68	41
Electrical supplies, heating/cooling equipment	346	250	113	127	9	52	66	11
Roofing and gutters	456	259	114	130	26	25	80	15
Insulation, remodeling, and finishing room or basement	1,243	1,006	260	661	104	399	158	85
Miscellaneous supplies and equipment	1,519	1,190	656	472	74	166	232	61
Rented dwellings	139,237	54,591	18,281	31,201	11,076	15,675	4,451	5,109
Rent	135,280	52,501	17,676	29,833	10,438	15,184	4,210	4,992
Rent as pay	1,631	894	225	614	287	204	123	55
Maintenance, repairs, and insurance	2,325	1,196	380	755	350	287	117	61
Tenant's insurance	749	357	151	187	75	82	30	18
Maintenance and repair services	1,001	485	137	318	157	98	63	29
Maintenance and repair commodities	576	354	92	249	118	107	25	13
Other lodging	43,282	30,526	11,670	16,371	1,722	7,689	6,960	2,485
Owned vacation homes	7,267	4,897	2,268	2,220	194	1,023	1,004	409
Expenses for other properties	15,217	10,555	3,549	5,839	638	2,827	2,374	1,167

Aggregate expenditures in 1988 for shelter and utilities, by married couples with and without children.

(continued from previous page)	all cu's	all married couples	married couple only	all married couples with children	AGE OF OLDEST CHILD			other married couples
					under 6	6 to 17	18 or older	
Housing while attending school	3,441	2,357	308	1,988	18	552	1,419	61
Lodging while out-of-town	17,357	12,716	5,545	6,323	873	3,288	2,162	848
UTILITIES, FUELS, AND PUBLIC SERVICES	**$165,763**	**$109,214**	**$37,878**	**$62,351**	**$10,782**	**$31,187**	**$20,382**	**$8,985**
Natural gas	**22,174**	**14,384**	**5,030**	**8,087**	**1,435**	**3,845**	**2,807**	**1,266**
Electricity	**67,240**	**45,539**	**15,557**	**26,443**	**4,380**	**13,843**	**8,220**	**3,538**
Fuel oil and other fuels	**9,273**	**6,594**	**2,700**	**3,471**	**568**	**1,558**	**1,345**	**423**
Fuel oil	5,702	3,952	1,551	2,089	343	880	866	312
Coal	338	270	113	153	31	64	58	5
Bottled gas	2,282	1,674	732	852	139	420	293	90
Wood and other fuels	951	698	305	377	55	193	128	16
Telephone	**50,945**	**31,083**	**10,652**	**17,640**	**3,374**	**8,403**	**5,863**	**2,791**
Water and other public services	**16,131**	**11,615**	**3,939**	**6,710**	**1,025**	**3,538**	**2,147**	**966**
Water and sewerage maintenance	12,361	8,863	3,029	5,073	759	2,725	1,589	761
Trash and garbage collection	3,622	2,624	874	1,562	259	764	539	189
Septic tank cleaning	128	128	36	75	7	49	19	17

Note: Expenditures listed for items in a given category may not add to the total for that category because the listing is incomplete. "Maintenance and repair services," for example, includes "other maintenance and repair services," which is omitted here. Numbers may not add to total due to rounding. Other married couples include extended family members or unrelated persons in addition to the married couple. The "all cu's" aggregates will differ slightly from table to table because they are the sums of the aggregates in each row. In this table they include aggregates for single parents, single persons, and other types of consumer units, in addition to all married couples. Aggregates for "all married couples" and "all married couples with children" are sums of the appropriate aggregates in each row. *See Appendix B for information on mortgage principle reduction.

CHAPTER

4

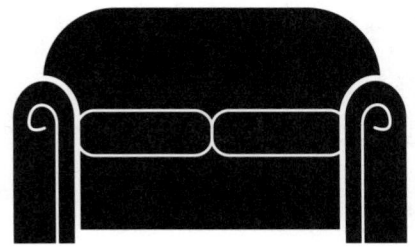

Household Operations and Furnishings

The average household devoted 31 percent of its expenditures to housing in 1988, up 1 percentage point since 1984. More than three-quarters of the average housing budget is allocated to homeownership, rent, utilities, and public services. Household furnishings and equipment account for 13 percent of the average housing budget. Household services and supplies each account for 5 percent of housing expenditures.

The budget share devoted to household supplies, and furnishings and equipment declined between 1984 and 1988. The share going to household services rose, due to increased spending on personal services such as child care and elder care.

Five-year trends for household operations and furnishings

	1984	1985	1986	1987	1988	change 1984 to 1988
Share of household expenditures devoted to housing, share of housing expenditures devoted to household operations and furnishing items, and change in share, 1984 to 1988.						
Housing, share of household expenditures	*30.4%*	*30.2%*	*30.6%*	*31.0%*	*31.2%*	*0.8%*
*Housing, expenditures**	*100.0%*	*100.0%*	*100.0%*	*100.0%*	*100.0%*	*0.0%*
HOUSING	**100.0%**	**100.0%**	**100.0%**	**100.0%**	**100.0%**	**0.0%**
HOUSEHOLD SERVICES	**4.7%**	**4.9%**	**4.9%**	**4.9%**	**4.9%**	**0.2%**
Personal services	1.9	2.2	2.3	2.2	2.1	0.2
Other household services	2.8	2.7	2.6	2.7	2.8	0.0
HOUSEKEEPING SUPPLIES	**4.6%**	**4.6%**	**4.3%**	**4.5%**	**4.5%**	**-0.1%**
Laundry and cleaning supplies	1.3	1.3	1.3	1.3	1.3	0.0
Other household products	2.0	1.9	1.7	1.8	1.8	-0.2
Postage and stationery	1.3	1.4	1.3	1.4	1.4	0.1
HOUSEHOLD FURNISHINGS AND EQUIPMENT	**13.9%**	**13.2%**	**13.7%**	**13.6%**	**13.4%**	**-0.5%**
Household textiles	1.3	1.4	1.4	1.2	1.2	-0.1
Furniture	4.0	4.0	4.2	4.2	4.0	0.0
Floor coverings	1.2	1.0	0.8	0.9	0.8	-0.4
Major appliances	2.1	1.9	2.1	2.1	2.1	-0.1
Small appliances, miscellaneous housewares	1.0	0.8	0.8	0.8	0.7	-0.3
Miscellaneous household equipment	4.2	4.1	4.4	4.5	4.6	0.4

Housing expenditures also include those for shelter and utilities (see page 52). Note: Numbers may not add to total due to rounding.

PART I
Spending by age for household operations and furnishings

The youngest households have well below-average spending on household services, supplies, and furnishings and equipment. Laundering and cleaning of household textiles, and infant's furniture are the only items on which householders under age 25 spend more than the average.

Among 25-to-34 year-olds, spending on household services, and furnishing and equipment is above average. These starting-out households have the highest expenditures for such items as sofas, vacuum cleaners, infant's furniture, and appliance rentals. They devote more than twice the average amount of dollars to personal services, mostly child care.

Overall, householders aged 35 to 44 spend the most on household services. They spend 57 percent more than the average household on personal services, mostly child care, and 17 percent more than average on other kinds of household services. Their spending on furnishing and equipment items is consistently high and they outspend the others on such things as kitchen and dining room linens, outdoor furniture, flatware, glassware, closet and storage fixtures, and luggage.

Householders aged 45 to 54 no longer have high day care costs, so their expenses for household personal services fall below average. But 45-to-54-year-olds spend more than average on other services such as housekeeping, appliance repair, and upholstering. And this age group spends the most on household furnishings and equipment.

Householders aged 55 or older spend less than average on personal services although their expenditures on elder care and care for the handicapped are well above average. Spending is also exceptionally high in the older age groups on many services like lawn and garden care and furniture upholstering. The peak spenders on sewing materials for household items, portable dishwashers, and living room chairs are aged 55 to 64. Householders aged 65 to 74 outspend the others on window air conditions and the oldest household are the biggest spenders on bathroom linens.

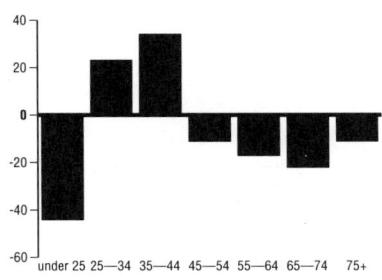

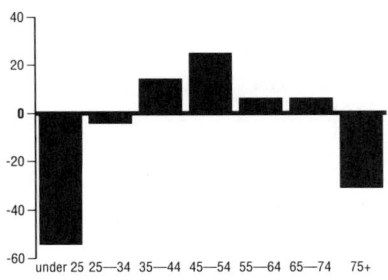

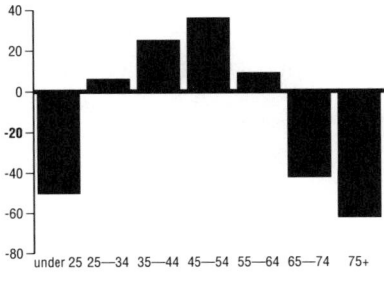

0 = average spending

Average expenditures

	all cu's	under 25	25 to 34	35 to 44	45 to 54	55 to 64	65 to 74	75+
Number of consumer units (in thousands)	94,862	7,216	21,985	19,911	13,601	12,546	11,319	8,284
Average number of persons per cu	2.6	1.8	2.8	3.3	2.9	2.2	2.0	1.5
Average total before-tax income	$28,540.00	$14,827.00	$28,318.00	$36,428.00	$39,934.00	$29,979.00	$20,704.00	$13,707.00
Total average annual expenditures	$25,891.85	$16,373.17	$25,770.27	$33,077.72	$33,204.87	$25,765.35	$20,119.90	$13,339.49
Housing, average annual expenditures	$8,078.63	$4,746.39	$8,469.29	$10,466.69	$9,672.11	$7,756.96	$6,177.84	$4,681.58
HOUSEHOLD SERVICES	**$394.12**	**$141.29**	**$483.46**	**$528.49**	**$349.34**	**$327.31**	**$306.35**	**$348.96**
Personal services	**171.19**	**97.48**	**362.43**	**268.61**	**58.32**	**42.36**	**23.35**	**76.09**
Babysitting	71.51	52.32	181.82	99.62	25.15	2.54	4.57	0.00
Care for elderly, invalids, handicapped, etc	12.42	0.00	-	1.43	6.95	19.90	15.82	75.16
Day care centers, nursery and preschools	87.25	45.15	180.45	167.56	26.22	19.92	2.96	0.93
Other household services	**222.93**	**43.81**	**121.03**	**259.88**	**291.02**	**284.95**	**283.00**	**272.87**
Housekeeping services	76.80	7.11	33.03	95.68	119.31	107.48	64.50	108.78
Gardening, lawn care service	50.35	2.21	15.78	49.85	59.04	63.93	99.42	83.37
Water softening service	2.68	-	2.81	4.72	2.10	2.77	2.06	1.02
Dry cleaning/laundering of household textiles	6.51	8.42	8.36	6.71	7.02	5.02	4.01	4.36
Moving, storage, and freight express	29.28	9.18	28.62	47.31	34.17	30.11	15.88	14.30
Appliance repair	16.21	3.33	10.11	15.40	21.85	20.60	27.99	13.50
Reupholstering and furniture repair	14.74	5.95	4.04	10.02	21.81	25.99	24.48	20.20
Repairs and rental of equipment/power tools ..	5.47	0.51	2.69	5.44	6.89	8.04	7.93	7.70
Appliance rental	2.16	2.10	3.46	1.96	2.05	2.11	1.69	-
HOUSEKEEPING SUPPLIES	**$360.94**	**$165.53**	**$347.13**	**$411.38**	**$449.67**	**$383.00**	**$381.60**	**$248.50**
Laundry and cleaning supplies	**100.73**	**54.83**	**98.78**	**119.17**	**134.17**	**108.64**	**86.62**	**55.04**
Soaps and detergents	59.26	33.79	59.35	71.61	75.76	61.34	52.75	30.85
Other household products	**147.21**	**57.81**	**140.29**	**174.67**	**191.89**	**161.26**	**133.52**	**107.18**
Cleansing/toilet tissue, paper towels/napkins ..	49.87	22.24	41.82	56.82	66.71	55.94	54.31	36.73
Lawn and garden supplies	33.60	6.97	36.63	40.26	33.09	35.88	29.62	39.32
Postage and stationery	**113.00**	**52.89**	**108.06**	**117.54**	**123.62**	**113.09**	**161.47**	**86.28**
Stationery, stationery supplies, giftwrap	50.42	27.66	48.89	58.42	56.38	44.40	73.26	23.47
Postage	62.58	25.24	59.17	59.12	67.24	68.70	88.21	62.81
HOUSEHOLD FURNISHINGS/EQUIP. ...	**$1,083.41**	**$538.85**	**$1,151.63**	**$1,356.72**	**$1,468.66**	**$1,182.73**	**$733.13**	**$414.70**
Household textiles	**93.97**	**56.41**	**93.34**	**101.70**	**122.16**	**106.42**	**70.99**	**76.38**
Bathroom linens	13.08	6.55	13.13	13.41	13.74	19.32	4.51	20.11
Bedroom linens	35.07	34.84	40.70	28.81	40.00	43.54	20.64	33.35
Kitchen and dining room linens	5.57	0.70	3.69	8.47	9.88	5.10	3.63	4.66
Curtains and draperies	27.78	4.63	26.69	34.67	44.88	21.59	29.38	13.36
Sewing materials for household items	9.70	8.52	6.96	11.89	9.91	14.16	10.32	4.32
Slipcovers, decorative pillows, other linens.....	2.77	1.17	2.16	4.46	3.75	2.71	2.51	0.59

Average annual expenditures for household operations and furnishings, by age of reference person.

(continued from previous page)	all cu's	under 25	25 to 34	35 to 44	45 to 54	55 to 64	65 to 74	75+
Furniture	**326.01**	**195.48**	**370.76**	**430.32**	**440.73**	**331.77**	**174.32**	**80.40**
Mattress and springs	42.85	29.59	45.36	55.04	63.95	42.84	21.24	13.37
Other bedroom furniture	44.69	30.19	48.36	64.36	55.84	53.95	17.93	4.53
Sofas	68.18	55.49	89.22	82.09	81.28	62.05	38.15	18.79
Living room chairs	34.00	18.95	34.66	36.01	39.41	45.23	27.76	23.20
Living room tables	19.33	13.71	23.74	23.45	25.60	17.28	12.34	4.94
Kitchen and dining room furniture	56.64	18.70	64.09	88.89	93.27	43.60	17.70	5.22
Infants' furniture	6.77	8.88	11.86	6.25	5.99	5.35	3.84	-
Outdoor furniture	12.57	1.12	10.50	23.75	17.23	14.88	4.45	1.06
Occasional furniture	40.98	18.86	42.97	50.49	58.17	46.58	30.91	9.18
Carpet, rugs, and other floor coverings	**65.34**	**27.40**	**43.51**	**82.46**	**109.55**	**104.61**	**37.10**	**18.51**
Major appliances	**168.60**	**47.56**	**172.00**	**204.31**	**196.59**	**206.47**	**145.36**	**108.16**
Built-in dishwashers, garbage disposals, hoods	11.01	0.89	6.84	14.38	19.31	8.17	14.62	8.53
Portable dishwashers	1.63	0.00	1.82	2.35	1.07	2.68	0.00	2.37
Refrigerators and freezers	49.14	9.86	53.55	60.06	39.24	71.30	42.14	37.69
Washing machines and dryers	37.33	16.70	41.33	45.05	52.62	34.74	27.43	18.32
Stoves and ovens	22.18	2.55	17.46	29.49	30.66	30.56	21.40	8.77
Microwave ovens	14.10	9.42	14.06	14.25	18.07	21.56	8.35	8.02
Window air conditioners	10.49	2.49	6.45	10.13	10.27	15.56	17.15	12.60
Electric floor cleaning equipment	14.47	5.05	19.34	15.79	14.70	16.08	8.89	11.44
Sewing machines	5.52	0.60	5.86	7.36	9.50	4.38	4.97	-
Small appliances and misc. housewares	**60.50**	**37.90**	**47.08**	**91.26**	**79.03**	**64.84**	**48.04**	**22.99**
Housewares	39.32	24.55	29.65	63.39	50.72	41.21	28.72	13.99
China and dinnerware	12.34	6.56	10.27	16.36	18.39	15.19	9.27	3.15
Flatware	3.39	1.89	3.15	5.55	2.92	4.47	2.29	0.80
Glassware	10.87	5.24	6.97	26.37	9.01	7.86	7.73	2.13
Nonelectric cookware	11.20	10.04	7.63	13.45	18.45	11.65	8.18	7.56
Small electrical kitchen appliances	13.79	9.66	11.80	17.75	17.30	16.64	12.37	5.02
Portable heating and cooling equipment	7.39	3.68	5.63	10.12	11.02	7.00	6.95	3.98
Miscellaneous household equipment	**368.99**	**174.09**	**424.93**	**446.67**	**520.59**	**368.61**	**257.32**	**108.26**
Clocks	4.96	2.50	4.82	3.16	11.94	3.24	5.68	1.97
Lamps and lighting fixtures	25.59	11.03	30.41	20.43	49.95	13.53	34.85	2.19
Telephones, accessories, answering devices	13.26	7.02	14.33	17.72	9.72	24.90	8.27	-
Lawn and garden equipment	47.65	1.04	40.58	62.10	66.16	50.80	58.93	21.64
Power and hand tools	26.41	13.66	32.80	28.29	44.30	20.52	20.54	2.52
Indoor plants and fresh flowers	36.46	8.84	38.46	41.95	45.67	51.54	31.07	11.77
Closet and storage items	5.19	-	6.68	11.27	3.07	3.43	3.07	0.61
Luggage	8.42	6.63	6.88	12.07	11.78	8.81	6.72	1.51
Business equipment for home use	6.16	2.49	4.22	7.18	16.01	4.48	3.20	2.48

Note: Expenditures listed for items in a given category may not add to the total for that category because the listing is incomplete. "Other household services," for example, includes "other services," which is omitted here. Expenditures are not given (-) when the amount is too small to be reliable. Numbers may not add to total due to rounding.

Share of spending

	all cu's	under 25	25 to 34	35 to 44	45 to 54	55 to 64	65 to 74	75+
Number of consumer units (in thousands)	94,862	7,216	21,985	19,911	13,601	12,546	11,319	8,284
Average number of persons per cu	2.6	1.8	2.8	3.3	2.9	2.2	2.0	1.5
Average total before-tax income	$28,540	$14,827	$28,318	$36,428	$39,934	$29,979	$20,704	$13,707
TOTAL AVERAGE ANNUAL EXPENDITURES	100.00%	100.00%	100.00%	100.00%	100.00%	100.00%	100.00%	100.00%
HOUSING, AVERAGE ANNUAL EXPENDITURES	31.20%	28.99%	32.86%	31.64%	29.13%	30.11%	30.71%	35.10%
HOUSEHOLD SERVICES	1.52%	0.86%	1.88%	1.60%	1.05%	1.27%	1.52%	2.62%
Personal services	0.66	0.60	1.41	0.81	0.18	0.16	0.12	0.57
Babysitting	0.28	0.32	0.71	0.30	0.08	0.01	0.02	0.00
Care for elderly, invalids, handicapped, etc.	0.05	0.00	-	0.00	0.02	0.08	0.08	0.56
Day care centers, nursery and preschools	0.34	0.28	0.70	0.51	0.08	0.08	0.01	0.01
Other household services	0.86	0.27	0.47	0.79	0.88	1.11	1.41	2.05
Housekeeping services	0.30	0.04	0.13	0.29	0.36	0.42	0.32	0.82
Gardening, lawn care service	0.19	0.01	0.06	0.15	0.18	0.25	0.49	0.62
Water softening service	0.01	-	0.01	0.01	0.01	0.01	0.01	0.01
Dry cleaning/laundering of household textiles	0.03	0.05	0.03	0.02	0.02	0.02	0.02	0.03
Moving, storage, and freight express	0.11	0.06	0.11	0.14	0.10	0.12	0.08	0.11
Appliance repair	0.06	0.02	0.04	0.05	0.07	0.08	0.14	0.10
Reupholstering and furniture repair	0.06	0.04	0.02	0.03	0.07	0.10	0.12	0.15
Repairs and rental of equipment/power tools	0.02	0.00	0.01	0.02	0.02	0.03	0.04	0.06
Appliance rental	0.01	0.01	0.01	0.01	0.01	0.01	0.01	-
HOUSEKEEPING SUPPLIES	1.39%	1.01%	1.35%	1.24%	1.35%	1.49%	1.90%	1.86%
Laundry and cleaning supplies	0.39	0.33	0.38	0.36	0.40	0.42	0.43	0.41
Soaps and detergents	0.23	0.21	0.23	0.22	0.23	0.24	0.26	0.23
Other household products	0.57	0.35	0.54	0.53	0.58	0.63	0.66	0.80
Cleansing/toilet tissue, paper towels/napkins	0.19	0.14	0.16	0.17	0.20	0.22	0.27	0.28
Lawn and garden supplies	0.13	0.04	0.14	0.12	0.10	0.14	0.15	0.29
Postage and stationery	0.44	0.32	0.42	0.36	0.37	0.44	0.80	0.65
Stationery, stationery supplies, giftwrap	0.19	0.17	0.19	0.18	0.17	0.17	0.36	0.18
Postage	0.24	0.15	0.23	0.18	0.20	0.27	0.44	0.47
HOUSEHOLD FURNISHINGS/EQUIP.	4.18%	3.29%	4.47%	4.10%	4.42%	4.59%	3.64%	3.11%
Household textiles	0.36	0.34	0.36	0.31	0.37	0.41	0.35	0.57
Bathroom linens	0.05	0.04	0.05	0.04	0.04	0.07	0.02	0.15
Bedroom linens	0.14	0.21	0.16	0.09	0.12	0.17	0.10	0.25
Kitchen and dining room linens	0.02	0.00	0.01	0.03	0.03	0.02	0.02	0.03
Curtains and draperies	0.11	0.03	0.10	0.10	0.14	0.08	0.15	0.10
Sewing materials for household items	0.04	0.05	0.03	0.04	0.03	0.05	0.05	0.03
Slipcovers, decorative pillows, other linens	0.01	0.01	0.01	0.01	0.01	0.01	0.01	0.00

Percent of total average annual expenditures spent on household operations and furnishings, by age of reference person.

(continued from previous page)

	all cu's	under 25	25 to 34	35 to 44	45 to 54	55 to 64	65 to 74	75+
Furniture	**1.26**	**1.19**	**1.44**	**1.30**	**1.33**	**1.29**	**0.87**	**0.60**
Mattress and springs	0.17	0.18	0.18	0.17	0.19	0.17	0.11	0.10
Other bedroom furniture	0.17	0.18	0.19	0.19	0.17	0.21	0.09	0.03
Sofas	0.26	0.34	0.35	0.25	0.24	0.24	0.19	0.14
Living room chairs	0.13	0.12	0.13	0.11	0.12	0.18	0.14	0.17
Living room tables	0.07	0.08	0.09	0.07	0.08	0.07	0.06	0.04
Kitchen and dining room furniture	0.22	0.11	0.25	0.27	0.28	0.17	0.09	0.04
Infants' furniture	0.03	0.05	0.05	0.02	0.02	0.02	0.02	-
Outdoor furniture	0.05	0.01	0.04	0.07	0.05	0.06	0.02	0.01
Occasional furniture	0.16	0.12	0.17	0.15	0.18	0.18	0.15	0.07
Carpet, rugs, and other floor coverings	**0.25**	**0.17**	**0.17**	**0.25**	**0.33**	**0.41**	**0.18**	**0.14**
Major appliances	**0.65**	**0.29**	**0.67**	**0.62**	**0.59**	**0.80**	**0.72**	**0.81**
Built-in dishwashers, garbage disposals, hoods	0.04	0.01	0.03	0.04	0.06	0.03	0.07	0.06
Portable dishwashers	0.01	0.00	0.01	0.01	0.00	0.01	0.00	0.02
Refrigerators and freezers	0.19	0.06	0.21	0.18	0.12	0.28	0.21	0.28
Washing machines and dryers	0.14	0.10	0.16	0.14	0.16	0.13	0.14	0.14
Stoves and ovens	0.09	0.02	0.07	0.09	0.09	0.12	0.11	0.07
Microwave ovens ..	0.05	0.06	0.05	0.04	0.05	0.08	0.04	0.06
Window air conditioners	0.04	0.02	0.03	0.03	0.03	0.06	0.09	0.09
Electric floor cleaning equipment	0.06	0.03	0.08	0.05	0.04	0.06	0.04	0.09
Sewing machines	0.02	0.00	0.02	0.02	0.03	0.02	0.02	-
Small appliances/miscellaneous housewares	**0.23**	**0.23**	**0.18**	**0.28**	**0.24**	**0.25**	**0.24**	**0.17**
Housewares	0.15	0.15	0.12	0.19	0.15	0.16	0.14	0.10
China and other dinnerware	0.05	0.04	0.04	0.05	0.06	0.06	0.05	0.02
Flatware	0.01	0.01	0.01	0.02	0.01	0.02	0.01	0.01
Glassware	0.04	0.03	0.03	0.08	0.03	0.03	0.04	0.02
Nonelectric cookware	0.04	0.06	0.03	0.04	0.06	0.05	0.04	0.06
Small electrical kitchen appliances	0.05	0.06	0.05	0.05	0.05	0.06	0.06	0.04
Portable heating and cooling equipment	0.03	0.02	0.02	0.03	0.03	0.03	0.03	0.03
Miscellaneous household equipment	**1.43**	**1.06**	**1.65**	**1.35**	**1.57**	**1.43**	**1.28**	**0.81**
Clocks	0.02	0.02	0.02	0.01	0.04	0.01	0.03	0.01
Lamps and lighting fixtures	0.10	0.07	0.12	0.06	0.15	0.05	0.17	0.02
Telephones, accessories, and answering devices	0.05	0.04	0.06	0.05	0.03	0.10	0.04	-
Lawn and garden equipment	0.18	0.01	0.16	0.19	0.20	0.20	0.29	0.16
Power and hand tools	0.10	0.08	0.13	0.09	0.13	0.08	0.10	0.02
Indoor plants and fresh flowers	0.14	0.05	0.15	0.13	0.14	0.20	0.15	0.09
Closet and storage items	0.02	-	0.03	0.03	0.01	0.01	0.02	0.00
Luggage	0.03	0.04	0.03	0.04	0.04	0.03	0.03	0.01
Business equipment for home use	0.02	0.02	0.02	0.02	0.05	0.02	0.02	0.02

Note: Expenditures listed for items in a given category may not add to the total for that category because the listing is incomplete. "Other household services," for example, includes "other services," which is omitted here. Expenditures are not given (-) when the amount is too small to be reliable. Numbers may not add to total due to rounding.

Indexed expenditures

	all cu's	under 25	25 to 34	35 to 44	45 to 54	55 to 64	65 to 74	75+
Number of consumer units (in thousands)	94,862	7,216	21,985	19,911	13,601	12,546	11,319	8,284
Average number of persons per cu	2.6	1.8	2.8	3.3	2.9	2.2	2.0	1.5
Average total before-tax income	$28,540	$14,827	$28,318	$36,428	$39,934	$29,979	$20,704	$13,707
TOTAL AVERAGE ANNUAL EXPENDITURES	100	63	100	128	128	100	78	52
HOUSING, AVERAGE ANNUAL EXPENDITURES	100	59	105	130	120	96	76	58
HOUSEHOLD SERVICES	100	36	123	134	89	83	78	89
Personal services	100	57	212	157	34	25	14	44
Babysitting	100	73	254	139	35	4	6	0
Care for elderly, invalids, handicapped, etc.	100	0	-	12	56	160	127	605
Day care centers, nursery and preschools	100	52	207	192	30	23	3	1
Other household services	100	20	54	117	131	128	127	122
Housekeeping services	100	9	43	125	155	140	84	142
Gardening, lawn care service	100	4	31	99	117	127	197	166
Water softening service	100	-	105	176	78	103	77	38
Dry cleaning/laundering of household textiles	100	129	128	103	108	77	62	67
Moving, storage, and freight express	100	31	98	162	117	103	54	49
Appliance repair	100	21	62	95	135	127	173	83
Reupholstering and furniture repair	100	40	27	68	148	176	166	137
Repairs and rental of equipment/power tools ..	100	9	49	99	126	147	145	141
Appliance rental	100	97	160	91	95	98	78	-
HOUSEKEEPING SUPPLIES	100	46	96	114	125	106	106	69
Laundry and cleaning supplies	100	54	98	118	133	108	86	55
Soaps and detergents	100	57	100	121	128	104	89	52
Other household products	100	39	95	119	130	110	91	73
Cleansing/toilet tissue, paper towels/napkins ..	100	45	84	114	134	112	109	74
Lawn and garden supplies	100	21	109	120	98	107	88	117
Postage and stationery	100	47	96	104	109	100	143	76
Stationery, stationery supplies, giftwrap	100	55	97	116	112	88	145	47
Postage	100	40	95	94	107	110	141	100
HOUSEHOLD FURNISHINGS/EQUIP.	100	50	106	125	136	109	68	38
Household textiles	100	60	99	108	130	113	76	81
Bathroom linens	100	50	100	103	105	148	34	154
Bedroom linens	100	99	116	82	114	124	59	95
Kitchen and dining room linens	100	13	66	152	177	92	65	84
Curtains and draperies	100	17	96	125	162	78	106	48
Sewing materials for household items	100	88	72	123	102	146	106	45
Slipcovers, decorative pillows, other linens.....	100	42	78	161	135	98	91	21

Indexed average annual expenditures for household operations and furnishings, by age of reference person.

(continued from previous page)	all cu's	under 25	25 to 34	35 to 44	45 to 54	55 to 64	65 to 74	75+
Furniture	**100**	**60**	**114**	**132**	**135**	**102**	**53**	**25**
Mattress and springs	100	69	106	128	149	100	50	31
Other bedroom furniture	100	68	108	144	125	121	40	10
Sofas	100	81	131	120	119	91	56	28
Living room chairs	100	56	102	106	116	133	82	68
Living room tables	100	71	123	121	132	89	64	26
Kitchen and dining room furniture	100	33	113	157	165	77	31	9
Infants' furniture	100	131	175	92	88	79	57	-
Outdoor furniture	100	9	84	189	137	118	35	8
Occasional furniture	100	46	105	123	142	114	75	22
Carpet, rugs, and other floor coverings	**100**	**42**	**67**	**126**	**168**	**160**	**57**	**28**
Major appliances	**100**	**28**	**102**	**121**	**117**	**122**	**86**	**64**
Built-in dishwashers, garbage disposals, hoods	100	8	62	131	175	74	133	77
Portable dishwashers	100	0	112	144	66	164	0	145
Refrigerators and freezers	100	20	109	122	80	145	86	77
Washing machines and dryers	100	45	111	121	141	93	73	49
Stoves and ovens	100	11	79	133	138	138	96	40
Microwave ovens	100	67	100	101	128	153	59	57
Window air conditioners	100	24	61	97	98	148	163	120
Electric floor cleaning equipment	100	35	134	109	102	111	61	79
Sewing machines	100	11	106	133	172	79	90	-
Small appliances/miscellaneous housewares	**100**	**63**	**78**	**151**	**131**	**107**	**79**	**38**
Housewares	100	62	75	161	129	105	73	36
China and dinnerware	100	53	83	133	149	123	75	26
Flatware	100	56	93	164	86	132	68	24
Glassware	100	48	64	243	83	72	71	20
Nonelectric cookware	100	90	68	120	165	104	73	68
Small electrical kitchen appliances	100	70	86	129	125	121	90	36
Portable heating and cooling equipment	100	50	76	137	149	95	94	54
Miscellaneous household equipment	**100**	**47**	**115**	**121**	**141**	**100**	**70**	**29**
Clocks	100	50	97	64	241	65	115	40
Lamps and lighting fixtures	100	43	119	80	195	53	136	9
Telephones, accessories, answering devices	100	53	108	134	73	188	62	-
Lawn and garden equipment	100	2	85	130	139	107	124	45
Power and hand tools	100	52	124	107	168	78	78	10
Indoor plants and fresh flowers	100	24	105	115	125	141	85	32
Closet and storage items	100	-	129	217	59	66	59	12
Luggage	100	79	82	143	140	105	80	18
Business equipment for home use	100	40	69	117	260	73	52	40

Note: Expenditures are not given (-) when the amount is too small to be reliable. An index of 100 represents the average for all consumer units. An index of 132 means that the average for the subgroup is 32 percent above the average for all consumer units. An index of 68 indicates spending that is 32 percent below the overall average.

Aggregate expenditures, 1988

Aggregate expenditures in 1988 for household operations and furnishings, by age of reference person.

	all cu's	under 25	25 to 34	35 to 44	45 to 54	55 to 64	65 to 74	75+
Number of consumer units (in thousands)	94,862	7,216	21,985	19,911	13,601	12,546	11,319	8,284
Average number of persons per cu	2.6	1.8	2.8	3.3	2.9	2.2	2.0	1.5
Aggregate before-tax income (in millions)	$2,722,037	$106,992	$622,571	$725,318	$543,142	$376,117	$234,349	$113,549
TOTAL AGGREGATE EXPENDITURES (in millions)	$2,456,432	$118,149	$566,559	$658,610	$451,619	$323,252	$227,737	$110,504
HOUSING, AGG. EXPENDITURES (in millions)	$766,428	$34,250	$186,197	$208,402	$131,550	$97,319	$69,927	$38,782
HOUSEHOLD SERVICES	$37,387	$1,020	$10,629	$10,523	$4,751	$4,106	$3,468	$2,891
Personal services	16,239	703	7,968	5,348	793	531	264	630
Babysitting	6,784	378	3,997	1,984	342	32	52	0
Care for elderly, invalids, handicapped, etc. ...	1,174	0	-	28	95	250	179	623
Day care centers, nursery and preschools	8,277	326	3,967	3,336	357	250	34	8
Other household services	21,148	316	2,661	5,174	3,958	3,575	3,203	2,260
Housekeeping services	7,285	51	726	1,905	1,623	1,348	730	901
Gardening, lawn care service	4,776	16	347	993	803	802	1,125	691
Water softening service	251	-	62	94	29	35	23	8
Dry cleaning/laundering of household textiles	618	61	184	134	95	63	45	36
Moving, storage, and freight express	2,778	66	629	942	465	378	180	118
Appliance repair	1,537	24	222	307	297	258	317	112
Reupholstering and furniture repair	1,398	43	89	200	297	326	277	167
Repairs and rental of equipment/power tools ..	519	4	59	108	94	101	90	64
Appliance rental	204	15	76	39	28	26	19	-
HOUSEKEEPING SUPPLIES	$34,316	$1,194	$7,632	$8,191	$6,116	$4,805	$4,319	$2,059
Laundry and cleaning supplies	9,564	396	2,172	2,373	1,825	1,363	980	456
Soaps and detergents	5,627	244	1,305	1,426	1,030	770	597	256
Other household products	14,012	417	3,084	3,478	2,610	2,023	1,511	888
Cleansing/toilet tissue, paper towels, napkins .	4,739	160	919	1,131	907	702	615	304
Lawn and garden supplies	3,218	50	805	802	450	450	335	326
Postage and stationery	10,740	382	2,376	2,340	1,681	1,419	1,828	715
Stationery, stationery supplies, giftwrap	4,785	200	1,075	1,163	767	557	829	194
Postage	5,955	182	1,301	1,177	915	862	998	520
HOUSEHOLD FURNISHINGS/EQUIP. ...	$102,768	$3,888	$25,319	$27,014	$19,975	$14,839	$8,298	$3,435
Household textiles	8,917	407	2,052	2,025	1,661	1,335	804	633
Bathroom linens	1,250	47	289	267	187	242	51	167
Bedroom linens	3,320	251	895	574	544	546	234	276
Kitchen and dining room linens	533	5	81	169	134	64	41	39
Curtains and draperies	2,635	33	587	690	610	271	333	111
Sewing materials for household items	916	61	153	237	135	178	117	36
Slipcovers, decorative pillows, other linens.....	263	8	47	89	51	34	28	5

Aggregate expenditures in 1988 for household operations and furnishings, by age of reference person.

(continued from previous page)	all cu's	under 25	25 to 34	35 to 44	45 to 54	55 to 64	65 to 74	75+
Furniture	**30,926**	**1,411**	**8,151**	**8,568**	**5,994**	**4,162**	**1,973**	**666**
Mattress and springs	4,065	214	997	1,096	870	537	240	111
Other bedroom furniture	4,239	218	1,063	1,281	759	677	203	38
Sofas	6,468	400	1,962	1,634	1,105	778	432	156
Living room chairs	3,226	137	762	717	536	567	314	192
Living room tables	1,833	99	522	467	348	217	140	41
Kitchen and dining room furniture	5,373	135	1,409	1,770	1,269	547	200	43
Infants' furniture	641	64	261	124	81	67	43	-
Outdoor furniture	1,192	8	231	473	234	187	50	9
Occasional furniture	3,888	136	945	1,005	791	584	350	76
Carpet, rugs, and other floor coverings	**6,172**	**198**	**957**	**1,642**	**1,490**	**1,312**	**420**	**153**
Major appliances	**15,998**	**343**	**3,781**	**4,068**	**2,674**	**2,590**	**1,645**	**896**
Built-in dishwashers, garbage disposals, hoods	1,044	6	150	286	263	103	165	71
Portable dishwashers	155	0	40	47	15	34	0	20
Refrigerators and freezers	4,662	71	1,177	1,196	534	895	477	312
Washing machines and dryers	3,540	121	909	897	716	436	310	152
Stoves and ovens	2,105	18	384	587	417	383	242	73
Microwave ovens	1,338	68	309	284	246	270	95	66
Window air conditioners	995	18	142	202	140	195	194	104
Electric floor cleaning equipment	1,373	36	425	314	200	202	101	95
Sewing machines	520	4	129	147	129	55	56	-
Small appliances/miscellaneous housewares	**5,748**	**273**	**1,035**	**1,817**	**1,075**	**813**	**544**	**190**
Housewares	3,739	177	652	1,262	690	517	325	116
China and dinnerware	1,171	47	226	326	250	191	105	26
Flatware	322	14	69	111	40	56	26	7
Glassware	1,042	38	153	525	123	99	87	18
Nonelectric cookware	1,060	72	168	268	251	146	93	63
Small electrical kitchen appliances	1,308	70	259	353	235	209	140	42
Portable heating and cooling equipment	701	27	124	201	150	88	79	33
Miscellaneous household equipment	**35,007**	**1,256**	**9,342**	**8,894**	**7,081**	**4,625**	**2,913**	**897**
Clocks	471	18	106	63	162	41	64	16
Lamps and lighting fixtures	2,417	80	669	407	679	170	394	18
Telephones, accessories, answering devices	1,257	51	315	353	132	312	94	-
Lawn and garden equipment	4,520	8	892	1,236	900	637	667	179
Power and hand tools	2,496	99	721	563	603	257	232	21
Indoor plants and fresh flowers	3,462	64	846	835	621	647	352	98
Closet and storage items	496	-	147	224	42	43	35	5
Luggage	799	48	151	240	160	111	76	13
Business equipment for home use	584	18	93	143	218	56	36	21

Note: Expenditures listed for items in a given category may not add to the total for that category because the listing is incomplete. "Other household services," for example, includes "other services," which is omitted here. Expenditures are not given (-) when the amount is too small to be reliable. Numbers may not add to total due to rounding. The "all cu's" aggregates will differ slightly from table to table because they are the sums of the aggregates in each row.

Aggregate expenditures, 1995

Aggregate expenditures for household operations and furnishings, by age of householder in 1995 (in 1988 dollars).

	all households	under 25	25 to 34	35 to 44	45 to 54	55 to 64	65 to 74	75+
Number of households (in thousands)	100,308	4,316	19,927	23,916	18,035	12,223	12,006	9,876
HOUSING, AGGREGATE EXPENDITURES IN 1995 (in millions)	$829,231	$20,485	$168,768	$250,321	$174,437	$94,813	$74,171	$46,235
HOUSEHOLD SERVICES	$40,309	$610	$9,634	$12,639	$6,300	$4,001	$3,678	$3,446
Personal services	16,668	421	7,222	6,424	1,052	518	280	751
Babysitting	6,771	226	3,623	2,383	454	31	55	0
Care for elderly, invalids, handicapped, etc.	1,335	0	-	34	125	243	190	742
Day care centers, nursery and preschools	8,559	195	3,596	4,007	473	243	36	9
Other household services	23,640	189	2,412	6,215	5,249	3,483	3,398	2,695
Housekeeping services	8,291	31	658	2,288	2,152	1,314	774	1,074
Gardening, lawn care service	5,379	10	314	1,192	1,065	781	1,194	823
Water softening service	275	-	56	113	38	34	25	10
Dry cleaning/laundering of household textiles	643	36	167	160	127	61	48	43
Moving, storage, and freight express	3,058	40	570	1,131	616	368	191	141
Appliance repair	1,699	14	201	368	394	252	336	133
Reupholstering and furniture repair	1,550	26	81	240	393	318	294	199
Repairs and rental of equipment/power tools ..	580	2	54	130	124	98	95	76
Appliance rental	208	9	69	47	37	26	20	-
HOUSEKEEPING SUPPLIES	$37,297	$714	$6,917	$9,839	$8,110	$4,681	$4,581	$2,454
Laundry and cleaning supplies	10,386	237	1,968	2,850	2,420	1,328	1,040	544
Soaps and detergents	6,095	146	1,183	1,713	1,366	750	633	305
Other household products	15,316	250	2,796	4,177	3,461	1,971	1,603	1,059
Cleansing/toilet tissue, paper towels/napkins ..	5,190	96	833	1,359	1,203	684	652	363
Lawn and garden supplies	3,502	30	730	963	597	439	356	388
Postage and stationery	11,595	228	2,153	2,811	2,229	1,382	1,939	852
Stationery, stationery supplies, giftwrap	5,162	119	974	1,397	1,017	543	880	232
Postage	6,434	109	1,179	1,414	1,213	840	1,059	620
HOUSEHOLD FURNISHINGS/EQUIP. ...	$111,563	$2,326	$22,949	$32,447	$26,487	$14,457	$8,802	$4,096
Household textiles	9,646	243	1,860	2,432	2,203	1,301	852	754
Bathroom linens	1,347	28	262	321	248	236	54	199
Bedroom linens	3,481	150	811	689	721	532	248	329
Kitchen and dining room linens	609	3	74	203	178	62	44	46
Curtains and draperies	2,939	20	532	829	809	264	353	132
Sewing materials for household items	978	37	139	284	179	173	124	43
Slipcovers, decorative pillows, other linens291	5	43	107	68	33	30	6	

Aggregate expenditures for household operations and furnishings, by age of householder in 1995 (in 1988 dollars).

(continued from previous page)	all households	under 25	25 to 34	35 to 44	45 to 54	55 to 64	65 to 74	75+
Furniture	**33,414**	**844**	**7,388**	**10,292**	**7,949**	**4,055**	**2,093**	**794**
Mattress and springs	4,412	128	904	1,316	1,153	524	255	132
Other bedroom furniture	4,560	130	964	1,539	1,007	659	215	45
Sofas	6,849	239	1,778	1,963	1,466	758	458	186
Living room chairs	3,460	82	691	861	711	553	333	229
Living room tables	1,963	59	473	561	462	211	148	49
Kitchen and dining room furniture	5,963	81	1,277	2,126	1,682	533	213	52
Infants' furniture	644	38	236	149	108	65	46	-
Outdoor furniture	1,339	5	209	568	311	182	53	10
Occasional furniture	4,225	81	856	1,208	1,049	569	371	91
Carpet, rugs, and other floor coverings	**6,840**	**118**	**867**	**1,972**	**1,976**	**1,279**	**445**	**183**
Major appliances	**17,402**	**205**	**3,427**	**4,886**	**3,546**	**2,524**	**1,745**	**1,068**
Built-in dishwashers, garbage disposals, hoods	1,192	4	136	344	348	100	176	84
Portable dishwashers	168	0	36	56	19	33	0	23
Refrigerators and freezers	5,003	43	1,067	1,436	708	871	506	372
Washing machines and dryers	3,857	72	824	1,077	949	425	329	181
Stoves and ovens	2,334	11	348	705	553	374	257	87
Microwave ovens	1,431	41	280	341	326	264	100	79
Window air conditioners	1,087	11	129	242	185	190	206	124
Electric floor cleaning equipment	1,466	22	385	378	265	197	107	113
Sewing machines	580	3	117	176	171	54	60	-
Small appliances/miscellaneous housewares	**6,306**	**164**	**938**	**2,183**	**1,425**	**793**	**577**	**227**
Housewares	4,114	106	591	1,516	915	504	345	138
China and dinnerware	1,284	28	205	391	332	186	111	31
Flatware	346	8	63	133	53	55	27	8
Glassware	1,165	23	139	631	162	96	93	21
Nonelectric cookware	1,165	43	152	322	333	142	98	75
Small electrical kitchen appliances	1,415	42	235	425	312	203	149	50
Portable heating and cooling equipment	777	16	112	242	199	86	83	39
Miscellaneous household equipment	**37,954**	**751**	**8,468**	**10,683**	**9,389**	**4,506**	**3,089**	**1,069**
Clocks	525	11	96	76	215	40	68	19
Lamps and lighting fixtures	2,648	48	606	489	901	165	418	22
Telephones, accessories, answering devices	1,319	30	286	424	175	304	99	-
Lawn and garden equipment	5,034	4	809	1,485	1,193	621	708	214
Power and hand tools	2,710	59	654	677	799	251	247	25
Indoor plants and fresh flowers	3,751	38	766	1,003	824	630	373	116
Closet and storage items	543	-	133	270	55	42	37	6
Luggage	870	29	137	289	212	108	81	15
Business equipment for home use	673	11	84	172	289	55	38	24

Note: Expenditures listed for items in a given category may not add to the total for that category because the listing is incomplete. "Other household services," for example, includes "other services," which is omitted here. Expenditures are not given (-) when the amount is too small to be reliable. Numbers may not add to total due to rounding. Households are used here because the number of consumer units in 1995 and 2000 is not available. Household projections are from the Census Bureau. Projections show how annual aggregate expenditures will change as the number of households in the age groups changes in 1995 and 2000. Projections are based on the average annual expenditures in 1988 and have not been adjusted for price increases or for changes in expenditure patterns.

Aggregate expenditures, 2000

Aggregate expenditures for household operations and furnishings, by age of householder in 2000 (in 1988 dollars).								
	all households	under 25	25 to 34	35 to 44	45 to 54	55 to 64	65 to 74	75+
Number of households (in thousands)	105,933	4,442	18,004	25,339	21,603	13,903	11,516	11,126
HOUSING, AGGREGATE EXPENDITURES IN 2000 (in millions)	$878,803	$21,083	$152,481	$265,215	$208,947	$107,845	$71,144	$52,087
HOUSEHOLD SERVICES	$42,231	$628	$8,704	$13,391	$7,547	$4,551	$3,528	$3,883
Personal services	16,729	433	6,525	6,806	1,260	589	269	847
Babysitting	6,661	232	3,273	2,524	543	35	53	0
Care for elderly, invalids, handicapped, etc.	1,481	0	-	36	150	277	182	836
Day care centers, nursery and preschools	8,583	201	3,249	4,246	566	277	34	10
Other household services	25,502	195	2,179	6,585	6,287	3,962	3,259	3,036
Housekeeping services	9,076	32	595	2,424	2,577	1,494	743	1,210
Gardening, lawn care service	5,794	10	284	1,263	1,275	889	1,145	928
Water softening service	289	-	51	120	45	39	24	11
Dry cleaning/laundering of household textiles	674	37	151	170	152	70	46	49
Moving, storage, and freight express	3,254	41	515	1,199	738	419	183	159
Appliance repair	1,818	15	182	390	472	286	322	150
Reupholstering and furniture repair	1,692	26	73	254	471	361	282	225
Repairs and rental of equipment/power tools ..	626	2	48	138	149	112	91	86
Appliance rental	214	9	62	50	44	29	19	-
HOUSEKEEPING SUPPLIES	$39,607	$735	$6,250	$10,424	$9,714	$5,325	$4,395	$2,765
Laundry and cleaning supplies	11,060	244	1,778	3,020	2,898	1,510	998	612
Soaps and detergents	6,473	150	1,069	1,815	1,637	853	607	343
Other household products	16,326	257	2,526	4,426	4,145	2,242	1,538	1,192
Cleansing/toilet tissue, paper towels/napkins ..	5,544	99	753	1,440	1,441	778	625	409
Lawn and garden supplies	3,703	31	659	1,020	715	499	341	437
Postage and stationery	12,221	235	1,946	2,978	2,671	1,572	1,859	960
Stationery, stationery supplies, giftwrap	5,423	123	880	1,480	1,218	617	844	261
Postage	6,798	112	1,065	1,498	1,453	955	1,016	699
HOUSEHOLD FURNISHINGS/EQUIP. ...	$118,733	$2,394	$20,734	$34,378	$31,727	$16,443	$8,443	$4,614
Household textiles	10,294	251	1,680	2,577	2,639	1,480	818	850
Bathroom linens	1,446	29	236	340	297	269	52	224
Bedroom linens	3,696	155	733	730	864	605	238	371
Kitchen and dining room linens	662	3	66	215	213	71	42	52
Curtains and draperies.......................................	3,136	21	481	879	970	300	338	149
Sewing materials for household items	1,042	38	125	301	214	197	119	48
Slipcovers, decorative pillows, other linens.....	311	5	39	113	81	38	29	7

Aggregate expenditures for household operations and furnishings, by age of householder in 2000 (in 1988 dollars).

(continued from previous page)	all households	under 25	25 to 34	35 to 44	45 to 54	55 to 64	65 to 74	75+
Furniture	**35,483**	**868**	**6,675**	**10,904**	**9,521**	**4,613**	**2,007**	**895**
Mattress and springs	4,713	131	817	1,395	1,382	596	245	149
Other bedroom furniture	4,849	134	871	1,631	1,206	750	206	50
Sofas	7,200	246	1,606	2,080	1,756	863	439	209
Living room chairs	3,679	84	624	912	851	629	320	258
Living room tables	2,073	61	427	594	553	240	142	55
Kitchen and dining room furniture	6,372	83	1,154	2,252	2,015	606	204	58
Infants' furniture	659	39	214	158	129	74	44	-
Outdoor furniture	1,438	5	189	602	372	207	51	12
Occasional furniture	4,499	84	774	1,279	1,257	648	356	102
Carpet, rugs, and other floor coverings	**7,449**	**122**	**783**	**2,089**	**2,367**	**1,454**	**427**	**206**
Major appliances	**18,480**	**211**	**3,097**	**5,177**	**4,247**	**2,871**	**1,674**	**1,203**
Built-in dishwashers, garbage disposals, hoods	1,285	4	123	364	417	114	168	95
Portable dishwashers	179	0	33	60	23	37	0	26
Refrigerators and freezers	5,273	44	964	1,522	848	991	485	419
Washing machines and dryers	4,099	74	744	1,142	1,137	483	316	204
Stoves and ovens	2,504	11	314	747	662	425	246	98
Microwave ovens	1,532	42	253	361	390	300	96	89
Window air conditioners	1,160	11	116	257	222	216	197	140
Electric floor cleaning equipment	1,542	22	348	400	318	224	102	127
Sewing machines	618	3	106	186	205	61	57	-
Small appliances/miscellaneous housewares	**6,746**	**168**	**848**	**2,312**	**1,707**	**901**	**553**	**256**
Housewares	4,404	109	534	1,606	1,096	573	331	156
China and dinnerware	1,379	29	185	415	397	211	107	35
Flatware	366	8	57	141	63	62	26	9
Glassware	1,234	23	125	668	195	109	89	24
Nonelectric cookware	1,262	45	137	341	399	162	94	84
Small electrical kitchen appliances	1,509	43	212	450	374	231	142	56
Portable heating and cooling equipment	834	16	101	256	238	97	80	44
Miscellaneous household equipment	**40,281**	**773**	**7,650**	**11,318**	**11,246**	**5,125**	**2,963**	**1,205**
Clocks	568	11	87	80	258	45	65	22
Lamps and lighting fixtures	2,807	49	548	518	1,079	188	401	24
Telephones, accessories, answering devices	1,390	31	258	449	210	346	95	-
Lawn and garden equipment	5,364	5	731	1,574	1,429	706	679	241
Power and hand tools	2,875	61	591	717	957	285	237	28
Indoor plants and fresh flowers	3,987	39	692	1,063	987	717	358	131
Closet and storage items	562	-	120	286	66	48	35	7
Luggage	930	29	124	306	254	122	77	17
Business equipment for home use	742	11	76	182	346	62	37	28

Note: Expenditures listed for items in a given category may not add to the total for that category because the listing is incomplete. "Other household services," for example, includes "other services," which is omitted here. Expenditures are not given (-) when the amount is too small to be reliable. Numbers may not add to total due to rounding. Households are used here because the number of consumer units in 1995 and 2000 is not available. Household projections are from the Census Bureau. Projections show how annual aggregate expenditures will change as the number of households in the age groups changes in 1995 and 2000. Projections are based on the average annual expenditures in 1988 and have not been adjusted for price increases or for changes in expenditure patterns.

PART II
Spending by income for household operations and furnishings

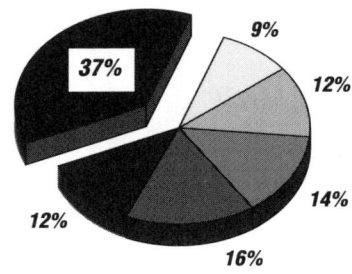

The highest-income households account for the largest share of the market for household services...

9%
37%
12%
12%
14%
16%

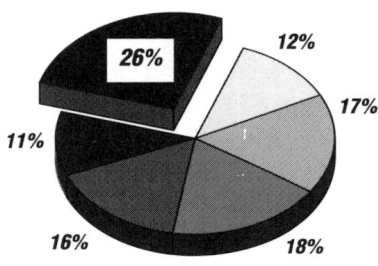

...and for housekeeping supplies...

26%
12%
11%
17%
16%
18%

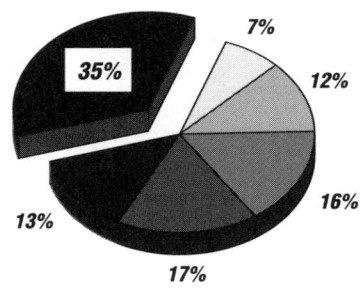

...and for household furnishings.

35%
7%
13%
12%
17%
16%

☐ under $10,000	■ $30,000–39,999
■ $10,000–19,999	■ $40,000–49,999
■ $20,000–29,999	■ $50,000 and over

Overall, housing expenditures increase by 283 percent from the lowest to the highest income households. Spending on furniture, however, increases by over 1000 percent and spending on household services by 520 percent. Items for which spending is most responsive to rising income are day care and housekeeping services, kitchen and dining room furniture, outdoor furniture, floor coverings, glassware, lamps, and lighting fixtures.

Because their spending is so great, the 12 million households with incomes of $50,000 or more are, by far, the largest single market for household services and products. All told they spent $32 billion on furnishings and equipment in 1988, and $12 billion on household services, accounting for 35 and 37 percent, respectively, of those markets. Households with incomes between $30,000 and $50,000 accounted for nearly 30 percent more of the household furnishings, equipment, and services markets.

The low-end market

Households with incomes under $30,000 spend below-average or just average amounts on household services, supplies, furnishings, and equipment. Those in the lowest income groups, under $10,000, spend more than average on just three items—care for the elderly and infirm, appliance rentals, and window air conditioners.

Households bringing in between $10,000 and $20,000 a year spend more than average on cleaning household textiles, appliance rentals, portable dishwashers, sewing machines, clocks, and lighting fixtures. Those with incomes of $20,000 to $30,000 spend 20 percent less than the average household on services and 11 percent less on furnishings and equipment. Their spending on housekeeping supplies is just average.

The high-end market

Households in the highest income bracket spend 147 percent more than the average household on household services, 135 percent more on furnishings and equipment, and 75 percent more on housekeeping supplies.

Households in the $40,000 to $50,000 income group spend 37 percent more than average on household services, despite below-average expenditures on such items as housekeeping services, furniture upholstering and repair, and appliance rentals. These households spend 24 percent more than the average household on housekeeping supplies and 46 percent more on furnishings and equipment. They are big buyers of infant furniture, portable dishwashers, lawn and garden equipment, and hand and power tools, spending at least twice the average amount on those items.

Spending on babysitting is highest among households with incomes of $30,000 to $40,000. This, together with other child care expenses, pushes their personal-services spending 56 percent above average. This groups spends 18 percent more than the average household on housekeeping supplies and 26 percent more on furnishings and equipment. Their spending is at least 50 percent above average for floor coverings, stoves and ovens, lamps and lighting fixtures, hand and power tools, and business equipment for the home.

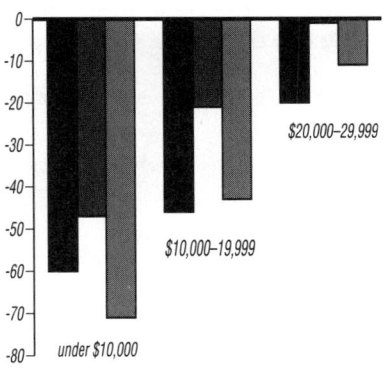

Lower-income households spend less than the average household on these products and services...

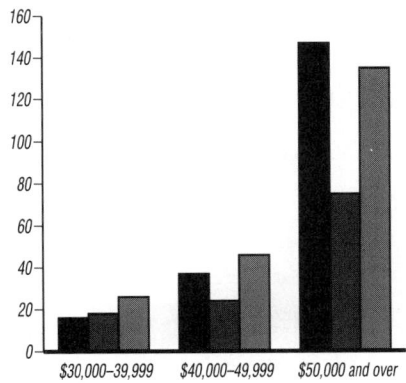

...while higher-income households are above-average spenders.

0 = average spending

■ *Household services*
■ *Housekeeping supplies*
■ *Household furnishings/equipment*

Average expenditures

(consumer units include complete income reporters only)	all cu's	under $10,000	$10,000 to $19,999	$20,000 to $29,999	$30,000 to $39,999	$40,000 to $49,999	$50,000 and over
Number of consumer units (in thousands)	81,354	18,809	17,652	14,586	10,901	7,198	12,209
Average number of persons per cu	2.6	1.8	2.3	2.7	2.9	3.2	3.1
Average number of earners per cu	1.4	0.7	1.0	1.5	1.8	2.0	2.1
TOTAL AVERAGE ANNUAL EXPENDITURES	$26,389.07	$11,269.43	$18,078.25	$24,896.36	$31,659.60	$37,562.00	$52,320.19
HOUSING, AVERAGE ANNUAL EXPENDITURES	$8,069.13	$4,108.61	$5,705.41	$7,511.85	$9,260.40	$10,608.79	$15,719.12
HOUSEHOLD SERVICES	**$387.45**	**$153.81**	**$211.05**	**$310.21**	**$448.86**	**$530.72**	**$955.30**
Personal services	**176.53**	**54.01**	**99.77**	**166.06**	**275.08**	**311.41**	**321.27**
Babysitting	74.62	14.21	49.52	85.19	133.19	114.65	115.47
Care for elderly, invalids, handicapped, etc.	11.66	27.64	2.36	4.58	1.46	-	24.66
Day care centers, nursery and preschools	90.25	12.16	47.90	76.28	140.43	196.28	181.13
Other household services	**210.92**	**99.80**	**111.28**	**144.16**	**173.78**	**219.78**	**634.03**
Housekeeping services	67.76	24.24	30.07	28.84	41.53	50.94	269.17
Gardening, lawn care service	49.60	25.50	25.22	30.40	31.13	53.69	159.01
Water softening service	2.81	-	1.81	2.19	2.95	4.10	7.63
Dry cleaning and laundering of household textiles	6.41	5.01	6.53	7.07	7.10	8.62	5.66
Moving, storage, and freight express	26.46	13.06	10.61	23.78	32.08	46.84	56.17
Appliance repair	16.44	8.34	13.57	18.93	20.85	17.46	25.57
Reupholstering and furniture repair	13.85	7.31	8.01	13.68	15.55	11.69	32.30
Repairs and rental of equipment and power tools	5.92	1.98	4.36	4.90	6.20	9.08	13.38
Appliance rental	2.08	3.73	3.46	1.01	1.16	0.52	0.54
HOUSEKEEPING SUPPLIES	**$382.82**	**$201.64**	**$302.72**	**$383.43**	**$451.24**	**$475.45**	**$670.22**
Laundry and cleaning supplies	**106.44**	**60.11**	**91.59**	**109.27**	**131.66**	**129.47**	**162.63**
Soaps and detergents	62.10	37.73	53.45	63.11	78.35	77.19	89.28
Other household products	**157.48**	**65.72**	**121.04**	**149.94**	**183.61**	**201.65**	**316.09**
Cleansing and toilet tissue, paper towels and napkins	52.12	28.92	44.04	51.88	64.86	67.41	80.71
Lawn and garden supplies	37.47	12.30	31.13	39.79	33.12	25.27	95.48
Postage and stationery	**118.89**	**75.81**	**90.09**	**124.23**	**135.97**	**144.33**	**191.50**
Stationery, stationery supplies, and giftwraps	54.40	39.93	33.08	45.35	55.09	74.49	105.20
Postage	64.49	35.88	57.01	78.88	80.87	69.84	86.30
HOUSEHOLD FURNISHINGS/EQUIPMENT	**$1,102.32**	**$323.82**	**$630.47**	**$982.28**	**$1,385.76**	**$1,612.00**	**$2,590.97**
Household textiles	**97.11**	**36.09**	**64.64**	**96.28**	**104.56**	**122.28**	**220.32**
Bathroom linens	13.69	4.92	12.19	9.71	18.83	13.05	30.80
Bedroom linens	38.11	17.81	31.77	36.81	33.56	50.47	77.56
Kitchen and dining room linens	5.74	-	3.64	4.03	6.56	7.12	15.73
Curtains and draperies	26.56	7.84	8.50	28.90	26.44	39.44	71.25
Sewing materials for household items	10.32	3.07	6.27	14.65	15.39	9.43	19.15
Slipcovers, decorative pillows, and other linens	2.69	0.75	2.28	2.17	3.77	2.78	5.83

Average annual expenditures for household operations and furnishings, by total before-tax income of consumer unit.

(continued from previous page)	all cu's	under $10,000	$10,000 to $19,999	$20,000 to $29,999	$30,000 to $39,999	$40,000 to $49,999	$50,000 and over
Furniture	**319.44**	**74.88**	**169.79**	**261.90**	**378.37**	**433.38**	**861.57**
Mattress and springs	41.86	9.41	25.23	39.28	57.01	62.91	93.05
Other bedroom furniture	39.75	10.44	21.09	22.88	52.21	62.05	107.77
Sofas	65.44	17.66	39.01	58.54	83.34	108.08	144.37
Living room chairs	35.91	11.97	25.97	40.43	31.79	44.77	80.20
Living room tables	20.16	6.48	10.79	15.21	26.54	27.03	50.94
Kitchen and dining room furniture	58.64	9.31	24.15	22.79	61.09	56.39	226.46
Infants' furniture	7.01	1.84	3.50	4.57	8.94	14.79	16.63
Outdoor furniture	12.57	1.74	2.50	12.51	10.65	19.59	41.43
Occasional furniture	38.12	6.03	17.54	45.67	46.80	37.77	100.73
Carpet, rugs, and other floor coverings	**70.23**	**10.62**	**23.71**	**74.77**	**110.80**	**113.46**	**164.89**
Major appliances	**172.90**	**72.68**	**121.88**	**169.54**	**213.08**	**240.59**	**328.70**
Dishwashers (built-in), garbage disposals, hoods	10.29	2.26	5.59	9.73	10.34	19.20	24.86
Portable dishwashers	1.64	-	1.92	1.22	-	3.87	4.10
Refrigerators and freezers	50.47	20.10	31.21	53.01	68.04	56.70	102.71
Washing machines and dryers	39.05	20.93	28.50	34.99	49.68	64.40	62.65
Stoves and ovens	22.42	9.34	12.44	18.75	35.24	32.07	47.54
Microwave ovens	14.28	4.35	12.27	14.97	18.79	17.89	25.47
Window air conditioners	10.66	10.77	10.43	10.71	8.66	4.25	17.96
Electric floor cleaning equipment	14.62	5.52	9.64	19.58	17.20	17.77	25.74
Sewing machines	6.08	1.48	6.60	6.21	2.84	8.29	13.83
Small appliances and miscellaneous housewares	**60.51**	**22.65**	**38.79**	**46.50**	**71.00**	**77.96**	**148.46**
Housewares	39.14	14.28	23.48	26.52	45.46	47.51	105.70
China and other dinnerware	12.14	4.40	6.18	9.47	17.76	19.00	26.87
Flatware	3.44	1.05	1.45	3.30	2.32	3.40	11.15
Glassware	9.79	2.63	2.77	4.54	11.70	9.13	36.70
Nonelectric cookware	12.14	5.44	11.49	7.98	12.53	13.45	27.64
Small electrical kitchen appliances	14.17	4.54	8.84	13.81	17.74	21.71	29.49
Portable heating and cooling equipment	7.20	3.83	6.47	6.17	7.80	8.73	13.26
Miscellaneous household equipment	**382.11**	**106.90**	**211.66**	**333.29**	**507.95**	**624.34**	**867.02**
Clocks	5.46	3.28	5.88	4.27	3.57	7.24	10.26
Lamps and lighting fixtures	28.40	3.23	30.60	21.24	50.72	42.07	46.18
Telephones, accessories, and answering devices	11.48	4.35	4.81	12.46	9.99	12.46	32.29
Lawn and garden equipment	49.12	19.24	30.49	40.12	60.08	100.17	92.96
Power and hand tools	28.06	6.60	9.34	43.32	82.63	151.20	49.34
Indoor plants and fresh flowers	41.42	12.79	28.74	24.78	34.12	74.01	110.87
Closet and storage items	4.62	-	0.82	1.25	4.26	4.50	18.01
Luggage	8.72	2.73	4.15	6.02	9.30	14.24	23.99
Business equipment for home use	6.20	1.97	2.79	5.13	9.35	7.42	15.40

Note: Expenditures listed for items in a given category may not add to the total for that category because the listing is incomplete. "Other household services," for example, includes "other services," which is omitted here. Expenditures are not given (-) when the amount is too small to be reliable. Total expenditure exceeds total income in some categories due to a number of factors including the underreporting of income, borrowing, and the use of savings. Numbers may not add to total due to rounding.

Share of spending

(consumer units include complete income reporters only)	all cu's	under $10,000	$10,000 to $19,999	$20,000 to $29,999	$30,000 to $39,999	$40,000 to $49,999	$50,000 and over
Number of consumer units (in thousands)	81,354	18,809	17,652	14,586	10,901	7,198	12,209
Average number of persons per cu	2.6	1.8	2.3	2.7	2.9	3.2	3.1
Average number of earners per cu	1.4	0.7	1.0	1.5	1.8	2.0	2.1
TOTAL AVERAGE ANNUAL EXPENDITURES	100.00%	100.00%	100.00%	100.00%	100.00%	100.00%	100.00%
HOUSING, AVERAGE ANNUAL EXPENDITURES	30.58%	36.46%	31.56%	30.17%	29.25%	28.24%	30.04%
HOUSEHOLD SERVICES	**1.47%**	**1.36%**	**1.17%**	**1.25%**	**1.42%**	**1.41%**	**1.83%**
Personal services	**0.67**	**0.48**	**0.55**	**0.67**	**0.87**	**0.83**	**0.61**
Babysitting	0.28	0.13	0.27	0.34	0.42	0.31	0.22
Care for elderly, invalids, handicapped, etc.	0.04	0.25	0.01	0.02	0.00	-	0.05
Day care centers, nursery and preschools	0.34	0.11	0.26	0.31	0.44	0.52	0.35
Other household services	**0.80**	**0.89**	**0.62**	**0.58**	**0.55**	**0.59**	**1.21**
Housekeeping services	0.26	0.22	0.17	0.12	0.13	0.14	0.51
Gardening, lawn care service	0.19	0.23	0.14	0.12	0.10	0.14	0.30
Water softening service	0.01	-	0.01	0.01	0.01	0.01	0.01
Dry cleaning and laundering of household textiles	0.02	0.04	0.04	0.03	0.02	0.02	0.01
Moving, storage, and freight express	0.10	0.12	0.06	0.10	0.10	0.12	0.11
Appliance repair	0.06	0.07	0.08	0.08	0.07	0.05	0.05
Reupholstering and furniture repair	0.05	0.06	0.04	0.05	0.05	0.03	0.06
Repairs and rental of equipment and power tools	0.02	0.02	0.02	0.02	0.02	0.02	0.03
Appliance rental	0.01	0.03	0.02	0.00	0.00	0.00	0.00
HOUSEKEEPING SUPPLIES	**1.45%**	**1.79%**	**1.67%**	**1.54%**	**1.43%**	**1.27%**	**1.28%**
Laundry and cleaning supplies	**0.40**	**0.53**	**0.51**	**0.44**	**0.42**	**0.34**	**0.31**
Soaps and detergents	0.24	0.33	0.30	0.25	0.25	0.21	0.17
Other household products	**0.60**	**0.58**	**0.67**	**0.60**	**0.58**	**0.54**	**0.60**
Cleansing and toilet tissue, paper towels and napkins	0.20	0.26	0.24	0.21	0.20	0.18	0.15
Lawn and garden supplies	0.14	0.11	0.17	0.16	0.10	0.07	0.18
Postage and stationery	**0.45**	**0.67**	**0.50**	**0.50**	**0.43**	**0.38**	**0.37**
Stationery, stationery supplies, and giftwrap	0.21	0.35	0.18	0.18	0.17	0.20	0.20
Postage	0.24	0.32	0.32	0.32	0.26	0.19	0.16
HOUSEHOLD FURNISHINGS AND EQUIPMENT	**4.18%**	**2.87%**	**3.49%**	**3.95%**	**4.38%**	**4.29%**	**4.95%**
Household textiles	**0.37**	**0.32**	**0.36**	**0.39**	**0.33**	**0.33**	**0.42**
Bathroom linens	0.05	0.04	0.07	0.04	0.06	0.03	0.06
Bedroom linens	0.14	0.16	0.18	0.15	0.11	0.13	0.15
Kitchen and dining room linens	0.02	-	0.02	0.02	0.02	0.02	0.03
Curtains and draperies	0.10	0.07	0.05	0.12	0.08	0.10	0.14
Sewing materials for household items	0.04	0.03	0.03	0.06	0.05	0.03	0.04
Slipcovers, decorative pillows, and other linens	0.01	0.01	0.01	0.01	0.01	0.01	0.01

Percent of total average annual expenditures spent on household operations and furnishings, by total before-tax income of consumer unit.

(continued from previous page)	all cu's	under $10,000	$10,000 to $19,999	$20,000 to $29,999	$30,000 to $39,999	$40,000 to $49,999	$50,000 and over
Furniture	**1.21**	**0.66**	**0.94**	**1.05**	**1.20**	**1.15**	**1.65**
Mattress and springs	0.16	0.08	0.14	0.16	0.18	0.17	0.18
Other bedroom furniture	0.15	0.09	0.12	0.09	0.16	0.17	0.21
Sofas	0.25	0.16	0.22	0.24	0.26	0.29	0.28
Living room chairs	0.14	0.11	0.14	0.16	0.10	0.12	0.15
Living room tables	0.08	0.06	0.06	0.06	0.08	0.07	0.10
Kitchen and dining room furniture	0.22	0.08	0.13	0.09	0.19	0.15	0.43
Infants' furniture	0.03	0.02	0.02	0.02	0.03	0.04	0.03
Outdoor furniture	0.05	0.02	0.01	0.05	0.03	0.05	0.08
Occasional furniture	0.14	0.05	0.10	0.18	0.15	0.10	0.19
Carpet, rugs, and other floor coverings	**0.27**	**0.09**	**0.13**	**0.30**	**0.35**	**0.30**	**0.32**
Major appliances	**0.66**	**0.64**	**0.67**	**0.68**	**0.67**	**0.64**	**0.63**
Built-in dishwashers, garbage disposals, hoods	0.04	0.02	0.03	0.04	0.03	0.05	0.05
Portable dishwashers	0.01	-	0.01	0.00	-	0.01	0.01
Refrigerators and freezers	0.19	0.18	0.17	0.21	0.21	0.15	0.20
Washing machines and dryers	0.15	0.19	0.16	0.14	0.16	0.17	0.12
Stoves and ovens	0.08	0.08	0.07	0.08	0.11	0.09	0.09
Microwave ovens	0.05	0.04	0.07	0.06	0.06	0.05	0.05
Window air conditioners	0.04	0.10	0.06	0.04	0.03	0.01	0.03
Electric floor cleaning equipment	0.06	0.05	0.05	0.08	0.05	0.05	0.05
Sewing machines	0.02	0.01	0.04	0.02	0.01	0.02	0.03
Small appliances and miscellaneous housewares	**0.23**	**0.20**	**0.21**	**0.19**	**0.22**	**0.21**	**0.28**
Housewares	0.15	0.13	0.13	0.11	0.14	0.13	0.20
China and other dinnerware	0.05	0.04	0.03	0.04	0.06	0.05	0.05
Flatware	0.01	0.01	0.01	0.01	0.01	0.01	0.02
Glassware	0.04	0.02	0.02	0.02	0.04	0.02	0.07
Nonelectric cookware	0.05	0.05	0.06	0.03	0.04	0.04	0.05
Small electrical kitchen appliances	0.05	0.04	0.05	0.06	0.06	0.06	0.06
Portable heating and cooling equipment	0.03	0.03	0.04	0.02	0.02	0.02	0.03
Miscellaneous household equipment	**1.45**	**0.95**	**1.17**	**1.34**	**1.60**	**1.66**	**1.66**
Clocks	0.02	0.03	0.03	0.02	0.01	0.02	0.02
Lamps and lighting fixtures	0.11	0.03	0.17	0.09	0.16	0.11	0.09
Telephones, accessories, and answering devices	0.04	0.04	0.03	0.05	0.03	0.03	0.06
Lawn and garden equipment	0.19	0.17	0.17	0.16	0.19	0.27	0.18
Power and hand tools	0.11	0.06	0.05	0.17	0.26	0.40	0.09
Indoor plants and fresh flowers	0.16	0.11	0.16	0.10	0.11	0.20	0.21
Closet and storage items	0.02	-	0.00	0.01	0.01	0.01	0.03
Luggage	0.03	0.02	0.02	0.02	0.03	0.04	0.05
Business equipment for home use	0.02	0.02	0.02	0.02	0.03	0.02	0.03

Note: Expenditures listed for items in a given category may not add to the total for that category because the listing is incomplete. "Other household services," for example, includes "other services," which is omitted here. Expenditures are not given (-) when the amount is too small to be reliable. Numbers may not add to total due to rounding.

Indexed expenditures

Indexed average annual expenditures for household operations and furnishings, by total before-tax income of consumer unit.							
(consumer units include complete income reporters only)	all cu's	under $10,000	$10,000 to $19,999	$20,000 to $29,999	$30,000 to $39,999	$40,000 to $49,999	$50,000 and over
Number of consumer units (in thousands)	81,354	18,809	17,652	14,586	10,901	7,198	12,209
Average number of persons per cu	2.6	1.8	2.3	2.7	2.9	3.2	3.1
Average number of earners per cu	1.4	0.7	1.0	1.5	1.8	2.0	2.1
TOTAL AVERAGE ANNUAL EXPENDITURES	100	43	69	94	120	142	198
HOUSING, AVERAGE ANNUAL EXPENDITURES	100	51	71	93	115	131	195
HOUSEHOLD SERVICES	100	40	54	80	116	137	247
Personal services	100	31	57	94	156	176	182
Babysitting	100	19	66	114	178	154	155
Care for elderly, invalids, handicapped, etc.	100	237	20	39	13	-	211
Day care centers, nursery and preschools	100	13	53	85	156	217	201
Other household services	100	47	53	68	82	104	301
Housekeeping services	100	36	44	43	61	75	397
Gardening, lawn care service	100	51	51	61	63	108	321
Water softening service	100	-	65	78	105	146	272
Dry cleaning and laundering of household textiles	100	78	102	110	111	134	88
Moving, storage, and freight express	100	49	40	90	121	177	212
Appliance repair	100	51	83	115	127	106	156
Reupholstering and furniture repair	100	53	58	99	112	84	233
Repairs and rental of equipment and power tools	100	33	74	83	105	153	226
Appliance rental	100	179	167	49	56	25	26
HOUSEKEEPING SUPPLIES	100	53	79	100	118	124	175
Laundry and cleaning supplies	100	56	86	103	124	122	153
Soaps and detergents	100	61	86	102	126	124	144
Other household products	100	42	77	95	117	128	201
Cleansing and toilet tissue, paper towels and napkins	100	55	84	100	124	129	155
Lawn and garden supplies	100	33	83	106	88	67	255
Postage and stationery	100	64	76	104	114	121	161
Stationery, stationery supplies, and giftwraps	100	73	61	83	101	137	193
Postage	100	56	88	122	125	108	134
HOUSEHOLD FURNISHINGS/EQUIPMENT	100	29	57	89	126	146	235
Household textiles	100	37	67	99	108	126	227
Bathroom linens	100	36	89	71	138	95	225
Bedroom linens	100	47	83	97	88	132	204
Kitchen and dining room linens	100	-	63	70	114	124	274
Curtains and draperies	100	30	32	109	100	148	268
Sewing materials for household items	100	30	61	142	149	91	186
Slipcovers, decorative pillows, and other linens	100	28	85	81	140	103	217

Indexed average annual expenditures for household operations and furnishings, by total before-tax income of consumer unit.

(continued from previous page)	all cu's	under $10,000	$10,000 to $19,999	$20,000 to $29,999	$30,000 to $39,999	$40,000 to $49,999	$50,000 and over
Furniture	100	23	53	82	118	136	270
Mattress and springs	100	22	60	94	136	150	222
Other bedroom furniture	100	26	53	58	131	156	271
Sofas	100	27	60	89	127	165	221
Living room chairs	100	33	72	113	89	125	223
Living room tables	100	32	54	75	132	134	253
Kitchen and dining room furniture	100	16	41	39	104	96	386
Infants' furniture	100	26	50	65	128	211	237
Outdoor furniture	100	14	20	100	85	156	330
Occasional furniture	100	16	46	120	123	99	264
Carpet, rugs, and other floor coverings	100	15	34	106	158	162	235
Major appliances	100	42	70	98	123	139	190
Dishwashers (built-in), garbage disposals, hoods	100	22	54	95	100	187	242
Portable dishwashers	100	-	117	74	-	236	250
Refrigerators and freezers	100	40	62	105	135	112	204
Washing machines and dryers	100	54	73	90	127	165	160
Stoves and ovens	100	42	55	84	157	143	212
Microwave ovens	100	30	86	105	132	125	178
Window air conditioners	100	101	98	100	81	40	168
Electric floor cleaning equipment	100	38	66	134	118	122	176
Sewing machines	100	24	109	102	47	136	227
Small appliances and miscellaneous housewares	100	37	64	77	117	129	245
Housewares	100	36	60	68	116	121	270
China and other dinnerware	100	36	51	78	146	157	221
Flatware	100	31	42	96	67	99	324
Glassware	100	27	28	46	120	93	375
Nonelectric cookware	100	45	95	66	103	111	228
Small electrical kitchen appliances	100	32	62	97	125	153	208
Portable heating and cooling equipment	100	53	90	86	108	121	184
Miscellaneous household equipment	100	28	55	87	133	163	227
Clocks	100	60	108	78	65	133	188
Lamps and lighting fixtures	100	11	108	75	179	148	163
Telephones, accessories, and answering devices	100	38	42	109	87	109	281
Lawn and garden equipment	100	39	62	82	122	204	189
Power and hand tools	100	24	33	154	294	539	176
Indoor plants and fresh flowers	100	31	69	60	82	179	268
Closet and storage items	100	-	18	27	92	97	390
Luggage	100	31	48	69	107	163	275
Business equipment for home use	100	32	45	83	151	120	248

Note: Expenditures are not given (-) when the amount is too small to be reliable. An index of 100 represents the average for all consumer units. An index of 132 means that the average for the subgroup is 32 percent above the average for all consumer units. An index of 68 indicates spending that is 32 percent below the overall average.

Aggregate expenditures, 1988

Aggregate expenditures in 1988 for household operations and furnishings, by total before-tax income of consumer unit.

(consumer units include complete income reporters only)	all cu's	under $10,000	$10,000 to $19,999	$20,000 to $29,999	$30,000 to $39,999	$40,000 to $49,999	$50,000 and over
Number of consumer units (in thousands)	81,354	18,809	17,652	14,586	10,901	7,198	12,209
Average number of persons per cu	2.6	1.8	2.3	2.7	2.9	3.2	3.1
Average number of earners per cu	1.4	0.7	1.0	1.5	1.8	2.0	2.1
TOTAL AGGREGATE EXPENDITURES (in millions)	$2,148,492	$211,967	$319,117	$363,138	$345,121	$270,371	$638,777
HOUSING, AGGREGATE EXPENDITURES (in millions)	$656,783	$77,279	$100,712	$109,568	$100,948	$76,362	$191,915
HOUSEHOLD SERVICES	**$31,520**	**$2,893**	**$3,725**	**$4,525**	**$4,893**	**$3,820**	**$11,663**
Personal services	**14,362**	**1,016**	**1,761**	**2,422**	**2,999**	**2,242**	**3,922**
Babysitting	6,071	267	874	1,243	1,452	825	1,410
Care for elderly, invalids, handicapped, etc.	945	520	42	67	16	-	301
Day care centers, nursery and preschools	7,342	229	845	1,113	1,531	1,413	2,211
Other household services	**17,161**	**1,877**	**1,964**	**2,103**	**1,894**	**1,582**	**7,741**
Housekeeping services	5,513	456	531	421	453	367	3,286
Gardening, lawn care service	4,035	480	445	443	339	386	1,941
Water softening service	219	-	32	32	32	30	93
Dry cleaning and laundering of household textiles	521	94	115	103	77	62	69
Moving, storage, and freight express	2,152	246	187	347	350	337	686
Appliance repair	1,338	157	240	276	227	126	312
Reupholstering and furniture repair	1,126	137	141	200	170	84	394
Repairs and rental of equipment and power tools	482	37	77	71	68	65	163
Appliance rental	169	70	61	15	13	4	7
HOUSEKEEPING SUPPLIES	**$31,253**	**$3,793**	**$5,344**	**$5,593**	**$4,919**	**$3,422**	**$8,183**
Laundry and cleaning supplies	**8,694**	**1,131**	**1,617**	**1,594**	**1,435**	**932**	**1,986**
Soaps and detergents	5,073	710	943	921	854	556	1,090
Other household products	**12,872**	**1,236**	**2,137**	**2,187**	**2,002**	**1,451**	**3,859**
Cleansing and toilet tissue, paper towels and napkins	4,256	544	777	757	707	485	985
Lawn and garden supplies	3,070	231	550	580	361	182	1,166
Postage and stationery	**9,687**	**1,426**	**1,590**	**1,812**	**1,482**	**1,039**	**2,338**
Stationery, stationery supplies, and giftwraps	4,418	751	584	661	601	536	1,284
Postage	5,270	675	1,006	1,151	882	503	1,054
HOUSEHOLD FURNISHINGS/EQUIPMENT	**$89,890**	**$6,091**	**$11,129**	**$14,328**	**$15,106**	**$11,603**	**$31,633**
Household textiles	**7,934**	**679**	**1,141**	**1,404**	**1,140**	**880**	**2,690**
Bathroom linens	1,125	93	215	142	205	94	376
Bedroom linens	3,109	335	561	537	366	363	947
Kitchen and dining room linens	438	-	64	59	72	51	192
Curtains and draperies	2,161	148	150	422	288	284	870
Sewing materials for household items	851	58	111	214	168	68	234
Slipcovers, decorative pillows, and other linens	218	14	40	32	41	20	71

Aggregate expenditures in 1988 for household operations and furnishings, by total before-tax income of consumer unit.

(continued from previous page)	all cu's	under $10,000	$10,000 to $19,999	$20,000 to $29,999	$30,000 to $39,999	$40,000 to $49,999	$50,000 and over
Furniture	**25,989**	**1,408**	**2,997**	**3,820**	**4,125**	**3,119**	**10,519**
Mattress and springs	3,406	177	445	573	621	453	1,136
Other bedroom furniture	3,234	196	372	334	569	447	1,316
Sofas	5,324	332	689	854	908	778	1,763
Living room chairs	2,921	225	459	590	347	322	979
Living room tables	1,640	122	191	222	289	195	622
Kitchen and dining room furniture	4,771	175	426	332	666	406	2,765
Infants' furniture	570	35	62	67	97	106	203
Outdoor furniture	1,022	33	44	182	116	141	506
Occasional furniture	3,101	113	310	666	510	272	1,230
Carpet, rugs, and other floor coverings	**5,747**	**200**	**419**	**1,091**	**1,208**	**817**	**2,013**
Major appliances	**14,059**	**1,367**	**2,152**	**2,473**	**2,323**	**1,732**	**4,013**
Dishwashers (built-in), garbage disposals, hoods	837	42	99	142	113	138	304
Portable dishwashers	130	-	34	18	-	28	50
Refrigerators and freezers	4,106	378	551	773	742	408	1,254
Washing machines and dryers	3,177	394	503	510	542	464	765
Stoves and ovens	1,864	176	220	273	384	231	580
Microwave ovens	1,161	82	217	218	205	129	311
Window air conditioners	887	203	184	156	94	31	219
Electric floor cleaning equipment	1,189	104	170	286	187	128	314
Sewing machines	495	28	117	91	31	60	169
Small appliances and miscellaneous housewares	**4,937**	**426**	**685**	**678**	**774**	**561**	**1,813**
Housewares	3,198	269	414	387	496	342	1,290
China and other dinnerware	988	83	109	138	194	137	328
Flatware	279	20	26	48	25	24	136
Glassware	806	50	49	66	128	66	448
Nonelectric cookware	992	102	203	116	137	97	337
Small electrical kitchen appliances	1,153	85	156	201	193	156	360
Portable heating and cooling equipment	586	72	114	90	85	63	162
Miscellaneous household equipment	**31,225**	**2,011**	**3,736**	**4,861**	**5,537**	**4,494**	**10,585**
Clocks	444	62	104	62	39	52	125
Lamps and lighting fixtures	2,330	61	540	310	553	303	564
Telephones, accessories, and answering devices	941	82	85	182	109	90	394
Lawn and garden equipment	3,996	362	538	585	655	721	1,135
Power and hand tools	3,512	124	165	632	901	1,088	602
Indoor plants and fresh flowers	3,368	241	507	361	372	533	1,354
Closet and storage items	331	-	14	18	46	32	220
Luggage	709	51	73	88	101	102	293
Business equipment for home use	505	37	49	75	102	53	188

Note: Expenditures listed for items in a given category may not add to the total for that category because the listing is incomplete. "Other household services," for example, includes "other services," which is omitted here. Expenditures are not given (-) when the amount is too small to be reliable. Numbers may not add to total due to rounding. The "all cu's" aggregates will differ slightly from table to table because they are the sums of the aggregates in each row.

PART III
Spending by type of household for household operations and furnishings

Married couples are the largest market for household services...

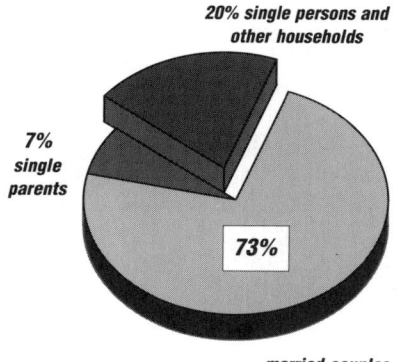

20% single persons and other households

7% single parents

73%

married couples

...and for housekeeping supplies...

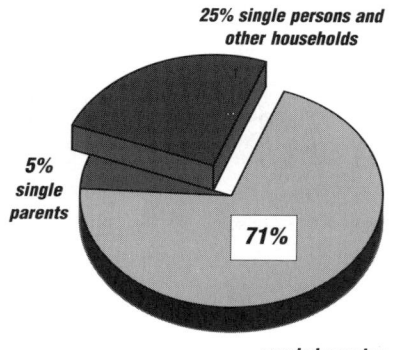

25% single persons and other households

5% single parents

71%

married couples

...and for household furnishings.

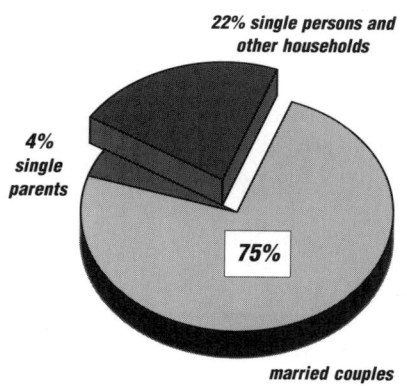

22% single persons and other households

4% single parents

75%

married couples

High child-care costs boost the household service spending of single parents to 18 percent more than the average for all households. This is the only item in this category on which single parents spend more than average. Most of the time, it's married couples who spend the most. Married couples spend 33 percent more than the average household on household services, 28 percent more than average on household supplies, and 36 percent more on furnishings and equipment.

Married couples are 55 percent of all households, but they account for 73 percent of the household services market, 71 percent of the housekeeping supplies market, and 75 percent of the furnishings and equipment market. The 37 million people who live alone or in "other" households* are 39 percent of the total, but only 20 percent of the market for household services and no more than 25 percent of the supplies, furnishings, and equipment markets. Single parents make up just 6 percent of all households, but their share of the household services market is 7 percent.

Among married couples, those with children account for the largest share of housing expenditures. They are 69 percent of the married-couple market for household services, 58 percent of the household supplies market, and 56 percent of the furnishings and equipment market. Married couples without children account for most of the remaining expenditures by married couples on household services, supplies, furnishing, and equipment. The small number of couples who live with extended family members or unrelated people, account for just 7 percent of the the expenditures of all couples on household services, supplies, furnishings, and equipment.

Married-couple market

Married couples without children at home don't spend a lot on personal services but their spending on other kinds of household services is 39 percent more than average. They spend more than other households on gardening and lawn care, appliance repairs, and upholstering and furniture repairs. These empty-nesters and childless couples are the biggest spenders on living room chairs, outdoor furniture, floor coverings, stoves and ovens, and nonelectric cookware.

Child care boosts the personal service spending of married couples with children under age 18. Spending on this category peaks among couples with children under age 6, at 210 percent above average. Married couples living

In this analysis, single-person households are grouped with "other" households. "Other" households are unrelated people living together and families that are not married-couple or single- parent families, such as siblings. Single-person households account for 72 percent of the households in this category.

with extended family members or unrelated people spend the most on services for the elderly and handicapped.

Married couples with preschoolers spend 137 percent more than the average household on moving and shipping services. They are also the biggest buyers of infants' furniture. Their spending on all furniture is 63 percent above average and they spend twice the average amount on sewing machines.

Parents of school-aged children outspend all others on housekeeping services. They spend 84 percent more than average on kitchen and dining room linens, 114 percent more than average on kitchen and dining room furniture, and 116 percent more on closet and storage items. Couples with children aged 18 or older at home are the biggest spenders on housewares such as china, glassware, and flatware. They also spend 112 percent more than the average household on lawn and garden equipment.

Other household markets

Although they generally spend less than average on housing items, single parents spend 136 percent more than the average household on baby sitting, and 88 percent more than average on day care and preschools. They spend well above average on such items as cleaning household textiles, appliance rentals, slipcovers and decorative pillows, washing machines and dryers, and vacuum cleaners.

Single-person and "other" households spend just half the average amount on household services, although they spend 101 percent more than average on care for the elderly or handicapped. They spend 18 percent more than the average household on telephones, telephone accessories, and answering machines, outspending both single parents and married couples on these items.

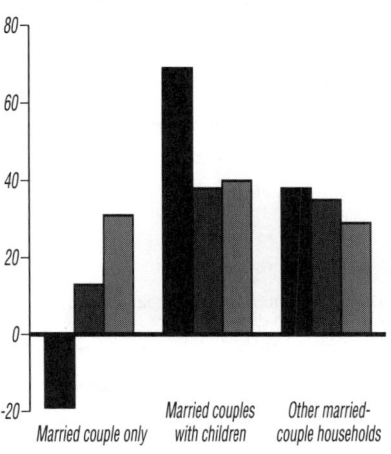

Married couples with children spend well above average for household services...

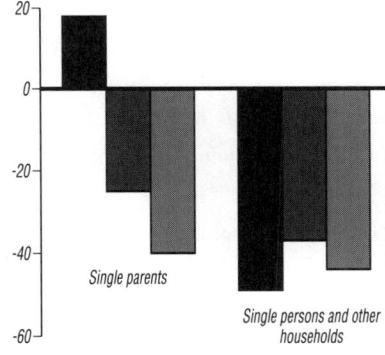

...so do single parents.

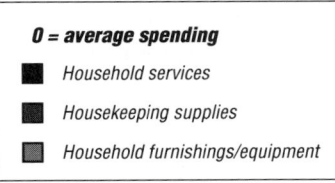

0 = average spending

- Household services
- Housekeeping supplies
- Household furnishings/equipment

Average expenditures

	all cu's	married couples	single parents	single persons and other cu's
Number of consumer units (in thousands)	94,862	52,010	5,716	37,136
Average number of persons per cu	2.6	3.3	2.9	1.5
Average number of earners per cu	1.4	1.7	1.0	0.9
Average total before-tax income	$28,540.00	$37,299.00	$16,276.00	$18,509.00
TOTAL AVERAGE ANNUAL EXPENDITURES	$25,891.85	$32,314.50	$18,615.80	$17,950.80
HOUSING, AVERAGE ANNUAL EXPENDITURES	$8,078.63	$9,731.21	$7,112.65	$5,902.84
HOUSEHOLD SERVICES	**$394.12**	**$522.74**	**$466.51**	**$202.82**
Personal services	**171.19**	**236.16**	**333.22**	**55.24**
Babysitting	71.51	105.57	168.78	8.84
Care for elderly, invalids, handicapped, etc.	12.42	4.81	-	24.93
Day care centers, nursery and preschools	87.25	125.78	164.07	21.47
Other household services	**222.93**	**286.57**	**133.29**	**147.59**
Housekeeping services	76.80	104.60	33.72	44.49
Gardening, lawn care service	50.35	61.81	13.76	39.94
Water softening service	2.68	3.72	3.77	1.05
Dry cleaning and laundering of household textiles	6.51	5.97	10.54	6.65
Moving, storage, and freight express	29.28	32.42	44.62	22.53
Appliance repair	16.21	22.27	6.55	9.20
Reupholstering and furniture repair	14.74	19.86	7.34	8.70
Repairs and rental of equipment and power tools	5.47	8.14	0.85	2.45
Appliance rental	2.16	2.53	3.09	1.51
HOUSEKEEPING SUPPLIES	**$360.94**	**$462.95**	**$270.69**	**$227.30**
Laundry and cleaning supplies	**100.73**	**130.70**	**98.37**	**57.80**
Soaps and detergents	59.26	75.45	64.77	35.04
Other household products	**147.21**	**192.73**	**103.08**	**88.15**
Cleansing and toilet tissue, paper towels and napkins	49.87	64.08	35.93	31.46
Lawn and garden supplies	33.60	43.10	27.26	20.85
Postage and stationery	**113.00**	**139.51**	**69.24**	**81.35**
Stationery, stationery supplies, and giftwrap	50.42	67.76	28.65	28.68
Postage	62.58	71.76	40.59	52.67
HOUSEHOLD FURNISHINGS/EQUIPMENT	**$1,083.41**	**$1,471.47**	**$645.17**	**$602.08**
Household textiles	**93.97**	**121.13**	**66.87**	**59.43**
Bathroom linens	13.08	15.12	5.68	11.25
Bedroom linens	35.07	41.23	34.97	26.18
Kitchen and dining room linens	5.57	8.13	1.01	2.56
Curtains and draperies	27.78	39.60	16.08	13.02
Sewing materials for household items	9.70	13.36	5.39	5.06
Slipcovers, decorative pillows, and other linens	2.77	3.68	3.73	1.35

Average annual expenditures for household operations and furnishings, by type of consumer unit.

(continued from previous page)

	all cu's	married couples	single parents	single persons and other cu's
Furniture	**326.01**	**440.93**	**178.47**	**187.77**
Mattress and springs	42.85	51.97	29.89	32.07
Other bedroom furniture	44.69	56.75	38.59	28.73
Sofas	68.18	91.00	32.17	41.76
Living room chairs	34.00	45.79	13.23	20.70
Living room tables	19.33	26.03	7.20	11.80
Kitchen and dining room furniture	56.64	82.45	21.37	25.93
Infants' furniture	6.77	10.44	3.22	2.17
Outdoor furniture	12.57	19.43	6.97	3.82
Occasional furniture	40.98	57.06	25.83	20.79
Carpet, rugs, and other floor coverings	**65.34**	**100.24**	**33.33**	**20.85**
Major appliances	**168.60**	**221.93**	**137.99**	**98.55**
Dishwashers (built-in), garbage disposals, hoods	11.01	17.65	1.56	3.15
Portable dishwashers	1.63	2.53	0.00	0.62
Refrigerators and freezers	49.14	64.68	37.55	29.16
Washing machines and dryers	37.33	44.68	42.63	26.20
Stoves and ovens	22.18	31.18	23.05	9.45
Microwave ovens	14.10	17.67	5.19	10.50
Window air conditioners	10.49	12.10	6.16	8.90
Electric floor cleaning equipment	14.47	17.78	19.38	9.09
Sewing machines	5.52	9.05	2.32	1.07
Small appliances and miscellaneous housewares	**60.50**	**79.42**	**30.14**	**38.28**
Housewares	39.32	52.29	17.73	24.09
China and other dinnerware	12.34	16.30	6.12	7.75
Flatware	3.39	3.89	1.67	2.95
Glassware	10.87	13.91	3.79	7.55
Nonelectric cookware	11.20	16.16	5.58	4.90
Small electrical kitchen appliances	13.79	17.97	7.66	8.88
Portable heating and cooling equipment	7.39	9.16	4.75	5.31
Miscellaneous household equipment	**368.99**	**507.83**	**198.38**	**197.19**
Clocks	4.96	5.58	1.39	4.64
Lamps and lighting fixtures	25.59	37.67	10.87	10.39
Telephones, accessories, and answering devices	13.26	12.56	3.91	15.67
Lawn and garden equipment	47.65	73.71	23.40	14.88
Power and hand tools	26.41	37.10	26.62	13.61
Indoor plants and fresh flowers	36.46	44.02	18.32	28.30
Closet and storage items	5.19	7.75	0.87	2.14
Luggage	8.42	10.59	5.65	5.81
Business equipment for home use	6.16	8.75	6.94	2.41

Note: Expenditures listed for items in a given category may not add to the total for that category because the listing is incomplete. "Other household services," for example, includes "other services," which is omitted here. Expenditures are not given (-) when the amount is too small to be reliable. Numbers may not add to total due to rounding. "Single parents" is one-parent consumer units with a child or children under age 18 living at home. "Other cu's" includes persons living with unrelated persons and families other than married-couple and single-parent families.

Share of spending

	all cu's	married couples	single parents	single persons and other cu's
Number of consumer units (in thousands)	94,862	52,010	5,716	37,136
Average number of persons per cu	2.6	3.3	2.9	1.5
Average number of earners per cu	1.4	1.7	1.0	0.9
Average total before-tax income	$28,540	$37,299	$16,276	$18,509
TOTAL AVERAGE ANNUAL EXPENDITURES	100.00%	100.00%	100.00%	100.00%
HOUSING, AVERAGE ANNUAL EXPENDITURES	31.20%	30.11%	38.21%	32.88%
HOUSEHOLD SERVICES	**1.52%**	**1.62%**	**2.51%**	**1.13%**
Personal services	**0.66**	**0.73**	**1.79**	**0.31**
Babysitting	0.28	0.33	0.91	0.05
Care for elderly, invalids, handicapped, etc.	0.05	0.01	-	0.14
Day care centers, nursery and preschools	0.34	0.39	0.88	0.12
Other household services	**0.86**	**0.89**	**0.72**	**0.82**
Housekeeping services	0.30	0.32	0.18	0.25
Gardening, lawn care service	0.19	0.19	0.07	0.22
Water softening service	0.01	0.01	0.02	0.01
Dry cleaning and laundering of household textiles	0.03	0.02	0.06	0.04
Moving, storage, and freight express	0.11	0.10	0.24	0.13
Appliance repair	0.06	0.07	0.04	0.05
Reupholstering and furniture repair	0.06	0.06	0.04	0.05
Repairs and rental of equipment and power tools	0.02	0.03	0.00	0.01
Appliance rental	0.01	0.01	0.02	0.01
HOUSEKEEPING SUPPLIES	**1.39%**	**1.43%**	**1.45%**	**1.27%**
Laundry and cleaning supplies	**0.39**	**0.40**	**0.53**	**0.32**
Soaps and detergents	0.23	0.23	0.35	0.20
Other household products	**0.57**	**0.60**	**0.55**	**0.49**
Cleansing and toilet tissue, paper towels and napkins	0.19	0.20	0.19	0.18
Lawn and garden supplies	0.13	0.13	0.15	0.12
Postage and stationery	**0.44**	**0.43**	**0.37**	**0.45**
Stationery, stationery supplies, and giftwrap	0.19	0.21	0.15	0.16
Postage	0.24	0.22	0.22	0.29
HOUSEHOLD FURNISHINGS AND EQUIPMENT	**4.18%**	**4.55%**	**3.47%**	**3.35%**
Household textiles	**0.36**	**0.37**	**0.36**	**0.33**
Bathroom linens	0.05	0.05	0.03	0.06
Bedroom linens	0.14	0.13	0.19	0.15
Kitchen and dining room linens	0.02	0.03	0.01	0.01
Curtains and draperies	0.11	0.12	0.09	0.07
Sewing materials for household items	0.04	0.04	0.03	0.03
Slipcovers, decorative pillows, and other linens	0.01	0.01	0.02	0.01

Percent of total average annual expenditures spent on household operations and furnishings, by type of consumer unit.

(continued from previous page)

	all cu's	married couples	single parents	single persons and other cu's
Furniture	**1.26**	**1.36**	**0.96**	**1.05**
Mattress and springs	0.17	0.16	0.16	0.18
Other bedroom furniture	0.17	0.18	0.21	0.16
Sofas	0.26	0.28	0.17	0.23
Living room chairs	0.13	0.14	0.07	0.12
Living room tables	0.07	0.08	0.04	0.07
Kitchen and dining room furniture ...	0.22	0.26	0.11	0.14
Infants' furniture	0.03	0.03	0.02	0.01
Outdoor furniture	0.05	0.06	0.04	0.02
Occasional furniture	0.16	0.18	0.14	0.12
Carpet, rugs, and other floor coverings ...	**0.25**	**0.31**	**0.18**	**0.12**
Major appliances	**0.65**	**0.69**	**0.74**	**0.55**
Built-in dishwashers, garbage disposals, hoods ...	0.04	0.05	0.01	0.02
Portable dishwashers	0.01	0.01	0.00	0.00
Refrigerators and freezers	0.19	0.20	0.20	0.16
Washing machines and dryers	0.14	0.14	0.23	0.15
Stoves and ovens	0.09	0.10	0.12	0.05
Microwave ovens	0.05	0.05	0.03	0.06
Window air conditioners	0.04	0.04	0.03	0.05
Electric floor cleaning equipment ...	0.06	0.06	0.10	0.05
Sewing machines	0.02	0.03	0.01	0.01
Small appliances and miscellaneous housewares ...	**0.23**	**0.25**	**0.16**	**0.21**
Housewares	0.15	0.16	0.10	0.13
China and other dinnerware	0.05	0.05	0.03	0.04
Flatware	0.01	0.01	0.01	0.02
Glassware	0.04	0.04	0.02	0.04
Nonelectric cookware	0.04	0.05	0.03	0.03
Small electrical kitchen appliances ...	0.05	0.06	0.04	0.05
Portable heating and cooling equipment ...	0.03	0.03	0.03	0.03
Miscellaneous household equipment ...	**1.43**	**1.57**	**1.07**	**1.10**
Clocks	0.02	0.02	0.01	0.03
Lamps and lighting fixtures	0.10	0.12	0.06	0.06
Telephones, accessories, and answering devices ...	0.05	0.04	0.02	0.09
Lawn and garden equipment	0.18	0.23	0.13	0.08
Power and hand tools	0.10	0.11	0.14	0.08
Indoor plants and fresh flowers ...	0.14	0.14	0.10	0.16
Closet and storage items	0.02	0.02	0.00	0.01
Luggage	0.03	0.03	0.03	0.03
Business equipment for home use ...	0.02	0.03	0.04	0.01

Note: Expenditures listed for items in a given category may not add to the total for that category because the listing is incomplete. "Other household services," for example, includes "other services," which is omitted here. Expenditures are not given (-) when the amount is too small to be reliable. Numbers may not add to total due to rounding. "Single parents" is one-parent consumer units with a child or children under age 18 living at home. "Other cu's" includes persons living with unrelated persons and families other than married-couple and single-parent families.

Indexed expenditures

	all cu's	married couples	single parents	single persons and other cu's
Number of consumer units (in thousands)	94,862	52,010	5,716	37,136
Average number of persons per cu	2.6	3.3	2.9	1.5
Average number of earners per cu	1.4	1.7	1.0	0.9
Average total before-tax income	$28,540	$37,299	$16,276	$18,509
TOTAL AVERAGE ANNUAL EXPENDITURES	100	125	72	69
HOUSING, AVERAGE ANNUAL EXPENDITURES	100	120	88	73
HOUSEHOLD SERVICES	100	133	118	51
Personal services	100	138	195	32
Babysitting	100	148	236	12
Care for elderly, invalids, handicapped, etc.	100	39	-	201
Day care centers, nursery and preschools	100	144	188	25
Other household services	100	129	60	66
Housekeeping services	100	136	44	58
Gardening, lawn care service	100	123	27	79
Water softening service	100	139	141	39
Dry cleaning and laundering of household textiles	100	92	162	102
Moving, storage, and freight express	100	111	152	77
Appliance repair	100	137	40	57
Reupholstering and furniture repair	100	135	50	59
Repairs and rental of equipment and power tools	100	149	16	45
Appliance rental	100	117	143	70
HOUSEKEEPING SUPPLIES	100	128	75	63
Laundry and cleaning supplies	100	130	98	57
Soaps and detergents	100	127	109	59
Other household products	100	131	70	60
Cleansing and toilet tissue, paper towels and napkins	100	128	72	63
Lawn and garden supplies	100	128	81	62
Postage and stationery	100	123	61	72
Stationery, stationery supplies, and giftwrap	100	134	57	57
Postage	100	115	65	84
HOUSEHOLD FURNISHINGS/EQUIPMENT	100	136	60	56
Household textiles	100	129	71	63
Bathroom linens	100	116	43	86
Bedroom linens	100	118	100	75
Kitchen and dining room linens	100	146	18	46
Curtains and draperies	100	143	58	47
Sewing materials for household items	100	138	56	52
Slipcovers, decorative pillows, and other linens	100	133	135	49

HOUSEHOLD
OPERATIONS

Indexed average annual expenditures for household operations and furnishings, by type of consumer unit.

(continued from previous page)

	all cu's	married couples	single parents	single persons and other cu's
Furniture	**100**	**135**	**55**	**58**
Mattress and springs	100	121	70	75
Other bedroom furniture	100	127	86	64
Sofas	100	133	47	61
Living room chairs	100	135	39	61
Living room tables	100	135	37	61
Kitchen and dining room furniture	100	146	38	46
Infants' furniture	100	154	48	32
Outdoor furniture	100	155	55	30
Occasional furniture	100	139	63	51
Carpet, rugs, and other floor coverings	**100**	**153**	**51**	**32**
Major appliances	**100**	**132**	**82**	**58**
Dishwashers (built-in), garbage disposals, hoods	100	160	14	29
Portable dishwashers	100	155	0	38
Refrigerators and freezers	100	132	76	59
Washing machines and dryers	100	120	114	70
Stoves and ovens	100	141	104	43
Microwave ovens	100	125	37	74
Window air conditioners	100	115	59	85
Electric floor cleaning equipment	100	123	134	63
Sewing machines	100	164	42	19
Small appliances and miscellaneous housewares ...	**100**	**131**	**50**	**63**
Housewares	100	133	45	61
China and other dinnerware	100	132	50	63
Flatware	100	115	49	87
Glassware	100	128	35	69
Nonelectric cookware	100	144	50	44
Small electrical kitchen appliances	100	130	56	64
Portable heating and cooling equipment	100	124	64	72
Miscellaneous household equipment	**100**	**138**	**54**	**53**
Clocks	100	113	28	94
Lamps and lighting fixtures	100	147	42	41
Telephones, accessories, and answering devices	100	95	29	118
Lawn and garden equipment	100	155	49	31
Power and hand tools	100	140	101	52
Indoor plants and fresh flowers	100	121	50	78
Closet and storage items	100	149	17	41
Luggage	100	126	67	69
Business equipment for home use	100	142	113	39

Note: An index of 100 represents the average for all consumer units. An index of 132 means that the average for the subgroup is 32 percent above the average for all consumer units. An index of 68 indicates spending that is 32 percent below the overall average. Expenditures are not given (-) when the amount is too small to be reliable. "Single parents" is one-parent consumer units with a child or children under age 18 living at home. "Other cu's" includes persons living with unrelated persons and families other than married-couple and single-parent families.

Aggregate expenditures, 1988

Aggregate expenditures in 1988 for household operations and furnishings, by type of consumer unit.

	all cu's	married couples	single parents	single persons and other cu's
Number of consumer units (in thousands)	94,862	52,010	5,716	37,136
Average number of persons per cu	2.6	3.3	2.9	1.5
Average number of earners per cu	1.4	1.7	1.0	0.9
Aggregate before-tax income (in millions)	$2,720,305	$1,939,921	$93,034	$687,350
TOTAL AGGREG. EXPENDITURES (in millions)	$2,453,706	$1,680,677	$106,408	$666,621
HOUSING, AGGREG. EXPENDITURES (in millions)	$765,984	$506,120	$40,656	$219,208
HOUSEHOLD SERVICES	$37,386	$27,188	$2,667	$7,532
Personal services	16,239	12,283	1,905	2,051
Babysitting	6,784	5,491	965	328
Care for elderly, invalids, handicapped, etc.	1,176	250	-	926
Day care centers, nursery and preschools	8,277	6,542	938	797
Other household services	21,147	14,905	762	5,481
Housekeeping services	7,285	5,440	193	1,652
Gardening, lawn care service	4,777	3,215	79	1,483
Water softening service	254	193	22	39
Dry cleaning and laundering of household textiles	618	310	60	247
Moving, storage, and freight express	2,778	1,686	255	837
Appliance repair	1,537	1,158	37	342
Reupholstering and furniture repair	1,398	1,033	42	323
Repairs and rental of equipment and power tools	519	423	5	91
Appliance rental	205	132	18	56
HOUSEKEEPING SUPPLIES	$34,066	$24,078	$1,547	$8,441
Laundry and cleaning supplies	9,506	6,798	562	2,146
Soaps and detergents	5,596	3,924	370	1,301
Other household products	13,887	10,024	589	3,274
Cleansing and toilet tissue, paper towels and napkins	4,706	3,333	205	1,168
Lawn and garden supplies	3,172	2,242	156	774
Postage and stationery	10,673	7,256	396	3,021
Stationery, stationery supplies, and giftwrap	4,753	3,524	164	1,065
Postage	5,920	3,732	232	1,956
HOUSEHOLD FURNISHINGS/EQUIPMENT	$102,578	$76,531	$3,688	$22,359
Household textiles	8,889	6,300	382	2,207
Bathroom linens	1,237	786	32	418
Bedroom linens	3,316	2,144	200	972
Kitchen and dining room linens	524	423	6	95
Curtains and draperies	2,635	2,060	92	484
Sewing materials for household items	914	695	31	188
Slipcovers, decorative pillows, and other linens	263	191	21	50

HOUSEHOLD
OPERATIONS

Aggregate expenditures in 1988 for household operations and furnishings, by type of consumer unit.

(continued from previous page)	all cu's	married couples	single parents	single persons and other cu's
Furniture	**30,926**	**22,933**	**1,020**	**6,973**
Mattress and springs	4,065	2,703	171	1,191
Other bedroom furniture	4,239	2,952	221	1,067
Sofas	6,468	4,733	184	1,551
Living room chairs	3,226	2,382	76	769
Living room tables	1,833	1,354	41	438
Kitchen and dining room furniture	5,373	4,288	122	963
Infants' furniture	642	543	18	81
Outdoor furniture	1,192	1,011	40	142
Occasional furniture	3,887	2,968	148	772
Carpet, rugs, and other floor coverings	**6,178**	**5,213**	**191**	**774**
Major appliances	**15,991**	**11,543**	**789**	**3,660**
Dishwashers (built-in), garbage disposals, hoods	1,044	918	9	117
Portable dishwashers	155	132	0	23
Refrigerators and freezers	4,662	3,364	215	1,083
Washing machines and dryers	3,540	2,324	244	973
Stoves and ovens	2,104	1,622	132	351
Microwave ovens	1,339	919	30	390
Window air conditioners	995	629	35	331
Electric floor cleaning equipment	1,373	925	111	338
Sewing machines	524	471	13	40
Small appliances and miscellaneous housewares	**5,724**	**4,131**	**172**	**1,422**
Housewares	3,716	2,720	101	895
China and other dinnerware	1,171	848	35	288
Flatware	321	202	10	110
Glassware	1,025	723	22	280
Nonelectric cookware	1,054	840	32	182
Small electrical kitchen appliances	1,308	935	44	330
Portable heating and cooling equipment	701	476	27	197
Miscellaneous household equipment	**34,869**	**26,412**	**1,134**	**7,323**
Clocks	470	290	8	172
Lamps and lighting fixtures	2,407	1,959	62	386
Telephones, accessories, and answering devices	1,258	653	22	582
Lawn and garden equipment	4,520	3,834	134	553
Power and hand tools	2,587	1,930	152	505
Indoor plants and fresh flowers	3,445	2,289	105	1,051
Closet and storage items	488	403	5	79
Luggage	799	551	32	216
Business equipment for home use	584	455	40	89

Note: Expenditures listed for items in a given category may not add to the total for that category because the listing is incomplete. "Other household services," for example, includes "other services," which is omitted here. Expenditures are not given (-) when the amount is too small to be reliable. Numbers may not add to total due to rounding. The "all cu's" aggregates will differ slightly from table to table because they are the sums of the aggregates in each row. "Single parents" is one-parent consumer units with a child or children under age 18 living at home. "Other cu's" includes persons living with unrelated persons and families other than married-couple and single-parent families.

Average expenditures

Average annual expenditures for household operations and furnishings, by married couples with and without children.

	all cu's	all married couples	married couple only	all married couples with children	AGE OF OLDEST CHILD under 6	AGE OF OLDEST CHILD 6 to 17	AGE OF OLDEST CHILD 18 or older	other married couples
Number of consumer units (in thousands)	94862	52010	20227	28100	5858	14194	8047	3684
Average number of persons per cu	2.6	3.3	2	3.9	3.5	4.1	3.9	5.1
Average number of earners per cu	1.4	1.7	1.2	2.1	1.7	1.9	2.7	2.4
Average total before-tax income	$28,540.00	$37,299.00	$33,825.00	$39,354.00	$34,318.00	$38,039.00	$45,596.00	$40,846.00
TOTAL AVERAGE ANNUAL EXPENDITURES	$25,891.85	$32,314.50	$27,954.50	$35,015.30	$30,942.80	$35,248.40	$37,763.90	$35,739.60
HOUSING, AVERAGE ANNUAL EXPENDITURES	$8,078.63	$9,731.21	$8,452.92	$10,541.90	$10,807.80	$10,850.20	$9,819.12	$10,567.30
HOUSEHOLD SERVICES	**$394.12**	**$522.74**	**$319.46**	**$666.53**	**$1,220.73**	**$643.90**	**$302.96**	**$542.06**
Personal services	**171.19**	**236.16**	**8.90**	**400.26**	**981.89**	**365.29**	**38.52**	**232.25**
Babysitting	71.51	105.57	0.71	180.33	454.32	162.91	11.59	111.13
Care for elderly, invalids, handicapped, etc.	12.42	4.81	5.19	0.55	0.50	-	0.94	35.21
Day care centers, nursery and preschools	87.25	125.78	3.00	219.38	527.07	202.03	25.99	85.91
Other household services	**222.93**	**286.57**	**310.55**	**266.28**	**238.85**	**278.61**	**264.43**	**309.81**
Housekeeping services	76.80	104.60	101.81	104.99	74.46	120.31	100.19	116.90
Gardening, lawn care service	50.35	61.81	79.57	50.32	36.89	49.57	61.40	52.00
Water softening service	2.68	3.72	2.47	4.22	2.72	6.66	1.01	6.76
Dry cleaning/laundering of household textiles	6.51	5.97	6.38	5.03	6.07	5.09	4.17	11.02
Moving, storage, and freight express	29.28	32.42	29.78	34.02	69.45	31.85	12.04	34.82
Appliance repair	16.21	22.27	24.98	20.24	15.41	18.00	27.69	22.91
Reupholstering and furniture repair	14.74	19.86	26.46	15.37	7.61	11.43	27.98	17.89
Repairs and rental of equipment/power tools	5.47	8.14	8.99	7.52	1.84	6.97	12.62	8.20
Appliance rental	2.16	2.53	1.57	3.00	1.57	5.07	-	4.31
HOUSEKEEPING SUPPLIES	**$360.94**	**$462.95**	**$409.37**	**$498.55**	**$476.69**	**$491.26**	**$533.02**	**$488.33**
Laundry and cleaning supplies	**100.73**	**130.70**	**98.79**	**145.80**	**125.23**	**154.51**	**147.28**	**194.85**
Soaps and detergents	59.26	75.45	55.41	84.55	70.51	91.46	83.63	118.76
Other household products	**147.21**	**192.73**	**174.05**	**208.32**	**212.05**	**204.90**	**211.71**	**176.12**
Cleansing/toilet tissue, paper towels/napkins	49.87	64.08	56.27	69.36	52.31	70.21	83.27	66.99
Lawn and garden supplies	33.60	43.10	42.60	43.53	66.15	38.00	33.85	42.64
Postage and stationery	**113.00**	**139.51**	**136.53**	**144.43**	**139.41**	**131.85**	**174.02**	**117.36**
Stationery, stationery supplies, and giftwrap	50.42	67.76	55.84	79.18	72.96	68.88	105.32	45.32
Postage	62.58	71.76	80.69	65.25	66.45	62.97	68.70	72.04
HOUSEHOLD FURNISHINGS/EQUIP.	**$1,083.41**	**$1,471.47**	**$1,418.86**	**$1,518.57**	**$1,497.52**	**$1,515.18**	**$1,548.81**	**$1,399.49**
Household textiles	**93.97**	**121.13**	**118.66**	**119.72**	**124.92**	**101.89**	**152.05**	**146.84**
Bathroom linens	13.08	15.12	12.65	14.06	13.73	13.80	14.86	38.07
Bedroom linens	35.07	41.23	35.08	45.08	42.86	29.89	77.29	46.11
Kitchen and dining room linens	5.57	8.13	8.60	8.06	4.15	10.23	7.31	6.04
Curtains and draperies	27.78	39.60	44.37	35.74	47.77	33.97	30.13	42.77
Sewing materials for household items	9.70	13.36	13.95	13.06	14.79	9.39	18.78	12.28
Slipcovers, decorative pillows, other linens	2.77	3.68	4.01	3.73	1.63	4.61	3.68	1.57

Average annual expenditures for household operations and furnishings, by married couples with and without children.

(continued from previous page)	all cu's	all married couples	married couple only	all married couples with children	AGE OF OLDEST CHILD			other married couples
					under 6	6 to 17	18 or older	
Furniture	326.01	440.93	404.59	476.02	531.97	494.53	402.64	372.76
Mattress and springs	42.85	51.97	49.05	56.43	65.81	52.67	56.23	34.07
Other bedroom furniture	44.69	56.75	52.58	61.13	64.66	70.14	42.68	46.30
Sofas	68.18	91.00	70.83	107.02	146.72	98.53	93.08	79.59
Living room chairs	34.00	45.79	50.32	42.62	42.43	38.14	50.67	44.98
Living room tables	19.33	26.03	27.59	26.63	23.76	25.82	30.15	12.90
Kitchen and dining room furniture	56.64	82.45	67.61	93.18	83.81	121.04	50.87	82.04
Infants' furniture	6.77	10.44	8.20	11.48	37.40	4.10	5.62	14.86
Outdoor furniture	12.57	19.43	24.26	17.20	15.90	18.08	16.59	9.92
Occasional furniture	40.98	57.06	54.17	60.33	51.47	66.01	56.74	48.08
Carpet, rugs, and other floor coverings	65.34	100.24	100.10	98.98	86.19	77.31	151.05	110.96
Major appliances	168.60	221.93	209.89	230.64	231.64	232.30	226.52	221.64
Built-in dishwashers, garbage disposals, hoods	11.01	17.65	18.90	17.40	13.81	17.80	19.30	12.77
Portable dishwashers	1.63	2.53	1.67	2.63	2.72	3.13	1.65	6.56
Refrigerators and freezers	49.14	64.68	70.73	58.49	68.11	57.05	54.04	78.73
Washing machines and dryers	37.33	44.68	32.81	54.22	38.73	51.27	70.74	37.02
Stoves and ovens	22.18	31.18	37.41	27.81	34.31	30.76	17.89	22.68
Microwave ovens	14.10	17.67	16.23	18.27	16.95	18.91	18.09	20.98
Window air conditioners	10.49	12.10	13.10	12.39	12.71	10.71	15.09	4.47
Electric floor cleaning equipment	14.47	17.78	10.86	23.13	28.73	19.01	26.31	14.94
Sewing machines	5.52	9.05	8.17	8.30	11.95	9.91	2.80	19.59
Small appliances and misc. housewares	60.50	79.42	76.72	83.31	69.82	76.08	107.47	63.81
Housewares	39.32	52.29	49.43	56.10	50.01	47.12	77.96	38.19
China and other dinnerware	12.34	16.30	14.56	17.15	7.65	18.97	20.88	19.43
Flatware	3.39	3.89	3.17	4.45	3.89	4.22	5.26	3.62
Glassware	10.87	13.91	10.26	17.73	18.56	10.40	31.56	4.39
Nonelectric cookware	11.20	16.16	19.16	14.80	17.79	11.76	18.10	9.61
Small electrical kitchen appliances	13.79	17.97	17.01	18.39	11.24	20.99	19.01	20.00
Portable heating and cooling equipment	7.39	9.16	10.28	8.82	8.57	7.97	10.51	5.62
Miscellaneous household equipment	368.99	507.83	508.89	509.90	452.98	533.08	509.08	483.49
Clocks	4.96	5.58	5.64	5.30	1.20	7.43	4.53	7.45
Lamps and lighting fixtures	25.59	37.67	47.45	31.39	15.33	29.76	49.30	31.22
Telephones, accessories, answering devices	13.26	12.56	11.18	13.82	6.85	19.42	8.92	10.42
Lawn and garden equipment	47.65	73.71	68.88	75.20	55.62	68.67	100.98	88.81
Power and hand tools	26.41	37.10	42.30	34.84	17.53	36.65	44.92	25.32
Indoor plants and fresh flowers	36.46	44.02	37.92	43.15	47.17	46.68	32.46	86.47
Closet and storage items	5.19	7.75	6.69	8.80	4.89	11.21	7.57	5.45
Luggage	8.42	10.59	9.48	11.83	9.00	10.78	15.76	7.21
Business equipment for home use	6.16	8.75	6.50	10.24	4.58	11.83	11.57	9.68

Note: Expenditures listed for items in a given category may not add to the total for that category because the listing is incomplete. "Other household services," for example, includes "other services," which is omitted here. Other married couples include extended family members or unrelated persons in addition to the married couple. Expenditures are not given (-) when the amount is too small to be reliable. Numbers may not add to total due to rounding.

Share of spending

	all cu's	all married couples	married couple only	all married couples with children	AGE OF OLDEST CHILD			other married couples
					under 6	6 to 17	18 or older	
Number of consumer units (in thousands)	94,862	52,010	20,227	28,100	5,858	14,194	8,047	3,684
Average number of persons per cu	2.6	3.3	2.0	3.9	3.5	4.1	3.9	5.1
Average number of earners per cu	1.4	1.7	1.2	2.1	1.7	1.9	2.7	2.4
Average total before-tax income	$28,540	$37,299	$33,825	$39,354	$34,318	$38,039	$45,596	$40,846
TOTAL AVERAGE ANNUAL EXPENDITURES	100.00%	100.00%	100.00%	100.00%	100.00%	100.00%	100.00%	100.00%
HOUSING, AVERAGE ANNUAL EXPENDITURES	31.20%	30.11%	30.24%	30.11%	34.93%	30.78%	26.00%	29.57%
HOUSEHOLD SERVICES	**1.52%**	**1.62%**	**1.14%**	**1.90%**	**3.95%**	**1.83%**	**0.80%**	**1.52%**
Personal services	**0.66**	**0.73**	**0.03**	**1.14**	**3.17**	**1.04**	**0.10**	**0.65**
Babysitting	0.28	0.33	0.00	0.52	1.47	0.46	0.03	0.31
Care for elderly, invalids, handicapped, etc.	0.05	0.01	0.02	0.00	0.00	-	0.00	0.10
Day care centers, nursery and preschools	0.34	0.39	0.01	0.63	1.70	0.57	0.07	0.24
Other household services	**0.86**	**0.89**	**1.11**	**0.76**	**0.77**	**0.79**	**0.70**	**0.87**
Housekeeping services	0.30	0.32	0.36	0.30	0.24	0.34	0.27	0.33
Gardening, lawn care service	0.19	0.19	0.28	0.14	0.12	0.14	0.16	0.15
Water softening service	0.01	0.01	0.01	0.01	0.01	0.02	0.00	0.02
Dry cleaning/laundering of household textiles	0.03	0.02	0.02	0.01	0.02	0.01	0.01	0.03
Moving, storage, and freight express	0.11	0.10	0.11	0.10	0.22	0.09	0.03	0.10
Appliance repair	0.06	0.07	0.09	0.06	0.05	0.05	0.07	0.06
Reupholstering and furniture repair	0.06	0.06	0.09	0.04	0.02	0.03	0.07	0.05
Repairs and rental of equipment/power tools	0.02	0.03	0.03	0.02	0.01	0.02	0.03	0.02
Appliance rental	0.01	0.01	0.01	0.01	0.01	0.01	-	0.01
HOUSEKEEPING SUPPLIES	**1.39%**	**1.43%**	**1.46%**	**1.42%**	**1.54%**	**1.39%**	**1.41%**	**1.37%**
Laundry and cleaning supplies	**0.39**	**0.40**	**0.35**	**0.42**	**0.40**	**0.44**	**0.39**	**0.55**
Soaps and detergents	0.23	0.23	0.20	0.24	0.23	0.26	0.22	0.33
Other household products	**0.57**	**0.60**	**0.62**	**0.59**	**0.69**	**0.58**	**0.56**	**0.49**
Cleansing/toilet tissue, paper towels/napkins	0.19	0.20	0.20	0.20	0.17	0.20	0.22	0.19
Lawn and garden supplies	0.13	0.13	0.15	0.12	0.21	0.11	0.09	0.12
Postage and stationery	**0.44**	**0.43**	**0.49**	**0.41**	**0.45**	**0.37**	**0.46**	**0.33**
Stationery, stationery supplies, and giftwrap	0.19	0.21	0.20	0.23	0.24	0.20	0.28	0.13
Postage	0.24	0.22	0.29	0.19	0.21	0.18	0.18	0.20
HOUSEHOLD FURNISHINGS/EQUIP.	**4.18%**	**4.55%**	**5.08%**	**4.34%**	**4.84%**	**4.30%**	**4.10%**	**3.92%**
Household textiles	**0.36**	**0.37**	**0.42**	**0.34**	**0.40**	**0.29**	**0.40**	**0.41**
Bathroom linens	0.05	0.05	0.05	0.04	0.04	0.04	0.04	0.11
Bedroom linens	0.14	0.13	0.13	0.13	0.14	0.08	0.20	0.13
Kitchen and dining room linens	0.02	0.03	0.03	0.02	0.01	0.03	0.02	0.02
Curtains and draperies	0.11	0.12	0.16	0.10	0.15	0.10	0.08	0.12
Sewing materials for household items	0.04	0.04	0.05	0.04	0.05	0.03	0.05	0.03
Slipcovers, decorative pillows, other linens	0.01	0.01	0.01	0.01	0.01	0.01	0.01	0.00

Percent of total average annual expenditures spent on household operations and furnishings, by married couples with and without children.

(continued from previous page)

	all cu's	all married couples	married couple only	all married couples with children	AGE OF OLDEST CHILD			other married couples
					under 6	6 to 17	18 or older	
Furniture	**1.26**	**1.36**	**1.45**	**1.36**	**1.72**	**1.40**	**1.07**	**1.04**
Mattress and springs	0.17	0.16	0.18	0.16	0.21	0.15	0.15	0.10
Other bedroom furniture	0.17	0.18	0.19	0.17	0.21	0.20	0.11	0.13
Sofas	0.26	0.28	0.25	0.31	0.47	0.28	0.25	0.22
Living room chairs	0.13	0.14	0.18	0.12	0.14	0.11	0.13	0.13
Living room tables	0.07	0.08	0.10	0.08	0.08	0.07	0.08	0.04
Kitchen and dining room furniture	0.22	0.26	0.24	0.27	0.27	0.34	0.13	0.23
Infants' furniture	0.03	0.03	0.03	0.03	0.12	0.01	0.01	0.04
Outdoor furniture	0.05	0.06	0.09	0.05	0.05	0.05	0.04	0.03
Occasional furniture	0.16	0.18	0.19	0.17	0.17	0.19	0.15	0.13
Carpet, rugs, and other floor coverings	**0.25**	**0.31**	**0.36**	**0.28**	**0.28**	**0.22**	**0.40**	**0.31**
Major appliances	**0.65**	**0.69**	**0.75**	**0.66**	**0.75**	**0.66**	**0.60**	**0.62**
Built-in dishwashers, garbage disposals, hoods	0.04	0.05	0.07	0.05	0.04	0.05	0.05	0.04
Portable dishwashers	0.01	0.01	0.01	0.01	0.01	0.01	0.00	0.02
Refrigerators and freezers	0.19	0.20	0.25	0.17	0.22	0.16	0.14	0.22
Washing machines and dryers	0.14	0.14	0.12	0.15	0.13	0.15	0.19	0.10
Stoves and ovens	0.09	0.10	0.13	0.08	0.11	0.09	0.05	0.06
Microwave ovens	0.05	0.05	0.06	0.05	0.05	0.05	0.05	0.06
Window air conditioners	0.04	0.04	0.05	0.04	0.04	0.03	0.04	0.01
Electric floor cleaning equipment	0.06	0.06	0.04	0.07	0.09	0.05	0.07	0.04
Sewing machines	0.02	0.03	0.03	0.02	0.04	0.03	0.01	0.05
Small appliances/miscellaneous housewares	**0.23**	**0.25**	**0.27**	**0.24**	**0.23**	**0.22**	**0.28**	**0.18**
Housewares	0.15	0.16	0.18	0.16	0.16	0.13	0.21	0.11
China and other dinnerware	0.05	0.05	0.05	0.05	0.02	0.05	0.06	0.05
Flatware	0.01	0.01	0.01	0.01	0.01	0.01	0.01	0.01
Glassware	0.04	0.04	0.04	0.05	0.06	0.03	0.08	0.01
Nonelectric cookware	0.04	0.05	0.07	0.04	0.06	0.03	0.05	0.03
Small electrical kitchen appliances	0.05	0.06	0.06	0.05	0.04	0.06	0.05	0.06
Portable heating and cooling equipment	0.03	0.03	0.04	0.03	0.03	0.02	0.03	0.02
Miscellaneous household equipment	**1.43**	**1.57**	**1.82**	**1.46**	**1.46**	**1.51**	**1.35**	**1.35**
Clocks...	0.02	0.02	0.02	0.02	0.00	0.02	0.01	0.02
Lamps and lighting fixtures	0.10	0.12	0.17	0.09	0.05	0.08	0.13	0.09
Telephones, accessories, answering devices	0.05	0.04	0.04	0.04	0.02	0.06	0.02	0.03
Lawn and garden equipment	0.18	0.23	0.25	0.21	0.18	0.19	0.27	0.25
Power and hand tools	0.10	0.11	0.15	0.10	0.06	0.10	0.12	0.07
Indoor plants and fresh flowers	0.14	0.14	0.14	0.12	0.15	0.13	0.09	0.24
Closet and storage items	0.02	0.02	0.02	0.03	0.02	0.03	0.02	0.02
Luggage	0.03	0.03	0.03	0.03	0.03	0.03	0.04	0.02
Business equipment for home use	0.02	0.03	0.02	0.03	0.01	0.03	0.03	0.03

Note: Expenditures listed for items in a given category may not add to the total for that category because the listing is incomplete. "Other household services," for example, includes "other services," which is omitted here. Other married couples include extended family members or unrelated persons in addition to the married couple. Expenditures are not given (-) when the amount is too small to be reliable. Numbers may not add to total due to rounding.

Indexed expenditures

	all cu's	all married couples	married couple only	all married couples with children	AGE OF OLDEST CHILD			other married couples
					under 6	6 to 17	18 or older	
Number of consumer units (in thousands)	94,862	52,010	20,227	28,100	5,858	14,194	8,047	3,684
Average number of persons per cu	2.6	3.3	2.0	3.9	3.5	4.1	3.9	5.1
Average number of earners per cu	1.4	1.7	1.2	2.1	1.7	1.9	2.7	2.4
Average total before-tax income	$28,540	$37,299	$33,825	$39,354	$34,318	$38,039	$45,596	$40,846
TOTAL AVERAGE ANNUAL EXPENDITURES	100	125	108	135	120	136	146	138
HOUSING, AVERAGE ANNUAL EXPENDITURES	100	120	105	130	134	134	122	131
HOUSEHOLD SERVICES	100	133	81	169	310	163	77	138
Personal services	100	138	5	234	574	213	23	136
Babysitting	100	148	1	252	635	228	16	155
Care for elderly, invalids, handicapped, etc.	100	39	42	4	4	-	8	283
Day care centers, nursery and preschools	100	144	3	251	604	232	30	98
Other household services	100	129	139	119	107	125	119	139
Housekeeping services	100	136	133	137	97	157	130	152
Gardening, lawn care service	100	123	158	100	73	98	122	103
Water softening service	100	139	92	157	101	249	38	252
Dry cleaning/laundering of household textiles	100	92	98	77	93	78	64	169
Moving, storage, and freight express	100	111	102	116	237	109	41	119
Appliance repair	100	137	154	125	95	111	171	141
Reupholstering and furniture repair	100	135	180	104	52	78	190	121
Repairs and rental of equipment/power tools	100	149	164	137	34	127	231	150
Appliance rental	100	117	73	139	73	235	-	200
HOUSEKEEPING SUPPLIES	100	128	113	138	132	136	148	135
Laundry and cleaning supplies	100	130	98	145	124	153	146	193
Soaps and detergents	100	127	94	143	119	154	141	200
Other household products	100	131	118	142	144	139	144	120
Cleansing/toilet tissue, paper towels/napkins	100	128	113	139	105	141	167	134
Lawn and garden supplies	100	128	127	130	197	113	101	127
Postage and stationery	100	123	121	128	123	117	154	104
Stationery, stationery supplies, and giftwrap	100	134	111	157	145	137	209	90
Postage	100	115	129	104	106	101	110	115
HOUSEHOLD FURNISHINGS/EQUIP.	100	136	131	140	138	140	143	129
Household textiles	100	129	126	127	133	108	162	156
Bathroom linens	100	116	97	107	105	106	114	291
Bedroom linens	100	118	100	129	122	85	220	131
Kitchen and dining room linens	100	146	154	145	75	184	131	108
Curtains and draperies	100	143	160	129	172	122	108	154
Sewing materials for household items	100	138	144	135	152	97	194	127
Slipcovers, decorative pillows, other linens	100	133	145	135	59	166	133	57

Indexed average annual expenditures for household furnishings and operations, by married couples with and without children.

(continued from previous page)

	all cu's	all married couples	married couple only	all married couples with children	AGE OF OLDEST CHILD			other married couples
					under 6	6 to 17	18 or older	
Furniture	100	**135**	**124**	**146**	**163**	**152**	**124**	**114**
Mattress and springs	100	121	114	132	154	123	131	80
Other bedroom furniture	100	127	118	137	145	157	96	104
Sofas	100	133	104	157	215	145	137	117
Living room chairs	100	135	148	125	125	112	149	132
Living room tables	100	135	143	138	123	134	156	67
Kitchen and dining room furniture	100	146	119	165	148	214	90	145
Infants' furniture	100	154	121	170	552	61	83	219
Outdoor furniture	100	155	193	137	126	144	132	79
Occasional furniture	100	139	132	147	126	161	138	117
Carpet, rugs, and other floor coverings	100	**153**	**153**	**151**	**132**	**118**	**231**	**170**
Major appliances	100	**132**	**124**	**137**	**137**	**138**	**134**	**131**
Built-in dishwashers, garbage disposals, hoods	100	160	172	158	125	162	175	116
Portable dishwashers	100	155	102	161	167	192	101	402
Refrigerators and freezers	100	132	144	119	139	116	110	160
Washing machines and dryers	100	120	88	145	104	137	189	99
Stoves and ovens	100	141	169	125	155	139	81	102
Microwave ovens	100	125	115	130	120	134	128	149
Window air conditioners	100	115	125	118	121	102	144	43
Electric floor cleaning equipment	100	123	75	160	199	131	182	103
Sewing machines	100	164	148	150	216	180	51	355
Small appliances/miscellaneous housewares	100	**131**	**127**	**138**	**115**	**126**	**178**	**105**
Housewares	100	133	126	143	127	120	198	97
China and other dinnerware	100	132	118	139	62	154	169	157
Flatware	100	115	94	131	115	124	155	107
Glassware	100	128	94	163	171	96	290	40
Nonelectric cookware	100	144	171	132	159	105	162	86
Small electrical kitchen appliances	100	130	123	133	82	152	138	145
Portable heating and cooling equipment	100	124	139	119	116	108	142	76
Miscellaneous household equipment	100	**138**	**138**	**138**	**123**	**144**	**138**	**131**
Clocks	100	113	114	107	24	150	91	150
Lamps and lighting fixtures	100	147	185	123	60	116	193	122
Telephones, accessories, answering devices	100	95	84	104	52	146	67	79
Lawn and garden equipment	100	155	145	158	117	144	212	186
Power and hand tools	100	140	160	132	66	139	170	96
Indoor plants and fresh flowers	100	121	104	118	129	128	89	237
Closet and storage items	100	149	129	170	94	216	146	105
Luggage	100	126	113	140	107	128	187	86
Business equipment for home use	100	142	106	166	74	192	188	157

Note: An index of 100 represents the average for all consumer units. An index of 132 means that the average for the subgroup is 32 percent above the average for all consumer units. An index of 68 indicates spending that is 32 percent below the overall average. Other married couples include extended family members or unrelated persons in addition to the married couple. Expenditures are not given (-) when the amount is too small to be reliable.

Aggregate expenditures, 1988

Aggregate expenditures in 1988 for household operations and furnishings, by married couples with and without children.

	all cu's	all married couples	married couple only	all married couples with children	AGE OF OLDEST CHILD			other married couples
					under 6	6 to 17	18 or older	
Number of consumer units (in thousands)	94,862	52,010	20,227	28,100	5,858	14,194	8,047	3,684
Average number of persons per cu	2.6	3.3	2.0	3.9	3.5	4.1	3.9	5.1
Average number of earners per cu	1.4	1.7	1.2	2.1	1.7	1.9	2.7	2.4
Aggregate before-tax income (in millions)	$2,722,910	$1,942,526	$684,178	$1,107,871	$201,035	$539,926	$366,911	$150,477
TOTAL AGG. EXPENDITURES (in millions)	$2,455,594	$1,682,565	$565,436	$985,465	$181,263	$500,316	$303,886	$131,665
HOUSING, AGG. EXPENDITURES (in millions)	$766,105	$506,241	$170,977	$296,334	$63,312	$154,008	$79,014	$38,930
HOUSEHOLD SERVICES	**$37,386**	**$27,187**	**$6,462**	**$18,728**	**$7,151**	**$9,140**	**$2,438**	**$1,997**
Personal services	**16,239**	**12,282**	**180**	**11,247**	**5,752**	**5,185**	**310**	**856**
Babysitting	6,784	5,491	14	5,067	2,661	2,312	93	409
Care for elderly, invalids, handicapped, etc.	1,172	246	105	11	3	-	8	130
Day care centers, nursery and preschools	8,277	6,542	61	6,164	3,088	2,868	209	316
Other household services	**21,147**	**14,904**	**6,281**	**7,482**	**1,399**	**3,955**	**2,128**	**1,141**
Housekeeping services	7,285	5,440	2,059	2,950	436	1,708	806	431
Gardening, lawn care service	4,777	3,215	1,609	1,414	216	704	494	192
Water softening service	254	193	50	119	16	95	8	25
Dry cleaning/laundering of household textiles	618	311	129	141	36	72	34	41
Moving, storage, and freight express	2,778	1,686	602	956	407	452	97	128
Appliance repair	1,537	1,158	505	569	90	255	223	84
Reupholstering and furniture repair	1,398	1,033	535	432	45	162	225	66
Repairs and rental of equipment/power tools	519	423	182	211	11	99	102	30
Appliance rental	203	129	32	81	9	72	-	16
HOUSEKEEPING SUPPLIES	**$34,122**	**$24,134**	**$8,280**	**$14,055**	**$2,792**	**$6,973**	**$4,289**	**$1,799**
Laundry and cleaning supplies	**9,537**	**6,828**	**1,998**	**4,112**	**734**	**2,193**	**1,185**	**718**
Soaps and detergents	5,614	3,942	1,121	2,384	413	1,298	673	438
Other household products	**13,886**	**10,024**	**3,521**	**5,854**	**1,242**	**2,908**	**1,704**	**649**
Cleansing/toilet tissue, paper towels/napkins	4,732	3,358	1,138	1,973	306	997	670	247
Lawn and garden supplies	3,148	2,218	862	1,199	388	539	272	157
Postage and stationery	**10,699**	**7,282**	**2,762**	**4,088**	**817**	**1,871**	**1,400**	**432**
Stationery, stationery supplies, and giftwrap	4,778	3,549	1,129	2,253	427	978	848	167
Postage	5,921	3,733	1,632	1,836	389	894	553	265
HOUSEHOLD FURNISHINGS/EQUIP.	**$102,644**	**$76,597**	**$28,699**	**$42,742**	**$8,772**	**$21,506**	**$12,463**	**$5,156**
Household textiles	**8,932**	**6,343**	**2,400**	**3,402**	**732**	**1,446**	**1,224**	**541**
Bathroom linens	1,242	792	256	396	80	196	120	140
Bedroom linens	3,349	2,177	710	1,297	251	424	622	170
Kitchen and dining room linens	525	425	174	228	24	145	59	22
Curtains and draperies	2,635	2,059	897	1,004	280	482	242	158
Sewing materials for household items	917	698	282	371	87	133	151	45
Slipcovers, decorative pillows, other linens	263	191	81	105	10	65	30	6

Aggregate expenditures in 1988 for household operations and furnishings, by married couples with and without children.

(continued from previous page)	all cu's	all married couples	married couple only	all married couples with children	AGE OF OLDEST CHILD			other married couples
					under 6	6 to 17	18 or older	
Furniture	**30,926**	**22,933**	**8,184**	**13,376**	**3,116**	**7,019**	**3,240**	**1,373**
Mattress and springs	4,065	2,703	992	1,586	386	748	452	126
Other bedroom furniture	4,239	2,952	1,064	1,718	379	996	343	171
Sofas	6,468	4,733	1,433	3,007	859	1,399	749	293
Living room chairs	3,226	2,381	1,018	1,198	249	541	408	166
Living room tables	1,833	1,354	558	748	139	366	243	48
Kitchen and dining room furniture	5,373	4,288	1,368	2,618	491	1,718	409	302
Infants' furniture	642	543	166	323	219	58	45	55
Outdoor furniture	1,192	1,011	491	483	93	257	133	37
Occasional furniture	3,888	2,968	1,096	1,695	302	937	457	177
Carpet, rugs, and other floor coverings	**6,216**	**5,251**	**2,025**	**2,818**	**505**	**1,097**	**1,215**	**409**
Major appliances	**15,987**	**11,539**	**4,245**	**6,477**	**1,357**	**3,297**	**1,823**	**817**
Built-in dishwashers, garbage disposals, hoods	1,044	918	382	489	81	253	155	47
Portable dishwashers	155	132	34	74	16	44	13	24
Refrigerators and freezers	4,662	3,364	1,431	1,644	399	810	435	290
Washing machines and dryers	3,541	2,324	664	1,524	227	728	569	136
Stoves and ovens	2,104	1,622	757	782	201	437	144	84
Microwave ovens	1,338	919	328	513	99	268	146	77
Window air conditioners	995	629	265	348	74	152	121	16
Electric floor cleaning equipment	1,373	925	220	650	168	270	212	55
Sewing machines	524	471	165	233	70	141	23	72
Small appliances/miscellaneous housewares	**5,734**	**4,141**	**1,552**	**2,354**	**409**	**1,080**	**865**	**235**
Housewares	3,726	2,730	1,000	1,589	293	669	627	141
China and other dinnerware	1,171	848	295	482	45	269	168	72
Flatware	322	202	64	125	23	60	42	13
Glassware	1,036	734	208	510	109	148	254	16
Nonelectric cookware	1,054	840	388	417	104	167	146	35
Small electrical kitchen appliances	1,308	934	344	517	66	298	153	74
Portable heating and cooling equipment	701	477	208	248	50	113	85	21
Miscellaneous household equipment	**34,848**	**26,391**	**10,293**	**14,317**	**2,654**	**7,567**	**4,097**	**1,781**
Clocks	471	290	114	149	7	105	36	27
Lamps and lighting fixtures	2,432	1,984	960	909	90	422	397	115
Telephones, accessories, answering devices	1,256	652	226	388	40	276	72	38
Lawn and garden equipment	4,520	3,834	1,393	2,113	326	975	813	327
Power and hand tools	2,591	1,933	856	984	103	520	361	93
Indoor plants and fresh flowers	3,441	2,286	767	1,200	276	663	261	319
Closet and storage items	489	404	135	249	29	159	61	20
Luggage	799	551	192	333	53	153	127	27
Business equipment for home use	584	455	131	288	27	168	93	36

Note: Expenditures listed for items in a given category may not add to the total for that category because the listing is incomplete. "Other household services," for example, includes "other services," which is omitted here. Other married couples include extended family members or unrelated persons in addition to the married couple. Expenditures are not given (-) when the amount is too small to be reliable. Numbers may not add to total due to rounding. The "all cu's" aggregates will differ slightly from table to table because they are the sums of the aggregates in each row. In this table they include aggregates for single parents, single persons, and other types of consumer units, in addition to all married couples. Aggregates for "all married couples" and "all married couples with children" are sums of the appropriate aggregates in each row.

5

Apparel and Apparel Services

The share of household expenditures devoted to this category was relatively stable from 1984 to 1988. Each year, households allotted about 6 percent of their budgets to clothing and clothing-related items.

One-third of apparel expenditures in 1988 went to women's clothing, a smaller share than in other years. Men's and boy's clothing were also allocated a smaller share of the apparel budget in 1988 than in 1984. These declines were small and inconsistent, from year to year, over the five-year period. Girls' clothing, babies' clothing, and apparel products and services were allocated a larger share of apparel expenditures in 1984 than in 1988.

Five-year spending trends for apparel and apparel services

	1984	1985	1986	1987	1988	change 1984 to 1988
Share of household expenditures devoted to apparel and apparel services, share of apparel and apparel services expenditures devoted to apparel and apparel services items, and change in share, 1984 to 1988.						
Apparel and apparel services,						
Share of household expenditures	*6.0%*	*6.0%*	*5.6%*	*5.9%*	*5.8%*	*-0.2%*
Apparel and apparel services, expenditures	*100.0%*	*100.0%*	*100.0%*	*100.0%*	*100.0%*	*0.0%*
WOMEN AND GIRLS	**39.7%**	**40.8%**	**40.4%**	**40.9%**	**39.4%**	**-0.3%**
Women, aged 16 and older	33.7	35.1	35.1	35.3	33.0	-0.7
Girls, aged 2 to 15	6.0	5.7	5.3	5.6	6.4	0.4
MEN AND BOYS	**26.5%**	**25.6%**	**25.5%**	**25.0%**	**26.1%**	**-0.4%**
Men, aged 16 and older	21.2	21.3	20.7	20.4	20.9	-0.3
Boys, aged 2 to 15	5.3	4.3	4.9	4.6	5.2	-0.1
BABIES, UNDER AGE 2	**3.8%**	**3.9%**	**4.2%**	**4.0%**	**4.2%**	**0.4%**
FOOTWEAR	**14.0%**	**13.0%**	**12.4%**	**12.7%**	**13.2%**	**-0.8%**
OTHER APPAREL PRODUCTS AND SERVICES	**16.0%**	**16.5%**	**17.5%**	**17.4%**	**17.3%**	**1.3%**

Note: Numbers may not add to total due to rounding.

PART I
Spending by age for apparel and apparel services

Americans spend 6 percent of their household budgets on clothing. One-third of this spending is for women's clothing, but men's clothing and shoes also take sizable chunks.

Once again, middle-aged householders are the big spenders. Householders aged 35 to 44 spend 35 percent more than average on apparel, and those aged 45 to 54 spend 42 percent more than average. Their spending on women's and men's clothing, shoes, and related clothing products and services exceeds the average by as much as 65 percent. Together, these age groups account for nearly half the entire apparel market—spending $69 billion in 1988. By 2000, their share of the market should surpass 50 percent.

As parents of young children, householders aged 35 to 44 spend more than double the average on children's clothing, but they spend only 7 percent more than average on baby clothes. Their spending on women's and men's clothes, shoes, and other apparel products and services is at least 20 percent above average.

It is no surprise that householders aged 25 to 34 spend nearly double the average amount on baby clothes. But even though 73 percent of women aged 25 to 34 are in the labor force, spending on women's clothes is 14 percent below average for this age group.

Both the youngest and the oldest householders spend less than average on clothing, except for selected items. Those under age 25 spend more than average only on men's sportswear, women's shoes, rented clothing, and coin-operated laundry and dry cleaning. Among 55-to-64-year-olds, spending is above average only for men's clothing. Among householders aged 75 or older, spending is above average only for men's and women's sleepwear.

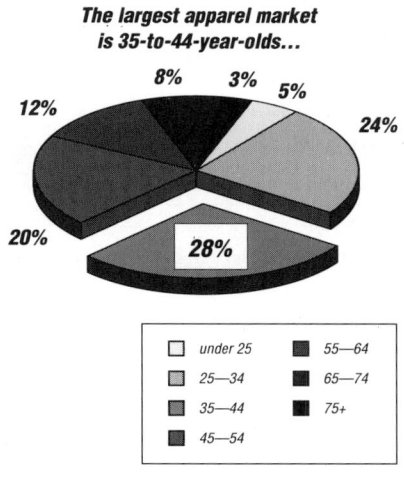

The largest apparel market is 35-to-44-year-olds...

□ under 25	■ 55—64
■ 25—34	■ 65—74
■ 35—44	■ 75+
■ 45—54	

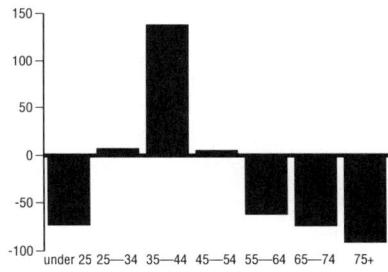

...they spend far more than the average household on girls' clothing...

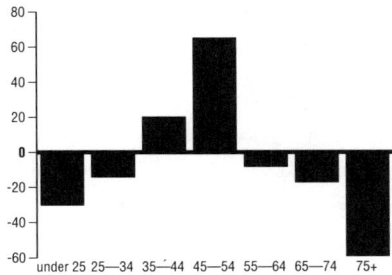

...but the peak spenders on women's clothing are older.

0 = average spending

Average expenditures

	all cu's	under 25	25 to 34	35 to 44	45 to 54	55 to 64	65 to 74	75+
Number of consumer units (in thousands)	94,862	7,216	21,985	19,911	13,601	12,546	11,319	8,284
Average number of persons per cu	2.6	1.8	2.8	3.3	2.9	2.2	2.0	1.5
Average total before-tax income	$28,540.00	$14,827.00	$28,318.00	$36,428.00	$39,934.00	$29,979.00	$20,704.00	$13,707.00
TOTAL AVERAGE ANNUAL EXPENDITURES	$25,891.85	$16,373.17	$25,770.27	$33,077.72	$33,204.87	$25,765.35	$20,119.90	$13,339.49
APPAREL AND APPAREL SERVICES, AVERAGE ANNUAL EXPENDITURES	$1,489.09	$1,042.48	$1,504.30	$2,015.18	$2,112.11	$1,355.08	$976.78	$450.83
WOMEN'S APPAREL	**$491.84**	**$345.97**	**$423.49**	**$590.91**	**$809.70**	**$453.33**	**$407.29**	**$203.63**
Coats and jackets	32.32	18.02	24.09	32.51	65.32	33.80	29.50	11.98
Dresses	80.87	70.63	63.36	84.39	158.67	64.31	68.16	38.20
Suits, sportcoats, and tailored jackets	30.51	14.63	29.00	41.39	38.00	28.63	30.25	13.03
Sweaters and vests	35.68	24.43	29.70	53.94	45.60	30.95	32.38	13.56
Shirts, blouses, and tops	80.01	55.44	67.23	90.82	142.10	73.74	64.58	35.81
Skirts	27.10	20.01	22.59	36.60	47.55	15.42	20.70	15.69
Pants	62.87	54.03	59.07	81.17	96.31	54.60	44.53	17.67
Shorts and shorts sets	12.85	14.29	16.58	16.14	20.34	6.51	3.53	3.48
Active sportswear	23.62	22.25	19.33	29.04	42.29	18.89	19.48	3.95
Sleepwear	21.29	6.86	18.68	22.55	28.50	22.86	23.68	21.37
Undergarments	25.28	12.96	17.80	28.60	39.29	37.13	23.33	8.59
Hosiery	25.32	21.88	27.85	31.22	33.73	23.48	15.79	9.48
Accessories	33.09	10.50	26.80	42.02	48.19	42.99	31.34	10.69
GIRLS' APPAREL	**$94.86**	**$25.52**	**$101.83**	**$225.31**	**$99.54**	**$35.84**	**$24.43**	**$8.78**
Coats and jackets	7.88	2.34	8.76	17.82	7.20	4.19	2.52	0.53
Dresses and suits	12.12	4.75	13.53	26.48	12.10	4.68	5.15	1.10
Shirts, blouses, and sweaters	27.34	6.96	25.02	74.40	30.16	5.13	5.14	2.90
Skirts, pants, shorts and short sets	22.49	5.05	26.22	51.63	20.96	9.52	6.73	1.40
Active sportswear	8.58	1.37	9.90	18.11	11.67	4.54	1.49	-
Underwear and sleepwear	5.69	1.00	6.22	12.93	5.36	2.48	2.33	0.96
Hosiery	4.40	0.79	5.92	8.55	6.57	1.63	-	0.67
Accessories	4.30	3.00	4.09	10.29	3.05	3.11	0.79	0.83
MEN'S APPAREL	**$310.52**	**$218.71**	**$310.76**	**$384.08**	**$431.66**	**$376.21**	**$189.12**	**$73.73**
Suits	44.25	22.30	46.44	49.94	59.14	51.83	41.25	11.98
Sportcoats	16.80	6.72	17.44	23.07	23.80	19.20	10.19	2.69
Coats and jackets	25.85	3.76	33.06	27.71	27.86	51.65	8.59	2.38
Underwear	9.71	5.73	6.24	15.46	10.31	12.60	10.76	1.71
Hosiery	9.52	5.80	11.76	10.05	11.28	9.34	7.81	5.39
Nightwear	2.88	-	1.73	4.68	3.35	2.71	3.43	2.92
Accessories	22.38	13.71	20.36	26.63	31.32	28.58	14.16	12.14
Sweaters and vests	18.44	15.74	16.29	24.91	29.73	18.56	9.78	4.07
Active sportswear	11.97	15.00	11.93	15.36	17.60	9.56	7.40	1.90

Average annual expenditures for apparel and apparel services, by age of reference person.

(continued from previous page)	all cu's	under 25	25 to 34	35 to 44	45 to 54	55 to 64	65 to 74	75+
Shirts	71.20	54.85	62.27	94.10	121.73	56.52	54.35	14.44
Pants, shorts, and short sets	73.89	72.48	79.29	86.93	89.70	112.81	20.48	12.64
Uniforms	2.92	2.17	3.08	4.42	4.58	2.26	-	1.20
BOYS' APPAREL	**$77.02**	**$14.40**	**$78.50**	**$169.09**	**$85.40**	**$47.91**	**$24.34**	**$18.66**
Coats and jackets	8.12	-	9.25	19.38	12.24	1.90	-	-
Sweaters	3.86	0.85	4.49	8.08	4.30	1.69	1.56	-
Shirts	19.64	3.89	20.72	42.79	20.72	12.51	7.38	3.44
Underwear	1.59	-	2.59	2.95	1.49	0.64	-	0.53
Nightwear	2.68	2.26	2.84	4.21	2.52	3.06	0.90	1.21
Hosiery	3.74	0.81	3.92	8.35	3.57	2.27	0.95	1.73
Accessories	2.64	0.74	2.96	5.70	3.52	1.16	0.57	-
Suits, sportcoats, and vests	2.92	-	4.05	4.82	3.34	3.78	-	-
Pants, shorts, and shorts sets	26.34	4.46	22.19	59.33	29.76	17.12	11.10	10.48
Uniforms and active sportswear	5.22	0.89	5.00	13.02	3.78	3.63	1.57	0.58
BABIES' APPAREL	**$62.38**	**$58.74**	**$122.89**	**$66.89**	**$48.99**	**$41.26**	**$19.63**	**$7.27**
Coats, jackets, and snowsuits	3.46	3.33	5.85	3.11	3.22	3.48	1.90	0.51
Outerwear including dresses	15.09	13.69	21.44	15.57	15.89	15.69	9.20	4.04
Underwear	34.95	33.62	81.48	38.23	19.86	15.38	4.57	1.43
Nightwear	3.24	2.71	4.53	3.28	4.50	2.65	1.92	0.77
Accessories and hosiery	3.54	2.64	5.86	4.35	3.71	2.49	1.54	-
FOOTWEAR	**$195.67**	**$161.16**	**$182.82**	**$247.07**	**$278.25**	**$178.91**	**$158.28**	**$73.42**
Women's	95.79	102.90	66.35	96.95	162.33	90.39	98.43	53.37
Girls'	16.99	1.67	30.18	36.51	9.59	3.93	3.84	1.68
Men's	66.00	51.31	70.99	71.28	93.70	76.95	44.94	16.55
Boys'	16.89	5.27	15.30	42.34	12.63	7.63	11.06	1.82
OTHER APPAREL PRODUCTS/SERVICES	**$256.81**	**$217.97**	**$284.01**	**$331.81**	**$358.57**	**$221.60**	**$153.70**	**$65.35**
Fabric, patterns, notions for making clothes	9.79	3.95	8.86	9.91	15.43	10.82	12.39	2.76
Watches	21.83	15.97	24.19	31.45	31.87	13.86	12.87	5.38
Jewelry	107.96	86.78	112.45	146.36	160.50	99.88	61.89	11.11
Shoe repair and other shoe services	3.32	1.50	3.03	4.21	5.51	3.30	2.06	1.68
Watch and jewelry repair services	5.49	2.56	3.54	6.86	6.73	7.55	6.52	3.32
Coin-operated laundry and dry cleaning	33.34	66.06	52.17	36.44	24.45	16.29	13.49	14.94
Professional laundry, dry cleaning, storage	64.55	33.08	69.82	84.82	98.08	59.47	35.67	21.43
Apparel alteration and repair services	6.08	3.24	4.94	7.30	8.48	5.60	6.81	4.44
Clothing rental	4.45	4.84	5.01	4.47	7.53	4.84	2.00	-

Note: Women and men include all persons aged 16 and older, girls and boys are aged 2 to 15, and babies are under age 2. Expenditures are not given (-) when the amount is too small to be reliable. Expenditures listed for a given category may not add to the total for that category because the listing is incomplete. "Men's apparel," for example, includes "other clothing," which is omitted here. Numbers may not add to total due to rounding.

Share of spending

	all cu's	under 25	25 to 34	35 to 44	45 to 54	55 to 64	65 to 74	75+
Number of consumer units (in thousands)	94,862	7,216	21,985	19,911	13,601	12,546	11,319	8,284
Average number of persons per cu	2.6	1.8	2.8	3.3	2.9	2.2	2.0	1.5
Average total before-tax income	$28,540	$14,827	$28,318	$36,428	$39,934	$29,979	$20,704	$13,707
TOTAL AVERAGE ANNUAL EXPENDITURES	100.00%	100.00%	100.00%	100.00%	100.00%	100.00%	100.00%	100.00%
APPAREL AND APPAREL SERVICES, AVERAGE ANNUAL EXPENDITURES	5.75%	6.37%	5.84%	6.09%	6.36%	5.26%	4.85%	3.38%
WOMEN'S APPAREL	**1.90%**	**2.11%**	**1.64%**	**1.79%**	**2.44%**	**1.76%**	**2.02%**	**1.53%**
Coats and jackets	0.12	0.11	0.09	0.10	0.20	0.13	0.15	0.09
Dresses	0.31	0.43	0.25	0.26	0.48	0.25	0.34	0.29
Suits, sportcoats, and tailored jackets	0.12	0.09	0.11	0.13	0.11	0.11	0.15	0.10
Sweaters and vests	0.14	0.15	0.12	0.16	0.14	0.12	0.16	0.10
Shirts, blouses, and tops	0.31	0.34	0.26	0.27	0.43	0.29	0.32	0.27
Skirts	0.10	0.12	0.09	0.11	0.14	0.06	0.10	0.12
Pants	0.24	0.33	0.23	0.25	0.29	0.21	0.22	0.13
Shorts and shorts sets	0.05	0.09	0.06	0.05	0.06	0.03	0.02	0.03
Active sportswear	0.09	0.14	0.08	0.09	0.13	0.07	0.10	0.03
Sleepwear	0.08	0.04	0.07	0.07	0.09	0.09	0.12	0.16
Undergarments	0.10	0.08	0.07	0.09	0.12	0.14	0.12	0.06
Hosiery	0.10	0.13	0.11	0.09	0.10	0.09	0.08	0.07
Accessories	0.13	0.06	0.10	0.13	0.15	0.17	0.16	0.08
GIRLS' APPAREL	**0.37%**	**0.16%**	**0.40%**	**0.68%**	**0.30%**	**0.14%**	**0.12%**	**0.07%**
Coats and jackets	0.03	0.01	0.03	0.05	0.02	0.02	0.01	0.00
Dresses and suits	0.05	0.03	0.05	0.08	0.04	0.02	0.03	0.01
Shirts, blouses, and sweaters	0.11	0.04	0.10	0.22	0.09	0.02	0.03	0.02
Skirts, pants, shorts and short sets	0.09	0.03	0.10	0.16	0.06	0.04	0.03	0.01
Active sportswear	0.03	0.01	0.04	0.05	0.04	0.02	0.01	-
Underwear and sleepwear	0.02	0.01	0.02	0.04	0.02	0.01	0.01	0.01
Hosiery	0.02	0.00	0.02	0.03	0.02	0.01	-	0.01
Accessories	0.02	0.02	0.02	0.03	0.01	0.01	0.00	0.01
MEN'S APPAREL	**1.20%**	**1.34%**	**1.21%**	**1.16%**	**1.30%**	**1.46%**	**0.94%**	**0.55%**
Suits	0.17	0.14	0.18	0.15	0.18	0.20	0.21	0.09
Sportcoats	0.06	0.04	0.07	0.07	0.07	0.07	0.05	0.02
Coats and jackets	0.10	0.02	0.13	0.08	0.08	0.20	0.04	0.02
Underwear	0.04	0.03	0.02	0.05	0.03	0.05	0.05	0.01
Hosiery	0.04	0.04	0.05	0.03	0.03	0.04	0.04	0.04
Nightwear	0.01	-	0.01	0.01	0.01	0.01	0.02	0.02
Accessories	0.09	0.08	0.08	0.08	0.09	0.11	0.07	0.09
Sweaters and vests	0.07	0.10	0.06	0.08	0.09	0.07	0.05	0.03
Active sportswear	0.05	0.09	0.05	0.05	0.05	0.04	0.04	0.01

Percent of total average annual expenditures spent on apparel and apparel services, by age of reference person.

(continued from previous page)	all cu's	under 25	25 to 34	35 to 44	45 to 54	55 to 64	65 to 74	75+
Shirts	0.27	0.33	0.24	0.28	0.37	0.22	0.27	0.11
Pants, short, and short sets	0.29	0.44	0.31	0.26	0.27	0.44	0.10	0.09
Uniforms	0.01	0.01	0.01	0.01	0.01	0.01	-	0.01
BOYS' APPAREL	**0.30%**	**0.09%**	**0.30%**	**0.51%**	**0.26%**	**0.19%**	**0.12%**	**0.14%**
Coats and jackets	0.03	-	0.04	0.06	0.04	0.01	-	-
Sweaters	0.01	0.01	0.02	0.02	0.01	0.01	0.01	-
Shirts	0.08	0.02	0.08	0.13	0.06	0.05	0.04	0.03
Underwear	0.01	-	0.01	0.01	0.00	0.00	-	0.00
Nightwear	0.01	0.01	0.01	0.01	0.01	0.01	0.00	0.01
Hosiery	0.01	0.00	0.02	0.03	0.01	0.01	0.00	0.01
Accessories	0.01	0.00	0.01	0.02	0.01	0.00	0.00	-
Suits, sportcoats, and vests	0.01	-	0.02	0.01	0.01	0.01	-	-
Pants, shorts, and shorts sets	0.10	0.03	0.09	0.18	0.09	0.07	0.06	0.08
Uniforms and active sportswear	0.02	0.01	0.02	0.04	0.01	0.01	0.01	0.00
BABIES' APPAREL	**0.24%**	**0.36%**	**0.48%**	**0.20%**	**0.15%**	**0.16%**	**0.10%**	**0.05%**
Coats, jackets, and snowsuits	0.01	0.02	0.02	0.01	0.01	0.01	0.01	0.00
Outerwear including dresses	0.06	0.08	0.08	0.05	0.05	0.06	0.05	0.03
Underwear	0.13	0.21	0.32	0.12	0.06	0.06	0.02	0.01
Nightwear	0.01	0.02	0.02	0.01	0.01	0.01	0.01	0.01
Accessories and hosiery	0.01	0.02	0.02	0.01	0.01	0.01	0.01	-
FOOTWEAR	**0.76%**	**0.98%**	**0.71%**	**0.75%**	**0.84%**	**0.69%**	**0.79%**	**0.55%**
Women's	0.37	0.63	0.26	0.29	0.49	0.35	0.49	0.40
Girls'	0.07	0.01	0.12	0.11	0.03	0.02	0.02	0.01
Men's	0.25	0.31	0.28	0.22	0.28	0.30	0.22	0.12
Boys'	0.07	0.03	0.06	0.13	0.04	0.03	0.05	0.01
OTHER APPAREL PRODUCTS/SERVICES	**0.99%**	**1.33%**	**1.10%**	**1.00%**	**1.08%**	**0.86%**	**0.76%**	**0.49%**
Fabric, patterns, notions for making clothes	0.04	0.02	0.03	0.03	0.05	0.04	0.06	0.02
Watches	0.08	0.10	0.09	0.10	0.10	0.05	0.06	0.04
Jewelry	0.42	0.53	0.44	0.44	0.48	0.39	0.31	0.08
Shoe repair and other shoe services	0.01	0.01	0.01	0.01	0.02	0.01	0.01	0.01
Watch and jewelry repair services	0.02	0.02	0.01	0.02	0.02	0.03	0.03	0.02
Coin-operated laundry and dry cleaning	0.13	0.40	0.20	0.11	0.07	0.06	0.07	0.11
Professional laundry, dry cleaning, storage	0.25	0.20	0.27	0.26	0.30	0.23	0.18	0.16
Apparel alteration and repair services	0.02	0.02	0.02	0.02	0.03	0.02	0.03	0.03
Clothing rental	0.02	0.03	0.02	0.01	0.02	0.02	0.01	-

Note: Women and men include all persons aged 16 and older, girls and boys are aged 2 to 15, and babies are under age 2. Expenditures are not given (-) when the amount is too small to be reliable. Expenditures listed for a given category may not add to the total for that category because the listing is incomplete. "Men's apparel," for example, includes "other clothing," which is omitted here. Numbers may not add to total due to rounding.

Indexed expenditures

	all cu's	under 25	25 to 34	35 to 44	45 to 54	55 to 64	65 to 74	75+
Indexed average annual expenditures for apparel and apparel services, by age of reference person.								
Number of consumer units (in thousands)	94,862	7,216	21,985	19,911	13,601	12,546	11,319	8,284
Average number of persons per cu	2.6	1.8	2.8	3.3	2.9	2.2	2.0	1.5
Average total before-tax income	$28,540	$14,827	$28,318	$36,428	$39,934	$29,979	$20,704	$13,707
TOTAL AVERAGE ANNUAL EXPENDITURES	100	63	100	128	128	100	78	52
APPAREL AND APPAREL SERVICES, AVERAGE ANNUAL EXPENDITURES	100	70	101	135	142	91	66	30
WOMEN'S APPAREL	**100**	**70**	**86**	**120**	**165**	**92**	**83**	**41**
Coats and jackets	100	56	75	101	202	105	91	37
Dresses	100	87	78	104	196	80	84	47
Suits, sportcoats, and tailored jackets	100	48	95	136	125	94	99	43
Sweaters and vests	100	68	83	151	128	87	91	38
Shirts, blouses, and tops	100	69	84	114	178	92	81	45
Skirts	100	74	83	135	175	57	76	58
Pants	100	86	94	129	153	87	71	28
Shorts and shorts sets	100	111	129	126	158	51	27	27
Active sportswear	100	94	82	123	179	80	82	17
Sleepwear	100	32	88	106	134	107	111	100
Undergarments	100	51	70	113	155	147	92	34
Hosiery	100	86	110	123	133	93	62	37
Accessories	100	32	81	127	146	130	95	32
GIRLS' APPAREL	**100**	**27**	**107**	**238**	**105**	**38**	**26**	**9**
Coats and jackets	100	30	111	226	91	53	32	7
Dresses and suits	100	39	112	218	100	39	42	9
Shirts, blouses, and sweaters	100	25	92	272	110	19	19	11
Skirts, pants, shorts and short sets	100	22	117	230	93	42	30	6
Active sportswear	100	16	115	211	136	53	17	-
Underwear and sleepwear	100	18	109	227	94	44	41	17
Hosiery	100	18	135	194	149	37	-	15
Accessories	100	70	95	239	71	72	18	19
MEN'S APPAREL	**100**	**70**	**100**	**124**	**139**	**121**	**61**	**24**
Suits	100	50	105	113	134	117	93	27
Sportcoats	100	40	104	137	142	114	61	16
Coats and jackets	100	15	128	107	108	200	33	9
Underwear	100	59	64	159	106	130	111	18
Hosiery	100	61	124	106	118	98	82	57
Nightwear	100	-	60	163	116	94	119	101
Accessories	100	61	91	119	140	128	63	54
Sweaters and vests	100	85	88	135	161	101	53	22
Active sportswear	100	125	100	128	147	80	62	16

Indexed average annual expenditures for apparel and apparel services, by age of reference person.

(continued from previous page)	all cu's	under 25	25 to 34	35 to 44	45 to 54	55 to 64	65 to 74	75+
Shirts	100	77	87	132	171	79	76	20
Pants, shorts, and short sets	100	98	107	118	121	153	28	17
Uniforms	100	74	105	151	157	77	-	41
BOYS' APPAREL	**100**	**19**	**102**	**220**	**111**	**62**	**32**	**24**
Coats and jackets	100	-	114	239	151	23	-	-
Sweaters	100	22	116	209	111	44	40	-
Shirts	100	20	105	218	105	64	38	18
Underwear	100	-	163	186	94	40	-	33
Nightwear	100	84	106	157	94	114	34	45
Hosiery	100	22	105	223	95	61	25	46
Accessories	100	28	112	216	133	44	22	-
Suits, sportcoats, and vests	100	-	139	165	114	129	-	-
Pants, shorts, and shorts sets	100	17	84	225	113	65	42	40
Uniforms and active sportswear	100	17	96	249	72	70	30	11
BABIES' APPAREL	**100**	**94**	**197**	**107**	**79**	**66**	**31**	**12**
Coats, jackets, and snowsuits	100	96	169	90	93	101	55	15
Outerwear including dresses	100	91	142	103	105	104	61	27
Underwear	100	96	233	109	57	44	13	4
Nightwear	100	84	140	101	139	82	59	24
Accessories and hosiery	100	75	166	123	105	70	44	-
FOOTWEAR	**100**	**82**	**93**	**126**	**142**	**91**	**81**	**38**
Women's	100	107	69	101	169	94	103	56
Girls'	100	10	178	215	56	23	23	10
Men's	100	78	108	108	142	117	68	25
Boys'	100	31	91	251	75	45	65	11
OTHER APPAREL PRODUCTS/SERVICES	**100**	**85**	**111**	**129**	**140**	**86**	**60**	**25**
Fabric, patterns, notions for making clothes	100	40	91	101	158	111	127	28
Watches	100	73	111	144	146	63	59	25
Jewelry	100	80	104	136	149	93	57	10
Shoe repair and other shoe services	100	45	91	127	166	99	62	51
Watch and jewelry repair services	100	47	64	125	123	138	119	60
Coin-operated laundry and dry cleaning	100	198	156	109	73	49	40	45
Professional laundry, dry cleaning, storage	100	51	108	131	152	92	55	33
Apparel alteration and repair services	100	53	81	120	139	92	112	73
Clothing rental	100	109	113	100	169	109	45	-

Note: Women and men include all persons aged 16 and older, girls and boys are aged 2 to 15, and babies are under age 2. Expenditures are not given (-) when the amount is too small to be reliable. An index of 100 represents the average for all consumer units. An index of 132 means that the average for the subgroup is 32 percent above the average for all consumer units. An index of 68 indicates spending that is 32 percent below the overall average.

Aggregate expenditures, 1988

Aggregate expenditures in 1988 for apparel and apparel services, by age of reference person.

	all cu's	under 25	25 to 34	35 to 44	45 to 54	55 to 64	65 to 74	75+
Number of consumer units (in thousands)	94,862	7,216	21,985	19,911	13,601	12,546	11,319	8,284
Average number of persons per cu	2.6	1.8	2.8	3.3	2.9	2.2	2.0	1.5
Aggregate before-tax income (in millions)	$2,722,037	$106,992	$622,571	$725,318	$543,142	$376,117	$234,349	$113,549
TOTAL AGGREGATE EXPENDITURES (in millions)	$2,456,432	$118,149	$566,559	$658,610	$451,619	$323,252	$227,737	$110,504
APPAREL AND APPAREL SERVICES, AGGREGATE EXPENDITURES (in millions)	$141,237	$7,523	$33,072	$40,124	$28,727	$17,001	$11,056	$3,735
WOMEN'S APPAREL	**$46,570**	**$2,497**	**$9,310**	**$11,766**	**$11,013**	**$5,687**	**$4,610**	**$1,687**
Coats and jackets	3,053	130	530	647	888	424	334	99
Dresses	7,636	510	1,393	1,680	2,158	807	772	316
Suits, sportcoats, and tailored jackets	2,894	106	638	824	517	359	342	108
Sweaters and vests	3,391	176	653	1,074	620	388	367	112
Shirts, blouses, and tops	7,572	400	1,478	1,808	1,933	925	731	297
Skirts	2,574	144	497	729	647	193	234	130
Pants	5,950	390	1,299	1,616	1,310	685	504	146
Shorts and shorts sets	1,216	103	365	321	277	82	40	29
Active sportswear	2,229	161	425	578	575	237	220	33
Sleepwear	2,029	50	411	449	388	287	268	177
Undergarments	2,390	94	391	569	534	466	264	71
Hosiery	2,402	158	612	622	459	295	179	79
Accessories	3,140	76	589	837	655	539	355	89
GIRLS' APPAREL	**$9,062**	**$184**	**$2,239**	**$4,486**	**$1,354**	**$450**	**$277**	**$73**
Coats and jackets	748	17	193	355	98	53	29	4
Dresses and suits	1,150	34	297	527	165	59	58	9
Shirts, blouses, and sweaters	2,638	50	550	1,481	410	64	58	24
Skirts, pants, shorts and short sets	2,133	36	576	1,028	285	119	76	12
Active sportswear	821	10	218	361	159	57	17	-
Underwear and sleepwear	540	7	137	257	73	31	26	8
Hosiery	421	6	130	170	89	20	-	6
Accessories	413	22	90	205	41	39	9	7
MEN'S APPAREL	**$29,400**	**$1,578**	**$6,832**	**$7,647**	**$5,871**	**$4,720**	**$2,141**	**$611**
Suits	4,197	161	1,021	994	804	650	467	99
Sportcoats	1,593	48	383	459	324	241	115	22
Coats and jackets	2,450	27	727	552	379	648	97	20
Underwear	921	41	137	308	140	158	122	14
Hosiery	904	42	259	200	153	117	88	45
Nightwear	274	-	38	93	46	34	39	24
Accessories	2,122	99	448	530	426	359	160	101
Sweaters and vests	1,749	114	358	496	404	233	111	34
Active sportswear	1,135	108	262	306	239	120	84	16

Aggregate expenditures for apparel and apparel services in 1988, by age of reference person.

(continued from previous page)	all cu's	under 25	25 to 34	35 to 44	45 to 54	55 to 64	65 to 74	75+
Shirts	6,738	396	1,369	1,874	1,656	709	615	120
Pants, shorts, and short sets	6,969	523	1,743	1,731	1,220	1,415	232	105
Uniforms	272	16	68	88	62	28	-	10
BOYS' APPAREL	**$7,389**	**$104**	**$1,726**	**$3,367**	**$1,162**	**$601**	**$276**	**$155**
Coats and jackets	780	-	203	386	166	24	-	-
Sweaters	363	6	99	161	58	21	18	-
Shirts	1,886	28	456	852	282	157	84	28
Underwear	148	-	57	59	20	8	-	4
Nightwear	255	16	62	84	34	38	10	10
Hosiery	360	6	86	166	49	28	11	14
Accessories	253	5	65	113	48	15	6	-
Suits, sportcoats, and vests	278	-	89	96	45	47	-	-
Pants, shorts, and shorts sets	2,533	32	488	1,181	405	215	126	87
Uniforms and active sportswear	495	6	110	259	51	46	18	5
BABIES' APPAREL	**$5,924**	**$424**	**$2,702**	**$1,332**	**$666**	**$518**	**$222**	**$60**
Coats, jackets, and snowsuits	328	24	129	62	44	44	22	4
Outerwear including dresses	1,431	99	471	310	216	197	104	33
Underwear	3,322	243	1,791	761	270	193	52	12
Nightwear	307	20	100	65	61	33	22	6
Accessories and hosiery	334	19	129	87	50	31	17	-
FOOTWEAR	**$18,531**	**$1,163**	**$4,019**	**$4,919**	**$3,784**	**$2,245**	**$1,792**	**$608**
Women's	9,030	743	1,459	1,930	2,208	1,134	1,114	442
Girls'	1,640	12	664	727	130	49	43	14
Men's	6,236	370	1,561	1,419	1,274	965	509	137
Boys'	1,625	38	336	843	172	96	125	15
OTHER APPAREL PRODUCTS/SERVICES	**$24,362**	**$1,573**	**$6,244**	**$6,607**	**$4,877**	**$2,780**	**$1,740**	**$541**
Fabric, patterns, notions for making clothes	929	29	195	197	210	136	140	23
Watches	2,071	115	532	626	433	174	146	45
Jewelry	10,241	626	2,472	2,914	2,183	1,253	701	92
Shoe repair and other shoe services	315	11	67	84	75	41	23	14
Watch and jewelry repair services	520	18	78	137	92	95	74	28
Coin-operated laundry and dry cleaning	3,163	477	1,147	726	333	204	153	124
Professional laundry, dry cleaning, storage	6,124	239	1,535	1,689	1,334	746	404	178
Apparel alteration and repair services	577	23	109	145	115	70	77	37
Clothing rental	420	35	110	89	102	61	23	-

Note: Women and men include all persons aged 16 and older, girls and boys are aged 2 to 15, and babies are under age 2. Expenditures are not given (-) when the amount is too small to be reliable. Expenditures listed for a given category may not add to the total for that category because the listing is incomplete. "Men's apparel," for example, includes "other clothing," which is omitted here. Numbers may not add to total due to rounding. The "all cu's" aggregates will differ slightly from table to table because they are the sums of the aggregates in each row.

Aggregate expenditures, 1995

Aggregate expenditures for apparel and apparel services, by age of householder in 1995 (in 1988 dollars).

	all households	under 25	25 to 34	35 to 44	45 to 54	55 to 64	65 to 74	75+
Number of households (in thousands)	100,308	4,316	19,927	23,916	18,035	12,233	12,006	9,876
APPAREL AND APPAREL SERVICES, AGGREGATE EXPENDITURES IN 1995 (in millions)	$153,519	$4,499	$29,976	$48,195	$38,092	$16,577	$11,727	$4,452
WOMEN'S APPAREL	$51,114	$1,493	$8,439	$14,132	$14,603	$5,546	$4,890	$2,011
Coats and jackets	3,399	78	480	778	1,178	413	354	118
Dresses	8,430	305	1,263	2,018	2,862	787	818	377
Suits, sportcoats, and tailored jackets	3,158	63	578	990	685	350	363	129
Sweaters and vests	3,711	105	592	1,290	822	379	389	134
Shirts, blouses, and tops	8,345	239	1,340	2,172	2,563	902	775	354
Skirts	2,862	86	450	875	858	189	249	155
Pants	6,466	233	1,177	1,941	1,737	668	535	175
Shorts and shorts sets	1,301	62	330	386	367	80	42	34
Active sportswear	2,442	96	385	695	763	231	234	39
Sleepwear	2,230	30	372	539	514	280	284	211
Undergarments	2,622	56	355	684	709	454	280	85
Hosiery	2,575	94	555	747	608	287	190	94
Accessories	3,461	45	534	1,005	869	526	376	106
GIRLS' APPAREL	$10,141	$110	$2,029	$5,389	$1,795	$438	$293	$87
Coats and jackets	827	10	175	426	130	51	30	5
Dresses and suits	1,272	21	270	633	218	57	62	11
Shirts, blouses, and sweaters	3,005	30	499	1,779	544	63	62	29
Skirts, pants, shorts and short sets	2,368	22	522	1,235	378	116	81	14
Active sportswear	920	6	197	433	210	56	18	-
Underwear and sleepwear	602	4	124	309	97	30	28	9
Hosiery	471	3	118	204	118	20	-	7
Accessories	451	13	82	246	55	38	9	8
MEN'S APPAREL	$31,708	$944	$6,193	$9,186	$7,785	$4,602	$2,271	$728
Suits	4,530	96	925	1,194	1,067	634	495	118
Sportcoats	1,741	29	348	552	429	235	122	27
Coats and jackets	2,599	16	659	663	502	632	103	24
Underwear	1,005	25	124	370	186	154	129	17
Hosiery	964	25	234	240	203	114	94	53
Nightwear	310	-	34	112	60	33	41	29
Accessories	2,306	59	406	637	565	350	170	120
Sweaters and vests	1,909	68	325	596	536	227	117	40
Active sportswear	1,212	65	238	367	317	117	89	19

Aggregate expenditures for apparel and apparel services, by age of householder in 1995 (in 1988 dollars).

(continued from previous page)	all households	under 25	25 to 34	35 to 44	45 to 54	55 to 64	65 to 74	75+
Shirts	7,410	237	1,241	2,250	2,195	691	653	143
Pants, shorts, and short sets	7,340	313	1,580	2,079	1,618	1,380	246	125
Uniforms	299	9	61	106	83	28	-	12
BOYS' APPAREL	**$8,273**	**$62**	**$1,564**	**$4,044**	**$1,540**	**$586**	**$292**	**$184**
Coats and jackets	892	-	184	463	221	23	-	-
Sweaters	403	4	89	193	78	21	19	-
Shirts	2,102	17	413	1,023	374	153	89	34
Underwear	162	-	52	71	27	8	-	5
Nightwear	273	10	57	101	45	37	11	12
Hosiery	402	3	78	200	64	28	11	17
Accessories	283	3	59	136	63	14	7	-
Suits, sportcoats, and vests	302	-	81	115	60	46	-	-
Pants, shorts, and shorts sets	2,863	19	442	1,419	537	209	133	104
Uniforms and active sportswear	552	4	100	311	68	44	19	6
BABIES' APPAREL	**$5,998**	**$254**	**$2,449**	**$1,600**	**$884**	**$505**	**$236**	**$72**
Coats, jackets, and snowsuits	334	14	117	74	58	43	23	5
Outerwear including dresses	1,488	59	427	372	287	192	110	40
Underwear	3,298	145	1,624	914	358	188	55	14
Nightwear	325	12	90	78	81	32	23	8
Accessories and hosiery	348	11	117	104	67	30	18	-
FOOTWEAR	**$20,080**	**$696**	**$3,643**	**$5,909**	**$5,018**	**$2,189**	**$1,900**	**$725**
Women's	9,827	444	1,322	2,319	2,928	1,106	1,182	527
Girls'	1,766	7	601	873	173	48	46	17
Men's	6,675	221	1,415	1,705	1,690	941	540	163
Boys'	1,812	23	305	1,013	228	93	133	18
OTHER APPAREL PRODUCTS/SERVICES	**$26,204**	**$941**	**$5,659**	**$7,936**	**$6,467**	**$2,711**	**$1,845**	**$645**
Fabric, patterns, notions for making clothes	1,017	17	177	237	278	132	149	27
Watches	2,255	69	482	752	575	170	155	53
Jewelry	11,085	375	2,241	3,500	2,895	1,222	743	110
Shoe repair and other shoe services	349	6	60	101	99	40	25	17
Watch and jewelry repair services	570	11	71	164	121	92	78	33
Coin-operated laundry and dry cleaning	3,146	285	1,040	871	441	199	162	148
Professional laundry, dry cleaning, storage	6,699	143	1,391	2,029	1,769	727	428	212
Apparel alteration and repair services	634	14	98	175	153	69	82	44
Clothing rental	447	21	100	107	136	59	24	-

Note: Households are used here because projections of the number of consumer units in 1995 and 2000 are not available. Projections show how annual aggregate expenditures will change as the number of households in the age groups changes in 1995 and 2000. Household projections are from the Census Bureau. Projections are based on the average annual expenditures in 1988 and have not been adjusted for price increases or for changes in expenditure patterns. Women and men include all persons aged 16 and older, girls and boys are aged 2 to 15, and babies are under age 2. Expenditures are not given (-) when the amount is too small to be reliable. Expenditures listed for a given category may not add to the total for that category because the listing is incomplete. "Men's apparel," for example, includes "other clothing," which is omitted here. Numbers may not add to total due to rounding.

Aggregate expenditures, 2000

	all households	under 25	25 to 34	35 to 44	45 to 54	55 to 64	65 to 74	75+
Aggregate expenditures for apparel and apparel services, by age of householder in 2000 (in 1988 dollars).								
Number of households (in thousands)	105,933	4,442	18,004	25,339	21,603	13,903	11,516	11,126
APPAREL AND APPAREL SERVICES								
AGGREGATE EXPENDITURES IN 2000 (in millions)	$163,509	$4,631	$27,083	$51,063	$45,628	$18,840	$11,249	$5,016
WOMEN'S APPAREL	$54,885	$1,537	$7,625	$14,973	$17,492	$6,303	$4,690	$2,266
Coats and jackets	3,692	80	434	824	1,411	470	340	133
Dresses	9,125	314	1,141	2,138	3,428	894	785	425
Suits, sportcoats, and tailored jackets	3,348	65	522	1,049	821	398	348	145
Sweaters and vests	3,949	109	535	1,367	985	430	373	151
Shirts, blouses, and tops	8,995	246	1,210	2,301	3,070	1,025	744	398
Skirts	3,078	89	407	927	1,027	214	238	175
Pants	6,909	240	1,063	2,057	2,081	759	513	197
Shorts and shorts sets	1,380	63	299	409	439	91	41	39
Active sportswear	2,627	99	348	736	914	263	224	44
Sleepwear	2,382	30	336	571	616	318	273	238
Undergarments	2,832	58	320	725	849	516	269	96
Hosiery	2,732	97	501	791	729	326	182	105
Accessories	3,712	47	483	1,065	1,041	598	361	119
GIRLS' APPAREL	$10,684	$113	$1,833	$5,709	$2,150	$498	$281	$98
Coats and jackets	868	10	158	452	156	58	29	6
Dresses and suits	1,334	21	244	671	261	65	59	12
Shirts, blouses, and sweaters	3,181	31	450	1,885	652	71	59	32
Skirts, pants, shorts and short sets	2,481	22	472	1,308	453	132	78	16
Active sportswear	976	6	178	459	252	63	17	-
Underwear and sleepwear	632	4	112	328	116	34	27	11
Hosiery	499	4	107	217	142	23	-	7
Accessories	475	13	74	261	66	43	9	9
MEN'S APPAREL	$33,852	$972	$5,595	$9,732	$9,325	$5,230	$2,178	$820
Suits	$4,807	99	836	1,265	1,278	721	475	133
Sportcoats	1,857	30	314	585	514	267	117	30
Coats and jackets	2,759	17	595	702	602	718	99	26
Underwear	1,070	25	112	392	223	175	124	19
Hosiery	1,016	26	212	255	244	130	90	60
Nightwear	332	-	31	119	72	38	39	32
Accessories	2,474	61	367	675	677	397	163	135
Sweaters and vests	2,053	70	293	631	642	258	113	45
Active sportswear	1,290	67	215	389	380	133	85	21

Aggregate expenditures for apparel and apparel services, by age of householder in 2000 (in 1988 dollars).

(continued from previous page)	all households	under 25	25 to 34	35 to 44	45 to 54	55 to 64	65 to 74	75+
Shirts	7,951	244	1,121	2,384	2,630	786	626	161
Pants, shorts, and short sets	7,835	322	1,428	2,203	1,938	1,568	236	141
Uniforms	321	10	55	112	99	31	-	13
BOYS' APPAREL	**$8,761**	**$64**	**$1,413**	**$4,285**	**$1,845**	**$666**	**$280**	**$208**
Coats and jackets	948	-	167	491	264	26	-	-
Sweaters	424	4	81	205	93	23	18	-
Shirts	2,219	17	373	1,084	448	174	85	38
Underwear	168	-	47	75	32	9	-	6
Nightwear	289	10	51	107	54	43	10	13
Hosiery	425	4	71	212	77	32	11	19
Accessories	300	3	53	144	76	16	7	-
Suits, sportcoats, and vests	320	-	73	122	72	53	-	-
Pants, shorts, and shorts sets	3,048	20	400	1,503	643	238	128	117
Uniforms and active sportswear	581	4	90	330	82	50	18	6
BABIES' APPAREL	**$6,107**	**$261**	**$2,213**	**$1,695**	**$1,058**	**$574**	**$226**	**$81**
Coats, jackets, and snowsuits	344	15	105	79	70	48	22	6
Outerwear including dresses	1,554	61	386	395	343	218	106	45
Underwear	3,296	149	1,467	969	429	214	53	16
Nightwear	341	12	82	83	97	37	22	9
Accessories and hosiery	360	12	106	110	80	35	18	-
FOOTWEAR	**$21,406**	**$716**	**$3,291**	**$6,261**	**$6,011**	**$2,487**	**$1,823**	**$817**
Women's	10,599	457	1,195	2,457	3,507	1,257	1,134	594
Girls'	1,801	7	543	925	207	55	44	19
Men's	7,108	228	1,278	1,806	2,024	1,070	518	184
Boys'	1,898	23	275	1,073	273	106	127	20
OTHER APPAREL PRODUCTS/SERVICES	**$27,813**	**$968**	**$5,113**	**$8,408**	**$7,746**	**$3,081**	**$1,770**	**$727**
Fabric, patterns, notions for making clothes	1,085	18	160	251	333	150	143	31
Watches	2,393	71	436	797	688	193	148	60
Jewelry	11,811	385	2,025	3,709	3,467	1,389	713	124
Shoe repair and other shoe services	375	7	55	107	119	46	24	19
Watch and jewelry repair services	611	11	64	174	145	105	75	37
Coin-operated laundry and dry cleaning	3,232	293	939	923	528	226	155	166
Professional laundry, dry cleaning, storage	7,148	147	1,257	2,149	2,119	827	411	238
Apparel alteration and repair services	677	14	89	185	183	78	78	49
Clothing rental	478	21	90	113	163	67	23	-

Note: Households are used here because projections of the number of consumer units in 1990 and 2000 are not available. Projections show how annual aggregate expenditures will change as the number of households in the age groups change from 1990 to 2000. Household projections are from the Census Bureau. Projections are based on the average annual expenditures in 1988 and have not been adjusted for price increases or for changes in expenditure patterns. Women and men include all persons aged 16 and older, girls and boys are aged 2 to 15, and babies are under age 2. Expenditures are not given (-) when the amount is too small to be reliable. Expenditures listed for a given category may not add to the total for that category because the listing is incomplete. "Men's apparel," for example, includes "other clothing," which is omitted here. Numbers may not add to total due to rounding.

PART II
Spending by income for apparel and apparel services

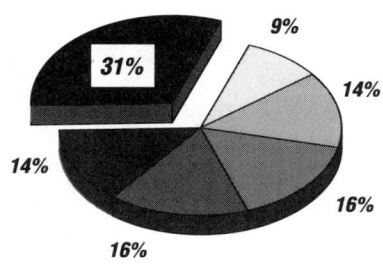

Households with incomes of $50,000 or more account for almost one-third of the apparel market

☐ under $10,000	■ $30,000–39,999
■ $10,000–19,999	■ $40,000–49,999
■ $20,000–29,999	■ $50,000 and over

From the lowest to the highest income households, spending on men's clothing increases by 610 percent; spending on boys' clothing by 520 percent; spending on girls' clothing by 500 percent; and spending on women's clothing by 330 percent. Adult clothing items for which spending climbs the fastest are suits, sportscoats, and jackets. Jewelry expenditures increase by more than 1800 percent and professional laundry and dry cleaning bills by 1000 percent.

Spending on clothing, shoes, jewelry, dry cleaning, and other clothes and related services rises from an average of $234 a year for the lowest income households to $993 a year for those in the $50,000 and over income bracket. But households with incomes of $40,000 to $50,000 spend the largest share of their total budget on clothing—6.4 percent, versus 5.8 percent for the average household.

The 12 million households with incomes of $50,000 or more spent $39 billion on apparel and apparel services in 1988. Together with their counterparts in the $30,000 to $50,000 income group they comprise 61 percent of the national apparel market. Less than 40 percent of the apparel market is accounted for by households with incomes under $30,000 although they do spend $49 billion for clothing, shoes, and other apparel items.

The low-end market

Households with incomes under $30,000 spend less than average on clothes. In the lowest income group, apparel spending is fully 60 percent below the norm. Spending by households in the $10,000 to $20,000 income group is 36 percent below average. But both of these groups spend more than the average household at the laundromat.

Households with incomes of $20,000 to $30,000 spend just 9 percent less than the average household on clothing. For selected items, like girls' coats and jackets, men's and boys' sleepwear, and clothing rentals, their spending is well above average.

The high-end market

Households with incomes of $30,000 or more spend more than average on men's, women's and children's clothing, shoes, and related clothing products and services. In the $30,000 to $40,000 income group, households spend about 25 percent more than average on women's and girls' clothes and some 7 to 8 percent more than average on men's and boy's clothes. This group spends the most on women's pants and active sportswear, boys' underwear, and babies' outerwear.

Below-average spending on apparel is the norm for lower-income households.

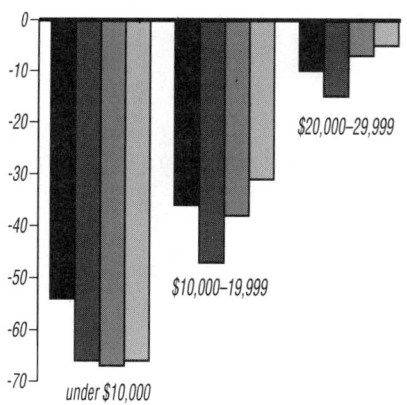

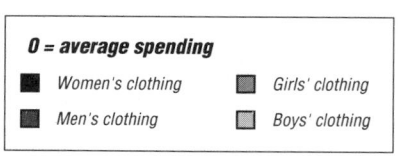

0 = average spending	
■ Women's clothing	■ Girls' clothing
■ Men's clothing	☐ Boys' clothing

Spending on women's clothing is 52 percent above average among households with incomes of $40,000 to $50,000. They spend nearly 80 percent more than the average household on girls' clothes and 60 percent more than the norm on men's, boy's, and babies' clothing. This group also spends more than any other on shoes. But there are a few items, like adult nightwear and boy's underwear, for which this group's spending is below average.

With their average spending amounting to nearly $1,000 a year, households in the $50,000 plus income group spend more than twice the average on clothing. They spend more than twice the average amount on women's suits, dresses and skirts, and three times the average on men's suits and sports coats. Their spending is below average only on boys' nightwear and trips to the laundromat.

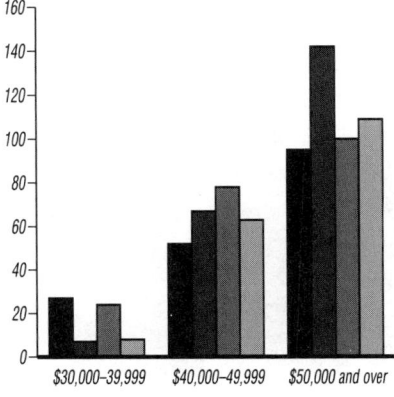

With incomes of $30,000 or more, high-end households spend above average on apparel.

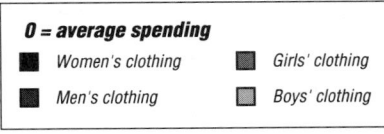

0 = average spending
- ■ Women's clothing
- ■ Men's clothing
- ■ Girls' clothing
- ■ Boys' clothing

Average expenditures

(consumer units include complete income reporters only)	all cu's	under $10,000	$10,000 to $19,999	$20,000 to $29,999	$30,000 to $39,999	$40,000 to $49,999	$50,000 and over
Number of consumer units (in thousands)	81,354	18,809	17,652	14,586	10,901	7,198	12,209
Average number of persons per cu	2.6	1.8	2.3	2.7	2.9	3.2	3.1
Average number of earners per cu	1.4	0.7	1.0	1.5	1.8	2.0	2.1
TOTAL AVERAGE ANNUAL EXPENDITURES	$26,389.07	$11,269.43	$18,078.25	$24,896.36	$31,659.60	$37,562.00	$52,320.19
APPAREL AND APPAREL SERVICES, AVERAGE ANNUAL EXPENDITURES	$1,537.27	$615.68	$979.03	$1,406.15	$1,847.24	$2,396.00	$3,154.03
WOMEN'S APPAREL	**$509.83**	**$233.53**	**$325.74**	**$458.04**	**$648.56**	**$773.35**	**$992.62**
Coats and jackets	33.49	18.95	11.23	21.91	41.71	80.18	66.72
Dresses	83.27	50.74	51.51	65.67	81.62	111.38	185.83
Suits, sportcoats, and tailored jackets	28.88	10.36	12.23	24.07	36.63	34.99	76.52
Sweaters and vests	36.74	13.01	29.19	42.26	35.17	62.71	63.75
Shirts, blouses, and tops	85.55	41.94	60.78	72.57	113.40	126.51	156.36
Skirts	29.28	11.17	18.07	25.37	22.72	59.17	65.45
Pants	66.85	32.27	41.62	64.99	108.85	94.87	107.29
Shorts and shorts sets	14.23	4.81	10.93	11.30	21.45	27.91	22.87
Active sportswear	23.13	6.87	13.19	24.37	46.07	37.59	33.33
Sleepwear	22.57	7.88	18.38	23.09	28.70	16.87	49.94
Undergarments	24.38	11.25	18.44	21.01	35.71	28.83	45.68
Hosiery	25.85	11.49	19.68	25.51	32.18	34.56	46.47
Accessories	34.46	12.76	20.46	32.04	43.27	54.45	72.36
GIRLS' APPAREL	**$99.08**	**$33.12**	**$61.16**	**$92.41**	**$122.63**	**$176.67**	**$197.71**
Coats and jackets	7.95	3.65	4.28	10.81	8.51	12.90	13.03
Dresses and suits	12.02	4.34	8.16	10.60	14.15	20.78	24.03
Shirts, blouses, and sweaters	30.19	10.30	13.27	28.93	36.40	55.73	67.22
Skirts, pants, shorts and short sets	22.78	8.30	17.00	23.06	31.02	36.73	37.53
Active sportswear	9.32	1.90	6.59	6.23	9.77	22.73	19.94
Underwear and sleepwear	5.92	2.01	4.64	5.32	8.10	8.51	11.05
Hosiery	4.88	1.66	3.41	3.94	7.41	11.90	6.67
Accessories	4.08	0.61	3.34	2.18	3.59	5.04	12.81
MEN'S APPAREL	**$318.80**	**$108.30**	**$170.08**	**$271.44**	**$340.48**	**$533.15**	**$772.68**
Suits	41.20	8.38	14.64	30.69	36.93	63.99	133.12
Sportcoats	15.57	2.33	4.51	7.90	17.97	25.65	53.04
Coats and jackets	29.30	8.11	9.78	22.27	26.54	54.07	86.61
Underwear	9.72	4.92	9.29	7.71	13.05	10.40	17.16
Hosiery	10.34	3.45	8.81	9.30	11.24	20.53	17.50
Nightwear	2.89	0.98	1.11	4.49	4.01	1.80	6.37
Accessories	22.88	9.07	12.32	15.23	20.45	47.19	56.32
Sweaters and vests	17.65	6.40	7.09	13.16	18.88	25.26	50.07
Active sportswear	12.10	4.63	5.20	11.75	13.46	18.24	29.10

Average annual expenditures for apparel and apparel services, by total before-tax income of consumer unit.

(continued from previous page)	all cu's	under $10,000	$10,000 to $19,999	$20,000 to $29,999	$30,000 to $39,999	$40,000 to $49,999	$50,000 and over
Shirts	74.17	28.98	50.13	68.02	88.29	133.41	139.09
Pants, shorts, and short sets	79.05	29.35	44.65	78.24	84.72	125.83	175.97
Uniforms	3.16	1.37	1.99	2.05	4.00	6.58	6.18
BOYS' APPAREL	**$81.86**	**$27.54**	**$56.58**	**$78.09**	**$88.56**	**$133.33**	**$171.25**
Coats and jackets	9.48	3.15	7.18	10.54	5.87	10.64	23.83
Sweaters	3.73	1.74	2.30	2.37	5.37	3.86	8.97
Shirts	20.55	6.13	13.14	15.76	26.30	45.42	39.42
Underwear	1.55	-	0.70	1.61	4.81	1.15	2.25
Nightwear	2.79	1.10	1.70	4.28	3.30	6.20	2.71
Hosiery	3.99	1.77	4.16	4.63	3.97	2.81	7.29
Accessories	2.77	1.34	0.95	1.61	1.39	6.89	7.66
Suits, sportcoats, and vests	3.00	-	1.17	2.93	1.45	11.49	6.29
Pants, shorts, and shorts sets	28.61	10.69	22.46	30.20	29.30	34.07	60.01
Uniforms and active sportswear	5.10	1.16	2.64	3.84	6.38	10.48	11.92
BABIES' APPAREL	**$63.60**	**$26.44**	**$40.95**	**$68.75**	**$96.77**	**$104.17**	**$95.15**
Coats, jackets, and snowsuits	3.17	1.52	2.10	2.70	5.66	3.78	5.18
Outerwear including dresses	14.98	5.11	10.37	16.35	20.21	21.64	26.63
Underwear	36.68	16.51	23.59	40.50	58.19	65.47	47.23
Nightwear	3.19	1.14	1.76	3.93	4.80	4.48	5.32
Accessories and hosiery	3.47	1.45	1.77	3.71	5.09	5.59	6.13
FOOTWEAR	**$204.13**	**$96.65**	**$171.24**	**$203.00**	**$253.61**	**$332.12**	**$299.98**
Women's	104.54	58.00	86.33	97.66	124.35	156.11	162.71
Girls'	18.46	5.48	14.04	10.56	20.33	52.31	31.94
Men's	62.95	23.03	57.77	78.61	78.10	109.06	72.77
Boys'	18.19	10.14	13.11	16.18	30.82	14.64	32.55
OTHER APPAREL PRODUCTS/SERVICES	**$259.97**	**$90.09**	**$153.28**	**$234.41**	**$296.64**	**$343.22**	**$624.63**
Fabric, patterns, and notions for making clothes	10.27	4.47	7.24	11.32	11.01	13.74	19.58
Watches	21.65	7.10	14.44	17.82	29.45	32.67	45.59
Jewelry	110.35	16.39	51.39	94.40	127.09	153.93	318.74
Shoe repair and other shoe services	3.46	1.34	1.64	3.19	4.34	4.75	8.11
Watch and jewelry repair services	5.72	1.38	2.86	5.51	8.94	10.91	10.88
Coin-operated laundry and dry cleaning	34.25	38.99	45.08	41.09	28.11	27.33	12.67
Professional laundry, dry cleaning, and storage	63.47	16.59	25.30	48.60	75.46	88.10	183.42
Apparel alteration and repair services	6.05	2.53	2.94	4.69	6.48	6.95	16.68
Clothing rental	4.77	1.31	2.39	7.80	5.77	4.83	8.96

Note: Women and men include all persons aged 16 and older, girls and boys are aged 2 to 15, and babies are under age 2. Expenditures are not given (-) when the amount is too small to be reliable. Expenditures listed for a given category may not add to the total for that category because the listing is incomplete. "Men's apparel," for example, includes "other clothing," which is omitted here. Total expenditure exceeds total income in some income categories due to a number of factors including the underreporting of income, borrowing, and the use of savings. Numbers may not add to total due to rounding.

Share of spending

Percent of total average annual expenditures spent on apparel and apparel services, by total before-tax income of consumer unit.

(consumer units include complete income reporters only)	all cu's	under $10,000	$10,000 to $19,999	$20,000 to $29,999	$30,000 to $39,999	$40,000 to $49,999	$50,000 and over
Number of consumer units (in thousands)	81,354	18,809	17,652	14,586	10,901	7,198	12,209
Average number of persons per cu	2.6	1.8	2.3	2.7	2.9	3.2	3.1
Average number of earners per cu	1.4	0.7	1.0	1.5	1.8	2.0	2.1
TOTAL AVERAGE ANNUAL EXPENDITURES	100.00%	100.00%	100.00%	100.00%	100.00%	100.00%	100.00%
APPAREL AND APPAREL SERVICES,							
AVERAGE ANNUAL EXPENDITURES	5.83%	5.46%	5.42%	5.65%	5.83%	6.38%	6.03%
WOMEN'S APPAREL	**1.93%**	**2.07%**	**1.80%**	**1.84%**	**2.05%**	**2.06%**	**1.90%**
Coats and jackets	0.13	0.17	0.06	0.09	0.13	0.21	0.13
Dresses	0.32	0.45	0.28	0.26	0.26	0.30	0.36
Suits, sportcoats, and tailored jackets	0.11	0.09	0.07	0.10	0.12	0.09	0.15
Sweaters and vests	0.14	0.12	0.16	0.17	0.11	0.17	0.12
Shirts, blouses, and tops	0.32	0.37	0.34	0.29	0.36	0.34	0.30
Skirts	0.11	0.10	0.10	0.10	0.07	0.16	0.13
Pants	0.25	0.29	0.23	0.26	0.34	0.25	0.21
Shorts and shorts sets	0.05	0.04	0.06	0.05	0.07	0.07	0.04
Active sportswear	0.09	0.06	0.07	0.10	0.15	0.10	0.06
Sleepwear	0.09	0.07	0.10	0.09	0.09	0.04	0.10
Undergarments	0.09	0.10	0.10	0.08	0.11	0.08	0.09
Hosiery	0.10	0.10	0.11	0.10	0.10	0.09	0.09
Accessories	0.13	0.11	0.11	0.13	0.14	0.14	0.14
GIRLS' APPAREL	**0.38%**	**0.29%**	**0.34%**	**0.37%**	**0.39%**	**0.47%**	**0.38%**
Coats and jackets	0.03	0.03	0.02	0.04	0.03	0.03	0.02
Dresses and suits	0.05	0.04	0.05	0.04	0.04	0.06	0.05
Shirts, blouses, and sweaters	0.11	0.09	0.07	0.12	0.11	0.15	0.13
Skirts, pants, shorts and short sets	0.09	0.07	0.09	0.09	0.10	0.10	0.07
Active sportswear	0.04	0.02	0.04	0.03	0.03	0.06	0.04
Underwear and sleepwear	0.02	0.02	0.03	0.02	0.03	0.02	0.02
Hosiery	0.02	0.01	0.02	0.02	0.02	0.03	0.01
Accessories	0.02	0.01	0.02	0.01	0.01	0.01	0.02
MEN'S APPAREL	**1.21%**	**0.96%**	**0.94%**	**1.09%**	**1.08%**	**1.42%**	**1.48%**
Suits	0.16	0.07	0.08	0.12	0.12	0.17	0.25
Sportcoats	0.06	0.02	0.02	0.03	0.06	0.07	0.10
Coats and jackets	0.11	0.07	0.05	0.09	0.08	0.14	0.17
Underwear	0.04	0.04	0.05	0.03	0.04	0.03	0.03
Hosiery	0.04	0.03	0.05	0.04	0.04	0.05	0.03
Nightwear	0.01	0.01	0.01	0.02	0.01	0.00	0.01
Accessories	0.09	0.08	0.07	0.06	0.06	0.13	0.11
Sweaters and vests	0.07	0.06	0.04	0.05	0.06	0.07	0.10
Active sportswear	0.05	0.04	0.03	0.05	0.04	0.05	0.06

Percent of total average annual expenditures spent on apparel and apparel services, by total before-tax income of consumer unit.

(continued from previous page)	all cu's	under $10,000	$10,000 to $19,999	$20,000 to $29,999	$30,000 to $39,999	$40,000 to $49,999	$50,000 and over
Shirts	0.28	0.26	0.28	0.27	0.28	0.36	0.27
Pants, short, and short sets	0.30	0.26	0.25	0.31	0.27	0.33	0.34
Uniforms	0.01	0.01	0.01	0.01	0.01	0.02	0.01
BOYS' APPAREL	**0.31%**	**0.24%**	**0.31%**	**0.31%**	**0.28%**	**0.35%**	**0.33%**
Coats and jackets	0.04	0.03	0.04	0.04	0.02	0.03	0.05
Sweaters	0.01	0.02	0.01	0.01	0.02	0.01	0.02
Shirts	0.08	0.05	0.07	0.06	0.08	0.12	0.08
Underwear	0.01	-	0.00	0.01	0.02	0.00	0.00
Nightwear	0.01	0.01	0.01	0.02	0.01	0.02	0.01
Hosiery	0.02	0.02	0.02	0.02	0.01	0.01	0.01
Accessories	0.01	0.01	0.01	0.01	0.00	0.02	0.01
Suits, sportcoats, and vests	0.01	-	0.01	0.01	0.00	0.03	0.01
Pants, shorts, and shorts sets	0.11	0.09	0.12	0.12	0.09	0.09	0.11
Uniforms and active sportswear	0.02	0.01	0.01	0.02	0.02	0.03	0.02
BABIES' APPAREL	**0.24%**	**0.23%**	**0.23%**	**0.28%**	**0.31%**	**0.28%**	**0.18%**
Coats, jackets, and snowsuits	0.01	0.01	0.01	0.01	0.02	0.01	0.01
Outerwear including dresses	0.06	0.05	0.06	0.07	0.06	0.06	0.05
Underwear	0.14	0.15	0.13	0.16	0.18	0.17	0.09
Nightwear	0.01	0.01	0.01	0.02	0.02	0.01	0.01
Accessories and hosiery	0.01	0.01	0.01	0.01	0.02	0.01	0.01
FOOTWEAR	**0.77%**	**0.86%**	**0.95%**	**0.82%**	**0.80%**	**0.88%**	**0.57%**
Women's	0.40	0.51	0.48	0.39	0.39	0.42	0.31
Girls'	0.07	0.05	0.08	0.04	0.06	0.14	0.06
Men's	0.24	0.20	0.32	0.32	0.25	0.29	0.14
Boys'	0.07	0.09	0.07	0.06	0.10	0.04	0.06
OTHER APPAREL PRODUCTS/SERVICES	**0.99%**	**0.80%**	**0.85%**	**0.94%**	**0.94%**	**0.91%**	**1.19%**
Fabric, patterns, and notions for making clothes	0.04	0.04	0.04	0.05	0.03	0.04	0.04
Watches	0.08	0.06	0.08	0.07	0.09	0.09	0.09
Jewelry	0.42	0.15	0.28	0.38	0.40	0.41	0.61
Shoe repair and other shoe services	0.01	0.01	0.01	0.01	0.01	0.01	0.02
Watch and jewelry repair services	0.02	0.01	0.02	0.02	0.03	0.03	0.02
Coin-operated laundry and dry cleaning	0.13	0.35	0.25	0.17	0.09	0.07	0.02
Professional laundry, dry cleaning, and storage	0.24	0.15	0.14	0.20	0.24	0.23	0.35
Apparel alteration and repair services	0.02	0.02	0.02	0.02	0.02	0.02	0.03
Clothing rental	0.02	0.01	0.01	0.03	0.02	0.01	0.02

Note: Women and men include all persons aged 16 and older, girls and boys are aged 2 to 15, and babies are under age 2. Expenditures are not given (-) when the amount is too small to be reliable. Expenditures listed for a given category may not add to the total for that category because the listing is incomplete. "Men's apparel," for example, includes "other clothing," which is omitted here. Numbers may not add to total due to rounding.

Indexed expenditures

Indexed average annual expenditures for apparel and apparel services, by total before-tax income of consumer unit.

(consumer units include complete income reporters only)	all cu's	under $10,000	$10,000 to $19,999	$20,000 to $29,999	$30,000 to $39,999	$40,000 to $49,999	$50,000 and over
Number of consumer units (in thousands)	81,354	18,809	17,652	14,586	10,901	7,198	12,209
Average number of persons per cu	2.6	1.8	2.3	2.7	2.9	3.2	3.1
Average number of earners per cu	1.4	0.7	1.0	1.5	1.8	2.0	2.1
TOTAL AVERAGE ANNUAL EXPENDITURES	100	43	69	94	120	142	198
APPAREL AND APPAREL SERVICES,							
AVERAGE ANNUAL EXPENDITURES	100	40	64	91	120	156	205
WOMEN'S APPAREL	**100**	**46**	**64**	**90**	**127**	**152**	**195**
Coats and jackets	100	57	34	65	125	239	199
Dresses	100	61	62	79	98	134	223
Suits, sportcoats, and tailored jackets	100	36	42	83	127	121	265
Sweaters and vests	100	35	79	115	96	171	174
Shirts, blouses, and tops	100	49	71	85	133	148	183
Skirts	100	38	62	87	78	202	224
Pants	100	48	62	97	163	142	160
Shorts and shorts sets	100	34	77	79	151	196	161
Active sportswear	100	30	57	105	199	163	144
Sleepwear	100	35	81	102	127	75	221
Undergarments	100	46	76	86	146	118	187
Hosiery	100	44	76	99	124	134	180
Accessories	100	37	59	93	126	158	210
GIRLS' APPAREL	**100**	**33**	**62**	**93**	**124**	**178**	**200**
Coats and jackets	100	46	54	136	107	162	164
Dresses and suits	100	36	68	88	118	173	200
Shirts, blouses, and sweaters	100	34	44	96	121	185	223
Skirts, pants, shorts and short sets	100	36	75	101	136	161	165
Active sportswear	100	20	71	67	105	244	214
Underwear and sleepwear	100	34	78	90	137	144	187
Hosiery	100	34	70	81	152	244	137
Accessories	100	15	82	53	88	124	314
MEN'S APPAREL	**100**	**34**	**53**	**85**	**107**	**167**	**242**
Suits	100	20	36	74	90	155	323
Sportcoats	100	15	29	51	115	165	341
Coats and jackets	100	28	33	76	91	185	296
Underwear	100	51	96	79	134	107	177
Hosiery	100	33	85	90	109	199	169
Nightwear	100	34	38	155	139	62	220
Accessories	100	40	54	67	89	206	246
Sweaters and vests	100	36	40	75	107	143	284
Active sportswear	100	38	43	97	111	151	241

Indexed average annual expenditures for apparel and apparel services, by total before-tax income of consumer unit.

(continued from previous page)	all cu's	under $10,000	$10,000 to $19,999	$20,000 to $29,999	$30,000 to $39,999	$40,000 to $49,999	$50,000 and over
Shirts	100	39	68	92	119	180	188
Pants, shorts, and short sets	100	37	56	99	107	159	223
Uniforms	100	43	63	65	127	208	196
BOYS' APPAREL	**100**	**34**	**69**	**95**	**108**	**163**	**209**
Coats and jackets	100	33	76	111	62	112	251
Sweaters	100	47	62	64	144	103	240
Shirts	100	30	64	77	128	221	192
Underwear	100	-	45	104	310	74	145
Nightwear	100	40	61	153	118	222	97
Hosiery	100	44	104	116	99	70	183
Accessories	100	49	34	58	50	249	277
Suits, sportcoats, and vests	100	-	39	98	48	383	210
Pants, shorts, and shorts sets	100	37	79	106	102	119	210
Uniforms and active sportswear	100	23	52	75	125	205	234
BABIES' APPAREL	**100**	**42**	**64**	**108**	**152**	**164**	**150**
Coats, jackets, and snowsuits	100	48	66	85	179	119	163
Outerwear including dresses	100	34	69	109	135	144	178
Underwear	100	45	64	110	159	178	129
Nightwear	100	36	55	123	150	140	167
Accessories and hosiery	100	42	51	107	147	161	177
FOOTWEAR	**100**	**47**	**84**	**99**	**124**	**163**	**147**
Women's	100	55	83	93	119	149	156
Girls'	100	30	76	57	110	283	173
Men's	100	37	92	125	124	173	116
Boys'	100	56	72	89	169	80	179
OTHER APPAREL PRODUCTS/SERVICES	**100**	**35**	**59**	**90**	**114**	**132**	**240**
Fabric, patterns, and notions for making clothes	100	43	70	110	107	134	191
Watches	100	33	67	82	136	151	211
Jewelry	100	15	47	86	115	139	289
Shoe repair and other shoe services	100	39	47	92	125	137	234
Watch and jewelry repair services	100	24	50	96	156	191	190
Coin-operated laundry and dry cleaning	100	114	132	120	82	80	37
Professional laundry, dry cleaning, and storage	100	26	40	77	119	139	289
Apparel alteration and repair services	100	42	49	78	107	115	276
Clothing rental	100	27	50	164	121	101	188

Note: Women and men include all persons aged 16 and older, girls and boys are aged 2 to 15, and babies are under age 2. Expenditures are not given (-) when the amount is too small to be reliable. An index of 100 represents the average for all consumer units. An index of 132 means that the average for the subgroup is 32 percent above the average for all consumer units. An index of 68 indicates spending that is 32 percent below the overall average.

Aggregate expenditures, 1988

Aggregate expenditures in 1988 for apparel and apparel services, by total before-tax income of consumer unit.

(consumer units include complete income reporters only)	all cu's	under $10,000	$10,000 to $19,999	$20,000 to $29,999	$30,000 to $39,999	$40,000 to $49,999	$50,000 and over
Number of consumer units (in thousands)	81,354	18,809	17,652	14,586	10,901	7,198	12,209
Average number of persons per cu	2.6	1.8	2.3	2.7	2.9	3.2	3.1
Average number of earners per cu	1.4	0.7	1.0	1.5	1.8	2.0	2.1
TOTAL AGGREGATE EXPENDITURES (in millions)	$2,148,492	$211,967	$319,117	$363,138	$345,121	$270,371	$638,777
APPAREL AND APPAREL SERVICES, AGGREGATE EXPENDITURES (in millions)	$125,263	$11,580	$17,282	$20,510	$20,137	$17,246	$38,508
WOMEN'S APPAREL	$41,579	$4,393	$5,750	$6,681	$7,070	$5,567	$12,119
Coats and jackets	2,721	356	198	320	455	577	815
Dresses	6,782	954	909	958	890	802	2,269
Suits, sportcoats, and tailored jackets	2,347	195	216	351	399	252	934
Sweaters and vests	2,989	245	515	616	383	451	778
Shirts, blouses, and tops	6,976	789	1,073	1,059	1,236	911	1,909
Skirts	2,372	210	319	370	248	426	799
Pants	5,469	607	735	948	1,187	683	1,310
Shorts and shorts sets	1,162	90	193	165	234	201	279
Active sportswear	1,897	129	233	355	502	271	407
Sleepwear	1,853	148	324	337	313	121	610
Undergarments	1,998	212	326	306	389	208	558
Hosiery	2,103	216	347	372	351	249	567
Accessories	2,816	240	361	467	472	392	883
GIRLS' APPAREL	$8,073	$623	$1,080	$1,348	$1,337	$1,272	$2,414
Coats and jackets	647	69	76	158	93	93	159
Dresses and suits	978	82	144	155	154	150	293
Shirts, blouses, and sweaters	2,469	194	234	422	397	401	821
Skirts, pants, shorts and short sets	1,853	156	300	336	338	264	458
Active sportswear	757	36	116	91	107	164	243
Underwear and sleepwear	482	38	82	78	88	61	135
Hosiery	397	31	60	57	81	86	81
Accessories	334	11	59	32	39	36	156
MEN'S APPAREL	$25,981	$2,037	$3,002	$3,959	$3,712	$3,838	$9,434
Suits	3,352	158	258	448	403	461	1,625
Sportcoats	1,267	44	80	115	196	185	648
Coats and jackets	2,386	153	173	325	289	389	1,057
Underwear	796	93	164	112	142	75	210
Hosiery	840	65	156	136	123	148	214
Nightwear	238	18	20	65	44	13	78
Accessories	1,860	171	217	222	223	340	688
Sweaters and vests	1,436	120	125	192	206	182	611
Active sportswear	984	87	92	171	147	131	356

Aggregate expenditures in 1988 for apparel and apparel services, by total before-tax income of consumer unit.

(continued from previous page)	all cu's	under $10,000	$10,000 to $19,999	$20,000 to $29,999	$30,000 to $39,999	$40,000 to $49,999	$50,000 and over
Shirts	6,043	545	885	992	962	960	1,698
Pants, shorts, and short sets	6,459	552	788	1,141	924	906	2,148
Uniforms	257	26	35	30	44	47	75
BOYS' APPAREL	**$6,672**	**$518**	**$999**	**$1,139**	**$965**	**$960**	**$2,091**
Coats and jackets	771	59	127	154	64	77	291
Sweaters	304	33	41	35	59	28	110
Shirts	1,672	115	232	230	287	327	481
Underwear	124	-	12	23	52	8	27
Nightwear	227	21	30	62	36	45	33
Hosiery	327	33	73	68	43	20	89
Accessories	224	25	17	23	15	50	94
Suits, sportcoats, and vests	239	-	21	43	16	83	77
Pants, shorts, and shorts sets	2,335	201	397	440	319	245	733
Uniforms and active sportswear	415	22	47	56	70	75	146
BABIES' APPAREL	**$5,189**	**$497**	**$723**	**$1,003**	**$1,055**	**$750**	**$1,162**
Coats, jackets, and snowsuits	257	29	37	39	62	27	63
Outerwear including dresses	1,219	96	183	238	220	156	325
Underwear	3,000	311	416	591	634	471	577
Nightwear	259	21	31	57	52	32	65
Accessories and hosiery	283	27	31	54	55	40	75
FOOTWEAR	**$16,619**	**$1,818**	**$3,023**	**$2,961**	**$2,765**	**$2,391**	**$3,662**
Women's	8,505	1,091	1,524	1,424	1,356	1,124	1,987
Girls'	1,493	103	248	154	222	377	390
Men's	5,124	433	1,020	1,147	851	785	888
Boys'	1,497	191	231	236	336	105	397
OTHER APPAREL PRODUCTS/SERVICES	**$21,150**	**$1,695**	**$2,706**	**$3,419**	**$3,234**	**$2,470**	**$7,626**
Fabric, patterns, and notions for making clothes	835	84	128	165	120	99	239
Watches	1,761	134	255	260	321	235	557
Jewelry	8,977	308	907	1,377	1,385	1,108	3,891
Shoe repair and other shoe services	281	25	29	47	47	34	99
Watch and jewelry repair services	466	26	51	80	97	79	133
Coin-operated laundry and dry cleaning	2,786	733	796	599	306	197	155
Professional laundry, dry cleaning, and storage	5,164	312	447	709	823	634	2,239
Apparel alteration and repair services	492	48	52	68	71	50	204
Clothing rental	388	25	42	114	63	35	109

Note: Women and men include all persons aged 16 and older, girls and boys are aged 2 to 15, and babies are under age 2. Expenditures are not given (-) when the amount is too small to be reliable. Expenditures listed for a given category may not add to the total for that category because the listing is incomplete. "Men's apparel," for example, includes "other clothing," which is omitted here. Numbers may not add to total due to rounding. The "all cu's" aggregates will differ slightly from table to table because they are the sums of the aggregates in each row.

PART III
Spending by type of household for apparel and apparel services

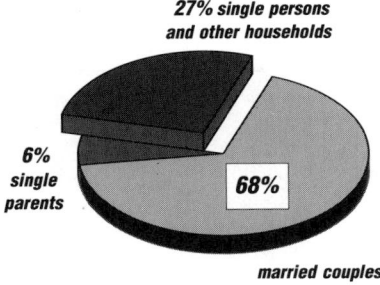

Married couples account for more than two-thirds of the apparel market.

27% single persons and other households

6% single parents

68% married couples

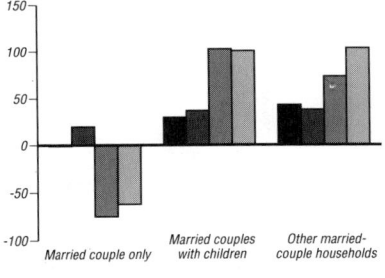

Childless couples and empty-nesters spend far below average on children's clothes...

Married couple only / Married couples with children / Other married-couple households

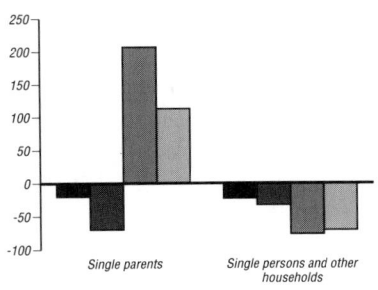

...while single parents spend far above average on children's clothes.

Single parents / Single persons and other households

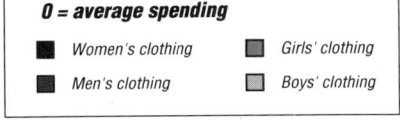

0 = average spending

- ■ Women's clothing
- ■ Men's clothing
- ■ Girls' clothing
- ■ Boys' clothing

Married couples typically spend much more than the average on household products and services while everyone else spends much less than average. Single parents, however, outspend married couples (even those with children) on children's clothing and shoes.

Overall, single parents spend 7 percent less than the average household on clothing, accessories, and clothing-related services—20 percent less than average on women's clothing and 70 percent less on men's clothing. But they spend more than three times the average amount on girls' clothes and more than twice the average amount on boys' clothes. Single parents spend more than other types of households at the laundromat and their clothing rental bills are 54 percent above average.

Single-person and "other" households* spend less than average on all clothing items except men's shoes and laundromats. Overall, their spending on clothing is 32 percent below average. Married couples spend 23 percent more than the average on clothing. They spend less than the average on just one item, laundromats.

The 52 million married-couple households spent more than $95 billion on clothing, accessories, and clothing-related services in 1988, accounting for 68 percent of the market. Single-person and "other" households accounted for another 27 percent of the market, spending $38 billion. Single parents spent just $8 billion—6 percent of the apparel market.

Married couples without children at home spend more than average on men's clothing and accessories. Couples with preschoolers spend 473 percent more on baby clothes than the average household, and they spend above average amounts on women's sportswear, men's and boys' clothing, children's shoes. Their overall clothing expenditures are 18 percent above average.

Married couples with school-aged children spend well above average amounts on clothing and accessories for all family members. Above-average spending among married couples with children aged 18 or older is concentrated in the women's and men's wear categories. These households are also the peak spenders on jewelry, jewelry repairs, shoe repairs, and clothing rentals. Couples who live with extended family members or unrelated people spend the most on clothes—fully 55 percent more than average. They are big buyers of clothing for adults, children, and babies. They also spend more than the other types of households on shoes.

In this analysis, single-person households are grouped with "other" households. "Other" households are unrelated people living together and families that are not married-couple or single-parent families, such as siblings. Single-person households account for 72 percent of the households in this category.

Average expenditures

	all cu's	married couples	single parents	single persons and other cu's
Number of consumer units (in thousands)	94,862	52,010	5,716	37,136
Average number of persons per cu	2.6	3.3	2.9	1.5
Average number of earners per cu	1.4	1.7	1.0	0.9
Average total before-tax income	$28,540.00	$37,229.00	$16,276.00	$18,509.00
TOTAL AVERAGE ANNUAL EXPENDITURES	$25,891.85	$32,314.50	$18,615.80	$17,950.80
APPAREL AND APPAREL SERVICES, AVERAGE ANNUAL EXPENDITURES	$1,489.09	$1,828.95	$1,383.12	$1,019.19
WOMEN'S APPAREL	**$491.84**	**$582.21**	**$392.60**	**$376.67**
Coats and jackets	32.32	40.19	17.86	23.15
Dresses	80.87	98.77	76.60	55.66
Suits, sportcoats, and tailored jackets	30.51	35.01	19.75	25.85
Sweaters and vests	35.68	42.56	16.38	28.68
Shirts, blouses, and tops	80.01	90.43	70.38	66.41
Skirts	27.10	32.92	9.87	21.30
Pants	62.87	70.54	83.15	48.72
Shorts and shorts sets	12.85	17.03	15.87	6.35
Active sportswear	23.62	30.40	11.26	15.72
Sleepwear	21.29	23.79	8.02	19.70
Undergarments	25.28	30.67	11.52	19.60
Hosiery	25.32	27.87	30.35	20.98
Accessories	33.09	40.42	21.02	24.35
GIRLS' APPAREL	**$94.86**	**$124.93**	**$291.02**	**$22.26**
Coats and jackets	7.88	10.23	20.75	2.61
Dresses and suits	12.12	16.66	23.55	3.99
Shirts, blouses, and sweaters	27.34	33.37	121.44	4.33
Skirts, pants, shorts and short sets	22.49	30.33	58.04	6.02
Active sportswear	8.58	11.91	23.25	1.52
Underwear and sleepwear	5.69	7.68	13.94	1.64
Hosiery	4.40	6.03	14.82	-
Accessories	4.30	5.70	9.83	1.45
MEN'S APPAREL	**$310.52**	**$404.57**	**$94.57**	**$208.86**
Suits	44.25	59.27	7.38	28.88
Sportcoats	16.80	21.44	1.94	12.58
Coats and jackets	25.85	38.78	2.55	10.71
Underwear	9.71	11.91	5.69	7.14
Hosiery	9.52	12.15	3.49	6.64
Nightwear	2.88	3.13	2.51	2.57
Accessories	22.38	29.35	3.36	15.19
Sweaters and vests	18.44	23.05	9.31	13.39
Active sportswear	11.97	14.77	3.39	9.37

Average annual expenditures for apparel and apparel services, by type of consumer unit.

(continued from previous page)

	all cu's	married couples	single parents	single persons and other cu's
Shirts	71.20	89.75	14.94	52.96
Pants, short, and short sets	73.89	96.05	39.04	47.16
Uniforms	2.92	3.90	0.90	1.86
BOYS' APPAREL	**$77.02**	**$105.80**	**$163.84**	**$22.42**
Coats and jackets	8.12	11.60	10.25	2.78
Sweaters	3.86	5.31	9.97	0.88
Shirts	19.64	26.50	51.73	4.86
Underwear	1.59	2.34	3.33	-
Nightwear	2.68	3.55	2.63	1.44
Hosiery	3.74	5.39	8.75	0.60
Accessories	2.64	4.02	4.68	-
Suits, sportcoats, and vests	2.92	4.79	0.76	0.55
Pants, shorts, and shorts sets	26.34	28.59	60.22	8.53
Uniforms and active sportswear	5.22	7.74	8.38	1.21
BABIES' APPAREL	**$62.38**	**$92.18**	**$63.69**	**$19.69**
Coats, jackets, and snowsuits	3.46	4.98	2.21	1.52
Outerwear including dresses	15.09	21.60	8.34	6.99
Underwear	34.95	52.61	48.03	7.47
Nightwear	3.24	4.58	1.42	1.65
Accessories and hosiery	3.54	4.67	1.89	1.16
FOOTWEAR	**$195.67**	**$223.30**	**$191.48**	**$156.40**
Women's	95.79	104.72	87.70	84.11
Girls'	16.99	24.04	44.89	2.57
Men's	66.00	71.27	17.41	65.78
Boys'	16.89	23.26	41.49	3.94
OTHER APPAREL PRODUCTS/SERVICES	**$256.81**	**$295.97**	**$185.92**	**$212.89**
Fabric, patterns, and notions for making clothes	9.79	13.34	6.86	5.29
Watches	21.83	25.51	21.25	16.77
Jewelry	107.96	134.47	43.60	80.73
Shoe repair and other shoe services	3.32	3.98	2.20	2.56
Watch and jewelry repair	5.49	7.02	2.12	3.86
Coin-operated laundry and dry cleaning	33.34	23.60	60.95	42.72
Professional laundry, dry cleaning, and storage	64.55	75.36	40.13	53.18
Apparel alteration and repair services	6.08	6.84	1.96	5.65
Clothing rental	4.45	5.84	6.84	2.14

Note: Women and men include all persons aged 16 and older, girls and boys are aged 2 to 15, and babies are under age 2. Expenditures are not given (-) when the amount is too small to be reliable. Expenditures listed for a given category may not add to the total for that category because the listing is incomplete. "Men's apparel," for example, includes "other clothing," which is omitted here. Numbers may not add to total due to rounding. "Single parents" is one-parent consumer units with a child or children under age 18 living at home. "Other cu's" includes persons living with unrelated persons and families other than married-couple and single-parent families.

Share of spending

	all cu's	married couples	single parents	single persons and other cu's
Percent of total average annual expenditures spent on apparel and apparel services, by type of consumer unit.				
Number of consumer units (in thousands)	94,862	52,010	5,716	37,136
Average number of persons per cu	2.6	3.3	2.9	1.5
Average total before-tax income	$28,540	$37,229	$16,276	$18,509
TOTAL AVERAGE ANNUAL EXPENDITURES	100.00%	100.00%	100.00%	100.00%
APPAREL AND APPAREL SERVICES, ANNUAL AVERAGE EXPENDITURES	5.75%	5.66%	7.43%	5.68%
WOMEN'S APPAREL	**1.90%**	**1.80%**	**2.11%**	**2.10%**
Coats and jackets	0.12	0.12	0.10	0.13
Dresses	0.31	0.31	0.41	0.31
Suits, sportcoats, and tailored jackets	0.12	0.11	0.11	0.14
Sweaters and vests	0.14	0.13	0.09	0.16
Shirts, blouses, and tops	0.31	0.28	0.38	0.37
Skirts	0.10	0.10	0.05	0.12
Pants	0.24	0.22	0.45	0.27
Shorts and shorts sets	0.05	0.05	0.09	0.04
Active sportswear	0.09	0.09	0.06	0.09
Sleepwear	0.08	0.07	0.04	0.11
Undergarments	0.10	0.09	0.06	0.11
Hosiery	0.10	0.09	0.16	0.12
Accesories	0.13	0.13	0.11	0.14
GIRLS' APPAREL	**0.37%**	**0.39%**	**1.56%**	**0.12%**
Coats and jackets	0.03	0.03	0.11	0.01
Dresses and suits	0.05	0.05	0.13	0.02
Shirts, blouses, and sweaters	0.11	0.10	0.65	0.02
Skirts, pants, shorts and short sets	0.09	0.09	0.31	0.03
Active sportswear	0.03	0.04	0.12	0.01
Underwear and sleepwear	0.02	0.02	0.07	0.01
Hosiery	0.02	0.02	0.08	-
Accessories	0.02	0.02	0.05	0.01
MEN'S APPAREL	**1.20%**	**1.25%**	**0.51%**	**1.16%**
Suits	0.17	0.18	0.04	0.16
Sportscoats	0.06	0.07	0.01	0.07
Coats and jackets	0.10	0.12	0.01	0.06
Underwear	0.04	0.04	0.03	0.04
Hosiery	0.04	0.04	0.02	0.04
Nightwear	0.01	0.01	0.01	0.01
Accessories	0.09	0.09	0.02	0.08
Sweaters and vests	0.07	0.07	0.05	0.07
Active sportswear	0.05	0.05	0.02	0.05

Percent of total average annual expenditures spent on apparel and apparel services, by type of consumer unit.

(continued from previous page)	all cu's	married couples	single parents	single persons and other cu's
Shirts	0.27	0.28	0.08	0.30
Pants, short, and short sets	0.29	0.30	0.21	0.26
Uniforms	0.01	0.01	0.00	0.01
BOYS' APPAREL	**0.30%**	**0.33%**	**0.88%**	**0.12%**
Coats and jackets	0.03	0.04	0.06	0.02
Sweaters	0.01	0.02	0.05	0.00
Shirts	0.08	0.08	0.28	0.03
Underwear	0.01	0.01	0.02	-
Nightwear	0.01	0.01	0.01	0.01
Hosiery	0.01	0.02	0.05	0.00
Accessories	0.01	0.01	0.03	-
Suits, sportcoats, and vests	0.01	0.01	0.00	0.00
Pants, shorts, and shorts sets	0.10	0.09	0.32	0.05
Uniforms and active sportswear	0.02	0.02	0.05	0.01
BABIES' APPAREL	**0.24%**	**0.29%**	**0.34%**	**0.11%**
Coats, jackets, and snowsuits	0.01	0.02	0.01	0.01
Outerwear including dresses	0.06	0.07	0.04	0.04
Underwear	0.13	0.16	0.26	0.04
Nightwear	0.01	0.01	0.01	0.01
Accessories and hosiery	0.01	0.01	0.01	0.01
FOOTWEAR	**0.76%**	**0.69%**	**1.03%**	**0.87%**
Women's	0.37	0.32	0.47	0.47
Girls'	0.07	0.07	0.24	0.01
Men's	0.25	0.22	0.09	0.37
Boys'	0.07	0.07	0.22	0.02
OTHER APPAREL PRODUCTS/SERVICES	**0.99%**	**0.92%**	**1.00%**	**1.19%**
Fabric, patterns, and notions for making clothes	0.04	0.04	0.04	0.03
Watches	0.08	0.08	0.11	0.09
Jewelry	0.42	0.42	0.23	0.45
Shoe repair and other shoe services	0.01	0.01	0.01	0.01
Watch and jewelry repair services	0.02	0.02	0.01	0.02
Coin-operated laundry and dry cleaning	0.13	0.07	0.33	0.24
Professional laundry, dry cleaning, and storage	0.25	0.23	0.22	0.30
Apparel alteration and repair services	0.02	0.02	0.01	0.03
Clothing rental	0.02	0.02	0.04	0.01

Note: Women and men include all persons aged 16 and older, girls and boys are aged 2 to 15, and babies are under age 2. Expenditures are not given (-) when the amount is too small to be reliable. Expenditures listed for a given category may not add to the total for that category because the listing is incomplete. "Men's apparel," for example, includes "other clothing," which is omitted here. Numbers may not add to total due to rounding. "Single parents" is one-parent consumer units with a child or children under age 18 living at home. "Other cu's" includes persons living with unrelated persons and families other than married-couple and single-parent families.

Indexed expenditures

	all cu's	married couples	single parents	single persons and other cu's
Number of consumer units (in thousands)	94,862	52,010	5,716	37,136
Average number of persons per cu	2.6	3.3	2.9	1.5
Average number of earners per cu	1.4	1.7	1.0	0.9
Average total before-tax income	$28,540	$37,229	$16,276	$18,509
TOTAL AVERAGE ANNUAL EXPENDITURES	100	125	72	69
APPAREL AND APPAREL SERVICES, AVERAGE ANNUAL EXPENDITURES	100	123	93	68
WOMEN'S APPAREL	**100**	**118**	**80**	**77**
Coats and jackets	100	124	55	72
Dresses	100	122	95	69
Suits, sportcoats, and tailored jackets	100	115	65	85
Sweaters and vests	100	119	46	80
Shirts, blouses, and tops	100	113	88	83
Skirts	100	121	36	79
Pants	100	112	132	77
Shorts and shorts sets	100	133	124	49
Active sportswear	100	129	48	67
Sleepwear	100	112	38	93
Undergarments	100	121	46	78
Hosiery	100	110	120	83
Accessories	100	122	64	74
GIRLS' APPAREL	**100**	**132**	**307**	**23**
Coats and jackets	100	130	263	33
Dresses and suits	100	137	194	33
Shirts, blouses, and sweaters	100	122	444	16
Skirts, pants, shorts and short sets	100	135	258	27
Active sportswear	100	139	271	18
Underwear and sleepwear	100	135	245	29
Hosiery	100	137	337	-
Accessories	100	133	229	34
MEN'S APPAREL	**100**	**130**	**30**	**67**
Suits	100	134	17	65
Sportcoats	100	128	12	75
Coats and jackets	100	150	10	41
Underwear	100	123	59	74
Hosiery	100	128	37	70
Nightwear	100	109	87	89
Accessories	100	131	15	68
Sweaters and vests	100	125	50	73
Active sportswear	100	123	28	78

Indexed average annual expenditures for apparel and apparel services, by type of consumer unit.

(continued from previous page)

	all cu's	married couples	single parents	single persons and other cu's
Shirts	100	126	21	74
Pants, short, and short sets	100	130	53	64
Uniforms	100	134	31	64
BOYS' APPAREL	**100**	**137**	**213**	**29**
Coats and jackets	100	143	126	34
Sweaters	100	138	258	23
Shirts	100	135	263	25
Underwear	100	147	209	-
Nightwear	100	132	98	54
Hosiery	100	144	234	16
Accessories	100	152	177	-
Suits, sportcoats, and vests	100	164	26	19
Pants, shorts, and shorts sets	100	109	229	32
Uniforms and active sportswear	100	148	161	23
BABIES' APPAREL	**100**	**148**	**102**	**32**
Coats, jackets, and snowsuits	100	144	64	44
Outerwear including dresses	100	143	55	46
Underwear	100	151	137	21
Nightwear	100	141	44	51
Accessories and hosiery	100	132	53	33
FOOTWEAR	**100**	**114**	**98**	**80**
Women's	100	109	92	88
Girls'	100	141	264	15
Men's	100	108	26	100
Boys'	100	138	246	23
OTHER APPAREL PRODUCTS/SERVICES	**100**	**115**	**72**	**83**
Fabric, patterns, and notions for making clothes	100	136	70	54
Watches	100	117	97	77
Jewelry	100	125	40	75
Shoe repair and other shoe services	100	120	66	77
Watch and jewelry repair	100	128	39	70
Coin-operated laundry and dry cleaning	100	71	183	128
Professional laundry, dry cleaning, and storage	100	117	62	82
Apparel alteration and repair services	100	113	32	93
Clothing rental	100	131	154	48

Note: An index of 100 represents the average for all consumer units. An index of 132 means that the average for the subgroup is 32 percent above the average for all consumer units. An index of 68 indicates spending that is 32 percent below the overall average. Women and men include all persons aged 16 and older, girls and boys are aged 2 to 15, and babies are under age 2. Expenditures are not given (-) when the amount is too small to be reliable. "Single parents" is one-parent consumer units with a child or children under age 18 living at home. "Other cu's" includes persons living with unrelated persons and families other than married-couple and single-parent families.

Aggregate expenditures, 1988

Aggregate expenditures in 1988 for apparel and apparel services, by type of consumer unit.

	all cu's	married couples	single parents	single persons and other cu's
Number of consumer units (in thousands)	94,862	52,010	5,716	37,136
Average number of persons per cu	2.6	3.3	2.9	1.5
Average number of earners per cu	1.4	1.7	1.0	0.9
Aggregate before-tax income (in millions)	$2,716,664	$1,936,280	$93,034	$687,350
TOTAL AGGREGATE EXPENDITURES (in millions)	$2,453,706	$1,680,677	$106,408	$666,621
APPAREL AND APPAREL SERVICES,				
AGGREGATE EXPENDITURES (in millions)	$140,878	$95,124	$7,906	$37,849
WOMEN'S APPAREL	**$46,513**	**$30,281**	**$2,244**	**$13,988**
Coats and jackets	3,052	2,090	102	860
Dresses	7,642	5,137	438	2,067
Suits, sportcoats, and tailored jackets	2,894	1,821	113	960
Sweaters and vests	3,372	2,214	94	1,065
Shirts, blouses, and tops	7,572	4,703	402	2,466
Skirts	2,560	1,712	56	791
Pants	5,953	3,669	475	1,809
Shorts and shorts sets	1,212	886	91	236
Active sportswear	2,229	1,581	64	584
Sleepwear	2,015	1,237	46	732
Undergarments	2,389	1,595	66	728
Hosiery	2,402	1,450	173	779
Accessories	3,127	2,102	120	904
GIRLS' APPAREL	**$8,988**	**$6,498**	**$1,663**	**$827**
Coats and jackets	748	532	119	97
Dresses and suits	1,149	866	135	148
Shirts, blouses, and sweaters	2,591	1,736	694	161
Skirts, pants, shorts and short sets	2,133	1,577	332	224
Active sportswear	809	619	133	56
Underwear and sleepwear	540	399	80	61
Hosiery	399	314	85	-
Accessories	406	296	56	54
MEN'S APPAREL	**$29,338**	**$21,042**	**$541**	**$7,756**
Suits	4,197	3,083	42	1,072
Sportcoats	1,593	1,115	11	467
Coats and jackets	2,429	2,017	15	398
Underwear	917	619	33	265
Hosiery	898	632	20	247
Nightwear	273	163	14	95
Accessories	2,110	1,526	19	564
Sweaters and vests	1,749	1,199	53	497
Active sportswear	1,136	768	19	348

Aggregate expenditures in 1988 for apparel and apparel services, by type of consumer unit.

(continued from previous page)

	all cu's	married couples	single parents	single persons and other cu's
Shirts	6,720	4,668	85	1,967
Pants, short, and short sets	6,970	4,996	223	1,751
Uniforms	277	203	5	69
BOYS' APPAREL	**$7,272**	**$5,503**	**$937**	**$833**
Coats and jackets	765	603	59	103
Sweaters	366	276	57	33
Shirts	1,854	1,378	296	180
Underwear	141	122	19	-
Nightwear	253	185	15	53
Hosiery	353	280	50	22
Accessories	236	209	27	-
Suits, sportcoats, and vests	274	249	4	20
Pants, shorts, and shorts sets	2,148	1,487	344	317
Uniforms and active sportswear	495	403	48	45
BABIES' APPAREL	**$5,890**	**$4,794**	**$364**	**$731**
Coats, jackets, and snowsuits	328	259	13	56
Outerwear including dresses	1,431	1,123	48	260
Underwear	3,288	2,736	275	277
Nightwear	308	238	8	61
Accessories and hosiery	297	243	11	43
FOOTWEAR	**$18,516**	**$11,614**	**$1,094**	**$5,808**
Women's	9,071	5,446	501	3,124
Girls'	1,602	1,250	257	95
Men's	6,249	3,707	100	2,443
Boys'	1,593	1,210	237	146
OTHER APPAREL PRODUCTS/SERVICES	**$24,362**	**$15,393**	**$1,063**	**$7,906**
Fabric, patterns, and notions for making clothes	929	694	39	196
Watches	2,071	1,327	121	623
Jewelry	10,241	6,994	249	2,998
Shoe repair and other shoe services	315	207	13	95
Watch and jewelry repair	521	365	12	143
Coin-operated laundry and dry cleaning	3,162	1,227	348	1,586
Professional laundry, dry cleaning, and storage	6,124	3,919	229	1,975
Apparel alteration and repair services	577	356	11	210
Clothing rental	422	304	39	79

Note: Women and men include all persons aged 16 and older, girls and boys are aged 2 to 15, and babies are under age 2. Expenditures are not given (-) when the amount is too small to be reliable. Expenditures listed for a given category may not add to the total for that category because the listing is incomplete. "Men's apparel," for example, includes "other clothing," which is omitted here. Numbers may not add to total due to rounding. "Single parents" is one-parent consumer units with a child or children under age 18 living at home. "Other cu's" includes persons living with unrelated persons and families other than married-couple and single-parent families. The "all cu's" aggregates will differ slightly from table to table because they are the sums of the aggregates in each row.

Average expenditures

	all cu's	all married couples	married couple only	all married couples with children	AGE OF OLDEST CHILD under 6	AGE OF OLDEST CHILD 6 to 17	AGE OF OLDEST CHILD 18 or older	other married couples
Number of consumer units (in thousands)	94,862	52,010	20,227	28,100	5,858	14,194	8,047	3,684
Average number of persons per cu	2.6	3.3	2.0	3.9	3.5	4.1	3.9	5.1
Average number of earners per cu	1.4	1.7	1.2	2.1	1.7	1.9	2.7	2.4
Average total before-tax income	$28,540.00	$37,229.00	$33,825.00	$39,354.00	$34,318.00	$38,039.00	$45,596.00	$40,846.00
TOTAL AVERAGE ANNUAL EXPENDITURES	$25,891.85	$32,314.50	$27,954.50	$35,015.30	$30,942.80	$35,248.40	$37,763.90	$35,739.60
APPAREL AND APPAREL SERVICES, AVERAGE ANNUAL EXPENDITURES	$1,489.09	$1,828.95	$1,395.08	$2,082.94	$1,764.14	$2,181.98	$2,170.88	$2,300.69
WOMEN'S APPAREL	**$491.84**	**$582.21**	**$485.95**	**$636.97**	**$480.88**	**$636.04**	**$779.97**	**$702.02**
Coats and jackets	32.32	40.19	35.21	41.47	40.27	39.70	46.09	58.76
Dresses	80.87	98.77	80.73	109.76	75.40	112.27	136.17	115.31
Suits, sportcoats, and tailored jackets	30.51	35.01	40.85	30.01	31.29	27.18	34.03	41.52
Sweaters and vests	35.68	42.56	40.37	40.28	31.94	33.64	61.09	73.49
Shirts, blouses, and tops	80.01	90.43	67.12	102.85	63.77	105.09	134.10	126.13
Skirts	27.10	32.92	22.61	39.61	28.64	36.49	55.84	39.20
Pants	62.87	70.54	55.45	77.76	80.17	78.55	73.99	100.29
Shorts and shorts sets	12.85	17.03	10.85	20.99	19.86	23.81	16.42	21.18
Active sportswear	23.62	30.40	25.62	33.63	18.11	44.73	25.74	32.23
Sleepwear	21.29	23.79	19.86	28.23	20.54	23.22	45.22	11.00
Undergarments	25.28	30.67	25.40	35.33	15.92	30.64	62.39	23.80
Hosiery	25.32	27.87	26.64	28.68	25.82	26.63	34.38	28.51
Accessories	33.09	40.42	34.03	46.26	29.13	51.99	50.52	30.57
GIRLS' APPAREL	**$94.86**	**$124.93**	**$23.48**	**$193.01**	**$82.89**	**$305.23**	**$74.44**	**$163.87**
Coats and jackets	7.88	10.23	1.76	15.64	8.13	24.69	5.15	15.40
Dresses and suits	12.12	16.66	3.26	23.81	15.76	36.01	8.15	35.76
Shirts, blouses, and sweaters	27.34	33.37	7.56	51.31	16.14	80.36	25.71	39.35
Skirts, pants, shorts and short sets	22.49	30.33	3.89	47.94	17.76	80.14	13.09	41.22
Active sportswear	8.58	11.91	2.60	19.64	5.82	30.80	10.08	4.03
Underwear and sleepwear	5.69	7.68	1.47	11.58	6.06	18.32	3.71	11.98
Hosiery	4.40	6.03	0.66	9.81	6.52	14.21	4.06	6.84
Accessories	4.30	5.70	1.97	8.43	5.94	12.80	2.01	5.42
MEN'S APPAREL	**$310.52**	**$404.57**	**$372.62**	**$424.55**	**$317.55**	**$395.85**	**$570.37**	**$429.13**
Suits	44.25	59.27	57.40	60.35	44.17	56.60	78.76	61.25
Sportcoats	16.80	21.44	18.61	22.82	15.97	22.00	29.25	26.45
Coats and jackets	25.85	38.78	49.79	31.30	25.04	38.35	23.02	34.88
Underwear	9.71	11.91	10.96	12.58	6.50	12.87	17.55	11.98
Hosiery	9.52	12.15	11.18	12.78	9.02	14.83	12.15	12.75
Nightwear	2.88	3.13	4.74	1.89	1.38	2.70	0.78	3.68
Accessories	22.38	29.35	36.88	24.78	17.42	24.00	33.05	22.35
Sweaters and vests	18.44	23.05	18.47	26.50	17.72	22.00	40.83	21.93
Active sportswear	11.97	14.77	14.17	15.38	12.78	13.79	20.08	13.37

Average annual expenditures for apparel and apparel services, by married couples with and without children.

(continued from previous page)	all cu's	all married couples	married couple only	all married couples with children	AGE OF OLDEST CHILD			other married couples
					under 6	6 to 17	18 or older	
Shirts	71.20	89.75	64.35	107.14	63.22	97.69	166.03	97.74
Pants, short, and short sets	73.89	96.05	81.70	103.92	100.91	85.30	143.68	116.17
Uniforms	2.92	3.90	3.59	4.10	2.50	4.90	3.86	4.05
BOYS' APPAREL	**$77.02**	**$105.80**	**$29.07**	**$154.84**	**$110.80**	**$211.70**	**$82.20**	**$157.19**
Coats and jackets	8.12	11.60	2.05	17.24	5.38	28.23	6.23	21.79
Sweaters	3.86	5.31	1.41	7.66	3.23	10.99	4.99	8.80
Shirts	19.64	26.50	9.37	36.53	27.12	50.33	17.69	45.48
Underwear	1.59	2.34	-	3.28	4.71	4.11	-	6.98
Nightwear	2.68	3.55	-	5.35	10.73	4.48	2.16	6.94
Hosiery	3.74	5.39	1.55	8.13	6.67	10.27	5.20	5.69
Accessories	2.64	4.02	1.40	5.43	2.89	8.90	0.87	7.93
Suits, sportcoats, and vests	2.92	4.79	1.69	6.81	5.85	8.74	3.86	6.59
Pants, shorts, and shorts sets	26.34	28.59	7.10	43.88	32.13	55.81	30.89	30.75
Uniforms and active sportswear	5.22	7.74	2.08	11.56	4.70	17.76	5.61	9.64
BABIES' APPAREL	**$62.38**	**$92.18**	**$34.09**	**$127.51**	**$357.47**	**$69.98**	**$41.83**	**$143.86**
Coats, jackets, and snowsuits	3.46	4.98	2.72	5.68	19.29	2.00	2.28	12.02
Outerwear including dresses	15.09	21.60	14.40	24.55	63.61	13.23	16.08	38.79
Underwear	34.95	52.61	9.88	81.16	230.54	45.59	15.43	71.57
Nightwear	3.24	4.58	2.88	5.48	13.86	3.09	3.60	6.96
Accessories and hosiery	3.54	4.67	2.79	5.58	15.77	2.69	3.26	8.10
FOOTWEAR	**$195.67**	**$223.30**	**$165.85**	**$247.35**	**$158.74**	**$273.96**	**$275.38**	**$363.96**
Women's	95.79	104.72	92.19	101.38	68.89	105.21	123.45	204.32
Girls'	16.99	24.04	3.53	37.41	41.31	49.25	10.31	35.95
Men's	66.00	71.27	65.14	74.51	23.01	76.96	116.69	80.81
Boys'	16.89	23.26	4.99	34.04	25.54	42.54	24.93	42.88
OTHER APPAREL PRODUCTS/SVCS.	**$256.81**	**$295.97**	**$284.02**	**$298.71**	**$255.82**	**$289.21**	**$346.69**	**$340.67**
Fabric, patterns, notions for making clothes	9.79	13.34	13.94	12.98	10.72	13.09	14.45	12.76
Watches	21.83	25.51	17.40	29.19	28.95	30.44	27.15	41.98
Jewelry	107.96	134.47	139.67	127.55	99.51	114.99	170.11	158.80
Shoe repair and other shoe services	3.32	3.98	3.86	4.21	3.64	3.83	5.28	2.93
Watch and jewelry repair	5.49	7.02	6.64	7.79	4.11	9.11	8.14	3.20
Coin-operated laundry and dry cleaning	33.34	23.60	19.87	24.26	36.20	26.90	10.93	39.08
Professional laundry, dry cleaning, storage	64:55	75.36	72.18	78.46	63.58	78.12	89.90	69.06
Apparel alteration and repair services	6.08	6.84	6.89	7.02	5.20	6.98	8.41	5.19
Clothing rental	4.45	5.84	3.56	7.25	3.91	5.74	12.32	7.67

Note: Women and men include all persons aged 16 and older, girls and boys are aged 2 to 15, and babies are under age 2. Expenditures are not given (-) when the amount is too small to be reliable. Expenditures listed for a given category may not add to the total for that category because the listing is incomplete. "Men's apparel," for example, includes "other clothing," which is omitted here. Numbers may not add to total due to rounding. Other married couples include extended family members or unrelated persons in addition to the married couple.

Share of spending

	all cu's	all married couples	married couple only	all married couples with children	AGE OF OLDEST CHILD			other married couples
					under 6	6 to 17	18 or older	
Number of consumer units (in thousands)	94,862	52,010	20,227	28,100	5,858	14,194	8,047	3,684
Average number of persons per cu	2.6	3.3	2.0	3.9	3.5	4.1	3.9	5.1
Average number of earners per cu	1.4	1.7	1.2	2.1	1.7	1.9	2.7	2.4
Average total before-tax income	$28,540	$37,229	$33,825	$39,354	$34,318	$38,039	$45,596	$40,846
TOTAL AVERAGE ANNUAL EXPENDITURES	100.00%	100.00%	100.00%	100.00%	100.00%	100.00%	100.00%	100.00%
APPAREL AND APPAREL SERVICES, AVERAGE ANNUAL EXPENDITURES	5.75%	5.66%	4.99%	5.95%	5.70%	6.19%	5.75%	6.44%
WOMEN'S APPAREL	**1.90%**	**1.80%**	**1.74%**	**1.82%**	**1.55%**	**1.80%**	**2.07%**	**1.96%**
Coats and jackets	0.12	0.12	0.13	0.12	0.13	0.11	0.12	0.16
Dresses	0.31	0.31	0.29	0.31	0.24	0.32	0.36	0.32
Suits, sportcoats, and tailored jackets	0.12	0.11	0.15	0.09	0.10	0.08	0.09	0.12
Sweaters and vests	0.14	0.13	0.14	0.12	0.10	0.10	0.16	0.21
Shirts, blouses, and tops	0.31	0.28	0.24	0.29	0.21	0.30	0.36	0.35
Skirts	0.10	0.10	0.08	0.11	0.09	0.10	0.15	0.11
Pants	0.24	0.22	0.20	0.22	0.26	0.22	0.20	0.28
Shorts and shorts sets	0.05	0.05	0.04	0.06	0.06	0.07	0.04	0.06
Active sportswear	0.09	0.09	0.09	0.10	0.06	0.13	0.07	0.09
Sleepwear	0.08	0.07	0.07	0.08	0.07	0.07	0.12	0.03
Undergarments	0.10	0.09	0.09	0.10	0.05	0.09	0.17	0.07
Hosiery	0.10	0.09	0.10	0.08	0.08	0.08	0.09	0.08
Accessories	0.13	0.13	0.12	0.13	0.09	0.15	0.13	0.09
GIRLS' APPAREL	**0.37%**	**0.39%**	**0.08%**	**0.55%**	**0.27%**	**0.87%**	**0.20%**	**0.46%**
Coats and jackets	0.03	0.03	0.01	0.04	0.03	0.07	0.01	0.04
Dresses and suits	0.05	0.05	0.01	0.07	0.05	0.10	0.02	0.10
Shirts, blouses, and sweaters	0.11	0.10	0.03	0.15	0.05	0.23	0.07	0.11
Skirts, pants, shorts and short sets	0.09	0.09	0.01	0.14	0.06	0.23	0.03	0.12
Active sportswear	0.03	0.04	0.01	0.06	0.02	0.09	0.03	0.01
Underwear and sleepwear	0.02	0.02	0.01	0.03	0.02	0.05	0.01	0.03
Hosiery	0.02	0.02	0.00	0.03	0.02	0.04	0.01	0.02
Accessories	0.02	0.02	0.01	0.02	0.02	0.04	0.01	0.02
MEN'S APPAREL	**1.20%**	**1.25%**	**1.33%**	**1.21%**	**1.03%**	**1.12%**	**1.51%**	**1.20%**
Suits	0.17	0.18	0.21	0.17	0.14	0.16	0.21	0.17
Sportcoats	0.06	0.07	0.07	0.07	0.05	0.06	0.08	0.07
Coats and jackets	0.10	0.12	0.18	0.09	0.08	0.11	0.06	0.10
Underwear	0.04	0.04	0.04	0.04	0.02	0.04	0.05	0.03
Hosiery	0.04	0.04	0.04	0.04	0.03	0.04	0.03	0.04
Nightwear	0.01	0.01	0.02	0.01	0.00	0.01	0.00	0.01
Accessories	0.09	0.09	0.13	0.07	0.06	0.07	0.09	0.06
Sweaters and vests	0.07	0.07	0.07	0.08	0.06	0.06	0.11	0.06
Active sportswear	0.05	0.05	0.05	0.04	0.04	0.04	0.05	0.04

Percent of total average annual expenditures spent on apparel and apparel services, by married couples with and without children.

(continued from previous page)	all cu's	all married couples	married couple only	all married couples with children	AGE OF OLDEST CHILD			other married couples
					under 6	6 to 17	18 or older	
Shirts	0.27	0.28	0.23	0.31	0.20	0.28	0.44	0.27
Pants, short, and short sets	0.29	0.30	0.29	0.30	0.33	0.24	0.38	0.33
Uniforms	0.01	0.01	0.01	0.01	0.01	0.01	0.01	0.01
BOYS' APPAREL	**0.30%**	**0.33%**	**0.10%**	**0.44%**	**0.36%**	**0.60%**	**0.22%**	**0.44%**
Coats and jackets........................	0.03	0.04	0.01	0.05	0.02	0.08	0.02	0.06
Sweaters	0.01	0.02	0.01	0.02	0.01	0.03	0.01	0.02
Shirts	0.08	0.08	0.03	0.10	0.09	0.14	0.05	0.13
Underwear	0.01	0.01	-	0.01	0.02	0.01	-	0.02
Nightwear	0.01	0.01	-	0.02	0.03	0.01	0.01	0.02
Hosiery	0.01	0.02	0.01	0.02	0.02	0.03	0.01	0.02
Accessories	0.01	0.01	0.01	0.02	0.01	0.03	0.00	0.02
Suits, sportcoats, and vests............................	0.01	0.01	0.01	0.02	0.02	0.02	0.01	0.02
Pants, shorts, and shorts sets	0.10	0.09	0.03	0.13	0.10	0.16	0.08	0.09
Uniforms and active sportswear	0.02	0.02	0.01	0.03	0.02	0.05	0.01	0.03
BABIES' APPAREL	**0.24%**	**0.29%**	**0.12%**	**0.36%**	**1.16%**	**0.20%**	**0.11%**	**0.40%**
Coats, jackets, and snowsuits	0.01	0.02	0.01	0.02	0.06	0.01	0.01	0.03
Outerwear including dresses	0.06	0.07	0.05	0.07	0.21	0.04	0.04	0.11
Underwear	0.13	0.16	0.04	0.23	0.75	0.13	0.04	0.20
Nightwear	0.01	0.01	0.01	0.02	0.04	0.01	0.01	0.02
Accessories and hosiery	0.01	0.01	0.01	0.02	0.05	0.01	0.01	0.02
FOOTWEAR	**0.76%**	**0.69%**	**0.59%**	**0.71%**	**0.51%**	**0.78%**	**0.73%**	**1.02%**
Women's	0.37	0.32	0.33	0.29	0.22	0.30	0.33	0.57
Girls'	0.07	0.07	0.01	0.11	0.13	0.14	0.03	0.10
Men's	0.25	0.22	0.23	0.21	0.07	0.22	0.31	0.23
Boys'	0.07	0.07	0.02	0.10	0.08	0.12	0.07	0.12
OTHER APPAREL PRODUCTS/SVCS.	**0.99%**	**0.92%**	**1.02%**	**0.85%**	**0.83%**	**0.82%**	**0.92%**	**0.95%**
Fabric, patterns, notions for making clothes	0.04	0.04	0.05	0.04	0.03	0.04	0.04	0.04
Watches	0.08	0.08	0.06	0.08	0.09	0.09	0.07	0.12
Jewelry	0.42	0.42	0.50	0.36	0.32	0.33	0.45	0.44
Shoe repair and other shoe services	0.01	0.01	0.01	0.01	0.01	0.01	0.01	0.01
Watch and jewelry repair	0.02	0.02	0.02	0.02	0.01	0.03	0.02	0.01
Coin-operated laundry and dry cleaning	0.13	0.07	0.07	0.07	0.12	0.08	0.03	0.11
Professional laundry, dry cleaning, storage	0.25	0.23	0.26	0.22	0.21	0.22	0.24	0.19
Apparel alteration and repair services	0.02	0.02	0.02	0.02	0.02	0.02	0.02	0.01
Clothing rental	0.02	0.02	0.01	0.02	0.01	0.02	0.03	0.02

Note: Women and men include all persons aged 16 and older, girls and boys are aged 2 to 15, and babies are under age 2. Expenditures are not given (-) when the amount is too small to be reliable. Expenditures listed for a given category may not add to the total for that category because the listing is incomplete. "Men's apparel," for example, includes "other clothing," which is omitted here. Numbers may not add to total due to rounding. Other married couples include extended family members or unrelated persons in addition to the married couple.

Indexed expenditures

	all cu's	all married couples	married couple only	all married couples with children	AGE OF OLDEST CHILD under 6	AGE OF OLDEST CHILD 6 to 17	AGE OF OLDEST CHILD 18 or older	other married couples
Number of consumer units (in thousands)	94,862	52,010	20,227	28,100	5,858	14,194	8,047	3,684
Average number of persons per cu	2.6	3.3	2.0	3.9	3.5	4.1	3.9	5.1
Average number of earners per cu	1.4	1.7	1.2	2.1	1.7	1.9	2.7	2.4
Average total before-tax income	$28,540	$37,229	$33,825	$39,354	$34,318	$38,039	$45,596	$40,846
TOTAL AVERAGE ANNUAL EXPENDITURES	100	125	108	135	120	136	146	138
APPAREL AND APPAREL SERVICES, AVERAGE ANNUAL EXPENDITURES	100	123	94	140	118	147	146	155
WOMEN'S APPAREL	100	118	99	130	98	129	159	143
Coats and jackets	100	124	109	128	125	123	143	182
Dresses	100	122	100	136	93	139	168	143
Suits, sportcoats, and tailored jackets	100	115	134	98	103	89	112	136
Sweaters and vests	100	119	113	113	90	94	171	206
Shirts, blouses, and tops	100	113	84	129	80	131	168	158
Skirts	100	121	83	146	106	135	206	145
Pants	100	112	88	124	128	125	118	160
Shorts and shorts sets	100	133	84	163	155	185	128	165
Active sportswear	100	129	108	142	77	189	109	136
Sleepwear	100	112	93	133	96	109	212	52
Undergarments	100	121	100	140	63	121	247	94
Hosiery	100	110	105	113	102	105	136	113
Accessories	100	122	103	140	88	157	153	92
GIRLS' APPAREL	100	132	25	203	87	322	78	173
Coats and jackets	100	130	22	198	103	313	65	195
Dresses and suits	100	137	27	196	130	297	67	295
Shirts, blouses, and sweaters	100	122	28	188	59	294	94	144
Skirts, pants, shorts and short sets	100	135	17	213	79	356	58	183
Active sportswear	100	139	30	229	68	359	117	47
Underwear and sleepwear	100	135	26	204	107	322	65	211
Hosiery	100	137	15	223	148	323	92	155
Accessories	100	133	46	196	138	298	47	126
MEN'S APPAREL	100	130	120	137	102	127	184	138
Suits	100	134	130	136	100	128	178	138
Sportcoats	100	128	111	136	95	131	174	157
Coats and jackets	100	150	193	121	97	148	89	135
Underwear	100	123	113	130	67	133	181	123
Hosiery	100	128	117	134	95	156	128	134
Nightwear	100	109	165	66	48	94	27	128
Accessories	100	131	165	111	78	107	148	100
Sweaters and vests	100	125	100	144	96	119	221	119
Active sportswear	100	123	118	128	107	115	168	112

Indexed average annual expenditures for apparel and apparel services, by married couples with and without children.

(continued from previous page)

	all cu's	all married couples	married couple only	all married couples with children	AGE OF OLDEST CHILD			other married couples
					under 6	6 to 17	18 or older	
Shirts	100	126	90	150	89	137	233	137
Pants, short, and short sets	100	130	111	141	137	115	194	157
Uniforms	100	134	123	140	86	168	132	139
BOYS' APPAREL	**100**	**137**	**38**	**201**	**144**	**275**	**107**	**204**
Coats and jackets	100	143	25	212	66	348	77	268
Sweaters	100	138	37	198	84	285	129	228
Shirts	100	135	48	186	138	256	90	232
Underwear	100	147	-	206	296	258	-	439
Nightwear	100	132	-	200	400	167	81	259
Hosiery	100	144	41	217	178	275	139	152
Accessories	100	152	53	206	109	337	33	300
Suits, sportcoats, and vests	100	164	58	233	200	299	132	226
Pants, shorts, and shorts sets	100	109	27	167	122	212	117	117
Uniforms and active sportswear	100	148	40	221	90	340	107	185
BABIES' APPAREL	**100**	**148**	**55**	**204**	**573**	**112**	**67**	**231**
Coats, jackets, and snowsuits	100	144	79	164	558	58	66	347
Outerwear including dresses	100	143	95	163	422	88	107	257
Underwear	100	151	28	232	660	130	44	205
Nightwear	100	141	89	169	428	95	111	215
Accessories and hosiery	100	132	79	158	445	76	92	229
FOOTWEAR	**100**	**114**	**85**	**126**	**81**	**140**	**141**	**186**
Women's	100	109	96	106	72	110	129	213
Girls'	100	141	21	220	243	290	61	212
Men's	100	108	99	113	35	117	177	122
Boys'	100	138	30	202	151	252	148	254
OTHER APPAREL PRODUCTS/SVCS.	**100**	**115**	**111**	**116**	**100**	**113**	**135**	**133**
Fabric, patterns, notions for making clothes	100	136	142	133	109	134	148	130
Watches	100	117	80	134	133	139	124	192
Jewelry	100	125	129	118	92	107	158	147
Shoe repair and other shoe services	100	120	116	127	110	115	159	88
Watch and jewelry repair	100	128	121	142	75	166	148	58
Coin-operated laundry and dry cleaning	100	71	60	73	109	81	33	117
Professional laundry, dry cleaning, storage	100	117	112	122	98	121	139	107
Apparel alteration and repair services	100	113	113	115	86	115	138	85
Clothing rental	100	131	80	163	88	129	277	172

Note: An index of 100 represents the average for all consumer units. An index of 132 means that the average for the subgroup is 32 percent above the average for all consumer units. An index of 68 indicates spending that is 32 percent below the overall average. Women and men include all persons aged 16 and older, girls and boys are aged 2 to 15, and babies are under age 2. Expenditures are not given (-) when the amount is too small to be reliable. Numbers may not add to total due to rounding. Other married couples include extended family members or unrelated persons in addition to the married couple.

Aggregate expenditures, 1988

Aggregate expenditures in 1988 for apparel and apparel services, by married couples with and without children.

	all cu's	all married couples	married couple only	all married couples with children	AGE OF OLDEST CHILD			other married couples
					under 6	6 to 17	18 or older	
Number of consumer units (in thousands)	94,862	52,010	20,227	28,100	5,858	14,194	8,047	3,684
Average number of persons per cu	2.6	3.3	2.0	3.9	3.5	4.1	3.9	5.1
Average number of earners per cu	1.4	1.7	1.2	2.1	1.7	1.9	2.7	2.4
Aggregate before-tax income (in millions)	$2,722,910	$1,942,526	$684,178	$1,107,871	$201,035	$539,926	$366,911	$150,477
TOTAL AGGREG. EXPENDITURES (in millions)	$2,455,594	$1,682,565	$565,436	$985,465	$181,263	$500,316	$303,886	$131,665
APPAREL AND APPAREL SERVICES, AGGREGATE EXPENDITURES (in millions)	$141,223	$95,468	$28,218	$58,774	$10,334	$30,971	$17,469	$8,476
WOMEN'S APPAREL	**$46,769**	**$30,537**	**$9,829**	**$18,121**	**$2,817**	**$9,028**	**$6,276**	**$2,586**
Coats and jackets	3,061	2,099	712	1,170	236	564	371	216
Dresses	7,694	5,189	1,633	3,131	442	1,594	1,096	425
Suits, sportcoats, and tailored jackets	2,895	1,822	826	843	183	386	274	153
Sweaters and vests	3,402	2,243	817	1,156	187	477	492	271
Shirts, blouses, and tops	7,635	4,767	1,358	2,944	374	1,492	1,079	465
Skirts	2,584	1,737	457	1,135	168	518	449	144
Pants	5,956	3,671	1,122	2,180	470	1,115	595	369
Shorts and shorts sets	1,210	884	219	586	116	338	132	78
Active sportswear	2,233	1,585	518	948	106	635	207	119
Sleepwear	2,033	1,256	402	814	120	330	364	41
Undergarments	2,425	1,632	514	1,030	93	435	502	88
Hosiery	2,402	1,450	539	806	151	378	277	105
Accessories	3,140	2,116	688	1,315	171	738	407	113
GIRLS' APPAREL	**$8,986**	**$6,496**	**$475**	**$5,417**	**$486**	**$4,332**	**$599**	**$604**
Coats and jackets	747	532	36	440	48	350	41	57
Dresses and suits	1,149	867	66	669	92	511	66	132
Shirts, blouses, and sweaters	2,595	1,740	153	1,442	95	1,141	207	145
Skirts, pants, shorts and short sets	2,133	1,577	79	1,347	104	1,138	105	152
Active sportswear	809	620	53	552	34	437	81	15
Underwear and sleepwear	540	399	30	325	35	260	30	44
Hosiery	416	311	13	273	38	202	33	25
Accessories	403	292	40	233	35	182	16	20
MEN'S APPAREL	**$29,483**	**$21,187**	**$7,537**	**$12,069**	**$1,860**	**$5,619**	**$4,590**	**$1,581**
Suits	4,197	3,083	1,161	1,696	259	803	634	226
Sportcoats	1,593	1,115	376	641	94	312	235	97
Coats and jackets	2,424	2,012	1,007	876	147	544	185	128
Underwear	925	628	222	362	38	183	141	44
Hosiery	901	634	226	361	53	210	98	47
Nightwear	272	162	96	53	8	38	6	14
Accessories	2,120	1,537	746	709	102	341	266	82
Sweaters and vests	1,749	1,199	374	745	104	312	329	81
Active sportswear	1,135	768	287	432	75	196	162	49

Aggregate expenditures in 1988 for apparel and apparel services, by married couples with and without children.

(continued from previous page)

	all cu's	all married couples	married couple only	all married couples with children	AGE OF OLDEST CHILD			other married couples
					under 6	6 to 17	18 or older	
Shirts	6,807	4,755	1,302	3,093	370	1,387	1,336	360
Pants, short, and short sets	7,013	5,039	1,653	2,958	591	1,211	1,156	428
Uniforms	277	203	73	115	15	70	31	15
BOYS' APPAREL	**$7,252**	**$5,482**	**$588**	**$4,315**	**$649**	**$3,005**	**$661**	**$579**
Coats and jackets	766	604	41	482	32	401	50	80
Sweaters	366	276	29	215	19	156	40	32
Shirts	1,849	1,373	190	1,016	159	714	142	168
Underwear	131	112	-	86	28	58	-	26
Nightwear	239	170	-	144	63	64	17	26
Hosiery	351	279	31	227	39	146	42	21
Accessories	235	208	28	150	17	126	7	29
Suits, sportcoats, and vests	273	248	34	189	34	124	31	24
Pants, shorts, and shorts sets	2,147	1,486	144	1,229	188	792	249	113
Uniforms and active sportswear	495	402	42	325	28	252	45	36
BABIES' APPAREL	**$5,739**	**$4,643**	**$690**	**$3,424**	**$2,094**	**$993**	**$337**	**$530**
Coats, jackets, and snowsuits	328	259	55	160	113	28	18	44
Outerwear including dresses	1,431	1,124	291	690	373	188	129	143
Underwear	3,137	2,585	200	2,122	1,351	647	124	264
Nightwear	307	238	58	154	81	44	29	26
Accessories and hosiery	297	243	56	157	92	38	26	30
FOOTWEAR	**$18,633**	**$11,730**	**$3,355**	**$7,034**	**$930**	**$3,889**	**$2,216**	**$1,341**
Women's	9,133	5,508	1,865	2,890	404	1,493	993	753
Girls'	1,580	1,228	71	1,024	242	699	83	132
Men's	6,324	3,781	1,318	2,166	135	1,092	939	298
Boys'	1,596	1,213	101	954	150	604	201	158
OTHER APPAREL PRODUCTS/SVCS.	**$24,362**	**$15,393**	**$5,745**	**$8,393**	**$1,499**	**$4,105**	**$2,790**	**$1,255**
Fabric, patterns, notions for making clothes	930	694	282	365	63	186	116	47
Watches	2,071	1,327	352	820	170	432	218	155
Jewelry	10,241	6,994	2,825	3,584	583	1,632	1,369	585
Shoe repair and other shoe services	315	207	78	118	21	54	42	11
Watch and jewelry repair	520	365	134	219	24	129	66	12
Coin-operated laundry and dry cleaning	3,163	1,228	402	682	212	382	88	144
Professional laundry, dry cleaning, storage	6,123	3,919	1,460	2,205	372	1,109	723	254
Apparel alteration and repair services	577	356	139	197	30	99	68	19
Clothing rental	422	304	72	204	23	81	99	28

Note: Women and men include all persons aged 16 and older, girls and boys are aged 2 to 15, and babies are under age 2. Expenditures are not given (-) when the amount is too small to be reliable. Expenditures listed for a given category may not add to the total for that category because the listing is incomplete. "Men's apparel," for example, includes "other clothing," which is omitted here. Numbers may not add to total due to rounding. Other married couples include extended family members or unrelated persons in addition to the married couple. The "all cu's" aggregates will differ slightly from table to table because they are the sums of the aggregates in each row. In this table they include aggregates for single parents, single persons, and other types of consumer units, in addition to all married couples. Aggregates for "all married couples" and "all married couples" with children are sums of the appropriate aggregates in each row.

6

Transportation

The average American household devotes 20 percent of its expenditures to transportation, a share that did not change between 1984 and 1988. There have been changes, however, in the way transportation dollars are allocated. And allocations could shift again as the relative prices of vehicles, gas and oil, insurance, and public transportation change.

During this period of decline and stability in the price of oil, spending on gas and oil, as a share of transportation expenditures, dropped from nearly 25 percent to just 18 percent. The share of the transportation budget allocated to public transportation also declined. Meanwhile, the share going to car and truck purchases increased by more than 4 percentage points. Insurance, vehicle finance charges, licenses, and vehicle rentals took a larger bite out of the average transportation budget in 1988 than in 1984.

Five-year spending trends for transportation

	1984	1985	1986	1987	1988	change 1984 to 1988
Share of household expenditures devoted to transportation, share of transportation expenditures devoted to transportation items, and change in share, 1984 to 1988.						
Transportation, share of household expenditures	*19.6%*	*19.5%*	*20.3%*	*18.8%*	*19.7%*	*0.1%*
Transportation, expenditures	*100.0%*	*100.0%*	*100.0%*	*100.0%*	*100.0%*	*0.0%*
VEHICLE PURCHASES	**42.1%**	**44.5%**	**48.3%**	**44.0%**	**46.4%**	**4.3%**
Cars and trucks, new (net outlay)	23.9	26.1	29.2	24.8	26.6	2.7
Cars and trucks, used (net outlay)..........................	17.6	17.6	18.4	18.7	19.3	1.7
Other vehicles	0.6	0.9	0.6	0.4	0.5	-0.1
GASOLINE AND MOTOR OIL	**24.6%**	**22.6%**	**18.9%**	**19.3%**	**18.3%**	**-6.3%**
OTHER VEHICLE EXPENSES	**27.4%**	**27.1%**	**27.7%**	**30.8%**	**29.9%**	**2.5%**
Vehicle finance charges	4.9	5.5	5.6	6.1	5.6	0.7
Maintenance and repairs	11.2	10.3	10.2	11.2	10.9	-0.3
Vehicle insurance	8.1	8.1	8.7	10.0	10.0	1.9
Vehicle rental, licenses, and other charges	3.1	3.1	3.3	3.5	3.5	0.4
PUBLIC TRANSPORTATION	**5.9%**	**5.8%**	**5.1%**	**5.9%**	**5.5%**	**-0.4%**

Note: Numbers may not add to total due to rounding.

PART I
Spending by age for transportation

Transportation gobbles up 20 percent of the typical household's budget. Of the $5,093 spent by the average household on transportation in 1988, 46 percent went for vehicles; 30 percent went for finance charges, maintenance, repair, and insurance; 18 percent was spent on gas and oil; and the remaining 5 percent went for public transportation.

Households headed by people under age 25 spend 14 percent less than average on cars and trucks. Householders under age 25 spend nearly 75 percent more than the average household on towing charges, and they also spend more than average on intracity transit and taxi fares.

Overall, householders aged 55 or older spend less than average on transportation. Their spending on vehicle purchases is at least 22 percent below average, for example. Householders aged 55 to 64 spend higher-than-average amounts on fuel, repairs and maintenance, and insurance. Households headed by people aged 65 or older spend more than average on intercity bus travel.

As with housing, the biggest spenders on transportation are householders aged 25 to 54. All told, they spent $338 billion in 1988, including $161 billion on vehicle purchases, $60 billion on gas and oil, $35 billion on maintenance and repairs, and $32 billion on insurance. These totals will increase during the 1990s as more baby boomers enter their late 40s and early 50s.

Householders aged 25 to 34 spend 9 percent more than the average household on new cars, and 53 percent more than average on new trucks. Householders aged 35 to 44 spend the most on leased vehicles, used cars and trucks, and maintenance and repairs. But households headed by 45-to-54-year-olds are the peak spenders on gasoline, vehicle finance charges, and insurance. They also hold a virtual monopoly on aircraft purchases.

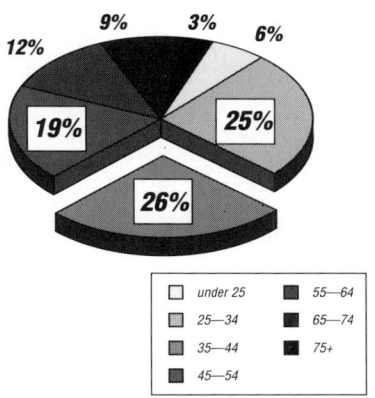

Householders aged 25 to 54 account for fully 70 percent of the transportation market...

under 25 | 55—64
25—34 | 65—74
35—44 | 75+
45—54

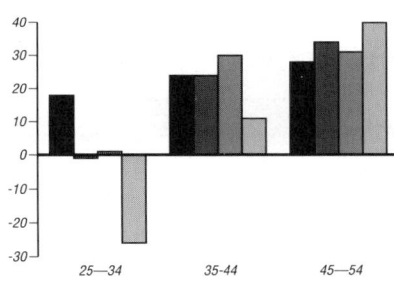

...and are generally above-average spenders on transportation...

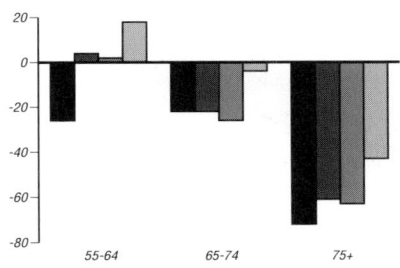

...while older householders spend less than the average household on most transportation items.

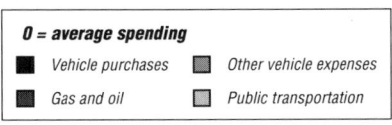

0 = average spending

Vehicle purchases | Other vehicle expenses
Gas and oil | Public transportation

Average expenditures

	all cu's	under 25	25 to 34	35 to 44	45 to 54	55 to 64	65 to 74	75+
Number of consumer units (in thousands)	*94,862*	*7,216*	*21,985*	*19,911*	*13,601*	*12,546*	*11,319*	*8,284*
Average number of persons per cu	*2.6*	*1.8*	*2.8*	*3.3*	*2.9*	*2.2*	*2.0*	*1.5*
Average total before-tax income	*$28,540.00*	*$14,827.00*	*$28,318.00*	*$36,428.00*	*$39,934.00*	*$29,979.00*	*$20,704.00*	*$13,707.00*
TOTAL AVERAGE ANNUAL EXPENDITURES	*$25,891.85*	*$16,373.17*	*$25,770.27*	*$33,077.72*	*$33,204.87*	*$25,765.35*	*$20,119.90*	*$13,339.49*
TRANSPORTATION, AVERAGE ANNUAL EXPENDITURES	*$5,092.81*	*$3,910.96*	*$5,479.19*	*$6,369.07*	*$6,641.16*	*$4,602.93*	*$3,974.95*	*$1,759.52*
VEHICLE PURCHASES (NET OUTLAY)	**$2,360.51**	**$2,038.56**	**$2,794.05**	**$2,930.84**	**$3,016.03**	**$1,749.42**	**$1,849.39**	**$667.18**
Cars and trucks, new	**1,355.10**	**1,158.59**	**1,651.10**	**1,518.29**	**1,640.01**	**1,082.22**	**1,187.25**	**523.39**
New cars	974.20	868.67	1,066.54	1,073.13	1,197.98	865.11	1,026.61	309.43
New trucks	380.91	289.92	584.55	445.17	442.03	217.11	160.64	213.97
Cars and trucks, used	**982.07**	**860.79**	**1,110.82**	**1,393.41**	**1,307.37**	**662.94**	**662.14**	**143.78**
Used cars	766.68	665.13	782.03	1,094.35	1,055.86	552.88	586.53	121.99
Used trucks	215.40	195.65	328.79	299.06	251.51	110.06	75.62	21.79
Other vehicles	**23.33**	**19.18**	**32.14**	**19.14**	**68.65**	**4.26**	**0.00**	**0.00**
Motorcycles	19.67	19.18	32.14	19.14	43.13	4.26	0.00	0.00
Aircraft	3.66	0.00	0.00	0.00	25.51	0.00	0.00	0.00
GASOLINE AND MOTOR OIL	**$931.97**	**$659.40**	**$922.65**	**$1,151.54**	**$1,248.37**	**$969.97**	**$728.64**	**$367.18**
Gasoline at home	**814.53**	**561.34**	**812.74**	**997.65**	**1,104.24**	**841.31**	**632.96**	**331.60**
Gasoline on out-of-town trips	**92.71**	**80.70**	**87.42**	**116.38**	**111.62**	**105.28**	**79.98**	**27.64**
Diesel fuel	**11.69**	**6.26**	**8.50**	**21.25**	**16.60**	**9.24**	**7.38**	**3.50**
Motor oil	**13.02**	**11.10**	**13.98**	**16.26**	**15.91**	**14.14**	**8.31**	**4.43**
OTHER VEHICLE EXPENSES	**$1,521.36**	**$1,023.28**	**$1,527.74**	**$1,977.91**	**$1,987.39**	**$1,553.17**	**$1,128.62**	**$567.16**
Vehicle finance charges	**283.56**	**191.87**	**357.51**	**370.50**	**397.54**	**234.33**	**154.22**	**22.70**
Cars	197.79	145.72	242.60	234.01	285.27	182.88	121.32	20.60
Trucks	69.50	41.13	102.42	108.54	82.41	39.60	21.95	2.09
Motorcycles, planes, and other vehicles	16.29	5.02	12.48	27.95	29.87	11.84	10.95	0.00
Repairs and maintenance	**552.66**	**361.20**	**523.64**	**743.92**	**665.67**	**586.59**	**442.39**	**253.28**
Body work	34.13	31.24	29.42	46.91	43.12	36.17	24.16	14.24
Clutch, transmission repair	34.75	19.18	35.88	47.29	42.63	34.60	26.27	14.01
Drive train repair	7.14	1.34	8.90	7.26	7.99	10.42	3.79	5.49
Brake repair and adjustment	37.74	23.18	40.89	51.64	41.13	39.36	26.88	15.53
Steering repair	11.19	11.85	10.64	13.52	12.02	9.29	11.09	8.16
Cooling system repair	22.70	11.71	20.47	27.20	26.36	25.99	24.46	14.06
Motor tune-up	40.31	28.51	39.78	49.83	44.85	48.51	33.44	18.60
Motor repair and replacement	61.81	48.75	62.87	77.04	79.32	66.40	35.14	34.54

Average annual expenditures for transportation, by age of reference person.

(continued from previous page)	all cu's	under 25	25 to 34	35 to 44	45 to 54	55 to 64	65 to 74	75+
Lubrication, oil change	24.52	16.62	21.25	26.07	28.99	30.34	28.65	14.58
Front end alignment, wheel balancing	9.08	3.93	8.51	11.25	13.07	9.14	8.74	3.70
Shock absorber replacement	6.38	2.47	6.67	7.89	8.81	6.75	4.56	3.36
Exhaust system repair	14.59	7.45	11.42	16.34	21.52	14.95	16.21	10.85
Electrical system repair	19.62	9.46	14.43	25.98	27.42	21.57	19.55	11.29
Tire replacement	85.02	57.80	79.24	118.82	107.16	84.09	65.99	33.92
Coolant, additives, brake/transmission fluids ..	7.07	5.99	7.11	9.27	8.65	6.56	5.51	2.93
Parts, equipment, accessories,								
and other vehicle products	78.28	45.07	79.72	120.78	92.26	85.01	42.86	18.57
Out-of-town, tire, other servicing and repairs ..	46.17	27.78	33.23	70.38	49.41	45.05	52.99	26.40
Auto repair service policy	8.70	2.59	9.68	12.18	8.37	9.85	8.32	2.36
Vehicle insurance	**507.72**	**363.88**	**454.01**	**606.65**	**699.68**	**564.90**	**428.19**	**244.74**
Vehicle leasing, renting, licensing,								
and other charges	**177.39**	**106.33**	**192.59**	**256.84**	**224.50**	**167.36**	**103.83**	**46.45**
Leased and rented vehicles	64.06	27.02	74.25	116.80	88.18	43.60	12.46	4.39
Cars	47.38	22.18	57.22	75.98	73.68	34.01	10.29	2.15
Trucks	15.85	3.80	15.77	39.31	14.28	9.39	1.37	2.24
State and local registration	63.65	36.54	63.06	78.09	74.58	70.70	61.92	27.89
Drivers' license	6.38	6.02	5.77	7.83	7.65	6.64	5.73	3.22
Vehicle inspection	6.06	3.45	5.67	7.06	7.44	6.84	5.71	3.99
Parking fees	21.31	17.63	25.84	26.69	27.86	21.83	9.60	4.00
Tolls	10.83	6.80	11.81	15.16	12.01	13.61	5.97	2.02
Towing charges	5.10	8.87	6.19	5.21	6.78	4.13	2.45	0.94
PUBLIC TRANSPORTATION	**$278.98**	**$189.73**	**$234.75**	**$308.78**	**$389.37**	**$330.38**	**$268.29**	**$158.01**
Airline fares	**186.43**	**104.63**	**163.66**	**206.00**	**265.28**	**223.85**	**174.45**	**101.35**
Intercity bus fares	**14.29**	**5.67**	**4.02**	**9.34**	**13.15**	**15.38**	**45.74**	**18.27**
Intercity train fares	**8.91**	**6.65**	**3.70**	**9.72**	**17.44**	**11.61**	**7.42**	**6.64**
Intracity mass transit fares	**44.08**	**51.32**	**48.91**	**47.13**	**59.08**	**52.10**	**18.44**	**15.85**
Taxi fares	**11.36**	**11.49**	**10.56**	**10.84**	**15.02**	**13.94**	**7.43**	**10.06**
Ship fares	**12.35**	**8.95**	**2.90**	**23.12**	**16.16**	**12.23**	**14.47**	**5.58**
School bus	**1.01**	**-**	**0.77**	**1.97**	**2.28**	**-**	**0.00**	**0.00**

Note: Expenditures are not given (-) when the amount is too small to be reliable. Expenditures listed for a given category may not add to the total for that category because the listing is incomplete. "Leased and rented vehicles," for example, includes "aircraft rental," which is omitted here. Numbers may not add to total due to rounding.

Share of spending

	all cu's	under 25	25 to 34	35 to 44	45 to 54	55 to 64	65 to 74	75+
Number of consumer units (in thousands)	94,862	7,216	21,985	19,911	13,601	12,546	11,319	8,284
Average number of persons per cu	2.6	1.8	2.8	3.3	2.9	2.2	2.0	1.5
Average total before-tax income	$28,540	$14,827	$28,318	$36,428	$39,934	$29,979	$20,704	$13,707
TOTAL AVERAGE ANNUAL EXPENDITURES	100.00%	100.00%	100.00%	100.00%	100.00%	100.00%	100.00%	100.00%
TRANSPORTATION, AVERAGE ANNUAL EXPENDITURES	19.67%	23.89%	21.26%	19.25%	20.00%	17.86%	19.76%	13.19%
VEHICLE PURCHASES (NET OUTLAY)	**9.12%**	**12.45%**	**10.84%**	**8.86%**	**9.08%**	**6.79%**	**9.19%**	**5.00%**
Cars and trucks, new	**5.23**	**7.08**	**6.41**	**4.59**	**4.94**	**4.20**	**5.90**	**3.92**
New cars	3.76	5.31	4.14	3.24	3.61	3.36	5.10	2.32
New trucks	1.47	1.77	2.27	1.35	1.33	0.84	0.80	1.60
Cars and trucks, used	**3.79**	**5.26**	**4.31**	**4.21**	**3.94**	**2.57**	**3.29**	**1.08**
Used cars	2.96	4.06	3.03	3.31	3.18	2.15	2.92	0.91
Used trucks	0.83	1.19	1.28	0.90	0.76	0.43	0.38	0.16
Other vehicles	**0.09**	**0.12**	**0.12**	**0.06**	**0.21**	**0.02**	**0.00**	**0.00**
Motorcycles	0.08	0.12	0.12	0.06	0.13	0.02	0.00	0.00
Aircraft	0.01	0.00	0.00	0.00	0.08	0.00	0.00	0.00
GASOLINE AND MOTOR OIL	**3.60%**	**4.03%**	**3.58%**	**3.48%**	**3.76%**	**3.76%**	**3.62%**	**2.75%**
Gasoline at home	**3.15**	**3.43**	**3.15**	**3.02**	**3.33**	**3.27**	**3.15**	**2.49**
Gasoline on out-of-town trips	**0.36**	**0.49**	**0.34**	**0.35**	**0.34**	**0.41**	**0.40**	**0.21**
Diesel fuel	**0.05**	**0.04**	**0.03**	**0.06**	**0.05**	**0.04**	**0.04**	**0.03**
Motor oil	**0.05**	**0.07**	**0.05**	**0.05**	**0.05**	**0.05**	**0.04**	**0.03**
OTHER VEHICLE EXPENSES	**5.88%**	**6.25%**	**5.93%**	**5.98%**	**5.99%**	**6.03%**	**5.61%**	**4.25%**
Vehicle finance charges	**1.10**	**1.17**	**1.39**	**1.12**	**1.20**	**0.91**	**0.77**	**0.17**
Cars	0.76	0.89	0.94	0.71	0.86	0.71	0.60	0.15
Trucks..	0.27	0.25	0.40	0.33	0.25	0.15	0.11	0.02
Motorcycles, planes, and other vehicles	0.06	0.03	0.05	0.08	0.09	0.05	0.05	0.00
Repairs and maintenance	**2.13**	**2.21**	**2.03**	**2.25**	**2.00**	**2.28**	**2.20**	**1.90**
Body work	0.13	0.19	0.11	0.14	0.13	0.14	0.12	0.11
Clutch, transmission repair	0.13	0.12	0.14	0.14	0.13	0.13	0.13	0.11
Drive train repair	0.03	0.01	0.03	0.02	0.02	0.04	0.02	0.04
Brake repair and adjustment	0.15	0.14	0.16	0.16	0.12	0.15	0.13	0.12
Steering repair	0.04	0.07	0.04	0.04	0.04	0.04	0.06	0.06
Cooling system repair	0.09	0.07	0.08	0.08	0.08	0.10	0.12	0.11
Motor tune-up	0.16	0.17	0.15	0.15	0.14	0.19	0.17	0.14
Motor repair and replacement	0.24	0.30	0.24	0.23	0.24	0.26	0.17	0.26

Percent of total average annual expenditures spent on transportation, by age of reference person.

(continued from previous page)	all cu's	under 25	25 to 34	35 to 44	45 to 54	55 to 64	65 to 74	75+
Lubrication, oil change	0.09	0.10	0.08	0.08	0.09	0.12	0.14	0.11
Front end alignment, wheel balancing	0.04	0.02	0.03	0.03	0.04	0.04	0.04	0.03
Shock absorber replacement	0.02	0.02	0.03	0.02	0.03	0.03	0.02	0.03
Exhaust system repair	0.06	0.05	0.04	0.05	0.06	0.06	0.08	0.08
Electrical system repair	0.08	0.06	0.06	0.08	0.08	0.08	0.10	0.08
Tire replacement	0.33	0.35	0.31	0.36	0.32	0.33	0.33	0.25
Coolant, additives, brake/transmission fluids ..	0.03	0.04	0.03	0.03	0.03	0.03	0.03	0.02
Parts, equipment, accessories and other vehicle products	0.30	0.28	0.31	0.37	0.28	0.33	0.21	0.14
Out-of-town, tire, other servicing and repairs ..	0.18	0.17	0.13	0.21	0.15	0.17	0.26	0.20
Auto repair service policy	0.03	0.02	0.04	0.04	0.03	0.04	0.04	0.02
Vehicle insurance	**1.96**	**2.22**	**1.76**	**1.83**	**2.11**	**2.19**	**2.13**	**1.83**
Vehicle leasing, renting, licensing, and other charges	**0.69**	**0.65**	**0.75**	**0.78**	**0.68**	**0.65**	**0.52**	**0.35**
Leased and rented vehicles	0.25	0.17	0.29	0.35	0.27	0.17	0.06	0.03
Cars	0.18	0.14	0.22	0.23	0.22	0.13	0.05	0.02
Trucks	0.06	0.02	0.06	0.12	0.04	0.04	0.01	0.02
State and local registration	0.25	0.22	0.24	0.24	0.22	0.27	0.31	0.21
Drivers' license	0.02	0.04	0.02	0.02	0.02	0.03	0.03	0.02
Vehicle inspection	0.02	0.02	0.02	0.02	0.02	0.03	0.03	0.03
Parking fees	0.08	0.11	0.10	0.08	0.08	0.08	0.05	0.03
Tolls	0.04	0.04	0.05	0.05	0.04	0.05	0.03	0.02
Towing charges	0.02	0.05	0.02	0.02	0.02	0.02	0.01	0.01
PUBLIC TRANSPORTATION	**1.08%**	**1.16%**	**0.91%**	**0.93%**	**1.17%**	**1.28%**	**1.33%**	**1.18%**
Airline fares	**0.72**	**0.64**	**0.64**	**0.62**	**0.80**	**0.87**	**0.87**	**0.76**
Intercity bus fares	**0.06**	**0.03**	**0.02**	**0.03**	**0.04**	**0.06**	**0.23**	**0.14**
Intercity train fares	**0.03**	**0.04**	**0.01**	**0.03**	**0.05**	**0.05**	**0.04**	**0.05**
Intracity mass transit fares	**0.17**	**0.31**	**0.19**	**0.14**	**0.18**	**0.20**	**0.09**	**0.12**
Taxi fares	**0.04**	**0.07**	**0.04**	**0.03**	**0.05**	**0.05**	**0.04**	**0.08**
Ship fares	**0.05**	**0.05**	**0.01**	**0.07**	**0.05**	**0.05**	**0.07**	**0.04**
School bus	**0.00**	**-**	**0.00**	**0.01**	**0.01**	**-**	**0.00**	**0.00**

Note: Expenditures are not given (-) when the amount is too small to be reliable. Expenditures listed for a given category may not add to the total for that category because the listing is incomplete. "Leased and rented vehicles," for example, includes "aircraft rental," which is omitted here. Numbers may not add to total due to rounding.

Indexed expenditures

	all cu's	under 25	25 to 34	35 to 44	45 to 54	55 to 64	65 to 74	75+
Number of consumer units (in thousands)	94,862	7,216	21,985	19,911	13,601	12,546	11,319	8,284
Average number of persons per cu	2.6	1.8	2.8	3.3	2.9	2.2	2.0	1.5
Average total before-tax income	$28,540	$14,827	$28,318	$36,428	$39,934	$29,979	$20,704	$13,707
TOTAL AVERAGE ANNUAL EXPENDITURES	100	63	100	128	128	100	78	52
TRANSPORTATION, AVERAGE ANNUAL EXPENDITURES	100	77	108	125	130	90	78	35
VEHICLE PURCHASES (NET OUTLAY)	100	86	118	124	128	74	78	28
Cars and trucks, new	100	85	122	112	121	80	88	39
New cars	100	89	109	110	123	89	105	32
New trucks	100	76	153	117	116	57	42	56
Cars and trucks, used	100	88	113	142	133	68	67	15
Used cars	100	87	102	143	138	72	77	16
Used trucks	100	91	153	139	117	51	35	10
Other vehicles	100	82	138	82	294	18	0	0
Motorcycles	100	98	163	97	219	22	0	0
Aircraft	100	0	0	0	697	0	0	0
GASOLINE AND MOTOR OIL	100	71	99	124	134	104	78	39
Gasoline at home	100	69	100	122	136	103	78	41
Gasoline on out-of-town trips	100	87	94	126	120	114	86	30
Diesel fuel	100	54	73	182	142	79	63	30
Motor oil	100	85	107	125	122	109	64	34
OTHER VEHICLE EXPENSES	100	67	100	130	131	102	74	37
Vehicle finance charges	100	68	126	131	140	83	54	8
Cars	100	74	123	118	144	92	61	10
Trucks	100	59	147	156	119	57	32	3
Motorcycles, planes, and other vehicles	100	31	77	172	183	73	67	0
Repairs and maintenance	100	65	95	135	120	106	80	46
Body work	100	92	86	137	126	106	71	42
Clutch, transmission repair	100	55	103	136	123	100	76	40
Drive train repair	100	19	125	102	112	146	53	77
Brake repair and adjustment	100	61	108	137	109	104	71	41
Steering repair	100	106	95	121	107	83	99	73
Cooling system repair	100	52	90	120	116	114	108	62
Motor tune-up	100	71	99	124	111	120	83	46
Motor repair and replacement	100	79	102	125	128	107	57	56

Indexed average annual expenditures for transportation, by age of reference person.

(continued from previous page)	all cu's	under 25	25 to 34	35 to 44	45 to 54	55 to 64	65 to 74	75+
Lubrication, oil change	100	68	87	106	118	124	117	59
Front end alignment, wheel balancing	100	43	94	124	144	101	96	41
Shock absorber replacement	100	39	105	124	138	106	71	53
Exhaust system repair	100	51	78	112	147	102	111	74
Electrical system repair	100	48	74	132	140	110	100	58
Tire replacement	100	68	93	140	126	99	78	40
Coolant, additives, brake/transmission fluids	100	85	101	131	122	93	78	41
Parts, equipment, accessories, and other vehicle products	100	58	102	154	118	109	55	24
Out-of-town, tire, other servicing and repairs	100	60	72	152	107	98	115	57
Auto repair service policy	100	30	111	140	96	113	96	27
Vehicle insurance	**100**	**72**	**89**	**119**	**138**	**111**	**84**	**48**
Vehicle leasing, renting, licensing, and other charges	**100**	**60**	**109**	**145**	**127**	**94**	**59**	**26**
Leased and rented vehicles	100	42	116	182	138	68	19	7
Cars	100	47	121	160	156	72	22	5
Trucks	100	24	99	248	90	59	9	14
State and local registration	100	57	99	123	117	111	97	44
Drivers' license	100	94	90	123	120	104	90	50
Vehicle inspection	100	57	94	117	123	113	94	66
Parking fees	100	83	121	125	131	102	45	19
Tolls	100	63	109	140	111	126	55	19
Towing charges	100	174	121	102	133	81	48	18
PUBLIC TRANSPORTATION	**100**	**68**	**84**	**111**	**140**	**118**	**96**	**57**
Airline fares	**100**	**56**	**88**	**110**	**142**	**120**	**94**	**54**
Intercity bus fares	**100**	**40**	**28**	**65**	**92**	**108**	**320**	**128**
Intercity train fares	**100**	**75**	**42**	**109**	**196**	**130**	**83**	**75**
Intracity mass transit fares	**100**	**116**	**111**	**107**	**134**	**118**	**42**	**36**
Taxi fares	**100**	**101**	**93**	**95**	**132**	**123**	**65**	**89**
Ship fares	**100**	**72**	**23**	**187**	**131**	**99**	**117**	**45**
School bus	**100**	**-**	**76**	**195**	**226**	**-**	**0**	**0**

Note: Expenditures are not given (-) when the amount is too small to be reliable. An index of 100 represents the average for all consumer units. An index of 132 means that the average for the subgroup is 32 percent above the average for all consumer units. An index of 68 indicates spending that is 32 percent below the overall average.

Aggregate expenditures, 1988

Aggregate expenditures in 1988 for transportation, by age of reference person.

	all cu's	under 25	25 to 34	35 to 44	45 to 54	55 to 64	65 to 74	75+
Number of consumer units (in thousands)	94,862	7,216	21,985	19,911	13,601	12,546	11,319	8,284
Average number of persons per cu	2.6	1.8	2.8	3.3	2.9	2.2	2.0	1.5
Aggregate before-tax income (in millions)	$2,722,037	$106,992	$622,571	$725,318	$543,142	$376,117	$234,349	$113,549
TOTAL AGGREGATE EXPENDITURES (in millions)	$2,456,432	$118,149	$566,559	$658,610	$451,619	$323,252	$227,737	$110,504
TRANSPORTATION, AGGREGATE EXPENDITURES (in millions)	$483,139	$28,221	$120,460	$126,815	$90,326	$57,748	$44,992	$14,576
VEHICLE PURCHASES (NET OUTLAY)	$223,923	$14,710	$61,427	$58,356	$41,021	$21,948	$20,933	$5,527
Cars and trucks, new	128,548	8,360	36,299	30,231	22,306	13,578	13,438	4,336
New cars	92,414	6,268	23,448	21,367	16,294	10,854	11,620	2,563
New trucks	36,134	2,092	12,851	8,864	6,012	2,724	1,818	1,773
Cars and trucks, used	93,162	6,211	24,421	27,744	17,782	8,317	7,495	1,191
Used cars	72,729	4,800	17,193	21,790	14,361	6,936	6,639	1,011
Used trucks	20,433	1,412	7,228	5,955	3,421	1,381	856	181
Other vehicles	2,213	138	707	381	934	53	0	0
Motorcycles	1,866	138	707	381	587	53	0	0
Aircraft	347	0	0	0	347	0	0	0
GASOLINE AND MOTOR OIL	$88,409	$4,758	$20,284	$22,928	$16,979	$12,169	$8,247	$3,042
Gasoline at home	77,268	4,051	17,868	19,864	15,019	10,555	7,164	2,747
Gasoline on out-of-town trips	8,795	582	1,922	2,317	1,518	1,321	905	229
Diesel fuel	1,109	45	187	423	226	116	84	29
Motor oil	1,236	80	307	324	216	177	94	37
OTHER VEHICLE EXPENSES	$144,343	$7,384	$33,587	$39,382	$27,030	$19,486	$12,775	$4,698
Vehicle finance charges	26,902	1,385	7,860	7,377	5,407	2,940	1,746	188
Cars	18,763	1,052	5,334	4,659	3,880	2,294	1,373	171
Trucks	6,593	297	2,252	2,161	1,121	497	248	17
Motorcycles, planes, and other vehicles	1,546	36	274	557	406	149	124	0
Repairs and maintenance	52,450	2,606	11,512	14,812	9,054	7,359	5,007	2,098
Body work	3,238	225	647	934	586	454	273	118
Clutch, transmission repair	3,296	138	789	942	580	434	297	116
Drive train repair	678	10	196	145	109	131	43	45
Brake repair and adjustment	3,581	167	899	1,028	559	494	304	129
Steering repair	1,062	86	234	269	163	117	126	68
Cooling system repair	2,154	84	450	542	359	326	277	116
Motor tune-up	3,824	206	875	992	610	609	379	154
Motor repair and replacement	5,864	352	1,382	1,534	1,079	833	398	286

Aggregate expenditures for transportation in 1988, by age of reference person.

(continued from previous page)	all cu's	under 25	25 to 34	35 to 44	45 to 54	55 to 64	65 to 74	75+
Lubrication, oil change	2,326	120	467	519	394	381	324	121
Front end alignment, wheel balancing	861	28	187	224	178	115	99	31
Shock absorber replacement	606	18	147	157	120	85	52	28
Exhaust system repair	1,384	54	251	325	293	188	183	90
Electrical system repair	1,861	68	317	517	373	271	221	94
Tire replacement	8,065	417	1,742	2,366	1,457	1,055	747	281
Coolant, additives, brake/transmission fluids ..	671	43	156	185	118	82	62	24
Parts, equipment, accessories, and other vehicle products	7,443	325	1,753	2,405	1,255	1,067	485	154
Out-of-town, tire, other servicing and repairs ..	4,388	200	731	1,401	672	565	600	219
Auto repair service policy	825	19	213	243	114	124	94	20
Vehicle insurance	**48,164**	**2,626**	**9,981**	**12,079**	**9,516**	**7,087**	**4,847**	**2,027**
Vehicle leasing, renting, licensing, and other charges	**16,828**	**767**	**4,234**	**5,114**	**3,053**	**2,100**	**1,175**	**385**
Leased and rented vehicles	6,077	195	1,632	2,326	1,199	547	141	36
Cars	4,494	160	1,258	1,513	1,002	427	116	18
Trucks	1,503	27	347	783	194	118	16	19
State and local registration	6,038	264	1,386	1,555	1,014	887	701	231
Drivers' license	605	43	127	156	104	83	65	27
Vehicle inspection	575	25	125	141	101	86	65	33
Parking fees	2,021	127	568	531	379	274	109	33
Tolls	1,029	49	260	302	163	171	68	17
Towing charges	483	64	136	104	92	52	28	8
PUBLIC TRANSPORTATION	**$26,465**	**$1,369**	**$5,161**	**$6,148**	**$5,296**	**$4,145**	**$3,037**	**$1,309**
Airline fares	**17,685**	**755**	**3,598**	**4,102**	**3,608**	**2,808**	**1,975**	**840**
Intercity bus fares	**1,356**	**41**	**88**	**186**	**179**	**193**	**518**	**151**
Intercity train fares	**845**	**48**	**81**	**194**	**237**	**146**	**84**	**55**
Intracity mass transit fares	**4,181**	**370**	**1,075**	**938**	**804**	**654**	**209**	**131**
Taxi fares	**1,078**	**83**	**232**	**216**	**204**	**175**	**84**	**83**
Ship fares	**1,172**	**65**	**64**	**460**	**220**	**153**	**164**	**46**
School bus	**87**	**-**	**17**	**39**	**31**	**-**	**0**	**0**

Note: Expenditures are not given (-) when the amount is too small to be reliable. Expenditures listed for a given category may not add to the total for that category because the listing is incomplete. "Leased and rented vehicles," for example, includes "aircraft rental," which is omitted here. Numbers may not add to total due to rounding. The "all cu's" aggregates will differ from table to table because they are the sums of the aggregates in each row.

Aggregate expenditures, 1995

Aggregate expenditures for transportation, by age of householder in 1995 (in 1988 dollars).

	all households	under 25	25 to 34	35 to 44	45 to 54	55 to 64	65 to 74	75+
Number of households (in thousands)	**100,308**	**4,316**	**19,927**	**23,916**	**18,035**	**12,223**	**12,006**	**9,876**
TRANSPORTATION, AGGREGATE EXPENDITURES IN 1995 (in millions)	**$519,521**	**$16,880**	**$109,184**	**$152,323**	**$119,773**	**$56,262**	**$47,723**	**$17,377**
VEHICLE PURCHASES (NET OUTLAY)	**$239,140**	**$8,798**	**$55,677**	**$70,094**	**$54,394**	**$21,383**	**$22,204**	**$6,589**
Cars and trucks, new	**136,442**	**5,000**	**32,901**	**36,311**	**29,578**	**13,228**	**14,254**	**5,169**
New cars	98,228	3,749	21,253	25,665	21,606	10,574	12,325	3,056
New trucks	38,214	1,251	11,648	10,647	7,972	2,654	1,929	2,113
Cars and trucks, used	**100,226**	**3,715**	**22,135**	**33,325**	**23,578**	**8,103**	**7,950**	**1,420**
Used cars	78,674	2,871	15,584	26,172	19,042	6,758	7,042	1,205
Used trucks	21,553	844	6,552	7,152	4,536	1,345	908	215
Other vehicles	**2,471**	**83**	**640**	**458**	**1,238**	**52**	**0**	**0**
Motorcycles	2,011	83	640	458	778	52	0	0
Aircraft	460	0	0	0	460	0	0	0
GASOLINE AND MOTOR OIL	**$95,516**	**$2,846**	**$18,386**	**$27,540**	**$22,514**	**$11,856**	**$8,748**	**$3,626**
Gasoline at home	**83,551**	**2,423**	**16,195**	**23,860**	**19,915**	**10,283**	**7,599**	**3,275**
Gasoline on out-of-town trips	**9,407**	**348**	**1,742**	**2,783**	**2,013**	**1,287**	**960**	**273**
Diesel fuel	**1,240**	**27**	**169**	**508**	**299**	**113**	**89**	**35**
Motor oil	**1,319**	**48**	**279**	**389**	**287**	**173**	**100**	**44**
OTHER VEHICLE EXPENSES	**$156,142**	**$4,416**	**$30,443**	**$47,304**	**$35,843**	**$18,984**	**$13,550**	**$5,601**
Vehicle finance charges	**28,923**	**828**	**7,124**	**8,861**	**7,170**	**2,864**	**1,852**	**224**
Cars	20,100	629	4,834	5,597	5,145	2,235	1,457	203
Trucks	7,069	178	2,041	2,596	1,486	484	264	21
Motorcycles, planes, and other vehicles	1,754	22	249	668	539	145	131	0
Repairs and maintenance	**56,773**	**1,559**	**10,435**	**17,792**	**12,005**	**7,170**	**5,311**	**2,501**
Body work	3,493	135	586	1,122	778	442	290	141
Clutch, transmission repair	3,574	83	715	1,131	769	423	315	138
Drive train repair	728	6	177	174	144	127	46	54
Brake repair and adjustment	3,849	100	815	1,235	742	481	323	153
Steering repair	1,131	51	212	323	217	114	133	81
Cooling system repair	2,335	51	408	651	475	318	294	139
Motor tune-up	4,094	123	793	1,192	809	593	401	184
Motor repair and replacement	6,311	210	1,253	1,842	1,431	812	422	341

Aggregate expenditures for transportation, by age of householder in 1995 (in 1988 dollars).

(continued from previous page)	all households	under 25	25 to 34	35 to 44	45 to 54	55 to 64	65 to 74	75+
Lubrication, oil change	2,500	72	423	623	523	371	344	144
Front end alignment, wheel balancing	945	17	170	269	236	112	105	37
Shock absorber replacement	662	11	133	189	159	83	55	33
Exhaust system repair	1,523	32	228	391	388	183	195	107
Electrical system repair	2,054	41	288	621	495	264	235	112
Tire replacement	8,758	249	1,579	2,842	1,933	1,028	792	335
Coolant, additives, brake/transmission fluids	721	26	142	222	156	80	66	29
Parts, equipment, accessories, and other vehicle products	8,073	195	1,589	2,889	1,664	1,039	515	183
Out-of-town, tire, other servicing and repairs	4,804	120	662	1,683	891	551	636	261
Auto repair service policy	890	11	193	291	151	120	100	23
Vehicle insurance	**52,208**	**1,571**	**9,047**	**14,509**	**12,619**	**6,905**	**5,141**	**2,417**
Vehicle leasing, renting, licensing, and other charges	**18,239**	**459**	**3,838**	**6,143**	**4,049**	**2,046**	**1,247**	**459**
Leased and rented vehicles	6,706	117	1,480	2,793	1,590	533	150	43
Cars	4,942	96	1,140	1,817	1,329	416	124	21
Trucks	1,682	16	314	940	258	115	16	22
State and local registration	6,510	158	1,257	1,868	1,345	864	743	275
Drivers' license	648	26	115	187	138	81	69	32
Vehicle inspection	622	15	113	169	134	84	69	39
Parking fees	2,153	76	515	638	502	267	115	40
Tolls	1,102	29	235	363	217	166	72	20
Towing charges	498	38	123	125	122	50	29	9
PUBLIC TRANSPORTATION	**$28,724**	**$819**	**$4,678**	**$7,385**	**$7,022**	**$4,038**	**$3,221**	**$1,561**
Airline fares	**19,255**	**452**	**3,261**	**4,927**	**4,784**	**2,736**	**2,094**	**1,001**
Intercity bus fares	**1,483**	**24**	**80**	**223**	**237**	**188**	**549**	**180**
Intercity train fares	**946**	**29**	**74**	**232**	**315**	**142**	**89**	**66**
Intracity mass transit fares	**4,404**	**221**	**975**	**1,127**	**1,066**	**637**	**221**	**157**
Taxi fares	**1,149**	**50**	**210**	**259**	**271**	**170**	**89**	**99**
Ship fares	**1,319**	**39**	**58**	**553**	**291**	**149**	**174**	**55**
School bus	**104**	**-**	**15**	**47**	**41**	**-**	**0**	**0**

Note: Expenditures are not given (-) when the amount is too small to be reliable. Expenditures listed for a given category may not add to the total for that category because the listing is incomplete. "Leased and rented vehicles," for example, includes "aircraft rental," which is omitted here. Numbers may not add to total due to rounding. Households are used here because the number of consumer units in 1995 and 2000 is not available. Household projections are from the Census Bureau. Projections show how annual aggregate expenditures will change as the number of households in the age groups changes in 1995 and 2000. Projections are based on the average annual expenditures in 1988 and have not been adjusted for price increases or for changes in expenditure patterns.

Aggregate expenditures, 2000

	all households	under 25	25 to 34	35 to 44	45 to 54	55 to 64	65 to 74	75+
Number of households (in thousands)	105,933	4,442	18,004	25,339	21,603	13,903	11,516	11,126
TRANSPORTATION, AGGREGATE EXPENDITURES IN 2000 (in millions)	$550,221	$17,372	$98,647	$161,386	$143,469	$63,995	$45,776	$19,576
VEHICLE PURCHASES (NET OUTLAY)	$251,822	$9,055	$50,304	$74,265	$65,155	$24,322	$21,298	$7,423
Cars and trucks, new	143,316	5,146	29,726	38,472	35,429	15,046	13,672	5,823
New cars	103,425	3,859	19,202	27,192	25,880	12,028	11,822	3,443
New trucks	39,890	1,288	10,524	11,280	9,549	3,018	1,850	2,381
Cars and trucks, used	105,815	3,824	19,999	35,308	28,243	9,217	7,625	1,600
Used cars	83,372	2,955	14,080	27,730	22,810	7,687	6,754	1,357
Used trucks	22,443	869	5,920	7,578	5,433	1,530	871	242
Other vehicles	2,691	85	579	485	1,483	59	0	0
Motorcycles	2,140	85	579	485	932	59	0	0
Aircraft	551	0	0	0	551	0	0	0
GASOLINE AND MOTOR OIL	$101,650	$2,929	$16,611	$29,179	$26,969	$13,485	$8,391	$4,085
Gasoline at home	88,936	2,493	14,633	25,279	23,855	11,697	7,289	3,689
Gasoline on out-of-town trips	9,985	358	1,574	2,949	2,411	1,464	921	308
Diesel fuel	1,330	28	153	538	359	128	85	39
Motor oil	1,398	49	252	412	344	197	96	49
OTHER VEHICLE EXPENSES	$166,004	$4,545	$27,505	$50,118	$42,934	$21,594	$12,997	$6,310
Vehicle finance charges	30,552	852	6,437	9,388	8,588	3,258	1,776	253
Cars	21,276	647	4,368	5,930	6,163	2,543	1,397	229
Trucks	7,384	183	1,844	2,750	1,780	551	253	23
Motorcycles, planes, and other vehicles	1,891	22	225	708	645	165	126	0
Repairs and maintenance	60,331	1,604	9,428	18,850	14,380	8,155	5,095	2,818
Body work	3,728	139	530	1,189	932	503	278	158
Clutch, transmission repair	3,790	85	646	1,198	921	481	303	156
Drive train repair	772	6	160	184	173	145	44	61
Brake repair and adjustment	4,066	103	736	1,309	889	547	310	173
Steering repair	1,194	53	192	343	260	129	128	91
Cooling system repair	2,479	52	369	689	569	361	282	156
Motor tune-up	4,341	127	716	1,263	969	674	385	207
Motor repair and replacement	6,726	217	1,132	1,952	1,714	923	405	384

Aggregate expenditures for transportation, by age of householder in 2000 (in 1988 dollars).

(continued from previous page)	all households	under 25	25 to 34	35 to 44	45 to 54	55 to 64	65 to 74	75+
Lubrication, oil change	2,657	74	383	661	626	422	330	162
Front end alignment, wheel balancing	1,007	17	153	285	282	127	101	41
Shock absorber replacement	705	11	120	200	190	94	53	37
Exhaust system repair	1,633	33	206	414	465	208	187	121
Electrical system repair	2,203	42	260	658	592	300	225	126
Tire replacement	9,316	257	1,427	3,011	2,315	1,169	760	377
Coolant, additives, brake/transmission fluids	764	27	128	235	187	91	63	33
Parts, equipment, accessories, and other vehicle products	8,571	200	1,435	3,060	1,993	1,182	494	207
Out-of-town, tire, other servicing and repairs	5,103	123	598	1,783	1,067	626	610	294
Auto repair service policy	934	12	174	309	181	137	96	26
Vehicle insurance	**55,785**	**1,616**	**8,174**	**15,372**	**15,115**	**7,854**	**4,931**	**2,723**
Vehicle leasing, renting, licensing, and other charges	**19,337**	**472**	**3,467**	**6,508**	**4,850**	**2,327**	**1,196**	**517**
Leased and rented vehicles	7,120	120	1,337	2,960	1,905	606	143	49
Cars	5,261	99	1,030	1,925	1,592	473	118	24
Trucks	1,777	17	284	996	308	131	16	25
State and local registration	6,894	162	1,135	1,979	1,611	983	713	310
Drivers' license	688	27	104	198	165	92	66	36
Vehicle inspection	662	15	102	179	161	95	66	44
Parking fees	2,280	78	465	676	602	304	111	45
Tolls	1,167	30	213	384	259	189	69	22
Towing charges	525	39	111	132	146	57	28	10
PUBLIC TRANSPORTATION	**$30,746**	**$843**	**$4,226**	**$7,824**	**$8,412**	**$4,593**	**$3,090**	**$1,758**
Airline fares	**20,611**	**465**	**2,947**	**5,220**	**5,731**	**3,112**	**2,009**	**1,128**
Intercity bus fares	**1,562**	**25**	**72**	**237**	**284**	**214**	**527**	**203**
Intercity train fares	**1,040**	**30**	**67**	**246**	**377**	**161**	**85**	**74**
Intracity mass transit fares	**4,692**	**228**	**881**	**1,194**	**1,276**	**724**	**212**	**176**
Taxi fares	**1,232**	**51**	**190**	**275**	**324**	**194**	**86**	**112**
Ship fares	**1,426**	**40**	**52**	**586**	**349**	**170**	**167**	**62**
School bus	**113**	**-**	**14**	**50**	**49**	**-**	**0**	**0**

Note: Expenditures are not given (-) when the amount is too small to be reliable. Expenditures listed for a given category may not add to the total for that category because the listing is incomplete. "Leased and rented vehicles," for example, includes "aircraft rental," which is omitted here. Numbers may not add to total due to rounding. Households are used here because the number of consumer units in 1995 and 2000 is not available. Household projections are from the Census Bureau. Projections show how annual aggregate expenditures will change as the number of households in the age groups changes in 1995 and 2000. Projections are based on the average annual expenditures in 1988 and have not been adjusted for price increases or for changes in expenditure patterns.

PART II
Spending by income for transportation

The highest-income households account for one-third of the market for new cars and trucks...

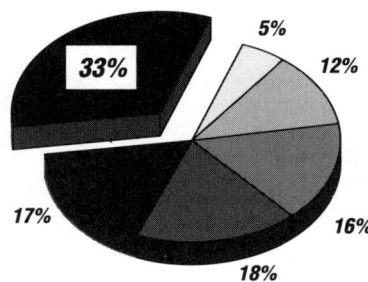

...nearly one-quarter of the market for used cars and trucks...

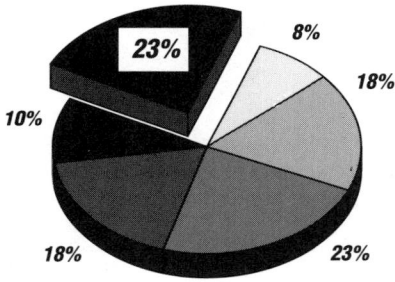

...and the largest share of the market for vehicle maintenance and repair.

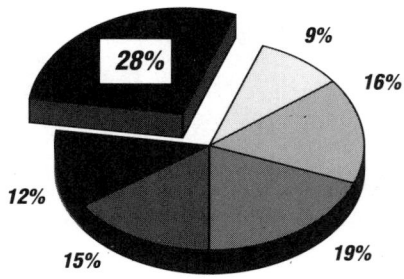

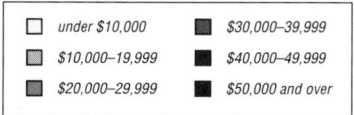

☐ under $10,000	◼ $30,000–39,999
◼ $10,000–19,999	◼ $40,000–49,999
◼ $20,000–29,999	◼ $50,000 and over

As household income climbs from the lowest to the highest income group, the average amount people spend on transportation increases by 470 percent. Those classy new automobiles don't come cheap and neither do repairs. Average spending on new cars climbs 1300 percent from the lowest to the highest income households; spending on maintenance and repairs increases by 370 percent; spending on public transportation by 460 percent. Other transportation items for which spending escalates rapidly with income are aircraft purchases, body work, shock absorber replacement, vehicle leasing and rentals, tolls, air fares, and ship fares.

One reason for the increase in spending on transportation with income is that the average number of vehicles per household rises with income. Households with incomes under $10,000 own an average of just one vehicle. Those with incomes of $50,000 or more own an average of three vehicles. Since they have so many vehicles, it is not surprising that the highest income households spend the most on nearly every transportation item with a few exceptions. The big spenders on used trucks, new and used motorcycles, towing charges, and intercity bus fares are households in the $20,000 to $40,000 income brackets.

Households with incomes of $50,000 or more spent $119 billion on transportation in 1988—28 percent of the national market. With spending of $129 billion, middle income households with incomes of $30,000 to $50,000 represent 30 percent of the market. Forty-two percent of the transportation market is accounted for by households with incomes under $30,000.

Low-end markets

Households with incomes under $30,000 spend more than average on only a few transportation items. Those with incomes of $20,000 to $30,000 spend only 4 percent more than the average for vehicles in general. But they are big spenders when it comes to used trucks and motorcycles. For all other major transportation categories, their spending is only slightly above average, and for public transportation it's 10 percent below average.

Among households in the $10,000 to $20,000 income group, spending on new and used vehicles is 34 percent below average. This group spends about 25 percent less than the average household on gas, oil, and maintenance and repairs.

Transportation spending is 67 percent below average for households with incomes under $10,000. They spend only one-quarter of the average amount on vehicles, half as much on gas and oil, and less than half as much on maintenance and repairs, insurance, leasing and licensing, and public transportation.

High-end markets

Transportation spending is 30 percent above average for households with incomes in the $30,000 to $40,000 range. Their spending is 36 percent above average for vehicles; 27 percent above average for gas, motor oil, and other vehicle-related items. Nevertheless, this group spends more than any other on towing and intercity buses.

With overall vehicle expenses 61 percent above average, households with incomes of $40,000 to $50,000 spend more than twice the average amount on new trucks and nearly 80 percent more on new cars. They are the peak spenders on motor oil, liquid additives like coolant, auto service repair policies, steering repairs, and exhaust system repairs. In the public transportation category, they spend well above-average amounts on airfare, intercity buses, taxis, and school buses.

Nearly 30 percent of the U.S. transportation market is accounted for by households with incomes of $50,000 or more. These households spend more than twice the average amount on new vehicles, other vehicles (primarily airplanes), vehicle leasing, public transportation, and several maintenance and repair items like body work and tune-ups. They pay parking fees and cruise fares that are about triple the average, airfares that are 168 percent more than average, and intercity bus fares that beat the average by 152 percent.

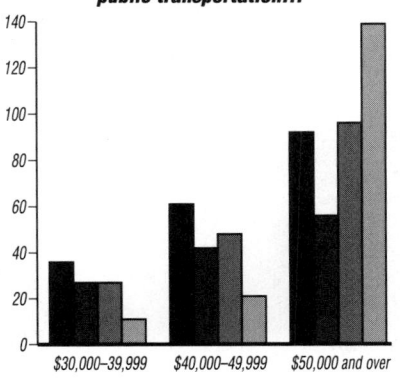

High-end households spend well above average for both private and public transportation...

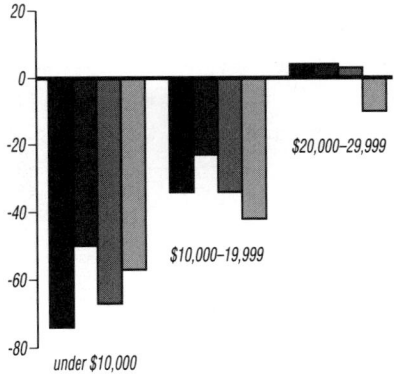

...while most low-end households do not.

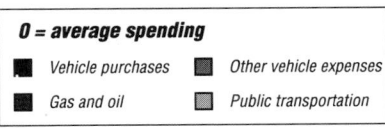

0 = average spending

- ■ Vehicle purchases
- ■ Gas and oil
- ■ Other vehicle expenses
- ■ Public transportation

Average expenditures

(consumer units include complete income reporters only)	all cu's	under $10,000	$10,000 to $19,999	$20,000 to $29,999	$30,000 to $39,999	$40,000 to $49,999	$50,000 and over
Number of consumer units (in thousands)	81,354	18,809	17,652	14,586	10,901	7,198	12,209
Average number of persons per cu	2.6	1.8	2.3	2.7	2.9	3.2	3.1
Average number of earners per cu	1.4	0.7	1.0	1.5	1.8	2.0	2.1
TOTAL AVERAGE ANNUAL EXPENDITURES	$26,389.07	$11,269.43	$18,078.25	$24,896.36	$31,659.60	$37,562.00	$52,320.19
TRANSPORTATION, AVERAGE ANNUAL EXPENDITURES	$5,140.21	$1,709.35	$3,459.41	$5,302.92	$6,704.50	$7,779.21	$9,714.71
VEHICLE PURCHASES (NET OUTLAY)	**$2,388.19**	**$609.75**	**$1,568.08**	**$2,485.58**	**$3,248.39**	**$3,839.91**	**$4,573.46**
Cars and trucks, new	**1,393.73**	**279.84**	**760.49**	**1,223.08**	**1,894.51**	**2,685.18**	**3,007.38**
New cars	991.60	158.28	566.77	782.66	1,565.37	1,777.93	2,163.34
New trucks	400.13	121.56	193.72	440.42	329.13	907.25	844.04
Cars and trucks, used	**971.12**	**326.73**	**793.85**	**1,221.87**	**1,330.29**	**1,132.30**	**1,504.86**
Used cars	754.27	247.23	629.62	863.43	974.26	926.36	1,287.37
Used trucks	216.85	79.50	164.24	358.44	356.03	205.94	217.49
Other vehicles	**25.34**	**3.19**	**13.74**	**40.63**	**23.59**	**22.43**	**61.22**
Motorcycles	21.07	3.19	13.74	40.64	23.59	22.43	32.80
Aircraft	4.27	0.00	0.00	0.00	0.00	0.00	28.42
GASOLINE AND MOTOR OIL	**$933.90**	**$467.29**	**$714.76**	**$974.84**	**$1,189.53**	**$1,328.42**	**$1,459.88**
Gasoline at home	**812.03**	**410.26**	**627.46**	**860.76**	**1,037.67**	**1,152.21**	**1,237.62**
Gasoline on out-of-town trips	**96.47**	**44.98**	**69.32**	**92.50**	**118.25**	**145.52**	**171.41**
Diesel fuel	**12.01**	**3.28**	**5.44**	**7.50**	**16.98**	**13.33**	**35.10**
Motor oil	**13.40**	**8.76**	**12.53**	**14.07**	**16.62**	**17.36**	**15.74**
OTHER VEHICLE EXPENSES	**$1,552.56**	**$518.74**	**$1,022.62**	**$1,603.36**	**$1,972.84**	**$2,290.12**	**$3,046.42**
Vehicle finance charges	**284.70**	**61.09**	**137.60**	**293.49**	**397.69**	**485.81**	**611.95**
Cars	196.25	45.97	109.87	200.40	275.36	306.48	412.11
Trucks	71.94	12.49	25.21	77.35	107.00	155.35	144.14
Motorcycles, planes, and other vehicles	16.52	2.64	2.52	15.75	15.33	23.98	55.71
Repairs and maintenance	**568.66**	**224.51**	**426.03**	**610.06**	**656.51**	**783.55**	**1,055.81**
Body work	34.71	9.22	26.07	38.37	32.79	33.62	84.44
Clutch, transmission repair	34.54	13.63	23.72	41.79	43.59	42.05	61.22
Drive train repair	7.58	2.21	3.06	12.07	6.41	10.31	16.45
Brake repair and adjustment	37.80	19.01	23.91	37.52	43.30	54.64	72.32
Steering repair	11.64	6.01	8.62	12.11	10.17	23.19	18.63
Cooling system repair	22.87	8.90	20.55	21.85	24.60	31.59	42.28
Motor tune-up	40.07	14.45	27.78	35.55	42.71	54.54	91.82
Motor repair and replacement	63.53	28.70	53.27	71.06	62.61	82.11	112.89

Average annual expenditures for transportation, by total before-tax income of consumer unit.

(continued from previous page)	all cu's	under $10,000	$10,000 to $19,999	$20,000 to $29,999	$30,000 to $39,999	$40,000 to $49,999	$50,000 and over
Lubrication, oil change	24.67	9.60	19.42	24.21	30.88	32.99	45.55
Front end alignment, wheel balancing	9.30	3.20	5.94	9.91	12.59	11.68	18.51
Shock absorber replacement	6.01	1.76	2.78	7.11	5.80	7.10	15.43
Exhaust system repair	14.55	7.99	11.99	16.15	16.86	22.09	19.92
Electrical system repair	20.35	10.66	13.80	22.14	19.66	34.50	34.88
Tire replacement	86.22	36.49	62.69	84.47	115.02	134.28	144.92
Coolant, additives, brake and transmission fluids	7.15	4.68	6.71	7.65	8.94	9.47	8.01
Parts, equipment, accessories, and other vehicle products	90.72	25.57	76.85	96.64	116.95	105.09	176.86
Out-of-town, tire, and other servicing and repairs	48.33	21.36	31.73	62.00	53.12	77.82	76.52
Auto repair service policy	8.54	-	7.11	9.44	10.51	16.46	14.61
Vehicle insurance	**515.06**	**182.09**	**358.64**	**544.70**	**665.71**	**728.25**	**958.57**
Vehicle leasing, renting, licensing, and other charges	**184.14**	**51.06**	**100.37**	**155.11**	**252.94**	**292.51**	**420.08**
Leased and rented vehicles	68.54	8.35	26.26	42.79	96.33	124.51	195.33
Cars	51.14	6.72	24.72	33.64	70.28	105.82	129.32
Trucks	16.50	1.63	1.37	8.47	24.58	18.19	62.63
State and local registration	67.04	24.40	47.40	70.39	96.23	99.31	112.03
Drivers' license	6.59	3.32	5.92	6.62	9.23	7.71	9.58
Vehicle inspection	6.33	3.14	4.85	6.17	8.61	9.70	9.56
Parking fees	20.50	6.02	7.93	14.30	23.35	30.90	59.74
Tolls	10.08	2.15	3.48	10.46	12.21	14.21	27.53
Towing charges	5.05	3.68	4.55	4.38	6.97	6.18	6.32
PUBLIC TRANSPORTATION	**$265.56**	**$113.57**	**$153.95**	**$239.14**	**$293.73**	**$320.76**	**$634.96**
Airline fares	**176.01**	**51.90**	**84.03**	**158.79**	**193.56**	**232.90**	**471.55**
Intercity bus fares	**14.30**	**13.42**	**9.56**	**12.41**	**27.86**	**10.82**	**14.74**
Intercity train fares	**9.04**	**5.27**	**4.60**	**8.18**	**4.87**	**14.49**	**22.78**
Intracity mass transit fares	**41.07**	**32.65**	**43.88**	**38.53**	**32.98**	**34.12**	**64.33**
Taxi fares	**10.75**	**6.11**	**7.24**	**10.89**	**14.27**	**13.13**	**18.24**
Ship fares	**13.00**	**3.69**	**3.87**	**9.46**	**19.05**	**12.55**	**39.62**
School bus	**0.86**	-	-	-	-	**1.70**	**2.48**

Note: Expenditures are not given (-) when the amount is too small to be reliable. Expenditures listed for a given category may not add to the total for that category because the listing is incomplete. "Leased and rented vehicles," for example, includes "aircraft rental," which is omitted here. Total expenditure exceeds total income in some income categories due to a number of factors including the underreporting of income, borrowing, and the use of savings. Numbers may not add to total due to rounding.

Share of spending

(consumer units include complete income reporters only)	all cu's	under $10,000	$10,000 to $19,999	$20,000 to $29,999	$30,000 to $39,999	$40,000 to $49,999	$50,000 and over
Number of consumer units (in thousands)	81,354	18,809	17,652	14,586	10,901	7,198	12,209
Average number of persons per cu	2.6	1.8	2.3	2.7	2.9	3.2	3.1
Average number of earners per cu	1.4	0.7	1.0	1.5	1.8	2.0	2.1
TOTAL AVERAGE ANNUAL EXPENDITURES	100.00%	100.00%	100.00%	100.00%	100.00%	100.00%	100.00%
TRANSPORTATION, AVERAGE ANNUAL EXPENDITURES	19.48%	15.17%	19.14%	21.30%	21.18%	20.71%	18.57%
VEHICLE PURCHASES (NET OUTLAY)	**9.05%**	**5.41%**	**8.67%**	**9.98%**	**10.26%**	**10.22%**	**8.74%**
Cars and trucks, new	**5.28**	**2.48**	**4.21**	**4.91**	**5.98**	**7.15**	**5.75**
New cars..	3.76	1.40	3.14	3.14	4.94	4.73	4.13
New trucks	1.52	1.08	1.07	1.77	1.04	2.42	1.61
Cars and trucks, used	**3.68**	**2.90**	**4.39**	**4.91**	**4.20**	**3.01**	**2.88**
Used cars	2.86	2.19	3.48	3.47	3.08	2.47	2.46
Used trucks	0.82	0.71	0.91	1.44	1.12	0.55	0.42
Other vehicles	**0.10**	**0.03**	**0.08**	**0.16**	**0.07**	**0.06**	**0.12**
Motorcycles	0.08	0.03	0.08	0.16	0.07	0.06	0.06
Aircraft	0.02	0.00	0.00	0.00	0.00	0.00	0.05
GASOLINE AND MOTOR OIL	**3.54%**	**4.15%**	**3.95%**	**3.92%**	**3.76%**	**3.54%**	**2.79%**
Gasoline at home	**3.08**	**3.64**	**3.47**	**3.46**	**3.28**	**3.07**	**2.37**
Gasoline on out-of-town trips...................................	**0.37**	**0.40**	**0.38**	**0.37**	**0.37**	**0.39**	**0.33**
Diesel fuel	**0.05**	**0.03**	**0.03**	**0.03**	**0.05**	**0.04**	**0.07**
Motor oil	**0.05**	**0.08**	**0.07**	**0.06**	**0.05**	**0.05**	**0.03**
OTHER VEHICLE EXPENSES	**5.88%**	**4.60%**	**5.66%**	**6.44%**	**6.23%**	**6.10%**	**5.82%**
Vehicle finance charges	**1.08**	**0.54**	**0.76**	**1.18**	**1.26**	**1.29**	**1.17**
Cars	0.74	0.41	0.61	0.80	0.87	0.82	0.79
Trucks...	0.27	0.11	0.14	0.31	0.34	0.41	0.28
Motorcycles, planes, and other vehicles	0.06	0.02	0.01	0.06	0.05	0.06	0.11
Repairs and maintenance	**2.15**	**1.99**	**2.36**	**2.45**	**2.07**	**2.09**	**2.02**
Body work	0.13	0.08	0.14	0.15	0.10	0.09	0.16
Clutch, transmission repair	0.13	0.12	0.13	0.17	0.14	0.11	0.12
Drive train repair	0.03	0.02	0.02	0.05	0.02	0.03	0.03
Brake repair and adjustment	0.14	0.17	0.13	0.15	0.14	0.15	0.14
Steering repair	0.04	0.05	0.05	0.05	0.03	0.06	0.04
Cooling system repair	0.09	0.08	0.11	0.09	0.08	0.08	0.08
Motor tune-up	0.15	0.13	0.15	0.14	0.13	0.15	0.18
Motor repair and replacement	0.24	0.25	0.29	0.29	0.20	0.22	0.22

Percent of total average annual expenditures spent on transportation, by total before-tax income of consumer unit.

(continued from previous page)	all cu's	under $10,000	$10,000 to $19,999	$20,000 to $29,999	$30,000 to $39,999	$40,000 to $49,999	$50,000 and over
Lubrication, oil change	0.09	0.09	0.11	0.10	0.10	0.09	0.09
Front end alignment, wheel balancing	0.04	0.03	0.03	0.04	0.04	0.03	0.04
Shock absorber replacement	0.02	0.02	0.02	0.03	0.02	0.02	0.03
Exhaust system repair	0.06	0.07	0.07	0.06	0.05	0.06	0.04
Electrical system repair	0.08	0.09	0.08	0.09	0.06	0.09	0.07
Tire replacement	0.33	0.32	0.35	0.34	0.36	0.36	0.28
Coolant, additives, brake and transmission fluids	0.03	0.04	0.04	0.03	0.03	0.03	0.02
Parts, equipment, accessories and other vehicle products	0.34	0.23	0.43	0.39	0.37	0.28	0.34
Out-of-town, tire, and other servicing and repairs	0.18	0.19	0.18	0.25	0.17	0.21	0.15
Auto repair service policy	0.03	-	0.04	0.04	0.03	0.04	0.03
Vehicle insurance	**1.95**	**1.62**	**1.98**	**2.19**	**2.10**	**1.94**	**1.83**
Vehicle leasing, renting, licensing, and other charges	**0.70**	**0.45**	**0.56**	**0.62**	**0.80**	**0.78**	**0.80**
Leased and rented vehicles	0.26	0.07	0.15	0.17	0.30	0.33	0.37
Cars	0.19	0.06	0.14	0.14	0.22	0.28	0.25
Trucks	0.06	0.01	0.01	0.03	0.08	0.05	0.12
State and local registration	0.25	0.22	0.26	0.28	0.30	0.26	0.21
Drivers' license	0.02	0.03	0.03	0.03	0.03	0.02	0.02
Vehicle inspection	0.02	0.03	0.03	0.02	0.03	0.03	0.02
Parking fees	0.08	0.05	0.04	0.06	0.07	0.08	0.11
Tolls	0.04	0.02	0.02	0.04	0.04	0.04	0.05
Towing charges	0.02	0.03	0.03	0.02	0.02	0.02	0.01
PUBLIC TRANSPORTATION	**1.01%**	**1.01%**	**0.85%**	**0.96%**	**0.93%**	**0.85%**	**1.21%**
Airline fares	**0.67**	**0.46**	**0.46**	**0.64**	**0.61**	**0.62**	**0.90**
Intercity bus fares	**0.05**	**0.12**	**0.05**	**0.05**	**0.09**	**0.03**	**0.03**
Intercity train fares	**0.03**	**0.05**	**0.03**	**0.03**	**0.02**	**0.04**	**0.04**
Intracity mass transit fares	**0.16**	**0.29**	**0.24**	**0.15**	**0.10**	**0.09**	**0.12**
Taxi fares	**0.04**	**0.05**	**0.04**	**0.04**	**0.05**	**0.03**	**0.03**
Ship fares	**0.05**	**0.03**	**0.02**	**0.04**	**0.06**	**0.03**	**0.08**
School bus	**0.00**	-	-	-	-	**0.00**	**0.00**

Note: Expenditures are not given (-) when the amount is too small to be reliable. Expenditures listed for a given category may not add to the total for that category because the listing is incomplete. "Leased and rented vehicles," for example, includes "aircraft rental," which is omitted here. Numbers may not add to total due to rounding.

Indexed expenditures

Indexed average annual expenditures for transportation, by total before-tax income of consumer unit.

(consumer units include complete income reporters only)	all cu's	under $10,000	$10,000 to $19,999	$20,000 to $29,999	$30,000 to $39,999	$40,000 to $49,999	$50,000 and over
Number of consumer units (in thousands)	81,354	18,809	17,652	14,586	10,901	7,198	12,209
Average number of persons per cu	2.6	1.8	2.3	2.7	2.9	3.2	3.1
Average number of earners per cu	1.4	0.7	1.0	1.5	1.8	2.0	2.1
TOTAL AVERAGE ANNUAL EXPENDITURES	100	43	69	94	120	142	198
TRANSPORTATION, AVERAGE ANNUAL EXPENDITURES	100	33	67	103	130	151	189
VEHICLE PURCHASES (NET OUTLAY)	100	26	66	104	136	161	192
Cars and trucks, new	100	20	55	88	136	193	216
New cars	100	16	57	79	158	179	218
New trucks	100	30	48	110	82	227	211
Cars and trucks, used	100	34	82	126	137	117	155
Used cars	100	33	83	114	129	123	171
Used trucks	100	37	76	165	164	95	100
Other vehicles	100	13	54	160	93	89	242
Motorcycles	100	15	65	193	112	106	156
Aircraft	100	0	0	0	0	0	666
GASOLINE AND MOTOR OIL	100	50	77	104	127	142	156
Gasoline at home	100	51	77	106	128	142	152
Gasoline on out-of-town trips	100	47	72	96	123	151	178
Diesel fuel	100	27	45	62	141	111	292
Motor oil	100	65	94	105	124	130	117
OTHER VEHICLE EXPENSES	100	33	66	103	127	148	196
Vehicle finance charges	100	21	48	103	140	171	215
Cars	100	23	56	102	140	156	210
Trucks	100	17	35	108	149	216	200
Motorcycles, planes, and other vehicles	100	16	15	95	93	145	337
Repairs and maintenance	100	39	75	107	115	138	186
Body work	100	27	75	111	94	97	243
Clutch, transmission repair	100	39	69	121	126	122	177
Drive train repair	100	29	40	159	85	136	217
Brake repair and adjustment	100	50	63	99	115	145	191
Steering repair	100	52	74	104	87	199	160
Cooling system repair	100	39	90	96	108	138	185
Motor tune-up	100	36	69	89	107	136	229
Motor repair and replacement	100	45	84	112	99	129	178

Indexed average annual expenditures for transportation, by total before-tax income of consumer unit.

(continued from previous page)	all cu's	under $10,000	$10,000 to $19,999	$20,000 to $29,999	$30,000 to $39,999	$40,000 to $49,999	$50,000 and over
Lubrication, oil change	100	39	79	98	125	134	185
Front end alignment, wheel balancing	100	34	64	107	135	126	199
Shock absorber replacement	100	29	46	118	97	118	257
Exhaust system repair	100	55	82	111	116	152	137
Electrical system repair	100	52	68	109	97	170	171
Tire replacement	100	42	73	98	133	156	168
Coolant, additives, brake and transmission fluids	100	65	94	107	125	132	112
Parts, equipment, accessories, and other vehicle products	100	28	85	107	129	116	195
Out-of-town, tire, and other servicing and repairs	100	44	66	128	110	161	158
Auto repair service policy	100	-	83	111	123	193	171
Vehicle insurance	**100**	**35**	**70**	**106**	**129**	**141**	**186**
Vehicle leasing, renting, licensing, and other charges	**100**	**28**	**55**	**84**	**137**	**159**	**228**
Leased and rented vehicles	100	12	38	62	141	182	285
Cars	100	13	48	66	137	207	253
Trucks	100	10	8	51	149	110	380
State and local registration	100	36	71	105	144	148	167
Drivers' license	100	50	90	100	140	117	145
Vehicle inspection	100	50	77	97	136	153	151
Parking fees	100	29	39	70	114	151	291
Tolls	100	21	35	104	121	141	273
Towing charges	100	73	90	87	138	122	125
PUBLIC TRANSPORTATION	**100**	**43**	**58**	**90**	**111**	**121**	**239**
Airline fares	**100**	**29**	**48**	**90**	**110**	**132**	**268**
Intercity bus fares	**100**	**94**	**67**	**87**	**195**	**76**	**103**
Intercity train fares	**100**	**58**	**51**	**90**	**54**	**160**	**252**
Intracity mass transit fares	**100**	**80**	**107**	**94**	**80**	**83**	**157**
Taxi fares	**100**	**57**	**67**	**101**	**133**	**122**	**170**
Ship fares	**100**	**28**	**30**	**73**	**147**	**97**	**305**
School bus	**100**	-	-	-	-	**198**	**288**

Note: Expenditures are not given (-) when the amount is too small to be reliable. An index of 100 represents the average for all consumer units. An index of 132 means that the average for the subgroup is 32 percent above the average for all consumer units. An index of 68 indicates spending that is 32 percent below the overall average.

Aggregate expenditures, 1988

(consumer units include complete income reporters only)	all cu's	under $10,000	$10,000 to $19,999	$20,000 to $29,999	$30,000 to $39,999	$40,000 to $49,999	$50,000 and over
Number of consumer units (in thousands)	81,354	18,809	17,652	14,586	10,901	7,198	12,20
Average number of persons per cu	2.6	1.8	2.3	2.7	2.9	3.2	3.1
Average number of earners per cu	1.4	0.7	1.0	1.5	1.8	2.0	2.1
TOTAL AGGREGATE EXPENDITURES (in millions)	$2,148,492	$211,967	$319,117	$363,138	$345,121	$270,371	$638,777
TRANSPORTATION, AGGREGATE EXPENDITURES (in millions)	$418,253	$32,151	$61,066	$77,348	$73,086	$55,995	$118,607
VEHICLE PURCHASES (NET OUTLAY)	$194,291	$11,469	$27,680	$36,255	$35,411	$27,640	$55,837
Cars and trucks, new	113,225	5,264	13,424	17,840	20,652	19,328	36,717
New cars	80,671	2,977	10,005	11,416	17,064	12,798	26,412
New trucks	32,553	2,286	3,420	6,424	3,588	6,530	10,305
Cars and trucks, used	79,005	6,145	14,013	17,822	14,501	8,150	18,373
Used cars	61,364	4,650	11,114	12,594	10,620	6,668	15,718
Used trucks	17,641	1,495	2,899	5,228	3,881	1,482	2,655
Other vehicles	2,061	60	243	593	257	161	747
Motorcycles	1,714	60	243	593	257	161	400
Aircraft	347	0	0	0	0	0	347
GASOLINE AND MOTOR OIL	$75,978	$8,789	$12,617	$14,219	$12,967	$9,562	$17,824
Gasoline at home	66,063	7,716	11,076	12,555	11,312	8,294	15,110
Gasoline on out-of-town trips	7,848	846	1,224	1,349	1,289	1,047	2,093
Diesel fuel	977	62	96	109	185	96	429
Motor oil	1,089	165	221	205	181	125	192
OTHER VEHICLE EXPENSES	$126,379	$9,757	$18,051	$23,387	$21,506	$16,484	$37,194
Vehicle finance charges	23,162	1,149	2,429	4,281	4,335	3,497	7,471
Cars	15,966	865	1,939	2,923	3,002	2,206	5,031
Trucks	5,852	235	445	1,128	1,166	1,118	1,760
Motorcycles, planes, and other vehicles	1,344	50	44	230	167	173	680
Repairs and maintenance	46,328	4,223	7,520	8,898	7,157	5,640	12,890
Body work	2,824	173	460	560	357	242	1,031
Clutch, transmission repair	2,810	256	419	610	475	303	747
Drive train repair	617	42	54	176	70	74	201
Brake repair and adjustment	3,075	358	422	547	472	393	883
Steering repair	947	113	152	177	111	167	227
Cooling system repair	1,861	167	363	319	268	227	516
Motor tune-up	3,260	272	490	519	466	393	1,121
Motor repair and replacement	5,169	540	940	1,036	683	591	1,378

Aggregate expenditures in 1988 for transportation, by total before-tax income of consumer unit.

(continued from previous page)	all cu's	under $10,000	$10,000 to $19,999	$20,000 to $29,999	$30,000 to $39,999	$40,000 to $49,999	$50,000 and over
Lubrication, oil change	2,007	181	343	353	337	237	556
Front end alignment, wheel balancing	757	60	105	145	137	84	226
Shock absorber replacement	489	33	49	104	63	51	188
Exhaust system repair	1,184	150	212	236	184	159	243
Electrical system repair	1,656	201	244	323	214	248	426
Tire replacement	7,015	686	1,107	1,232	1,254	967	1,769
Coolant, additives, brake and transmission fluids	581	88	118	112	97	68	98
Parts, equipment, accessories, and other vehicle products	7,438	481	1,357	1,410	1,275	756	2,159
Out-of-town, tire, and other servicing and repairs	3,940	402	560	904	579	560	934
Auto repair service policy	675	-	126	138	115	118	178
Vehicle insurance	**41,903**	**3,425**	**6,331**	**7,945**	**7,257**	**5,242**	**11,703**
Vehicle leasing, renting, licensing, and other charges	**14,986**	**960**	**1,772**	**2,262**	**2,757**	**2,105**	**5,129**
Leased and rented vehicles	5,576	157	463	624	1,050	896	2,385
Cars	4,160	126	436	491	766	762	1,579
Trucks	1,342	31	24	124	268	131	765
State and local registration	5,454	459	837	1,027	1,049	715	1,368
Drivers' license	537	62	104	97	101	55	117
Vehicle inspection	515	59	86	90	94	70	117
Parking fees	1,668	113	140	209	255	222	729
Tolls	826	40	61	153	133	102	336
Towing charges	411	69	80	64	76	44	77
PUBLIC TRANSPORTATION	**$21,605**	**$2,136**	**$2,718**	**$3,488**	**$3,202**	**$2,309**	**$7,752**
Airline fares	**14,319**	**976**	**1,483**	**2,316**	**2,110**	**1,676**	**5,757**
Intercity bus fares	**1,164**	**252**	**169**	**181**	**304**	**78**	**180**
Intercity train fares	**735**	**99**	**81**	**119**	**53**	**104**	**278**
Intracity mass transit fares	**3,341**	**614**	**775**	**562**	**360**	**246**	**785**
Taxi fares	**874**	**115**	**128**	**159**	**156**	**95**	**223**
Ship fares	**1,057**	**69**	**68**	**138**	**208**	**90**	**484**
School bus	**43**	**-**	**-**	**-**	**-**	**12**	**30**

Note: Expenditures are not given (-) when the amount is too small to be reliable. Expenditures listed for a given category may not add to the total for that category because the listing is incomplete. "Leased and rented vehicles," for example, includes "aircraft rental," which is omitted here. Numbers may not add to total due to rounding. The "all cu's" aggregates will differ slightly from table to table because they are the sums of the aggregates in each row.

PART III
Spending by type of household for transportation

Married couples account for over 70 percent of the market for new cars and trucks...

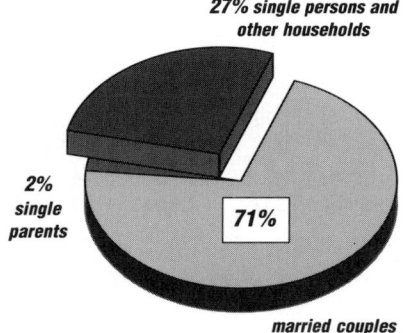

...nearly three-quarters of the market for used cars and trucks...

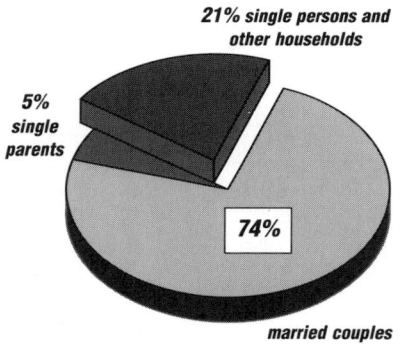

...and the majority of spending on vehicle maintenance and repairs.

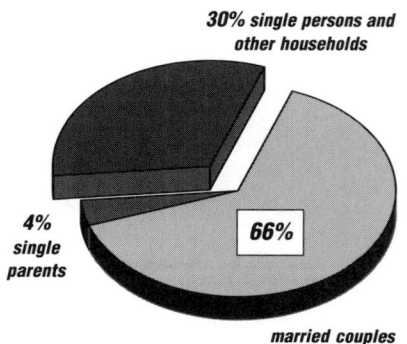

Married couples spent over $339 billion on transportation in 1988, accounting for 70 percent of the transportation market. They own an average of 2.6 vehicles and devote 20 percent of their household budget to transportation. Just 5 percent of those dollars go to public transportation, while the rest are evenly split between vehicle purchases and other vehicle expenses.

People who live alone and "other" households* are another 26 percent of the market. Together they spent $127 billion on transportation with 45 percent of that devoted to vehicle purchases; 31 percent going to maintenance, leasing, insurance and licensing; 18 percent to gas and oil; and 7 percent to public transportation. They own an average of 1.3 cars, trucks, or other vehicles.

Only 3 percent of the transportation market is accounted for by single parents, although they are 6 percent of all households. About 15 percent of their budget is devoted to this category, and 40 percent of those transportation dollars are allocated to vehicle purchases, mostly used cars.

Married-couple market

Empty-nesters and childless couples spend only 12 percent more than average on transportation. But these households are the biggest spenders on new cars, air fares, and intercity bus and train trips. They spend 43 percent more than the average household on new cars and air fares, 94 percent more than average on intercity bus fares, and 6 percent more on intercity train fares. They spend less than average on used, rented, or leased vehicles; intracity mass transit; and taxi fares.

Overall, married couples with children spend 38 percent more than average on transportation. Spending in this category rises with the age of the children, from 23 percent more than average for households with preschoolers to fully 65 percent above average for households with children aged 18 or older. Married couples with older children at home outspend others on all major transportation categories except public transportation. They have below average spending only on auto service policies, intercity bus fares, and taxi fares.

Households with school-aged children are the peak spenders on rented and leased vehicles. Those with children under age 6 spend more than any other type of household on new and used trucks and towing. Married

---

In this analysis, single-person households are grouped with "other" households. "Other" households are unrelated people living together and families that are not married-couple or single-parent families, such as siblings. Single-person households account for 72 percent of the households in this category.

couples living with extended family members or unrelated people spend 38 percent more than average on public transportation with spending on ship fares that is 215 percent above average.

Other household markets

Other types of households are typically below-average spenders and their spending on transportation is no exception. Single-person and "other" households spend 33 percent less than the average household on this category; single parents spend 44 percent less than average. Those who live alone or in "other" households, however, spend 22 percent more than average on taxi fares, 14 percent more on intercity bus fares and 5 percent more on mass transit fares. They also spend more than the average household on towing.

Single parents spend 16 percent more than average on towing and 17 percent more on leased and rented cars. They spend nearly twice the average amount on school bus fares and 38 percent more on mass transit fares.

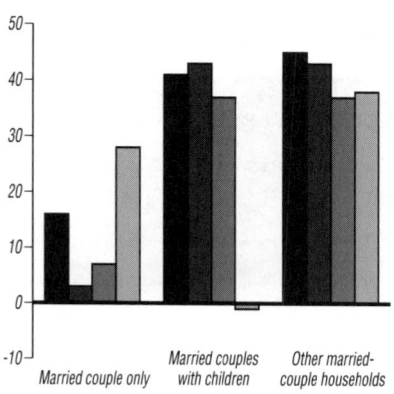

Married couples living with children outspend childless couples and empty-nesters for all categories except public transportation.

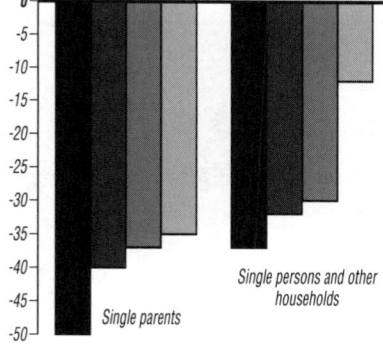

Single parents spend less than other households for all transportation categories.

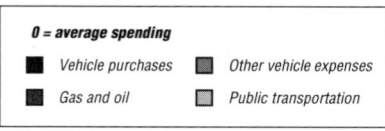

0 = average spending
- Vehicle purchases
- Gas and oil
- Other vehicle expenses
- Public transportation

Average expenditures

	all cu's	married couples	single parents	single persons and other cu's
Number of consumer units (in thousands)	94,862	52,010	5,716	37,136
Average number of persons per cu	2.6	3.3	2.9	1.5
Average number of earners per cu	1.4	1.7	1.0	0.9
Average total before-tax income	$28,540.00	$37,299.00	$16,276.00	$18,509.00
TOTAL AVERAGE ANNUAL EXPENDITURES	$25,891.85	$32,314.50	$18,615.80	$17,950.80
TRANSPORTATION, AVERAGE ANNUAL EXPENDITURES	$5,092.81	$6,523.20	$2,863.88	$3,431.44
VEHICLE PURCHASES (NET OUTLAY)	$2,360.51	$3,108.66	$1,174.00	$1,495.32
Cars and trucks, new	1,355.10	1,746.50	453.38	945.75
New cars	974.20	1,212.56	409.29	727.31
New trucks	380.91	533.94	44.09	218.43
Cars and trucks, used	982.07	1,331.56	714.06	533.85
Used cars	766.68	1,038.46	632.50	406.68
Used trucks	215.40	293.10	81.56	127.17
Other vehicles	23.33	30.60	6.57	15.73
Motorcycles	19.67	23.93	6.57	15.72
Aircraft	3.66	6.67	0.00	0.00
GASOLINE AND MOTOR OIL	$931.97	$1,188.09	$557.59	$630.89
Gasoline at home	814.53	1,034.48	506.02	553.99
Gasoline on out-of-town trips	92.71	120.93	37.67	61.65
Diesel fuel	11.69	16.47	4.56	6.10
Motor oil	13.02	16.21	9.34	9.15
OTHER VEHICLE EXPENSES	$1,521.36	$1,912.30	$951.89	$1,060.34
Vehicle finance charges	238.56	381.64	151.82	166.54
Cars	197.79	259.54	128.10	122.03
Trucks	69.50	98.10	22.99	36.61
Motorcycles, planes, and other vehicles	16.29	24.00	0.73	7.89
Repairs and maintenance	552.66	669.45	359.47	417.80
Body work	34.13	39.90	15.86	28.86
Clutch, transmission repair	34.75	40.67	25.41	27.88
Drive train repair	7.14	10.18	2.48	3.61
Brake repair and adjustment	37.74	43.80	30.53	30.37
Steering repair	11.19	13.25	7.08	8.94
Cooling system repair	22.70	26.97	9.47	18.77
Motor tune-up	40.31	48.20	22.41	32.01
Motor repair and replacement	61.81	75.08	34.89	47.38

Average annual expenditures for transportation, by type of consumer unit.

(continued from previous page)

	all cu's	married couples	single parents	single persons and other cu's
Lubrication, oil change	24.52	28.56	12.36	20.74
Front end alignment, wheel balancing	9.08	10.64	5.05	7.52
Shock absorber replacement	6.38	8.16	2.50	4.50
Exhaust system repair	14.59	18.33	8.31	10.32
Electrical system repair	19.62	23.43	15.93	14.85
Tire replacement	85.02	106.65	51.97	59.82
Coolant, additives, brake and transmission fluids	7.07	9.16	3.73	4.64
Parts, equipment, accessories, and other vehicle products	78.28	103.26	74.31	51.75
Out-of-town, tire, and other servicing and repairs	46.17	51.48	34.10	40.30
Auto repair service policy	8.70	11.59	3.06	5.52
Vehicle insurance	**507.72**	**642.20**	**320.57**	**348.19**
Vehicle leasing, renting, licensing, and other charges	**177.39**	**219.00**	**120.02**	**127.81**
Leased and rented vehicles	64.06	78.75	57.93	44.43
Cars	47.38	55.25	55.61	35.07
Trucks	15.85	22.61	2.32	8.45
State and local registration	63.65	82.19	30.28	42.83
Drivers' license	6.38	8.13	4.59	4.20
Vehicle inspection	6.06	7.64	4.23	4.13
Parking fees	21.31	23.31	12.35	19.88
Tolls	10.83	14.25	4.73	6.87
Towing charges	5.10	4.74	5.92	5.47
PUBLIC TRANSPORTATION	**$278.98**	**$314.16**	**$180.40**	**$244.89**
Airline fares	**186.43**	**222.82**	**90.76**	**150.20**
Intercity bus fares	**14.29**	**15.96**	**6.24**	**13.21**
Intercity train fares	**8.91**	**8.26**	**6.57**	**10.18**
Intracity mass transit fares	**44.08**	**40.66**	**60.89**	**46.28**
Taxi fares	**11.36**	**9.69**	**10.44**	**13.83**
Ship fares	**12.35**	**14.61**	**3.35**	**10.57**
School bus	**1.01**	**1.56**	**1.98**	**-**

Note: Expenditures are not given (-) when the amount is too small to be reliable. Expenditures listed for a given category may not add to the total for that category because the listing is incomplete. "Leased and rented vehicles," for example, includes "aircraft rental," which is omitted here. Numbers may not add to total due to rounding. "Single parents" is one-parent consumer units with a child or children under age 18 living at home. "Other cu's" includes persons living with unrelated persons and families other than married-couple and single-parent families.

Share of spending

	all cu's	married couples	single parents	single persons and other cu's
Number of consumer units (in thousands)	94,862	52,010	5,716	37,136
Average number of persons per cu	2.6	3.3	2.9	1.5
Average number of earners per cu	1.4	1.7	1.0	0.9
Average total before-tax income	$28,540	$37,299	$16,276	$18,509
TOTAL AVERAGE ANNUAL EXPENDITURES	100.00%	100.00%	100.00%	100.00%
TRANSPORTATION, AVERAGE ANNUAL EXPENDITURES	19.67%	20.19%	15.38%	19.12%
VEHICLE PURCHASES (NET OUTLAY)	**9.12%**	**9.62%**	**6.31%**	**8.33%**
Cars and trucks, new	**5.23**	**5.40**	**2.44**	**5.27**
New cars	3.76	3.75	2.20	4.05
New trucks	1.47	1.65	0.24	1.22
Cars and trucks, used	**3.79**	**4.12**	**3.84**	**2.97**
Used cars	2.96	3.21	3.40	2.27
Used trucks	0.83	0.91	0.44	0.71
Other vehicles	**0.09**	**0.09**	**0.04**	**0.09**
Motorcycles	0.08	0.07	0.04	0.09
Aircraft	0.01	0.02	0.00	0.00
GASOLINE AND MOTOR OIL	**3.60%**	**3.68%**	**3.00%**	**3.51%**
Gasoline at home	**3.15**	**3.20**	**2.72**	**3.09**
Gasoline on out-of-town trips	**0.36**	**0.37**	**0.20**	**0.34**
Diesel fuel	**0.05**	**0.05**	**0.02**	**0.03**
Motor oil	**0.05**	**0.05**	**0.05**	**0.05**
OTHER VEHICLE EXPENSES	**5.88%**	**5.92%**	**5.11%**	**5.91%**
Vehicle finance charges	**0.92**	**1.18**	**0.82**	**0.93**
Cars	0.76	0.80	0.69	0.68
Trucks	0.27	0.30	0.12	0.20
Motorcycles, planes, and other vehicles	0.06	0.07	0.00	0.04
Repairs and maintenance	**2.13**	**2.07**	**1.93**	**2.33**
Body work	0.13	0.12	0.09	0.16
Clutch, transmission repair	0.13	0.13	0.14	0.16
Drive train repair	0.03	0.03	0.01	0.02
Brake repair and adjustment	0.15	0.14	0.16	0.17
Steering repair	0.04	0.04	0.04	0.05
Cooling system repair	0.09	0.08	0.05	0.10
Motor tune-up	0.16	0.15	0.12	0.18
Motor repair and replacement	0.24	0.23	0.19	0.26

Percent of total average annual expenditures spent on transportation, by type of consumer unit.

(continued from previous page)

	all cu's	married couples	single parents	single persons and other cu's
Lubrication, oil change	0.09	0.09	0.07	0.12
Front end alignment, wheel balancing	0.04	0.03	0.03	0.04
Shock absorber replacement	0.02	0.03	0.01	0.03
Exhaust system repair	0.06	0.06	0.04	0.06
Electrical system repair	0.08	0.07	0.09	0.08
Tire replacement	0.33	0.33	0.28	0.33
Coolant, additives, brake and transmission fluids	0.03	0.03	0.02	0.03
Parts, equipment, accessories and other vehicle products	0.30	0.32	0.40	0.29
Out-of-town, tire, and other servicing and repairs	0.18	0.16	0.18	0.22
Auto repair service policy	0.03	0.04	0.02	0.03
Vehicle insurance	**1.96**	**1.99**	**1.72**	**1.94**
Vehicle leasing, renting, licensing, and other charges	**0.69**	**0.68**	**0.64**	**0.71**
Leased and rented vehicles	0.25	0.24	0.31	0.25
Cars	0.18	0.17	0.30	0.20
Trucks	0.06	0.07	0.01	0.05
State and local registration	0.25	0.25	0.16	0.24
Drivers' license	0.02	0.03	0.02	0.02
Vehicle inspection	0.02	0.02	0.02	0.02
Parking fees	0.08	0.07	0.07	0.11
Tolls	0.04	0.04	0.03	0.04
Towing charges	0.02	0.01	0.03	0.03
PUBLIC TRANSPORTATION	**1.08%**	**0.97%**	**0.97%**	**1.36%**
Airline fares	**0.72**	**0.69**	**0.49**	**0.84**
Intercity bus fares	**0.06**	**0.05**	**0.03**	**0.07**
Intercity train fares	**0.03**	**0.03**	**0.04**	**0.06**
Intracity mass transit fares	**0.17**	**0.13**	**0.33**	**0.26**
Taxi fares	**0.04**	**0.03**	**0.06**	**0.08**
Ship fares	**0.05**	**0.05**	**0.02**	**0.06**
School bus	**0.00**	**0.00**	**0.01**	**-**

Note: Expenditures are not given (-) when the amount is too small to be reliable. Expenditures listed for a given category may not add to the total for that category because the listing is incomplete. "Leased and rented vehicles," for example, includes "aircraft rental," which is omitted here. Numbers may not add to total due to rounding. "Single parents" is one-parent consumer units with a child or children under age 18 living at home. "Other cu's" includes persons living with unrelated persons and families other than married-couple and single-parent families.

Indexed expenditures

	all cu's	married couples	single parents	single persons and other cu's
Number of consumer units (in thousands)	94,862	52,010	5,716	37,136
Average number of persons per cu	2.6	3.3	2.9	1.5
Average number of earners per cu	1.4	1.7	1.0	0.9
Average total before-tax income	$28,540	$37,299	$16,276	$18,509
TOTAL AVERAGE ANNUAL EXPENDITURES	100	125	72	69
TRANSPORTATION, AVERAGE ANNUAL EXPENDITURES	100	128	56	67
VEHICLE PURCHASES (NET OUTLAY)	100	132	50	63
Cars and trucks, new	100	129	33	70
New cars	100	124	42	75
New trucks	100	140	12	57
Cars and trucks, used	100	136	73	54
Used cars	100	135	82	53
Used trucks	100	136	38	59
Other vehicles	100	131	28	67
Motorcycles	100	122	33	80
Aircraft	100	182	0	0
GASOLINE AND MOTOR OIL	100	127	60	68
Gasoline at home	100	127	62	68
Gasoline on out-of-town trips	100	130	41	66
Diesel fuel	100	141	39	52
Motor oil	100	125	72	70
OTHER VEHICLE EXPENSES	100	126	63	70
Vehicle finance charges	100	160	64	70
Cars	100	131	65	62
Trucks	100	141	33	53
Motorcycles, planes, and other vehicles	100	147	4	48
Repairs and maintenance	100	121	65	76
Body work	100	117	46	85
Clutch, transmission repair	100	117	73	80
Drive train repair	100	143	35	51
Brake repair and adjustment	100	116	81	80
Steering repair	100	118	63	80
Cooling system repair	100	119	42	83
Motor tune-up	100	120	56	79
Motor repair and replacement	100	121	56	77

Indexed average annual expenditures for transportation, by type of consumer unit.

(continued from previous page)

	all cu's	married couples	single parents	single persons and other cu's
Lubrication, oil change	100	116	50	85
Front end alignment, wheel balancing	100	117	56	83
Shock absorber replacement	100	128	39	71
Exhaust system repair	100	126	57	71
Electrical system repair	100	119	81	76
Tire replacement	100	125	61	70
Coolant, additives, brake and transmission fluids	100	130	53	66
Parts, equipment, accessories, and other vehicle products	100	132	95	66
Out-of-town, tire, and other servicing and repairs	100	112	74	87
Auto repair service policy	100	133	35	63
Vehicle insurance	**100**	**126**	**63**	**69**
Vehicle leasing, renting, licensing, and other charges	**100**	**123**	**68**	**72**
Leased and rented vehicles	100	123	90	69
Cars	100	117	117	74
Trucks	100	143	15	53
State and local registration	100	129	48	67
Drivers' license	100	127	72	66
Vehicle inspection	100	126	70	68
Parking fees	100	109	58	93
Tolls	100	132	44	63
Towing charges	100	93	116	107
PUBLIC TRANSPORTATION	**100**	**113**	**65**	**88**
Airline fares	**100**	**120**	**49**	**81**
Intercity bus fares	**100**	**112**	**44**	**92**
Intercity train fares	**100**	**93**	**74**	**114**
Intracity mass transit fares	**100**	**92**	**138**	**105**
Taxi fares	**100**	**85**	**92**	**122**
Ship fares	**100**	**118**	**27**	**86**
School bus	**100**	**154**	**196**	-

Note: An index of 100 represents the average for all consumer units. An index of 132 means that the average for the subgroup is 32 percent above the average for all consumer units. An index of 68 indicates spending that is 32 percent below the overall average. Expenditures are not given (-) when the amount is too small to be reliable. "Single parents" is one-parent consumer units with a child or children under age 18 living at home. "Other cu's" includes persons living with unrelated persons and families other than married-couple and single-parent families.

Aggregate expenditures, 1988

	all cu's	married couples	single parents	single persons and other cu's
Number of consumer units (in thousands)	94,862	52,010	5,716	37,136
Average number of persons per cu	2.6	3.3	2.9	1.5
Average number of earners per cu	1.4	1.7	1.0	0.9
Aggregate before-tax income (in millions)	$2,720,305	$1,939,921	$93,034	$687,350
TOTAL AGGREGATE EXPENDITURES (in millions)	$2,453,706	$1,680,677	$106,408	$666,621
TRANSPORTATION, AGGREGATE EXPENDITURES (in millions)	$483,072	$339,272	$16,370	$127,430
VEHICLE PURCHASES (NET OUTLAY)	**$223,922**	**$161,681**	**$6,711**	**$55,530**
Cars and trucks, new	**128,548**	**90,835**	**2,592**	**35,121**
New cars	92,414	63,065	2,340	27,009
New trucks	36,134	27,770	252	8,112
Cars and trucks, used	**93,161**	**69,254**	**4,082**	**19,825**
Used cars	72,728	54,010	3,615	15,102
Used trucks	20,433	15,244	466	4,723
Other vehicles	**2,213**	**1,592**	**38**	**584**
Motorcycles	1,866	1,245	38	584
Aircraft	347	347	0	0
GASOLINE AND MOTOR OIL	**$88,408**	**$61,793**	**$3,187**	**$23,429**
Gasoline at home	**77,269**	**53,803**	**2,892**	**20,573**
Gasoline on out-of-town trips	**8,794**	**6,290**	**215**	**2,289**
Diesel fuel	**1,109**	**857**	**26**	**227**
Motor oil	**1,236**	**843**	**53**	**340**
OTHER VEHICLE EXPENSES	**$144,277**	**$99,459**	**$5,441**	**$39,377**
Vehicle finance charges	**26,902**	**19,849**	**868**	**6,185**
Cars	18,763	13,499	732	4,532
Trucks	6,593	5,102	131	1,360
Motorcycles, planes, and other vehicles	1,545	1,248	4	293
Repairs and maintenance	**52,388**	**34,818**	**2,055**	**15,515**
Body work	3,238	2,075	91	1,072
Clutch, transmission repair	3,296	2,115	145	1,035
Drive train repair	678	529	14	134
Brake repair and adjustment	3,580	2,278	175	1,128
Steering repair	1,062	689	40	332
Cooling system repair	2,154	1,403	54	697
Motor tune-up	3,824	2,507	128	1,189
Motor repair and replacement	5,864	3,905	199	1,760

Aggregate expenditures in 1988 for transportation, by type of consumer unit.

(continued from previous page)

	all cu's	married couples	single parents	single persons and other cu's
Lubrication, oil change	2,326	1,485	71	770
Front end alignment, wheel balancing	862	553	29	279
Shock absorber replacement	606	424	14	167
Exhaust system repair	1,384	953	47	383
Electrical system repair	1,861	1,219	91	551
Tire replacement	8,065	5,547	297	2,221
Coolant, additives, brake and transmission fluids	670	476	21	172
Parts, equipment, accessories, and other vehicle products	7,717	5,371	425	1,922
Out-of-town, tire, and other servicing and repairs	4,369	2,677	195	1,497
Auto repair service policy	825	603	17	205
Vehicle insurance	**48,164**	**33,401**	**1,832**	**12,930**
Vehicle leasing, renting, licensing, and other charges	**16,823**	**11,390**	**686**	**4,746**
Leased and rented vehicles	6,077	4,096	331	1,650
Cars	4,494	2,874	318	1,302
Trucks	1,503	1,176	13	314
State and local registration	6,038	4,275	173	1,591
Drivers' license	605	423	26	156
Vehicle inspection	575	397	24	153
Parking fees	2,021	1,212	71	738
Tolls	1,023	741	27	255
Towing charges	484	247	34	203
PUBLIC TRANSPORTATION	**$26,465**	**$16,339**	**$1,031**	**$9,094**
Airline fares	**17,685**	**11,589**	**519**	**5,578**
Intercity bus fares	**1,356**	**830**	**36**	**491**
Intercity train fares	**845**	**430**	**38**	**378**
Intracity mass transit fares	**4,181**	**2,115**	**348**	**1,719**
Taxi fares	**1,077**	**504**	**60**	**514**
Ship fares	**1,172**	**760**	**19**	**393**
School bus	**92**	**81**	**11**	**-**

Note: Expenditures are not given (-) when the amount is too small to be reliable. Expenditures listed for a given category may not add to the total for that category because the listing is incomplete. "Leased and rented vehicles," for example, includes "aircraft rental," which is omitted here. Numbers may not add to total due to rounding. "Single parents" is one-parent consumer units with a child or children under age 18 living at home. "Other cu's" includes persons living with unrelated persons and families other than married-couple and single-parent families. The "all cu's" aggregates will differ slightly from table to table because they are the sums of the aggregates in each row.

Average expenditures

	all cu's	all married couples	married couple only	all married couples with children	AGE OF OLDEST CHILD			other married couples
					under 6	6 to 17	18 or older	
Number of consumer units (in thousands)	94,862	52,010	20,227	28,100	5,858	14,194	8,047	3,684
Average number of persons per cu	2.6	3.3	2.0	3.9	3.5	4.1	3.9	5.1
Average number of earners per cu	1.4	1.7	1.2	2.1	1.7	1.9	2.7	2.4
Average total before-tax income	$28,540.00	$37,299.00	$33,825.00	$39,354.00	$34,318.00	$38,039.00	$45,596.00	$40,846.00
Total average annual expenditures	$25,891.85	$32,314.50	$27,954.50	$35,015.30	$30,942.80	$35,248.40	$37,763.90	$35,739.60
TRANSPORTATION, AVERAGE ANNUAL EXPENDITURES	$5,092.81	$6,523.20	$5,695.45	$7,027.62	$6,248.32	$6,569.40	$8,412.25	$7,220.26
VEHICLE PURCHASES (NET OUTLAY)	$2,360.51	$3,108.66	$2,743.47	$3,330.24	$3,224.05	$3,054.24	$3,894.37	$3,423.65
Cars and trucks, new	1,355.10	1,746.50	1,871.85	1,673.00	1,960.54	1,471.27	1,819.49	1,618.89
New cars	974.20	1,212.56	1,388.54	1,070.88	1,069.50	997.81	1,200.78	1,326.99
New trucks	380.91	533.94	483.31	602.11	891.04	473.46	618.72	291.90
Cars and trucks, used	982.07	1,331.56	855.48	1,614.17	1,214.51	1,571.91	1,979.66	1,789.86
Used cars	766.68	1,038.46	679.29	1,238.82	795.81	1,159.43	1,701.36	1,482.23
Used trucks	215.40	293.10	176.20	375.35	418.69	412.48	278.30	307.63
Other vehicles	23.33	30.60	16.14	43.07	49.00	11.06	95.22	14.90
Motorcycles	19.67	23.93	16.13	30.72	49.00	11.07	52.09	14.90
Aircraft	3.66	6.67	0.00	12.35	0.00	0.00	43.12	0.00
GASOLINE AND MOTOR OIL	$931.97	$1,188.09	$964.14	$1,330.82	$1,053.65	$1,279.15	$1,623.73	$1,328.99
Gasoline at home	814.53	1,034.48	818.46	1,172.99	935.66	1,119.71	1,439.73	1,164.00
Gasoline on out-of-town trips	92.71	120.93	122.18	119.73	96.33	120.32	135.70	123.32
Diesel fuel	11.69	16.47	10.60	19.72	6.74	21.48	26.04	24.02
Motor oil	13.02	16.21	12.91	18.39	14.93	17.63	22.25	17.65
OTHER VEHICLE EXPENSES	$1,521.36	$1,912.30	$1,632.09	$2,091.59	$1,768.05	$1,970.03	$2,550.61	$2,082.98
Vehicle finance charges	238.56	381.64	286.54	437.68	411.86	400.55	521.99	476.38
Cars	197.79	259.54	208.97	285.37	257.14	241.16	383.90	340.21
Trucks	69.50	98.10	52.14	128.71	142.73	129.48	117.16	116.89
Motorcycles, planes, and other vehicles	16.29	24.00	25.43	23.60	11.99	29.90	20.93	19.28
Repairs and maintenance	552.66	669.45	599.06	723.03	601.78	699.35	861.99	647.23
Body work	34.13	39.90	36.16	42.89	39.21	38.95	52.53	37.58
Clutch, transmission repair	34.75	40.67	33.93	47.64	33.54	41.64	68.48	24.57
Drive train repair	7.14	10.18	10.48	10.43	13.74	8.19	11.97	6.65
Brake repair and adjustment	37.74	43.80	35.09	49.59	39.72	49.59	56.84	47.45
Steering repair	11.19	13.25	12.52	13.71	12.97	13.51	14.60	13.83
Cooling system repair	22.70	26.97	25.71	27.14	29.48	23.18	32.41	32.62
Motor tune-up	40.31	48.20	47.71	48.18	41.34	47.69	54.03	51.05
Motor repair and replacement	61.81	75.08	62.77	85.18	96.77	78.66	88.23	65.64

Average annual expenditures for transportation, by married couples with and without children.

(continued from previous page)

	all cu's	all married couples	married couple only	all married couples with children	AGE OF OLDEST CHILD			other married couples
					under 6	6 to 17	18 or older	
Lubrication, oil change	24.52	28.56	31.25	26.41	24.50	25.18	29.96	30.16
Front end alignment, wheel balancing	9.08	10.64	9.18	11.69	8.14	9.81	17.59	10.66
Shock absorber replacement	6.38	8.16	8.62	7.91	7.30	8.38	7.52	7.50
Exhaust system repair	14.59	18.33	17.35	19.34	16.96	17.80	23.78	16.03
Electrical system repair	19.62	23.43	21.55	25.03	23.46	20.25	34.60	21.56
Tire replacement	85.02	106.65	85.50	122.20	92.45	122.36	143.56	104.19
Coolant, additives, brake/transmission fluids ..	7.07	9.16	6.69	10.70	8.16	10.59	12.74	10.95
Parts, equipment, accessories,								
and other vehicle products	78.28	103.26	96.05	108.86	57.13	116.79	140.35	100.11
Out-of-town, tire, other servicing and repairs ..	46.17	51.48	47.96	55.19	39.89	56.23	65.59	42.40
Auto repair service policy	8.70	11.59	10.54	10.68	17.00	10.06	7.19	24.26
Vehicle insurance	**507.72**	**642.20**	**552.83**	**689.66**	**540.62**	**616.76**	**926.76**	**770.86**
Vehicle leasing, renting, licensing,								
and other charges	**177.39**	**219.00**	**193.66**	**241.20**	**213.79**	**253.36**	**239.88**	**188.51**
Leased and rented vehicles	64.06	78.75	60.50	95.01	90.81	101.63	86.39	54.96
Cars	47.38	55.25	42.42	65.79	69.08	64.78	65.15	45.43
Trucks	15.85	22.61	17.41	28.05	20.04	35.39	20.95	9.54
State and local registration	63.65	82.19	77.30	85.42	70.39	91.15	86.26	84.38
Drivers' license	6.38	8.13	8.06	8.21	6.17	8.15	9.81	7.91
Vehicle inspection	6.06	7.64	7.70	7.27	5.38	6.94	9.22	10.14
Parking fees	21.31	23.31	22.41	25.24	23.03	25.38	26.59	13.62
Tolls	10.83	14.25	15.21	14.18	9.54	15.94	14.64	9.14
Towing charges	5.10	4.74	2.49	5.88	8.47	4.18	6.98	8.36
PUBLIC TRANSPORTATION	**$278.98**	**$314.16**	**$355.75**	**$274.98**	**$202.57**	**$265.99**	**$343.55**	**$384.65**
Airline fares	**186.43**	**222.82**	**267.27**	**187.70**	**150.78**	**188.69**	**212.83**	**246.71**
Intercity bus fares	**14.29**	**15.96**	**27.75**	**7.63**	**1.98**	**7.72**	**11.56**	**14.74**
Intercity train fares	**8.91**	**8.26**	**9.42**	**7.44**	**1.17**	**8.97**	**9.29**	**8.14**
Intracity mass transit fares	**44.08**	**40.66**	**28.71**	**45.77**	**39.37**	**31.15**	**76.23**	**67.31**
Taxi fares	**11.36**	**9.69**	**9.83**	**9.92**	**5.42**	**11.18**	**10.96**	**7.24**
Ship fares	**12.35**	**14.61**	**11.90**	**13.38**	**1.27**	**14.17**	**20.80**	**38.93**
School bus	**1.01**	**1.56**	**-**	**2.55**	**2.36**	**3.38**	**1.23**	**1.19**

Note: Expenditures are not given (-) when the amount is too small to be reliable. Expenditures listed for a given category may not add to the total for that category because the listing is incomplete. "Leased and rented vehicles," for example, includes "aircraft rental," which is omitted here. Numbers may not add to total due to rounding. Other married couples include extended family members or unrelated persons in addition to the married couple.

Share of spending

	all cu's	all married couples	married couple only	all married couples with children	AGE OF OLDEST CHILD			other married couples
					under 6	6 to 17	18 or older	
Number of consumer units (in thousands)	94,862	52,010	20,227	28,100	5,858	14,194	8,047	3,684
Average number of persons per cu	2.6	3.3	2.0	3.9	3.5	4.1	3.9	5.1
Average number of earners per cu	1.4	1.7	1.2	2.1	1.7	1.9	2.7	2.4
Average total before-tax income	$28,540	$37,299	$33,825	$39,354	$34,318	$38,039	$45,596	$40,846
TOTAL AVERAGE ANNUAL EXPENDITURES	100.00%	100.00%	100.00%	100.00%	100.00%	100.00%	100.00%	100.00%
TRANSPORTATION, AVERAGE ANNUAL EXPENDITURES	19.67%	20.19%	20.37%	20.07%	20.19%	18.64%	22.28%	20.20%
VEHICLE PURCHASES (NET OUTLAY)	**9.12%**	**9.62%**	**9.81%**	**9.51%**	**10.42%**	**8.66%**	**10.31%**	**9.58%**
Cars and trucks, new	**5.23**	**5.40**	**6.70**	**4.78**	**6.34**	**4.17**	**4.82**	**4.53**
New cars	3.76	3.75	4.97	3.06	3.46	2.83	3.18	3.71
New trucks	1.47	1.65	1.73	1.72	2.88	1.34	1.64	0.82
Cars and trucks, used	**3.79**	**4.12**	**3.06**	**4.61**	**3.93**	**4.46**	**5.24**	**5.01**
Used cars	2.96	3.21	2.43	3.54	2.57	3.29	4.51	4.15
Used trucks	0.83	0.91	0.63	1.07	1.35	1.17	0.74	0.86
Other vehicles	**0.09**	**0.09**	**0.06**	**0.12**	**0.16**	**0.03**	**0.25**	**0.04**
Motorcycles	0.08	0.07	0.06	0.09	0.16	0.03	0.14	0.04
Aircraft	0.01	0.02	0.00	0.04	0.00	0.00	0.11	0.00
GASOLINE AND MOTOR OIL	**3.60%**	**3.68%**	**3.45%**	**3.80%**	**3.41%**	**3.63%**	**4.30%**	**3.72%**
Gasoline at home	**3.15**	**3.20**	**2.93**	**3.35**	**3.02**	**3.18**	**3.81**	**3.26**
Gasoline on out-of-town trips	**0.36**	**0.37**	**0.44**	**0.34**	**0.31**	**0.34**	**0.36**	**0.35**
Diesel fuel	**0.05**	**0.05**	**0.04**	**0.06**	**0.02**	**0.06**	**0.07**	**0.07**
Motor oil	**0.05**	**0.05**	**0.05**	**0.05**	**0.05**	**0.05**	**0.06**	**0.05**
OTHER VEHICLE EXPENSES	**5.88%**	**5.92%**	**5.84%**	**5.97%**	**5.71%**	**5.59%**	**6.75%**	**5.83%**
Vehicle finance charges	**0.92**	**1.18**	**1.03**	**1.25**	**1.33**	**1.14**	**1.38**	**1.33**
Cars	0.76	0.80	0.75	0.81	0.83	0.68	1.02	0.95
Trucks	0.27	0.30	0.19	0.37	0.46	0.37	0.31	0.33
Motorcycles, planes, and other vehicles	0.06	0.07	0.09	0.07	0.04	0.08	0.06	0.05
Repairs and maintenance	**2.13**	**2.07**	**2.14**	**2.06**	**1.94**	**1.98**	**2.28**	**1.81**
Body work	0.13	0.12	0.13	0.12	0.13	0.11	0.14	0.11
Clutch, transmission repair	0.13	0.13	0.12	0.14	0.11	0.12	0.18	0.07
Drive train repair	0.03	0.03	0.04	0.03	0.04	0.02	0.03	0.02
Brake repair and adjustment	0.15	0.14	0.13	0.14	0.13	0.14	0.15	0.13
Steering repair	0.04	0.04	0.04	0.04	0.04	0.04	0.04	0.04
Cooling system repair	0.09	0.08	0.09	0.08	0.10	0.07	0.09	0.09
Motor tune-up	0.16	0.15	0.17	0.14	0.13	0.14	0.14	0.14
Motor repair and replacement	0.24	0.23	0.22	0.24	0.31	0.22	0.23	0.18

Percent of total average annual expenditures spent on transportation, by married couples with and without children.

(continued from previous page)

	all cu's	all married couples	married couple only	all married couples with children	AGE OF OLDEST CHILD under 6	AGE OF OLDEST CHILD 6 to 17	AGE OF OLDEST CHILD 18 or older	other married couples
Lubrication, oil change	0.09	0.09	0.11	0.08	0.08	0.07	0.08	0.08
Front end alignment, wheel balancing	0.04	0.03	0.03	0.03	0.03	0.03	0.05	0.03
Shock absorber replacement	0.02	0.03	0.03	0.02	0.02	0.02	0.02	0.02
Exhaust system repair	0.06	0.06	0.06	0.06	0.05	0.05	0.06	0.04
Electrical system repair	0.08	0.07	0.08	0.07	0.08	0.06	0.09	0.06
Tire replacement	0.33	0.33	0.31	0.35	0.30	0.35	0.38	0.29
Coolant, additives, brake/transmission fluids	0.03	0.03	0.02	0.03	0.03	0.03	0.03	0.03
Parts, equipment, accessories and other vehicle products	0.30	0.32	0.34	0.31	0.18	0.33	0.37	0.28
Out-of-town, tire, other servicing and repairs	0.18	0.16	0.17	0.16	0.13	0.16	0.17	0.12
Auto repair service policy	0.03	0.04	0.04	0.03	0.05	0.03	0.02	0.07
Vehicle insurance	**1.96**	**1.99**	**1.98**	**1.97**	**1.75**	**1.75**	**2.45**	**2.16**
Vehicle leasing, renting, licensing, and other charges	**0.69**	**0.68**	**0.69**	**0.69**	**0.69**	**0.72**	**0.64**	**0.53**
Leased and rented vehicles	0.25	0.24	0.22	0.27	0.29	0.29	0.23	0.15
Cars	0.18	0.17	0.15	0.19	0.22	0.18	0.17	0.13
Trucks	0.06	0.07	0.06	0.08	0.06	0.10	0.06	0.03
State and local registration	0.25	0.25	0.28	0.24	0.23	0.26	0.23	0.24
Drivers' license	0.02	0.03	0.03	0.02	0.02	0.02	0.03	0.02
Vehicle inspection	0.02	0.02	0.03	0.02	0.02	0.02	0.02	0.03
Parking fees	0.08	0.07	0.08	0.07	0.07	0.07	0.07	0.04
Tolls	0.04	0.04	0.05	0.04	0.03	0.05	0.04	0.03
Towing charges	0.02	0.01	0.01	0.02	0.03	0.01	0.02	0.02
PUBLIC TRANSPORTATION	**1.08%**	**0.97%**	**1.27%**	**0.79%**	**0.65%**	**0.75%**	**0.91%**	**1.08%**
Airline fares	**0.72**	**0.69**	**0.96**	**0.54**	**0.49**	**0.54**	**0.56**	**0.69**
Intercity bus fares	**0.06**	**0.05**	**0.10**	**0.02**	**0.01**	**0.02**	**0.03**	**0.04**
Intercity train fares	**0.03**	**0.03**	**0.03**	**0.02**	**0.00**	**0.03**	**0.02**	**0.02**
Intracity mass transit fares	**0.17**	**0.13**	**0.10**	**0.13**	**0.13**	**0.09**	**0.20**	**0.19**
Taxi fares	**0.04**	**0.03**	**0.04**	**0.03**	**0.02**	**0.03**	**0.03**	**0.02**
Ship fares	**0.05**	**0.05**	**0.04**	**0.04**	**0.00**	**0.04**	**0.06**	**0.11**
School bus	**0.00**	**0.00**	**-**	**0.01**	**0.01**	**0.01**	**0.00**	**0.00**

Note: Expenditures are not given (-) when the amount is too small to be reliable. Expenditures listed for a given category may not add to the total for that category because the listing is incomplete. "Leased and rented vehicles," for example, includes "aircraft rental," which is omitted here. Numbers may not add to total due to rounding. Other married couples include extended family members or unrelated persons in addition to the married couple.

Indexed expenditures

	all cu's	all married couples	married couple only	all married couples with children	AGE OF OLDEST CHILD			other married couples
					under 6	6 to 17	18 or older	
Number of consumer units (in thousands)	94,862	52,010	20,227	28,100	5,858	14,194	8,047	3,684
Average number of persons per cu	2.6	3.3	2.0	3.9	3.5	4.1	3.9	5.1
Average number of earners per cu	1.4	1.7	1.2	2.1	1.7	1.9	2.7	2.4
Average total before-tax income	$28,540	$37,299	$33,825	$39,354	$34,318	$38,039	$45,596	$40,846
TOTAL AVERAGE ANNUAL EXPENDITURES	100	125	108	135	120	136	146	138
TRANSPORTATION, AVERAGE ANNUAL EXPENDITURES	100	128	112	138	123	129	165	142
VEHICLE PURCHASES (NET OUTLAY)	100	132	116	141	137	129	165	145
Cars and trucks, new	100	129	138	123	145	109	134	119
New cars	100	124	143	110	110	102	123	136
New trucks	100	140	127	158	234	124	162	77
Cars and trucks, used	100	136	87	164	124	160	202	182
Used cars	100	135	89	162	104	151	222	193
Used trucks	100	136	82	174	194	191	129	143
Other vehicles	100	131	69	185	210	47	408	64
Motorcycles	100	122	82	156	249	56	265	76
Aircraft	100	182	0	337	0	0	1178	0
GASOLINE AND MOTOR OIL	100	127	103	143	113	137	174	143
Gasoline at home	100	127	100	144	115	137	177	143
Gasoline on out-of-town trips	100	130	132	129	104	130	146	133
Diesel fuel	100	141	91	169	58	184	223	205
Motor oil	100	125	99	141	115	135	171	136
OTHER VEHICLE EXPENSES	100	126	107	137	116	129	168	137
Vehicle finance charges	100	160	120	183	173	168	219	200
Cars	100	131	106	144	130	122	194	172
Trucks	100	141	75	185	205	186	169	168
Motorcycles, planes, and other vehicles	100	147	156	145	74	184	128	118
Repairs and maintenance	100	121	108	131	109	127	156	117
Body work	100	117	106	126	115	114	154	110
Clutch, transmission repair	100	117	98	137	97	120	197	71
Drive train repair	100	143	147	146	192	115	168	93
Brake repair and adjustment	100	116	93	131	105	131	151	126
Steering repair	100	118	112	123	116	121	130	124
Cooling system repair	100	119	113	120	130	102	143	144
Motor tune-up	100	120	118	120	103	118	134	127
Motor repair and replacement	100	121	102	138	157	127	143	106
Lubrication, oil change	100	116	127	108	100	103	122	123

Indexed average annual expenditures for transportation, by married couples with and without children.

(continued from previous page)	all cu's	all married couples	married couple only	all married couples with children	AGE OF OLDEST CHILD			other married couples
					under 6	6 to 17	18 or older	
Front end alignment, wheel balancing	100	117	101	129	90	108	194	117
Shock absorber replacement	100	128	135	124	114	131	118	118
Exhaust system repair	100	126	119	133	116	122	163	110
Electrical system repair	100	119	110	128	120	103	176	110
Tire replacement	100	125	101	144	109	144	169	123
Coolant, additives, brake/transmission fluids ..	100	130	95	151	115	150	180	155
Parts, equipment, accessories, and other vehicle products	100	132	123	139	73	149	179	128
Out-of-town, tire, other servicing and repairs ..	100	112	104	120	86	122	142	92
Auto repair service policy	100	133	121	123	195	116	83	279
Vehicle insurance	**100**	**126**	**109**	**136**	**106**	**121**	**183**	**152**
Vehicle leasing, renting, licensing, and other charges	**100**	**123**	**109**	**136**	**121**	**143**	**135**	**106**
Leased and rented vehicles	100	123	94	148	142	159	135	86
Cars	100	117	90	139	146	137	138	96
Trucks	100	143	110	177	126	223	132	60
State and local registration	100	129	121	134	111	143	136	133
Drivers' license	100	127	126	129	97	128	154	124
Vehicle inspection	100	126	127	120	89	115	152	167
Parking fees	100	109	105	118	108	119	125	64
Tolls	100	132	140	131	88	147	135	84
Towing charges	100	93	49	115	166	82	137	164
PUBLIC TRANSPORTATION	**100**	**113**	**128**	**99**	**73**	**95**	**123**	**138**
Airline fares	**100**	**120**	**143**	**101**	**81**	**101**	**114**	**132**
Intercity bus fares	**100**	**112**	**194**	**53**	**14**	**54**	**81**	**103**
Intercity train fares	**100**	**93**	**106**	**84**	**13**	**101**	**104**	**91**
Intracity mass transit fares	**100**	**92**	**65**	**104**	**89**	**71**	**173**	**153**
Taxi fares	**100**	**85**	**87**	**87**	**48**	**98**	**96**	**64**
Ship fares	**100**	**118**	**96**	**108**	**10**	**115**	**168**	**315**
School bus	**100**	**154**	**-**	**252**	**234**	**335**	**122**	**118**

Note: An index of 100 represents the average for all consumer units. An index of 132 means that the average for the subgroup is 32 percent above the average for all consumer units. An index of 68 indicates spending that is 32 percent below the overall average. Expenditures are not given (-) when the amount is too small to be reliable. Other married couples include extended family members or unrelated persons in addition to the married couple.

Aggregate expenditures, 1988

Aggregate expenditures in 1988 for transportation, by married couples with and without children.

	all cu's	all married couples	married couple only	all married couples with children	AGE OF OLDEST CHILD			other married couples
					under 6	6 to 17	18 or older	
Number of consumer units (in thousands)	94,862	52,010	20,227	28,100	5,858	14,194	8,047	3,684
Average number of persons per cu	2.6	3.3	2.0	3.9	3.5	4.1	3.9	5.1
Average number of earners per cu	1.4	1.7	1.2	2.1	1.7	1.9	2.7	2.4
Aggregate before-tax income (in millions)	$2,722,910	$1,942,526	$684,178	$1,107,871	$201,035	$539,926	$366,911	$150,477
TOTAL AGGREG. EXPENDITURES (in millions)	$2,455,594	$1,682,565	$565,436	$985,465	$181,263	$500,316	$303,886	$131,665
TRANSPORTATION, AGGREGATE EXPENDITURES (in millions)	$483,143	$339,343	$115,202	$197,542	$36,603	$93,246	$67,693	$26,599
VEHICLE PURCHASES (NET OUTLAY)	$223,922	$161,681	$55,492	$93,576	$18,886	$43,352	$31,338	$12,613
Cars and trucks, new	128,548	90,835	37,862	47,009	11,485	20,883	14,641	5,964
New cars	92,414	63,065	28,086	30,091	6,265	14,163	9,663	4,889
New trucks	36,134	27,770	9,776	16,919	5,220	6,720	4,979	1,075
Cars and trucks, used	93,161	69,254	17,304	45,357	7,115	22,312	15,930	6,594
Used cars	72,728	54,010	13,740	34,810	4,662	16,457	13,691	5,461
Used trucks	20,433	15,244	3,564	10,547	2,453	5,855	2,239	1,133
Other vehicles	2,213	1,592	326	1,210	287	157	766	55
Motorcycles	1,866	1,244	326	863	287	157	419	55
Aircraft	347	347	0	347	0	0	347	0
GASOLINE AND MOTOR OIL	$88,408	$61,792	$19,502	$37,395	$6,172	$18,156	$13,066	$4,896
Gasoline at home	77,268	53,803	16,555	32,960	5,481	15,893	11,586	4,288
Gasoline on out-of-town trips	8,795	6,290	2,471	3,364	564	1,708	1,092	454
Diesel fuel	1,109	857	214	554	39	305	210	88
Motor oil	1,236	843	261	517	87	250	179	65
OTHER VEHICLE EXPENSES	$144,348	$99,531	$33,012	$58,845	$10,357	$27,963	$20,525	$7,674
Vehicle finance charges	26,902	19,849	5,796	12,299	2,413	5,685	4,200	1,755
Cars	18,763	13,499	4,227	8,019	1,506	3,423	3,089	1,253
Trucks	6,593	5,102	1,055	3,617	836	1,838	943	431
Motorcycles, planes, and other vehicles	1,546	1,248	514	663	70	424	168	71
Repairs and maintenance	52,460	34,890	12,117	20,388	3,525	9,927	6,936	2,384
Body work	3,238	2,075	731	1,205	230	553	423	138
Clutch, transmission repair	3,296	2,115	686	1,339	196	591	551	91
Drive train repair	678	530	212	293	80	116	96	24
Brake repair and adjustment	3,581	2,279	710	1,394	233	704	457	175
Steering repair	1,062	689	253	385	76	192	117	51
Cooling system repair	2,154	1,403	520	763	173	329	261	120
Motor tune-up	3,824	2,507	965	1,354	242	677	435	188
Motor repair and replacement	5,864	3,905	1,270	2,393	567	1,117	710	242

Aggregate expenditures in 1988 for transportation, by married couples with and without children.

(continued from previous page)	all cu's	all married couples	married couple only	all married couples with children	AGE OF OLDEST CHILD			other married couples
					under 6	6 to 17	18 or older	
Lubrication, oil change	2,326	1,485	632	742	144	357	241	111
Front end alignment, wheel balancing	862	553	186	328	48	139	142	39
Shock absorber replacement	606	424	174	222	43	119	61	28
Exhaust system repair	1,384	953	351	543	99	253	191	59
Electrical system repair	1,861	1,219	436	703	137	287	278	79
Tire replacement	8,065	5,547	1,729	3,434	542	1,737	1,155	384
Coolant, additives, brake/transmission fluids	670	476	135	301	48	150	103	40
Parts, equipment, accessories, and other vehicle products	7,780	5,433	1,943	3,122	335	1,658	1,129	369
Out-of-town, tire, other servicing and repairs	4,377	2,686	970	1,560	234	798	528	156
Auto repair service policy	825	603	213	300	100	143	58	89
Vehicle insurance	**48,164**	**33,401**	**11,182**	**19,379**	**3,167**	**8,754**	**7,458**	**2,840**
Vehicle leasing, renting, licensing, and other charges	**16,823**	**11,391**	**3,917**	**6,779**	**1,252**	**3,596**	**1,930**	**694**
Leased and rented vehicles	6,077	4,096	1,224	2,670	532	1,443	695	202
Cars	4,494	2,874	858	1,848	405	919	524	167
Trucks	1,503	1,176	352	788	117	502	169	35
State and local registration	6,038	4,275	1,564	2,400	412	1,294	694	311
Drivers' license	605	423	163	231	36	116	79	29
Vehicle inspection	575	397	156	204	32	99	74	37
Parking fees	2,021	1,213	453	709	135	360	214	50
Tolls	1,023	741	308	400	56	226	118	34
Towing charges	483	246	50	165	50	59	56	31
PUBLIC TRANSPORTATION	**$26,465**	**$16,339**	**$7,196**	**$7,727**	**$1,187**	**$3,775**	**$2,765**	**$1,417**
Airline fares	**17,686**	**11,589**	**5,406**	**5,274**	**883**	**2,678**	**1,713**	**909**
Intercity bus fares	**1,356**	**830**	**561**	**214**	**12**	**110**	**93**	**54**
Intercity train fares	**845**	**429**	**191**	**209**	**7**	**127**	**75**	**30**
Intracity mass transit fares	**4,182**	**2,115**	**581**	**1,286**	**231**	**442**	**613**	**248**
Taxi fares	**1,077**	**504**	**199**	**279**	**32**	**159**	**88**	**27**
Ship fares	**1,172**	**760**	**241**	**376**	**7**	**201**	**167**	**143**
School bus	**87**	**76**	**-**	**72**	**14**	**48**	**10**	**4**

Note: Expenditures are not given (-) when the amount is too small to be reliable. Expenditures listed for a given category may not add to the total for that category because the listing is incomplete. "Leased and rented vehicles," for example, includes "aircraft rental," which is omitted here. Numbers may not add to total due to rounding. Other married couples include extended family members or unrelated persons in addition to the married couple. The "all cu's" aggregates will differ slightly from table to table because they are the sums of the aggregates in each row. In this table they include aggregates for single parents, single persons, and other types of consumer units, in addition to all married couples. Aggregates for "all married couples" and "all married couples with children" are sums of the appropriate aggregates in each row.

CHAPTER
7

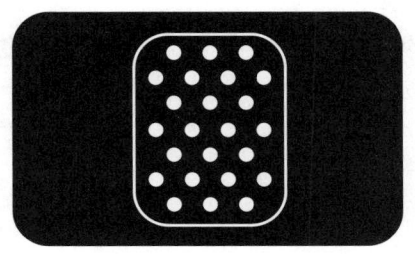

Health Care

The average household devoted 5 percent of its expenditures to health care in 1988. That share varied from year to year during the previous four years and wound up just slightly higher in 1988 than in 1984. Health care will take a larger share of the household budget in the 1990s as employers and insurers continue to shift more of their costs to consumers.

The share of health care expenditures allocated to health insurance dropped from 1984 to 1986 and then gained nearly 4 percentage points in the next two years. Drugs took a larger share of the health care budget in 1988 than in 1984 while the share devoted to medical services shrank 2.5 percentage points. The health care budget share going to medical supplies rose for four years before dropping back to its 1984 level in 1988.

Five-year spending trends for health care

	1984	1985	1986	1987	1988	change 1984 to 1988
Share of household expenditures devoted to health care, share of health care expenditures devoted to health care items, and change in share, 1984 to 1988.						
Health care, share of household expenditures	4.8%	4.7%	4.8%	4.6%	5.0%	0.2%
Health care, expenditures	100.0%	100.0%	100.0%	100.0%	100.0%	0.0%
HEALTH INSURANCE	35.3%	33.8%	32.7%	34.5%	36.5%	1.2%
MEDICAL SERVICES	43.3%	44.8%	44.2%	41.1%	40.8%	-2.5%
DRUGS	15.9%	16.1%	16.9%	17.9%	17.2%	1.3%
MEDICAL SUPPLIES	5.5%	5.4%	6.1%	6.4%	5.5%	0.0%

Note: Numbers may not add to total due to rounding.

PART II
Spending by age for health care

Health care is the only category in which expenditures do not peak in middle-age. The share of household spending devoted to health care rises from 3 percent among householders aged 25 to 34 to fully 17 percent among householders aged 75 or older. Householders under age 35 spend more than average only on selected health care items, such as therapy and out-patient hospital services. By age 35 to 44, households are spending more than average on medical services and supplies. Health insurance premiums are higher than average starting at age 55.

From age 55 on, householders are spending more than average on most health care products and services except eyeglasses. Those aged 65 or older spend at least double the national average on supplemental insurance, prescription drugs, and medical equipment.

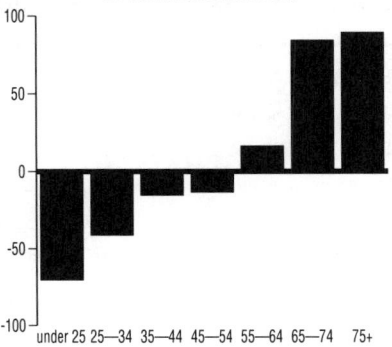

Householders aged 55 or older spend more than the average household on health insurance...

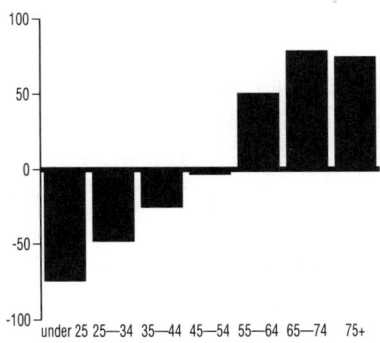

...and on drugs...

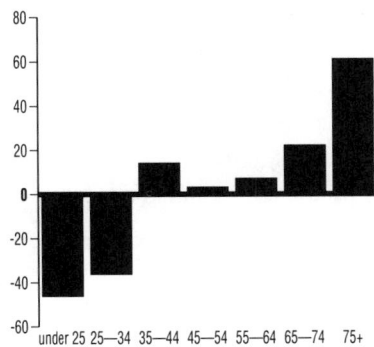

...while those aged 35 or older spend more than average on medical services.

0 = average spending

Average expenditures

Average annual expenditures for health care, by age of reference person.

	all cu's	under 25	25 to 34	35 to 44	45 to 54	55 to 64	65 to 74	75+
Number of consumer units (in thousands)	*94,862*	*7,216*	*21,985*	*19,911*	*13,601*	*12,546*	*11,319*	*8,284*
Average number of persons per cu	*2.6*	*1.8*	*2.8*	*3.3*	*2.9*	*2.2*	*2.0*	*1.5*
Average total before-tax income	*$28,540.00*	*$14,827.00*	*$28,318.00*	*$36,428.00*	*$39,934.00*	*$29,979.00*	*$20,704.00*	*$13,707.00*
TOTAL AVERAGE ANNUAL EXPENDITURES	*$25,891.85*	*$16,373.17*	*$25,770.27*	*$33,077.72*	*$33,204.87*	*$25,765.35*	*$20,119.90*	*$13,339.49*
HEALTH CARE, AVER. ANNUAL EXPENDITURES	*$1,297.68*	*$522.64*	*$780.65*	*$1,253.31*	*$1,257.77*	*$1,518.45*	*$2,004.71*	*$2,229.72*
HEALTH INSURANCE	**$474.39**	**$143.46**	**$279.22**	**$404.92**	**$410.73**	**$549.96**	**$871.86**	**$894.59**
Commercial health insurance	166.27	77.23	129.76	196.49	193.93	224.22	165.88	135.40
Blue Cross/Blue Shield	120.93	34.19	66.97	97.06	105.27	171.51	191.94	249.09
Health maintenance plans (HMOs)	46.39	19.98	46.27	63.06	45.99	51.44	48.56	19.66
Medicare payments	77.03	0.87	2.46	6.71	18.68	42.20	321.16	325.22
Commercial medicare supplements/ other health insurance	63.79	11.19	33.76	41.59	46.86	60.59	144.33	165.21
MEDICAL SERVICES	**$529.34**	**$285.92**	**$340.26**	**$604.34**	**$534.56**	**$564.28**	**$645.06**	**$852.61**
Physician's services	153.86	82.02	140.42	193.71	180.43	53.20	180.06	229.31
Dental services	151.97	31.07	96.82	211.22	190.18	190.26	156.81	133.89
Eye care services	22.03	8.15	11.82	20.54	27.33	31.42	33.08	26.72
Service by other than physician	22.63	6.27	14.90	28.93	30.82	22.86	25.08	25.15
Lab test, x-rays	25.82	14.35	13.89	25.38	32.55	35.92	34.77	29.95
Nursing, therapy, misc. medical services	3.84	5.88	-	1.69	4.46	16.07	6.95	3.38
Hospital room	59.71	61.06	32.54	59.37	41.67	132.64	42.92	73.53
Hospital services other than room	35.53	41.74	19.16	27.93	18.33	51.59	47.03	80.02
Care in convalescent or nursing home	40.55	31.43	1.76	11.72	0.61	11.44	106.70	239.98
Other medical services	13.42	3.95	8.95	23.85	8.48	18.87	11.66	10.68
DRUGS	**$223.20**	**$58.05**	**$116.12**	**$167.24**	**$218.99**	**$334.60**	**$397.35**	**$387.29**
Non-prescription drugs	61.85	20.77	47.12	55.71	79.60	93.70	68.23	66.67
Prescription drugs	161.35	37.29	69.00	111.53	139.39	240.90	329.12	320.63
MEDICAL SUPPLIES	**$70.74**	**$35.20**	**$45.05**	**$76.80**	**$93.19**	**$69.62**	**$90.44**	**$95.22**
Eyeglasses	44.65	25.90	31.03	52.28	66.39	49.55	48.96	29.78
Topicals and dressings	13.28	8.62	11.46	17.78	17.54	12.67	12.84	5.92
Medical equipment for general use	5.26	-	1.17	1.71	4.77	2.43	14.68	21.34
Supportive/convalescent medical equipment	5.23	0.55	1.24	4.78	4.20	4.53	12.96	13.18
Rental of medical equipment	-	-	-	-	-	-	1.00	2.07
Hearing aids	1.84	0.00	0.00	0.00	0.00	0.00	0.00	22.92

Note: Expenditures are not given (-) when the amount is too small to be reliable. Numbers may not add to total due to rounding.

Share of spending

Percent of total average annual expenditures spent on health care, by age of reference person.

	all cu's	under 25	25 to 34	35 to 44	45 to 54	55 to 64	65 to 74	75+
Number of consumer units (in thousands)	*94,862*	*7,216*	*21,985*	*19,911*	*13,601*	*12,546*	*11,319*	*8,284*
Average number of persons per cu	*2.6*	*1.8*	*2.8*	*3.3*	*2.9*	*2.2*	*2.0*	*1.5*
Average total before-tax income	*$28,540*	*$14,827*	*$28,318*	*$36,428*	*$39,934*	*$29,979*	*$20,704*	*$13,707*
TOTAL AVERAGE ANNUAL EXPENDITURES	*100.00%*	*100.00%*	*100.00%*	*100.00%*	*100.00%*	*100.00%*	*100.00%*	*100.00%*
HEALTH CARE, AVERAGE ANNUAL EXPENDITURES	*5.01%*	*3.19%*	*3.03%*	*3.79%*	*3.79%*	*5.89%*	*9.96%*	*16.72%*
HEALTH INSURANCE	**1.83%**	**0.88%**	**1.08%**	**1.22%**	**1.24%**	**2.13%**	**4.33%**	**6.71%**
Commercial health insurance	0.64	0.47	0.50	0.59	0.58	0.87	0.82	1.02
Blue Cross/Blue Shield	0.47	0.21	0.26	0.29	0.32	0.67	0.95	1.87
Health maintenance plans (HMO's)	0.18	0.12	0.18	0.19	0.14	0.20	0.24	0.15
Medicare payments	0.30	0.01	0.01	0.02	0.06	0.16	1.60	2.44
Commercial medicare supplements/ other health insurance	0.25	0.07	0.13	0.13	0.14	0.24	0.72	1.24
MEDICAL SERVICES	**2.04%**	**1.75%**	**1.32%**	**1.83%**	**1.61%**	**2.19%**	**3.21%**	**6.39%**
Physician's services	0.59	0.50	0.54	0.59	0.54	0.21	0.89	1.72
Dental services	0.59	0.19	0.38	0.64	0.57	0.74	0.78	1.00
Eye care services	0.09	0.05	0.05	0.06	0.08	0.12	0.16	0.20
Service by other than physician	0.09	0.04	0.06	0.09	0.09	0.09	0.12	0.19
Lab test, x-rays	0.10	0.09	0.05	0.08	0.10	0.14	0.17	0.22
Nursing, therapy, misc. medical services	0.01	0.04	-	0.01	0.01	0.06	0.03	0.03
Hospital room	0.23	0.37	0.13	0.18	0.13	0.51	0.21	0.55
Hospital services other than room	0.14	0.25	0.07	0.08	0.06	0.20	0.23	0.60
Care in convalescent or nursing home	0.16	0.19	0.01	0.04	0.00	0.04	0.53	1.80
Other medical services	0.05	0.02	0.03	0.07	0.03	0.07	0.06	0.08
DRUGS	**0.86%**	**0.35%**	**0.45%**	**0.51%**	**0.66%**	**1.30%**	**1.97%**	**2.90%**
Non-prescription drugs	0.24	0.13	0.18	0.17	0.24	0.36	0.34	0.50
Prescription drugs	0.62	0.23	0.27	0.34	0.42	0.93	1.64	2.40
MEDICAL SUPPLIES	**0.27%**	**0.21%**	**0.17%**	**0.23%**	**0.28%**	**0.27%**	**0.45%**	**0.71%**
Eyeglasses	0.17	0.16	0.12	0.16	0.20	0.19	0.24	0.22
Topicals and dressings	0.05	0.05	0.04	0.05	0.05	0.05	0.06	0.04
Medical equipment for general use	0.02	-	0.00	0.01	0.01	0.01	0.07	0.16
Supportive/convalescent medical equipment	0.02	0.00	0.00	0.01	0.01	0.02	0.06	0.10
Rental of medical equipment	-	-	-	-	-	-	0.00	0.02
Hearing aids	0.01	0.00	0.00	0.00	0.00	0.00	0.00	0.17

Note: Expenditures are not given (-) when the amount is too small to be reliable. Numbers may not add to total due to rounding.

Indexed expenditures

Indexed average annual expenditures for health care, by age of reference person.

	all cu's	under 25	25 to 34	35 to 44	45 to 54	55 to 64	65 to 74	75+
Number of consumer units (in thousands)	**94,862**	**7,216**	**21,985**	**19,911**	**13,601**	**12,546**	**11,319**	**8,284**
Average number of persons per cu	**2.6**	**1.8**	**2.8**	**3.3**	**2.9**	**2.2**	**2.0**	**1.5**
Average total before-tax income	**$28,540**	**$14,827**	**$28,318**	**$36,428**	**$39,934**	**$29,979**	**$20,704**	**$13,707**
TOTAL AVERAGE ANNUAL EXPENDITURES	**100**	**63**	**100**	**128**	**128**	**100**	**78**	**52**
HEALTH CARE, AVERAGE ANNUAL EXPENDITURES	**100**	**40**	**60**	**97**	**97**	**117**	**154**	**172**
HEALTH INSURANCE	**100**	**30**	**59**	**85**	**87**	**116**	**184**	**189**
Commercial health insurance	100	46	78	118	117	135	100	81
Blue Cross/Blue Shield	100	28	55	80	87	142	159	206
Health maintenance plans (HMOs)	100	43	100	136	99	111	105	42
Medicare payments	100	1	3	9	24	55	417	422
Commercial medicare supplements/ other health insurance	100	18	53	65	73	95	226	259
MEDICAL SERVICES	**100**	**54**	**64**	**114**	**101**	**107**	**122**	**161**
Physician's services	100	53	91	126	117	35	117	149
Dental services	100	20	64	139	125	125	103	88
Eye care services	100	37	54	93	124	143	150	121
Service by other than physician	100	28	66	128	136	101	111	111
Lab test, x-rays	100	56	54	98	126	139	135	116
Nursing, therapy, misc. medical services	100	153	-	44	116	418	181	88
Hospital room	100	102	54	99	70	222	72	123
Hospital services other than room	100	117	54	79	52	145	132	225
Care in convalescent or nursing home	100	78	4	29	2	28	263	592
Other medical services	100	29	67	178	63	141	87	80
DRUGS	**100**	**26**	**52**	**75**	**98**	**150**	**178**	**174**
Non-prescription drugs	100	34	76	90	129	151	110	108
Prescription drugs	100	23	43	69	86	149	204	199
MEDICAL SUPPLIES	**100**	**50**	**64**	**109**	**132**	**98**	**128**	**135**
Eyeglasses	100	58	69	117	149	111	110	67
Topicals and dressings	100	65	86	134	132	95	97	45
Medical equipment for general use	100	-	22	33	91	46	279	406
Supportive/convalescent medical equipment	100	11	24	91	80	87	248	252
Rental of medical equipment	100	-	-	-	-	-	-	-
Hearing aids	100	0	0	0	0	0	0	1246

Note: Expenditures are not given (-) when the amount is too small to be reliable. An index of 100 represents the average for all consumer units. An index of 132 means that the average for the subgroup is 32 percent above the average for all consumer units. An index of 68 indicates spending that is 32 percent below the overall aveage.

Aggregate expenditures, 1988

Aggregate expenditures in 1988 for health care, by age of reference person.

	all cu's	under 25	25 to 34	35 to 44	45 to 54	55 to 64	65 to 74	75+
Number of consumer units (in thousands)	94,862	7,216	21,985	19,911	13,601	12,546	11,319	8,284
Average number of persons per cu	2.6	1.8	2.8	3.3	2.9	2.2	2.0	1.5
Aggregate before-tax income (in millions)	$2,722,037	$106,992	$622,571	$725,318	$543,142	$376,117	$234,349	$113,549
TOTAL AGGREGATE EXPENDITURES (in millions)	$2,456,432	$118,149	$566,559	$658,610	$451,619	$323,252	$227,737	$110,504
HEALTH CARE, AGG. EXPENDITURES (in millions)	$123,208	$3,771	$17,163	$24,955	$17,107	$19,050	$22,691	$18,471
HEALTH INSURANCE	$45,002	$1,035	$6,139	$8,062	$5,586	$6,900	$9,869	$7,411
Commercial health insurance	15,772	557	2,853	3,912	2,638	2,813	1,878	1,122
Blue Cross/Blue Shield	11,471	247	1,472	1,933	1,432	2,152	2,173	2,063
Health maintenance plans (HMOs)	4,400	144	1,017	1,256	626	645	550	163
Medicare payments	7,307	6	54	134	254	529	3,635	2,694
Commercial medicare supplements/ other health insurance	6,051	81	742	828	637	760	1,634	1,369
MEDICAL SERVICES	$50,291	$2,063	$7,481	$12,033	$7,271	$7,079	$7,301	$7,063
Physician's services	14,595	592	3,087	3,857	2,454	667	2,038	1,900
Dental services	14,416	224	2,129	4,206	2,587	2,387	1,775	1,109
Eye care services	2,089	59	260	409	372	394	374	221
Service by other than physician	2,147	45	328	576	419	287	284	208
Lab test, x-rays	2,449	104	305	505	443	451	394	248
Nursing, therapy, misc. medical services	445	42	-	34	61	202	79	28
Hospital room	5,664	441	715	1,182	567	1,664	486	609
Hospital services other than room	3,370	301	421	556	249	647	532	663
Care in convalescent or nursing home	3,846	227	39	233	8	144	1,208	1,988
Other medical services	1,273	29	197	475	115	237	132	88
DRUGS	$21,184	$419	$2,553	$3,330	$2,978	$4,198	$4,498	$3,208
Non-prescription drugs	5,878	150	1,036	1,109	1,083	1,176	772	552
Prescription drugs	15,306	269	1,517	2,221	1,896	3,022	3,725	2,656
MEDICAL SUPPLIES	$6,727	$254	$990	$1,529	$1,267	$873	$1,024	$789
Eyeglasses	4,236	187	682	1,041	903	622	554	247
Topicals and dressings	1,260	62	252	354	239	159	145	49
Medical equipment for general use	498	-	26	34	65	30	166	177
Supportive/convalescent medical equipment ...	496	4	27	95	57	57	147	109
Rental of medical equipment	28	-	-	-	-	-	11	17
Hearing aids	190	0	0	0	0	0	0	190

Note: Expenditures are not given (-) when the amount is too small to be reliable. Numbers may not add to total due to rounding. The "all cu's" aggregates will differ slightly from table to table because they are the sums of the aggregates in each row.

Aggregate expenditures, 1995

Aggregate expenditures for health care, by age of householder in 1995 (in 1988 dollars).

	all households	under 25	25 to 34	35 to 44	45 to 54	55 to 64	65 to 74	75+
Number of households (in thousands)	100,308	4,316	19,927	23,916	18,035	12,233	12,006	9,876
HEALTH CARE, AGGREGATE EXPENDITURES IN 1995 (in millions)	$135,134	$2,256	$15,556	$29,974	$22,684	$18,575	$24,069	$22,021
HEALTH INSURANCE	$49,305	$619	$5,564	$9,684	$7,408	$6,728	$10,468	$8,835
Commercial health insurance	17,187	333	2,586	4,699	3,498	2,743	1,992	1,337
Blue Cross/Blue Shield	12,564	148	1,335	2,321	1,899	2,098	2,304	2,460
Health maintenance plans (HMOs)	4,752	86	922	1,508	829	629	583	194
Medicare payments	8,134	4	49	160	337	516	3,856	3,212
Commercial medicare supplements/ other health insurance	6,666	48	673	995	845	741	1,733	1,632
MEDICAL SERVICES	$55,176	$1,234	$6,780	$14,453	$9,641	$6,903	$7,745	$8,420
Physician's services	16,116	354	2,798	4,633	3,254	651	2,162	2,265
Dental services	16,077	134	1,929	5,052	3,430	2,327	1,883	1,322
Eye care services	2,300	35	236	491	493	384	397	264
Service by other than physician	2,401	27	297	692	556	280	301	248
Lab test, x-rays	2,685	62	277	607	587	439	417	296
Nursing, therapy, misc. medical services	460	25	-	40	80	197	83	33
Hospital room	5,947	264	648	1,420	752	1,623	515	726
Hospital services other than room	3,547	180	382	668	331	631	565	790
Care in convalescent or nursing home	4,253	136	35	280	11	140	1,281	2,370
Other medical services	1,395	17	178	570	153	231	140	105
DRUGS	$23,202	$251	$2,314	$4,000	$3,949	$4,093	$4,771	$3,825
Non-prescription drugs	6,420	90	939	1,332	1,436	1,146	819	658
Prescription drugs	16,782	161	1,375	2,667	2,514	2,947	3,951	3,167
MEDICAL SUPPLIES	$7,445	$152	$898	$1,837	$1,681	$852	$1,086	$940
Eyeglasses	4,666	112	618	1,250	1,197	606	588	294
Topicals and dressings	1,375	37	228	425	316	155	154	58
Medical equipment for general use	567	-	23	41	86	30	176	211
Supportive/convalescent medical equipment	558	2	25	114	76	55	156	130
Rental of medical equipment	32	-	-	-	-	-	12	20
Hearing aids	226	0	0	0	0	0	0	226

Note: Expenditures are not given (-) when the amount is too small to be reliable. Numbers may not add to total due to rounding. Households are used here because the number of consumer units in 1995 and 2000 is not available. Household projections are from the Census Bureau. Projections show how annual aggregate expenditures will change as the number of households in the age groups changes in 1995 and 2000. Projections are based on the average annual expenditures in 1988 and have not been adjusted for price increases or for changes in expenditure patterns.

Aggregate expenditures, 2000

Aggregate expenditures for health care, by age of householder in 2000 (in 1988 dollars).

	all households	under 25	25 to 34	35 to 44	45 to 54	55 to 64	65 to 74	75+
Number of households (in thousands)	105,933	4,442	18,004	25,339	21,603	13,903	11,516	11,126
HEALTH CARE, AGGREGATE EXPENDITURES IN 2000 (in millions)	$141,524	$2,322	$14,055	$31,758	$27,172	$21,111	$23,086	$22,021
HEALTH INSURANCE	**$51,319**	**$637**	**$5,027**	**$10,260**	**$8,873**	**$7,646**	**$10,040**	**$8,835**
Commercial health insurance	18,212	343	2,336	4,979	4,189	3,117	1,910	1,337
Blue Cross/Blue Shield	13,146	152	1,206	2,459	2,274	2,385	2,210	2,460
Health maintenance plans (HMOs)	4,982	89	833	1,598	994	715	559	194
Medicare payments	8,119	4	44	170	404	587	3,698	3,212
Commercial medicare supplements/ other health insurance	6,860	50	608	1,054	1,012	842	1,662	1,632
MEDICAL SERVICES	**$57,952**	**$1,270**	**$6,126**	**$15,313**	**$11,548**	**$7,845**	**$7,429**	**$8,420**
Physician's services	16,777	364	2,528	4,908	3,898	740	2,074	2,265
Dental services	17,115	138	1,743	5,352	4,108	2,645	1,806	1,322
Eye care services	2,442	36	213	520	590	437	381	264
Service by other than physician	2,550	28	268	733	666	318	289	248
Lab test, x-rays	2,856	64	250	643	703	499	400	296
Nursing, therapy, misc. medical services	502	26	-	43	96	223	80	33
Hospital room	6,326	271	586	1,504	900	1,844	494	726
Hospital services other than room	3,683	185	345	708	396	717	542	790
Care in convalescent or nursing home	4,239	140	32	297	13	159	1,229	2,370
Other medical services	1,468	18	161	604	183	262	134	105
DRUGS	**$24,370**	**$258**	**$2,091**	**$4,238**	**$4,731**	**$4,652**	**$4,576**	**$3,825**
Non-prescription drugs	6,819	92	848	1,412	1,720	1,303	786	658
Prescription drugs	17,551	166	1,242	2,826	3,011	3,349	3,790	3,167
MEDICAL SUPPLIES	**$7,876**	**$156**	**$811**	**$1,946**	**$2,013**	**$968**	**$1,042**	**$940**
Eyeglasses	4,979	115	559	1,325	1,434	689	564	294
Topicals and dressings	1,457	38	206	451	379	176	148	58
Medical equipment for general use	581	-	21	43	103	34	169	211
Supportive/convalescent medical equipment	579	2	22	121	91	63	149	130
Rental of medical equipment	32	-	-	-	-	-	12	20
Hearing aids	226	0	0	0	0	0	0	226

Note: Expenditures are not given (-) when the amount is too small to be reliable. Numbers may not add to total due to rounding. Households are used here because the number of consumer units in 1995 and 2000 is not available. Household projections are from the Census Bureau. Projections show how annual aggregate expenditures will change as the number of households in the age groups changes in 1995 and 2000. Projections are based on the average annual expenditures in 1988 and have not been adjusted for price increases or for changes in expenditure patterns.

PART II
Spending by income for health care

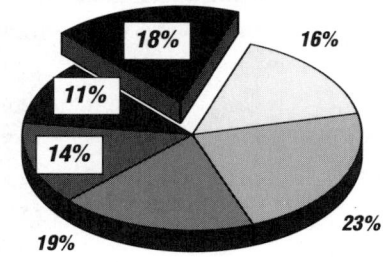

Households with incomes of $30,000 or more account for just 43 percent of out-of-pocket health care expenditures...

18%   16%
11%
14%
23%
19%

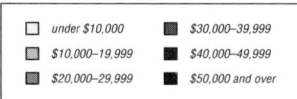

□ under $10,000   ■ $30,000–39,999
■ $10,000–19,999   ■ $40,000–49,999
■ $20,000–29,999   ■ $50,000 and over

...although they're generally above-average spenders on health care.

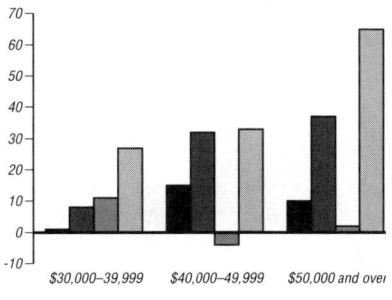

$30,000–39,999 $40,000–49,999 $50,000 and over

Lower-income households spend more than the average household on some categories of health care.

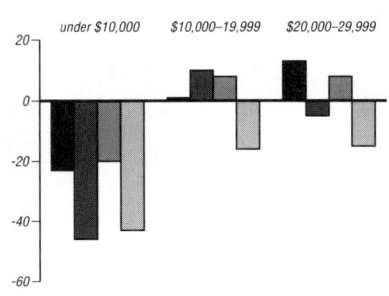

under $10,000 $10,000–19,999 $20,000–29,999

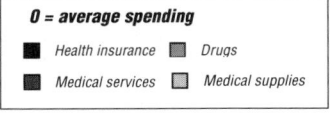

0 = average spending

■ Health insurance   ■ Drugs
■ Medical services   □ Medical supplies

Because a large share of health care costs are paid by employers and insurance companies, out-of-pocket spending for health care doesn't climb steeply with income. From the lowest to the highest income households, however, spending on nursing, therapy, and dental services; eyeglasses; and services delivered by someone other than a physician increase quickly—by at least 300 percent.

The lowest income group spent an average of $858 on health care in 1988 while the highest income group spent less than twice as much—$1,568. Insurance, medical services and supplies, and drugs, however, all take a much bigger bite out of the spending dollar of low-income households.

In terms of out-of-pocket costs, the largest health care market is households with incomes under $30,000. This group spent $59 billion on health care products and services in 1988—57 percent of the market. Together, higher income households spent $45 billion on health care.

Each of the income groups has relatively high expenses for some health care product or service. Only those with incomes under $10,000 spend less than the average household on health care although their spending on medical equipment, convalescent or nursing homes, and Medicare is above average.

Among households with incomes of $10,000 to $20,000, health care spending is just 5 percent above average. But because nearly 30 percent of all households headed by a person aged 75 or older fall into this income bracket, this group spends more than twice the average amount on convalescent or nursing home care, and on hospital services other than rooms. Their expenses for Medicare, hospital rooms, and prescription drugs are also relatively high.

Households in the $20,000 to $30,000 income group spend 4 percent more than the average household on health care, with well above-average expenses for commercial health insurance, HMO's, and medical services delivered by someone other than a doctor. Those in the $30,000 to $40,000 income group spend more than average on medical services, drugs, and supplies.

In the highest income groups, health care spending is below average for Medicare, convalescent or nursing homes, prescription drugs, and general-use medical equipment. But households with incomes of $40,000 to $50,000 spend more than any others on commercial insurance and HMO's, as well as on doctors' services and hospital rooms. The highest income households are the big spenders for dental, eye care, nursing, and therapy services.

Average expenditures

Average annual expenditures for health care, by total before-tax income of consumer unit.

Consumer units include complete income reporters only.	all cu's	under $10,000	$10,000 to $19,999	$20,000 to $29,999	$30,000 to $39,999	$40,000 to $49,999	$50,000 and over
Number of consumer units (in thousands)	81,354	18,809	17,652	14,586	10,901	7,198	12,209
Average number of persons per cu	2.6	1.8	2.3	2.7	2.9	3.2	3.1
Average number of earners per cu	1.4	0.7	1.0	1.5	1.8	2.0	2.1
TOTAL AVERAGE ANNUAL EXPENDITURES	$26,389.07	$11,269.43	$18,078.25	$24,896.36	$31,659.60	$37,562.00	$52,320.19
HEALTH CARE, AVERAGE ANNUAL EXPENDITURES	$1,282.43	$857.74	$1,343.83	$1,328.49	$1,367.25	$1,531.77	$1,567.75
HEALTH INSURANCE	**$473.36**	**$362.36**	**$477.43**	**$537.14**	**$475.48**	**$543.90**	**$518.80**
Commercial health insurance	165.28	73.45	142.67	208.24	195.72	255.42	207.76
Blue Cross/Blue Shield	116.52	96.11	112.27	127.18	114.09	111.37	146.61
Health maintenance plans (HMOs)	48.48	16.91	35.18	57.95	67.51	84.53	66.81
Medicare payments	78.60	117.36	117.22	71.71	41.13	31.51	32.52
Commercial medicare supplements/other health insurance	64.48	58.53	70.10	72.07	57.02	61.07	65.10
MEDICAL SERVICES	**$512.73**	**$274.89**	**$564.12**	**$487.31**	**$551.59**	**$676.69**	**$700.64**
Physician's services	149.19	81.08	152.70	160.54	202.90	205.76	154.17
Dental services	150.89	56.00	104.16	150.62	192.81	211.77	291.66
Eye care services	22.70	13.18	19.10	24.89	24.45	24.55	37.32
Service by other than physician	22.62	7.40	10.90	32.64	33.87	28.23	37.72
Lab test, x-rays	26.78	15.92	26.26	26.95	25.75	28.61	43.93
Nursing, therapy, and miscellaneous medical services	4.21	3.53	0.66	1.59	1.80	1.01	20.02
Hospital room	54.96	24.32	72.01	50.56	28.43	95.50	82.57
Hospital services other than room	26.61	13.12	54.88	28.85	22.89	39.94	0.00
Care in convalescent or nursing home	40.86	44.10	118.29	4.48	2.60	18.57	14.65
Other medical services	13.86	16.04	8.60	6.19	16.09	22.77	20.00
DRUGS	**$225.58**	**$180.26**	**$242.53**	**$243.50**	**$250.24**	**$216.93**	**$231.03**
Non-prescription drugs	65.79	39.84	64.96	74.26	86.34	75.99	72.99
Prescription drugs	159.49	140.42	177.58	169.24	163.91	140.94	158.04
MEDICAL SUPPLIES	**$71.06**	**$40.23**	**$59.75**	**$60.54**	**$89.93**	**$94.24**	**$117.28**
Eyeglasses	45.18	17.99	37.48	44.92	56.67	64.90	76.60
Topicals and dressings	14.40	6.11	11.11	11.38	19.22	24.24	25.72
Medical equipment for general use	5.29	9.56	4.57	1.83	4.67	4.14	5.12
Supportive/convalescent medical equipment	5.70	5.80	6.23	2.02	8.91	0.65	9.30
Rental of medical equipment	0.50	0.77	-	-	-	-	0.55

Note: Expenditures are not given (-) when the amount is too small to be reliable. Numbers may not add to total due to rounding. Total expenditure exceeds total income in some income categories due to a number of factors including underreporting of income, borrowing, and the use of savings. Expenditures for hearing aids are not available by income.

Share of spending

Percent of total average annual expenditures spent on health care, by total before-tax income of consumer unit.

(consumer units include complete income reporters only)	all cu's	under $10,000	$10,000 to $19,999	$20,000 to $29,999	$30,000 to $39,999	$40,000 to $49,999	$50,000 and over
Number of consumer units (in thousands)	81,354	18,809	17,652	14,586	10,901	7,198	12,209
Average number of persons per cu	2.6	1.8	2.3	2.7	2.9	3.2	3.1
Average number of earners per cu	1.4	0.7	1.0	1.5	1.8	2.0	2.1
TOTAL AVERAGE ANNUAL EXPENDITURES	100.00%	100.00%	100.00%	100.00%	100.00%	100.00%	100.00%
HEALTH CARE, AVERAGE ANNUAL EXPENDITURES	4.86%	7.61%	7.43%	5.34%	4.32%	4.08%	3.00%
HEALTH INSURANCE	**1.79%**	**3.22%**	**2.64%**	**2.16%**	**1.50%**	**1.45%**	**0.99%**
Commercial health insurance	0.63	0.65	0.79	0.84	0.62	0.68	0.40
Blue Cross/Blue Shield	0.44	0.85	0.62	0.51	0.36	0.30	0.28
Health maintenance plans (HMO's)	0.18	0.15	0.19	0.23	0.21	0.23	0.13
Medicare payments	0.30	1.04	0.65	0.29	0.13	0.08	0.06
Commercial medicare supplements/other health insurance	0.24	0.52	0.39	0.29	0.18	0.16	0.12
MEDICAL SERVICES	**1.94%**	**2.44%**	**3.12%**	**1.96%**	**1.74%**	**1.80%**	**1.34%**
Physician's services	0.57	0.72	0.84	0.64	0.64	0.55	0.29
Dental services	0.57	0.50	0.58	0.60	0.61	0.56	0.56
Eye care services	0.09	0.12	0.11	0.10	0.08	0.07	0.07
Service by other than physician	0.09	0.07	0.06	0.13	0.11	0.08	0.07
Lab test, x-rays	0.10	0.14	0.15	0.11	0.08	0.08	0.08
Nursing, therapy, and miscellaneous medical services	0.02	0.03	0.00	0.01	0.01	0.00	0.04
Hospital room	0.21	0.22	0.40	0.20	0.09	0.25	0.16
Hospital services other than room	0.10	0.12	0.30	0.12	0.07	0.11	0.00
Care in convalescent or nursing home	0.15	0.39	0.65	0.02	0.01	0.05	0.03
Other medical services	0.05	0.14	0.05	0.02	0.05	0.06	0.04
DRUGS	**0.85%**	**1.60%**	**1.34%**	**0.98%**	**0.79%**	**0.58%**	**0.44%**
Non-prescription drugs	0.25	0.35	0.36	0.30	0.27	0.20	0.14
Prescription drugs	0.60	1.25	0.98	0.68	0.52	0.38	0.30
MEDICAL SUPPLIES	**0.27%**	**0.36%**	**0.33%**	**0.24%**	**0.28%**	**0.25%**	**0.22%**
Eyeglasses	0.17	0.16	0.21	0.18	0.18	0.17	0.15
Topicals and dressings	0.05	0.05	0.06	0.05	0.06	0.06	0.05
Medical equipment for general use	0.02	0.08	0.03	0.01	0.01	0.01	0.01
Supportive/convalescent medical equipment	0.02	0.05	0.03	0.01	0.03	0.00	0.02
Rental of medical equipment	0.00	0.01	-	-	-	-	0.00

Note: Expenditures are not given (-) when the amount is too small to be reliable. Numbers may not add to total due to rounding. Expenditures for hearing aids are not available by income.

Indexed expenditures

Indexed average annual expenditures for health care, by total before-tax income of consumer unit.

Consumer units include complete income reporters only.	all cu's	under $10,000	$10,000 to $19,999	$20,000 to $29,999	$30,000 to $39,999	$40,000 to $49,999	$50,000 and over
Number of consumer units (in thousands)	81,354	18,809	17,652	14,586	10,901	7,198	12,209
Average number of persons per cu	2.6	1.8	2.3	2.7	2.9	3.2	3.1
Average number of earners per cu	1.4	0.7	1.0	1.5	1.8	2.0	2.1
TOTAL AVERAGE ANNUAL EXPENDITURES	100	43	69	94	120	142	198
HEALTH CARE, AVERAGE ANNUAL EXPENDITURES	100	67	105	104	107	119	122
HEALTH INSURANCE	**100**	**77**	**101**	**113**	**100**	**115**	**110**
Commercial health insurance	100	44	86	126	118	155	126
Blue Cross/Blue Shield	100	82	96	109	98	96	126
Health maintenance plans (HMOs)	100	35	73	120	139	174	138
Medicare payments	100	149	149	91	52	40	41
Commercial medicare supplements/other health insurance	100	91	109	112	88	95	101
MEDICAL SERVICES	**100**	**54**	**110**	**95**	**108**	**132**	**137**
Physician's services	100	54	102	108	136	138	103
Dental services	100	37	69	100	128	140	193
Eye care services	100	58	84	110	108	108	164
Service by other than physician	100	33	48	144	150	125	167
Lab test, x-rays	100	59	98	101	96	107	164
Nursing, therapy, and miscellaneous medical services	100	84	16	38	43	24	476
Hospital room	100	44	131	92	52	174	150
Hospital services other than room	100	49	206	108	86	150	0
Care in convalescent or nursing home	100	108	290	11	6	45	36
Other medical services	100	116	62	45	116	164	144
DRUGS	**100**	**80**	**108**	**108**	**111**	**96**	**102**
Non-prescription drugs	100	61	99	113	131	116	111
Prescription drugs	100	88	111	106	103	88	99
MEDICAL SUPPLIES	**100**	**57**	**84**	**85**	**127**	**133**	**165**
Eyeglasses	100	40	83	99	125	144	170
Topicals and dressings	100	42	77	79	133	168	179
Medical equipment for general use	100	181	86	35	88	78	97
Supportive/convalescent medical equipment	100	102	109	35	156	11	163
Rental of medical equipment	100	153	-	-	-	-	110

Note: Expenditures are not given (-) when the amount is too small to be reliable. An index of 100 represents the average for all consumer units. An index of 132 means that the average for the subgroup is 32 percent above the average for all consumer units. An index of 68 indicates spending that is 32 percent below the overall average. Expenditures for hearing aids are not available by income.

Aggregate expenditures, 1988

Aggregate expenditures in 1988 for health care, by total before-tax income of consumer unit.

Consumer units include complete income reporters only.	all cu's	under $10,000	$10,000 to $19,999	$20,000 to $29,999	$30,000 to $39,999	$40,000 to $49,999	$50,000 and over
Number of consumer units (in thousands)	81,354	18,809	17,652	14,586	10,901	7,198	12,209
Average number of persons per cu	2.6	1.8	2.3	2.7	2.9	3.2	3.1
Average number of earners per cu	1.4	0.7	1.0	1.5	1.8	2.0	2.1
TOTAL AGGREGATE EXPENDITURES (in millions)	$2,148,492	$211,967	$319,117	$363,138	$345,121	$270,371	$638,777
HEALTH CARE, AGGREGATE EXPENDITURES (in millions)	$104,303	$16,133	$23,721	$19,377	$14,904	$11,026	$19,141
HEALTH INSURANCE	**$38,510**	**$6,816**	**$8,428**	**$7,835**	**$5,183**	**$3,915**	**$6,334**
Commercial health insurance	13,446	1,382	2,518	3,037	2,134	1,839	2,537
Blue Cross/Blue Shield	9,480	1,808	1,982	1,855	1,244	802	1,790
Health maintenance plans (HMOs)	3,944	318	621	845	736	608	816
Medicare payments	6,395	2,207	2,069	1,046	448	227	397
Commercial medicare supplements/other health insurance	5,245	1,101	1,237	1,051	622	440	795
MEDICAL SERVICES	**$41,674**	**$5,170**	**$9,958**	**$7,108**	**$6,013**	**$4,871**	**$8,554**
Physician's services	12,137	1,525	2,696	2,342	2,212	1,481	1,882
Dental services	12,276	1,053	1,839	2,197	2,102	1,524	3,561
Eye care services	1,847	248	337	363	267	177	456
Service by other than physician	1,840	139	192	476	369	203	461
Lab test, x-rays	2,179	299	463	393	281	206	536
Nursing, therapy, and miscellaneous medical services	373	66	12	23	20	7	244
Hospital room	4,471	457	1,271	737	310	687	1,008
Hospital services other than room	2,173	247	969	421	250	287	0
Care in convalescent or nursing home	3,324	829	2,088	65	28	134	179
Other medical services	1,127	302	152	90	175	164	244
DRUGS	**$18,333**	**$3,390**	**$4,281**	**$3,552**	**$2,728**	**$1,561**	**$2,821**
Non-prescription drugs	5,358	749	1,147	1,083	941	547	891
Prescription drugs	12,975	2,641	3,135	2,469	1,787	1,014	1,930
MEDICAL SUPPLIES	**$5,785**	**$757**	**$1,055**	**$883**	**$980**	**$678**	**$1,432**
Eyeglasses	3,675	338	662	655	618	467	935
Topicals and dressings	1,175	115	196	166	210	174	314
Medical equipment for general use	430	180	81	27	51	30	63
Supportive/convalescent medical equipment	464	109	110	29	97	5	114
Rental of medical equipment	21	14	-	-	-	-	7

Note: Expenditures are not given (-) when the amount is too small to be reliable. Numbers may not add to total due to rounding. The "all cu's" aggregates will differ slightly from table to table because they are the sums of the aggregates in each row. Expenditures for hearing aids are not available by income.

PART III
Spending by type of household for health care

As with other product and service categories, married couples are the biggest share of the health care market...

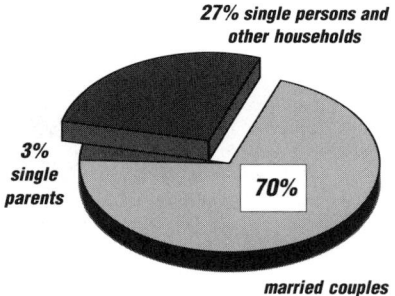

27% single persons and other households

3% single parents

70%

married couples

...but those with children are not the top spenders.

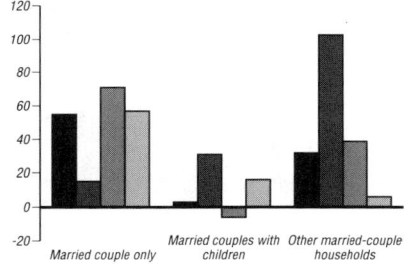

Married couple only

Married couples with children

Other married-couple households

Single parents spend far less than the average household on health care.

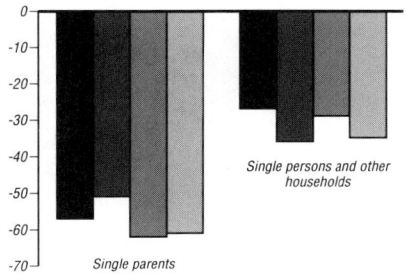

Single persons and other households

Single parents

0 = average spending

■ Health insurance   ■ Drugs

■ Medical services   ▧ Medical supplies

Married couples spent $1,658 on health care in 1988, nearly twice as much as single-person and "other" households* and three times as much as single parents. Together, married-couple households paid $86 billion for health care in 1988, accounting for 70 percent of the out-of-pocket health care market. Single-person and "other" households spent $34 billion, accounting for another 27 percent of the market. Although single parents are 6 percent of all households, they account for just 3 percent of the health care market, spending $3 billion on health care products and services in 1988.

Married couples spend 28 percent more than the average household on health care. Their spending is below average only for convalescent or nursing home care. People who live alone or in "other" households, many of them elderly, spend 30 percent less than the average household on health care, with above average spending for two items—Medicare and nursing homes. Single parents spend 55 percent less than the average household on health care. They spend less than average on all health care items except unspecified medical services.

Health care is the one category in which empty-nesters and other childless couples outspend married couples with children. Married couples with no children at home spend 42 percent more than the average household on health care, while those with children spend 14 percent more than average. The highest spending households, however, are married couples who live with extended family members or unrelated people. Their health care expenditures are 61 percent above average.

*In this analysis, single-person households are grouped with "other" households. "Other" households are unrelated people living together and families that are not married-couple or single-parent families, such as siblings. Single-person households account for 72 percent of the households in this category.

Average expenditures

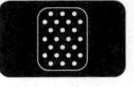
Average annual expenditures for health care, by type of consumer unit.

	all cu's	married couples	single parents	single persons and other cu's
Number of consumer units (in thousands)	*94,862*	*52,010*	*5,716*	*37,136*
Average number of persons per cu	*2.6*	*3.3*	*2.9*	*1.5*
Average number of earners per cu	*1.4*	*1.7*	*1.0*	*0.9*
Average total before-tax income	*$28,540.00*	*$37,299.00*	*$16,276.00*	*$18,509.00*
TOTAL AVERAGE ANNUAL EXPENDITURES	*$25,891.85*	*$32,314.50*	*$18,615.80*	*$17,950.80*
HEALTH CARE, AVERAGE ANNUAL EXPENDITURES	*$1,297.68*	*$1,657.91*	*$577.88*	*$902.84*
HEALTH INSURANCE	**$474.39**	**$594.21**	**$204.89**	**$348.06**
Commercial health insurance	166.27	222.47	99.60	97.82
Blue Cross/Blue Shield	120.93	148.14	51.65	93.47
Health maintenance plans (HMOs)	46.39	60.87	31.82	28.35
Medicare payments	77.03	84.05	2.84	78.61
Commercial medicare supplements/other health insurance	63.79	78.68	18.99	49.82
MEDICAL SERVICES	**$529.34**	**$686.89**	**$260.60**	**$350.07**
Physician's services	153.86	197.80	94.58	101.44
Dental services	151.97	205.34	91.25	86.56
Eye care services	22.03	28.46	10.54	14.78
Service by other than physician	22.63	26.99	4.90	19.26
Lab test, x-rays	25.82	34.51	10.60	16.00
Nursing, therapy, and miscellaneous medical services	3.84	6.34	-	0.90
Hospital room	59.71	90.47	10.46	24.19
Hospital services other than room	35.53	50.62	17.32	17.20
Care in convalescent or nursing home	40.55	31.88	1.97	58.63
Other medical services	13.42	14.47	18.78	11.02
DRUGS	**$223.20**	**$283.87**	**$84.98**	**$158.68**
Non-prescription drugs	61.85	79.58	37.60	39.92
Prescription drugs	161.35	204.29	47.38	118.76
MEDICAL SUPPLIES	**$70.74**	**$92.94**	**$27.41**	**$46.04**
Eyeglasses	44.65	57.70	22.51	29.79
Topicals and dressings	13.28	17.89	3.08	8.17
Medical equipment for general use	5.26	5.83	1.41	5.05
Supportive/convalescent medical equipment	5.23	7.73	-	2.49
Rental of medical equipment	-	-	-	0.54
Hearing aids	1.84	3.30	0.00	0.00

Note: Expenditures are not given (-) when the amount is too small to be reliable. Numbers may not add to total due to rounding. "Single parents" is one-parent consumer units with a child or children under age 18 living at home. "Other cu's" includes persons living with unrelated persons and families other than married-couple and single-parent families.

Share of spending

Percent of total average annual expenditures spent on health care, by type of consumer unit.

	all cu's	married couples	single parents	single persons and other cu's
Number of consumer units (in thousands)	94,862	52,010	5,716	37,136
Average number of persons per cu	2.6	3.3	2.9	1.5
Average total before-tax income	$28,540	$37,299	$16,276	$18,509
TOTAL AVERAGE ANNUAL EXPENDITURES	100.00%	100.00%	100.00%	100.00%
HEALTH CARE, AVERAGE ANNUAL EXPENDITURES	5.01%	5.13%	3.10%	5.03%
HEALTH INSURANCE	**1.83%**	**1.84%**	**1.10%**	**1.94%**
Commercial health insurance	0.64	0.69	0.54	0.54
Blue Cross/Blue Shield	0.47	0.46	0.28	0.52
Health maintenance plans (HMOs)	0.18	0.19	0.17	0.16
Medicare payments	0.30	0.26	0.02	0.44
Commercial medicare supplements/other health insurance	0.25	0.24	0.10	0.28
MEDICAL SERVICES	**2.04%**	**2.13%**	**1.40%**	**1.95%**
Physician's services	0.59	0.61	0.51	0.57
Dental services	0.59	0.64	0.49	0.48
Eye care services	0.09	0.09	0.06	0.08
Service by other than physician	0.09	0.08	0.03	0.11
Lab test, x-rays	0.10	0.11	0.06	0.09
Nursing, therapy, and miscellaneous medical services	0.01	0.02	-	0.01
Hospital room	0.23	0.28	0.06	0.13
Hospital services other than room	0.14	0.16	0.09	0.10
Care in convalescent or nursing home	0.16	0.10	0.01	0.33
Other medical services	0.05	0.04	0.10	0.06
DRUGS	**0.86%**	**0.88%**	**0.46%**	**0.88%**
Non-prescription drugs	0.24	0.25	0.20	0.22
Prescription drugs	0.62	0.63	0.25	0.66
MEDICAL SUPPLIES	**0.27%**	**0.29%**	**0.15%**	**0.26%**
Eyeglasses	0.17	0.18	0.12	0.17
Topicals and dressings	0.05	0.06	0.02	0.05
Medical equipment for general use	0.02	0.02	0.01	0.03
Supportive/convalescent medical equipment	0.02	0.02	-	0.01
Rental of medical equipment	-	-	-	0.00
Hearing aids	0.01	0.01	0.00	0.00

Note: Expenditures are not given (-) when the amount is too small to be reliable. Numbers may not add to total due to rounding. "Single parents" is one-parent consumer units with a child or children under age 18 living at home. "Other cu's" includes persons living with unrelated persons and families other than married-couple and single-parent families.

Indexed expenditures

Indexed average annual expenditures for health care, by type of consumer unit.

	all cu's	married couples	single parents	single persons and other cu's
Number of consumer units (in thousands)	**94,862**	**52,010**	**5,716**	**37,136**
Average number of persons per cu	*2.6*	*3.3*	*2.9*	*1.5*
Average number of earners per cu	*1.4*	*1.7*	*1.0*	*0.9*
Average total before-tax income	*$28,540*	*$37,299*	*$16,276*	*$18,509*
TOTAL AVERAGE ANNUAL EXPENDITURES	*100*	*125*	*72*	*69*
HEALTH CARE, AVERAGE ANNUAL EXPENDITURES	*100*	*128*	*45*	*70*
HEALTH INSURANCE	**100**	**125**	**43**	**73**
Commercial health insurance	100	134	60	59
Blue Cross/Blue Shield	100	123	43	77
Health maintenance plans (HMOs)	100	131	69	61
Medicare payments	100	109	4	102
Commercial medicare supplements/other health insurance	100	123	30	78
MEDICAL SERVICES	**100**	**130**	**49**	**66**
Physician's services	100	129	61	66
Dental services	100	135	60	57
Eye care services	100	129	48	67
Service by other than physician	100	119	22	85
Lab test, x-rays	100	134	41	62
Nursing, therapy, and miscellaneous medical services	100	165	-	23
Hospital room	100	152	18	41
Hospital services other than room	100	142	49	48
Care in convalescent or nursing home	100	79	5	145
Other medical services	100	108	140	82
DRUGS	**100**	**127**	**38**	**71**
Non-prescription drugs	100	129	61	65
Prescription drugs	100	127	29	74
MEDICAL SUPPLIES	**100**	**131**	**39**	**65**
Eyeglasses	100	129	50	67
Topicals and dressings	100	135	23	62
Medical equipment for general use	100	111	27	96
Supportive/convalescent medical equipment	100	148	-	48
Rental of medical equipment	100	-	-	-
Hearing aids	100	179	0	0

Note: An index of 100 represents the average for all consumer units. An index of 132 means that the average for the subgroup is 32 percent above the average for all consumer units. An index of 68 indicates spending that is 32 percent below the overall average. Expenditures are not given (-) when the amount is too small to be reliable. "Single parents" is one-parent consumer units with a child or children under age 18 living at home. "Other cu's" includes persons living with unrelated persons and families other than married-couple and single-parent families.

Aggregate expenditures, 1988

Aggregate expenditures in 1988 for health care, by type of consumer unit.

	all cu's	married couples	single parents	single persons and other cu's
Number of consumer units (in thousands)	94,862	52,010	5,716	37,136
Average number of persons per cu	2.6	3.3	2.9	1.5
Average number of earners per cu	1.4	1.7	1.0	0.9
Aggregate before-tax income (in millions)	$2,720,305	$1,939,921	$93,034	$687,350
TOTAL AGGREGATE EXPENDITURES (in millions)	$2,453,706	$1,680,677	$106,408	$666,621
HEALTH CARE, AGGREGATE EXPENDITURES (in millions)	$123,059	$86,228	$3,303	$33,528
HEALTH INSURANCE	**$45,002**	**$30,905**	**$1,171**	**$12,926**
Commercial health insurance	15,773	11,571	569	3,633
Blue Cross/Blue Shield	11,471	7,705	295	3,471
Health maintenance plans (HMOs)	4,401	3,166	182	1,053
Medicare payments	7,307	4,371	16	2,919
Commercial medicare supplements/other health insurance	6,051	4,092	109	1,850
MEDICAL SERVICES	**$50,215**	**$35,725**	**$1,490**	**$13,000**
Physician's services	14,595	10,288	541	3,767
Dental services	14,416	10,680	522	3,214
Eye care services	2,089	1,480	60	549
Service by other than physician	2,147	1,404	28	715
Lab test, x-rays	2,450	1,795	61	594
Nursing, therapy, and miscellaneous medical services	363	330	-	33
Hospital room	5,663	4,705	60	898
Hospital services other than room	3,370	2,633	99	639
Care in convalescent or nursing home	3,847	1,658	11	2,177
Other medical services	1,269	753	107	409
DRUGS	**$21,143**	**$14,764**	**$486**	**$5,893**
Non-prescription drugs	5,836	4,139	215	1,482
Prescription drugs	15,306	10,625	271	4,410
MEDICAL SUPPLIES	**$6,700**	**$4,834**	**$157**	**$1,710**
Eyeglasses	4,236	3,001	129	1,106
Topicals and dressings	1,251	930	18	303
Medical equipment for general use	499	303	8	188
Supportive/convalescent medical equipment	494	402	-	92
Rental of medical equipment	20	-	-	20
Hearing aids	172	172	0	0

Note: Expenditures are not given (-) when the amount is too small to be reliable. Numbers may not add to total due to rounding. "Single parents" is one-parent consumer units with a child or children under age 18 living at home. "Other cu's" includes persons living with unrelated persons and families other than married-couple and single-parent families. The "all cu's" aggregates will differ slightly from table to table because they are the sums of the aggregates in each row.

Average expenditures

Average annual expenditures for health care, by married couples with and without children.

	all cu's	all married couples	married couple only	all married couples with children	AGE OF OLDEST CHILD			other married couples
					under 6	6 to 17	18 or older	
Number of consumer units (in thousands)	94,862	52,010	20,227	28,100	5,858	14,194	8,047	3,684
Average number of persons per cu	2.6	3.3	2	3.9	3.5	4.1	3.9	5.1
Average number of earners per cu	1.4	1.7	1.2	2.1	1.7	1.9	2.7	2.4
Average total before-tax income	$28,540.00	$37,299.00	$33,825.00	$39,354.00	$34,318.00	$38,039.00	$45,596.00	$40,846.00
TOTAL AVERAGE ANNUAL EXPENDITURES	$25,891.85	$32,314.50	$27,954.50	$35,015.30	$30,942.80	$35,248.40	$37,763.90	$35,739.60
HEALTH CARE, AVER. ANNUAL EXPENDITURES	$1,297.68	$1,657.91	$1,836.52	$1,473.05	$1,206.02	$1,478.52	$1,659.02	$2,086.48
HEALTH INSURANCE	**$474.39**	**$594.21**	**$735.14**	**$488.31**	**$413.63**	**$470.69**	**$573.76**	**$628.18**
Commercial health insurance	166.27	222.47	218.77	228.77	205.60	226.48	249.69	194.71
Blue Cross/Blue Shield	120.93	148.14	185.20	120.42	107.87	108.72	150.21	156.12
Health maintenance plans (HMOs)	46.39	60.87	50.35	64.94	72.69	67.37	55.01	87.55
Medicare payments	77.03	84.05	169.20	18.28	0.00	5.67	53.82	118.24
Commercial medicare supplements/ other health insurance	63.79	78.68	111.63	55.90	27.48	62.46	65.02	71.56
MEDICAL SERVICES	**$529.34**	**$686.89**	**$608.46**	**$692.57**	**$575.55**	**$730.41**	**$711.00**	**$1,074.18**
Physician's services	153.86	197.80	122.54	243.36	248.27	242.46	241.37	263.48
Dental services	151.97	205.34	205.21	206.40	98.93	255.85	197.39	198.04
Eye care services	22.03	28.46	34.00	24.16	15.10	20.14	37.84	30.84
Service by other than physician	22.63	26.99	30.08	24.69	16.75	23.69	32.22	27.63
Lab test, x-rays	25.82	34.51	37.07	30.96	18.71	26.18	48.32	47.50
Nursing, therapy, misc. medical services	3.84	6.34	4.32	8.41	-	1.64	26.24	1.61
Hospital room	59.71	90.47	56.17	93.28	103.64	103.78	67.23	257.39
Hospital services other than room	35.53	50.62	29.64	44.93	63.78	40.02	39.86	209.19
Care in convalescent or nursing home	40.55	31.88	71.59	3.36	0.00	3.50	5.55	31.43
Other medical services	13.42	14.47	17.84	13.02	10.05	13.14	14.98	7.06
DRUGS	**$223.20**	**$283.87**	**$382.06**	**$209.77**	**$156.14**	**$194.43**	**$277.54**	**$309.27**
Non-prescription drugs	61.85	79.58	95.44	68.92	55.91	72.20	74.29	73.11
Prescription drugs	161.35	204.29	286.62	140.85	100.23	122.23	203.24	236.16
MEDICAL SUPPLIES	**$70.74**	**$92.94**	**$110.85**	**$82.40**	**$60.70**	**$82.98**	**$96.72**	**$74.86**
Eyeglasses	44.65	57.70	60.90	57.09	32.15	58.24	76.21	44.75
Topicals and dressings	13.28	17.89	16.47	18.37	16.67	21.81	13.06	22.27
Medical equipment for general use	5.26	5.83	11.32	2.35	1.82	1.65	3.98	2.18
Supportive/convalescent medical equipment	5.23	7.73	13.21	4.16	9.72	1.05	5.61	4.82
Rental of medical equipment	-	-	0.52	-	-	-	0.86	0.83
Hearing aids	1.84	3.30	8.44	0.00	0.00	0.00	0.00	0.00

Note: Expenditures are not given (-) when the amount is too small to be reliable. Numbers may not add to total due to rounding. Other married couples include extended family members or unrelated persons in addition to the married couple.

Share of spending

HEALTH CARE

Percent of total average annual expenditures spent on health care, by married couples with and without children.

	all cu's	all married couples	married couple only	all married couples with children	AGE OF OLDEST CHILD			other married couples
					under 6	6 to 17	18 or older	
Number of consumer units (in thousands)	94,862	52,010	20,227	28,100	5,858	14,194	8,047	3,684
Average number of persons per cu	2.6	3.3	2	3.9	3.5	4.1	3.9	5.1
Average total before-tax income	$28,540	$37,299	$33,825	$39,354	$34,318	$38,039	$45,596	$40,846
TOTAL AVERAGE ANNUAL EXPENDITURES	100.00%	100.00%	100.00%	100.00%	100.00%	100.00%	100.00%	100.00%
HEALTH CARE, AVER. ANNUAL EXPENDITURES	5.01%	5.13%	6.57%	4.21%	3.90%	4.19%	4.39%	5.84%
HEALTH INSURANCE	**1.83%**	**1.84%**	**2.63%**	**1.39%**	**1.34%**	**1.34%**	**1.52%**	**1.76%**
Commercial health insurance	0.64	0.69	0.78	0.65	0.66	0.64	0.66	0.54
Blue Cross/Blue Shield	0.47	0.46	0.66	0.34	0.35	0.31	0.40	0.44
Health maintenance plans (HMOs)	0.18	0.19	0.18	0.19	0.23	0.19	0.15	0.24
Medicare payments	0.30	0.26	0.61	0.05	0.00	0.02	0.14	0.33
Commercial medicare supplements/ other health insurance	0.25	0.24	0.40	0.16	0.09	0.18	0.17	0.20
MEDICAL SERVICES	**2.04%**	**2.13%**	**2.18%**	**1.98%**	**1.86%**	**2.07%**	**1.88%**	**3.01%**
Physician's services	0.59	0.61	0.44	0.70	0.80	0.69	0.64	0.74
Dental services	0.59	0.64	0.73	0.59	0.32	0.73	0.52	0.55
Eye care services	0.09	0.09	0.12	0.07	0.05	0.06	0.10	0.09
Service by other than physician	0.09	0.08	0.11	0.07	0.05	0.07	0.09	0.08
Lab test, x-rays	0.10	0.11	0.13	0.09	0.06	0.07	0.13	0.13
Nursing, therapy, misc. medical services	0.01	0.02	0.02	0.02	-	0.00	0.07	0.00
Hospital room	0.23	0.28	0.20	0.27	0.33	0.29	0.18	0.72
Hospital services other than room	0.14	0.16	0.11	0.13	0.21	0.11	0.11	0.59
Care in convalescent or nursing home	0.16	0.10	0.26	0.01	0.00	0.01	0.01	0.09
Other medical services	0.05	0.04	0.06	0.04	0.03	0.04	0.04	0.02
DRUGS	**0.86%**	**0.88%**	**1.37%**	**0.60%**	**0.50%**	**0.55%**	**0.73%**	**0.87%**
Non-prescription drugs	0.24	0.25	0.34	0.20	0.18	0.20	0.20	0.20
Prescription drugs	0.62	0.63	1.03	0.40	0.32	0.35	0.54	0.66
MEDICAL SUPPLIES	**0.27%**	**0.29%**	**0.40%**	**0.24%**	**0.20%**	**0.24%**	**0.26%**	**0.21%**
Eyeglasses	0.17	0.18	0.22	0.16	0.10	0.17	0.20	0.13
Topicals and dressings	0.05	0.06	0.06	0.05	0.05	0.06	0.03	0.06
Medical equipment for general use	0.02	0.02	0.04	0.01	0.01	0.00	0.01	0.01
Supportive/convalescent medical equipment	0.02	0.02	0.05	0.01	0.03	0.00	0.01	0.01
Rental of medical equipment	-	-	0.00	-	-	-	0.00	0.00
Hearing aids	0.01	0.01	0.03	0.00	0.00	0.00	0.00	0.00

Note: Expenditures are not given (-) when the amount is too small to be reliable. Numbers may not add to total due to rounding. Other married couples include extended family members or unrelated persons in addition to the married couple.

Indexed expenditures

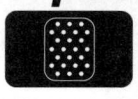
Indexed average annual expenditures for health care, by married couples with and without children.

	all cu's	all married couples	married couple only	all married couples with children	AGE OF OLDEST CHILD			other married couples
					under 6	6 to 17	18 or older	
Number of consumer units (in thousands)	94,862	52,010	20,227	28,100	5,858	14,194	8,047	3,684
Average number of persons per cu	2.6	3.3	2	3.9	3.5	4.1	3.9	5.1
Average number of earners per cu	1.4	1.7	1.2	2.1	1.7	1.9	2.7	2.4
Average total before-tax income	$28,540	$37,299	$33,825	$39,354	$34,318	$38,039	$45,596	$40,846
TOTAL AVERAGE ANNUAL EXPENDITURES	100	125	108	135	120	136	146	138
HEALTH CARE, AVER. ANNUAL EXPENDITURES	100	128	142	114	93	114	128	161
HEALTH INSURANCE	**100**	**125**	**155**	**103**	**87**	**99**	**121**	**132**
Commercial health insurance	100	134	132	138	124	136	150	117
Blue Cross/Blue Shield	100	123	153	100	89	90	124	129
Health maintenance plans (HMOs)	100	131	109	140	157	145	119	189
Medicare payments	100	109	220	24	0	7	70	153
Commercial medicare supplements/ other health insurance	100	123	175	88	43	98	102	112
MEDICAL SERVICES	**100**	**130**	**115**	**131**	**109**	**138**	**134**	**203**
Physician's services	100	129	80	158	161	158	157	171
Dental services	100	135	135	136	65	168	130	130
Eye care services	100	129	154	110	69	91	172	140
Service by other than physician	100	119	133	109	74	105	142	122
Lab test, x-rays	100	134	144	120	72	101	187	184
Nursing, therapy, misc. medical services	100	165	113	219	-	43	683	42
Hospital room	100	152	94	156	174	174	113	431
Hospital services other than room	100	142	83	126	180	113	112	589
Care in convalescent or nursing home	100	79	177	8	0	9	14	78
Other medical services	100	108	133	97	75	98	112	53
DRUGS	**100**	**127**	**171**	**94**	**70**	**87**	**124**	**139**
Non-prescription drugs	100	129	154	111	90	117	120	118
Prescription drugs	100	127	178	87	62	76	126	146
MEDICAL SUPPLIES	**100**	**131**	**157**	**116**	**86**	**117**	**137**	**106**
Eyeglasses	100	129	136	128	72	130	171	100
Topicals and dressings	100	135	124	138	126	164	98	168
Medical equipment for general use	100	111	215	45	35	31	76	41
Supportive/convalescent medical equipment	100	148	253	80	186	20	107	92
Rental of medical equipment	100	-	-	-	-	-	-	-
Hearing aids	100	179	459	0	0	0	0	0

Note: An index of 100 represents the average for all consumer units. An index of 132 means that the average for the subgroup is 32 percent above the average for all consumer units. An index of 68 indicates spending that is 32 percent below the overall average. Expenditures are not given (-) when the amount is too small to be reliable. Other married couples include extended family members or unrelated persons in addition to the married couple.

Aggregate expenditures, 1988

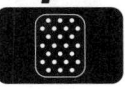

Aggregate expenditures in 1988 for health care, by married couples with and without children.

	all cu's	all married couples	married couple only	all married couples with children	AGE OF OLDEST CHILD			other married couples
					under 6	6 to 17	18 or older	
Number of consumer units (in thousands)	94,862	52,010	20,227	28,100	5,858	14,194	8,047	3,684
Average number of persons per cu	2.6	3.3	2	3.9	3.5	4.1	3.9	5.1
Average number of earners per cu	1.4	1.7	1.2	2.1	1.7	1.9	2.7	2.4
Aggregate before-tax income (in millions)	$2,722,910	$1,942,526	$684,178	$1,107,871	$201,035	$539,926	$366,911	$150,477
TOTAL AGGREG. EXPENDITURES (in millions)	$2,455,594	$1,682,565	$565,436	$985,465	$181,263	$500,316	$303,886	$131,665
HEALTH CARE, AGGREGATE EXPENDITURES (in millions)	$123,066	$86,235	$37,147	$41,401	$7,065	$20,986	$13,350	$7,687
HEALTH INSURANCE	**$45,002**	**$30,905**	**$14,870**	**$13,721**	**$2,423**	**$6,681**	**$4,617**	**$2,314**
Commercial health insurance	15,773	11,571	4,425	6,428	1,204	3,215	2,009	717
Blue Cross/Blue Shield	11,471	7,705	3,746	3,384	632	1,543	1,209	575
Health maintenance plans (HMOs)	4,400	3,166	1,018	1,825	426	956	443	323
Medicare payments	7,307	4,372	3,422	514	0	80	433	436
Commercial medicare supplements/ other health insurance	6,051	4,092	2,258	1,571	161	887	523	264
MEDICAL SERVICES	**$50,215**	**$35,725**	**$12,307**	**$19,460**	**$3,372**	**$10,367**	**$5,721**	**$3,957**
Physician's services	14,595	10,287	2,479	6,838	1,454	3,441	1,942	971
Dental services	14,416	10,680	4,151	5,799	580	3,632	1,588	730
Eye care services	2,089	1,480	688	679	88	286	304	114
Service by other than physician	2,147	1,404	608	694	98	336	259	102
Lab test, x-rays	2,450	1,795	750	870	110	372	389	175
Nursing, therapy, misc. medical services	360	327	87	234	-	23	211	6
Hospital room	5,664	4,706	1,136	2,621	607	1,473	541	948
Hospital services other than room	3,370	2,633	600	1,262	374	568	321	771
Care in convalescent or nursing home	3,847	1,658	1,448	94	0	50	45	116
Other medical services	1,269	753	361	366	59	187	121	26
DRUGS..	**$21,154**	**$14,775**	**$7,728**	**$5,908**	**$915**	**$2,760**	**$2,233**	**$1,139**
Non-prescription drugs	5,847	4,150	1,930	1,950	328	1,025	598	269
Prescription drugs	15,306	10,625	5,797	3,958	587	1,735	1,635	870
MEDICAL SUPPLIES	**$6,696**	**$4,830**	**$2,242**	**$2,312**	**$356**	**$1,178**	**$778**	**$276**
Eyeglasses	4,260	3,025	1,232	1,628	188	827	613	165
Topicals and dressings	1,249	927	333	512	98	310	105	82
Medical equipment for general use	499	303	229	66	11	23	32	8
Supportive/convalescent medical equipment ...	494	402	267	117	57	15	45	18
Rental of medical equipment	41	21	11	7	-	-	7	3
Hearing aids	171	171	171	0	0	0	0	0

Note: Expenditures are not given (-) when the amount is too small to be reliable. Numbers may not add to total due to rounding. Other married couples include extended family members or unrelated persons in addition to the married couple. The "all cu's" aggregates will differ slightly from table to table because they are the sums of the aggregates in each row. In this table they include aggregates for single parents, single persons, and other types of consumer units, in addition to all married couples. Aggregates for "all married couples" and "all married couples with children" are sums of the appropriate aggregates in each row.

CHAPTER

8

Entertainment

The average American household spent a slightly larger share of its expenditures on entertainment in 1988 than in 1984. The way the entertainment budget was spent, however, changed a lot.

Consumers are shifting their spending toward the kinds of entertainment that they can schedule themselves. Fees and admissions took a smaller bite out of the entertainment dollar in 1988 than in 1984. But TV, radio, sound equipment, and other supplies and equipment such as boats, camping gear, and sports equipment gained a larger share of the entertainment budget. The share of the entertainment budget that went to toys, pets, and playground equipment dropped by less than 1 percentage point during this time period.

Five-year spending trends for entertainment

	1984	1985	1986	1987	1988	change 1984 to 1988
Share of household expenditures devoted to entertainment, share of entertainment expenditures devoted to entertainment items, and change in share, 1984 to 1988.						
Entertainment, share of household expenditures	4.8%	5.0%	4.8%	4.9%	5.1%	0.3%
Entertainment, expenditures	100.0%	100.0%	100.0%	100.0%	100.0%	0.0%
FEES AND ADMISSIONS	29.7%	27.4%	26.8%	27.1%	26.6%	-3.1%
TELEVISION, RADIO, AND SOUND EQUIPMENT	30.5%	31.7%	32.3%	31.8%	31.3%	0.8%
PETS, TOYS, AND PLAYGROUND EQUIPMENT	18.0%	18.2%	17.6%	18.3%	17.3%	-0.7%
OTHER ENTERTAINMENT SUPPLIES, EQUIPMENT, AND SERVICES	21.8%	22.7%	23.3%	22.9%	24.8%	3.0%

Note: Numbers may not add to total due to rounding.

PART I
Spending by age for entertainment

American households spent $126 billion having fun in 1988. The average household devotes about 5 percent of its spending to entertainment, and spending is higher than average among householders aged 25 to 54.

The biggest partiers are households headed by people aged 35 to 44. Their overall spending on entertainment is nearly 50 percent above average, and they spend at least twice as much as the average household on recreational lessons, home video game equipment, musical instruments, nonmotorized boats, winter sports equipment, and arcade games.

Older middle-aged households are also big consumers of entertainment. Households headed by 45-to-54-year-olds spend 37 percent more than average on fees and admissions, and they spend 80 percent more than the average household on sporting events. They are the biggest buyers of radios, boat docking space and services, and photographic equipment.

Householders aged 25 to 34 spend only 5 percent more on entertainment than the average household. They spend much more than average on supplies and medicines for pets; VCR, radio, and sound equipment rentals; and sound equipment purchases.

Householders under age 25 spend almost four times more than the average household on tape recorders and players. They also spend above average on TV rentals and bicycles. Overall, however, the entertainment spending of the youngest households is 28 percent below average. Households in the 55-to-64 age group spend less than average on entertainment in general, but they spend more than average on color TV consoles, recreational vehicles, and docking fees.

Householders aged 65 to 74 spend twice as much as the average household on recreational vehicles. And they must treat their grandchildren to playground equipment, because they spend 60 percent more than the average household on this item.

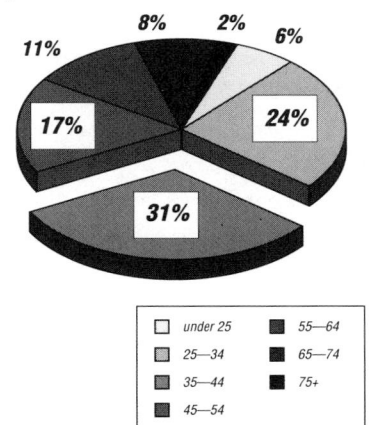

Middle-aged householders account for 72 percent of the entertainment market.

8% 2% 6%
11% 17% 24% 31%

□ under 25	■ 55—64
25—34	■ 65—74
35—44	■ 75+
■ 45—54	

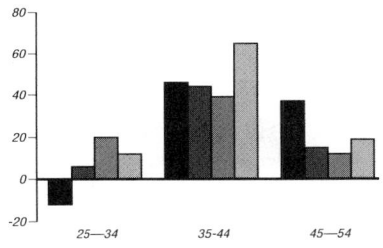

Households headed by 35-to-54-year-olds spend more than the average household on all categories of entertainment...

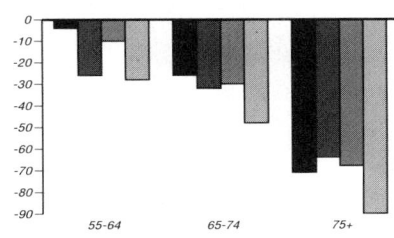

...while those aged 55 or older spend less than average on all categories of entertainment

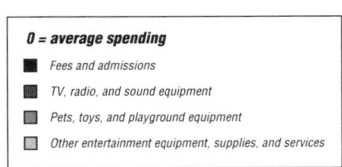

0 = average spending
■ Fees and admissions
■ TV, radio, and sound equipment
Pets, toys, and playground equipment
Other entertainment equipment, supplies, and services

Average expenditures

	all cu's	under 25	25 to 34	35 to 44	45 to 54	55 to 64	65 to 74	75+
Number of consumer units (in thousands)	94,862	7,216	21,985	19,911	13,601	12,546	11,319	8,284
Average number of persons per cu	2.6	1.8	2.8	3.3	2.9	2.2	2.0	1.5
Average total before-tax income	$28,540.00	$14,827.00	$28,318.00	$36,428.00	$39,934.00	$29,979.00	$20,704.00	$13,707.00
TOTAL AVERAGE ANNUAL EXPENDITURES	$25,891.85	$16,373.17	$25,770.27	$33,077.72	$33,204.87	$25,765.35	$20,119.90	$13,339.49
ENTERTAINMENT, AVERAGE ANNUAL EXPENDITURES	$1,328.68	$960.76	$1,395.72	$1,975.38	$1,614.90	$1,135.80	$880.78	$351.22
FEES AND ADMISSIONS	$353.16	$247.24	$310.21	$514.10	$484.76	$339.91	$261.90	$101.28
Club membership dues and fees	79.45	38.87	62.25	93.42	108.02	104.41	81.74	39.03
Participant sports fees	45.69	36.57	46.06	67 .06	44.87	42.01	39.52	16.64
Participant sports fees, out-of-town trips	18.32	17.10	15.81	27.89	24.38	14.86	14.63	3.33
Movie, theater, opera, ballet, other admissions	60.65	70.26	63.13	82.04	83.72	51.15	30.83	11.52
Movie, other out-of-town admissions	26.02	15.70	19.03	35.27	41.23	29.32	20.70	8.62
Sporting event admissions	20.73	14.93	23.41	26.17	37.22	13.15	11.14	3.12
Sporting event, out-of-town admissions	26.02	15.70	19.03	35.27	41.23	29.32	20.70	8.62
Recreational lesson fees	40.52	15.58	32.99	94.90	50.66	17.97	16.35	2.10
Recreational entrance fees, other out-of-town expenses	35.76	22.54	28.50	52.06	53.42	37.72	26.30	8.30
TELEVISION, RADIO, SOUND EQUIP.	$415.52	$349.10	$441.90	$596.67	$479.33	$350.17	$284.25	$141.50
Television	291.96	193.25	291.02	391.47	332.56	296.60	244.69	132.97
Community antenna or cable TV	136.89	70.74	136.85	173.72	157.01	144.77	123.36	79.66
Black and white TV	2.48	0.00	-	10.07	0.00	2.85	0.00	0.00
Color TV, console	22.72	31.98	18.73	23.10	13.86	32.40	29.49	15.03
Color TV, portable and table model	44.06	40.06	43.64	52.19	61.37	42.39	33.23	17.99
VCRs and video disc players	46.72	32.21	53.22	64.70	57.64	45.91	30.95	3.79
Video cassettes, tapes, and discs	12.80	4.41	10.90	23.02	15.79	10.47	9.31	3.92
Video games hardware and software	14.60	6.85	18.89	30.21	11.76	7.53	5.08	0.80
Repair of TV, radio, and sound equipment	10.02	3.65	6.77	12.44	12.52	9.33	13.01	11.16
Rental of TVs	1.67	3.34	1.79	2.01	2.63	0.95	-	0.62
Radios and sound equipment	123.56	155.85	150.88	205.20	146.77	53.57	39.56	8.53
Radios	4.57	1.73	5.32	5.19	12.90	0.74	1.35	0.00
Tape recorders and players	9.29	35.43	6.77	18.52	0.00	1.17	6.89	0.00
Sound components and component systems	28.28	43.35	42.26	36.71	36.72	11.10	5.53	1.90
Sound equipment accessories	3.79	1.94	1.55	12.48	1.34	2.82	-	1.31
Records, tapes, needles, and styli	29.22	44.57	34.70	39.20	36.90	19.72	11.11	3.83
Rental of VCR, radio, sound equipment	1.45	2.68	2.19	1.95	1.74	-	-	-
Musical instruments and accessories	21.91	6.56	23.57	48.82	28.38	6.61	5.81	0.78
Rental and repair of musical instruments	2.14	-	1.95	4.99	1.94	-	2.42	0.00
Rental of video cassettes, tapes, discs, and films	22.58	19.27	32.47	37.52	25.21	10.76	5.35	-

Average annual expenditures for entertainment, by age of reference person.

(continued from previous page)	all cu's	under 25	25 to 34	35 to 44	45 to 54	55 to 64	65 to 74	75+
PETS, TOYS, PLAYGROUND EQUIP.	$230.22	$116.32	$275.83	$320.00	$258.53	$207.65	$162.09	$74.50
Pets	127.45	56.72	132.55	159.40	165.96	129.84	109.05	58.23
Pet food	62.23	25.10	55.05	75.01	80.71	73.42	66.17	31.01
Pet supplies and medicines	20.99	18.11	39.04	17.52	21.19	14.29	6.47	13.92
Pet services	10.86	2.08	8.57	17.60	18.74	7.89	9.06	2.42
Veterinarian services	33.38	11.42	29.89	49.28	45.31	34.24	27.35	10.89
Toys, games, hobbies, and tricycles	100.00	58.98	139.82	155.79	91.37	76.29	48.60	16.27
Playground equipment	2.76	0.62	3.47	4.82	1.19	1.51	4.44	0.00
OTHER ENTERTAINMENT EQUIP., SUPPLIES, AND SERVICES	$329.78	$248.09	$367.78	$544.61	$392.29	$238.07	$172.54	$33.95
Boats and trailers without motors	22.91	0.74	19.53	63.47	16.40	12.64	5.87	3.19
Boats and boat trailers	16.17	0.74	10.64	48.94	9.33	10.92	3.74	1.71
Trailers and other attachable campers	6.74	0.00	8.90	14.54	7.08	1.71	2.13	1.48
Motorized sports vehicles	137.23	110.52	157.78	220.20	142.61	102.70	91.58	12.40
Camper coach and other vehicles	41.77	0.55	58.58	25.64	9.91	76.41	85.11	12.40
Motor boats	95.46	109.97	99.19	194.55	132.70	26.29	6.46	0.00
Sports vehicle rentals	2.29	1.24	3.15	3.24	2.06	1.34	2.17	0.57
Outboard motors	1.16	-	0.87	0.95	1.58	0.63	3.49	0.00
Docking fees	4.92	1.59	1.42	5.86	13.53	7.35	2.36	-
Sports equipment	87.81	68.89	105.30	147.03	103.18	57.63	34.14	9.31
Athletic gear, game tables, exercise equipment	35.06	29.84	40.26	55.03	37.54	29.18	19.88	3.35
Bicycles	11.69	16.30	16.31	20.60	9.61	5.30	2.00	-
Camping equipment	3.17	1.77	3.07	4.87	5.21	2.65	0.95	1.00
Hunting and fishing equipment	15.37	9.59	19.08	26.40	18.04	9.75	6.03	0.93
Winter sports equipment	6.05	4.58	5.95	12.36	9.22	2.09	-	0.99
Water sports/miscellaneous sports equipment .	14.41	5.79	18.73	24.88	20.33	7.36	3.92	0.61
Rental and repair of sports equipment	2.06	1.03	1.90	2.88	3.23	1.32	0.94	2.14
Photographic equip., supplies, and services	67.42	58.16	74.68	91.13	102.91	53.70	32.83	7.88
Film	19.70	14.92	22.12	26.63	27.97	15.56	12.31	3.60
Film processing	24.98	18.91	29.71	33.49	35.94	19.86	13.14	3.21
Photographic equipment	14.88	9.80	16.46	21.10	25.65	10.60	6.32	0.62
Photographer fees	7.07	14.53	5.81	9.31	12.77	5.24	-	-
Pinball and electronic video games	3.84	6.33	3.41	8.39	5.32	-	-	-

Note: Expenditures are not given (-) when the amount is too small to be reliable. Expenditures listed for a given category may not add to the total for that category because the listing is incomplete. "Photographic equipment, supplies, and services," for example, includes "other photographic supplies," which is omitted here. Numbers may not add to total due to rounding.

Share of spending

	all cu's	under 25	25 to 34	35 to 44	45 to 54	55 to 64	65 to 74	75+
Number of consumer units (in thousands)	94,862	7,216	21,985	19,911	13,601	12,546	11,319	8,284
Average number of persons per cu	2.6	1.8	2.8	3.3	2.9	2.2	2.0	1.5
Average total before-tax income	$28,540	$14,827	$28,318	$36,428	$39,934	$29,979	$20,704	$13,707
TOTAL AVERAGE ANNUAL EXPENDITURES	100.00%	100.00%	100.00%	100.00%	100.00%	100.00%	100.00%	100.00%
ENTERTAINMENT, AVERAGE ANNUAL EXPENDITURES	5.13%	5.87%	5.42%	5.97%	4.86%	4.41%	4.38%	2.63%
FEES AND ADMISSIONS	1.36%	1.51%	1.20%	1.55%	1.46%	1.32%	1.30%	0.76%
Club membership dues and fees	0.31	0.24	0.24	0.28	0.33	0.41	0.41	0.29
Participant sports fees	0.18	0.22	0.18	-	0.14	0.16	0.20	0.12
Participant sports fees, out-of-town trips	0.07	0.10	0.06	0.08	0.07	0.06	0.07	0.02
Movie, theater, opera, ballet, other admissions	0.23	0.43	0.24	0.25	0.25	0.20	0.15	0.09
Movie, other out-of-town admissions	0.10	0.10	0.07	0.11	0.12	0.11	0.10	0.06
Sporting event admissions	0.08	0.09	0.09	0.08	0.11	0.05	0.06	0.02
Sporting event, out-of-town admissions	0.10	0.10	0.07	0.11	0.12	0.11	0.10	0.06
Recreational lesson fees	0.16	0.10	0.13	0.29	0.15	0.07	0.08	0.02
Recreational entrance fees, other out-of-town expenses	0.14	0.14	0.11	0.16	0.16	0.15	0.13	0.06
TELEVISION, RADIO, SOUND EQUIP.	1.60%	2.13%	1.71%	1.80%	1.44%	1.36%	1.41%	1.06%
Television	1.13	1.18	1.13	1.18	1.00	1.15	1.22	1.00
Community antenna or cable TV	0.53	0.43	0.53	0.53	0.47	0.56	0.61	0.60
Black and white TV	0.01	0.00	-	0.03	0.00	0.01	0.00	0.00
Color TV, console	0.09	0.20	0.07	0.07	0.04	0.13	0.15	0.11
Color TV, portable and table model	0.17	0.24	0.17	0.16	0.18	0.16	0.17	0.13
VCRs and video disc players	0.18	0.20	0.21	0.20	0.17	0.18	0.15	0.03
Video cassettes, tapes, and discs	0.05	0.03	0.04	0.07	0.05	0.04	0.05	0.03
Video games hardware and software	0.06	0.04	0.07	0.09	0.04	0.03	0.03	0.01
Repair of TV, radio, and sound equipment	0.04	0.02	0.03	0.04	0.04	0.04	0.06	0.08
Rental of TVs	0.01	0.02	0.01	0.01	0.01	0.00	-	0.00
Radios and sound equipment	0.48	0.95	0.59	0.62	0.44	0.21	0.20	0.06
Radios	0.02	0.01	0.02	0.02	0.04	0.00	0.01	0.00
Tape recorders and players	0.04	0.22	0.03	0.06	0.00	0.00	0.03	0.00
Sound components and component systems	0.11	0.26	0.16	0.11	0.11	0.04	0.03	0.01
Sound equipment accessories	0.01	0.01	0.01	0.04	0.00	0.01	-	0.01
Records, tapes, needles, and styli	0.11	0.27	0.13	0.12	0.11	0.08	0.06	0.03
Rental of VCR, radio, sound equipment	0.01	0.02	0.01	0.01	0.01	-	-	-
Musical instruments and accessories	0.08	0.04	0.09	0.15	0.09	0.03	0.03	0.01
Rental and repair of musical instruments	0.01	-	0.01	0.02	0.01	-	0.01	0.00
Rental of video cassettes, tapes, discs, and films	0.09	0.12	0.13	0.11	0.08	0.04	0.03	-

Percent of total average annual expenditures spent on entertainment, by age of reference person.

(continued from previous page)	all cu's	under 25	25 to 34	35 to 44	45 to 54	55 to 64	65 to 74	75+
PETS, TOYS, PLAYGROUND EQUIP.	**0.89%**	**0.71%**	**1.07%**	**0.97%**	**0.78%**	**0.81%**	**0.81%**	**0.56%**
Pets	**0.49**	**0.35**	**0.51**	**0.48**	**0.50**	**0.50**	**0.54**	**0.44**
Pet food	0.24	0.15	0.21	0.23	0.24	0.28	0.33	0.23
Pet supplies and medicines	0.08	0.11	0.15	0.05	0.06	0.06	0.03	0.10
Pet services	0.04	0.01	0.03	0.05	0.06	0.03	0.05	0.02
Veterinarian services	0.13	0.07	0.12	0.15	0.14	0.13	0.14	0.08
Toys, games, hobbies, and tricycles	**0.39**	**0.36**	**0.54**	**0.47**	**0.28**	**0.30**	**0.24**	**0.12**
Playground equipment	**0.01**	**0.00**	**0.01**	**0.01**	**0.00**	**0.01**	**0.02**	**0.00**
OTHER ENTERTAINMENT EQUIP., SUPPLIES, AND SERVICES	**1.27%**	**1.52%**	**1.43%**	**1.65%**	**1.18%**	**0.92%**	**0.86%**	**0.25%**
Boats and trailers without motors	**0.09**	**0.00**	**0.08**	**0.19**	**0.05**	**0.05**	**0.03**	**0.02**
Boats and boat trailers	0.06	0.00	0.04	0.15	0.03	0.04	0.02	0.01
Trailers and other attachable campers	0.03	0.00	0.03	0.04	0.02	0.01	0.01	0.01
Motorized sports vehicles	**0.53**	**0.68**	**0.61**	**0.67**	**0.43**	**0.40**	**0.46**	**0.09**
Camper coach and other vehicles	0.16	0.00	0.23	0.08	0.03	0.30	0.42	0.09
Motor boats	0.37	0.67	0.38	0.59	0.40	0.10	0.03	0.00
Sports vehicle rentals	**0.01**	**0.01**	**0.01**	**0.01**	**0.01**	**0.01**	**0.01**	**0.00**
Outboard motors	**0.00**	**-**	**0.00**	**0.00**	**0.00**	**0.00**	**0.02**	**0.00**
Docking fees	**0.02**	**0.01**	**0.01**	**0.02**	**0.04**	**0.03**	**0.01**	**-**
Sports equipment	**0.34**	**0.42**	**0.41**	**0.44**	**0.31**	**0.22**	**0.17**	**0.07**
Athletic gear, game tables, exercise equipment	0.14	0.18	0.16	0.17	0.11	0.11	0.10	0.03
Bicycles	0.05	0.10	0.06	0.06	0.03	0.02	0.01	-
Camping equipment	0.01	0.01	0.01	0.01	0.02	0.01	0.00	0.01
Hunting and fishing equipment	0.06	0.06	0.07	0.08	0.05	0.04	0.03	0.01
Winter sports equipment	0.02	0.03	0.02	0.04	0.03	0.01	-	0.01
Water sports/miscellaneous sports equipment .	0.06	0.04	0.07	0.08	0.06	0.03	0.02	0.00
Rental and repair of sports equipment	0.01	0.01	0.01	0.01	0.01	0.01	0.00	0.02
Photographic equip., supplies, and services	**0.26**	**0.36**	**0.29**	**0.28**	**0.31**	**0.21**	**0.16**	**0.06**
Film	0.08	0.09	0.09	0.08	0.08	0.06	0.06	0.03
Film processing	0.10	0.12	0.12	0.10	0.11	0.08	0.07	0.02
Photographic equipment	0.06	0.06	0.06	0.06	0.08	0.04	0.03	0.00
Photographer fees	0.03	0.09	0.02	0.03	0.04	0.02	-	-
Pinball and electronic video games	**0.01**	**0.04**	**0.01**	**0.03**	**0.02**	**-**	**-**	**-**

Note: Expenditures are not given (-) when the amount is too small to be reliable. Expenditures listed for a given category may not add to the total for that category because the listing is incomplete. "Photographic equipment, supplies, and services," for example, includes "other photographic supplies," which is omitted here. Numbers may not add to total due to rounding.

Indexed expenditures

	all cu's	under 25	25 to 34	35 to 44	45 to 54	55 to 64	65 to 74	75+
Number of consumer units (in thousands)	94,862	7,216	21,985	19,911	13,601	12,546	11,319	8,284
Average number of persons per cu	2.6	1.8	2.8	3.3	2.9	2.2	2.0	1.5
Average total before-tax income	$28,540	$14,827	$28,318	$36,428	$39,934	$29,979	$20,704	$13,707
TOTAL AVERAGE ANNUAL EXPENDITURES	100	63	100	128	128	100	78	52
ENTERTAINMENT, AVERAGE ANNUAL EXPENDITURES	100	72	105	149	122	85	66	26
FEES AND ADMISSIONS	100	70	88	146	137	96	74	29
Club membership dues and fees	100	49	78	118	136	131	103	49
Participant sports fees	100	80	101	-	98	92	86	36
Participant sports fees, out-of-town trips	100	93	86	152	133	81	80	18
Movie, theater, opera, ballet, other admissions	100	116	104	135	138	84	51	19
Movie, other out-of-town admissions	100	60	73	136	158	113	80	33
Sporting event admissions	100	72	113	126	180	63	54	15
Sporting event, out-of-town admissions	100	60	73	136	158	113	80	33
Recreational lesson fees	100	38	81	234	125	44	40	5
Recreational entrance fees, other out-of-town expenses	100	63	80	146	149	105	74	23
TELEVISION, RADIO, SOUND EQUIP.	100	84	106	144	115	84	68	34
Television	100	66	100	134	114	102	84	46
Community antenna or cable TV	100	52	100	127	115	106	90	58
Black and white TV	100	0	-	406	0	115	0	0
Color TV, console	100	141	82	102	61	143	130	66
Color TV, portable and table model	100	91	99	118	139	96	75	41
VCRs and video disc players	100	69	114	138	123	98	66	8
Video cassettes, tapes, and discs	100	34	85	180	123	82	73	31
Video games hardware and software	100	47	129	207	81	52	35	5
Repair of TV, radio, and sound equipment	100	36	68	124	125	93	130	111
Rental of TVs	100	200	107	120	157	57	-	37
Radios and sound equipment	100	126	122	166	119	43	32	7
Radios	100	38	116	114	282	16	30	0
Tape recorders and players	100	381	73	199	0	13	74	0
Sound components and component systems	100	153	149	130	130	39	20	7
Sound equipment accessories	100	51	41	329	35	74	-	35
Records, tapes, needles, and styli	100	153	119	134	126	67	38	13
Rental of VCR, radio, sound equipment	100	185	151	134	120	-	-	-
Musical instruments and accessories	100	30	108	223	130	30	27	4
Rental and repair of musical instruments	100	-	91	233	91	-	113	0
Rental of video cassettes, tapes, discs, and films	100	85	144	166	112	48	24	-

Indexed average annual expenditures for entertainment, by age of reference person.

(continued from previous page)	all cu's	under 25	25 to 34	35 to 44	45 to 54	55 to 64	65 to 74	75+
PETS, TOYS, PLAYGROUND EQUIP.	**100**	**51**	**120**	**139**	**112**	**90**	**70**	**32**
Pets	**100**	**45**	**104**	**125**	**130**	**102**	**86**	**46**
Pet food	100	40	88	121	130	118	106	50
Pet supplies and medicines	100	86	186	83	101	68	31	66
Pet services	100	19	79	162	173	73	83	22
Veterinarian services	100	34	90	148	136	103	82	33
Toys, games, hobbies, and tricycles	**100**	**59**	**140**	**156**	**91**	**76**	**49**	**16**
Playground equipment	**100**	**22**	**126**	**175**	**43**	**55**	**161**	**0**
OTHER ENTERTAINMENT EQUIP., SUPPLIES, AND SERVICES	**100**	**75**	**112**	**165**	**119**	**72**	**52**	**10**
Boats and trailers without motors	**100**	**3**	**85**	**277**	**72**	**55**	**26**	**14**
Boats and boat trailers	100	5	66	303	58	68	23	11
Trailers and other attachable campers	100	0	132	216	105	25	32	22
Motorized sports vehicles	**100**	**81**	**115**	**160**	**104**	**75**	**67**	**9**
Camper coach and other vehicles	100	1	140	61	24	183	204	30
Motor boats	100	115	104	204	139	28	7	0
Sports vehicle rentals	**100**	**54**	**138**	**141**	**90**	**59**	**95**	**25**
Outboard motors	**100**	-	**75**	**82**	**136**	**54**	**301**	**0**
Docking fees	**100**	**32**	**29**	**119**	**275**	**149**	**48**	-
Sports equipment	**100**	**78**	**120**	**167**	**118**	**66**	**39**	**11**
Athletic gear, game tables, exercise equipment	100	85	115	157	107	83	57	10
Bicycles	100	139	140	176	82	45	17	-
Camping equipment	100	56	97	154	164	84	30	32
Hunting and fishing equipment	100	62	124	172	117	63	39	6
Winter sports equipment	100	76	98	204	152	35	-	16
Water sports/miscellaneous sports equipment .	100	40	130	173	141	51	27	4
Rental and repair of sports equipment	100	50	92	140	157	64	46	104
Photographic equip., supplies, and services	**100**	**86**	**111**	**135**	**153**	**80**	**49**	**12**
Film	100	76	112	135	142	79	62	18
Film processing	100	76	119	134	144	80	53	13
Photographic equipment	100	66	111	142	172	71	42	4
Photographer fees	100	206	82	132	181	74	-	-
Pinball and electronic video games	**100**	**165**	**89**	**218**	**139**	-	-	-

Note: Expenditures are not given (-) when the amount is too small to be reliable. An index of 100 represents the average for all consumer units. An index of 132 means that the average for the subgroup is 32 percent above the average for all consumer units. An index of 68 indicates spending that is 32 percent below the overall average.

Aggregate expenditures, 1988

	all cu's	under 25	25 to 34	35 to 44	45 to 54	55 to 64	65 to 74	75+
Number of consumer units (in thousands)	94,862	7,216	21,985	19,911	13,601	12,546	11,319	8,284
Average number of persons per cu	2.6	1.8	2.8	3.3	2.9	2.2	2.0	1.5
Aggregate before-tax income (in millions)	$2,722,037	$106,992	$622,571	$725,318	$543,142	$376,117	$234,349	$113,549
TOTAL AGGREGATE EXPENDITURES (in millions)	$2,456,432	$118,149	$566,559	$658,610	$451,619	$323,252	$227,737	$110,504
ENTERTAINMENT, AGGREGATE EXPENDITURES (in millions)	$126,043	$6,933	$30,685	$39,332	$21,964	$14,250	$9,970	$2,910
FEES AND ADMISSIONS	$33,501	$1,784	$6,820	$10,236	$6,593	$4,265	$2,964	$839
Club membership dues and fees	7,537	280	1,369	1,860	1,469	1,310	925	323
Participant sports fees	2,999	264	1,013	-	610	527	447	138
Participant sports fees, out-of-town trips	1,738	123	348	555	332	186	166	28
Movie, theater, opera, ballet, other admissions	5,753	507	1,388	1,633	1,139	642	349	95
Movie, other out-of-town admissions	2,468	113	418	702	561	368	234	71
Sporting event admissions	1,967	108	515	521	506	165	126	26
Sporting event, out-of-town admissions	2,468	113	418	702	561	368	234	71
Recreational lesson fees	3,844	112	725	1,890	689	225	185	17
Recreational entrance fees, other out-of-town expenses	3,392	163	627	1,037	727	473	298	69
TELEVISION, RADIO, SOUND EQUIP.	$39,417	$2,519	$9,715	$11,880	$6,519	$4,393	$3,217	$1,172
Television	27,703	1,394	6,398	7,795	4,523	3,721	2,770	1,102
Community antenna or cable TV	12,986	510	3,009	3,459	2,135	1,816	1,396	660
Black and white TV	236	0	-	201	0	36	0	0
Color TV, console	2,156	231	412	460	189	406	334	125
Color TV, portable and table model	4,179	289	959	1,039	835	532	376	149
VCRs and video disc players	4,432	232	1,170	1,288	784	576	350	31
Video cassettes, tapes, and discs	1,214	32	240	458	215	131	105	32
Video games hardware and software	1,385	49	415	602	160	94	58	7
Repair of TV, radio, and sound equipment	950	26	149	248	170	117	147	92
Rental of TVs	156	24	39	40	36	12	-	5
Radios and sound equipment	11,714	1,125	3,317	4,086	1,996	672	448	71
Radios	433	12	117	103	175	9	15	0
Tape recorders and players	866	256	149	369	0	15	78	0
Sound components and component systems	2,690	313	929	731	499	139	63	16
Sound equipment accessories	361	14	34	248	18	35	-	11
Records, tapes, needles, and styli	2,772	322	763	781	502	247	126	32
Rental of VCR, radio, sound equipment	130	19	48	39	24	-	-	-
Musical instruments and accessories	2,079	47	518	972	386	83	66	6
Rental and repair of musical instruments	196	-	43	99	26	-	27	0
Rental of video cassettes, tapes, discs, and films	2,138	139	714	747	343	135	61	-

Aggregate expenditures in 1988 for entertainment, by age of reference person.

(continued from previous page)

	all cu's	under 25	25 to 34	35 to 44	45 to 54	55 to 64	65 to 74	75+
PETS, TOYS, PLAYGROUND EQUIP.	**$21,848**	**$839**	**$6,064**	**$6,372**	**$3,516**	**$2,605**	**$1,835**	**$617**
Pets	**12,100**	**409**	**2,914**	**3,174**	**2,257**	**1,629**	**1,234**	**482**
Pet food	5,910	181	1,210	1,494	1,098	921	749	257
Pet supplies and medicines	1,994	131	858	349	288	179	73	115
Pet services	1,030	15	188	350	255	99	103	20
Veterinarian services	3,166	82	657	981	616	430	310	90
Toys, games, hobbies, and tricycles	**9,486**	**426**	**3,074**	**3,102**	**1,243**	**957**	**550**	**135**
Playground equipment	**262**	**4**	**76**	**96**	**16**	**19**	**50**	**0**
OTHER ENTERTAINMENT EQUIP., SUPPLIES, AND SERVICES	**$31,276**	**$1,790**	**$8,086**	**$10,844**	**$5,336**	**$2,987**	**$1,953**	**$281**
Boats and trailers without motors	**2,173**	**5**	**429**	**1,264**	**223**	**159**	**66**	**26**
Boats and boat trailers	1,534	5	234	974	127	137	42	14
Trailers and other attachable campers	639	0	196	290	96	21	24	12
Motorized sports vehicles	**13,018**	**798**	**3,469**	**4,384**	**1,940**	**1,288**	**1,037**	**103**
Camper coach and other vehicles	3,962	4	1,288	511	135	959	963	103
Motor boats	9,056	794	2,181	3,874	1,805	330	73	0
Sports vehicle rentals	**217**	**9**	**69**	**65**	**28**	**17**	**25**	**5**
Outboard motors	**107**	**-**	**19**	**19**	**21**	**8**	**40**	**0**
Docking fees	**462**	**11**	**31**	**117**	**184**	**92**	**27**	**-**
Sports equipment	**8,330**	**497**	**2,315**	**2,928**	**1,403**	**723**	**386**	**77**
Athletic gear, game tables, exercise equipment	3,326	215	885	1,096	511	366	225	28
Bicycles	1,106	118	359	410	131	66	23	-
Camping equipment	300	13	67	97	71	33	11	8
Hunting and fishing equipment	1,458	69	419	526	245	122	68	8
Winter sports equipment	570	33	131	246	125	26	-	8
Water sports/miscellaneous sports equipment .	1,367	42	412	495	277	92	44	5
Rental and repair of sports equipment	195	7	42	57	44	17	11	18
Photographic equip., supplies, and services	**6,386**	**420**	**1,642**	**1,814**	**1,400**	**674**	**372**	**65**
Film	1,869	108	486	530	380	195	139	30
Film processing	2,370	136	653	667	489	249	149	27
Photographic equipment	1,411	71	362	420	349	133	72	5
Photographer fees	657	105	128	185	174	66	-	-
Pinball and electronic video games	**360**	**46**	**75**	**167**	**72**	**-**	**-**	**-**

Note: Expenditures are not given (-) when the amount is too small to be reliable. Expenditures listed for a given category may not add to the total for that category because the listing is incomplete. "Photographic equipment, supplies, and services," for example, includes "other photographic supplies," which is omitted here. Numbers may not add to total due to rounding. The "all cu's" aggregates will differ slightly from table to table because they are the sums of the aggregates in each row.

Aggregate expenditures, 1995

Aggregate expenditures for entertainment, by age of householder in 1995 (in 1988 dollars).

	all households	under 25	25 to 34	35 to 44	45 to 54	55 to 64	65 to 74	75+
Number of households (in thousands)	100,308	4,316	19,927	23,916	18,035	12,223	12,006	9,876
ENTERTAINMENT, AGGREGATE EXPENDITURES IN 1995 (in millions)	$136,253	$4,147	$27,813	$47,243	$29,125	$13,883	$10,575	$3,469
FEES AND ADMISSIONS	$36,586	$1,067	$6,182	$12,295	$8,743	$4,155	$3,144	$1,000
Club membership dues and fees	8,234	168	1,240	2,234	1,948	1,276	981	385
Participant sports fees	3,037	158	918	-	809	513	474	164
Participant sports fees, out-of-town trips	1,886	74	315	667	440	182	176	33
Movie, theater, opera, ballet, other admissions	6,142	303	1,258	1,962	1,510	625	370	114
Movie, other out-of-town admissions	2,726	68	379	844	744	358	249	85
Sporting event admissions	2,153	64	466	626	671	161	134	31
Sporting event, out-of-town admissions	2,726	68	379	844	744	358	249	85
Recreational lesson fees	4,345	67	657	2,270	914	220	196	21
Recreational entrance fees, other out-of-town expenses	3,732	97	568	1,245	963	461	316	82
TELEVISION, RADIO, SOUND EQUIP.	$42,317	$1,507	$8,806	$14,270	$8,645	$4,280	$3,413	$1,397
Television	29,870	834	5,799	9,362	5,998	3,625	2,938	1,313
Community antenna or cable TV	14,056	305	2,727	4,155	2,832	1,770	1,481	787
Black and white TV	276	0	-	241	0	35	0	0
Color TV, console	2,212	138	373	552	250	396	354	148
Color TV, portable and table model	4,492	173	870	1,248	1,107	518	399	178
VCRs and video disc players	4,757	139	1,061	1,547	1,040	561	372	37
Video cassettes, tapes, and discs	1,350	19	217	551	285	128	112	39
Video games hardware and software	1,502	30	376	723	212	92	61	8
Repair of TV, radio, and sound equipment	1,054	16	135	298	226	114	156	110
Rental of TVs	163	14	36	48	47	12	-	6
Radios and sound equipment	12,448	673	3,007	4,908	2,647	655	475	84
Radios	496	7	106	124	233	9	16	0
Tape recorders and players	828	153	135	443	0	14	83	0
Sound components and component systems	2,790	187	842	878	662	136	66	19
Sound equipment accessories	409	8	31	298	24	34	-	13
Records, tapes, needles, and styli	2,899	192	691	938	665	241	133	38
Rental of VCR, radio, sound equipment	133	12	44	47	31	-	-	-
Musical instruments and accessories	2,336	28	470	1,168	512	81	70	8
Rental and repair of musical instruments	222	-	39	119	35	-	29	0
Rental of video cassettes, tapes, discs, and films	2,278	83	647	897	455	132	64	-

Aggregate expenditures for entertainment, by age of householder in 1995 (in 1988 dollars).

(continued from previous page)	all households	under 25	25 to 34	35 to 44	45 to 54	55 to 64	65 to 74	75+
PETS, TOYS, PLAYGROUND EQUIP.	$23,534	$502	$5,496	$7,653	$4,663	$2,538	$1,946	$736
Pets	13,163	245	2,641	3,812	2,993	1,587	1,309	575
Pet food	6,453	108	1,097	1,794	1,456	897	794	306
Pet supplies and medicines	2,047	78	778	419	382	175	78	137
Pet services	1,168	9	171	421	338	96	109	24
Veterinarian services	3,495	49	596	1,179	817	419	328	108
Toys, games, hobbies, and tricycles	10,091	255	2,786	3,726	1,648	932	583	161
Playground equipment	280	3	69	115	21	18	53	0
OTHER ENTERTAINMENT EQUIP., SUPPLIES, AND SERVICES	$33,816	$1,071	$7,329	$13,025	$7,075	$2,910	$2,072	$335
Boats and trailers without motors	2,463	3	389	1,518	296	154	70	32
Boats and boat trailers	1,749	3	212	1,170	168	133	45	17
Trailers and other attachable campers	714	0	177	348	128	21	26	15
Motorized sports vehicles	13,937	477	3,144	5,266	2,572	1,255	1,100	122
Camper coach and other vehicles	4,040	2	1,167	613	179	934	1,022	122
Motor boats	9,896	475	1,977	4,653	2,393	321	78	0
Sports vehicle rentals	231	5	63	77	37	16	26	6
Outboard motors	118	-	17	23	28	8	42	0
Docking fees	537	7	28	140	244	90	28	-
Sports equipment	8,979	297	2,098	3,516	1,861	704	410	92
Athletic gear, game tables, exercise equipment	3,553	129	802	1,316	677	357	239	33
Bicycles	1,150	70	325	493	173	65	24	-
Camping equipment	333	8	61	116	94	32	11	10
Hunting and fishing equipment	1,579	41	380	631	325	119	72	9
Winter sports equipment	636	20	119	296	166	26	-	10
Water sports/miscellaneous sports equipment .	1,503	25	373	595	367	90	47	6
Rental and repair of sports equipment	218	4	38	69	58	16	11	21
Photographic equip., supplies, and services	6,903	251	1,488	2,179	1,856	656	394	78
Film	2,020	64	441	637	504	190	148	36
Film processing	2,555	82	592	801	648	243	158	32
Photographic equipment	1,549	42	328	505	463	130	76	6
Photographer fees	696	63	116	223	230	64	-	-
Pinball and electronic video games	392	27	68	201	96	-	-	-

Note: Expenditures are not given (-) when the amount is too small to be reliable. Expenditures listed for a given category may not add to the total for that category because the listing is incomplete. "Photographic equipment, supplies, and services," for example, includes "other photographic supplies," which is omitted here. Numbers may not add to total due to rounding. Households are used here because the number of consumer units in 1995 and 2000 is not available. Household projections are from the Census Bureau. Projections show how annual aggregate expenditures will change as the number of households in the age groups changes in 1995 and 2000. Projections are based on the average annual expenditures in 1988 and have not been adjusted for price increases or for changes in expenditure patterns.

Aggregate expenditures, 2000

Aggregate expenditures for entertainment, by age of householder in 2000 (in 1988 dollars).

	all households	under 25	25 to 34	35 to 44	45 to 54	55 to 64	65 to 74	75+
Number of households (in thousands)	105,933	4,442	18,004	25,339	21,603	13,903	11,516	11,126
ENTERTAINMENT, AGGREGATE								
EXPENDITURES IN 2000 (in millions)	$144,179	$4,268	$25,129	$50,054	$34,887	$15,791	$10,143	$3,908
FEES AND ADMISSIONS	$39,051	$1,098	$5,585	$13,027	$10,472	$4,726	$3,016	$1,127
Club membership dues and fees	8,821	173	1,121	2,367	2,334	1,452	941	434
Participant sports fees	3,185	162	829	-	969	584	455	185
Participant sports fees, out-of-town trips	2,006	76	285	707	527	207	168	37
Movie, theater, opera, ballet, other admissions	6,530	312	1,137	2,079	1,809	711	355	128
Movie, other out-of-town admissions	2,939	70	343	894	891	408	238	96
Sporting event admissions	2,301	66	421	663	804	183	128	35
Sporting event, out-of-town admissions	2,939	70	343	894	891	408	238	96
Recreational lesson fees	4,624	69	594	2,405	1,094	250	188	23
Recreational entrance fees,								
other out-of-town expenses	4,006	100	513	1,319	1,154	524	303	92
TELEVISION, RADIO, SOUND EQUIP.	$44,697	$1,551	$7,956	$15,119	$10,355	$4,868	$3,273	$1,574
Television	31,623	858	5,240	9,919	7,184	4,124	2,818	1,479
Community antenna or cable TV	14,892	314	2,464	4,402	3,392	2,013	1,421	886
Black and white TV	295	0	-	255	0	40	0	0
Color TV, console	2,321	142	337	585	299	450	340	167
Color TV, portable and table model	4,784	178	786	1,322	1,326	589	383	200
VCRs and video disc players	5,023	143	958	1,639	1,245	638	356	42
Video cassettes, tapes, and discs	1,437	20	196	583	341	146	107	44
Video games hardware and software	1,562	30	340	765	254	105	59	9
Repair of TV, radio, and sound equipment	1,127	16	122	315	270	130	150	124
Rental of TVs	175	15	32	51	57	13	-	7
Radios and sound equipment	13,074	692	2,716	5,200	3,171	745	456	95
Radios...	539	8	96	132	279	10	16	0
Tape recorders and players	844	157	122	469	0	16	79	0
Sound components and component systems	2,916	193	761	930	793	154	64	21
Sound equipment accessories.........................	435	9	28	316	29	39	-	15
Records, tapes, needles, and styli	3,058	198	625	993	797	274	128	43
Rental of VCR, radio, sound equipment	138	12	39	49	38	-	-	-
Musical instruments and accessories	2,471	29	424	1,237	613	92	67	9
Rental and repair of musical instruments	231	-	35	126	42	-	28	0
Rental of video cassettes, tapes, discs, and films	2,377	86	585	951	545	150	62	-

Aggregate expenditures for entertainment, by age of householder in 2000 (in 1988 dollars).

(continued from previous page)	all households	under 25	25 to 34	35 to 44	45 to 54	55 to 64	65 to 74	75+
PETS, TOYS, PLAYGROUND EQUIP.	**$24,759**	**$517**	**$4,966**	**$8,108**	**$5,585**	**$2,887**	**$1,867**	**$829**
Pets	**13,972**	**252**	**2,386**	**4,039**	**3,585**	**1,805**	**1,256**	**648**
Pet food	6,875	111	991	1,901	1,744	1,021	762	345
Pet supplies and medicines	2,113	80	703	444	458	199	75	155
Pet services	1,255	9	154	446	405	110	104	27
Veterinarian services	3,729	51	538	1,249	979	476	315	121
Toys, games, hobbies, and tricycles	**10,502**	**262**	**2,517**	**3,948**	**1,974**	**1,061**	**560**	**181**
Playground equipment	**285**	**3**	**62**	**122**	**26**	**21**	**51**	**0**
OTHER ENTERTAINMENT EQUIP., SUPPLIES, AND SERVICES	**$35,673**	**$1,102**	**$6,622**	**$13,800**	**$8,475**	**$3,310**	**$1,987**	**$378**
Boats and trailers without motors	**2,596**	**3**	**352**	**1,608**	**354**	**176**	**68**	**35**
Boats and boat trailers	1,850	3	192	1,240	202	152	43	19
Trailers and other attachable campers	746	0	160	368	153	24	25	16
Motorized sports vehicles	**14,612**	**491**	**2,841**	**5,580**	**3,081**	**1,428**	**1,055**	**138**
Camper coach and other vehicles	4,101	2	1,055	650	214	1,062	980	138
Motor boats	10,511	488	1,786	4,930	2,867	366	74	0
Sports vehicle rentals	**239**	**6**	**57**	**82**	**45**	**19**	**25**	**6**
Outboard motors	**123**	**-**	**16**	**24**	**34**	**9**	**40**	**0**
Docking fees	**603**	**7**	**26**	**148**	**292**	**102**	**27**	**-**
Sports equipment	**9,454**	**306**	**1,896**	**3,726**	**2,229**	**801**	**393**	**104**
Athletic gear, game tables, exercise equipment	3,735	133	725	1,394	811	406	229	37
Bicycles	1,192	72	294	522	208	74	23	-
Camping equipment	358	8	55	123	113	37	11	11
Hunting and fishing equipment	1,660	43	344	669	390	136	69	10
Winter sports equipment	680	20	107	313	199	29	-	11
Water sports/miscellaneous sports equipment .	1,587	26	337	630	439	102	45	7
Rental and repair of sports equipment	235	5	34	73	70	18	11	24
Photographic equip., supplies, and services	**7,348**	**258**	**1,345**	**2,309**	**2,223**	**747**	**378**	**88**
Film	2,142	66	398	675	604	216	142	40
Film processing	2,707	84	535	849	776	276	151	36
Photographic equipment	1,656	44	296	535	554	147	73	7
Photographer fees	754	65	105	236	276	73	-	-
Pinball and electronic video games	**417**	**28**	**61**	**213**	**115**	**-**	**-**	**-**

Note: Expenditures are not given (-) when the amount is too small to be reliable. Expenditures listed for a given category may not add to the total for that category because the listing is incomplete. "Photographic equipment, supplies, and services," for example, includes "other photographic supplies," which is omitted here. Numbers may not add to total due to rounding. Households are used here because the number of consumer units in 1995 and 2000 is not available. Projections show how annual aggregate expenditures will change as the number of households in the age groups changes in 1995 and 2000. Household projections are from the Census Bureau. Projections are based on the average annual expenditures in 1988 and have not been adjusted for price increases or for changes in expenditure patterns.

PART II
Spending by income for entertainment

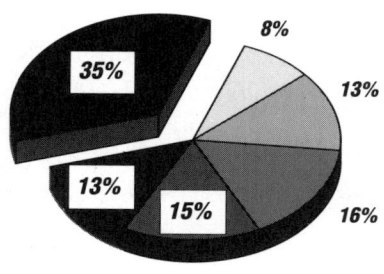

Households with incomes of $30,000 or more account for 63 percent of the entertainment market.

8%
13%
35%
13%
15%
16%

☐ under $10,000	■ $30,000–39,999
■ $10,000–19,999	■ $40,000–49,999
■ $20,000–29,999	■ $50,000 and over

Affluent households don't have a monopoly on fun, but they spend more for it. From the lowest to the highest income households, spending on entertainment increases by nearly 600 percent. Spending on out-of-town sporting event admissions, stereo components, pet services, sports equipment, and photographic equipment climbs by over 1000 percent. Expenditures on items like winter and water sports equipment, boats, trailers, and other sports vehicles are affected even more by income. Spending for these items is at least 2000 percent greater among households with incomes of $50,000 or more than in households with incomes under $10,000.

Households with incomes of $30,000 or more spent nearly $70 billion on entertainment in 1988—63 percent of all entertainment spending. A 35 percent share of the entertainment market is accounted for by households in the $50,000-plus bracket alone.

Annual spending on entertainment is just $454 for households with incomes under $10,000. That figure rises to fully $3,148 for the highest income group. The share of the household budget devoted to entertainment climbs from 4 to 6 percent as incomes rise.

The low-end market

Households with incomes of less than $10,000 spend more than the average household on only three entertainment items, two of which are rentals. These households spend about 50 percent more than average for TV, VCR, radio, and sound equipment rentals. They also spend 47 percent more than average on tape recorders and players.

Those with incomes of $10,000 to $20,000 spend more than average on TV rentals. They spend 29 percent more than average on camper coaches and 9 percent more than average on outboard motors. They spend less than average on all other entertainment items, with overall entertainment spending 39 percent below average.

The fun and games expenses for households with incomes between $20,000 and $30,000 are just 12 percent less than the average. There are many items for which they spend above-average amounts—out-of-town movies, sporting events, and entrance fees; sports equipment rentals and repairs; and photographer fees, for example.

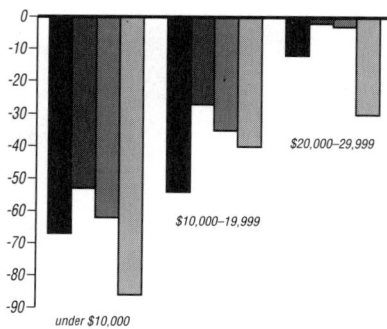

Households in the low-end market spend less than the average household on fun and games.

0
-10
-20
-30
-40 $20,000–29,999
-50
-60 $10,000–19,999
-70
-80
-90
under $10,000

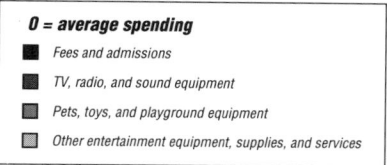

0 = average spending
■ Fees and admissions
■ TV, radio, and sound equipment
■ Pets, toys, and playground equipment
☐ Other entertainment equipment, supplies, and services

The high-end market

Households in the $30,000 to $40,000 income group spend well above average on pets, toys, and playground equipment. They also spend at least 50 percent more than the average household on radios, musical instruments, camping equipment, water sports equipment, and pinball and electronic video games. Households in the $40,000 to $50,000 income group spend almost 50 percent more than the average household on entertainment in general.

Renting entertainment equipment doesn't appeal much to the highest income group. Rentals are the only items for which households with incomes of $50,000 or more spend less than average amounts. Overall, they spend 133 percent more than the average household on entertainment, spending two or three times the average on boats, trailers, and winter sports equipment.

High-end households, especially those with incomes of $50,000 or more, spend more than others on all kinds of entertainment.

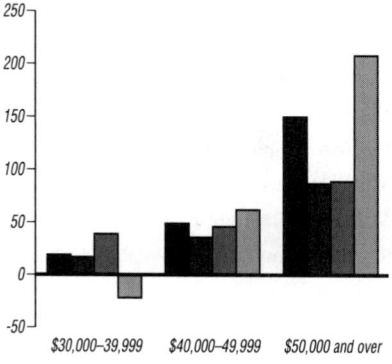

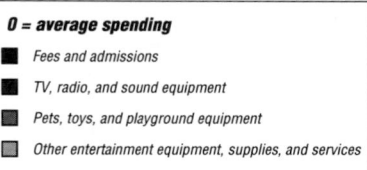

0 = average spending

■ *Fees and admissions*

■ *TV, radio, and sound equipment*

■ *Pets, toys, and playground equipment*

■ *Other entertainment equipment, supplies, and services*

Average expenditures

Average annual expenditures for entertainment, by total before-tax income of consumer unit.

(consumer units include complete income reporters only)	all cu's	under $10,000	$10,000 to $19,999	$20,000 to $29,999	$30,000 to $39,999	$40,000 to $49,999	$50,000 and over
Number of consumer units (in thousands)	81,354	18,809	17,652	14,586	10,901	7,198	12,209
Average number of persons per cu	2.6	1.8	2.3	2.7	2.9	3.2	3.1
Average number of earners per cu	1.4	0.7	1.0	1.5	1.8	2.0	2.1
TOTAL AVERAGE ANNUAL EXPENDITURES	$26,389.07	$11,269.43	$18,078.25	$24,896.36	$31,659.60	$37,562.00	$52,320.19
ENTERTAINMENT, AVERAGE ANNUAL EXPENDITURES	$1,348.90	$453.78	$827.32	$1,191.35	$1,510.43	$1,994.64	$3,148.34
FEES AND ADMISSIONS	$351.99	$116.24	$160.85	$309.51	$419.64	$525.52	$879.59
Club membership dues and fees	76.68	21.23	37.71	57.91	79.31	90.82	230.17
Participant sports fees	46.90	13.13	25.44	46.82	63.52	68.77	102.29
Participant sports fees, out-of-town trips	18.96	7.38	7.60	15.44	23.16	34.10	44.73
Movie, theater, opera, ballet, and other admissions	61.08	26.21	31.26	50.31	70.94	82.33	149.40
Movie and other out-of-town admissions	25.91	9.94	11.76	28.74	35.89	37.17	52.04
Sporting event admissions	19.63	6.48	8.48	17.81	18.39	41.10	46.63
Sporting event, out-of-town admissions	25.91	9.94	11.76	28.74	35.89	37.17	52.04
Recreational lesson fees	41.23	9.30	10.64	24.00	51.63	77.27	124.72
Recreational entrance fees, other out-of-town expenses	35.70	12.61	16.19	39.72	40.92	56.80	77.56
TELEVISION, RADIO, AND SOUND EQUIPMENT	$422.50	$196.92	$308.43	$416.12	$493.78	$576.29	$788.05
Television	295.95	143.23	235.86	299.91	344.82	398.08	509.85
Community antenna or cable TV	137.94	73.26	114.20	142.38	161.32	184.08	218.51
Black and white TV	2.84	0.00	-	1.95	0.00	0.00	16.41
Color TV, console	23.60	17.17	18.63	28.58	27.00	24.27	31.30
Color TV, portable and table model	43.50	25.78	36.92	48.29	39.51	54.93	71.38
VCRs and video disc players	47.70	11.53	37.34	41.57	69.42	66.10	95.51
Video cassettes, tapes, and discs	13.44	3.13	8.50	11.97	18.39	21.56	28.99
Video games hardware and software	14.88	4.15	6.57	16.27	17.25	31.40	29.94
Repair of TV, radio, and sound equipment	10.43	5.76	9.93	8.32	10.43	15.74	17.75
Rental of TVs	1.61	2.42	3.42	0.57	1.49	0.00	-
Radios and sound equipment	126.55	53.70	72.58	116.21	148.96	178.21	278.21
Radios	4.84	1.51	1.70	3.99	7.25	8.26	11.80
Tape recorders and players	10.50	15.43	7.21	0.51	0.96	9.12	27.49
Sound components and component systems	29.17	5.70	20.22	35.08	23.87	45.64	66.29
Sound equipment accessories	4.29	-	1.30	12.72	4.33	1.68	6.77
Records, tapes, needles, and styli	30.03	14.42	18.00	23.73	37.26	46.04	63.10
Rental of VCR, radio, sound equipment	1.59	2.36	1.10	1.98	1.54	-	1.40
Musical instruments and accessories	20.58	5.12	7.65	13.86	37.81	24.77	53.28
Rental and repair of musical instruments	2.12	1.14	0.70	1.62	1.95	4.09	5.25
Rental of video cassettes, tapes, discs, and films	23.27	7.77	14.36	22.74	33.76	38.22	42.49

Average annual expenditures for entertainment, by total before-tax income of consumer unit.

(continued from previous page)	all cu's	under $10,000	$10,000 to $19,999	$20,000 to $29,999	$30,000 to $39,999	$40,000 to $49,999	$50,000 and over
PETS, TOYS, AND PLAYGROUND EQUIPMENT	$242.26	$92.87	$157.12	$234.32	$336.90	$354.45	$457.26
Pets	136.31	59.14	97.10	125.55	183.79	180.80	259.08
Pet food	66.61	36.73	50.30	63.13	93.51	83.41	108.50
Pet supplies and medicines	25.23	8.07	23.53	24.37	29.83	28.53	49.96
Pet services	10.64	2.07	4.33	9.06	14.74	19.11	26.24
Veterinarian services	33.84	12.28	18.95	28.99	45.71	49.75	74.38
Toys, games, hobbies, and tricycles	102.96	33.62	59.72	107.09	149.80	167.96	187.24
Playground equipment	2.98	-	-	1.69	3.31	5.69	10.94
OTHER ENTERTAINMENT EQUIPMENT, SUPPLIES, AND SERVICES	$332.16	$47.75	$200.92	$231.39	$260.12	$538.39	$1,023.44
Boats and trailers without motors	24.02	0.67	1.22	22.31	7.09	46.24	96.99
Boats and boat trailers	18.32	0.65	0.98	18.35	4.76	33.83	73.57
Trailers and other attachable campers	5.70	-	-	3.96	2.34	12.41	23.42
Motorized sports vehicles	137.44	7.17	116.03	51.83	40.89	217.35	510.44
Camper coach and other vehicles	38.79	7.17	50.00	1.65	28.53	22.53	134.38
Motor boats	98.65	0.00	66.04	50.19	12.36	194.81	376.06
Sports vehicle rentals	2.33	1.07	-	1.43	1.14	3.90	8.13
Outboard motors	1.28	0.00	1.39	-	0.51	-	5.79
Docking fees	5.33	2.20	1.26	3.30	3.12	5.73	20.20
Sports equipment	86.67	18.18	39.33	82.59	113.75	136.51	211.99
Athletic gear, game tables, and exercise equipment	34.85	6.83	17.12	33.84	38.39	61.59	85.92
Bicycles	12.28	4.42	6.17	12.50	17.62	20.21	23.55
Camping equipment	3.26	1.18	1.34	1.45	4.94	4.43	9.21
Hunting and fishing equipment	15.91	2.99	8.11	15.40	22.84	24.90	36.25
Winter sports equipment	4.86	0.67	1.55	3.99	5.69	3.92	16.95
Water sports and miscellaneous sports equipment	13.20	1.51	3.83	12.31	22.46	17.71	34.87
Rental and repair of sports equipment	2.31	0.58	1.22	3.09	1.80	3.76	5.25
Photographic equipment, supplies, and services	69.61	17.97	37.56	67.06	83.07	119.31	157.10
Film	19.96	6.19	11.36	20.05	22.90	32.28	43.61
Film processing	25.21	7.36	12.81	23.97	28.28	41.48	59.82
Photographic equipment	15.43	2.71	6.15	13.04	20.47	25.46	40.91
Photographer fees	8.12	1.70	5.29	9.45	11.00	19.51	11.12
Pinball and electronic video games	3.78	-	2.98	2.34	9.38	8.74	4.45

Note: Expenditures are not given (-) when the amount is too small to be reliable. Expenditures listed for a given category may not add to the total for that category because the listing is incomplete. "Photographic equipment, supplies, and services," for example, includes "other photographic supplies," which is omitted here. Total expenditure exceeds total income in some income categories due to a number of factors including underreporting of income, borrowing, and the use of savings. Numbers may not add to total due to rounding.

Share of spending

(consumer units include complete income reporters only)	all cu's	under $10,000	$10,000 to $19,999	$20,000 to $29,999	$30,000 to $39,999	$40,000 to $49,999	$50,000 and over
Number of consumer units (in thousands)	81,354	18,809	17,652	14,586	10,901	7,198	12,209
Average number of persons per cu	2.6	1.8	2.3	2.7	2.9	3.2	3.1
Average number of earners per cu	1.4	0.7	1.0	1.5	1.8	2.0	2.1
TOTAL AVERAGE ANNUAL EXPENDITURES	100.00%	100.00%	100.00%	100.00%	100.00%	100.00%	100.00%
ENTERTAINMENT, AVERAGE ANNUAL EXPENDITURES	5.11%	4.03%	4.58%	4.79%	4.77%	5.31%	6.02%
FEES AND ADMISSIONS	1.33%	1.03%	0.89%	1.24%	1.33%	1.40%	1.68%
Club membership dues and fees	0.29	0.19	0.21	0.23	0.25	0.24	0.44
Participant sports fees	0.18	0.12	0.14	0.19	0.20	0.18	0.20
Participant sports fees, out-of-town trips	0.07	0.07	0.04	0.06	0.07	0.09	0.09
Movie, theater, opera, ballet, and other admissions	0.23	0.23	0.17	0.20	0.22	0.22	0.29
Movie and other out-of-town admissions	0.10	0.09	0.07	0.12	0.11	0.10	0.10
Sporting event admissions	0.07	0.06	0.05	0.07	0.06	0.11	0.09
Sporting event, out-of-town admissions	0.10	0.09	0.07	0.12	0.11	0.10	0.10
Recreational lesson fees	0.16	0.08	0.06	0.10	0.16	0.21	0.24
Recreational entrance fees, other out-of-town expenses	0.14	0.11	0.09	0.16	0.13	0.15	0.15
TELEVISION, RADIO, AND SOUND EQUIPMENT	1.60%	1.75%	1.71%	1.67%	1.56%	1.53%	1.51%
Television	1.12	1.27	1.30	1.20	1.09	1.06	0.97
Community antenna or cable TV	0.52	0.65	0.63	0.57	0.51	0.49	0.42
Black and white TV	0.01	0.00	-	0.01	0.00	0.00	0.03
Color TV, console	0.09	0.15	0.10	0.11	0.09	0.06	0.06
Color TV, portable and table model	0.16	0.23	0.20	0.19	0.12	0.15	0.14
VCRs and video disc players	0.18	0.10	0.21	0.17	0.22	0.18	0.18
Video cassettes, tapes, and discs	0.05	0.03	0.05	0.05	0.06	0.06	0.06
Video games hardware and software	0.06	0.04	0.04	0.07	0.05	0.08	0.06
Repair of TV, radio, and sound equipment	0.04	0.05	0.05	0.03	0.03	0.04	0.03
Rental of TVs	0.01	0.02	0.02	0.00	0.00	0.00	-
Radios and sound equipment	0.48	0.48	0.40	0.47	0.47	0.47	0.53
Radios	0.02	0.01	0.01	0.02	0.02	0.02	0.02
Tape recorders and players	0.04	0.14	0.04	0.00	0.00	0.02	0.05
Sound components and component systems	0.11	0.05	0.11	0.14	0.08	0.12	0.13
Sound equipment accessories	0.02	-	0.01	0.05	0.01	0.00	0.01
Records, tapes, needles, and styli	0.11	0.13	0.10	0.10	0.12	0.12	0.12
Rental of VCR, radio, sound equipment	0.01	0.02	0.01	0.01	0.00	-	0.00
Musical instruments and accessories	0.08	0.05	0.04	0.06	0.12	0.07	0.10
Rental and repair of musical instruments	0.01	0.01	0.00	0.01	0.01	0.01	0.01
Rental of video cassettes, tapes, discs, and films	0.09	0.07	0.08	0.09	0.11	0.10	0.08

Percent of total average annual expenditures spent on entertainment, by total before-tax income of consumer unit.

(continued from previous page)	*all cu's*	*under $10,000*	*$10,000 to $19,999*	*$20,000 to $29,999*	*$30,000 to $39,999*	*$40,000 to $49,999*	*$50,000 and over*
PETS, TOYS, AND PLAYGROUND EQUIPMENT	**0.92%**	**0.82%**	**0.87%**	**0.94%**	**1.06%**	**0.94%**	**0.87%**
Pets	**0.52**	**0.52**	**0.54**	**0.50**	**0.58**	**0.48**	**0.50**
Pet food	0.25	0.33	0.28	0.25	0.30	0.22	0.21
Pet supplies and medicines	0.10	0.07	0.13	0.10	0.09	0.08	0.10
Pet services	0.04	0.02	0.02	0.04	0.05	0.05	0.05
Veterinarian services	0.13	0.11	0.10	0.12	0.14	0.13	0.14
Toys, games, hobbies, and tricycles	**0.39**	**0.30**	**0.33**	**0.43**	**0.47**	**0.45**	**0.36**
Playground equipment	**0.01**	**-**	**-**	**0.01**	**0.01**	**0.02**	**0.02**
OTHER ENTERTAINMENT EQUIPMENT, SUPPLIES, AND SERVICES	**1.26%**	**0.42%**	**1.11%**	**0.93%**	**0.82%**	**1.43%**	**1.96%**
Boats and trailers without motors	**0.09**	**0.01**	**0.01**	**0.09**	**0.02**	**0.12**	**0.19**
Boats and boat trailers	0.07	0.01	0.01	0.07	0.02	0.09	0.14
Trailers and other attachable campers	0.02	-	-	0.02	0.01	0.03	0.04
Motorized sports vehicles	**0.52**	**0.06**	**0.64**	**0.21**	**0.13**	**0.58**	**0.98**
Camper coach and other vehicles	0.15	0.06	0.28	0.01	0.09	0.06	0.26
Motor boats	0.37	0.00	0.37	0.20	0.04	0.52	0.72
Sports vehicle rentals	**0.01**	**0.01**	**-**	**0.01**	**0.00**	**0.01**	**0.02**
Outboard motors	**0.00**	**0.00**	**0.01**	**-**	**0.00**	**-**	**0.01**
Docking fees	**0.02**	**0.02**	**0.01**	**0.01**	**0.01**	**0.02**	**0.04**
Sports equipment	**0.33**	**0.16**	**0.22**	**0.33**	**0.36**	**0.36**	**0.41**
Athletic gear, game tables, and exercise equipment	0.13	0.06	0.09	0.14	0.12	0.16	0.16
Bicycles	0.05	0.04	0.03	0.05	0.06	0.05	0.05
Camping equipment	0.01	0.01	0.01	0.01	0.02	0.01	0.02
Hunting and fishing equipment	0.06	0.03	0.04	0.06	0.07	0.07	0.07
Winter sports equipment	0.02	0.01	0.01	0.02	0.02	0.01	0.03
Water sports and miscellaneous sports equipment	0.05	0.01	0.02	0.05	0.07	0.05	0.07
Rental and repair of sports equipment	0.01	0.01	0.01	0.01	0.01	0.01	0.01
Photographic equipment, supplies, and services	**0.26**	**0.16**	**0.21**	**0.27**	**0.26**	**0.32**	**0.30**
Film	0.08	0.05	0.06	0.08	0.07	0.09	0.08
Film processing	0.10	0.07	0.07	0.10	0.09	0.11	0.11
Photographic equipment	0.06	0.02	0.03	0.05	0.06	0.07	0.08
Photographer fees	0.03	0.02	0.03	0.04	0.03	0.05	0.02
Pinball and electronic video games	**0.01**	**-**	**0.02**	**0.01**	**0.03**	**0.02**	**0.01**

Note: Expenditures are not given (-) when the amount is too small to be reliable. Expenditures listed for a given category may not add to the total for that category because the listing is incomplete. "Photographic equipment, supplies, and services," for example, includes "other photographic supplies," which is omitted here. Numbers may not add to total due to rounding.

Indexed expenditures

Indexed average annual expenditures for entertainment, by total before-tax income of consumer unit.							
(consumer units include complete income reporters only)	all cu's	under $10,000	$10,000 to $19,999	$20,000 to $29,999	$30,000 to $39,999	$40,000 to $49,999	$50,000 and over
Number of consumer units (in thousands)	81,354	18,809	17,652	14,586	10,901	7,198	12,209
Average number of persons per cu	2.6	1.8	2.3	2.7	2.9	3.2	3.1
Average number of earners per cu	1.4	0.7	1.0	1.5	1.8	2.0	2.1
TOTAL AVERAGE ANNUAL EXPENDITURES	100	43	69	94	120	142	198
ENTERTAINMENT, AVERAGE ANNUAL EXPENDITURES	100	34	61	88	112	148	233
FEES AND ADMISSIONS	100	33	46	88	119	149	250
Club membership dues and fees	100	28	49	76	103	118	300
Participant sports fees	100	28	54	100	135	147	218
Participant sports fees, out-of-town trips	100	39	40	81	122	180	236
Movie, theater, opera, ballet, and other admissions	100	43	51	82	116	135	245
Movie and other out-of-town admissions	100	38	45	111	139	143	201
Sporting event admissions	100	33	43	91	94	209	238
Sporting event, out-of-town admissions	100	38	45	111	139	143	201
Recreational lesson fees	100	23	26	58	125	187	302
Recreational entrance fees, other out-of-town expenses	100	35	45	111	115	159	217
TELEVISION, RADIO, AND SOUND EQUIPMENT	100	47	73	98	117	136	187
Television	100	48	80	101	117	135	172
Community antenna or cable TV	100	53	83	103	117	133	158
Black and white TV	100	0	-	69	0	0	578
Color TV, console	100	73	79	121	114	103	133
Color TV, portable and table model	100	59	85	111	91	126	164
VCRs and video disc players	100	24	78	87	146	139	200
Video cassettes, tapes, and discs	100	23	63	89	137	160	216
Video games hardware and software	100	28	44	109	116	211	201
Repair of TV, radio, and sound equipment	100	55	95	80	100	151	170
Rental of TVs	100	151	212	35	93	0	-
Radios and sound equipment	100	42	57	92	118	141	220
Radios	100	31	35	82	150	171	244
Tape recorders and players	100	147	69	5	9	87	262
Sound components and component systems	100	20	69	120	82	156	227
Sound equipment accessories	100	-	30	297	101	39	158
Records, tapes, needles, and styli	100	48	60	79	124	153	210
Rental of VCR, radio, sound equipment	100	148	69	125	97	-	88
Musical instruments and accessories	100	25	37	67	184	120	259
Rental and repair of musical instruments	100	54	33	76	92	193	248
Rental of video cassettes, tapes, discs, and films	100	33	62	98	145	164	183

Indexed average annual expenditures for entertainment, by total before-tax income of consumer unit.

(continued from previous page)

	all cu's	under $10,000	$10,000 to $19,999	$20,000 to $29,999	$30,000 to $39,999	$40,000 to $49,999	$50,000 and over
PETS, TOYS, AND PLAYGROUND EQUIPMENT	100	38	65	97	139	146	189
Pets	100	43	71	92	135	133	190
Pet food	100	55	76	95	140	125	163
Pet supplies and medicines	100	32	93	97	118	113	198
Pet services	100	19	41	85	139	180	247
Veterinarian services	100	36	56	86	135	147	220
Toys, games, hobbies, and tricycles	100	33	58	104	145	163	182
Playground equipment	100	-	-	57	111	191	367
OTHER ENTERTAINMENT EQUIPMENT, SUPPLIES, AND SERVICES	100	14	60	70	78	162	308
Boats and trailers without motors	100	3	5	93	30	193	404
Boats and boat trailers	100	4	5	100	26	185	402
Trailers and other attachable campers	100	-	-	69	41	218	411
Motorized sports vehicles	100	5	84	38	30	158	371
Camper coach and other vehicles	100	18	129	4	74	58	346
Motor boats	100	0	67	51	13	197	381
Sports vehicle rentals	100	46	-	61	49	167	349
Outboard motors	100	0	109	-	40	-	452
Docking fees	100	41	24	62	59	108	379
Sports equipment	100	21	45	95	131	158	245
Athletic gear, game tables, and exercise equipment	100	20	49	97	110	177	247
Bicycles	100	36	50	102	143	165	192
Camping equipment	100	36	41	44	152	136	283
Hunting and fishing equipment	100	19	51	97	144	157	228
Winter sports equipment	100	14	32	82	117	81	349
Water sports and miscellaneous sports equipment	100	11	29	93	170	134	264
Rental and repair of sports equipment	100	25	53	134	78	163	227
Photographic equipment, supplies, and services	100	26	54	96	119	171	226
Film	100	31	57	100	115	162	218
Film processing	100	29	51	95	112	165	237
Photographic equipment	100	18	40	85	133	165	265
Photographer fees	100	21	65	116	135	240	137
Pinball and electronic video games	100	-	79	62	248	231	118

Note: Expenditures are not given (-) when the amount is too small to be reliable. An index of 100 represents the average for all consumer units. An index of 132 means that the average for the subgroup is 32 percent above the average for all consumer units. An index of 68 indicates spending that is 32 percent below the overall average.

Aggregate expenditures, 1988

(consumer units include complete income reporters only)	all cu's	under $10,000	$10,000 to $19,999	$20,000 to $29,999	$30,000 to $39,999	$40,000 to $49,999	$50,000 and over
Number of consumer units (in thousands)	81,354	18,809	17,652	14,586	10,901	7,198	12,209
Average number of persons per cu	2.6	1.8	2.3	2.7	2.9	3.2	3.1
Average number of earners per cu	1.4	0.7	1.0	1.5	1.8	2.0	2.1
TOTAL AGGREGATE EXPENDITURES (in millions)	$2,148,492	$211,967	$319,117	$363,138	$345,121	$270,371	$638,777
ENTERTAINMENT, AGGREGATE EXPENDITURES (in millions)	$109,777	$8,535	$14,604	$17,377	$16,465	$14,357	$38,438
FEES AND ADMISSIONS	$28,636	$2,186	$2,839	$4,515	$4,574	$3,783	$10,739
Club membership dues and fees	6,238	399	666	845	865	654	2,810
Participant sports fees	3,815	247	449	683	692	495	1,249
Participant sports fees, out-of-town trips	1,542	139	134	225	252	245	546
Movie, theater, opera, ballet, and other admissions	4,969	493	552	734	773	593	1,824
Movie and other out-of-town admissions	2,108	187	208	419	391	268	635
Sporting event admissions	1,597	122	150	260	200	296	569
Sporting event, out-of-town admissions	2,108	187	208	419	391	268	635
Recreational lesson fees	3,355	175	188	350	563	556	1,523
Recreational entrance fees, other out-of-town expenses	2,904	237	286	579	446	409	947
TELEVISION, RADIO, AND SOUND EQUIPMENT	$34,370	$3,704	$5,444	$6,070	$5,383	$4,148	$9,621
Television	24,081	2,694	4,163	4,374	3,759	2,865	6,225
Community antenna or cable TV	11,222	1,378	2,016	2,077	1,759	1,325	2,668
Black and white TV	229	0	-	28	0	0	200
Color TV, console	1,920	323	329	417	294	175	382
Color TV, portable and table model	3,538	485	652	704	431	395	871
VCRs and video disc players	3,881	217	659	606	757	476	1,166
Video cassettes, tapes, and discs	1,093	59	150	175	200	155	354
Video games hardware and software	1,211	78	116	237	188	226	366
Repair of TV, radio, and sound equipment	849	108	175	121	114	113	217
Rental of TVs	131	46	60	8	16	0	-
Radios and sound equipment	10,289	1,010	1,281	1,695	1,624	1,283	3,397
Radios	399	28	30	58	79	59	144
Tape recorders and players	837	290	127	7	10	66	336
Sound components and component systems	2,374	107	357	512	260	329	809
Sound equipment accessories	350	-	23	186	47	12	83
Records, tapes, needles, and styli	2,443	271	318	346	406	331	770
Rental of VCR, radio, sound equipment	126	44	19	29	17	-	17
Musical instruments and accessories	1,675	96	135	202	412	178	650
Rental and repair of musical instruments	172	21	12	24	21	29	64
Rental of video cassettes, tapes, discs, and films	1,893	146	254	332	368	275	519

Aggregate expenditures in 1988 for entertainment, by total before-tax income of consumer unit.

(continued from previous page)	all cu's	under $10,000	$10,000 to $19,999	$20,000 to $29,999	$30,000 to $39,999	$40,000 to $49,999	$50,000 and over
PETS, TOYS, AND PLAYGROUND EQUIPMENT	**$19,745**	**$1,747**	**$2,774**	**$3,418**	**$3,673**	**$2,551**	**$5,583**
Pets	**11,126**	**1,112**	**1,714**	**1,831**	**2,003**	**1,301**	**3,163**
Pet food	5,444	691	888	921	1,019	600	1,325
Pet supplies and medicines	2,063	152	415	355	325	205	610
Pet services	866	39	76	132	161	138	320
Veterinarian services	2,753	231	334	423	498	358	908
Toys, games, hobbies, and tricycles	**8,377**	**632**	**1,054**	**1,562**	**1,633**	**1,209**	**2,286**
Playground equipment	**235**	**-**	**-**	**25**	**36**	**41**	**134**
OTHER ENTERTAINMENT EQUIPMENT, SUPPLIES, AND SERVICES	**$27,026**	**$898**	**$3,547**	**$3,375**	**$2,836**	**$3,875**	**$12,495**
Boats and trailers without motors	**1,954**	**13**	**22**	**325**	**77**	**333**	**1,184**
Boats and boat trailers	1,491	12	17	268	52	244	898
Trailers and other attachable campers	459	-	-	58	26	89	286
Motorized sports vehicles	**11,181**	**135**	**2,048**	**756**	**446**	**1,564**	**6,232**
Camper coach and other vehicles	3,155	135	883	24	311	162	1,641
Motor boats	8,026	0	1,166	732	135	1,402	4,591
Sports vehicle rentals	**181**	**20**	**-**	**21**	**12**	**28**	**99**
Outboard motors	**101**	**0**	**25**	**-**	**6**	**-**	**71**
Docking fees	**434**	**41**	**22**	**48**	**34**	**41**	**247**
Sports equipment	**7,052**	**342**	**694**	**1,205**	**1,240**	**983**	**2,588**
Athletic gear, game tables, and exercise equipment	2,835	128	302	494	418	443	1,049
Bicycles	999	83	109	182	192	145	288
Camping equipment	265	22	24	21	54	32	112
Hunting and fishing equipment	1,295	56	143	225	249	179	443
Winter sports equipment	395	13	27	58	62	28	207
Water sports and miscellaneous sports equipment	1,074	28	68	180	245	127	426
Rental and repair of sports equipment	188	11	22	45	20	27	64
Photographic equipment, supplies, and services	**5,661**	**338**	**663**	**978**	**906**	**859**	**1,918**
Film	1,624	116	200	292	250	232	532
Film processing	2,051	138	226	350	308	299	730
Photographic equipment	1,256	51	109	190	223	183	499
Photographer fees	659	32	93	138	120	140	136
Pinball and electronic video games	**306**	**-**	**53**	**34**	**102**	**63**	**54**

Note: Expenditures are not given (-) when the amount is too small to be reliable. Expenditures listed for a given category may not add to the total for that category because the listing is incomplete. "Photographic equipment, supplies, and services," for example, includes "other photographic supplies," which is omitted here. Numbers may not add to total due to rounding. The "all cu's" aggregates will differ slightly from table to table because they are the sums of the aggregates in each row.

PART III
Spending by type of household for entertainment

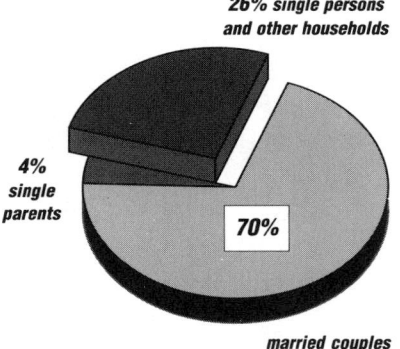

Married couples account for 55 percent of all households, but 70 percent of the entertainment market...

26% single persons and other households

4% single parents

70%

married couples

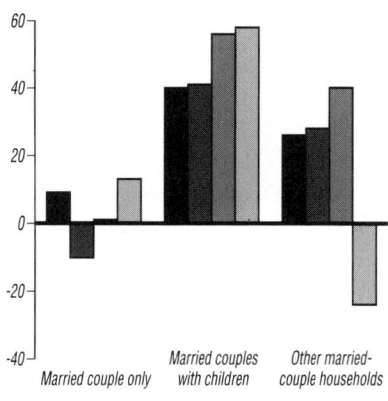

...and married couples living with children are the biggest entertainment spenders of all.

Married couple only

Married couples with children

Other married-couple households

0 = average spending

- Fees and admissions
- TV, radio, and sound equipment
- Pets, toys, and playground equipment
- Other entertainment equipment, supplies, and services

Married couples outspend other households on nearly every category of household products and services, including entertainment. The average married-couple household spends $1,700 a year on entertainment, single parents spend $920, and single-person and "other" households* spend $870.

Together, the 52 million married couple households spent more than $88 billion on having fun in 1988. They account for 70 percent of the entertainment market, while single-person and "other" households account for 26 percent of the market, and single parents for the remaining 4 percent.

Married-couple market

When it comes to fun and games, married couples with school-aged children are the big spenders. These households spend 64 percent more than average on entertainment, with below-average spending on only two items—TV rentals and camper coaches. They spend three or four times more than average on recreational lessons, radios, video games, sound equipment accessories, musical instrument repairs, boats without motors, boat trailers, and camping trailers.

Married couples with preschoolers and those with children aged 18 or older at home spend about 30 percent more than the average household on entertainment. Households with children under age 6 spend less than average on fees and admissions, but 73 percent more than average on pets, toys, and playground equipment. They are also the peak spenders on VCRs purchases, tape recorders and players, VCR and sound equipment rentals, camper coaches, fishing and hunting equipment, film, and film processing.

Married couples with children aged 18 or older at home spend more than other households on fees and admissions. They are also big spenders on black and white TVs, TV rentals, records, tapes, and turntable needles and styli. They spend 54 percent more than average on veterinary services, 88 percent more than average on sports vehicle rentals, 96 percent more on photographic equipment, and 123 percent more on camping equipment.

Empty-nesters and childless couples spend just 3 percent more than average on entertainment. But they spend 149 percent more than the average household on camper coaches, 57 percent more on outboard motors, and 48 percent more on club memberships and fees.

---

*In this analysis, single-person households are grouped with "other" households. "Other" households are unrelated people living together and families that are not married-couple or single-parent families, such as siblings. Single-person households account for 72 percent of the households in this category.

Other household markets

People who live alone or in "other" households spend 35 percent less than the average household on entertainment. Their spending is above average for only TV rentals and sound systems. Single parents spend more than the average on cable TV, video games, TV rentals, toys, games, tricycles, bicycles, camping equipment, photographers fees, and pinball games.

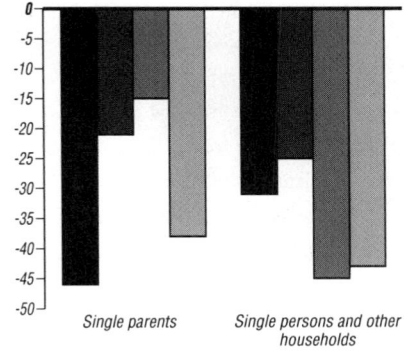

Single persons and other households spend less than others on all entertainment categories except fees and admissions.

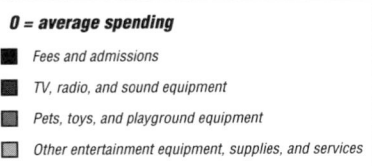

0 = average spending

■ Fees and admissions

■ TV, radio, and sound equipment

■ Pets, toys, and playground equipment

□ Other entertainment equipment, supplies, and services

Average expenditures

	all cu's	married couples	single parents	single persons and other cu's
Number of consumer units (in thousands)	94,862	52,010	5,716	37,136
Average number of persons per cu	2.6	3.3	2.9	1.5
Average number of earners per cu	1.4	1.7	1.0	0.9
Average total before-tax income	$28,540.00	$37,299.00	$16,276.00	$18,509.00
TOTAL AVERAGE ANNUAL EXPENDITURES	$25,891.85	$32,314.50	$18,615.80	$17,950.80
ENTERTAINMENT, AVERAGE ANNUAL EXPENDITURES	$1,328.68	$1,700.17	$920.34	$869.57
FEES AND ADMISSIONS	$353.16	$448.26	$189.06	$245.22
Club membership dues and fees	79.45	107.55	38.13	46.45
Participant sports fees	45.69	59.19	23.44	30.22
Participant sports fees, out-of-town trips	18.32	21.51	10.55	15.04
Movie, theater, opera, ballet, and other admissions	60.65	64.64	44.56	57.54
Movie, other out-of-town admissions	26.02	32.44	11.54	19.25
Sporting event admissions	20.73	26.55	8.34	14.48
Sporting event, out-of-town admissions	26.02	32.44	11.54	19.25
Recreational lesson fees	40.52	58.73	25.94	17.28
Recreational entrance fees, other out-of-town expenses	35.76	45.22	15.04	25.70
TELEVISION, RADIO, AND SOUND EQUIPMENT	$415.52	$500.29	$329.59	$309.69
Television	291.96	354.60	253.11	210.15
Community antenna or cable TV	136.89	161.46	141.74	101.74
Black and white TV	2.48	3.85	0.00	0.87
Color TV, console	22.72	29.79	6.01	15.41
Color TV, portable and table model	44.06	50.79	42.63	34.84
VCRs and video disc players	46.72	59.60	28.76	31.46
Video cassettes, tapes, and discs	12.80	15.83	7.03	9.43
Video games hardware and software	14.60	19.98	17.91	6.55
Repair of TV, radio, and sound equipment	10.02	12.14	7.09	7.51
Rental of TVs	1.67	1.15	1.94	2.35
Radios and sound equipment	123.56	145.69	76.47	99.54
Radios	4.57	6.13	3.34	2.50
Tape recorders and players	9.29	10.31	1.62	8.97
Sound components and component systems	28.28	28.61	12.96	30.18
Sound equipment accessories	3.79	6.37	-	0.56
Records, tapes, needles, and styli	29.22	30.54	18.69	29.00
Rental of VCR, radio, sound equipment	1.45	1.58	1.45	1.27
Musical instruments and accessories	21.91	29.52	17.96	11.86
Rental and repair of musical instruments	2.14	3.01	0.99	1.09
Rental of video cassettes, tapes, discs, and films	22.58	29.02	18.99	14.11

Average annual expenditures for entertainment, by type of consumer unit.

(continued from previous page)

	all cu's	married couples	single parents	single persons and other cu's
PETS, TOYS, AND PLAYGROUND EQUIPMENT	$230.22	$306.75	$196.15	$127.08
Pets	127.45	163.09	85.94	82.75
Pet food	62.23	78.87	46.41	40.59
Pet supplies and medicines	20.99	29.88	5.64	10.47
Pet services	10.86	14.83	8.58	5.65
Veterinarian services	33.38	39.51	25.31	26.03
Toys, games, hobbies, and tricycles	100.00	139.03	110.15	43.78
Playground equipment	2.76	4.64	-	0.55
OTHER ENTERTAINMENT EQUIPMENT, SUPPLIES, AND SERVICES	$329.78	$444.87	$205.54	$187.58
Boats and trailers without motors	22.91	33.80	3.50	10.64
Boats and boat trailers	16.17	23.24	3.50	8.22
Trailers and other attachable campers	6.74	10.56	0.00	2.42
Motorized sports vehicles	137.23	185.51	70.10	79.94
Camper coach and other vehicles	41.77	70.49	4.28	7.30
Motor boats	95.46	115.02	65.82	72.63
Sports vehicle rentals	2.29	2.50	-	2.29
Outboard motors	1.16	2.06	0.00	-
Docking fees	4.92	6.70	4.25	2.52
Sports equipment	87.81	115.94	60.71	52.58
Athletic gear, game tables, and exercise equipment	35.06	46.70	27.41	19.93
Bicycles	11.69	12.51	16.09	9.86
Camping equipment	3.17	4.46	3.23	1.34
Hunting and fishing equipment	15.37	21.33	6.95	8.32
Winter sports equipment	6.05	7.71	2.05	4.35
Water sports and miscellaneous sports equipment	14.41	20.67	4.76	7.13
Rental and repair of sports equipment	2.06	2.55	-	1.66
Photographic equipment, supplies, and services	67.42	91.11	61.94	35.00
Film	19.70	26.33	12.92	11.46
Film processing	24.98	33.87	12.86	14.40
Photographic equipment	14.88	20.18	9.95	8.21
Photographer fees	7.07	9.60	25.94	0.54
Pinball and electronic video games	3.84	4.39	4.80	2.91

Note: Expenditures are not given (-) when the amount is too small to be reliable. Expenditures listed for a given category may not add to the total for that category because the listing is incomplete. "Photographic equipment, supplies, and services," for example, includes "other photographic supplies, which is omitted here. Numbers may not add to total due to rounding. "Single parents" is one-parent consumer units with a child or children under age 18 living at home. "Other cu's" includes persons living with unrelated persons and families other than married-couple and single-parent families.

Share of spending

	all cu's	married couples	single parents	single persons and other cu's
Number of consumer units (in thousands)	*94,862*	*52,010*	*5,716*	*37,136*
Average number of persons per cu	*2.6*	*3.3*	*2.9*	*1.5*
Average total before-tax income	*$28,540*	*$37,299*	*$16,276*	*$18,509*
TOTAL AVERAGE ANNUAL EXPENDITURES	*100.00%*	*100.00%*	*100.00%*	*100.00%*
ENTERTAINMENT, AVERAGE ANNUAL EXPENDITURES	*5.13%*	*5.26%*	*4.94%*	*4.84%*
FEES AND ADMISSIONS	**1.36%**	**1.39%**	**1.02%**	**1.37%**
Club membership dues and fees	0.31	0.33	0.20	0.26
Participant sports fees	0.18	0.18	0.13	0.17
Participant sports fees, out-of-town trips	0.07	0.07	0.06	0.08
Movie, theater, opera, ballet, and other admissions	0.23	0.20	0.24	0.32
Movie, other out-of-town admissions	0.10	0.10	0.06	0.11
Sporting event admissions	0.08	0.08	0.04	0.08
Sporting event, out-of-town admissions	0.10	0.10	0.06	0.11
Recreational lesson fees	0.16	0.18	0.14	0.10
Recreational entrance fees, other out-of-town expenses	0.14	0.14	0.08	0.14
TELEVISION, RADIO, AND SOUND EQUIPMENT	**1.60%**	**1.55%**	**1.77%**	**1.73%**
Television	**1.13**	**1.10**	**1.36**	**1.17**
Community antenna or cable TV	0.53	0.50	0.76	0.57
Black and white TV	0.01	0.01	0.00	0.00
Color TV, console	0.09	0.09	0.03	0.09
Color TV, portable and table model	0.17	0.16	0.23	0.19
VCRs and video disc players	0.18	0.18	0.15	0.18
Video cassettes, tapes, and discs	0.05	0.05	0.04	0.05
Video games hardware and software	0.06	0.06	0.10	0.04
Repair of TV, radio, and sound equipment	0.04	0.04	0.04	0.04
Rental of TVs	0.01	0.00	0.01	0.01
Radios and sound equipment	**0.48**	**0.45**	**0.41**	**0.55**
Radios	0.02	0.02	0.02	0.01
Tape recorders and players	0.04	0.03	0.01	0.05
Sound components and component systems	0.11	0.09	0.07	0.17
Sound equipment accessories	0.01	0.02	-	0.00
Records, tapes, needles, and styli	0.11	0.09	0.10	0.16
Rental of VCR, radio, sound equipment	0.01	0.00	0.01	0.01
Musical instruments and accessories	0.08	0.09	0.10	0.07
Rental and repair of musical instruments	0.01	0.01	0.01	0.01
Rental of video cassettes, tapes, discs, and films	0.09	0.09	0.10	0.08

Percent of total average annual expenditures spent on entertainment, by type of consumer unit.

(continued from previous page)

	all cu's	married couples	single parents	single persons and other cu's
PETS, TOYS, AND PLAYGROUND EQUIPMENT	**0.89%**	**0.95%**	**1.05%**	**0.71%**
Pets	**0.49**	**0.50**	**0.46**	**0.46**
Pet food	0.24	0.24	0.25	0.23
Pet supplies and medicines	0.08	0.09	0.03	0.06
Pet services	0.04	0.05	0.05	0.03
Veterinarian services	0.13	0.12	0.14	0.15
Toys, games, hobbies, and tricycles	**0.39**	**0.43**	**0.59**	**0.24**
Playground equipment	**0.01**	**0.01**	-	**0.00**
OTHER ENTERTAINMENT EQUIPMENT, SUPPLIES, AND SERVICES	**1.27%**	**1.38%**	**1.10%**	**1.04%**
Boats and trailers without motors	**0.09**	**0.10**	**0.02**	**0.06**
Boats and boat trailers	0.06	0.07	0.02	0.05
Trailers and other attachable campers	0.03	0.03	0.00	0.01
Motorized sports vehicles	**0.53**	**0.57**	**0.38**	**0.45**
Camper coach and other vehicles	0.16	0.22	0.02	0.04
Motor boats	0.37	0.36	0.35	0.40
Sports vehicle rentals	**0.01**	**0.01**	-	**0.01**
Outboard motors	**0.00**	**0.01**	**0.00**	-
Docking fees	**0.02**	**0.02**	**0.02**	**0.01**
Sports equipment	**0.34**	**0.36**	**0.33**	**0.29**
Athletic gear, game tables, and exercise equipment	0.14	0.14	0.15	0.11
Bicycles	0.05	0.04	0.09	0.05
Camping equipment	0.01	0.01	0.02	0.01
Hunting and fishing equipment	0.06	0.07	0.04	0.05
Winter sports equipment	0.02	0.02	0.01	0.02
Water sports and miscellaneous sports equipment	0.06	0.06	0.03	0.04
Rental and repair of sports equipment	0.01	0.01	-	0.01
Photographic equipment, supplies, and services	**0.26**	**0.28**	**0.33**	**0.19**
Film	0.08	0.08	0.07	0.06
Film processing	0.10	0.10	0.07	0.08
Photographic equipment	0.06	0.06	0.05	0.05
Photographer fees	0.03	0.03	0.14	0.00
Pinball and electronic video games	**0.01**	**0.01**	**0.03**	**0.02**

Note: Expenditures are not given (-) when the amount is too small to be reliable. Expenditures listed for a given category may not add to the total for that category because the listing is incomplete. "Photographic equipment, supplies, and services," for example, includes "other photographic supplies," which is omitted here. Numbers may not add to total due to rounding. "Single parents" is one-parent consumer units with a child or children under age 18 living at home. "Other cu's" includes persons living with unrelated persons and families other than married-couple and single-parent families.

Indexed expenditures

	all cu's	married couples	single parents	single persons and other cu's
Number of consumer units (in thousands)	94,862	52,010	5,716	37,136
Average number of persons per cu	2.6	3.3	2.9	1.5
Average number of earners per cu	1.4	1.7	1.0	0.9
Average total before-tax income	$28,540	$37,299	$16,276	$18,509
TOTAL AVERAGE ANNUAL EXPENDITURES	100	125	72	69
ENTERTAINMENT, AVERAGE ANNUAL EXPENDITURES	100	128	69	65
FEES AND ADMISSIONS	100	127	54	69
Club membership dues and fees	100	135	48	58
Participant sports fees	100	130	51	66
Participant sports fees, out-of-town trips	100	117	58	82
Movie, theater, opera, ballet, and other admissions	100	107	73	95
Movie, other out-of-town admissions	100	125	44	74
Sporting event admissions	100	128	40	70
Sporting event, out-of-town admissions	100	125	44	74
Recreational lesson fees	100	145	64	43
Recreational entrance fees, other out-of-town expenses	100	126	42	72
TELEVISION, RADIO, AND SOUND EQUIPMENT	100	120	79	75
Television	100	121	87	72
Community antenna or cable TV	100	118	104	74
Black and white TV	100	155	0	35
Color TV, console	100	131	26	68
Color TV, portable and table model	100	115	97	79
VCRs and video disc players	100	128	62	67
Video cassettes, tapes, and discs	100	124	55	74
Video games hardware and software	100	137	123	45
Repair of TV, radio, and sound equipment	100	121	71	75
Rental of TVs	100	69	116	141
Radios and sound equipment	100	118	62	81
Radios	100	134	73	55
Tape recorders and players	100	111	17	97
Sound components and component systems	100	101	46	107
Sound equipment accessories	100	168	-	15
Records, tapes, needles, and styli	100	105	64	99
Rental of VCR, radio, sound equipment	100	109	100	88
Musical instruments and accessories	100	135	82	54
Rental and repair of musical instruments	100	141	46	51
Rental of video cassettes, tapes, discs, and films	100	129	84	62

Indexed average annual expenditures for entertainment, by type of consumer unit.

(continued from previous page)	all cu's	married couples	single parents	single persons and other cu's
PETS, TOYS, AND PLAYGROUND EQUIPMENT	**100**	**133**	**85**	**55**
Pets	**100**	**128**	**67**	**65**
Pet food	100	127	75	65
Pet supplies and medicines	100	142	27	50
Pet services	100	137	79	52
Veterinarian services	100	118	76	78
Toys, games, hobbies, and tricycles	**100**	**139**	**110**	**44**
Playground equipment	**100**	**168**	-	**20**
OTHER ENTERTAINMENT EQUIPMENT, SUPPLIES, AND SERVICES	**100**	**135**	**62**	**57**
Boats and trailers without motors	**100**	**148**	**15**	**46**
Boats and boat trailers	100	144	22	51
Trailers and other attachable campers	100	157	0	36
Motorized sports vehicles	**100**	**135**	**51**	**58**
Camper coach and other vehicles	100	169	10	17
Motor boats	100	120	69	76
Sports vehicle rentals	**100**	**109**	-	**100**
Outboard motors	**100**	**178**	**0**	-
Docking fees	**100**	**136**	**86**	**51**
Sports equipment	**100**	**132**	**69**	**60**
Athletic gear, game tables, and exercise equipment	100	133	78	57
Bicycles	100	107	138	84
Camping equipment	100	141	102	42
Hunting and fishing equipment	100	139	45	54
Winter sports equipment	100	127	34	72
Water sports and miscellaneous sports equipment	100	143	33	49
Rental and repair of sports equipment	100	124	-	81
Photographic equipment, supplies, and services	**100**	**135**	**92**	**52**
Film	100	134	66	58
Film processing	100	136	51	58
Photographic equipment	100	136	67	55
Photographer fees	100	136	367	8
Pinball and electronic video games	**100**	**114**	**125**	**76**

Note: An index of 100 represents the average for all consumer units. An index of 132 means that the average for the subgroup is 32 percent above the average for all consumer units. An index of 68 indicates spending that is 32 percent below the overall average. Expenditures are not given (-) when the amount is too small to be reliable. "Single parents" is one-parent consumer units with a child or children under age 18 living at home. "Other cu's" includes persons living with unrelated persons and families other than married-couple and single-parent families.

Aggregate expenditures, 1988

	all cu's	married couples	single parents	single persons and other cu's
Number of consumer units (in thousands)	94,862	52,010	5,716	37,136
Average number of persons per cu	2.6	3.3	2.9	1.5
Average number of earners per cu	1.4	1.7	1.0	0.9
Aggregate before-tax income (in millions)	$2,720,305	$1,939,921	$93,034	$687,350
TOTAL AGGREGATE EXPENDITURES (in millions)	$2,453,706	$1,680,677	$106,408	$666,621
ENTERTAINMENT, AGGREGATE EXPENDITURES (in millions)	$125,979	$88,426	$5,261	$32,292
FEES AND ADMISSIONS	$33,501	$23,314	$1,081	$9,106
Club membership dues and fees	7,537	5,594	218	1,725
Participant sports fees	4,335	3,078	134	1,122
Participant sports fees, out-of-town trips	1,738	1,119	60	559
Movie, theater, opera, ballet, and other admissions	5,753	3,362	255	2,137
Movie, other out-of-town admissions	2,468	1,687	66	715
Sporting event admissions	1,966	1,381	48	538
Sporting event, out-of-town admissions	2,468	1,687	66	715
Recreational lesson fees	3,845	3,055	148	642
Recreational entrance fees, other out-of-town expenses	3,392	2,352	86	954
TELEVISION, RADIO, AND SOUND EQUIPMENT	$39,405	$26,020	$1,884	$11,501
Television	27,694	18,443	1,447	7,804
Community antenna or cable TV	12,986	8,398	810	3,778
Black and white TV	233	200	0	32
Color TV, console	2,156	1,549	34	572
Color TV, portable and table model	4,179	2,642	244	1,294
VCRs and video disc players	4,432	3,100	164	1,168
Video cassettes, tapes, and discs	1,214	823	40	350
Video games hardware and software	1,385	1,039	102	243
Repair of TV, radio, and sound equipment	951	631	41	279
Rental of TVs	158	60	11	87
Radios and sound equipment	11,711	7,577	437	3,697
Radios	431	319	19	93
Tape recorders and players	879	536	9	333
Sound components and component systems	2,683	1,488	74	1,121
Sound equipment accessories	352	331	-	21
Records, tapes, needles, and styli	2,772	1,588	107	1,077
Rental of VCR, radio, sound equipment	138	82	8	47
Musical instruments and accessories	2,078	1,535	103	440
Rental and repair of musical instruments	203	157	6	40
Rental of video cassettes, tapes, discs, and films	2,142	1,509	109	524

Aggregate expenditures in 1988 for entertainment, by type of consumer unit.

(continued from previous page)

	all cu's	married couples	single parents	single persons and other cu's
PETS, TOYS, AND PLAYGROUND EQUIPMENT	**$21,795**	**$15,954**	**$1,121**	**$4,719**
Pets	**12,047**	**8,482**	**491**	**3,073**
Pet food	5,875	4,102	265	1,507
Pet supplies and medicines	1,975	1,554	32	389
Pet services	1,030	771	49	210
Veterinarian services	3,166	2,055	145	967
Toys, games, hobbies, and tricycles	**9,486**	**7,231**	**630**	**1,626**
Playground equipment	**241**	**241**	-	**20**
OTHER ENTERTAINMENT EQUIPMENT, SUPPLIES, AND SERVICES	**$31,279**	**$23,138**	**$1,175**	**$6,966**
Boats and trailers without motors	**2,173**	**1,758**	**20**	**395**
Boats and boat trailers	1,534	1,209	20	305
Trailers and other attachable campers	639	549	0	90
Motorized sports vehicles	**13,018**	**9,648**	**401**	**2,969**
Camper coach and other vehicles	3,962	3,666	24	271
Motor boats	9,056	5,982	376	2,697
Sports vehicle rentals	**215**	**130**	-	**85**
Outboard motors	**107**	**107**	**0**	-
Docking fees	**466**	**348**	**24**	**94**
Sports equipment	**8,330**	**6,030**	**347**	**1,953**
Athletic gear, game tables, and exercise equipment	3,326	2,429	157	740
Bicycles	1,109	651	92	366
Camping equipment	300	232	18	50
Hunting and fishing equipment	1,458	1,109	40	309
Winter sports equipment	574	401	12	162
Water sports and miscellaneous sports equipment	1,367	1,075	27	265
Rental and repair of sports equipment	195	133	-	62
Photographic equipment, supplies, and services	**6,392**	**4,739**	**354**	**1,300**
Film	1,869	1,369	74	426
Film processing	2,370	1,762	74	535
Photographic equipment	1,411	1,050	57	305
Photographer fees	668	499	148	20
Pinball and electronic video games	**364**	**228**	**27**	**108**

Note: Expenditures are not given (-) when the amount is too small to be reliable. Expenditures listed for a given category may not add to the total for that category because the listing is incomplete. "Photographic equipment, supplies, and services," for example, includes "other photographic supplies," which is omitted here. Numbers may not add to total due to rounding. "Single parents" is one-parent consumer units with a child or children under age 18 living at home. "Other cu's" includes persons living with unrelated persons and families other than married-couple and single-parent families. The "all cu's" aggregates will differ slightly from table to table because they are the sums of the aggregates in each row.

Average expenditures

	all cu's	all married couples	married couple only	all married couples with children	AGE OF OLDEST CHILD			other married couples
					under 6	6 to 17	18 or older	
Number of consumer units (in thousands)	94,862	52,010	20,227	28,100	5,858	14,194	8,047	3,684
Average number of persons per cu	2.6	3.3	2	3.9	3.5	4.1	3.9	5.1
Average number of earners per cu	1.4	1.7	1.2	2.1	1.7	1.9	2.7	2.4
Average total before-tax income	$28,540.00	$37,299.00	$33,825.00	$39,354.00	$34,318.00	$38,039.00	$45,596.00	$40,846.00
TOTAL AVERAGE ANNUAL EXPENDITURES	$25,891.85	$32,314.50	$27,954.50	$35,015.30	$30,942.80	$35,248.40	$37,763.90	$35,739.60
ENTERTAINMENT, AVERAGE ANNUAL EXPENDITURES	$1,328.68	$1,700.17	$1,365.67	$1,960.90	$1,734.47	$2,174.81	$1,748.24	$1,548.83
FEES AND ADMISSIONS	$353.16	$448.26	$384.23	$494.86	$310.56	$540.67	$548.21	$444.38
Club membership dues and fees	79.45	107.55	117.33	103.84	77.27	94.17	140.24	82.17
Participant sports fees	45.69	59.19	56.65	63.03	60.37	65.18	61.18	43.78
Participant sports fees, out-of-town trips	18.32	21.51	21.92	21.36	17.02	22.97	21.69	20.36
Movie, theater, opera, ballet, other admissions	60.65	64.64	50.72	73.74	45.62	73.33	94.92	71.60
Movie, other out-of-town admissions	26.02	32.44	28.92	32.72	17.02	37.31	36.06	49.66
Sporting event admissions	20.73	26.55	19.57	31.45	16.70	32.27	40.73	27.55
Sporting event, out-of-town admissions	26.02	32.44	28.92	32.72	17.02	37.31	36.06	49.66
Recreational lesson fees	40.52	58.73	14.14	92.88	36.82	132.09	64.53	43.00
Recreational entrance fees, other out-of-town expenses	35.76	45.22	46.06	43.10	22.74	46.02	52.80	56.58
TELEVISION, RADIO, SOUND EQUIP.	$415.52	$500.29	$375.64	$585.95	$536.14	$625.23	$553.57	$531.57
Television	291.96	354.60	294.24	391.88	374.11	395.77	399.98	401.54
Community antenna or cable TV	136.89	161.46	143.97	173.48	148.90	179.65	180.49	165.81
Black and white TV	2.48	3.85	0.00	7.11	0.00	3.97	19.87	0.00
Color TV, console	22.72	29.79	29.49	30.43	42.86	24.01	32.71	26.48
Color TV, portable and table model	44.06	50.79	43.93	52.06	35.24	56.90	55.78	78.83
VCRs and video disc players	46.72	59.60	45.96	68.26	106.08	52.95	67.72	68.47
Video cassettes, tapes, and discs	12.80	15.83	13.39	16.75	14.11	19.00	14.72	22.27
Video games hardware and software	14.60	19.98	4.54	30.11	14.92	45.51	14.01	27.50
Repair of TV, radio, and sound equipment	10.02	12.14	12.72	11.91	9.75	12.60	12.27	10.73
Rental of TVs	1.67	1.15	-	1.77	2.26	1.20	2.43	1.44
Radios and sound equipment	123.56	145.69	81.40	194.06	162.03	229.46	153.59	130.04
Radios	4.57	6.13	1.94	9.16	0.00	14.83	6.25	6.19
Tape recorders and players	9.29	10.31	5.89	14.80	21.97	16.58	4.70	0.00
Sound components and component systems	28.28	28.61	22.12	32.63	21.67	33.91	38.32	34.06
Sound equipment accessories	3.79	6.37	1.85	10.23	4.45	15.50	5.04	1.66
Records, tapes, needles, and styli	29.22	30.54	21.86	35.65	26.09	35.37	43.09	33.75
Rental of VCR, radio, sound equipment	1.45	1.58	-	2.39	4.75	1.89	1.55	2.15
Musical instruments and accessories	21.91	29.52	10.21	46.06	45.77	63.75	15.07	9.35
Rental and repair of musical instruments	2.14	3.01	0.55	4.99	1.09	7.83	2.81	1.42
Rental of video cassettes, tapes, discs, films	22.58	29.02	15.28	37.98	36.23	39.74	36.15	36.19

Average annual expenditures for entertainment, by married couples with and without children.

(continued from previous page)

	all cu's	all married couples	married couple only	all married couples with children	AGE OF OLDEST CHILD			other married couples
					under 6	6 to 17	18 or older	
PETS, TOYS, PLAYGROUND EQUIP.	$230.22	$306.75	$231.72	$358.86	$399.00	$405.14	$247.72	$321.67
Pets	127.45	163.09	154.26	168.57	127.24	191.18	158.49	170.08
Pet food	62.23	78.87	81.29	75.54	53.68	81.36	83.95	91.54
Pet supplies and medicines	20.99	29.88	21.96	36.60	34.44	52.05	7.87	21.90
Pet services	10.86	14.83	14.06	14.94	8.53	17.31	15.43	18.19
Veterinarian services	33.38	39.51	36.95	41.49	30.59	40.46	51.24	38.44
Toys, games, hobbies, and tricycles	100.00	139.03	73.68	185.44	264.13	208.05	88.29	143.79
Playground equipment	2.76	4.64	3.77	4.85	7.62	5.91	0.95	7.81
OTHER ENTERTAINMENT EQUIP., SUPPLIES, AND SERVICES	$329.78	$444.87	$374.09	$521.23	$488.77	$603.77	$398.74	$251.21
Boats and trailers without motors	22.91	33.80	14.31	51.49	30.64	86.75	4.49	5.78
Boats and boat trailers	16.17	23.24	11.86	33.79	20.49	56.96	2.59	5.20
Trailers and other attachable campers	6.74	10.56	2.45	17.71	10.16	29.79	1.90	0.58
Motorized sports vehicles	137.23	185.51	203.23	195.82	216.84	218.46	140.59	9.61
Camper coach and other vehicles	41.77	70.49	104.03	55.59	203.65	21.33	8.24	0.00
Motor boats	95.46	115.02	99.19	140.24	13.20	197.14	132.35	9.61
Sports vehicle rentals	2.29	2.50	1.51	3.38	3.83	2.67	4.31	1.22
Outboard motors	1.16	2.06	1.82	1.09	0.95	1.21	0.98	10.73
Docking fees	4.92	6.70	5.33	7.32	-	5.09	16.33	9.49
Sports equipment	87.81	115.94	78.52	147.06	118.54	173.62	120.97	83.97
Athletic gear, game tables, exercise equipment	35.06	46.70	39.50	53.44	38.85	65.22	43.28	34.86
Bicycles	11.69	12.51	4.46	17.71	9.60	22.65	14.90	17.05
Camping equipment	3.17	4.46	2.64	6.11	3.52	6.62	7.08	1.90
Hunting and fishing equipment	15.37	21.33	16.81	25.68	31.58	26.73	19.55	12.93
Winter sports equipment	6.05	7.71	2.40	11.06	5.06	13.68	10.81	11.35
Water sports/miscellaneous sports equipment .	14.41	20.67	9.78	30.73	28.95	35.80	23.08	3.72
Rental and repair of sports equipment	2.06	2.55	2.94	2.32	0.97	2.91	2.27	2.17
Photographic equip., supplies, and services	67.42	91.11	67.30	104.48	113.59	100.17	104.86	119.72
Film	19.70	26.33	19.05	30.71	35.33	29.12	30.17	32.94
Film processing	24.98	33.87	24.51	39.27	49.56	34.89	39.51	44.04
Photographic equipment	14.88	20.18	14.68	21.92	18.21	19.37	29.11	37.07
Photographer fees	7.07	9.60	7.24	11.81	10.40	15.92	4.92	5.66
Pinball and electronic video games	3.84	4.39	1.74	6.84	3.18	9.74	4.43	-

Note: Expenditures are not given (-) when the amount is too small to be reliable. Expenditures listed for a given category may not add to the total for that category because the listing is incomplete. "Photographic equipment, supplies, and services," for example, includes "other photographic supplies," which is omitted here. Numbers may not add to total due to rounding. Other married couples include extended family members or unrelated persons in addition to the married couple.

Share of spending

	all cu's	all married couples	married couple only	all married couples with children	AGE OF OLDEST CHILD			other married couples
					under 6	6 to 17	18 or older	
Number of consumer units (in thousands)	94,862	52,010	20,227	28,100	5,858	14,194	8,047	3,684
Average number of persons per cu	2.6	3.3	2	3.9	3.5	4.1	3.9	5.1
Average total before-tax income	$28,540	$37,299	$33,825	$39,354	$34,318	$38,039	$45,596	$40,846
TOTAL AVERAGE ANNUAL EXPENDITURES	100.00%	100.00%	100.00%	100.00%	100.00%	100.00%	100.00%	100.00%
ENTERTAINMENT, AVERAGE ANNUAL EXPENDITURES	5.13%	5.26%	4.89%	5.60%	5.61%	6.17%	4.63%	4.33%
FEES AND ADMISSIONS	1.36%	1.39%	1.37%	1.41%	1.00%	1.53%	1.45%	1.24%
Club membership dues and fees	0.31	0.33	0.42	0.30	0.25	0.27	0.37	0.23
Participant sports fees	0.18	0.18	0.20	0.18	0.20	0.18	0.16	0.12
Participant sports fees, out-of-town trips	0.07	0.07	0.08	0.06	0.06	0.07	0.06	0.06
Movie, theater, opera, ballet, other admissions	0.23	0.20	0.18	0.21	0.15	0.21	0.25	0.20
Movie, other out-of-town admissions	0.10	0.10	0.10	0.09	0.06	0.11	0.10	0.14
Sporting event admissions	0.08	0.08	0.07	0.09	0.05	0.09	0.11	0.08
Sporting event, out-of-town admissions	0.10	0.10	0.10	0.09	0.06	0.11	0.10	0.14
Recreational lesson fees	0.16	0.18	0.05	0.27	0.12	0.37	0.17	0.12
Recreational entrance fees, other out-of-town expenses	0.14	0.14	0.16	0.12	0.07	0.13	0.14	0.16
TELEVISION, RADIO, SOUND EQUIP.	1.60%	1.55%	1.34%	1.67%	1.73%	1.77%	1.47%	1.49%
Television	1.12	1.10	1.05	1.12	1.21	1.12	1.06	1.12
Community antenna or cable TV	0.53	0.50	0.52	0.50	0.48	0.51	0.48	0.46
Black and white TV	0.01	0.01	0.00	0.02	0.00	0.01	0.05	0.00
Color TV, console	0.09	0.09	0.11	0.09	0.14	0.07	0.09	0.07
Color TV, portable and table model	0.17	0.16	0.16	0.15	0.11	0.16	0.15	0.22
VCRs and video disc players	0.18	0.18	0.16	0.19	0.34	0.15	0.18	0.19
Video cassettes, tapes, and discs	0.05	0.05	0.05	0.05	0.05	0.05	0.04	0.06
Video games hardware and software	0.06	0.06	0.02	0.09	0.05	0.13	0.04	0.08
Repair of TV, radio, and sound equipment	0.04	0.04	0.05	0.03	0.03	0.04	0.03	0.03
Rental of TVs	0.01	0.00	-	0.01	0.01	0.00	0.01	0.00
Radios and sound equipment	0.48	0.45	0.29	0.55	0.52	0.65	0.41	0.36
Radios	0.02	0.02	0.01	0.03	0.00	0.04	0.02	0.02
Tape recorders and players	0.04	0.03	0.02	0.04	0.07	0.05	0.01	0.00
Sound components and component systems	0.11	0.09	0.08	0.09	0.07	0.10	0.10	0.10
Sound equipment accessories	0.01	0.02	0.01	0.03	0.01	0.04	0.01	0.00
Records, tapes, needles, and styli	0.11	0.09	0.08	0.10	0.08	0.10	0.11	0.09
Rental of VCR, radio, sound equipment	0.01	0.00	-	0.01	0.02	0.01	0.00	0.01
Musical instruments and accessories	0.08	0.09	0.04	0.13	0.15	0.18	0.04	0.03
Rental and repair of musical instruments	0.01	0.01	0.00	0.01	0.00	0.02	0.01	0.00
Rental of video cassettes, tapes, discs, films	0.09	0.09	0.05	0.11	0.12	0.11	0.10	0.10

Percent of total average annual expenditures spent on entertainment, by married couples with and without children.

(continued from previous page)

	all cu's	all married couples	married couple only	all married couples with children	AGE OF OLDEST CHILD			other married couples
					under 6	6 to 17	18 or older	
PETS, TOYS, PLAYGROUND EQUIP.	**0.89%**	**0.95%**	**0.83%**	**1.02%**	**1.29%**	**1.15%**	**0.66%**	**0.90%**
Pets	**0.49**	**0.50**	**0.55**	**0.48**	**0.41**	**0.54**	**0.42**	**0.48**
Pet food	0.24	0.24	0.29	0.22	0.17	0.23	0.22	0.26
Pet supplies and medicines	0.08	0.09	0.08	0.10	0.11	0.15	0.02	0.06
Pet services	0.04	0.05	0.05	0.04	0.03	0.05	0.04	0.05
Veterinarian services	0.13	0.12	0.13	0.12	0.10	0.11	0.14	0.11
Toys, games, hobbies, and tricycles	**0.38**	**0.43**	**0.26**	**0.53**	**0.85**	**0.59**	**0.23**	**0.40**
Playground equipment	**0.01**	**0.01**	**0.01**	**0.01**	**0.02**	**0.02**	**0.00**	**0.02**
OTHER ENTERTAINMENT EQUIP., SUPPLIES, AND SERVICES	**1.27%**	**1.38%**	**1.34%**	**1.49%**	**1.58%**	**1.71%**	**1.06%**	**0.70%**
Boats and trailers without motors	**0.09**	**0.10**	**0.05**	**0.15**	**0.10**	**0.25**	**0.01**	**0.02**
Boats and boat trailers	0.06	0.07	0.04	0.10	0.07	0.16	0.01	0.01
Trailers and other attachable campers	0.03	0.03	0.01	0.05	0.03	0.08	0.01	0.00
Motorized sports vehicles	**0.53**	**0.57**	**0.73**	**0.56**	**0.70**	**0.62**	**0.37**	**0.03**
Camper coach and other vehicles	0.16	0.22	0.37	0.16	0.66	0.06	0.02	0.00
Motor boats	0.37	0.36	0.35	0.40	0.04	0.56	0.35	0.03
Sports vehicle rentals	**0.01**	**0.01**	**0.01**	**0.01**	**0.01**	**0.01**	**0.01**	**0.00**
Outboard motors	**0.00**	**0.01**	**0.01**	**0.00**	**0.00**	**0.00**	**0.00**	**0.03**
Docking fees	**0.02**	**0.02**	**0.02**	**0.02**	**-**	**0.01**	**0.04**	**0.03**
Sports equipment	**0.34**	**0.36**	**0.28**	**0.42**	**0.38**	**0.49**	**0.32**	**0.23**
Athletic gear, game tables, exercise equipment	0.13	0.14	0.14	0.15	0.13	0.19	0.11	0.10
Bicycles	0.04	0.04	0.02	0.05	0.03	0.06	0.04	0.05
Camping equipment	0.01	0.01	0.01	0.02	0.01	0.02	0.02	0.01
Hunting and fishing equipment	0.06	0.07	0.06	0.07	0.10	0.08	0.05	0.04
Winter sports equipment	0.02	0.02	0.01	0.03	0.02	0.04	0.03	0.03
Water sports/miscellaneous sports equipment .	0.06	0.06	0.03	0.09	0.09	0.10	0.06	0.01
Rental and repair of sports equipment	0.01	0.01	0.01	0.01	0.00	0.01	0.01	0.01
Photographic equip., supplies, services	**0.26**	**0.28**	**0.24**	**0.30**	**0.37**	**0.28**	**0.28**	**0.33**
Film	0.08	0.08	0.07	0.09	0.11	0.08	0.08	0.09
Film processing	0.10	0.10	0.09	0.11	0.16	0.10	0.10	0.12
Photographic equipment	0.06	0.06	0.05	0.06	0.06	0.05	0.08	0.10
Photographer fees	0.03	0.03	0.03	0.03	0.03	0.05	0.01	0.02
Pinball and electronic video games	**0.01**	**0.01**	**0.01**	**0.02**	**0.01**	**0.03**	**0.01**	**-**

Note: Expenditures are not given (-) when the amount is too small to be reliable. Expenditures listed for a given category may not add to the total for that category because the listing is incomplete. "Photographic equipment, supplies, and services," for example, includes "other photographic supplies," which is omitted here. Numbers may not add to total due to rounding. Other married couples include extended family members or unrelated persons in addition to the married couple.

Indexed expenditures

	all cu's	all married couples	married couple only	all married couples with children	AGE OF OLDEST CHILD			other married couples
					under 6	6 to 17	18 or older	

Indexed average annual expenditures for entertainment, by married couples with and without children.

	all cu's	all married couples	married couple only	all married couples with children	under 6	6 to 17	18 or older	other married couples
Number of consumer units (in thousands)	94,862	52,010	20,227	28,100	5,858	14,194	8,047	3,684
Average number of persons per cu	2.6	3.3	2	3.9	3.5	4.1	3.9	5.1
Average number of earners per cu	1.4	1.7	1.2	2.1	1.7	1.9	2.7	2.4
Average total before-tax income	$28,540	$37,299	$33,825	$39,354	$34,318	$38,039	$45,596	$40,846
TOTAL AVERAGE ANNUAL EXPENDITURES	100	125	108	135	120	136	146	138
ENTERTAINMENT, AVERAGE ANNUAL EXPENDITURES	100	128	103	148	131	164	132	117
FEES AND ADMISSIONS	100	127	109	140	88	153	155	126
Club membership dues and fees	100	135	148	131	97	119	177	103
Participant sports fees	100	130	124	138	132	143	134	96
Participant sports fees, out-of-town trips	100	117	120	117	93	125	118	111
Movie, theater, opera, ballet, other admissions	100	107	84	122	75	121	157	118
Movie, other out-of-town admissions	100	125	111	126	65	143	139	191
Sporting event admissions	100	128	94	152	81	156	196	133
Sporting event, out-of-town admissions	100	125	111	126	65	143	139	191
Recreational lesson fees	100	145	35	229	91	326	159	106
Recreational entrance fees, other out-of-town expenses	100	126	129	121	64	129	148	158
TELEVISION, RADIO, SOUND EQUIP.	100	120	90	141	129	150	133	128
Television	100	121	101	134	128	136	137	138
Community antenna or cable TV	100	118	105	127	109	131	132	121
Black and white TV	100	155	0	287	0	160	801	0
Color TV, console	100	131	130	134	189	106	144	117
Color TV, portable and table model	100	115	100	118	80	129	127	179
VCRs and video disc players	100	128	98	146	227	113	145	147
Video cassettes, tapes, and discs	100	124	105	131	110	148	115	174
Video games hardware and software	100	137	31	206	102	312	96	188
Repair of TV, radio, and sound equipment	100	121	127	119	97	126	122	107
Rental of TVs	100	69	-	106	135	72	146	86
Radios and sound equipment	100	118	66	157	131	186	124	105
Radios	100	134	42	200	0	325	137	135
Tape recorders and players	100	111	63	159	236	178	51	0
Sound components and component systems	100	101	78	115	77	120	136	120
Sound equipment accessories	100	168	49	270	117	409	133	44
Records, tapes, needles, and styli	100	105	75	122	89	121	147	116
Rental of VCR, radio, sound equipment	100	109	-	165	328	130	107	148
Musical instruments and accessories	100	135	47	210	209	291	69	43
Rental and repair of musical instruments	100	141	26	233	51	366	131	66
Rental of video cassettes, tapes, discs, films	100	129	68	168	160	176	160	160

Indexed average annual expenditures for entertainment, by married couples with and without children.

(continued from previous page)

	all cu's	all married couples	married couple only	all married couples with children	AGE OF OLDEST CHILD			other married couples
					under 6	6 to 17	18 or older	
PETS, TOYS, PLAYGROUND EQUIP.	100	133	101	156	173	176	108	140
Pets	100	128	121	132	100	150	124	133
Pet food	100	127	131	121	86	131	135	147
Pet supplies and medicines	100	142	105	174	164	248	37	104
Pet services	100	137	129	138	79	159	142	167
Veterinarian services	100	118	111	124	92	121	154	115
Toys, games, hobbies, and tricycles	100	139	74	185	264	208	88	144
Playground equipment	100	168	137	176	276	214	34	283
OTHER ENTERTAINMENT EQUIP., SUPPLIES, AND SERVICES	100	135	113	158	148	183	121	76
Boats and trailers without motors	100	148	62	225	134	379	20	25
Boats and boat trailers	100	144	73	209	127	352	16	32
Trailers and other attachable campers	100	157	36	263	151	442	28	9
Motorized sports vehicles	100	135	148	143	158	159	102	7
Camper coach and other vehicles	100	169	249	133	488	51	20	0
Motor boats	100	120	104	147	14	207	139	10
Sports vehicle rentals	100	109	66	148	167	117	188	53
Outboard motors	100	178	157	94	82	104	84	925
Docking fees	100	136	108	149	-	103	332	193
Sports equipment	100	132	89	167	135	198	138	96
Athletic gear, game tables, exercise equipment	100	133	113	152	111	186	123	99
Bicycles	100	107	38	151	82	194	127	146
Camping equipment	100	141	83	193	111	209	223	60
Hunting and fishing equipment	100	139	109	167	205	174	127	84
Winter sports equipment	100	127	40	183	84	226	179	188
Water sports/miscellaneous sports equipment .	100	143	68	213	201	248	160	26
Rental and repair of sports equipment	100	124	143	113	47	141	110	105
Photographic equip., supplies, services	100	135	100	155	168	149	156	178
Film	100	134	97	156	179	148	153	167
Film processing	100	136	98	157	198	140	158	176
Photographic equipment	100	136	99	147	122	130	196	249
Photographer fees	100	136	102	167	147	225	70	80
Pinball and electronic video games	100	114	45	178	83	254	115	-

Note: An index of 100 represents the average for all consumer units. An index of 132 means that the average for the subgroup is 32 percent above the average for all consumer units. An index of 68 indicates spending that is 32 percent below the overall average. Expenditures are not given (-) when the amount is too small to be reliable. Other married couples include extended family members or unrelated persons in addition to the married couple.

Aggregate expenditures, 1988

	all cu's	all married couples	married couple only	all married couples with children	AGE OF OLDEST CHILD			other married couples
					under 6	6 to 17	18 or older	
Aggregate expenditures in 1988 for entertainment, by married couples with and without children.								
Number of consumer units (in thousands)	94,862	52,010	20,227	28,100	5,858	14,194	8,047	3,684
Average number of persons per cu	2.6	3.3	2	3.9	3.5	4.1	3.9	5.1
Average number of earners per cu	1.4	1.7	1.2	2.1	1.7	1.9	2.7	2.4
Aggregate before-tax income (in millions)	$2,722,910	$1,942,526	$684,178	$1,107,871	$201,035	$539,926	$366,911	$150,477
TOTAL AGGREG. EXPENDITURES (in millions)	$2,455,594	$1,682,565	$565,436	$985,465	$181,263	$500,316	$303,886	$131,665
ENTERTAINMENT, AGGREGATE EXPENDITURES (in millions)	$125,980	$88,427	$27,623	$55,098	$10,161	$30,869	$14,068	$5,706
FEES AND ADMISSIONS	$33,501	$23,314	$7,772	$13,905	$1,819	$7,674	$4,411	$1,637
Club membership dues and fees	7,537	5,594	2,373	2,918	453	1,337	1,129	303
Participant sports fees	4,335	3,078	1,146	1,771	354	925	492	161
Participant sports fees, out-of-town trips	1,737	1,119	443	600	100	326	175	75
Movie, theater, opera, ballet, other admissions	5,753	3,362	1,026	2,072	267	1,041	764	264
Movie, other out-of-town admissions	2,468	1,687	585	919	100	530	290	183
Sporting event admissions	1,966	1,381	396	884	98	458	328	101
Sporting event, out-of-town admissions	2,468	1,687	585	919	100	530	290	183
Recreational lesson fees	3,844	3,054	286	2,610	216	1,875	519	158
Recreational entrance fees, other out-of-town expenses	3,392	2,351	932	1,211	133	653	425	208
TELEVISION, RADIO, SOUND EQUIP.	$39,411	$26,026	$7,598	$16,470	$3,141	$8,875	$4,455	$1,958
Television	27,710	18,459	5,952	11,028	2,192	5,618	3,219	1,479
Community antenna or cable TV	12,986	8,398	2,912	4,875	872	2,550	1,452	611
Black and white TV	249	216	0	216	0	56	160	0
Color TV, console	2,156	1,549	596	855	251	341	263	98
Color TV, portable and table model	4,179	2,642	889	1,463	206	808	449	290
VCRs and video disc players	4,432	3,100	930	1,918	621	752	545	252
Video cassettes, tapes, and discs	1,214	824	271	471	83	270	118	82
Video games hardware and software	1,385	1,039	92	846	87	646	113	101
Repair of TV, radio, and sound equipment	951	632	257	335	57	179	99	40
Rental of TVs	153	55	-	50	13	17	20	5
Radios and sound equipment	11,701	7,568	1,646	5,442	949	3,257	1,236	479
Radios	435	323	39	261	0	210	50	23
Tape recorders and players	863	521	119	402	129	235	38	0
Sound components and component systems	2,684	1,490	447	917	127	481	308	125
Sound equipment accessories	351	330	37	287	26	220	41	6
Records, tapes, needles, and styli	2,752	1,568	442	1,002	153	502	347	124
Rental of VCR, radio, sound equipment	130	75	-	67	28	27	12	8
Musical instruments and accessories	2,078	1,535	207	1,294	268	905	121	34
Rental and repair of musical instruments	203	156	11	140	6	111	23	5
Rental of video cassettes, tapes, discs, films	2,142	1,510	309	1,067	212	564	291	133

Aggregate expenditures in 1988 for entertainment, by married couples with and without children.

(continued from previous page)

	all cu's	all married couples	married couple only	all married couples with children	AGE OF OLDEST CHILD			other married couples
					under 6	6 to 17	18 or older	
PETS, TOYS, PLAYGROUND EQUIP.	**$21,794**	**$15,953**	**$4,687**	**$10,081**	**$2,337**	**$5,751**	**$1,993**	**$1,185**
Pets	**12,045**	**8,481**	**3,120**	**4,734**	**745**	**2,714**	**1,275**	**627**
Pet food	5,899	4,126	1,644	2,145	314	1,155	676	337
Pet supplies and medicines	1,950	1,529	444	1,004	202	739	63	81
Pet services	1,030	771	284	420	50	246	124	67
Veterinarian services	3,166	2,055	747	1,166	179	574	412	142
Toys, games, hobbies, and tricycles	**9,486**	**7,231**	**1,490**	**5,211**	**1,547**	**2,953**	**710**	**530**
Playground equipment	**261**	**241**	**76**	**136**	**45**	**84**	**8**	**29**
OTHER ENTERTAINMENT EQUIP., SUPPLIES, AND SERVICES	**$31,275**	**$23,134**	**$7,567**	**$14,642**	**$2,863**	**$8,570**	**$3,209**	**$925**
Boats and trailers without motors	**2,173**	**1,758**	**289**	**1,447**	**179**	**1,231**	**36**	**21**
Boats and boat trailers	1,534	1,208	240	949	120	808	21	19
Trailers and other attachable campers	639	549	50	498	60	423	15	2
Motorized sports vehicles	**13,018**	**9,649**	**4,111**	**5,502**	**1,270**	**3,101**	**1,131**	**35**
Camper coach and other vehicles	3,962	3,666	2,104	1,562	1,193	303	66	0
Motor boats	9,056	5,982	2,006	3,941	77	2,798	1,065	35
Sports vehicle rentals	**215**	**130**	**31**	**95**	**22**	**38**	**35**	**4**
Outboard motors	**107**	**107**	**37**	**31**	**6**	**17**	**8**	**40**
Docking fees	**464**	**346**	**108**	**203**	**-**	**72**	**131**	**35**
Sports equipment	**8,329**	**6,030**	**1,588**	**4,132**	**694**	**2,464**	**973**	**309**
Athletic gear, game tables, exercise equipment	3,326	2,429	799	1,502	228	926	348	128
Bicycles	1,109	651	90	498	56	321	120	63
Camping equipment	300	232	53	172	21	94	57	7
Hunting and fishing equipment	1,458	1,109	340	722	185	379	157	48
Winter sports equipment	574	401	49	311	30	194	87	42
Water sports/miscellaneous sports equipment .	1,367	1,075	198	863	170	508	186	14
Rental and repair of sports equipment	195	133	59	65	6	41	18	8
Photographic equip., supplies, and services	**6,387**	**4,733**	**1,361**	**2,931**	**665**	**1,422**	**844**	**441**
Film	1,869	1,370	385	863	207	413	243	121
Film processing	2,370	1,761	496	1,103	290	495	318	162
Photographic equipment	1,411	1,049	297	616	107	275	234	137
Photographer fees	662	494	146	326	61	226	40	21
Pinball and electronic video games	**364**	**228**	**35**	**193**	**19**	**138**	**36**	**-**

Note: Expenditures are not given (-) when the amount is too small to be reliable. Expenditures listed for a given category may not add to the total for that category because the listing is incomplete. "Photographic equipment, supplies, and services," for example, includes "other photographic supplies," which is omitted here. Numbers may not add to total due to rounding. Other married couples include extended family members or unrelated persons in addition to the married couple. The "all cu's" aggregates will differ slightly from table to table because they are the sums of the aggregates in each row. In this table they include aggregates for single parents, single persons, and other types of consumer units, in addition to all married couples. Aggregates for "all married couples" and "all married couples with children" are sums of the appropriate aggregates in each row.

CHAPTER

9

Personal Care, Reading, Education, and Tobacco Products

Personal care products and services, including everything from shaving cream to hair cuts, was allocated the same share of expenditures in 1988 as in 1984—just over 1 percent. The budget share devoted to reading materials was also unchanged during that five-year period.

Between 1984 and 1988, the share of household expenditures devoted to education and to tobacco products moved up and down a little. Spending on cigarettes and other tobacco products is likely to decline during the 1990s. Cigarette smokers dropped from 32 to 29 percent of the adult population between 1983 and 1987 and are expected to be less than 25 percent of the population in 1990. The budget share devoted to education is likely to increase as the children of the baby boom continue with their schooling.

Five-year spending trends for personal care, reading, education, and tobacco products

Share of household expenditures devoted to personal care, reading, education, and tobacco products, and change in share, 1984 to 1988.						
	1984	1985	1986	1987	1988	change 1984 to 1988
Total average annual expenditures	100.0%	100.0%	100.0%	100.0%	100.0%	0.0%
PERSONAL CARE PRODUCTS AND SERVICES	1.3%	1.3%	1.3%	1.4%	1.3%	0.0%
READING	0.6%	0.6%	0.6%	0.6%	0.6%	0.0%
EDUCATION	1.4%	1.4%	1.3%	1.4%	1.3%	-0.1%
TOBACCO PRODUCTS AND SMOKING SUPPLIES	1.0%	0.9%	1.0%	1.0%	0.9%	-0.1%

PART I
Spending by age for personal care, reading, education, and tobacco products

Just over 1 percent of the average household budget is devoted to personal care products and services

Households headed by 35-to-54-year-olds spend the most on personal care products and services, with those in the 45-to-54 age group spending the most on women's personal care services. Householders aged 55 to 64 spend the most on oral hygiene products, while 35-to-44-year-olds outspend all others on hair accessories.

Householder aged 35 to 54 spent nearly $15 billion on personal care products and services in 1988. They account for fully 46 percent of the personal-care products and services market.

Reading

The average American household spends less than 1 percent of its budget on reading materials. Forty-three percent of expenditures for reading materials go to newspapers. Those aged 65 to 74 spend the most on newspapers, while householders aged 45 to 54 devote the most dollars to magazines and books. Spending on encyclopedias and other reference books peaks among 35-to-44-year-olds because so many have school-aged children.

Households headed by people aged 35 to 54 are 35 percent of American households but they account for 43 percent of the reading materials market. In 2000 they will account for 44 percent of households and 53 percent of the market for reading materials.

Education

Spending on items in this category reflects both the age of the student and the parent. Under-25-year-olds, for example, spend 144 percent more than the average household on college tuition. They also spend 328 percent more than average on college books and supplies. Householders aged 45 to 54 spend 135 percent more than the average household for college tuition. Spending on high school and elementary school tuition, books, and supplies is highest among those aged 35 to 44. Householders older than 55 or aged 25 to 34 spend less than average on education.

Householders aged 35 to 54 spent more than $18 billion on education in 1988. They accounted for 56 percent of the educational expenses market and will account for 69 percent of that market in 2000.

Tobacco

Spending on tobacco products and smoking supplies peaks among 45-to-54-year-olds. Those middle-aged householders spend 37 percent more than the average household on cigarettes and 72 percent more than average on other tobacco products. Households headed by someone under age 25 or 65 or older spend less than average on this category. They account for less than 20 percent of the tobacco and smoking supplies market.

Householders aged 35 to 64 spent more than $13 billion on tobacco and smoking supplies in 1988, accounting for 58 percent of the market for those products. Householders aged 25 to 34 spent $5 billion on cigarettes and other products in this category, accounting for another 24 percent of the market.

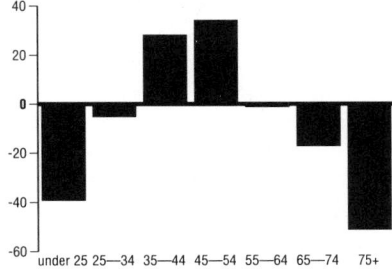

Middle-aged householders spend much more than the average household on personal care products and services...

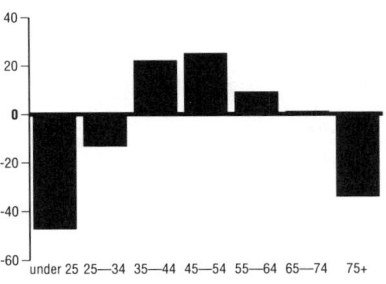

...and on reading materials...

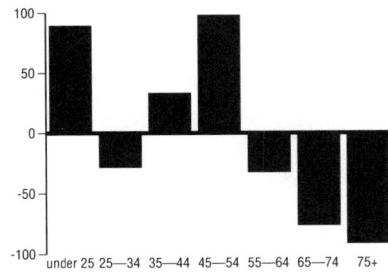

...they're joined by the youngest householders when it comes to education.

0 = average spending

Average expenditures

	all cu's	under 25	25 to 34	35 to 44	45 to 54	55 to 64	65 to 74	75+
Number of consumer units (in thousands)	94,862	7,216	21,985	19,911	13,601	12,546	11,319	8,284
Average number of persons per cu	2.6	1.8	2.8	3.3	2.9	2.2	2.0	1.5
Average total before-tax income	$28,540.00	$14,827.00	$28,318.00	$36,428.00	$39,934.00	$29,979.00	$20,704.00	$13,707.00
TOTAL AVERAGE ANNUAL EXPENDITURES	$25,891.85	$16,373.17	$25,770.27	$33,077.72	$33,204.87	$25,765.35	$20,119.90	$13,339.49
PERSONAL CARE PRODUCTS AND SERVICES	$333.52	$203.99	$318.38	$427.25	$446.22	$329.50	$275.68	$164.20
Personal care products	166.80	109.16	165.44	225.19	234.21	160.54	111.97	54.45
Hair care products	37.79	32.38	39.61	51.71	48.32	35.66	22.58	10.54
Hair accessories	3.95	2.01	5.74	6.50	3.65	2.92	1.44	0.52
Wigs and hairpieces	0.99	-	-	0.69	1.97	1.57	1.31	0.94
Oral hygiene products	16.77	9.42	14.43	18.37	21.71	22.21	15.48	10.82
Shaving products	8.02	4.70	9.06	10.67	11.06	6.25	6.15	2.11
Cosmetics, perfume, and bath products	72.52	42.23	67.56	100.91	108.87	69.67	50.38	18.91
Deodorant, feminine hygiene products, and miscellaneous items	21.71	14.20	23.45	28.16	32.78	18.02	11.83	9.30
Electrical personal care appliances	5.06	3.79	5.20	8.18	5.85	4.24	2.79	1.31
Personal care services	166.72	94.83	152.94	202.06	212.01	168.96	163.71	109.75
Personal care services/female	88.62	42.07	71.56	100.50	110.71	97.18	107.49	73.22
Personal care services/male	77.94	52.68	81.24	101.39	101.06	71.62	56.00	36.37
READING	$150.01	$79.86	$130.94	$182.86	$187.39	$163.65	$150.79	$99.72
Newspapers	64.51	26.14	47.05	68.83	75.65	81.04	83.74	64.31
Magazines	37.55	28.08	36.83	43.71	44.57	39.37	35.27	21.80
Books purchased through book clubs	10.06	3.02	9.61	13.42	14.52	10.86	8.48	2.95
Books not purchased through book clubs	34.33	21.07	32.54	48.63	50.75	31.43	22.07	10.41
Encyclopedia and other reference book sets	3.53	1.55	4.77	8.28	1.90	0.95	1.22	-
EDUCATION	$342.21	$646.40	$247.33	$454.29	$678.21	$233.51	$80.93	$30.55
College tuition	190.61	465.24	135.17	152.00	448.45	159.28	38.64	23.06
High school/elementary school tuition	57.65	11.50	30.98	154.67	97.16	20.59	3.43	0.79
Other school tuition	14.76	10.45	15.80	32.51	15.21	3.98	4.97	2.12
Books and supplies for college students	26.57	113.69	20.43	22.60	40.58	16.79	2.95	0.58

Average annual expenditures for personal care, reading, education, and tobacco products, by age of reference person.

(continued from previous page)	all cu's	under 25	25 to 34	35 to 44	45 to 54	55 to 64	65 to 74	75+
Books and supplies for high school and elementary students	6.04	1.63	5.68	14.78	7.64	1.34	1.85	-
Books and supplies for day care and nursery school	2.43	3.38	3.33	2.90	3.35	2.24	-	-
Miscellaneous school expenses and supplies	44.14	40.53	35.94	74.84	65.82	29.30	28.92	3.93
TOBACCO PRODUCTS AND SMOKING SUPPLIES	$241.94	$183.39	$246.44	$276.86	$333.59	$267.98	$185.14	$84.16
Cigarettes	224.00	159.99	232.79	262.42	305.98	250.25	165.74	69.37
Other tobacco products	15.40	13.19	12.59	10.49	26.47	16.56	17.40	13.97
Smoking accessories	2.54	10.21	1.05	3.95	1.13	1.18	1.99	0.82

Note: Expenditures are not given (-) when the amount is too small to be reliable. Expenditures listed for a given category may not add to the total for that category because the listing is incomplete. "Reading," for example, includes "newsletters," which is omitted here because all the expenditure amounts were too small to be reliable. Numbers may not add to total due to rounding.

Share of spending

	all cu's	under 25	25 to 34	35 to 44	45 to 54	55 to 64	65 to 74	75+
Number of consumer units (in thousands)	94,862	7,216	21,985	19,911	13,601	12,546	11,319	8,284
Average number of persons per cu	2.6	1.8	2.8	3.3	2.9	2.2	2.0	1.5
Average total before-tax income	$28,540	$14,827	$28,318	$36,428	$39,934	$29,979	$20,704	$13,707
TOTAL AVERAGE ANNUAL EXPENDITURES	100.00%	100.00%	100.00%	100.00%	100.00%	100.00%	100.00%	100.00%
PERSONAL CARE PRODUCTS AND SERVICES	1.29%	1.25%	1.24%	1.29%	1.34%	1.28%	1.37%	1.23%
Personal care products	0.64	0.67	0.64	0.68	0.71	0.62	0.56	0.41
Hair care products	0.15	0.20	0.15	0.16	0.15	0.14	0.11	0.08
Hair accessories	0.02	0.01	0.02	0.02	0.01	0.01	0.01	0.00
Wigs and hairpieces	0.00	-	-	0.00	0.01	0.01	0.01	0.01
Oral hygiene products	0.06	0.06	0.06	0.06	0.07	0.09	0.08	0.08
Shaving products	0.03	0.03	0.04	0.03	0.03	0.02	0.03	0.02
Cosmetics, perfume, and bath products	0.28	0.26	0.26	0.31	0.33	0.27	0.25	0.14
Deodorant, feminine hygiene products, and miscellaneous items	0.08	0.09	0.09	0.09	0.10	0.07	0.06	0.07
Electrical personal care appliances	0.02	0.02	0.02	0.02	0.02	0.02	0.01	0.01
Personal care services	0.64	0.58	0.59	0.61	0.64	0.66	0.81	0.82
Personal care services/female	0.34	0.26	0.28	0.30	0.33	0.38	0.53	0.55
Personal care services/male	0.30	0.32	0.32	0.31	0.30	0.28	0.28	0.27
READING	0.58%	0.49%	0.51%	0.55%	0.56%	0.64%	0.75%	0.75%
Newspapers	0.25	0.16	0.18	0.21	0.23	0.31	0.42	0.48
Magazines	0.15	0.17	0.14	0.13	0.13	0.15	0.18	0.16
Books purchased through book clubs	0.04	0.02	0.04	0.04	0.04	0.04	0.04	0.02
Books not purchased through book clubs	0.13	0.13	0.13	0.15	0.15	0.12	0.11	0.08
Encyclopedia and other reference book sets	0.01	0.01	0.02	0.03	0.01	0.00	0.01	-
EDUCATION	1.32%	3.95%	0.96%	1.37%	2.04%	0.91%	0.40%	0.23%
College tuition	0.74	2.84	0.52	0.46	1.35	0.62	0.19	0.17
High school/elementary school tuition	0.22	0.07	0.12	0.47	0.29	0.08	0.02	0.01
Other school tuition	0.06	0.06	0.06	0.10	0.05	0.02	0.02	0.02
Books and supplies for college students	0.10	0.69	0.08	0.07	0.12	0.07	0.01	0.00

Percent of total average annual expenditures spent on personal care, reading, education, and tobacco products, by age of reference person.

(continued from previous page)	all cu's	under 25	25 to 34	35 to 44	45 to 54	55 to 64	65 to 74	75+
Books and supplies for high school and elementary students	0.02	0.01	0.02	0.04	0.02	0.01	0.01	-
Books and supplies for day care and nursery school	0.01	0.02	0.01	0.01	0.01	0.01	-	-
Miscellaneous school expenses and supplies	0.17	0.25	0.14	0.23	0.20	0.11	0.14	0.03
TOBACCO PRODUCTS AND SMOKING SUPPLIES	0.93%	1.12%	0.96%	0.84%	1.00%	1.04%	0.92%	0.63%
Cigarettes	0.87	0.98	0.90	0.79	0.92	0.97	0.82	0.52
Other tobacco products	0.06	0.08	0.05	0.03	0.08	0.06	0.09	0.10
Smoking accessories	0.01	0.06	0.00	0.01	0.00	0.00	0.01	0.01

Note: Expenditures are not given (-) when the amount is too small to be reliable. Expenditures listed for a given category may not add to the total for that category because the listing is incomplete. "Reading," for example, includes "newsletters," which is omitted here because all the expenditure amounts were too small to be reliable. Numbers may not add to total due to rounding.

Indexed expenditures

	all cu's	under 25	25 to 34	35 to 44	45 to 54	55 to 64	65 to 74	75+
Number of consumer units (in thousands)	94,862	7,216	21,985	19,911	13,601	12,546	11,319	8,284
Average number of persons per cu	2.6	1.8	2.8	3.3	2.9	2.2	2.0	1.5
Average total before-tax income	$28,540	$14,827	$28,318	$36,428	$39,934	$29,979	$20,704	$13,707
TOTAL AVERAGE ANNUAL EXPENDITURES	100	63	100	128	128	100	78	52
PERSONAL CARE PRODUCTS AND SERVICES	**100**	**61**	**95**	**128**	**134**	**99**	**83**	**49**
Personal care products	**100**	**65**	**99**	**135**	**140**	**96**	**67**	**33**
Hair care products	100	86	105	137	128	94	60	28
Hair accessories	100	51	145	165	92	74	36	13
Wigs and hairpieces	100	-	-	70	199	159	132	95
Oral hygiene products	100	56	86	110	129	132	92	65
Shaving products	100	59	113	133	138	78	77	26
Cosmetics, perfume, and bath products	100	58	93	139	150	96	69	26
Deodorant, feminine hygiene products, and miscellaneous items	100	65	108	130	151	83	54	43
Electrical personal care appliances	100	75	103	162	116	84	55	26
Personal care services	**100**	**57**	**92**	**121**	**127**	**101**	**98**	**66**
Personal care services/female	100	47	81	113	125	110	121	83
Personal care services/male	100	68	104	130	130	92	72	47
READING	**100**	**53**	**87**	**122**	**125**	**109**	**101**	**66**
Newspapers	**100**	**41**	**73**	**107**	**117**	**126**	**130**	**100**
Magazines	**100**	**75**	**98**	**116**	**119**	**105**	**94**	**58**
Books purchased through book clubs	**100**	30	**96**	**133**	**144**	**108**	**84**	**29**
Books not purchased through book clubs	**100**	**61**	**95**	**142**	**148**	**92**	**64**	**30**
Encyclopedia and other reference book sets	**100**	**44**	**135**	**235**	**54**	**27**	**35**	-
EDUCATION	**100**	**189**	**72**	**133**	**198**	**68**	**24**	**9**
College tuition	**100**	**244**	**71**	**80**	**235**	**84**	**20**	**12**
High school/elementary school tuition	**100**	**20**	**54**	**268**	**169**	**36**	**6**	**1**
Other school tuition	**100**	**71**	**107**	**220**	**103**	**27**	**34**	**14**
Books and supplies for college students	**100**	**428**	**77**	**85**	**153**	**63**	**11**	**2**

Indexed average annual expenditures for personal care, reading, education, and tobacco products, by age of reference person.

(continued from previous page)	all cu's	under 25	25 to 34	35 to 44	45 to 54	55 to 64	65 to 74	75+
Books and supplies for high school and elementary students	100	27	94	245	126	22	31	-
Books and supplies for day care and nursery school	100	139	137	119	138	92	-	-
Miscellaneous school expenses and supplies	100	92	81	170	149	66	66	9
TOBACCO PRODUCTS AND SMOKING SUPPLIES	100	76	102	114	138	111	77	35
Cigarettes	100	71	104	117	137	112	74	31
Other tobacco products	100	86	82	68	172	108	113	91
Smoking accessories	100	402	41	156	44	46	78	32

Note: Expenditures are not given (-) when the amount is too small to be reliable. An index of 100 represents the average for all consumer units. An index of 132 means that the average for the subgroup is 32 percent above the average for all consumer units. An index of 68 indicates spending that is 32 percent below the overall average.

Aggregate expenditures, 1988

	all cu's	under 25	25 to 34	35 to 44	45 to 54	55 to 64	65 to 74	75+
Number of consumer units (in thousands)	94,862	7,216	21,985	19,911	13,601	12,546	11,319	8,284
Average number of persons per cu	2.6	1.8	2.8	3.3	2.9	2.2	2.0	1.5
Aggregate before-tax income (in millions)	$2,722,037	$106,992	$622,571	$725,318	$543,142	$376,117	$234,349	$113,549
TOTAL AGGREGATE EXPENDITURES (in millions)	$2,456,432	$118,149	$566,559	$658,610	$451,619	$323,252	$227,737	$110,504
PERSONAL CARE PRODUCTS AND SERVICES (in millions)	$31,662	$1,472	$7,000	$8,507	$6,069	$4,134	$3,120	$1,360
Personal care products	15,827	788	3,637	4,484	3,185	2,014	1,267	451
Hair care products	3,582	234	871	1,030	657	447	256	87
Hair accessories	377	15	126	129	50	37	16	4
Wigs and hairpieces	83	-	-	14	27	20	15	8
Oral hygiene products	1,590	68	317	366	295	279	175	90
Shaving products	761	34	199	212	150	78	70	17
Cosmetics, perfume, and bath products	6,881	305	1,485	2,009	1,481	874	570	157
Deodorant, feminine hygiene products, and miscellaneous items	2,062	102	516	561	446	226	134	77
Electrical personal care appliances	480	27	114	163	80	53	32	11
Personal care services	15,835	684	3,362	4,023	2,884	2,120	1,853	909
Personal care services/female	8,426	304	1,573	2,001	1,506	1,219	1,217	607
Personal care services/male	7,393	380	1,786	2,019	1,375	899	634	301
READING (in millions)	$14,231	$576	$2,879	$3,641	$2,549	$2,053	$1,707	$826
Newspapers	6,120	189	1,034	1,370	1,029	1,017	948	533
Magazines	3,563	203	810	870	606	494	399	181
Books purchased through book clubs	954	22	211	267	197	136	96	24
Books not purchased through book clubs	3,256	152	715	968	690	394	250	86
Encyclopedia and other reference book sets	332	11	105	165	26	12	14	-
EDUCATION (in millions)	$32,470	$4,664	$5,438	$9,045	$9,224	$2,930	$916	$253
College tuition	18,081	3,357	2,972	3,026	6,099	1,998	437	191
High school/elementary school tuition	5,469	83	681	3,080	1,321	258	39	7
Other school tuition	1,401	75	347	647	207	50	56	18
Books and supplies for college students	2,520	820	449	450	552	211	33	5

Aggregate expenditures for personal care, reading, education, and tobacco products in 1988, by age of reference person.

(continued from previous page)	all cu's	under 25	25 to 34	35 to 44	45 to 54	55 to 64	65 to 74	75+
Books and supplies for high school and elementary students	573	12	125	294	104	17	21	-
Books and supplies for day care and nursery school	229	24	73	58	46	28	-	-
Miscellaneous school expenses and supplies	4,195	292	790	1,490	895	368	327	33
TOBACCO PRODUCTS AND SMOKING SUPPLIES (in millions)	$22,946	$1,323	$5,418	$5,513	$4,537	$3,362	$2,096	$697
Cigarettes	21,249	1,154	5,118	5,225	4,162	3,140	1,876	575
Other tobacco products	1,461	95	277	209	360	208	197	116
Smoking accessories	235	74	23	79	15	15	23	7

Note: Expenditures are not given (-) when the amount is too small to be reliable. Expenditures listed for a given category may not add to the total for that category because the listing is incomplete. "Reading," for example, includes "newsletters," which is omitted here because all the expenditure amounts were too small to be reliable. Numbers may not add to total due to rounding. The "all cu's" aggregates will differ slightly from table to table because they are the sums of the aggregates in each row.

Aggregate expenditures, 1995

	all households	under 25	25 to 34	35 to 44	45 to 54	55 to 64	65 to 74	75+
Number of households (in thousands)	**100,308**	**4,316**	**19,927**	**23,916**	**18,035**	**12,233**	**12,006**	**9,876**
PERSONAL CARE PRODUCTS AND SERVICES (in millions)	**$34,453**	**$880**	**$6,344**	**$10,218**	**$8,048**	**$4,031**	**$3,310**	**$1,622**
Personal care products	**17,223**	**471**	**3,297**	**5,386**	**4,224**	**1,964**	**1,344**	**538**
care products	3,849	140	789	1,237	871	436	271	104
Hair accessories	402	9	114	155	66	36	17	5
Wigs and hairpieces	96	-	-	17	36	19	16	9
Oral hygiene products	1,723	41	288	439	392	272	186	107
Shaving products	827	20	181	255	199	76	74	21
Cosmetics, perfume, and bath products	7,549	182	1,346	2,413	1,963	852	605	187
Deodorant, feminine hygiene products, and miscellaneous items	2,248	61	467	673	591	220	142	92
Electrical personal care appliances	519	16	104	196	106	52	33	13
Personal care services	**17,229**	**409**	**3,048**	**4,832**	**3,824**	**2,067**	**1,966**	**1,084**
Personal care services/female	9,210	182	1,426	2,404	1,997	1,189	1,291	723
Personal care services/male	8,001	227	1,619	2,425	1,823	876	672	359
READING (in millions)	**$15,504**	**$345**	**$2,609**	**$4,373**	**$3,380**	**$2,002**	**$1,810**	**$985**
Newspapers	**6,693**	**113**	**938**	**1,646**	**1,364**	**991**	**1,005**	**635**
Magazines	**3,825**	**121**	**734**	**1,045**	**804**	**482**	**423**	**215**
Books purchased through book clubs	**1,051**	**13**	**191**	**321**	**262**	**133**	**102**	**29**
Books not purchased through book clubs	**3,570**	**91**	**648**	**1,163**	**915**	**384**	**265**	**103**
Encyclopedia and other reference book sets	**360**	**7**	**95**	**198**	**34**	**12**	**15**	**-**
EDUCATION (in millions)	**$34,945**	**$2,790**	**$4,929**	**$10,865**	**$12,232**	**$2,857**	**$972**	**$302**
College tuition	**19,065**	**2,008**	**2,694**	**3,635**	**8,088**	**1,948**	**464**	**228**
High school/elementary school tuition	**6,419**	**50**	**617**	**3,699**	**1,752**	**252**	**41**	**8**
Other school tuition	**1,541**	**45**	**315**	**778**	**274**	**49**	**60**	**21**
Books and supplies for college students	**2,417**	**491**	**407**	**541**	**732**	**205**	**35**	**6**

Aggregate expenditures for personal care, reading, education, and tobacco products, by age of householder in 1995 (in 1988 dollars).

(continued from previous page)	all households	under 25	25 to 34	35 to 44	45 to 54	55 to 64	65 to 74	75+
Books and supplies for high school and elementary students	650	7	113	353	138	16	22	-
Books and supplies for day care and nursery school	238	15	66	69	60	27	-	-
Miscellaneous school expenses and supplies	4,612	175	716	1,790	1,187	358	347	39
TOBACCO PRODUCTS AND SMOKING SUPPLIES (in millions)	$24,672	$792	$4,911	$6,621	$6,016	$3,278	$2,223	$831
Cigarettes	22,860	691	4,639	6,276	5,518	3,061	1,990	685
Other tobacco products	1,586	57	251	251	477	203	209	138
Smoking accessories	226	44	21	94	20	14	24	8

Note: Expenditures are not given (-) when the amount is too small to be reliable. Expenditures listed for a given category may not add to the total for that category because the listing is incomplete. "Reading," for example, includes "newsletters," which is omitted here because all the expenditure amounts were too small to be reliable. Numbers may not add to total due to rounding. Households are used here because the number of consumer units in 1995 and 2000 are not available. Household projections are from the Census Bureau. Projections show how annual aggregate expenditures will change as the number of households in the age groups changes in 1995 and 2000. Projections are based on the average annual expenditures in 1988 and have not been adjusted for price increases or for changes in expenditure patterns.

Aggregate expenditures, 2000

Number of households (in thousands)	all households 105,933	under 25 4,442	25 to 34 18,004	35 to 44 25,339	45 to 54 21,603	55 to 64 13,903	65 to 74 11,516	75+ 11,126
PERSONAL CARE PRODUCTS AND SERVICES (in millions)	**$36,687**	**$906**	**$5,732**	**$10,826**	**$9,640**	**$4,581**	**$3,175**	**$1,827**
Personal care products	**18,356**	**485**	**2,979**	**5,706**	**5,060**	**2,232**	**1,289**	**606**
Hair care products	4,084	144	713	1,310	1,044	496	260	117
Hair accessories	419	9	103	165	79	41	17	6
Wigs and hairpieces	107	-	-	17	43	22	15	10
Oral hygiene products	1,844	42	260	465	469	309	178	120
Shaving products	874	21	163	270	239	87	71	23
Cosmetics, perfume, and bath products	8,072	188	1,216	2,557	2,352	969	580	210
Deodorant, feminine hygiene products, and miscellaneous items	2,397	63	422	714	708	251	136	103
Electrical personal care appliances	550	17	94	207	126	59	32	15
Personal care services	**18,330**	**421**	**2,754**	**5,120**	**4,580**	**2,349**	**1,885**	**1,221**
Personal care services/female	9,817	187	1,288	2,547	2,392	1,351	1,238	815
Personal care services/male	8,494	234	1,463	2,569	2,183	996	645	405
READING (in millions)	**$16,515**	**$355**	**$2,357**	**$4,633**	**$4,048**	**$2,275**	**$1,736**	**$1,109**
Newspapers	**7,148**	**116**	**847**	**1,744**	**1,634**	**1,127**	**964**	**716**
Magazines	**4,054**	**125**	**663**	**1,108**	**963**	**547**	**406**	**243**
Books purchased through book clubs	**1,122**	**13**	**173**	**340**	**314**	**151**	**98**	**33**
Books not purchased through book clubs	**3,815**	**94**	**586**	**1,232**	**1,096**	**437**	**254**	**116**
Encyclopedia and other reference book sets	**371**	**7**	**86**	**210**	**41**	**13**	**14**	**-**
EDUCATION (in millions)	**$38,005**	**$2,871**	**$4,453**	**$11,511**	**$14,651**	**$3,246**	**$932**	**$340**
College tuition	**20,956**	**2,067**	**2,434**	**3,852**	**9,688**	**2,214**	**445**	**257**
High school/elementary school tuition	**6,962**	**51**	**558**	**3,919**	**2,099**	**286**	**39**	**9**
Other school tuition	**1,619**	**46**	**284**	**824**	**329**	**55**	**57**	**24**
Books and supplies for college students	**2,596**	**505**	**368**	**573**	**877**	**233**	**34**	**6**

Aggregate expenditures for personal care, reading, education, and tobacco products, by age of householder in 2000 (in 1988 dollars).

(continued from previous page)	all households	under 25	25 to 34	35 to 44	45 to 54	55 to 64	65 to 74	75+
Books and supplies for high school and elementary students	689	7	102	375	165	19	21	-
Books and supplies for day care and nursery school	252	15	60	73	72	31	-	-
Miscellaneous school expenses and supplies	4,930	180	647	1,896	1,422	407	333	44
TOBACCO PRODUCTS AND SMOKING SUPPLIES (in millions)	$26,268	$815	$4,437	$7,015	$7,207	$3,726	$2,132	$936
Cigarettes	24,321	711	4,191	6,649	6,610	3,479	1,909	772
Other tobacco products	1,709	59	227	266	572	230	200	155
Smoking accessories	237	45	19	100	24	16	23	9

Note: Expenditures are not given (-) when the amount is too small to be reliable. Expenditures listed for a given category may not add to the total for that category because the listing is incomplete. "Reading," for example, includes "newsletters," which is omitted here because all the expenditure amounts were too small to be reliable. Numbers may not add to total due to rounding. Households are used here because the number of consumer units in 1995 and 2000 are not available. Projections show how annual aggregate expenditures will change as the number of households in the age groups changes in 1995 and 2000. Household projections are from the Census Bureau. Projections are based on the average annual expenditures in 1988 and have not been adjusted for price increases or for changes in expenditure patterns.

PART II
Spending by income for personal care, reading, education, and tobacco products

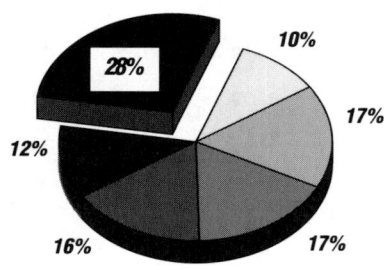

28%

10%

17%

12%

16%

17%

...28 percent of the market for reading materials...

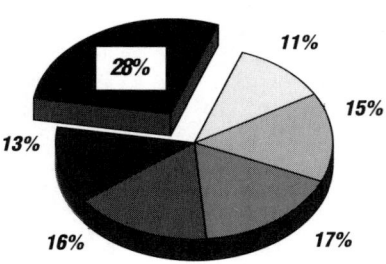

28%

11%

15%

13%

16%

17%

...and 39 percent of the education market.

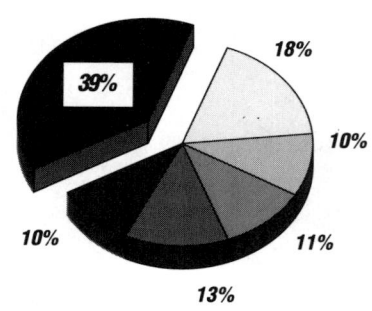

39%

18%

10%

10%

11%

13%

☐ under $10,000	■ $30,000–39,999
■ $10,000–19,999	■ $40,000–49,999
■ $20,000–29,999	■ $50,000 and over

Personal care

People in the highest income households spend over 300 percent more for personal care items than those in the lowest income households. Spending on personal care products rises faster than spending on personal care services, with spending on hair accessories, electrical personal care appliances, and shaving products leading the way.

This category claims an average of $151 a year from households with incomes under $10,000. For households at the top end of the income scale, the figure is $651.

Households with the highest incomes spent $8 billion on personal care products and services in 1988—28 percent of the total spending on these items. Households in the $30,000 to $50,000 income bracket accounted for another 28 percent of the market, while those with incomes below $30,000 are just 44 percent of the market.

Among households with incomes under $30,000 spending on most personal care items is less than average. But there are some exceptions. Households in the $10,000 to $20,000 income group spend more than average on shaving products. The $20,000 to $30,000 income group spends more than average on hair accessories, deodorant, and feminine hygiene products.

Households with incomes above $30,000 spend well above average on personal care products and services, but the biggest spenders are households with incomes of $50,000 or more.

Reading

From the lowest to the highest income households, spending on reading increases 310 percent. Book expenditures are most sensitive to income—spending on book club books climbs 720 percent and spending on non-book club books rises 500 percent between the lowest and highest income groups.By contrast, spending on newspapers increases 190 percent and magazine spending bumps up 350 percent.

Households with incomes of $30,000 or more account for fully 57 percent of the entire reading market, as well as two-thirds of the market for non-book club books, and nearly three-quarters of the market for reference book sets.

Education

Spending for education increases 240 percent from the lowest to the highest income households. Education items for which spending increases the fastest are elementary and high school tuition (up 1520 percent) and day care/nursery school books and supplies (up 360 percent).

The highest income households, those with incomes of $50,000 or more, account for nearly 40 percent of the total education market. Spending on books and supplies for day care and nursery school peaks among households with incomes of $30,000 to $40,000, while spending for all other education items peaks among those with incomes of $50,000 or more.

Tobacco products and smoking supplies

From the lowest to the highest income households, spending on tobacco and smoking supplies increases only 48 percent—less than any other product category.

The amount spent on tobacco products and smoking supplies varies from a low of $183 a year for households with incomes under $10,000 to a high of $293 among households in the $30,000 to $40,000 income group. Those high rollers spent 22 percent more than the average household on cigarettes and 18 percent more on other tobacco products like cigars and chewing tobacco. With total spending of $4 billion on cigarettes and other products, however, the $10,000 to $20,000 income group is the largest market for tobacco products.

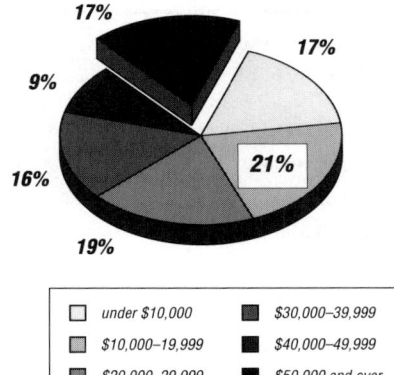

The biggest market for cigarettes and other tobacco products is households with incomes of $10,000 to $20,000.

17%   17%
9%
21%
16%
19%

☐ under $10,000   ■ $30,000–39,999
■ $10,000–19,999   ■ $40,000–49,999
■ $20,000–29,999   ■ $50,000 and over

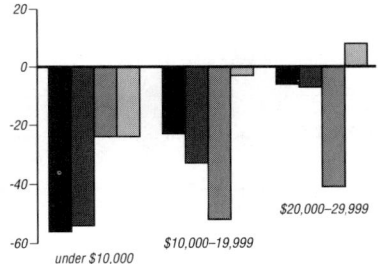

Some lower-income households spend more than the average household on tobacco...

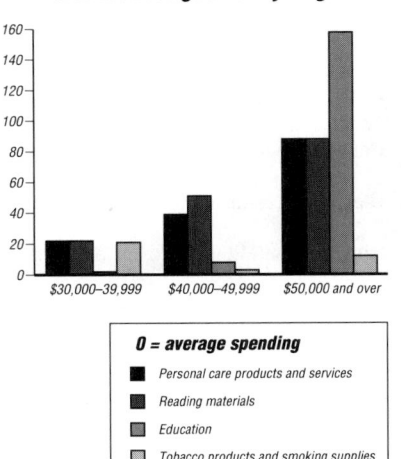

...higher-income households spend more than the average on everything.

0 = average spending
■ Personal care products and services
■ Reading materials
■ Education
☐ Tobacco products and smoking supplies

Average expenditures

(consumer units include complete income reporters only)	cu's	under $10,000	$10,000 to $19,999	$20,000 to $29,999	$30,000 to $39,999	$40,000 to $49,999	$50,000 and over
Number of consumer units (in thousands)	81,354	18,809	17,652	14,586	10,901	7,198	12,209
Average number of persons per cu	2.6	1.8	2.3	2.7	2.9	3.2	3.1
Average number of earners per cu	1.4	0.7	1.0	1.5	1.8	2.0	2.1
TOTAL AVERAGE ANNUAL EXPENDITURES	$26,389.07	$11,269.43	$18,078.25	$24,896.36	$31,659.60	$37,562.00	$52,320.19

	cu's	under $10,000	$10,000 to $19,999	$20,000 to $29,999	$30,000 to $39,999	$40,000 to $49,999	$50,000 and over
PERSONAL CARE PRODUCTS AND SERVICES	$345.68	$150.51	$264.48	$324.70	$420.30	$478.79	$651.43
Personal care products	179.05	76.73	150.74	169.79	198.77	245.49	335.33
Hair care products	40.57	17.36	35.67	37.36	41.43	56.30	77.75
Hair accessories	4.26	0.72	3.13	5.57	4.31	6.79	8.37
Wigs and hairpieces	1.07	0.76	0.67	0.59	1.50	-	2.71
Oral hygiene products	18.16	10.32	15.73	16.89	22.18	22.44	29.63
Shaving products	8.49	2.80	10.09	8.22	9.09	11.31	13.16
Cosmetics, perfume, and bath products	77.63	33.49	64.03	72.41	90.11	102.03	148.23
Deodorant, feminine hygiene products, and miscellaneous items	23.52	9.84	18.70	23.84	22.08	38.47	43.65
Electrical personal care appliances	5.35	1.44	2.71	4.92	8.07	7.80	11.83
Personal care services	166.63	73.79	113.74	154.91	221.54	233.30	316.10
Personal care services/female	89.35	38.38	60.15	83.46	127.40	112.04	174.08
Personal care services/male	77.12	35.39	53.43	71.27	93.93	120.95	141.78
READING	$152.49	$70.72	$102.92	$142.11	$185.46	$229.92	$287.41
Newspapers	63.99	36.84	50.33	63.85	72.82	84.18	105.97
Magazines	38.92	16.13	25.89	38.54	45.36	65.91	71.63
Books purchased through book clubs	10.63	2.64	7.73	8.86	15.44	16.33	21.60
Books not purchased through book clubs	35.24	13.21	18.31	28.28	48.03	54.12	79.39
Encyclopedia and other reference book sets	3.67	1.90	0.66	2.57	3.81	8.97	8.81
EDUCATION	$324.43	$246.80	$155.27	$190.35	$322.81	$349.24	$835.73
College tuition	176.75	166.21	71.06	99.69	186.76	125.89	458.90
High school/elementary school tuition	53.20	12.62	8.20	25.10	34.39	97.91	204.78
Other school tuition	15.29	10.53	12.62	9.00	13.94	21.58	31.48
Books and supplies for college students	26.56	34.32	21.76	16.63	24.53	16.65	41.08

Average annual expenditures for personal care, reading, education, and tobacco products, by total before-tax income of consumer unit.

(continued from previous page)	all cu's	under $10,000	$10,000 to $19,999	$20,000 to $29,999	$30,000 to $39,999	$40,000 to $49,999	$50,000 and over
Books and supplies for high school and elementary students	6.23	2.77	4.56	5.64	7.82	9.59	11.28
Books and supplies for day care and nursery school	2.52	1.05	1.51	1.30	6.04	2.25	4.76
Miscellaneous school expenses and supplies	76.67	56.39	61.89	55.26	81.67	101.61	135.82
TOBACCO PRODUCTS AND SMOKING SUPPLIES	$242.33	$183.33	$234.78	$262.82	$292.87	$249.43	$270.80
Cigarettes	224.61	170.06	215.19	244.22	273.20	230.82	251.80
Other tobacco products	15.28	11.33	14.96	16.00	17.99	17.73	17.12
Smoking accessories	2.44	1.95	4.64	2.60	1.69	0.88	1.37

Note: Expenditures are not given (-) when the amount is too small to be reliable. Expenditures listed for a given category may not add to the total for that category because the listing is incomplete. "Reading," for example, includes "newsletters, which is omitted here because all the expenditure amounts were too small to be reliable. Numbers may not add to total due to rounding. Total expenditure exceeds total income in some income categories due to a number of factors including underreporting of income, borrowing, and the use of savings.

Share of spending

Percent of total average annual expenditures spent on personal care, reading, education, and tobacco products, by total before-tax income of consumer unit.

(consumer units include complete income reporters only)	all cu's	under $10,000	$10,000 to $19,999	$20,000 to $29,999	$30,000 to $39,999	$40,000 to $49,999	$50,000 and over
Number of consumer units (in thousands)	81,354	18,809	17,652	14,586	10,901	7,198	12,209
Average number of persons per cu	2.6	1.8	2.3	2.7	2.9	3.2	3.1
Average number of earners per cu	1.4	0.7	1.0	1.5	1.8	2.0	2.1
TOTAL AVERAGE ANNUAL EXPENDITURES	100.00%	100.00%	100.00%	100.00%	100.00%	100.00%	100.00%
PERSONAL CARE PRODUCTS AND SERVICES	**1.31%**	**1.34%**	**1.46%**	**1.30%**	**1.33%**	**1.27%**	**1.25%**
Personal care products	**0.68**	**0.68**	**0.83**	**0.68**	**0.63**	**0.65**	**0.64**
Hair care products	0.15	0.15	0.20	0.15	0.13	0.15	0.15
Hair accessories	0.02	0.01	0.02	0.02	0.01	0.02	0.02
Wigs and hairpieces	0.00	0.01	0.00	0.00	0.00	-	0.01
Oral hygiene products	0.07	0.09	0.09	0.07	0.07	0.06	0.06
Shaving products	0.03	0.02	0.06	0.03	0.03	0.03	0.03
Cosmetics, perfume, and bath products	0.29	0.30	0.35	0.29	0.28	0.27	0.28
Deodorant, feminine hygiene products, and miscellaneous items	0.09	0.09	0.10	0.10	0.07	0.10	0.08
Electrical personal care appliances	0.02	0.01	0.02	0.02	0.03	0.02	0.02
Personal care services	**0.63**	**0.65**	**0.63**	**0.62**	**0.70**	**0.62**	**0.60**
Personal care services/female	0.34	0.34	0.33	0.34	0.40	0.30	0.33
Personal care services/male	0.29	0.31	0.30	0.29	0.30	0.32	0.27
READING	**0.58%**	**0.63%**	**0.57%**	**0.57%**	**0.59%**	**0.61%**	**0.55%**
Newspapers	**0.24**	**0.33**	**0.28**	**0.26**	**0.23**	**0.22**	**0.20**
Magazines	**0.15**	**0.14**	**0.14**	**0.15**	**0.14**	**0.18**	**0.14**
Books purchased through book clubs	**0.04**	**0.02**	**0.04**	**0.04**	**0.05**	**0.04**	**0.04**
Books not purchased through book clubs	**0.13**	**0.12**	**0.10**	**0.11**	**0.15**	**0.14**	**0.15**
Encyclopedia and other reference book sets	**0.01**	**0.02**	**0.00**	**0.01**	**0.01**	**0.02**	**0.02**
EDUCATION	**1.23%**	**2.19%**	**0.86%**	**0.76%**	**1.02%**	**0.93%**	**1.60%**
College tuition	**0.67**	**1.47**	**0.39**	**0.40**	**0.59**	**0.34**	**0.88**
High school/elementary school tuition	**0.20**	**0.11**	**0.05**	**0.10**	**0.11**	**0.26**	**0.39**
Other school tuition	**0.06**	**0.09**	**0.07**	**0.04**	**0.04**	**0.06**	**0.06**
Books and supplies for college students	**0.10**	**0.30**	**0.12**	**0.07**	**0.08**	**0.04**	**0.08**

Percent of total average annual expenditures spent on personal care, reading, education, and tobacco products, by total before-tax income of consumer unit.

(continued from previous page)	all cu's	under $10,000	$10,000 to $19,999	$20,000 to $29,999	$30,000 to $39,999	$40,000 to $49,999	$50,000 and over
Books and supplies for high school and elementary students	0.02	0.02	0.03	0.02	0.02	0.03	0.02
Books and supplies for day care and nursery school	0.01	0.01	0.01	0.01	0.02	0.01	0.01
Miscellaneous school expenses and supplies	0.29	0.50	0.34	0.22	0.26	0.27	0.26
TOBACCO PRODUCTS AND SMOKING SUPPLIES	0.92%	1.63%	1.30%	1.06%	0.93%	0.66%	0.52%
Cigarettes	0.85	1.51	1.19	0.98	0.86	0.61	0.48
Other tobacco products	0.06	0.10	0.08	0.06	0.06	0.05	0.03
Smoking accessories	0.01	0.02	0.03	0.01	0.01	0.00	0.00

Note: Expenditures are not given (-) when the amount is too small to be reliable. Expenditures listed for a given category may not add to the total for that category because the listing is incomplete. "Reading," for example, includes "newsletters," which is omitted here because all the expenditure amounts were too small to be reliable. Numbers may not add to total due to rounding.

Indexed expenditures

(consumer units include complete income reporters only)	all cu's	under $10,000	$10,000 to $19,999	$20,000 to $29,999	$30,000 to $39,999	$40,000 to $49,999	$50,000 and over
Number of consumer units (in thousands)	81,354	18,809	17,652	14,586	10,901	7,198	12,209
Average number of persons per cu	2.6	1.8	2.3	2.7	2.9	3.2	3.1
Average number of earners per cu	1.4	0.7	1.0	1.5	1.8	2.0	2.1
TOTAL AVERAGE ANNUAL EXPENDITURES	100	43	69	94	120	142	198
PERSONAL CARE PRODUCTS AND SERVICES	100	44	77	94	122	139	188
Personal care products	100	43	84	95	111	137	187
Hair care products	100	43	88	92	102	139	192
Hair accessories	100	17	73	131	101	159	196
Wigs and hairpieces	100	71	63	55	140	-	253
Oral hygiene products	100	57	87	93	122	124	163
Shaving products	100	33	119	97	107	133	155
Cosmetics, perfume, and bath products	100	43	82	93	116	131	191
Deodorant, feminine hygiene products, and miscellaneous items	100	42	80	101	94	164	186
Electrical personal care appliances	100	27	51	92	151	146	221
Personal care services	100	44	68	93	133	140	190
Personal care services/female	100	43	67	93	143	125	195
Personal care services/male	100	46	69	92	122	157	184
READING	100	46	67	93	122	151	188
Newspapers	100	58	79	100	114	132	166
Magazines	100	41	67	99	117	169	184
Books purchased through book clubs	100	25	73	83	145	154	203
Books not purchased through book clubs	100	37	52	80	136	154	225
Encyclopedia and other reference book sets	100	52	18	70	104	244	240
EDUCATION	100	76	48	59	100	108	258
College tuition	100	94	40	56	106	71	260
High school/elementary school tuition	100	24	15	47	65	184	385
Other school tuition	100	69	83	59	91	141	206
Books and supplies for college students	100	129	82	63	92	63	155

Indexed average annual expenditures for personal care, reading, education, and tobacco products, by total before-tax income of consumer unit.

(continued from previous page)	all cu's	under $10,000	$10,000 to $19,999	$20,000 to $29,999	$30,000 to $39,999	$40,000 to $49,999	$50,000 and over
Books and supplies for high school and elementary students	100	44	73	91	126	154	181
Books and supplies for day care and nursery school	100	41	60	52	240	89	189
Miscellaneous school expenses and supplies	100	74	81	72	107	133	177
TOBACCO PRODUCTS AND SMOKING SUPPLIES	100	76	97	108	121	103	112
Cigarettes	100	76	96	109	122	103	112
Other tobacco products	100	74	98	105	118	116	112
Smoking accessories	100	80	190	107	69	36	56

Note: Expenditures are not given (-) when the amount is too small to be reliable. An index of 100 represents the average for all consumer units. An index of 132 means that the average for the subgroup is 32 percent above the average for all consumer units. An index of 68 indicates spending that is 32 percent below the overall average.

Aggregate expenditures, 1988

(consumer units include complete income reporters only)	all cu's	under $10,000	$10,000 to $19,999	$20,000 to $29,999	$30,000 to $39,999	$40,000 to $49,999	$50,000 and over
Number of consumer units (in thousands)	81,354	18,809	17,652	14,586	10,901	7,198	12,209
Average number of persons per cu	2.6	1.8	2.3	2.7	2.9	3.2	3.1
Average number of earners per cu	1.4	0.7	1.0	1.5	1.8	2.0	2.1
TOTAL AGGREGATE EXPENDITURES (in millions)	$2,148,492	$211,967	$319,117	$363,138	$345,121	$270,371	$638,777
PERSONAL CARE PRODUCTS AND SERVICES (in millions)	**$28,217**	**$2,831**	**$4,669**	**$4,736**	**$4,582**	**$3,446**	**$7,953**
Personal care products	**14,608**	**1,443**	**2,661**	**2,477**	**2,167**	**1,767**	**4,094**
Hair care products	3,307	327	630	545	452	405	949
Hair accessories	348	13	55	81	47	49	102
Wigs and hairpieces	84	14	12	9	16	-	33
Oral hygiene products	1,483	194	278	246	242	162	362
Shaving products	692	53	178	120	99	81	161
Cosmetics, perfume, and bath products	6,343	630	1,130	1,056	982	734	1,810
Deodorant, feminine hygiene products, and miscellaneous items	1,913	185	330	348	241	277	533
Electrical personal care appliances	435	27	48	72	88	56	144
Personal care services	**13,609**	**1,388**	**2,008**	**2,260**	**2,415**	**1,679**	**3,859**
Personal care services/female	7,322	722	1,062	1,217	1,389	806	2,125
Personal care services/male	6,274	666	943	1,040	1,024	871	1,731
READING (in millions)	**$12,405**	**$1,330**	**$1,817**	**$2,073**	**$2,022**	**$1,655**	**$3,509**
Newspapers	**5,206**	**693**	**888**	**931**	**794**	**606**	**1,294**
Magazines	**3,166**	**303**	**457**	**562**	**494**	**474**	**875**
Books purchased through book clubs	**865**	**50**	**136**	**129**	**168**	**118**	**264**
Books not purchased through book clubs	**2,867**	**248**	**323**	**412**	**524**	**390**	**969**
Encyclopedia and other reference book sets	**298**	**36**	**12**	**37**	**42**	**65**	**108**
EDUCATION (in millions)	**$26,396**	**$4,642**	**$2,741**	**$2,776**	**$3,519**	**$2,514**	**$10,203**
College tuition	**14,379**	**3,126**	**1,254**	**1,454**	**2,036**	**906**	**5,603**
High school/elementary school tuition	**4,328**	**237**	**145**	**366**	**375**	**705**	**2,500**
Other school tuition	**1,244**	**198**	**223**	**131**	**152**	**155**	**384**
Books and supplies for college students	**2,161**	**645**	**384**	**243**	**267**	**120**	**502**

Aggregate expenditures in 1988 for personal care, reading, education, and tobacco products, by total before-tax income of consumer unit.

(continued from previous page)	all cu's	under $10,000	$10,000 to $19,999	$20,000 to $29,999	$30,000 to $39,999	$40,000 to $49,999	$50,000 and over
Books and supplies for high school and elementary students	507	52	80	82	85	69	138
Books and supplies for day care and nursery school	205	20	27	19	66	16	58
Miscellaneous school expenses and supplies	6,239	1,061	1,092	806	890	731	1,658
TOBACCO PRODUCTS AND SMOKING SUPPLIES (in millions)	$19,720	$3,448	$4,144	$3,833	$3,193	$1,795	$3,306
Cigarettes	18,273	3,199	3,798	3,562	2,978	1,661	3,074
Other tobacco products	1,243	213	264	233	196	128	209
Smoking accessories	198	37	82	38	18	6	17

Note: Expenditures are not given (-) when the amount is too small to be reliable. Expenditures listed for a given category may not add to the total for that category because the listing is incomplete. "Reading," for example, includes "newsletters," which is omitted here because all the expenditure amounts were too small to be reliable. Numbers may not add to total due to rounding. The "all cu's" aggregates will differ slightly from table to table because they are the sums of the aggregates in each row.

PART III *Spending by type of household for personal care, reading, education, and tobacco products*

Married couples with children at home spend far more than the average household on education.

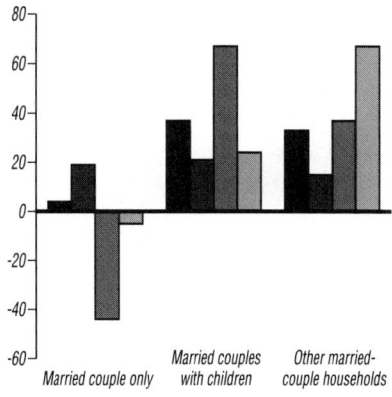

Single parents spend less than other kinds of households on reading materials and education.

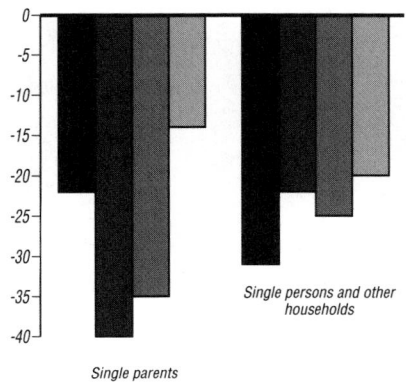

Single persons and other households

Single parents

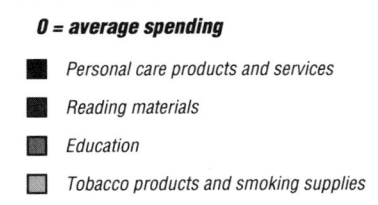

0 = average spending

◼ Personal care products and services

◼ Reading materials

◼ Education

◻ Tobacco products and smoking supplies

As with all other product and service categories, the personal care market is dominated by married couples. They spent over $21 billion on this category in 1988, and account for 68 percent of the personal care products and services market. Single-person and "other" households* spent $9 billion on these products and services, accounting for another 27 percent of the personal care market.

Married couples spend more than average on all items in this category, with overall spending 24 percent above average. Single parents spend 22 percent less than average on this category, while people who live alone or in "other" households spend 31 percent less than average. Single parents, however, spend well above average on hair care products and accessories.

Among married couples, those with children aged 18 or older are the peak spenders on personal care products and services, spending nearly 60 percent more than the average household. Married couples with school-aged children spend 42 percent more than average on this category, while those with preschoolers are average spenders.

Spending on tobacco is below average for married couples without children at home and for single-person,"other", and single-parent households. Spending on cigarettes rises from 3 percent above average for married couples with preschoolers to 41 percent above average for couples with children aged 18 or older. Married couples living with extended family members or unrelated people are the biggest spenders on tobacco products.

Reading and education

Married couples are the only households that spend more than average on reading materials. Couples without children at home spend 19 percent more than the average household on reading materials, while those with children at home spend 21 percent more than average. People who live alone or in "other" households and single parents spend less than average on all reading materials.

Sixty-seven percent of the education market is accounted for by married couples, 31 percent by single-person and "other" households. Married couples spend less than the average household on only books and supplies for college students and miscellaneous supplies. People who live alone or in "other" households (including many students) spend 25 percent more than the average household on college books and supplies and 122 percent more than average on tuition other than elementary, high school, and college tuition. Single parents are big spenders on books and supplies for elementary and high school students, with spending on that item 134 percent above average.

In this analysis, single-person households are grouped with "other" households. "Other" households are unrelated people living together and families that are not married-couple or single-parent families, such as siblings. Single-person households account for 72 percent of the households in this category.

Average expenditures

	all cu's	married couples	single parents	single persons and other cu's
Number of consumer units (in thousands)	94,862	52,010	5,716	37,136
Average number of persons per cu	2.6	3.3	2.9	1.5
Average number of earners per cu	1.4	1.7	1.0	0.9
Average total before-tax income	$28,540.00	$37,299.00	$16,276.00	$18,509.00
TOTAL AVERAGE ANNUAL EXPENDITURES	$25,891.85	$32,314.50	$18,615.80	$17,950.80
PERSONAL CARE PRODUCTS AND SERVICES	$333.52	$412.73	$259.34	$231.51
Personal care products	166.80	202.64	149.34	117.75
Hair care products	37.79	44.42	51.86	26.08
Hair accessories	3.95	4.83	4.92	2.53
Wigs and hairpieces	0.99	1.15	0.61	0.84
Oral hygiene products	16.77	20.39	11.91	12.28
Shaving products	8.02	10.27	3.77	5.40
Cosmetics, perfume, and bath products	72.52	87.67	50.34	54.00
Deodorant, feminine hygiene products, and miscellaneous items	21.71	27.75	21.64	13.00
Electrical personal care appliances	5.06	6.17	4.31	3.62
Personal care services	166.72	210.10	110.00	113.77
Personal care services/female	88.62	108.74	59.43	63.99
Personal care services/male	77.94	101.12	50.41	49.70
READING	$150.01	$180.07	$90.21	$117.12
Newspapers	64.51	78.20	38.19	49.39
Magazines	37.55	44.82	21.86	29.79
Books purchased through book clubs	10.06	12.26	6.54	7.52
Books not purchased through book clubs	34.33	39.37	21.75	29.19
Encyclopedia and other reference book sets	3.53	5.36	1.87	1.22
EDUCATION	$342.21	$416.28	$223.75	$256.68
College tuition	190.61	217.41	85.93	169.18
High school/elementary school tuition	57.65	93.92	35.07	10.33
Other school tuition	14.76	50.48	50.40	32.76
Books and supplies for college students	26.57	23.08	15.97	33.08

Average annual expenditures for personal care, reading, education, and tobacco products, by type of consumer unit.

(continued from previous page)	all cu's	married couples	single parents	single persons and other cu's
Books and supplies for high school and elementary students	6.04	8.48	14.14	1.38
Books and supplies for day care and nursery school	2.43	3.23	2.44	1.32
Miscellaneous school expenses and supplies	44.14	19.67	19.80	8.62
TOBACCO PRODUCTS AND SMOKING SUPPLIES	$241.94	$279.89	$208.59	$193.96
Cigarettes	224.00	256.57	204.36	181.41
Other tobacco products	15.40	21.61	3.53	8.54
Smoking accessories	2.54	1.71	0.69	4.01

Note: Expenditures listed for a given category may not add to the total for that category because the listing is incomplete. "Reading," for example, includes "newsletters," which is omitted here because all the expenditure amounts were too small to be reliable. Numbers may not add to total due to rounding. "Single parents" is one-parent consumer units with a child or children under age 18 living at home. "Other cu's" includes persons living with unrelated personsa and families other than married-couple and single-parent families.

Share of spending

	all cu's	married couples	single parents	single persons and other cu's
Number of consumer units (in thousands)	94,862	52,010	5,716	37,136
Average number of persons per cu	2.6	3.3	2.9	1.5
Average total before-tax income	$28,540	$37,299	$16,276	$18,509
TOTAL AVERAGE ANNUAL EXPENDITURES	100.00%	100.00%	100.00%	100.00%
PERSONAL CARE PRODUCTS AND SERVICES	**1.29%**	**1.28%**	**1.39%**	**1.29%**
Personal care products	**0.64**	**0.63**	**0.80**	**0.66**
Hair care products	0.15	0.14	0.28	0.15
Hair accessories	0.02	0.01	0.03	0.01
Wigs and hairpieces	0.00	0.00	0.00	0.00
Oral hygiene products	0.06	0.06	0.06	0.07
Shaving products	0.03	0.03	0.02	0.03
Cosmetics, perfume, and bath products	0.28	0.27	0.27	0.30
Deodorant, feminine hygiene products, and miscellaneous items	0.08	0.09	0.12	0.07
Electrical personal care appliances	0.02	0.02	0.02	0.02
Personal care services	**0.64**	**0.65**	**0.59**	**0.63**
Personal care services/female	0.34	0.34	0.32	0.36
Personal care services/male	0.30	0.31	0.27	0.28
READING	**0.58%**	**0.56%**	**0.48%**	**0.65%**
Newspapers	**0.25**	**0.24**	**0.21**	**0.28**
Magazines	**0.15**	**0.14**	**0.12**	**0.17**
Books purchased through book clubs	**0.04**	**0.04**	**0.04**	**0.04**
Books not purchased through book clubs	**0.13**	**0.12**	**0.12**	**0.16**
Encyclopedia and other reference book sets	**0.01**	**0.02**	**0.01**	**0.01**
EDUCATION	**1.32%**	**1.29%**	**1.20%**	**1.43%**
College tuition	**0.74**	**0.67**	**0.46**	**0.94**
High school/elementary school tuition	**0.22**	**0.29**	**0.19**	**0.06**
Other school tuition	**0.06**	**0.16**	**0.27**	**0.18**
Books and supplies for college students	**0.10**	**0.07**	**0.09**	**0.18**

Percent of total average annual expenditures spent on personal care, reading, education, and tobacco products, by type of consumer unit.

(continued from previous page)	all cu's	married couples	single parents	single persons and other cu's
Books and supplies for high school and elementary students	0.02	0.03	0.08	0.01
Books and supplies for day care and nursery school	0.01	0.01	0.01	0.01
Miscellaneous school expenses and supplies	0.17	0.06	0.11	0.05
TOBACCO PRODUCTS AND SMOKING SUPPLIES	0.93%	0.87%	1.12%	1.08%
Cigarettes	0.87	0.79	1.10	1.01
Other tobacco products	0.06	0.07	0.02	0.05
Smoking accessories	0.01	0.01	0.00	0.02

Note: Expenditures listed for a given category may not add to the total for that category because the listing is incomplete. "Reading," for example, includes "newsletters," which is omitted here because all the expenditure amounts were too small to be reliable. Numbers may not add to total due to rounding. "Single parents" is one-parent consumer units with a child or children under age 18 living at home. "Other cu's" includes persons living with unrelated persons and families other than married-couple and single-parent families.

Indexed expenditures

Indexed average annual expenditures for personal care, reading, education, and tobacco products, by type of consumer unit.

	all cu's	married couples	single parents	single persons and other cu's
Number of consumer units (in thousands)	94,862	52,010	5,716	37,136
Average number of persons per cu	2.6	3.3	2.9	1.5
Average number of earners per cu	1.4	1.7	1.0	0.9
Average total before-tax income	$28,540	$37,299	$16,276	$18,509
TOTAL AVERAGE ANNUAL EXPENDITURES	100	125	72	69
PERSONAL CARE PRODUCTS AND SERVICES	100	124	78	69
Personal care products	100	121	90	71
Hair care products	100	118	137	69
Hair accessories	100	122	125	64
Wigs and hairpieces	100	116	62	85
Oral hygiene products	100	122	71	73
Shaving products	100	128	47	67
Cosmetics, perfume, and bath products	100	121	69	74
Deodorant, feminine hygiene products, and miscellaneous items	100	128	100	60
Electrical personal care appliances	100	122	85	72
Personal care services	100	126	66	68
Personal care services/female	100	123	67	72
Personal care services/male	100	130	65	64
READING	100	120	60	78
Newspapers	100	121	59	77
Magazines	100	119	58	79
Books purchased through book clubs	100	122	65	75
Books not purchased through book clubs	100	115	63	85
Encyclopedia and other reference book sets	100	152	53	35
EDUCATION	100	122	65	75
College tuition	100	114	45	89
High school/elementary school tuition	100	163	61	18
Other school tuition	100	342	341	222
Books and supplies for college students	100	87	60	125

Indexed average annual expenditures for personal care, reading, education, and tobacco products, by type of consumer unit.

(continued from previous page)	all cu's	married couples	single parents	single persons and other cu's
Books and supplies for high school and elementary students	100	140	234	23
Books and supplies for day care and nursery school	100	133	100	54
Miscellaneous school expenses and supplies	100	45	45	20
TOBACCO PRODUCTS AND SMOKING SUPPLIES	100	116	86	80
Cigarettes	100	115	91	81
Other tobacco products	100	140	23	55
Smoking accessories	100	67	27	158

Note: An index of 100 represents the average for all consumer units. An index of 132 means that the average for the subgroup is 32 percent above the average for all consumer units. An index of 68 indicates spending that is 32 percent below the overall average. "Single parents" is one-parent consumer units with a child or children under age 18 living at home. "Other cu's" includes persons living with unrelated persons and families other than married-couple and single-parent families.

Aggregate expenditures, 1988

	all cu's	married couples	single parents	single persons and other cu's
Number of consumer units (in thousands)	94,862	52,010	5,716	37,136
Average number of persons per cu	2.6	3.3	2.9	1.5
Average number of earners per cu	1.4	1.7	1.0	0.9
Aggregate before-tax income	$2,720,305	$1,939,921	$93,034	$687,350
TOTAL AGGREGATE EXPENDITURES	$2,453,706	$1,680,677	$106,408	$666,621
PERSONAL CARE PRODUCTS AND SERVICES (in millions)	$31,546	$21,466	$1,482	$8,597
Personal care products	15,766	10,539	854	4,373
Hair care products	3,575	2,310	296	969
Hair accessories	373	251	28	94
Wigs and hairpieces	94	60	3	31
Oral hygiene products	1,585	1,060	68	456
Shaving products	756	534	22	201
Cosmetics, perfume, and bath products	6,853	4,560	288	2,005
Deodorant, feminine hygiene products, and miscellaneous items	2,050	1,443	124	483
Electrical personal care appliances	480	321	25	134
Personal care services	15,781	10,927	629	4,225
Personal care services/female	8,372	5,656	340	2,376
Personal care services/male	7,393	5,259	288	1,846
READING (in millions)	$14,230	$9,365	$516	$4,349
Newspapers	6,120	4,067	218	1,834
Magazines	3,562	2,331	125	1,106
Books purchased through book clubs	954	638	37	279
Books not purchased through book clubs	3,256	2,048	124	1,084
Encyclopedia and other reference book sets	335	279	11	45
EDUCATION (in millions)	$32,462	$21,651	$1,279	$9,532
College tuition	18,081	11,307	491	6,283
High school/elementary school tuition	5,469	4,885	200	384
Other school tuition	4,130	2,625	288	1,217
Books and supplies for college students	2,520	1,200	91	1,228

Aggregate expenditures in 1988 for personal care, reading, education, and tobacco products, by type of consumer unit.

(continued from previous page)

	all cu's	married couples	single parents	single persons and other cu's
Books and supplies for high school **and elementary students**	573	441	81	51
Books and supplies for day care **and nursery school**	231	168	14	49
Miscellaneous school expenses and supplies	1,456	1,023	113	320
TOBACCO PRODUCTS AND **SMOKING SUPPLIES (in millions)**	$22,952	$14,557	$1,192	$7,203
Cigarettes	21,249	13,344	1,168	6,737
Other tobacco products	1,461	1,124	20	317
Smoking accessories	242	89	4	149

Note: Expenditures listed for a given category may not add to the total for that category because the listing is incomplete. "Reading," for example, includes "newsletters," which is omitted here because all the expenditure amounts were too small to be reliable. Numbers may not add to total due to rounding. "Single parents" is one-parent consumer units with a child or children under age 18 living at home. "Other cu's" includes persons living with unrelated persons and families other than married-couple and single-parent families. The "all cu's" aggregates will differ slightly from table to table because they are the sums of the aggregates in each row.

Average expenditures

	all cu's	all married couples	married couple only	all married couples with children	AGE OF OLDEST CHILD			other married couples
					under 6	6 to 17	18 or older	
Number of consumer units (in thousands)	94,862	52,010	20,227	28,100	5,858	14,194	8,047	3,684
Average number of persons per cu	2.6	3.3	2	3.9	3.5	4.1	3.9	5.1
Average number of earners per cu	1.4	1.7	1.2	2.1	1.7	1.9	2.7	2.4
Average total before-tax income	$28,540.00	$37,299.00	$33,825.00	$39,354.00	$34,318.00	$38,039.00	$45,596.00	$40,846.00
TOTAL AVERAGE ANNUAL EXPENDITURES	$25,891.85	$32,314.50	$27,954.50	$35,015.30	$30,942.80	$35,248.40	$37,763.90	$35,739.60
PERSONAL CARE PRODUCTS AND SERVICES	$333.52	$412.73	$347.25	$456.24	$332.15	$473.97	$529.00	$442.64
Personal care products	166.80	202.64	157.81	232.02	178.95	236.56	271.04	227.07
Hair care products	37.79	44.42	33.12	52.46	37.74	54.46	61.92	45.48
Hair accessories	3.95	4.83	2.43	6.75	7.75	6.75	5.85	3.42
Wigs and hairpieces	0.99	1.15	-	1.62	-	0.84	3.91	1.52
Oral hygiene products	16.77	20.39	18.95	21.65	15.28	21.07	28.60	18.67
Shaving products	8.02	10.27	8.90	11.09	8.83	11.48	12.38	11.63
Cosmetics, perfume, and bath products	72.52	87.67	69.38	97.62	75.23	100.33	112.70	113.92
Deodorant, feminine hygiene products, and miscellaneous items	21.71	27.75	19.75	33.65	28.17	33.25	39.45	26.82
Electrical personal care appliances	5.06	6.17	4.87	7.17	5.56	8.37	6.24	5.62
Personal care services	166.72	210.10	189.44	224.22	153.20	237.42	257.96	215.58
Personal care services/female	88.62	108.74	109.54	108.73	68.05	118.64	126.21	104.12
Personal care services/male	77.94	101.12	79.70	115.23	85.13	118.47	131.43	111.11
READING	$150.01	$180.07	$178.31	$182.24	$149.73	$186.47	$198.41	$173.19
Newspapers	64.51	78.20	82.88	75.54	60.29	72.42	92.15	72.76
Magazines	37.55	44.82	46.04	44.16	39.13	44.15	47.82	43.22
Books purchased through book clubs	10.06	12.26	10.42	13.40	11.08	14.50	13.15	13.64
Books not purchased through book clubs	34.33	39.37	37.66	40.59	33.54	41.82	43.57	39.48
Encyclopedia and other reference book sets	3.53	5.36	1.30	8.44	5.25	13.57	1.72	4.09
EDUCATION	$342.21	$416.28	$192.14	$570.67	$142.09	$521.16	$969.04	$469.57
College tuition	190.61	217.41	148.18	270.06	49.82	122.12	691.36	195.94
High school/elementary school tuition	57.65	93.92	2.10	151.11	17.32	237.59	95.97	161.81
Other school tuition	14.76	50.48	18.88	72.20	53.63	84.12	63.78	58.59
Books and supplies for college students	26.57	23.08	12.80	30.82	13.73	15.28	70.67	20.52

Average annual expenditures for personal care, reading, education, and tobacco products, by married couples with and without children.

(continued from previous page)

	all cu's	all married couples	married couple only	all married couples with children	AGE OF OLDEST CHILD			other married couples
					under 6	6 to 17	18 or older	
Books and supplies for high school and elementary students	6.04	8.48	-	14.11	0.59	22.81	8.60	10.44
Books and supplies for day care and nursery school	2.43	3.23	1.34	4.36	1.28	5.38	4.83	4.95
Miscellaneous school expenses and supplies	44.14	19.67	8.54	27.99	5.71	33.86	33.85	17.31
TOBACCO PRODUCTS AND SMOKING SUPPLIES	$241.94	$279.89	$228.70	$300.38	$250.53	$293.22	$349.26	$404.66
Cigarettes	224.00	256.57	201.91	278.68	229.80	277.85	315.74	388.05
Other tobacco products	15.40	21.61	25.02	20.02	18.28	14.14	31.65	15.04
Smoking accessories	2.54	1.71	1.78	1.68	2.44	1.23	1.87	1.57

Note: Expenditures are not given (-) when the amount is too small to be reliable. Expenditures listed for a given category may not add to the total for that category because the listing is incomplete. "Reading," for example, includes "newsletters," which is omitted here because all the expenditure amounts were too small to be reliable. Other married couples include extended family members or unrelated persons in addition to the married couple. Numbers may not add to total due to rounding.

Share of spending

	all cu's	all married couples	married couple only	all married couples with children	AGE OF OLDEST CHILD under 6	AGE OF OLDEST CHILD 6 to 17	AGE OF OLDEST CHILD 18 or older	other married couples
Number of consumer units (in thousands)	94,862	52,010	20,227	28,100	5,858	14,194	8,047	3,684
Average number of persons per cu	2.6	3.3	2	3.9	3.5	4.1	3.9	5.1
Average total before-tax income	$28,540	$37,299	$33,825	$39,354	$34,318	$38,039	$45,596	$40,846
TOTAL AVERAGE ANNUAL EXPENDITURES	100.00%	100.00%	100.00%	100.00%	100.00%	100.00%	100.00%	100.00%
PERSONAL CARE PRODUCTS AND SERVICES	**1.29%**	**1.28%**	**1.24%**	**1.30%**	**1.07%**	**1.34%**	**1.40%**	**1.24%**
Personal care products	**0.64**	**0.63**	**0.56**	**0.66**	**0.58**	**0.67**	**0.72**	**0.64**
Hair care products	0.15	0.14	0.12	0.15	0.12	0.15	0.16	0.13
Hair accessories	0.02	0.01	0.01	0.02	0.03	0.02	0.02	0.01
Wigs and hairpieces	0.00	0.00	-	0.00	-	0.00	0.01	0.00
Oral hygiene products	0.06	0.06	0.07	0.06	0.05	0.06	0.08	0.05
Shaving products	0.03	0.03	0.03	0.03	0.03	0.03	0.03	0.03
Cosmetics, perfume, and bath products	0.28	0.27	0.25	0.28	0.24	0.28	0.30	0.32
Deodorant, feminine hygiene products, and miscellaneous items	0.08	0.09	0.07	0.10	0.09	0.09	0.10	0.08
Electrical personal care appliances	0.02	0.02	0.02	0.02	0.02	0.02	0.02	0.02
Personal care services	**0.64**	**0.65**	**0.68**	**0.64**	**0.50**	**0.67**	**0.68**	**0.60**
Personal care services/female	0.34	0.34	0.39	0.31	0.22	0.34	0.33	0.29
Personal care services/male	0.30	0.31	0.29	0.33	0.28	0.34	0.35	0.31
READING	**0.58%**	**0.56%**	**0.64%**	**0.52%**	**0.48%**	**0.53%**	**0.53%**	**0.48%**
Newspapers	**0.25**	**0.24**	**0.30**	**0.22**	**0.19**	**0.21**	**0.24**	**0.20**
Magazines	**0.15**	**0.14**	**0.16**	**0.13**	**0.13**	**0.13**	**0.13**	**0.12**
Books purchased through book clubs	**0.04**	**0.04**	**0.04**	**0.04**	**0.04**	**0.04**	**0.03**	**0.04**
Books not purchased through book clubs	**0.13**	**0.12**	**0.13**	**0.12**	**0.11**	**0.12**	**0.12**	**0.11**
Encyclopedia and other reference book sets	**0.01**	**0.02**	**0.00**	**0.02**	**0.02**	**0.04**	**0.00**	**0.01**
EDUCATION	**1.32%**	**1.29%**	**0.69%**	**1.63%**	**0.46%**	**1.48%**	**2.57%**	**1.31%**
College tuition	**0.74**	**0.67**	**0.53**	**0.77**	**0.16**	**0.35**	**1.83**	**0.55**
High school/elementary school tuition	**0.22**	**0.29**	**0.01**	**0.43**	**0.06**	**0.67**	**0.25**	**0.45**
Other school tuition	**0.06**	**0.16**	**0.07**	**0.21**	**0.17**	**0.24**	**0.17**	**0.16**
Books and supplies for college students	**0.10**	**0.07**	**0.05**	**0.09**	**0.04**	**0.04**	**0.19**	**0.06**

Percent of total average annual expenditures spent on personal care, reading, education, and tobacco products, by married couples with and without children.

(continued from previous page)

	all cu's	all married couples	married couple only	all married couples with children	AGE OF OLDEST CHILD			other married couples
					under 6	6 to 17	18 or older	
Books and supplies for high school and elementary students	0.02	0.03	-	0.04	0.00	0.06	0.02	0.03
Books and supplies for day care and nursery school	0.01	0.01	0.00	0.01	0.00	0.02	0.01	0.01
Miscellaneous school expenses and supplies	0.17	0.06	0.03	0.08	0.02	0.10	0.09	0.05
TOBACCO PRODUCTS AND SMOKING SUPPLIES	0.93%	0.87%	0.82%	0.86%	0.81%	0.83%	0.92%	1.13%
Cigarettes	0.87	0.79	0.72	0.80	0.74	0.79	0.84	1.09
Other tobacco products	0.06	0.07	0.09	0.06	0.06	0.04	0.08	0.04
Smoking accessories	0.01	0.01	0.01	0.00	0.01	0.00	0.00	0.00

Note: Expenditures are not given (-) when the amount is too small to be reliable. Expenditures listed for a given category may not add to the total for that category because the listing is incomplete. "Reading," for example, includes "newsletters," which is omitted here because all the expenditure amounts were too small to be reliable. Other married couples include extended family members or unrelated persons in addition to the married couple. Numbers may not add to total due to rounding.

Indexed expenditures

	all cu's	all married couples	married couple only	all married couples with children	AGE OF OLDEST CHILD			other married couples
					under 6	6 to 17	18 or older	
Number of consumer units (in thousands)	94,862	52,010	20,227	28,100	5,858	14,194	8,047	3,684
Average number of persons per cu	2.6	3.3	2	3.9	3.5	4.1	3.9	5.1
Average number of earners per cu	1.4	1.7	1.2	2.1	1.7	1.9	2.7	2.4
Average total before-tax income	$28,540	$37,299	$33,825	$39,354	$34,318	$38,039	$45,596	$40,846
TOTAL AVERAGE ANNUAL EXPENDITURES	100	125	108	135	120	136	146	138
PERSONAL CARE PRODUCTS AND SERVICES	100	124	104	137	100	142	159	133
Personal care products	100	121	95	139	107	142	162	136
Hair care products	100	118	88	139	100	144	164	120
Hair accessories	100	122	62	171	196	171	148	87
Wigs and hairpieces	100	116	-	164	-	85	395	154
Oral hygiene products	100	122	113	129	91	126	171	111
Shaving products	100	128	111	138	110	143	154	145
Cosmetics, perfume, and bath products	100	121	96	135	104	138	155	157
Deodorant, feminine hygiene products, and miscellaneous items	100	128	91	155	130	153	182	124
Electrical personal care appliances	100	122	96	142	110	165	123	111
Personal care services	100	126	114	134	92	142	155	129
Personal care services/female	100	123	124	123	77	134	142	117
Personal care services/male	100	130	102	148	109	152	169	143
READING	100	120	119	121	100	124	132	115
Newspapers	100	121	128	117	93	112	143	113
Magazines	100	119	123	118	104	118	127	115
Books purchased through book clubs	100	122	104	133	110	144	131	136
Books not purchased through book clubs	100	115	110	118	98	122	127	115
Encyclopedia and other reference book sets	100	152	37	239	149	384	49	116
EDUCATION	100	122	56	167	42	152	283	137
College tuition	100	114	78	142	26	64	363	103
High school/elementary school tuition	100	163	4	262	30	412	166	281
Other school tuition	100	342	128	489	363	570	432	397
Books and supplies for college students	100	87	48	116	52	58	266	77

Indexed average annual expenditures for personal care, reading, education, and tobacco products, by married couples with and without children.

(continued from previous page)	all cu's	all married couples	married couple only	all married couples with children	AGE OF OLDEST CHILD			other married couples
					under 6	6 to 17	18 or older	
Books and supplies for high school and elementary students	100	140	-	234	10	378	142	173
Books and supplies for day care and nursery school	100	133	55	179	53	221	199	204
Miscellaneous school expenses and supplies	100	45	19	63	13	77	77	39
TOBACCO PRODUCTS AND SMOKING SUPPLIES	100	116	95	124	104	121	144	167
Cigarettes	100	115	90	124	103	124	141	173
Other tobacco products	100	140	162	130	119	92	206	98
Smoking accessories	100	67	70	66	96	48	74	62

Note: An index of 100 represents the average for all consumer units. An index of 132 means that the average for the subgroup is 32 percent above the average for all consumer units. An index of 68 indicates spending that is 32 percent below the overall average. Expenditures are not given (-) when the amount is too small to be reliable. Other married couples include extended family members or unrelated persons in addition to the married couple.

Aggregate expenditures, 1988

Aggregate expenditures in 1988 for personal care, reading, education, and tobacco products, by married couples with and without children.

	all cu's	all married couples	married couple only	all married couples with children	AGE OF OLDEST CHILD			other married couples
					under 6	6 to 17	18 or older	
Number of consumer units (in thousands)	*94,862*	*52,010*	*20,227*	*28,100*	*5,858*	*14,194*	*8,047*	*3,684*
Average number of persons per cu	*2.6*	*3.3*	*2*	*3.9*	*3.5*	*4.1*	*3.9*	*5.1*
Average number of earners per cu	*1.4*	*1.7*	*1.2*	*2.1*	*1.7*	*1.9*	*2.7*	*2.4*
Aggregate before-tax income	*$2,722,910*	*$1,942,526*	*$684,178*	*$1,107,871*	*$201,035*	*$539,926*	*$366,911*	*$150,477*
TOTAL AGGREGATE EXPENDITURES	*$2,455,594*	*$1,682,565*	*$565,436*	*$985,465*	*$181,263*	*$500,316*	*$303,886*	*$131,665*
PERSONAL CARE PRODUCTS AND SERVICES (in millions)	**$31,664**	**$21,585**	**$7,024**	**$12,930**	**$1,946**	**$6,728**	**$4,257**	**$1,631**
Personal care products	**15,842**	**10,616**	**3,192**	**6,587**	**1,048**	**3,358**	**2,181**	**837**
Hair care products	3,595	2,330	670	1,492	221	773	498	168
Hair accessories	372	250	49	188	45	96	47	13
Wigs and hairpieces	84	49	-	43	-	12	31	6
Oral hygiene products	1,595	1,071	383	619	90	299	230	69
Shaving products	759	537	180	314	52	163	100	43
Cosmetics, perfume, and bath products	6,888	4,595	1,403	2,772	441	1,424	907	420
Deodorant, feminine hygiene products, and miscellaneous items	2,059	1,453	399	954	165	472	317	99
Electrical personal care appliances	480	321	99	202	33	119	50	21
Personal care services	**15,823**	**10,969**	**3,832**	**6,343**	**897**	**3,370**	**2,076**	**794**
Personal care services/female	8,414	5,697	2,216	3,098	399	1,684	1,016	384
Personal care services/male	7,393	5,259	1,612	3,238	499	1,682	1,058	409
READING (in millions)	**$14,230**	**$9,365**	**$3,607**	**$5,120**	**$877**	**$2,647**	**$1,597**	**$638**
Newspapers	**6,120**	**4,067**	**1,676**	**2,123**	**353**	**1,028**	**742**	**268**
Magazines	**3,562**	**2,331**	**931**	**1,241**	**229**	**627**	**385**	**159**
Books purchased through book clubs	**954**	**638**	**211**	**377**	**65**	**206**	**106**	**50**
Books not purchased through book clubs	**3,256**	**2,048**	**762**	**1,141**	**196**	**594**	**351**	**145**
Encyclopedia and other reference book sets	**335**	**279**	**26**	**237**	**31**	**193**	**14**	**15**
EDUCATION (in millions)	**$32,455**	**$21,644**	**$3,886**	**$16,028**	**$832**	**$7,397**	**$7,798**	**$1,730**
College tuition	**18,082**	**11,308**	**2,997**	**7,589**	**292**	**1,733**	**5,563**	**722**
High school/elementary school tuition	**5,469**	**4,885**	**42**	**4,246**	**101**	**3,372**	**772**	**596**
Other school tuition	**4,124**	**2,619**	**382**	**2,021**	**314**	**1,194**	**513**	**216**
Books and supplies for college students	**2,520**	**1,200**	**259**	**866**	**80**	**217**	**569**	**76**

Aggregate expenditures in 1988 for personal care, reading, education, and tobacco products, by married couples with and without children.

(continued from previous page)	all cu's	all married couples	married couple only	all married couples with children	AGE OF OLDEST CHILD			other married couples
					under 6	6 to 17	18 or older	
Books and supplies for high school and elementary students	566	434	-	396	3	324	69	38
Books and supplies for day care and nursery school	231	168	27	123	7	76	39	18
Miscellaneous school expenses and supplies	1,456	1,023	173	786	33	481	272	64
TOBACCO PRODUCTS AND SMOKING SUPPLIES (in millions)	$22,952	$14,557	$4,626	$8,440	$1,468	$4,162	$2,810	$1,491
Cigarettes	21,249	13,344	4,084	7,831	1,346	3,944	2,541	1,430
Other tobacco products	1,461	1,124	506	562	107	201	255	55
Smoking accessories	241	89	36	47	14	17	15	6

Note: Expenditures are not given (-) when the amount is too small to be reliable. Expenditures listed for a given category may not add to the total for that category because the listing is incomplete. "Reading," for example, includes "newsletters," which is omitted here because all the expenditure amounts were too small to be reliable. Other married couples include extended family members or unrelated persons in addition to the married couple. Numbers may not add to total due to rounding. The "all cu's" aggregates will differ slightly from table to table because they are the sums of the aggregates in each row. In this table they include aggregates for single parents, single persons, and other types of consumer units, in addition to all married couples. Aggregates for "all married couples" and "all married couples with children" are sums of the appropriate aggregates in each row.

10

Financial Products and Services, Cash Contributions, Gifts, and Other Items

Personal insurance, mainly life insurance, and cash contributions were allocated smaller expenditure shares in 1988 than in 1984. The share devoted to cash contributions, which include items such as alimony and cash gifts to household members, in addition to charitable contributions, also declined slightly.

Pensions and Social Security; gifts of products and services, and miscellaneous items such as funeral costs and legal fees each had small budget-share gains. Increases in the tax rate and tax base help to explain the bigger share allocated to Social Security.

Five-year spending trends for financial products and services, cash contributions, gifts, and miscellaneous items

Share of household expenditures devoted to financial products and services, cash contributions, gifts, and miscellaneous items, and change in share, 1984 to 1988.

	1984	1985	1986	1987	1988	change 1984 to 1988
Total average annual expenditures	100.0%	100.0%	100.0%	100.0%	100.0%	0.0%
LIFE INSURANCE, OTHER INSURANCES EXCEPT HEALTH	1.4%	1.2%	1.2%	1.2%	1.2%	-0.2%
PENSIONS AND SOCIAL SECURITY	7.3%	7.4%	7.7%	7.7%	7.5%	0.2%
CASH CONTRIBUTIONS	3.2%	3.4%	3.1%	3.0%	2.7%	-0.5%
GIFTS OF PRODUCTS AND SERVICES	3.0%	3.3%	3.0%	3.1%	3.2%	0.2%
MISCELLANEOUS ITEMS	2.1%	2.3%	2.2%	2.3%	2.2%	0.1%

Note: The amounts spent on gifts of products and services are also included in the expenditures for those items given elsewhere in the Consumer Expenditure Survey. The "miscellaneous" figure for 1988 on this table is different from others in this chapter because some items in "miscellaneous" are moved to the category "other financial products and services" in the detailed tables.

PART I
Spending by age for financial products and services, cash contributions, gifts, and other items

In the financial services category, the youngest householders spend more than average only on bank service fees. In the 25-to-34-age group, Social Security deductions, bank fees, and finance charges command above-average spending. Householders aged 65 to 74 make the largest contributions to churches, while those aged 75 or older spend the most on safety deposit boxes and gifts of cash.

Three percent of the average household budget is spent on gifts. Householders aged 45 to 54 are the most extravagant givers, as their gift spending is nearly 60 percent higher than average. In this category, younger households spend more than average only on gift watches and jewelry. Householders aged 35 to 44 spend more on baby clothes, while 65-to-74-year-olds favor appliances and houseware gifts.

Occupational expenses and legal fees are highest for householders aged 35 to 54. They account for over half of the total market for those items. Householders aged 65 to 74 spend more than others on funerals, cemetery lots, and vaults.

Householders aged 35 to 54 spend far more than the average household on financial products and services...

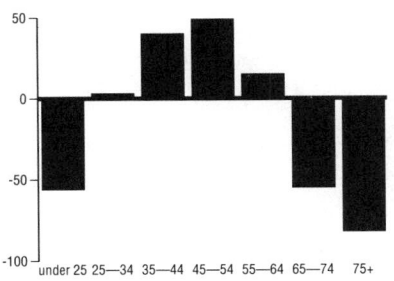

...while 45-to-64-year-olds outspend others on cash contributions...

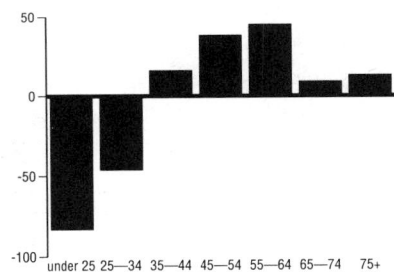

...and on gifts.

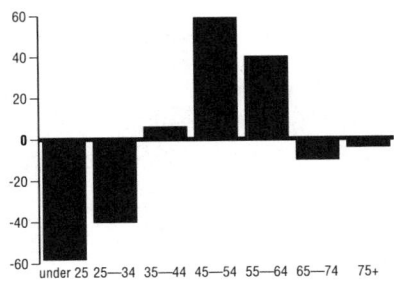

0 = average spending

Average expenditures

	all cu's	under 25	25 to 34	35 to 44	45 to 54	55 to 64	65 to 74	75+
Number of consumer units (in thousands)	94,862	7,216	21,985	19,911	13,601	12,546	11,319	8,284
Average number of persons per cu	2.6	1.8	2.8	3.3	2.9	2.2	2.0	1.5
Average total before-tax income	$28,540.00	$14,827.00	$28,318.00	$36,428.00	$39,934.00	$29,979.00	$20,704.00	$13,707.00
TOTAL AVERAGE ANNUAL EXPENDITURES	$25,891.85	$16,373.17	$25,770.27	$33,077.72	$33,204.87	$25,765.35	$20,119.90	$13,339.49
FINANCIAL PRODUCTS AND SERVICES	$2,511.27	$1,093.67	$2,575.53	$3,511.51	$3,753.64	$2,882.11	$1,127.99	$460.21
Life and other personal insurances except health	314.13	46.55	240.67	394.28	417.63	417.72	290.42	255.11
Retirement, pensions, Social Security	1,934.96	925.79	2,052.30	2,756.09	2,991.21	2,191.02	681.67	119.49
Deductions for government retirement	56.72	16.56	29.69	88.41	130.56	65.68	21.10	1.11
Deductions for railroad retirement	5.35	-	0.74	8.50	10.95	8.53	5.77	0.00
Deductions for private pensions	135.29	23.65	132.72	190.81	266.83	140.50	38.35	14.51
Deductions for self-employment IRAs and Keoghs	274.01	17.38	140.31	344.77	445.38	609.15	190.86	6.95
Deductions for Social Security	1,463.60	868.15	1,748.84	2,123.59	2,137.49	1,367.16	425.60	96.91
Other products and services	262.18	121.33	282.56	361.14	344.80	273.37	155.90	85.61
Accounting fees	41.68	8.01	27.41	46.02	46.23	72.18	43.45	42.32
Checking account fees and other bank services	24.33	25.19	29.32	33.29	29.62	19.73	10.23	6.38
Safety deposit box rentals	5.82	0.55	1.95	4.74	7.81	8.41	9.70	10.83
Finance charges other than auto and mortgage	190.35	87.58	223.88	277.09	261.14	173.05	92.52	26.08
CASH CONTRIBUTIONS	$693.36	$120.01	$374.92	$806.13	$956.57	$1,002.39	$753.21	$784.90
Contributions to non-cu member, including alimony and students at college	175.67	33.75	102.98	313.91	321.29	231.70	46.59	12.35
Cash gifts to non-cu member	135.30	20.64	39.17	57.45	150.92	253.87	234.30	336.95
Contributions to charities	64.35	8.64	34.66	74.07	90.07	114.77	51.63	67.08
Contributions to church	283.68	56.04	184.09	335.34	317.24	347.69	372.76	348.41
Contributions to educational organizations	16.76	-	5.28	14.06	30.18	36.87	25.54	3.70
Political contributions	10.65	-	5.98	5.51	32.60	10.86	13.46	4.26
GIFTS OF PRODUCTS AND SERVICES	$839.24	$393.27	$550.76	$885.57	$1,346.64	$1,141.93	$750.53	$711.01
Clothing for males aged 2 and older	69.63	20.90	48.34	53.87	86.21	170.83	62.17	31.90
Clothing for females aged 2 and older	79.76	56.23	58.97	77.60	151.32	90.51	71.50	33.53
Clothing for babies	26.94	16.40	26.49	36.99	38.31	35.80	18.68	6.73

Average annual expenditures for financial products and services, contributions, gifts, and miscellaneous items, by age of reference person.

(continued from previous page)	all cu's	under 25	25 to 34	35 to 44	45 to 54	55 to 64	65 to 74	75+
Jewelry and watches	25.67	27.52	33.60	25.09	35.78	19.49	21.88	2.36
Small appliances and housewares	16.76	9.71	15.08	16.90	24.57	22.06	18.36	3.78
Household textiles	9.66	0.61	8.64	6.03	14.09	18.86	9.32	8.12
All other non-cash gifts	610.82	261.90	359.64	669.09	996.36	784.38	548.62	624.59
MISCELLANEOUS ITEMS	$315.94	$95.64	$232.67	$421.88	$430.02	$326.18	$355.78	$215.09
Legal fees	99.76	27.99	87.31	179.57	120.92	96.72	46.58	46.08
Occupational expenses	89.07	41.08	79.26	141.24	141.16	59.76	27.98	73.84
Funeral expenses	47.12	5.55	8.14	29.00	51.86	77.22	128.99	65.10
Cemetery lots or vaults	21.28	1.12	3.37	7.67	22.05	18.82	93.56	22.79
Unspecified fees and personal services	58.71	19.90	54.59	64.40	94.03	73.66	58.67	7.28

Note: Expenditures are not given (-) when the amount is too small to be reliable. Numbers may not add to total due to rounding. The amounts spent on "gifts of products and services" are also included in the expenditures listed for the item elsewhere in the Consumer Expenditure Survey. Expenditures listed for items in a given category may not add to the total for that category because the listing is incomplete. "Cash contributions," for example, includes "other contributions," which is omitted here.

Share of spending

	all cu's	under 25	25 to 34	35 to 44	45 to 54	55 to 64	65 to 74	75+
Number of consumer units (in thousands)	94,862	7,216	21,985	19,911	13,601	12,546	11,319	8,284
Average number of persons per cu	2.6	1.8	2.8	3.3	2.9	2.2	2.0	1.5
Average total before-tax income	$28,540	$14,827	$28,318	$36,428	$39,934	$29,979	$20,704	$13,707
TOTAL AVERAGE ANNUAL EXPENDITURES	100.00%	100.00%	100.00%	100.00%	100.00%	100.00%	100.00%	100.00%
FINANCIAL PRODUCTS AND SERVICES	9.70%	6.68%	9.99%	10.62%	11.30%	11.19%	5.61%	3.45%
Life and other personal insurances except health	1.21	0.28	0.93	1.19	1.26	1.62	1.44	1.91
Retirement, pensions, Social Security	7.47	5.65	7.96	8.33	9.01	8.50	3.39	0.90
Deductions for government retirement	0.22	0.10	0.12	0.27	0.39	0.25	0.10	0.01
Deductions for railroad retirement	0.02	-	0.00	0.03	0.03	0.03	0.03	0.00
Deductions for private pensions	0.52	0.14	0.52	0.58	0.80	0.55	0.19	0.11
Deductions for self-employment IRAs and Keoghs	1.06	0.11	0.54	1.04	1.34	2.36	0.95	0.05
Deductions for Social Security	5.65	5.30	6.79	6.42	6.44	5.31	2.12	0.73
Other products and services	1.01	0.74	1.10	1.09	1.04	1.06	0.77	0.64
Accounting fees	0.16	0.05	0.11	0.14	0.14	0.28	0.22	0.32
Checking account fees and other bank services	0.09	0.15	0.11	0.10	0.09	0.08	0.05	0.05
Safety deposit box rentals	0.02	0.00	0.01	0.01	0.02	0.03	0.05	0.08
Finance charges other than auto and mortgage	0.74	0.53	0.87	0.84	0.79	0.67	0.46	0.20
CASH CONTRIBUTIONS	2.68%	0.73%	1.45%	2.44%	2.88%	3.89%	3.74%	5.88%
Contributions to non-CU member, including alimony and students at college	0.68	0.21	0.40	0.95	0.97	0.90	0.23	0.09
Cash gifts to non-CU member	0.52	0.13	0.15	0.17	0.45	0.99	1.16	2.53
Contributions to charities	0.25	0.05	0.13	0.22	0.27	0.45	0.26	0.50
Contributions to church	1.10	0.34	0.71	1.01	0.96	1.35	1.85	2.61
Contributions to educational organizations	0.06	-	0.02	0.04	0.09	0.14	0.13	0.03
Political contributions	0.04	-	0.02	0.02	0.10	0.04	0.07	0.03
GIFTS OF PRODUCTS AND SERVICES	3.24%	2.40%	2.14%	2.68%	4.06%	4.43%	3.73%	5.33%
Clothing for males aged 2 and older	0.27	0.13	0.19	0.16	0.26	0.66	0.31	0.24
Clothing for females aged 2 and older	0.31	0.34	0.23	0.23	0.46	0.35	0.36	0.25
Clothing for babies	0.10	0.10	0.10	0.11	0.12	0.14	0.09	0.05

Percent of total average annual expenditures spent on financial products and services, contributions, gifts, and miscellaneous items, by age of reference person.

(continued from previous page)	all cu's	under 25	25 to 34	35 to 44	45 to 54	55 to 64	65 to 74	75+
Jewelry and watches	0.10	0.17	0.13	0.08	0.11	0.08	0.11	0.02
Small appliances and housewares	0.06	0.06	0.06	0.05	0.07	0.09	0.09	0.03
Household textiles	0.04	0.00	0.03	0.02	0.04	0.07	0.05	0.06
All other non-cash gifts	2.36	1.60	1.40	2.02	3.00	3.04	2.73	4.68
MISCELLANEOUS ITEMS	1.22%	0.58%	0.90%	1.28%	1.30%	1.27%	1.77%	1.61%
Legal fees	0.39	0.17	0.34	0.54	0.36	0.38	0.23	0.35
Occupational expenses	0.34	0.25	0.31	0.43	0.43	0.23	0.14	0.55
Funeral expenses	0.18	0.03	0.03	0.09	0.16	0.30	0.64	0.49
Cemetery lots or vaults	0.08	0.01	0.01	0.02	0.07	0.07	0.47	0.17
Unspecified fees and personal services	0.23	0.12	0.21	0.19	0.28	0.29	0.29	0.05

Note: Expenditures are not given (-) when the amount is too small to be reliable. Numbers may not add to total due to rounding. The amounts spent on "gifts of products and services" are also included in the expenditures listed for the item elsewhere in the Consumer Expenditure Survey. Expenditures listed for items in a given category may not add to the total for that category because the listing is incomplete. "Cash contributions," for example, includes "other contributions," which is omitted here.

Indexed expenditures

	all cu's	under 25	25 to 34	35 to 44	45 to 54	55 to 64	65 to 74	75+
Number of consumer units (in thousands)	94,862	7,216	21,985	19,911	13,601	12,546	11,319	8,284
Average number of persons per cu	2.6	1.8	2.8	3.3	2.9	2.2	2.0	1.5
Average total before-tax income	$28,540	$14,827	$28,318	$36,428	$39,934	$29,979	$20,704	$13,707
TOTAL AVERAGE ANNUAL EXPENDITURES	100	63	100	128	128	100	78	52
FINANCIAL PRODUCTS AND SERVICES	100	44	103	140	149	115	45	18
Life and other personal insurances except health	100	15	77	126	133	133	92	81
Retirement, pensions, Social Security	100	48	106	142	155	113	35	6
Deductions for government retirement	100	29	52	156	230	116	37	2
Deductions for railroad retirement	100	-	14	159	205	159	108	0
Deductions for private pensions	100	17	98	141	197	104	28	11
Deductions for self-employment IRAs and Keoghs	100	6	51	126	163	222	70	3
Deductions for Social Security	100	59	119	145	146	93	29	7
Other products and services	100	46	108	138	132	104	59	33
Accounting fees	100	19	66	110	111	173	104	102
Checking account fees and other bank services	100	104	121	137	122	81	42	26
Safety deposit box rentals	100	9	34	81	134	145	167	186
Finance charges other than auto and mortgage	100	46	118	146	137	91	49	14
CASH CONTRIBUTIONS	100	17	54	116	138	145	109	113
Contributions to non-cu member, including alimony and students at college	100	19	59	179	183	132	27	7
Cash gifts to non-cu member	100	15	29	42	112	188	173	249
Contributions to charities	100	13	54	115	140	178	80	104
Contributions to church	100	20	65	118	112	123	131	123
Contributions to educational organizations	100	-	32	84	180	220	152	22
Political contributions	100	-	56	52	306	102	126	40
GIFTS OF PRODUCTS AND SERVICES	100	47	66	106	160	136	89	85
Clothing for males aged 2 and older	100	30	69	77	124	245	89	46
Clothing for females aged 2 and older	100	70	74	97	190	113	90	42
Clothing for babies	100	61	98	137	142	133	69	25

Indexed average annual expenditures for financial products and services, contributions, gifts, and miscellaneous items, by age of reference person.

(continued from previous page)	all cu's	under 25	25 to 34	35 to 44	45 to 54	55 to 64	65 to 74	75+
Jewelry and watches	100	107	131	98	139	76	85	9
Small appliances and housewares	100	58	90	101	147	132	110	23
Household textiles	100	6	89	62	146	195	96	84
All other non-cash gifts	100	43	59	110	163	128	90	102
MISCELLANEOUS ITEMS	100	30	74	134	136	103	113	68
Legal fees	100	28	88	180	121	97	47	46
Occupational expenses	100	46	89	159	158	67	31	83
Funeral expenses	100	12	17	62	110	164	274	138
Cemetery lots or vaults	100	5	16	36	104	88	440	107
Unspecified fees and personal services	100	34	93	110	160	125	100	12

Note: An index of 100 represents the average for all consumer units. An index of 132 means that the average for the subgroup is 32 percent above the average for all consumer units. An index of 68 indicates spending that is 32 percent below the overall average. Expenditures are not given (-) when the amount is too small to be reliable. The amounts spent on "gifts of products and services" are also included in the expenditures listed for the item elsewhere in the Consumer Expenditure Survey.

Aggregate expenditures, 1988

Aggregate expenditures in 1988 for financial products and services, contributions, gifts, and miscellaneous items, by age of reference person.

	all cu's	under 25	25 to 34	35 to 44	45 to 54	55 to 64	65 to 74	75+
Number of consumer units (in thousands)	94,862	7,216	21,985	19,911	13,601	12,546	11,319	8,284
Average number of persons per cu	2.6	1.8	2.8	3.3	2.9	2.2	2.0	1.5
Aggregate before-tax income (in millions)	$2,722,037	$106,992	$622,571	$725,318	$543,142	$376,117	$234,349	$113,549
TOTAL AGGREGATE EXPENDITURES (in millions)	$2,456,432	$118,149	$566,559	$658,610	$451,619	$323,252	$227,737	$110,504
FINANCIAL PRODUCTS AND SERVICES (in millions)	$238,225	$7,892	$56,623	$69,918	$51,053	$36,159	$12,768	$3,812
Life and other personal insurances except health	29,799	336	5,291	7,851	5,680	5,241	3,287	2,113
Retirement, pensions, Social Security	183,554	6,681	45,120	54,877	40,683	27,489	7,716	990
Deductions for government retirement	5,380	119	653	1,760	1,776	824	239	9
Deductions for railroad retirement	507	-	16	169	149	107	65	0
Deductions for private pensions	12,834	171	2,918	3,799	3,629	1,763	434	120
Deductions for self-employment IRAs and Keoghs	25,993	125	3,085	6,865	6,058	7,642	2,160	58
Deductions for Social Security	138,840	6,265	38,448	42,283	29,072	17,152	4,817	803
Other products and services	24,871	876	6,212	7,191	4,690	3,430	1,765	709
Accounting fees	3,953	58	603	916	629	906	492	351
Checking account fees and other bank services	2,308	182	645	663	403	248	116	53
Safety deposit box rentals	552	4	43	94	106	106	110	90
Finance charges other than auto and mortgage	18,057	632	4,922	5,517	3,552	2,171	1,047	216
CASH CONTRIBUTIONS (in millions)	$65,773	$866	$8,243	$16,051	$13,010	$12,576	$8,526	$6,502
Contributions to non-cu member, including alimony and students at college	16,664	244	2,264	6,250	4,370	2,907	527	102
Cash gifts to non-cu member	12,835	149	861	1,144	2,053	3,185	2,652	2,791
Contributions to charities	6,104	62	762	1,475	1,225	1,440	584	556
Contributions to church	26,911	404	4,047	6,677	4,315	4,362	4,219	2,886
Contributions to educational organizations	1,589	-	116	280	410	463	289	31
Political contributions	1,008	-	131	110	443	136	152	35
GIFTS OF PRODUCTS AND SERVICES (in millions)	$79,612	$2,838	$12,108	$17,633	$18,316	$14,327	$8,495	$5,890
Clothing for males aged 2 and older	6,570	151	1,063	1,073	1,173	2,143	704	264
Clothing for females aged 2 and older	7,528	406	1,296	1,545	2,058	1,136	809	278
Clothing for babies	2,675	118	582	737	521	449	211	56

Aggregate expenditures in 1988 for financial products and services, contributions, gifts, and miscellaneous items, by age of reference person.

(continued from previous page)	all cu's	under 25	25 to 34	35 to 44	45 to 54	55 to 64	65 to 74	75+
Jewelry and watches	2,435	199	739	500	487	245	248	20
Small appliances and housewares	1,588	70	332	336	334	277	208	31
Household textiles	915	4	190	120	192	237	105	67
All other non-cash gifts	57,895	1,890	7,907	13,322	13,551	9,841	6,210	5,174
MISCELLANEOUS ITEMS (in millions) ..	$29,955	$690	$5,115	$8,400	$5,849	$4,092	$4,027	$1,782
Legal fees	9,464	202	1,920	3,575	1,645	1,213	527	382
Occupational expenses	8,449	296	1,743	2,812	1,920	750	317	612
Funeral expenses	4,470	40	179	577	705	969	1,460	539
Cemetery lots or vaults	2,019	8	74	153	300	236	1,059	189
Unspecified fees and personal services	5,553	144	1,200	1,282	1,279	924	664	60

Note: Expenditures are not given (-) when the amount is too small to be reliable. Numbers may not add to total due to rounding. The amounts spent on "gifts of products and services" are also included in the expenditures listed for the item elsewhere in the Consumer Expenditure Survey. Expenditures listed for items in a given category may not add to the total for that category because the listing is incomplete. "Cash contributions," for example, includes "other contributions," which is omitted here. The "all cu's" aggregates will differ from table to table because they are the sums of the aggregates in each row.

Aggregate expenditures, 1995

Aggregate expenditures for financial products and services, contributions, gifts, and miscellaneous items, by age of householder in 1995 (in 1988 dollars).

	all households	under 25	25 to 34	35 to 44	45 to 54	55 to 64	65 to 74	75+
Number of households (in thousands)	**100,308**	**4,316**	**19,927**	**23,916**	**18,035**	**12,233**	**12,006**	**9,876**
FINANCIAL PRODUCTS AND SERVICES (in millions)	**$261,066**	**$4,720**	**$51,323**	**$83,981**	**$67,697**	**$35,257**	**$13,543**	**$4,545**
Life and other personal insurances except health	**33,075**	**201**	**4,796**	**9,430**	**7,532**	**5,110**	**3,487**	**2,519**
Retirement, pensions, Social Security	**200,920**	**3,996**	**40,896**	**65,915**	**53,946**	**26,803**	**8,184**	**1,180**
Deductions for government retirement	6,200	71	592	2,114	2,355	803	253	11
Deductions for railroad retirement	589	-	15	203	197	104	69	0
Deductions for private pensions	14,445	102	2,645	4,563	4,812	1,719	460	143
Deductions for self-employment IRAs and Keoghs	28,961	75	2,796	8,246	8,032	7,452	2,291	69
Deductions for Social Security	150,725	3,747	34,849	50,788	38,550	16,724	5,110	957
Other products and services	**27,071**	**524**	**5,631**	**8,637**	**6,218**	**3,344**	**1,872**	**845**
Accounting fees	4,338	35	546	1,101	834	883	522	418
Checking account fees and other bank services	2,451	109	584	796	534	241	123	63
Safety deposit box rentals	622	2	39	113	141	103	116	107
Finance charges other than auto and mortgage	19,661	378	4,461	6,627	4,710	2,117	1,111	258
CASH CONTRIBUTIONS (in millions)	**$73,577**	**$518**	**$7,471**	**$19,279**	**$17,252**	**$12,262**	**$9,043**	**$7,752**
Contributions to non-cu member, including alimony and students at college	**19,015**	**146**	**2,052**	**7,507**	**5,794**	**2,834**	**559**	**122**
Cash gifts to non-cu member	**14,212**	**89**	**781**	**1,374**	**2,722**	**3,106**	**2,813**	**3,328**
Contributions to charities	**6,810**	**37**	**691**	**1,771**	**1,624**	**1,404**	**620**	**662**
Contributions to church	**29,821**	**242**	**3,668**	**8,020**	**5,721**	**4,253**	**4,475**	**3,441**
Contributions to educational organizations	**1,780**	**-**	**105**	**336**	**544**	**451**	**307**	**37**
Political contributions	**1,175**	**-**	**119**	**132**	**588**	**133**	**162**	**42**
GIFTS OF PRODUCTS AND SERVICES (in millions)	**$84,182**	**$1,697**	**$10,975**	**$21,179**	**$24,287**	**$13,969**	**$9,011**	**$7,022**
Clothing for males aged 2 and older	**7,048**	**90**	**963**	**1,288**	**1,555**	**2,090**	**746**	**315**
Clothing for females aged 2 and older	**8,300**	**243**	**1,175**	**1,856**	**2,729**	**1,107**	**858**	**331**
Clothing for babies	**2,903**	**71**	**528**	**885**	**691**	**438**	**224**	**66**

Aggregate expenditures for financial products and services, contributions, gifts, and miscellaneous items, by age of householder in 1995 (in 1988 dollars).

(continued from previous page)	all households	under 25	25 to 34	35 to 44	45 to 54	55 to 64	65 to 74	75+
Jewelry and watches	2,558	119	670	600	645	238	263	23
Small appliances and housewares	1,717	42	300	404	443	270	220	37
Household textiles	996	3	172	144	254	231	112	80
All other non-cash gifts	64,619	1,130	7,167	16,002	17,969	9,595	6,587	6,168
MISCELLANEOUS ITEMS (in millions) ..	$33,280	$413	$4,636	$10,090	$7,755	$3,990	$4,271	$2,124
Legal fees	10,534	121	1,740	4,295	2,181	1,183	559	455
Occupational expenses	9,477	177	1,579	3,378	2,546	731	336	729
Funeral expenses	4,951	24	162	694	935	945	1,549	643
Cemetery lots or vaults	2,232	5	67	183	398	230	1,123	225
Unspecified fees and personal services	6,087	86	1,088	1,540	1,696	901	704	72

Note: Expenditures are not given (-) when the amount is too small to be reliable. Numbers may not add to total due to rounding. The amounts spent on "gifts of products and services" are also included in the expenditures listed for the item elsewhere in the Consumer Expenditure Survey. Expenditures listed for items in a given category may not add to the total for that category because the listing is incomplete. "Cash contributions," for example, includes "other contributions," which is omitted here. Households are used here because projections of the number of consumer units in 1995 and 2000 are not available. Projections show how annual aggregate expenditures will change as the number of households in the age groups changes in 1995 and 2000. Household projections are from the Census Bureau. Projections are based on the average annual expenditures in 1988 and have not been adjusted for price increases or for changes in expenditure patterns.

Aggregate expenditures, 2000

Number of households (in thousands)	all households 105,933	under 25 4,442	25 to 34 18,004	35 to 44 25,339	45 to 54 21,603	55 to 64 13,903	65 to 74 11,516	75+ 11,126
FINANCIAL PRODUCTS AND SERVICES (in millions)	**$279,476**	**$4,858**	**$46,370**	**$88,978**	**$81,090**	**$40,070**	**$12,990**	**$5,120**
Life and other personal insurances except health	**35,543**	**207**	**4,333**	**9,991**	**9,022**	**5,808**	**3,344**	**2,838**
Retirement, pensions, Social Security	**215,159**	**4,112**	**36,950**	**69,837**	**64,619**	**30,462**	**7,850**	**1,329**
Deductions for government retirement	6,837	74	535	2,240	2,820	913	243	12
Deductions for railroad retirement	650	-	13	215	237	119	66	0
Deductions for private pensions	15,650	105	2,389	4,835	5,764	1,953	442	161
Deductions for self-employment IRAs and Keoghs	31,705	77	2,526	8,736	9,622	8,469	2,198	77
Deductions for Social Security	160,315	3,856	31,486	53,810	46,176	19,008	4,901	1,078
Other products and services	**28,774**	**539**	**5,087**	**9,151**	**7,449**	**3,801**	**1,795**	**952**
Accounting fees	4,669	36	493	1,166	999	1,004	500	471
Checking account fees and other bank services	2,586	112	528	844	640	274	118	71
Safety deposit box rentals	676	2	35	120	169	117	112	120
Finance charges other than auto and mortgage	20,844	389	4,031	7,021	5,641	2,406	1,065	290
CASH CONTRIBUTIONS (in millions)	**$79,717**	**$533**	**$6,750**	**$20,427**	**$20,665**	**$13,936**	**$8,674**	**$8,733**
Contributions to non-cu member, including alimony and students at college	**20,794**	**150**	**1,854**	**7,954**	**6,941**	**3,221**	**537**	**137**
Cash gifts to non-cu member	**15,490**	**92**	**705**	**1,456**	**3,260**	**3,530**	**2,698**	**3,749**
Contributions to charities	**7,422**	**38**	**624**	**1,877**	**1,946**	**1,596**	**595**	**746**
Contributions to church	**31,917**	**249**	**3,314**	**8,497**	**6,853**	**4,834**	**4,293**	**3,876**
Contributions to educational organizations	**1,951**	**-**	**95**	**356**	**652**	**513**	**294**	**41**
Political contributions	**1,305**	**-**	**108**	**140**	**704**	**151**	**155**	**47**
GIFTS OF PRODUCTS AND SERVICES (in millions)	**$95,624**	**$1,747**	**$9,916**	**$22,439**	**$29,091**	**$15,876**	**$8,643**	**$7,911**
Clothing for males aged 2 and older	**7,636**	**93**	**870**	**1,365**	**1,862**	**2,375**	**716**	**355**
Clothing for females aged 2 and older	**9,002**	**250**	**1,062**	**1,966**	**3,269**	**1,258**	**823**	**373**
Clothing for babies	**3,102**	**73**	**477**	**937**	**828**	**498**	**215**	**75**

Aggregate expenditures for financial products and services, contributions, gifts, and miscellaneous items, by age of householder in 2000 (in 1988 dollars).

(continued from previous page)	all households	under 25	25 to 34	35 to 44	45 to 54	55 to 64	65 to 74	75+
Jewelry and watches	2,685	122	605	636	773	271	252	26
Small appliances and housewares	1,834	43	272	428	531	307	211	42
Household textiles	1,075	3	156	153	304	262	107	90
All other non-cash gifts	70,289	1,163	6,475	16,954	21,524	10,905	6,318	6,949
MISCELLANEOUS ITEMS (in millions)	$35,619	$425	$4,189	$10,690	$9,290	$4,535	$4,097	$2,393
Legal fees	11,252	124	1,572	4,550	2,612	1,345	536	513
Occupational expenses	10,212	182	1,427	3,579	3,049	831	322	822
Funeral expenses	5,310	25	147	735	1,120	1,074	1,485	724
Cemetery lots or vaults	2,329	5	61	194	476	262	1,077	254
Unspecified fees and personal services	6,515	88	983	1,632	2,031	1,024	676	81

Note: Expenditures are not given (-) when the amount is too small to be reliable. Numbers may not add to total due to rounding. The amounts spent on "gifts of products and services" are also included in the expenditures listed for the item elsewhere in the Consumer Expenditure Survey. Expenditures listed for items in a given category may not add to the total for that category because the listing is incomplete. "Cash contributions," for example, includes "other contributions," which is omitted here. Households are used here because projections of the number of consumer units in 1995 and 2000 are not available. Projections show how annual aggregate expenditures will change as the number of households in the age groups changes in 1995 and 2000. Household projections are from the Census Bureau. Projections are based on the average annual expenditures in 1988 and have not been adjusted for price increases or for changes in expenditure patterns.

PART II
Spending by income for financial products and services, cash contributions, gifts, and other items

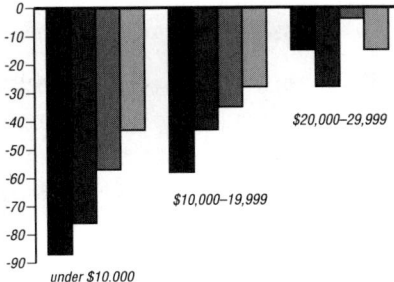

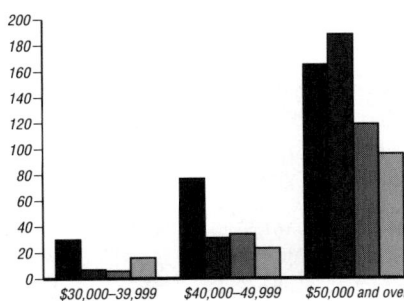

0 = average spending

- Financial products and services
- Cash contributions
- Gifts of products and services
- Miscellaneous items

High income households devote a much larger share of their budgets to financial products and services than low-income households. Households in the $50,000-plus income bracket spend over 14 percent of their budgets on things like life insurance, private pensions, and Social Security payments. In contrast, just 7 percent of the budgets of households with incomes of $10,000 to $20,000 goes to those items. Part of the reason for these differences is that Social Security and pension contributions are linked to income.

Annual average spending on financial products and services rises from $367 for the lowest income group to $7,429 for households with the highest incomes—an increase of nearly 2000 percent. Spending for financial products and services in general is below average for households with incomes under $30,000, and well above average among households with incomes of $30,000 or more. Nearly three-quarters of the market for these products is dominated by households with incomes of $30,000 or more.

Households with incomes under $30,000 spend above average amounts on just two items—checking account fees and finance charges other than those for auto loans and mortgages. Higher income households spend more than the average household on every financial product and service.

Cash contributions, gifts, and others

In general, households with incomes under $30,000 spend less than average on gifts and cash contributions. There are a few items for which their spending is above average, however. On gifts of jewelry and watches, funeral expenses, and cemetery lots or vaults, households in the lower income groups spend more than average. Since 87 percent of households headed by a person aged 75 or older have incomes under $30,000, it is no surpise that funeral expenses are above average for these income groups.

Households with incomes of $30,000 or more account for a major share of these markets. They are responsible for 69 percent of all cash contributions, 59 percent of gifts, and 56 percent of miscellaneous expenses including legal fees, occupational expenses, and funeral products and services.

Average expenditures

Average annual expenditures for financial products and services, contributions, gifts, and miscellaneous items, by total before-tax income of consumer unit.

(consumer units include complete income reporters only)	all cu's	under $10,000	$10,000 to $19,999	$20,000 to $29,999	$30,000 to $39,999	$40,000 to $49,999	$50,000 and over
Number of consumer units (in thousands)	81,354	18,809	17,652	14,586	10,901	7,198	12,209
Average number of persons per cu	2.6	1.8	2.3	2.7	2.9	3.2	3.1
Average number of earners per cu	1.4	0.7	1.0	1.5	1.8	2.0	2.1
TOTAL AVERAGE ANNUAL EXPENDITURES	$26,389.07	$11,269.43	$18,078.25	$24,896.36	$31,659.60	$37,562.00	$52,320.19
FINANCIAL PRODUCTS AND SERVICES	$2,806.56	$367.05	$1,166.50	$2,382.55	$3,642.22	$4,955.80	$7,429.44
Life and other personal insurances except health	324.17	107.96	204.36	301.69	354.87	494.30	729.64
Retirement, pensions, Social Security	2,208.19	177.05	799.92	1,795.89	2,911.44	4,048.02	6,153.42
Deductions for government retirement	65.36	1.13	14.06	48.33	82.39	119.99	211.42
Deductions for railroad retirement	6.23	-	0.62	-	19.12	16.29	13.24
Deductions for private pensions	156.10	1.02	24.68	84.28	160.98	328.55	564.77
Deductions for self-employment IRAs and Keoghs	297.28	28.78	55.89	181.88	333.32	494.25	1,049.52
Deductions for Social Security	1,683.21	145.84	704.66	1,481.16	2,315.63	3,088.94	4,314.48
Other products and services	274.20	82.04	162.22	284.97	375.91	413.48	546.38
Accounting fees	39.87	18.70	19.78	33.62	52.32	47.89	93.19
Checking account fees and other bank services	25.19	11.90	21.08	28.95	33.62	38.14	31.99
Safety deposit box rentals	5.69	3.14	3.85	5.05	5.86	6.20	12.59
Finance charges other than auto and mortgage	203.45	48.30	117.52	217.35	284.11	321.25	408.61
CASH CONTRIBUTIONS	$730.19	$174.51	$415.17	$529.28	$781.16	$956.30	$2,102.92
Contributions to non-cu member, including alimony and students at college	179.06	27.75	85.00	127.13	209.98	235.99	549.04
Cash gifts to non-cu member	149.99	34.36	62.23	109.45	161.57	162.57	485.66
Contributions to charities	69.16	14.97	25.21	32.84	65.78	99.80	244.53
Contributions to church	295.54	92.41	234.15	242.30	322.49	423.81	661.17
Contributions to educational organizations	17.97	3.58	1.86	2.95	12.56	12.48	89.44
Political contributions	7.29	-	1.29	2.38	6.73	10.74	30.82
GIFTS OF PRODUCTS AND SERVICES	$848.64	$362.58	$547.97	$818.10	$897.91	$1,134.16	$1,861.68
Clothing for males aged 2 and older	72.77	21.70	59.08	69.84	52.18	86.35	186.07
Clothing for females aged 2 and older	79.14	27.91	70.03	80.32	89.47	129.15	131.22
Clothing for babies	27.88	9.73	21.30	22.35	41.10	37.49	55.18

Average annual expenditures for financial products and services, contributions, gifts, and miscellaneous items, by total before-tax income of consumer unit.

(continued from previous page)	all cu's	under $10,000	$10,000 to $19,999	$20,000 to $29,999	$30,000 to $39,999	$40,000 to $49,999	$50,000 and over
Jewelry and watches	27.72	6.53	17.64	30.54	38.06	30.32	60.83
Small appliances and housewares	16.79	5.48	8.69	12.60	14.00	27.52	46.85
Household textiles	10.53	2.29	7.44	9.35	4.44	12.84	33.26
All other non-cash gifts	613.81	288.95	363.80	593.10	658.66	810.49	1,348.27
MISCELLANEOUS ITEMS	$284.76	$162.60	$206.25	$241.80	$331.43	$349.87	$559.24
Legal fees	104.50	37.42	66.67	109.06	133.34	62.67	255.98
Occupational expenses	90.26	23.26	41.85	50.40	131.46	184.94	218.49
Funeral expenses	49.32	71.69	62.52	57.05	13.57	49.05	18.62
Cemetery lots or vaults	17.66	23.28	19.71	12.86	13.74	12.52	18.29
Unspecified fees and personal services	23.02	6.95	15.50	12.43	39.32	40.69	47.86

Note: Expenditures are not given (-) when the amount is too small to be reliable. Numbers may not add to total due to rounding. Expenditures listed for items in a given category may not add to the total for that category because the listing is incomplete. "Cash contributions," for example, includes "other contributions," which is omitted here. The amounts spent on "gifts of products and services" are also included in the expenditures listed for the item elsewhere in the Consumer Expenditure Survey. Total expenditure exceeds total income in some income categories due to a number of factors including underreporting of income, borrowing, and the use of savings.

Share of spending

(consumer units include complete income reporters only)	all cu's	under $10,000	$10,000 to $19,999	$20,000 to $29,999	$30,000 to $39,999	$40,000 to $49,999	$50,000 and over
Number of consumer units (in thousands)	81,354	18,809	17,652	14,586	10,901	7,198	12,209
Average number of persons per cu	2.6	1.8	2.3	2.7	2.9	3.2	3.1
Average number of earners per cu	1.4	0.7	1.0	1.5	1.8	2.0	2.1
TOTAL AVERAGE ANNUAL EXPENDITURES	100.00%	100.00%	100.00%	100.00%	100.00%	100.00%	100.00%
FINANCIAL PRODUCTS AND SERVICES	10.64%	3.26%	6.45%	9.57%	11.50%	13.19%	14.20%
Life and other personal insurances except health	1.23	0.96	1.13	1.21	1.12	1.32	1.39
Retirement, pensions, Social Security	8.37	1.57	4.42	7.21	9.20	10.78	11.76
Deductions for government retirement	0.25	0.01	0.08	0.19	0.26	0.32	0.40
Deductions for railroad retirement	0.02	-	0.00	-	0.06	0.04	0.03
Deductions for private pensions	0.59	0.01	0.14	0.34	0.51	0.87	1.08
Deductions for self-employment IRAs and Keoghs	1.13	0.26	0.31	0.73	1.05	1.32	2.01
Deductions for Social Security	6.38	1.29	3.90	5.95	7.31	8.22	8.25
Other products and services	1.04	0.73	0.90	1.14	1.19	1.10	1.04
Accounting fees	0.15	0.17	0.11	0.14	0.17	0.13	0.18
Checking account fees and other bank services	0.10	0.11	0.12	0.12	0.11	0.10	0.06
Safety deposit box rentals	0.02	0.03	0.02	0.02	0.02	0.02	0.02
Finance charges other than auto and mortgage	0.77	0.43	0.65	0.87	0.90	0.86	0.78
CASH CONTRIBUTIONS	2.77%	1.55%	2.30%	2.13%	2.47%	2.55%	4.02%
Contributions to non-CU member, including alimony and students at college	0.68	0.25	0.47	0.51	0.66	0.63	1.05
Cash gifts to non-CU member	0.57	0.30	0.34	0.44	0.51	0.43	0.93
Contributions to charities	0.26	0.13	0.14	0.13	0.21	0.27	0.47
Contributions to church	1.12	0.82	1.30	0.97	1.02	1.13	1.26
Contributions to educational organizations	0.07	0.03	0.01	0.01	0.04	0.03	0.17
Political contributions	0.03	-	0.01	0.01	0.02	0.03	0.06
GIFTS OF PRODUCTS AND SERVICES	3.22%	3.22%	3.03%	3.29%	2.84%	3.02%	3.56%
Clothing for males aged 2 and older	0.28	0.19	0.33	0.28	0.16	0.23	0.36
Clothing for females aged 2 and older	0.30	0.25	0.39	0.32	0.28	0.34	0.25
Clothing for babies	0.11	0.09	0.12	0.09	0.13	0.10	0.11

Percent of total average annual expenditures spent on financial products and services, contributions, gifts, and miscellaneous items, by total before-tax income of consumer unit.

(continued from previous page)	all cu's	under $10,000	$10,000 to $19,999	$20,000 to $29,999	$30,000 to $39,999	$40,000 to $49,999	$50,000 and over
Jewelry and watches	0.11	0.06	0.10	0.12	0.12	0.08	0.12
Small appliances and housewares	0.06	0.05	0.05	0.05	0.04	0.07	0.09
Household textiles	0.04	0.02	0.04	0.04	0.01	0.03	0.06
All other non-cash gifts	2.33	2.56	2.01	2.38	2.08	2.16	2.58
MISCELLANEOUS ITEMS	1.08%	1.44%	1.14%	0.97%	1.05%	0.93%	1.07%
Legal fees	0.40	0.33	0.37	0.44	0.42	0.17	0.49
Occupational expenses	0.34	0.21	0.23	0.20	0.42	0.49	0.42
Funeral expenses	0.19	0.64	0.35	0.23	0.04	0.13	0.04
Cemetery lots or vaults	0.07	0.21	0.11	0.05	0.04	0.03	0.03
Unspecified fees and personal services	0.09	0.06	0.09	0.05	0.12	0.11	0.09

Note: Expenditures are not given (-) when the amount is too small to be reliable. Numbers may not add to total due to rounding. The amounts spent on "gifts of products and services" are also included in the expenditures listed for the item elsewhere in the Consumer Expenditure Survey. Expenditures listed for items in a given category may not add to the total for that category because the listing is incomplete. "Cash contributions," for example, includes "other contributions," which is omitted here.

Indexed expenditures

(consumer units include complete income reporters only)	all cu's	under $10,000	$10,000 to $19,999	$20,000 to $29,999	$30,000 to $39,999	$40,000 to $49,999	$50,000 and over
Number of consumer units (in thousands)	81,354	18,809	17,652	14,586	10,901	7,198	12,209
Average number of persons per cu	2.6	1.8	2.3	2.7	2.9	3.2	3.1
Average number of earners per cu	1.4	0.7	1.0	1.5	1.8	2.0	2.1
TOTAL AVERAGE ANNUAL EXPENDITURES	100	43	69	94	120	142	198
FINANCIAL PRODUCTS AND SERVICES	100	13	42	85	130	177	265
Life and other personal insurances except health	100	33	63	93	109	152	225
Retirement, pensions, Social Security	100	8	36	81	132	183	279
Deductions for government retirement	100	2	22	74	126	184	323
Deductions for railroad retirement	100	-	10	-	307	261	213
Deductions for private pensions	100	1	16	54	103	210	362
Deductions for self-employment IRAs and Keoghs	100	10	19	61	112	166	353
Deductions for Social Security	100	9	42	88	138	184	256
Other products and services	100	30	59	104	137	151	199
Accounting fees	100	47	50	84	131	120	234
Checking account fees and other bank services	100	47	84	115	133	151	127
Safety deposit box rentals	100	55	68	89	103	109	221
Finance charges other than auto and mortgage	100	24	58	107	140	158	201
CASH CONTRIBUTIONS	100	24	57	72	107	131	288
Contributions to non-cu member, including alimony and students at college	100	16	47	71	117	132	307
Cash gifts to non-cu member	100	23	41	73	108	108	324
Contributions to charities	100	22	36	47	95	144	354
Contributions to church	100	31	79	82	109	143	224
Contributions to educational organizations	100	20	10	16	70	69	498
Political contributions	100	-	18	33	92	147	423
GIFTS OF PRODUCTS AND SERVICES	100	43	65	96	106	134	219
Clothing for males aged 2 and older	100	30	81	96	72	119	256
Clothing for females aged 2 and older	100	35	88	101	113	163	166
Clothing for babies	100	35	76	80	147	134	198

Indexed average annual expenditures for financial products and services, contributions, gifts, and miscellaneous items, by total before-tax income of consumer unit.

(continued from previous page)

	all cu's	under $10,000	$10,000 to $19,999	$20,000 to $29,999	$30,000 to $39,999	$40,000 to $49,999	$50,000 and over
Jewelry and watches	100	24	64	110	137	109	219
Small appliances and housewares	100	33	52	75	83	164	279
Household textiles	100	22	71	89	42	122	316
All other non-cash gifts	100	47	59	97	107	132	220
MISCELLANEOUS ITEMS	100	57	72	85	116	123	196
Legal fees	100	36	64	104	128	60	245
Occupational expenses	100	26	46	56	146	205	242
Funeral expenses	100	145	127	116	28	99	38
Cemetery lots or vaults	100	132	112	73	78	71	104
Unspecified fees and personal services	100	30	67	54	171	177	208

Note: An index of 100 represents the average for all consumer units. An index of 132 means that the average for the subgroup is 32 percent above the average for all consumer units. An index of 68 indicates spending that is 32 percent below the overall average. Expenditures are not given (-) when the amount is too small to be reliable. The amounts spent on "gifts of products and services" are also included in the expenditures listed for the item elsewhere in the Consumer Expenditure Survey.

Aggregate expenditures, 1988

(consumer units include complete income reporters only)	all cu's	under $10,000	$10,000 to $19,999	$20,000 to $29,999	$30,000 to $39,999	$40,000 to $49,999	$50,000 and over
Number of consumer units (in thousands)	81,354	18,809	17,652	14,586	10,901	7,198	12,209
Average number of persons per cu	2.6	1.8	2.3	2.7	2.9	3.2	3.1
Average number of earners per cu	1.4	0.7	1.0	1.5	1.8	2.0	2.1
TOTAL AGGREGATE EXPENDITURES (in millions)	$2,148,492	$211,967	$319,117	$363,138	$345,121	$270,371	$638,777
FINANCIAL PRODUCTS AND SERVICES (in millions)	$228,329	$6,904	$20,591	$34,752	$39,704	$35,672	$90,706
Life and other personal insurances except health	26,373	2,031	3,607	4,400	3,868	3,558	8,908
Retirement, pensions, Social Security	179,648	3,330	14,120	26,195	31,738	29,138	75,127
Deductions for government retirement	5,317	21	248	705	898	864	2,581
Deductions for railroad retirement	498	-	11	-	208	117	162
Deductions for private pensions	12,699	19	436	1,229	1,755	2,365	6,895
Deductions for self-employment IRAs and Keoghs	24,186	541	987	2,653	3,634	3,558	12,814
Deductions for Social Security	136,938	2,743	12,439	21,604	25,243	22,234	52,675
Other products and services	22,308	1,543	2,864	4,157	4,098	2,976	6,671
Accounting fees	3,244	352	349	490	570	345	1,138
Checking account fees and other bank services	2,050	224	372	422	366	275	391
Safety deposit box rentals	463	59	68	74	64	45	154
Finance charges other than auto and mortgage	16,551	908	2,074	3,170	3,097	2,312	4,989
CASH CONTRIBUTIONS (in millions)	$59,404	$3,282	$7,329	$7,720	$8,515	$6,883	$25,675
Contributions to non-cu member, including alimony and students at college	14,568	522	1,500	1,854	2,289	1,699	6,703
Cash gifts to non-cu member	12,202	646	1,099	1,596	1,761	1,170	5,929
Contributions to charities	5,626	282	445	479	717	718	2,985
Contributions to church	24,044	1,738	4,133	3,534	3,515	3,051	8,072
Contributions to educational organizations	1,462	67	33	43	137	90	1,092
Political contributions	584	-	23	35	73	77	376
GIFTS OF PRODUCTS AND SERVICES (in millions)	$69,107	$6,820	$9,673	$11,933	$9,788	$8,164	$22,729
Clothing for males aged 2 and older	5,932	408	1,043	1,019	569	622	2,272
Clothing for females aged 2 and older	6,440	525	1,236	1,172	975	930	1,602
Clothing for babies	2,276	183	376	326	448	270	674

Aggregate expenditures in 1988 for financial products and services, contributions, gifts, and miscellaneous items, by total before-tax income of consumer unit.

(continued from previous page)	all cu's	under $10,000	$10,000 to $19,999	$20,000 to $29,999	$30,000 to $39,999	$40,000 to $49,999	$50,000 and over
Jewelry and watches	2,256	123	311	445	415	218	743
Small appliances and housewares	1,363	103	153	184	153	198	572
Household textiles	858	43	131	136	48	92	406
All other non-cash gifts	49,983	5,435	6,422	8,651	7,180	5,834	16,461
MISCELLANEOUS ITEMS (in millions)	$23,185	$3,058	$3,641	$3,527	$3,613	$2,518	$6,828
Legal fees	8,501	704	1,177	1,591	1,454	451	3,125
Occupational expenses	7,343	438	739	735	1,433	1,331	2,668
Funeral expenses	4,013	1,348	1,104	832	148	353	227
Cemetery lots or vaults	1,436	438	348	188	150	90	223
Unspecified fees and personal services	1,891	131	274	181	429	293	584

Note: Expenditures are not given (-) when the amount is too small to be reliable. Numbers may not add to total due to rounding. The amounts spent on "gifts of products and services" are also included in the expenditures listed for the item elsewhere in the Consumer Expenditure Survey. Expenditures listed for items in a given category may not add to the total for that category because the listing is incomplete. "Cash contributions," for example, includes "other contributions," which is omitted here. The "all cu's" aggregates will differ slightly from table to table because they are the sums of the aggregates in each row.

PART III
Spending by type of household for financial products and services, cash contributions, gifts, and other items

Married couples living with extended family members or unrelated people spend far more than the average household on gifts...

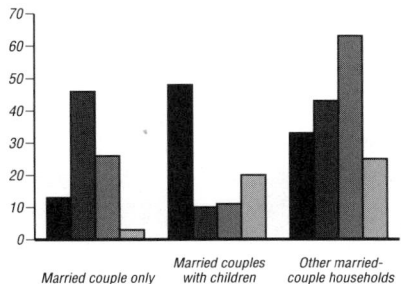

Married-couple households devote more than 10 percent of their budgets to financial products and services, an average of $3,358 a year. Over three-quarters of that amount goes to Social Security and other retirement and pension programs, while 14 percent is devoted to insurance other than health insurance. The remaining 9 percent is allocated to other products and services such as accountant and bank fees. Married couples spend 34 percent more than the average household on financial products and services.

Single parents, people who live alone, and people who live in "other" households allocate no more than 8 percent of their budgets to financial products and services. With an average of just one earner per household and relatively low incomes, it is not surprising that the spending of these households on Social Security and pensions is well below average, and well below that of married couples.

Married couples also outspend single persons, "other" households, and single parents on cash contributions, gifts, and miscellaneous products and services. Among married couples with children, spending on these categories generally increases with the age of their children. Empty-nesters and other childless couples spend more—46 percent more—than the average household on contributions. Married couples living with extended family members or unrelated people are the most generous gift-givers. They spend 63 percent more than the average household on gifts. They also spend more than other households on legal fees and funerals.

...while these households spend less than the average on gifts and other categories.

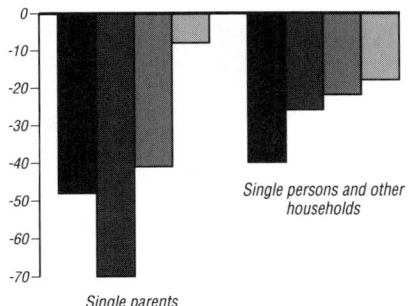

---

0 = average spending

■ Financial products and services

■ Cash contributions

▣ Gifts of products and services

▢ Miscellaneous items

In this analysis, single-person households are grouped with "other" households. "Other" households are unrelated people living together and families that are not married-couple or single-parent families, such as siblings. Single-person households account for 72 percent of the households in this category.

Average expenditures

Average annual expenditures for financial products and services, contributions, gifts, and miscellaneous items, by type of consumer unit.

	all cu's	married couples	single parents	single persons and other cu's
Number of consumer units (in thousands)	*94,862*	*52,010*	*5,716*	*37,136*
Average number of persons per cu	*2.6*	*3.3*	*2.9*	*1.5*
Average number of earners per cu	*1.4*	*1.7*	*1.0*	*0.9*
Average total before-tax income	*$28,540.00*	*$37,299.00*	*$16,276.00*	*$18,509.00*
TOTAL AVERAGE ANNUAL EXPENDITURES	*$25,891.85*	*$32,314.50*	*$18,615.80*	*$17,950.80*
FINANCIAL PRODUCTS AND SERVICES	$2,511.27	$3,358.44	$1,307.48	$1,510.08
Life and other personal insurances except health	314.13	462.08	153.24	131.68
Retirement, pensions, Social Security	1,934.96	2,578.66	981.65	1,180.17
Deductions for government retirement	56.72	78.53	45.15	27.94
Deductions for railroad retirement	5.35	7.92	-	2.55
Deductions for private pensions	135.29	186.68	57.67	75.26
Deductions for self-employment				
IRAs and Keoghs	274.01	371.61	70.30	168.67
Deductions for Social Security	1,463.60	1,933.91	808.50	905.75
Other products and services	262.18	317.70	172.59	198.23
Accounting fees	41.68	52.83	19.52	29.47
Checking account fees and other bank services	24.33	27.32	22.10	20.49
Safety deposit box rentals	5.82	7.48	1.98	4.10
Finance charges other than auto and mortgage	190.35	230.07	128.99	144.17
CASH CONTRIBUTIONS	$693.36	$875.39	$206.95	$513.29
Contributions to non-cu member, including alimony and students at college	175.67	170.09	99.20	195.25
Cash gifts to non-cu member	135.30	181.85	8.22	89.66
Contributions to charities	64.35	85.17	17.31	42.42
Contributions to church	283.68	391.32	71.40	165.61
Contributions to educational organizations	16.76	23.22	7.59	9.12
Political contributions	10.65	9.34	-	4.65
GIFTS OF PRODUCTS AND SERVICES	$839.24	$1,009.62	$493.06	$650.43
Clothing for males aged 2 and older :	69.63	88.94	12.84	50.46
Clothing for females aged 2 and older	79.76	94.88	61.87	60.71
Clothing for babies	26.94	37.69	17.54	13.12

Average annual expenditures for financial products and services, contributions, gifts, and miscellaneous items, by type of consumer unit.

(continued from previous page)

	all cu's	married couples	single parents	single persons and other cu's
Jewelry and watches	25.67	16.83	16.24	39.50
Small appliances and housewares	16.76	22.69	3.28	10.40
Household textiles	9.66	12.39	-	7.15
All other non-cash gifts	610.82	736.20	381.29	469.09
MISCELLANEOUS ITEMS	$315.94	$359.64	$289.64	$258.01
Legal fees	99.76	100.97	224.52	78.86
Occupational expenses	89.07	124.00	39.36	47.81
Funeral expenses	47.12	35.06	11.45	69.50
Cemetery lots or vaults	21.28	25.18	3.71	18.52
Unspecified fees and personal services	58.71	74.43	10.60	43.32

Note: Expenditures are not given (-) when the amount is too small to be reliable. Numbers may not add to total due to rounding. The amounts spent on "gifts of products and services" are also included in the expenditures listed for the item elsewhere in the Consumer Expenditure Survey. Expenditures listed for items in a given category may not add to the total for that category because the listing is incomplete. "Cash contributions," for example, includes "other contributions," which is omitted here. "Single parents" is one-parent consumer units with a child or children under age 18 living at home. "Other cu's" includes persons living with unrelated persons and families other than married-couple and single-parent families.

Share of spending

	all cu's	married couples	single parents	single persons and other cu's
Number of consumer units (in thousands)	94,862	52,010	5,716	37,136
Average number of persons per cu	2.6	3.3	2.9	1.5
Average total before-tax income	$28,540	$37,299	$16,276	$18,509
TOTAL AVERAGE ANNUAL EXPENDITURES	100.00%	100.00%	100.00%	100.00%
FINANCIAL PRODUCTS AND SERVICES	9.70%	10.39%	7.02%	8.41%
Life and other personal insurances except health	1.21	1.43	0.82	0.73
Retirement, pensions, Social Security	7.47	7.98	5.27	6.57
Deductions for government retirement	0.22	0.24	0.24	0.16
Deductions for railroad retirement	0.02	0.02	-	0.01
Deductions for private pensions	0.52	0.58	0.31	0.42
Deductions for self-employment IRAs and Keoghs	1.06	1.15	0.38	0.94
Deductions for Social Security	5.65	5.98	4.34	5.05
Other products and services	1.01	0.98	0.93	1.10
Accounting fees	0.16	0.16	0.10	0.16
Checking account fees and other bank services	0.09	0.08	0.12	0.11
Safety deposit box rentals	0.02	0.02	0.01	0.02
Finance charges other than auto and mortgage	0.74	0.71	0.69	0.80
CASH CONTRIBUTIONS	2.68%	2.71%	1.11%	2.86%
Contributions to non-CU member, including alimony and students at college	0.68	0.53	0.53	1.09
Cash gifts to non-CU member	0.52	0.56	0.04	0.50
Contributions to charities	0.25	0.26	0.09	0.24
Contributions to church	1.10	1.21	0.38	0.92
Contributions to educational organizations	0.06	0.07	0.04	0.05
Political contributions	0.04	0.03	-	0.03
GIFTS OF PRODUCTS AND SERVICES	3.24%	3.12%	2.65%	3.62%
Clothing for males aged 2 and older	0.27	0.28	0.07	0.28
Clothing for females aged 2 and older	0.31	0.29	0.33	0.34
Clothing for babies	0.10	0.12	0.09	0.07

Percent of total average annual expenditures spent on financial products and services, contributions, gifts, and miscellaneous items, by type of consumer unit.

(continued from previous page)

	all cu's	married couples	single parents	single persons and other cu's
Jewelry and watches	0.10	0.05	0.09	0.22
Small appliances and housewares	0.06	0.07	0.02	0.06
Household textiles	0.04	0.04	-	0.04
All other non-cash gifts	2.36	2.28	2.05	2.61
MISCELLANEOUS ITEMS	**1.22%**	**1.11%**	**1.56%**	**1.44%**
Legal fees	0.39	0.31	1.21	0.44
Occupational expenses	0.34	0.38	0.21	0.27
Funeral expenses	0.18	0.11	0.06	0.39
Cemetery lots or vaults	0.08	0.08	0.02	0.10
Unspecified fees and personal services	0.23	0.23	0.06	0.24

Note: Expenditures are not given (-) when the amount is too small to be reliable. Numbers may not add to total due to rounding. The amounts spent on "gifts of products and services" are also included in the expenditures listed for the item elsewhere in the Consumer Expenditure Survey. Expenditures listed for items in a given category may not add to the total for that category because the listing is incomplete. "Cash contributions," for example, includes "other contributions," which is omitted here. "Single parents" is one-parent consumer units with a child or children under age 18 living at home. "Other cu's" includes persons living with unrelated persons and families other than married-couple and single-parent families.

Indexed expenditures

	all cu's	married couples	single parents	single persons and other cu's
Number of consumer units (in thousands)	94,862	52,010	5,716	37,136
Average number of persons per cu	2.6	3.3	2.9	1.5
Average number of earners per cu	1.4	1.7	1.0	0.9
Average total before-tax income	$28,540	$37,299	$16,276	$18,509
TOTAL AVERAGE ANNUAL EXPENDITURES	100	125	72	69
FINANCIAL PRODUCTS AND SERVICES	100	134	52	60
Life and other personal insurances except health	100	147	49	42
Retirement, pensions, Social Security	100	133	51	61
Deductions for government retirement	100	138	80	49
Deductions for railroad retirement	100	148	-	48
Deductions for private pensions	100	138	43	56
Deductions for self-employment				
IRAs and Keoghs	100	136	26	62
Deductions for Social Security	100	132	55	62
Other products and services	100	121	66	76
Accounting fees	100	127	47	71
Checking account fees and other bank services	100	112	91	84
Safety deposit box rentals	100	129	34	70
Finance charges other than auto and mortgage	100	121	68	76
CASH CONTRIBUTIONS	100	126	30	74
Contributions to non-cu member, including alimony and students at college	100	97	56	111
Cash gifts to non-cu member	100	134	6	66
Contributions to charities	100	132	27	66
Contributions to church	100	138	25	58
Contributions to educational organizations	100	139	45	54
Political contributions	100	88	-	44
GIFTS OF PRODUCTS AND SERVICES	100	120	59	78
Clothing for males aged 2 and older	100	128	18	72
Clothing for females aged 2 and older	100	119	78	76
Clothing for babies	100	140	65	49

Indexed average annual expenditures for financial products and services, contributions, gifts, and miscellaneous items, by type of consumer unit.

(continued from previous page)

	all cu's	married couples	single parents	single persons and other cu's
Jewelry and watches	100	66	63	154
Small appliances and housewares	100	135	20	62
Household textiles	100	128	-	74
All other non-cash gifts	100	121	62	77
MISCELLANEOUS ITEMS	100	114	92	82
Legal fees	100	101	225	79
Occupational expenses	100	139	44	54
Funeral expenses	100	74	24	147
Cemetery lots or vaults	100	118	17	87
Unspecified fees and personal services	100	127	18	74

Note: Expenditures are not given (-) when the amount is too small to be reliable. Numbers may not add to total due to rounding. The amounts spent on "gifts of products and services" are also included in the expenditures listed for the item elsewhere in the Consumer Expenditure Survey. Expenditures listed for items in a given category may not add to the total for that category because the listing is incomplete. "Cash contributions," for example, includes "other contributions," which is omitted here. "Single parents" is one-parent consumer units with a child or children under age 18 living at home. "Other cu's" includes persons living with unrelated persons and families other than married-couple and single-parent families.

Aggregate expenditures, 1988

Aggregate expenditures in 1988 for financial products and services, contributions, gifts, and miscellaneous items, by type of consumer unit.

	all cu's	married couples	single parents	single persons and other cu's
Number of consumer units (in thousands)	94,862	52,010	5,716	37,136
Average number of persons per cu	2.6	3.3	2.9	1.5
Average number of earners per cu	1.4	1.7	1.0	0.9
Aggregate before-tax income	$2,720,305	$1,939,921	$93,034	$687,350
TOTAL AGGREGATE EXPENDITURES	$2,453,706	$1,680,677	$106,408	$666,621
FINANCIAL PRODUCTS AND SERVICES (in millions)	$238,224	$174,672	$7,474	$56,078
Life and other personal insurances except health	29,799	24,033	876	4,890
Retirement, pensions, Social Security	183,554	134,116	5,611	43,827
Deductions for government retirement	5,380	4,084	258	1,038
Deductions for railroad retirement	507	412	-	95
Deductions for private pensions	12,834	9,709	330	2,795
Deductions for self-employment				
IRAs and Keoghs	25,993	19,327	402	6,264
Deductions for Social Security	138,840	100,583	4,621	33,636
Other products and services	24,872	16,524	987	7,361
Accounting fees	3,954	2,748	112	1,094
Checking account fees and other bank services	2,308	1,421	126	761
Safety deposit box rentals	553	389	11	152
Finance charges other than auto and mortgage	18,057	11,966	737	5,354
CASH CONTRIBUTIONS (in millions)	$65,773	$45,529	$1,183	$19,062
Contributions to non-cu member, including alimony and students at college	16,664	8,846	567	7,251
Cash gifts to non-cu member	12,835	9,458	47	3,330
Contributions to charities	6,104	4,430	99	1,575
Contributions to church	26,911	20,353	408	6,150
Contributions to educational organizations	1,590	1,208	43	339
Political contributions	659	486	-	173
GIFTS OF PRODUCTS AND SERVICES (in millions)	$79,483	$52,510	$2,818	$24,154
Clothing for males aged 2 and older	6,573	4,626	73	1,874
Clothing for females aged 2 and older	7,543	4,935	354	2,255
Clothing for babies	2,548	1,960	100	487

Aggregate expenditures in 1988 for financial products and services, contributions, gifts, and miscellaneous items, by type of consumer unit.

(continued from previous page)

	all cu's	married couples	single parents	single persons and other cu's
Jewelry and watches	2,435	875	93	1,467
Small appliances and housewares.........................	1,585	1,180	19	386
Household textiles	910	644	-	266
All other non-cash gifts	57,889	38,290	2,179	17,420
MISCELLANEOUS ITEMS (in millions)	$29,942	$18,705	$1,656	$9,581
Legal fees..	9,463	5,251	1,283	2,929
Occupational expenses	8,450	6,449	225	1,775
Funeral expenses	4,470	1,823	65	2,581
Cemetery lots or vaults	2,019	1,310	21	688
Unspecified fees and personal services	5,540	3,871	61	1,609

Note: Expenditures are not given (-) when the amount is too small to be reliable. Numbers may not add to total due to rounding. The amounts spent on "gifts of products and services" are also included in the expenditures listed for the item elsewhere in the Consumer Expenditure Survey. Expenditures listed for items in a given category may not add to the total for that category because the listing is incomplete. "Cash contributions," for example, includes "other contributions," which is omitted here. "Single parents" is one-parent consumer units with a child or children under age 18 living at home. "Other cu's" includes persons living with unrelated persons and families other than married-couple and single-parent families. The "all cu's" aggregates will differ slightly from table to table because they are the sums of the aggregates in each row.

Average expenditures

Average annual expenditures for financial products and services, contributions, gifts, and miscellaneous items, by married couples with and without children.

	all cu's	all married couples	married couple only	all married couples with children	AGE OF OLDEST CHILD under 6	AGE OF OLDEST CHILD 6 to 17	AGE OF OLDEST CHILD 18 or older	other married couples
Number of consumer units (in thousands)	94,862	52,010	20,227	28,100	5,858	14,194	8,047	3,684
Average number of persons per cu	2.6	3.3	2	3.9	3.5	4.1	3.9	5.1
Average number of earners per cu	1.4	1.7	1.2	2.1	1.7	1.9	2.7	2.4
Average total before-tax income	$28,540.00	$37,299.00	$33,825.00	$39,354.00	$34,318.00	$38,039.00	$45,596.00	$40,846.00
TOTAL AVERAGE ANNUAL EXPENDITURES	$25,891.85	$32,314.50	$27,954.50	$35,015.30	$30,942.80	$35,248.40	$37,763.90	$35,739.60
FINANCIAL PRODUCTS AND SERVICES	$2,511.27	$3,358.44	$2,849.34	$3,725.91	$3,204.66	$3,723.28	$4,109.98	$3,350.68
Life and other personal insurances except health	314.13	462.08	460.17	470.52	356.86	481.46	533.95	408.21
Retirement, pensions, Social Security	1,934.96	2,578.66	2,126.80	2,902.08	2,501.55	2,877.55	3,236.93	2,592.61
Deductions for government retirement	56.72	78.53	77.18	81.24	63.67	66.12	120.70	65.32
Deductions for railroad retirement	5.35	7.92	5.86	10.45	3.66	9.93	16.32	0.00
Deductions for private pensions	135.29	186.68	136.54	233.25	186.32	216.44	297.06	106.80
Deductions for self-employment IRAs and Keoghs	274.01	371.61	439.12	322.07	181.00	318.02	431.92	378.83
Deductions for Social Security	1,463.60	1,933.91	1,468.11	2,255.07	2,066.90	2,267.04	2,370.94	2,041.66
Other products and services	262.18	317.70	262.37	353.31	346.25	364.27	339.10	349.86
Accounting fees	41.68	52.83	67.69	42.88	52.64	36.63	46.82	47.05
Checking account fees and other bank services	24.33	27.32	19.20	33.23	31.83	34.85	31.38	26.89
Safety deposit box rentals	5.82	7.48	11.20	4.93	3.46	4.56	6.63	6.50
Finance charges other than auto and mortgage	190.35	230.07	164.28	272.27	258.32	288.23	254.27	269.42
CASH CONTRIBUTIONS	$693.36	$875.39	$1,014.06	$760.01	$498.22	$730.78	$1,002.16	$994.15
Contributions to non-cu member, including alimony and students at college	175.67	170.09	151.20	184.48	124.37	100.45	376.48	164.04
Cash gifts to non-cu member	135.30	181.85	346.84	58.33	34.25	48.81	92.66	218.23
Contributions to charities	64.35	85.17	73.88	73.19	45.08	74.52	91.32	238.59
Contributions to church	283.68	391.32	380.64	403.44	278.10	461.83	391.68	357.46
Contributions to educational organizations	16.76	23.22	27.77	21.89	8.16	22.03	31.62	8.45
Political contributions	10.65	9.34	12.32	7.85	1.04	8.18	12.21	4.40
GIFTS OF PRODUCTS AND SERVICES	$839.24	$1,009.62	$1,055.21	$930.52	$842.82	$810.15	$1,210.47	$1,364.95
Clothing for males aged 2 and older	69.63	88.94	121.56	61.58	55.99	55.50	77.83	119.17
Clothing for females aged 2 and older	79.76	94.88	100.25	91.98	84.26	70.10	141.76	86.52
Clothing for babies	26.94	37.69	34.08	38.04	60.64	28.42	35.43	55.30

Average annual expenditures for financial products and services, contributions, gifts, and miscellaneous items, by married couples with and without children.

(continued from previous page)

	all cu's	all married couples	married couple only	all married couples with children	AGE OF OLDEST CHILD			other married couples
					under 6	6 to 17	18 or older	
Jewelry and watches	25.67	16.83	16.83	14.95	8.95	11.80	24.88	31.17
Small appliances and housewares	16.76	22.69	22.83	23.35	31.89	18.87	23.52	16.50
Household textiles	9.66	12.39	15.69	9.37	9.01	9.39	9.67	17.41
All other non-cash gifts	610.82	736.20	743.97	691.25	592.08	616.07	897.38	1,038.88
MISCELLANEOUS ITEMS	$315.94	$359.64	$325.28	$379.37	$254.68	$347.20	$531.50	$396.48
Legal fees	99.76	100.97	82.09	107.65	49.53	118.23	131.32	153.71
Occupational expenses	89.07	124.00	66.66	167.95	147.98	132.86	244.36	103.54
Funeral expenses	47.12	35.06	44.65	22.98	6.38	17.21	45.23	74.62
Cemetery lots or vaults	21.28	25.18	48.00	10.35	2.22	10.97	15.18	13.05
Unspecified fees and personal services	58.71	74.43	83.88	70.44	48.57	67.93	95.41	51.56

Note: The amounts spent on "gifts of products and services" are also included in the expenditures listed for the item elsewhere in the Consumer Expenditure Survey. Expenditures listed for items in a given category may not add to the total for that category because the listing is incomplete. "Cash contributions," for example, includes "other contributions," which is omitted here. Other married couples include extended family members or unrelated persons in addition to the married couple. Numbers may not add to total due to rounding.

Share of spending

	all cu's	all married couples	married couple only	all married couples with children	AGE OF OLDEST CHILD under 6	AGE OF OLDEST CHILD 6 to 17	AGE OF OLDEST CHILD 18 or older	other married couples
Number of consumer units (in thousands)	94,862	52,010	20,227	28,100	5,858	14,194	8,047	3,684
Average number of persons per cu	2.6	3.3	2	3.9	3.5	4.1	3.9	5.1
Average total before-tax income	$28,540	$37,299	$33,825	$39,354	$34,318	$38,039	$45,596	$40,846
TOTAL AVERAGE ANNUAL EXPENDITURES	100.00%	100.00%	100.00%	100.00%	100.00%	100.00%	100.00%	100.00%
FINANCIAL PRODUCTS AND SERVICES	**9.70%**	**10.39%**	**10.19%**	**10.64%**	**10.36%**	**10.56%**	**10.88%**	**9.38%**
Life and other personal insurances except health	**1.21**	**1.43**	**1.65**	**1.34**	**1.15**	**1.37**	**1.41**	**1.14**
Retirement, pensions, Social Security	**7.47**	**7.98**	**7.61**	**8.29**	**8.08**	**8.16**	**8.57**	**7.25**
Deductions for government retirement	0.22	0.24	0.28	0.23	0.21	0.19	0.32	0.18
Deductions for railroad retirement	0.02	0.02	0.02	0.03	0.01	0.03	0.04	0.00
Deductions for private pensions	0.52	0.58	0.49	0.67	0.60	0.61	0.79	0.30
Deductions for self-employment IRAs and Keoghs	1.06	1.15	1.57	0.92	0.58	0.90	1.14	1.06
Deductions for Social Security	5.65	5.98	5.25	6.44	6.68	6.43	6.28	5.71
Other products and services	**1.01**	**0.98**	**0.94**	**1.01**	**1.12**	**1.03**	**0.90**	**0.98**
Accounting fees	0.16	0.16	0.24	0.12	0.17	0.10	0.12	0.13
Checking account fees and other bank services	0.09	0.08	0.07	0.09	0.10	0.10	0.08	0.08
Safety deposit box rentals	0.02	0.02	0.04	0.01	0.01	0.01	0.02	0.02
Finance charges other than auto and mortgage	0.74	0.71	0.59	0.78	0.83	0.82	0.67	0.75
CASH CONTRIBUTIONS	**2.68%**	**2.71%**	**3.63%**	**2.17%**	**1.61%**	**2.07%**	**2.65%**	**2.78%**
Contributions to non-CU member, including alimony and students at college	**0.68**	**0.53**	**0.54**	**0.53**	**0.40**	**0.28**	**1.00**	**0.46**
Cash gifts to non-CU member	**0.52**	**0.56**	**1.24**	**0.17**	**0.11**	**0.14**	**0.25**	**0.61**
Contributions to charities	**0.25**	**0.26**	**0.26**	**0.21**	**0.15**	**0.21**	**0.24**	**0.67**
Contributions to church	**1.10**	**1.21**	**1.36**	**1.15**	**0.90**	**1.31**	**1.04**	**1.00**
Contributions to educational organizations	**0.06**	**0.07**	**0.10**	**0.06**	**0.03**	**0.06**	**0.08**	**0.02**
Political contributions	**0.04**	**0.03**	**0.04**	**0.02**	**0.00**	**0.02**	**0.03**	**0.01**
GIFTS OF PRODUCTS AND SERVICES	**3.24%**	**3.12%**	**3.77%**	**2.66%**	**2.72%**	**2.30%**	**3.21%**	**3.82%**
Clothing for males aged 2 and older	**0.27**	**0.28**	**0.43**	**0.18**	**0.18**	**0.16**	**0.21**	**0.33**
Clothing for females aged 2 and older	**0.31**	**0.29**	**0.36**	**0.26**	**0.27**	**0.20**	**0.38**	**0.24**
Clothing for babies	**0.10**	**0.12**	**0.12**	**0.11**	**0.20**	**0.08**	**0.09**	**0.15**

Percent of total average annual expenditures spent on financial products and services, contributions, gifts, and miscellaneous items, by married couples with and without children.

(continued from previous page)	all cu's	all married couples	married couple only	all married couples with children	AGE OF OLDEST CHILD			other married couples
					under 6	6 to 17	18 or older	
Jewelry and watches	0.10	0.05	0.06	0.04	0.03	0.03	0.07	0.09
Small appliances and housewares	0.06	0.07	0.08	0.07	0.10	0.05	0.06	0.05
Household textiles	0.04	0.04	0.06	0.03	0.03	0.03	0.03	0.05
All other non-cash gifts	2.36	2.28	2.66	1.97	1.91	1.75	2.38	2.91
MISCELLANEOUS ITEMS	1.22%	1.11%	1.16%	1.08%	0.82%	0.99%	1.41%	1.11%
Legal fees	0.39	0.31	0.29	0.31	0.16	0.34	0.35	0.43
Occupational expenses	0.34	0.38	0.24	0.48	0.48	0.38	0.65	0.29
Funeral expenses	0.18	0.11	0.16	0.07	0.02	0.05	0.12	0.21
Cemetery lots or vaults	0.08	0.08	0.17	0.03	0.01	0.03	0.04	0.04
Unspecified fees and personal services	0.23	0.23	0.30	0.20	0.16	0.19	0.25	0.14

Note: The amounts spent on "gifts of products and services" are also included in the expenditures listed for the item elsewhere in the Consumer Expenditure Survey. Expenditures listed for items in a given category may not add to the total for that category because the listing is incomplete. "Cash contributions," for example, includes "other contributions," which is omitted here. Other married couples include extended family members or unrelated persons in addition to the married couple. Numbers may not add to total due to rounding.

Indexed expenditures

	all cu's	all married couples	married couple only	all married couples with children	AGE OF OLDEST CHILD			other married couples
					under 6	6 to 17	18 or older	
Number of consumer units (in thousands)	94,862	52,010	20,227	28,100	5,858	14,194	8,047	3,684
Average number of persons per cu	2.6	3.3	2	3.9	3.5	4.1	3.9	5.1
Average number of earners per cu	1.4	1.7	1.2	2.1	1.7	1.9	2.7	2.4
Average total before-tax income	$28,540	$37,299	$33,825	$39,354	$34,318	$38,039	$45,596	$40,846
TOTAL AVERAGE ANNUAL EXPENDITURES	100	125	108	135	120	136	146	138
FINANCIAL PRODUCTS AND SERVICES	100	134	113	148	128	148	164	133
Life and other personal insurances except health	100	147	146	150	114	153	170	130
Retirement, pensions, Social Security	100	133	110	150	129	149	167	134
Deductions for government retirement	100	138	136	143	112	117	213	115
Deductions for railroad retirement	100	148	110	195	68	186	305	0
Deductions for private pensions	100	138	101	172	138	160	220	79
Deductions for self-employment IRAs and Keoghs	100	136	160	118	66	116	158	138
Deductions for Social Security	100	132	100	154	141	155	162	139
Other products and services	100	121	100	135	132	139	129	133
Accounting fees	100	127	162	103	126	88	112	113
Checking account fees and other bank services	100	112	79	137	131	143	129	111
Safety deposit box rentals	100	129	192	85	59	78	114	112
Finance charges other than auto and mortgage	100	121	86	143	136	151	134	142
CASH CONTRIBUTIONS	100	126	146	110	72	105	145	143
Contributions to non-cu member, including alimony and students at college	100	97	86	105	71	57	214	93
Cash gifts to non-cu member	100	134	256	43	25	36	68	161
Contributions to charities	100	132	115	114	70	116	142	371
Contributions to church	100	138	134	142	98	163	138	126
Contributions to educational organizations	100	139	166	131	49	131	189	50
Political contributions	100	88	116	74	10	77	115	41
GIFTS OF PRODUCTS AND SERVICES	100	120	126	111	100	97	144	163
Clothing for males aged 2 and older	100	128	175	88	80	80	112	171
Clothing for females aged 2 and older	100	119	126	115	106	88	178	108
Clothing for babies	100	140	127	141	225	105	132	205

Indexed average annual expenditures for financial products and services, contributions, gifts, and miscellaneous items, by married couples with and without children.

(continued from previous page)

	all cu's	all married couples	married couple only	all married couples with children	AGE OF OLDEST CHILD			other married couples
					under 6	6 to 17	18 or older	
Jewelry and watches	100	66	66	58	35	46	97	121
Small appliances and housewares	100	135	136	139	190	113	140	98
Household textiles	100	128	162	97	93	97	100	180
All other non-cash gifts	100	121	122	113	97	101	147	170
MISCELLANEOUS ITEMS	100	114	103	120	81	110	168	125
Legal fees	100	101	82	108	50	119	132	154
Occupational expenses	100	139	75	189	166	149	274	116
Funeral expenses	100	74	95	49	14	37	96	158
Cemetery lots or vaults	100	118	226	49	10	52	71	61
Unspecified fees and personal services	100	127	143	120	83	116	163	88

Note: An index of 100 represents the average for all consumer units. An index of 132 means that the average for the subgroup is 32 percent above the average for all consumer units. An index of 68 indicates spending that is 32 percent below the overall average. The amounts spent on "gifts of products and services" are also included in the expenditures listed for the item elsewhere in the Consumer Expenditure Survey. Other married couples include extended family or unrelated persons in addition to the married couple. Numbers may not add to total due to rounding.

Aggregate expenditures, 1988

Aggregate expenditures in 1988 for financial products and services, contributions, gifts, and miscellaneous items, by married couples with and without children.

	all cu's	all married couples	married couple only	all married couples with children	AGE OF OLDEST CHILD under 6	AGE OF OLDEST CHILD 6 to 17	AGE OF OLDEST CHILD 18 or older	other married couples
Number of consumer units (in thousands)	94,862	52,010	20,227	28,100	5,858	14,194	8,047	3,684
Average number of persons per cu	2.6	3.3	2	3.9	3.5	4.1	3.9	5.1
Average number of earners per cu	1.4	1.7	1.2	2.1	1.7	1.9	2.7	2.4
Aggregate before-tax income	$2,722,910	$1,942,526	$684,178	$1,107,871	$201,035	$539,926	$366,911	$150,477
TOTAL AGGREGATE EXPENDITURES	$2,455,594	$1,682,565	$565,436	$985,465	$181,263	$500,316	$303,886	$131,665
FINANCIAL PRODUCTS AND SERVICES (in millions)	$238,224	$174,672	$57,634	$104,694	$18,773	$52,848	$33,073	$12,344
Life and other personal insurances except health	29,799	24,033	9,308	13,221	2,090	6,834	4,297	1,504
Retirement, pensions, Social Security	183,553	134,116	43,019	81,546	14,654	40,844	26,048	9,551
Deductions for government retirement	5,380	4,085	1,561	2,283	373	939	971	241
Deductions for railroad retirement	507	412	119	294	21	141	131	0
Deductions for private pensions	12,834	9,709	2,762	6,554	1,091	3,072	2,390	393
Deductions for self-employment IRAs and Keoghs	25,993	19,328	8,882	9,050	1,060	4,514	3,476	1,396
Deductions for Social Security	138,839	100,582	29,695	63,365	12,108	32,178	19,079	7,521
Other products and services	24,871	16,523	5,307	9,928	2,028	5,170	2,729	1,289
Accounting fees	3,954	2,748	1,369	1,205	308	520	377	173
Checking account fees and other bank services	2,308	1,421	388	934	186	495	253	99
Safety deposit box rentals	552	389	227	138	20	65	53	24
Finance charges other than auto and mortgage	18,057	11,966	3,323	7,650	1,513	4,091	2,046	993
CASH CONTRIBUTIONS (in millions)	$65,774	$45,529	$20,511	$21,356	$2,919	$10,373	$8,064	$3,662
Contributions to non-cu member, including alimony and students at college	16,664	8,847	3,058	5,184	729	1,426	3,030	604
Cash gifts to non-cu member	12,835	9,459	7,016	1,639	201	693	746	804
Contributions to charities	6,104	4,430	1,494	2,057	264	1,058	735	879
Contributions to church	26,910	20,352	7,699	11,336	1,629	6,555	3,152	1,317
Contributions to educational organizations	1,590	1,208	562	615	48	313	254	31
Political contributions	659	486	249	220	6	116	98	16
GIFTS OF PRODUCTS AND SERVICES (in millions)	$79,522	$52,549	$21,344	$26,177	$4,937	$11,499	$9,741	$5,028
Clothing for males aged 2 and older	6,587	4,640	2,459	1,742	328	788	626	439
Clothing for females aged 2 and older	7,584	4,976	2,028	2,629	494	995	1,141	319
Clothing for babies	2,524	1,937	689	1,044	355	403	285	204

Aggregate expenditures in 1988 for financial products and services, contributions, gifts, and miscellaneous items, by married couples with and without children.

(continued from previous page)

	all cu's	all married couples	married couple only	all married couples with children	AGE OF OLDEST CHILD			other married couples
					under 6	6 to 17	18 or older	
Jewelry and watches	2,435	875	340	420	52	167	200	115
Small appliances and housewares	1,571	1,166	462	644	187	268	189	61
Household textiles	911	645	317	264	53	133	78	64
All other non-cash gifts	57,909	38,310	15,048	19,434	3,468	8,744	7,221	3,827
MISCELLANEOUS ITEMS (in millions) .	$29,974	$18,737	$6,579	$10,697	$1,492	$4,928	$4,277	$1,461
Legal fees	9,464	5,252	1,660	3,025	290	1,678	1,057	566
Occupational expenses	8,449	6,449	1,348	4,719	867	1,886	1,966	381
Funeral expenses	4,470	1,824	903	646	37	244	364	275
Cemetery lots or vaults	2,019	1,310	971	291	13	156	122	48
Unspecified fees and personal services	5,572	3,903	1,697	2,016	285	964	768	190

Note: The amounts spent on "gifts of products and services" are also included he expenditures listed for the item elsewhere in the Consumer Expenditure Survey. Expenditures listed for items in a given category may not add to the total for that category because the listing is incomplete. "Cash contributions," for example, includes "other contributions," which is omitted here. Other married couples include extended family members or unrelated persons in addition to the married couple. Numbers may not add to total due to rounding. The "all cu's" aggregates will differ slightly from table to table because they are the sums of the aggregates in each row. In this table they include aggregates for single parents, single persons, and other types of consumer units, in addition to allmarried couples. Aggregates for "all married couples" and "all married couples with children" are sums of the appropriate aggregates in each row.

11

Summary Tables, All Products and Services

The tables in this chapter show you, at a glance, expenditures for all product and service categories. Summaries of average annual expenditures and indexed average annual expenditures for the variables—age, income, and household type—that were detailed in chapters two through ten are included.

You will also find spending data organized by number of earners, household size, race, region of residence, and homeownership status. If you want to compare the spending of single-person households with that of larger households, for example, you can do that with the information in these tables.

Or, these tables will show you much much middle-aged householders with incomes of $30,000 to $40,000 spend on restaurant, carry-out, and other food prepared away from home. Summary tables for households in each age group, categorized by their income, are also in this chapter.

Age

In every major product and service category except health care, household spending is dominated by the middle-aged. Thanks to the aging baby boom, these age groups are scheduled to grow enormously during the 1990s. The number of households headed by 35-to-44-year-olds will climb nearly 20 percent during the decade, while householders aged 45 to 54 will increase by 50 percent.

The rise of the mature market has received a lot of attention, but it is important to remember that in sheer spending power, the 1990s will be a decade dominated by the middle. Businesses that market their products and services to the middle-aged will be well positioned for the rest of the decade.

Average annual expenditures in 1988 for all household products and services, by age of reference person.

	all cu's	under 25	25 to 34	35 to 44	45 to 54	55 to 64	65 to 74	75+
Number of consumer units (in thousands)	94,862	7,216	21,985	19,911	13,601	12,546	11,319	8,284
Average number of persons per cu	2.6	1.8	2.8	3.3	2.9	2.2	2.0	1.5
Average number of earners per cu	1.4	1.3	1.5	1.8	2.0	1.4	0.6	0.4
AVERAGE TOTAL BEFORE-TAX INCOME	$28,540	$14,827	$28,318	$36,428	$39,934	$29,979	$20,704	$13,707
AVERAGE ANNUAL EXPENDITURES	$25,892	$16,373	$25,770	$33,078	$33,205	$25,765	$20,120	$13,339
FOOD	$3,748	$2,455	$3,664	$4,636	$4,815	$3,952	$3,013	$1,939
Food at home	2,136	1,121	2,046	2,599	2,605	2,355	1,933	1,373
Cereals and bakery products	312	166	291	387	387	334	277	215
Meat, poultry, fish, and eggs	551	249	506	661	675	648	533	357
Dairy products	274	152	276	333	329	295	236	175
Fruits and vegetables	373	176	328	434	450	433	390	290
Other food at home	625	379	645	785	763	645	496	335
Food away from home	1,612	1,334	1,618	2,037	2,210	1,597	1,081	566
ALCOHOLIC BEVERAGES	$269	$312	$355	$281	$307	$239	$162	$89
HOUSING	$8,079	$4,746	$8,469	$10,467	$9,672	$7,757	$6,178	$4,682
Shelter	4,493	3,004	4,942	6,147	5,232	3,929	3,018	2,276
Owned dwellings	2,569	440	2,384	3,946	3,345	2,630	1,889	1,163
Mortgage interest	1,569	321	1,834	2,856	2,099	1,154	461	134
Property taxes	504	47	281	546	680	752	692	467
Maintenance, repairs, insurance, other expenses	496	72	269	544	567	725	736	562
Rented dwellings	1,468	2,396	2,253	1,519	1,179	770	772	937
Other lodging	456	168	305	682	708	529	358	176
Utilities, fuels, and public services	1,747	897	1,545	2,023	2,173	1,935	1,739	1,393
Household services	394	141	483	528	349	327	306	349
Personal services	171	97	362	269	58	42	23	76
Housekeeping supplies	361	166	347	411	450	383	382	249
Household furnishings and equipment	1,083	539	1,152	1,357	1,469	1,183	733	415
Household textiles	94	56	93	102	122	106	71	76
Furniture	326	195	371	430	441	332	174	80
Floor coverings	65	27	44	82	110	105	37	19

(continued from previous page)	all cu's	under 25	25 to 34	35 to 44	45 to 54	55 to 64	65 to 74	75+
Major appliances	169	48	172	204	197	206	145	108
Small appliances, miscellaneous								
housewares, equipment	429	212	472	538	600	434	305	131
APPAREL AND APPAREL SERVICES .	$1,489	$1,042	$1,504	$2,015	$2,112	$1,355	$977	$451
Men and boys	388	233	389	553	517	424	213	92
Men, aged 16 or older	311	219	311	384	432	376	189	74
Boys, aged 2 to 15	77	14	79	169	85	48	24	19
Women and girls	587	371	525	816	909	489	432	212
Women, aged 16 or older	492	346	423	591	810	453	407	204
Girls, aged 2 to 15	95	26	102	225	100	36	24	9
Babies, under age 2	62	59	123	67	49	41	20	7
Footwear	196	161	183	247	278	179	158	73
Other apparel products and services	257	218	284	332	359	222	154	65
TRANSPORTATION	$5,093	$3,911	$5,479	$6,369	$6,641	$4,603	$3,975	$1,760
Vehicle purchases (net outlay)	2,361	2,039	2,794	2,931	3,016	1,749	1,849	667
Cars and trucks, new	1,355	1,159	1,651	1,518	1,640	1,082	1,187	523
Cars and trucks, used	982	861	1,111	1,393	1,307	663	662	144
Gasoline and motor oil	932	659	923	1,152	1,248	970	729	367
Other vehicle expenses	1,521	1,023	1,528	1,978	1,987	1,553	1,129	567
Public transportation	279	190	235	309	389	330	268	158
HEALTH CARE	$1,298	$523	$777	$1,253	$1,258	$1,518	$2,005	$2,230
ENTERTAINMENT	$1,329	$961	$1,396	$1,975	$1,615	$1,136	$881	$351
Fees and admissions	353	247	310	514	485	340	262	101
Television, radios, sound equipment	416	349	442	597	479	350	284	141
Pets, toys, and playground equipment	230	116	276	320	259	208	162	75
Other entertainment supplies,								
equipment, services	330	248	368	545	392	238	173	34
PERSONAL CARE PDTS./SVCS	$334	$204	$318	$427	$446	$330	$276	$164
READING	$150	$80	$131	$183	$187	$164	$151	$100
EDUCATION	$342	$646	$247	$454	$678	$234	$81	$31
TOBACCO PDTS./SMOKING SUPPLIES	$242	$183	$246	$277	$334	$268	$185	$84
MISCELLANEOUS	$578	$217	$515	$783	$775	$600	$512	$301
CASH CONTRIBUTIONS	$693	$120	$375	$806	$957	$1,002	$753	$785
PERSONAL INSURANCE/PENSIONS	$2,249	$972	$2,293	$3,150	$3,409	$2,609	$972	$375
GIFTS OF PRODUCTS AND SERVICES .	$841	$394	$551	$880	$1,346	$1,142	$751	$712

Note: Average annual expenditures are based on the total number of consumer units, not just those that make purchases in the category. Numbers may not add to totals due to rounding and unlisted items in the subcategories. Expenditures for gifts of products and services are also included in the product or service category. Some items in "miscellaneous" are moved to the category "other financial products and services" in chapters 2 through 10.

Age

Indexed average annual expenditures in 1988 for all household products and services, by age of reference person.

	all cu's	under 25	25 to 34	35 to 44	45 to 54	55 to 64	65 to 74	75+
Number of consumer units (in thousands)	94,862	7,216	21,985	19,911	13,601	12,546	11,319	8,284
Average number of persons per cu	2.6	1.8	2.8	3.3	2.9	2.2	2.0	1.5
Average number of earners per cu	1.4	1.3	1.5	1.8	2.0	1.4	0.6	0.4
AVERAGE TOTAL BEFORE-TAX INCOME	$28,540	$14,827	$28,318	$36,428	$39,934	$29,979	$20,704	$13,707
AVERAGE ANNUAL EXPENDITURES	100	63	100	128	128	100	78	52
FOOD	100	66	98	124	128	105	80	52
Food at home	100	52	96	122	122	110	90	64
Cereals and bakery products	100	53	93	124	124	107	89	69
Meat, poultry, fish, and eggs	100	45	92	120	123	118	97	65
Dairy products	100	55	101	122	120	108	86	64
Fruits and vegetables	100	47	88	116	121	116	105	78
Other foods at home	100	61	103	126	122	103	79	54
Food away from home	100	83	100	126	137	99	67	35
ALCOHOLIC BEVERAGES	100	116	132	104	114	89	60	33
HOUSING	100	59	105	130	120	96	76	58
Shelter	100	67	110	137	116	87	67	51
Owned dwellings	100	17	93	154	130	102	74	45
Mortgage interest	100	20	117	182	134	74	29	9
Property taxes	100	9	56	108	135	149	137	93
Maintenance, repairs, insurance, other expenses	100	15	54	110	114	146	148	113
Rented dwellings	100	163	153	103	80	52	53	64
Other lodging	100	37	67	150	155	116	79	39
Utilities, fuels, and public services	100	51	88	116	124	111	100	80
Household services	100	36	123	134	89	83	78	89
Personal services	100	57	212	157	34	25	13	44
Housekeeping supplies	100	46	96	114	125	106	106	69
Household furnishings and equipment	100	50	106	125	136	109	68	38
Household textiles	100	60	99	109	130	113	76	81
Furniture	100	60	114	132	135	102	53	25
Floor coverings	100	42	68	126	169	162	57	29
Major appliances	100	28	102	121	117	122	86	64
Small appliances, miscellaneous housewares, equipment	100	49	110	125	140	101	71	31
APPAREL AND APPAREL SERVICES	100	70	101	135	142	91	66	30
Men and boys	100	60	100	143	133	109	55	24
Men, aged 16 or older	100	70	100	123	139	121	61	24
Boys, aged 2 to 15	100	18	103	219	110	62	31	25
Women and girls	100	63	89	139	155	83	74	36
Women, aged 16 or older	100	70	86	120	165	92	83	41
Girls, aged 2 to 15	100	27	107	237	105	38	25	9

(continued from previous page)

	all cu's	under 25	25 to 34	35 to 44	45 to 54	55 to 64	65 to 74	75+
Babies, under age 2	100	95	198	108	79	66	32	11
Footwear	100	82	93	126	142	91	81	37
Other apparel products and services	100	85	111	129	140	86	60	25
TRANSPORTATION	100	77	108	125	130	90	78	35
Vehicle purchases (net outlay)	100	86	118	124	128	74	78	28
Cars and trucks, new	100	86	122	112	121	80	88	39
Cars and trucks, used	100	88	113	142	133	68	67	15
Gasoline and motor oil	100	71	99	124	134	104	78	39
Other vehicle expenses	100	67	100	130	131	102	74	37
Public transportation	100	68	84	111	139	118	96	57
HEALTH CARE	100	40	60	97	97	117	154	172
ENTERTAINMENT	100	72	105	149	122	85	66	26
Fees and admissions	100	70	88	146	137	96	74	29
Television, radios, sound equipment	100	84	106	144	115	84	68	34
Pets, toys, and playground equipment	100	50	120	139	113	90	70	33
Other entertainment supplies, equipment, services	100	75	112	165	119	72	52	10
PERSONAL CARE PDTS./SVCS.	100	61	95	128	134	99	83	49
READING	100	53	87	122	125	109	101	67
EDUCATION	100	189	72	133	198	68	24	9
TOBACCO PDTS./SMOKING SUPPLIES	100	76	102	114	138	111	76	35
MISCELLANEOUS	100	38	89	135	134	104	89	52
CASH CONTRIBUTIONS	100	17	54	116	138	145	109	113
PERSONAL INSURANCE/PENSIONS	100	43	102	140	152	116	43	17
GIFTS OF PRODUCTS AND SERVICES	100	47	66	105	160	136	89	85

Note: Expenditures for gifts of products and services are also included in the product or service category. An index of 100 represents the average for all consumer units. Some items in "miscellaneous" are moved to the category "other financial products and services" in chapters 2 through 10. An index of 132 means that the average for the subgroup is 32 percent above the average for all consumer units. An index of 68 indicates spending that is 32 percent below the overall average.

Income

AVERAGE
EXPENDITURES

While spending for most products and services rises with income, it rises much faster in some categories than in others. Spending on financial products and services, for example, increases nearly 2000 percent from the lowest-income to the highest-income households, while spending on health care increases by just 83 percent. Sharply rising spending is an indication of a high-end market; smaller increases indicate flatter markets. Households that spend more than the average on most goods and services generally have incomes of $30,000 or more. In many spending categories, households with incomes of $50,000 or more claim large shares of the total market. Nearly 30 percent of the U.S. transportation market, 35 percent of the entertainment market, and 25 percent of the food market are accounted for by households in that income bracket. With the exception of alcohol, tobacco products, health care, and transportation, households with incomes under $30,000 are below-average spenders.

Average annual expenditures in 1988 for all household products and services, by before-tax income of consumer unit.

(consumer units include complete income reporters only)	all cu's	under $10,000	$10,000 to $19,999	$20,000 to $29,999	$30,000 to $39,999	$40,000 to $49,999	$50,000 and over
Number of consumer units (in thousands)	81,354	18,809	17,652	14,586	10,901	7,198	12,209
Average number of persons per cu	2.6	1.8	2.3	2.7	2.9	3.2	3.1
Average number of earners per cu	1.4	0.7	1.0	1.5	1.8	2.0	2.1
AVERAGE TOTAL BEFORE-TAX INCOME	$28,540	$5,530	$14,673	$24,591	$34,375	$44,331	$74,234
AVERAGE ANNUAL EXPENDITURES	$26,389	$11,269	$18,078	$24,896	$31,660	$37,562	$52,320
FOOD	$3,804	$2,019	$2,972	$3,765	$4,587	$5,282	$6,296
Food at home	2,177	1,371	1,877	2,174	2,557	2,907	3,110
Cereals and bakery products	317	202	270	321	375	417	450
Meat, poultry, fish, and eggs	560	361	513	542	636	700	812
Dairy products	278	171	241	287	338	365	383
Fruits and vegetables	376	252	331	366	442	487	526
Other foods at home	646	385	520	658	766	938	938
Food away from home	1,627	648	1,095	1,591	2,031	2,375	3,186
ALCOHOLIC BEVERAGES	$282	$141	$207	$291	$344	$353	$506
HOUSING	$8,069	$4,108	$5,70	$7,512	$9,260	$10,609	$15,719
Shelter	4,470	2,270	3,088	4,125	5,050	5,901	8,909
Owned dwellings	2,554	758	1,049	1,977	2,971	4,060	6,926
Mortgage interest	1,560	299	412	1,052	1,925	2,784	4,725
Property taxes	496	207	309	417	599	644	1,126
Maintenance, repairs, insurance, other expenses	497	252	327	508	446	633	1,075
Rented dwellings	1,469	1,380	1,764	1,805	1,564	1,249	825
Other lodging	447	132	274	343	516	592	1,158
Utilities, fuels, and public services	1,726	1,159	1,474	1,711	1,925	2,089	2,593
Household services	387	154	211	310	449	531	955
Personal services	177	54	100	166	275	311	321
Housekeeping supplies	383	202	303	383	451	475	670
Household furnishings and equipment	1,102	324	630	982	1,386	1,612	2,591
Household textiles	97	36	64	96	105	122	220
Furniture	319	75	170	262	378	433	862
Floor coverings	70	11	24	75	111	113	165

(continued from previous page)

	all cu's	under $10,000	$10,000 to $19,999	$20,000 to $29,999	$30,000 to $39,999	$40,000 to $49,999	$50,000 and over
Major appliances	173	73	122	170	213	241	329
Small appliances, misc. housewares, equipment	443	130	251	380	579	702	1,015
APPAREL AND APPAREL SERVICES	**$1,537**	**$616**	**$979**	**$1,406**	**$1,847**	**$2,396**	**$3,154**
Men and boys	**401**	**136**	**227**	**350**	**429**	**666**	**944**
Men, aged 16 or older	319	108	170	271	340	533	773
Boys, aged 2 to 15	82	27	57	78	89	133	171
Women and girls	**609**	**267**	**387**	**550**	**771**	**950**	**1,190**
Women, aged 16 or older	510	233	326	458	649	773	993
Girls, aged 2 to 15	99	33	61	92	123	177	198
Babies, under age 2	**64**	**26**	**41**	**69**	**97**	**104**	**95**
Footwear	**204**	**96**	**171**	**203**	**254**	**332**	**300**
Other apparel products and services	**260**	**90**	**153**	**234**	**297**	**343**	**625**
TRANSPORTATION	**$5,140**	**$1,709**	**$3,459**	**$5,303**	**$6,704**	**$7,779**	**$9,715**
Vehicle purchases (net outlay)	**2,388**	**610**	**1,568**	**2,486**	**3,248**	**3,840**	**4,573**
Cars and trucks (new)	1,392	280	761	1,223	1,895	2,685	3,007
Cars and trucks (used)	971	327	794	1,222	1,330	1,132	1,505
Gasoline and motor oil	**934**	**467**	**715**	**975**	**1,190**	**1,328**	**1,460**
Other vehicle expenses	**1,553**	**519**	**1,023**	**1,603**	**1,973**	**2,290**	**3,046**
Public transportation	**266**	**114**	**154**	**239**	**294**	**321**	**635**
HEALTH CARE	**$1,282**	**$858**	**$1,345**	**$1,328**	**$1,367**	**$1,532**	**$1,568**
ENTERTAINMENT	**$1,349**	**$454**	**$827**	**$1,191**	**$1,510**	**$1,995**	**$3,148**
Fees and admissions	**352**	**116**	**161**	**310**	**420**	**526**	**880**
Television, radios, sound equipment	**422**	**197**	**309**	**416**	**494**	**576**	**788**
Pets, toys, and playground equipment	**242**	**93**	**157**	**234**	**337**	**354**	**457**
Other entertainment supplies, equipment, services	**332**	**48**	**201**	**231**	**260**	**538**	**1,023**
PERSONAL CARE PRODUCTS AND SERVICES	**$346**	**$151**	**$264**	**$325**	**$420**	**$479**	**$651**
READING	**$152**	**$70**	**$103**	**$142**	**$185**	**$230**	**$287**
EDUCATION	**$324**	**$247**	**$155**	**$190**	**$323**	**$349**	**$836**
TOBACCO PRODUCTS AND SMOKING SUPPLIES	**$242**	**$183**	**$235**	**$263**	**$293**	**$249**	**$270**
MISCELLANEOUS	**$598**	**$253**	**$406**	**$553**	**$770**	**$811**	**$1,182**
CASH CONTRIBUTIONS	**$730**	**$175**	**$415**	**$529**	**$781**	**$956**	**$2,103**
PERSONAL INSURANCE AND PENSIONS	**$2,532**	**$285**	**$1,004**	**$2,098**	**$3,266**	**$4,542**	**$6,883**
GIFTS OF PRODUCTS AND SERVICES	**$850**	**$362**	**$547**	**$818**	**$897**	**$1,133**	**$1,861**

Note: Average annual expenditures are based on the total number of consumer units, not just those that make purchases in the category. Numbers may not add to totals due to rounding and unlisted items in the subcategories. Expenditures for gifts of products and services are also included in the product or service category. Some items in "miscellaneous" are moved to the category "other financial products and services" in chapters 2 through 10. Total expenditure exceeds total income in some income categories due to a number of factors including the underreporting of income, borrowing, and the use of savings.

Income

Indexed average annual expenditures in 1988 for all household products and services, by before-tax income of consumer unit.

(consumer units include complete income reporters only)	all cu's	under $10,000	$10,000 to $19,999	$20,000 to $29,999	$30,000 to $39,999	$40,000 to $49,999	$50,000 and over
Number of consumer units (in thousands)	81,354	18,809	17,652	14,586	10,901	7,198	12,209
Average number of persons per cu	2.6	1.8	2.3	2.7	2.9	3.2	3.1
Average number of earners per cu	1.4	0.7	1.0	1.5	1.8	2.0	2.1
AVERAGE TOTAL BEFORE-TAX INCOME	$28,540	$5,530	$14,673	$24,591	$34,375	$44,331	$74,234
AVERAGE ANNUAL EXPENDITURES	100	43	69	94	120	142	198
FOOD	100	53	78	99	121	139	166
Food at home	100	63	86	100	117	134	143
Cereals and bakery products	100	64	85	101	118	132	142
Meat, poultry, fish, and eggs	100	64	92	97	114	125	145
Dairy products	100	61	87	103	122	131	138
Fruits and vegetables	100	67	88	97	118	130	140
Other foods at home	100	60	80	102	119	145	145
Food away from home	100	40	67	98	125	146	196
ALCOHOLIC BEVERAGES	100	50	73	103	122	125	179
HOUSING	100	51	71	93	115	131	195
Shelter	100	51	69	92	113	132	199
Owned dwellings	100	30	41	77	116	159	271
Mortgage interest	100	19	26	67	123	178	303
Property taxes	100	42	62	84	121	130	227
Maintenance, repairs, insurance, other expenses	100	51	66	102	90	127	216
Rented dwellings	100	94	120	123	106	85	56
Other lodging	100	30	61	77	115	132	259
Utilities, fuels, and public services	100	67	85	99	112	121	150
Household services	100	40	55	80	116	137	247
Personal services	100	31	56	94	155	176	181
Housekeeping supplies	100	53	79	100	118	124	175
Household furnishings and equipment	100	29	57	89	126	146	235
Household textiles	100	38	66	99	108	126	227
Furniture	100	23	53	82	118	136	270
Floor coverings	100	15	34	107	159	161	236
Major appliances	100	42	70	98	123	139	190
Small appliances, misc. housewares, equipment	100	29	57	86	131	158	229
APPAREL AND APPAREL SERVICES	100	40	64	91	120	156	205
Men and boys	100	34	57	87	107	166	235
Men, aged 16 or older	100	34	53	85	107	167	242
Boys, aged 2 to 15	100	33	69	95	109	162	209
Women and girls	100	44	64	90	127	156	195
Women, aged 16 or older	100	46	64	90	127	152	195
Girls, aged 2 to 15	100	33	61	93	124	179	200

(continued from previous page)

	all cu's	under $10,000	$10,000 to $19,999	$20,000 to $29,999	$30,000 to $39,999	$40,000 to $49,999	$50,000 and over
Babies, under age 2	100	41	63	108	152	163	148
Footwear	100	47	84	100	125	163	147
Other apparel products and services	100	35	59	90	114	132	240
TRANSPORTATION	100	33	67	103	130	151	189
Vehicle purchases (net outlay)	100	26	66	104	136	161	191
Cars and trucks (new)	100	20	55	88	136	193	216
Cars and trucks (used)	100	34	82	126	137	117	155
Gasoline and motor oil......................................	100	50	77	104	127	142	156
Other vehicle expenses	100	33	66	103	127	147	196
Public transportation	100	43	58	90	111	121	239
HEALTH CARE	100	67	105	104	107	120	122
ENTERTAINMENT	100	34	61	88	112	148	233
Fees and admissions	100	33	46	88	119	149	250
Television, radios, sound equipment	100	47	73	99	117	136	187
Pets, toys, and playground equipment	100	38	65	97	139	146	189
Other entertainment supplies, equipment, services	100	14	60	70	78	162	308
PERSONAL CARE PRODUCTS AND SERVICES	100	44	76	94	121	138	188
READING	100	46	68	93	122	151	189
EDUCATION	100	76	48	59	100	108	258
TOBACCO PRODUCTS AND SMOKING SUPPLIES	100	76	97	109	121	103	112
MISCELLANEOUS...	100	42	68	92	129	136	198
CASH CONTRIBUTIONS	100	24	57	72	107	131	288
PERSONAL INSURANCE AND PENSIONS	100	11	40	83	129	179	272
GIFTS OF PRODUCTS AND SERVICES	100	43	64	96	106	133	219

Note: Expenditures for gifts of products and services are also included in the product or service category. Some items in "miscellaneous" are moved to the category "other financial products and services" in chapters 2 through 10. An index of 100 represents the average for all consumer units. An index of 132 means that the average for the subgroup is 32 percent above the average for all consumer units. An index of 68 indicates spending that is 32 percent below the overall average.

Number of earners

Households with multiple earners are the biggest spenders on all major product and service categories except alcohol and health care. Earners who live alone spend more than others on alcohol. Households with two or more people and no earners, mainly retirees, spend the most on health care.

The average income of households with more than one earner is at least $12,000 higher than that of single-earner households. Multiple-earner households are also larger than those with one or no earners, averaging more than three people per household. It's not surprising that the spending of these households is above average on every item except rent and cash contributions.

Average annual expenditures in 1988 for all household products and services, by number of earners in consumer unit.

	all cu's	SINGLE PERSONS		CONSUMER UNITS WITH TWO OR MORE PERSONS			
		no earner	1 earner	no earner	1 earner	2 earners	3+ earners
Number of consumer units (in thousands)	94,862	9,297	17,274	9,443	17,872	30,868	10,108
Average age of reference person	47.0	68.9	37.8	62.8	47.7	40.6	46.2
Average number of persons per cu	2.6	1.0	1.0	2.5	3.0	3.1	4.4
AVERAGE TOTAL BEFORE-TAX INCOME	$28,540	$8,825	$19,757	$15,876	$26,511	$38,742	$46,963
AVERAGE ANNUAL EXPENDITURES	$25,892	$10,327	$18,520	$16,943	$24,904	$33,013	$40,476
FOOD	$3,748	$1,637	$2,318	$2,811	$3,861	$4,534	$6,077
Food at home	2,136	1,080	943	2,049	2,468	2,521	3,374
Cereals and bakery products	312	160	134	311	355	364	510
Meat, poultry, fish, and eggs	551	264	217	570	660	638	896
Dairy products	274	140	121	249	320	327	428
Fruits and vegetables	373	231	168	389	428	430	559
Other foods at home	625	284	302	529	705	762	980
Food away from home	1,612	558	1,375	762	1,393	2,014	2,703
ALCOHOLIC BEVERAGES	$269	$105	$365	$121	$205	$317	$312
HOUSING	$8,079	$4,034	$6,033	$5,658	$8,236	$10,231	$10,629
Shelter	4,493	2,174	4,003	2,796	4,413	5,680	5,562
Owned dwellings	2,569	874	1,304	1,265	2,592	3,755	3,844
Mortgage interest	1,569	191	798	226	1,471	2,605	2,419
Property taxes	504	297	243	513	558	601	736
Maintenance, repairs, insurance, other expenses	496	386	263	526	563	549	688
Rented dwellings	1,468	1,195	2,336	1,024	1,416	1,391	977
Other lodging	456	105	363	508	405	535	742
Utilities, fuels, and public services	1,747	1,116	1,067	1,612	1,907	2,015	2,519
Household services	394	270	127	229	401	616	427
Personal services	171	74	14	25	165	352	125
Housekeeping supplies	361	196	194	335	401	430	522
Household furnishings and equipment	1,083	277	641	686	1,114	1,490	1,599
Household textiles	94	35	50	89	98	114	155
Furniture	326	51	224	156	366	461	432
Floor coverings	65	11	24	38	56	98	121

(continued from previous page)

	all cu's	SINGLE PERSONS		CONSUMER UNITS WITH TWO OR MORE PERSONS			
		no earner	1 earner	no earner	1 earner	2 earners	3+ earners
Major appliances	169	73	85	143	192	222	220
Small appliances, misc. housewares, equipment	429	107	259	260	403	596	671
APPAREL AND APPAREL SERVICES	**$1,489**	**$563**	**$1,065**	**$760**	**$1,345**	**$1,901**	**$2,571**
Men and boys	**388**	**80**	**274**	**174**	**322**	**516**	**724**
Men, aged 16 or older	311	75	261	138	209	415	579
Boys, aged 2 to 15	77	5	13	36	113	101	145
Women and girls	**587**	**305**	**365**	**307**	**562**	**718**	**1,051**
Women, aged 16 or older	492	299	351	266	411	578	927
Girls, aged 2 to 15	95	6	14	41	151	140	123
Babies, under age 2	**62**	**7**	**13**	**36**	**91**	**99**	**58**
Footwear	**196**	**92**	**160**	**137**	**158**	**229**	**343**
Other apparel products and services	**257**	**79**	**252**	**106**	**213**	**340**	**394**
TRANSPORTATION	**$5,093**	**$1,384**	**$3,467**	**$2,576**	**$4,631**	**$6,803**	**$9,215**
Vehicle purchases (net outlay)	**2,361**	**517**	**1,412**	**972**	**2,095**	**3,356**	**4,404**
Cars and trucks (new)	1,355	357	966	608	1,246	1,967	1,961
Cars and trucks (used)	982	160	425	364	835	1,367	2,352
Gasoline and motor oil	**932**	**288**	**642**	**559**	**889**	**1,185**	**1,672**
Other vehicle expenses	**1,521**	**437**	**1,130**	**854**	**1,357**	**1,973**	**2,712**
Public transportation	**279**	**142**	**284**	**191**	**291**	**289**	**427**
HEALTH CARE	**$1,298**	**$1,231**	**$621**	**$1,964**	**$1,344**	**$1,403**	**$1,493**
ENTERTAINMENT	**$1,329**	**$334**	**$1,070**	**$737**	**$1,230**	**$1,788**	**$1,990**
Fees and admissions	**353**	**95**	**329**	**175**	**321**	**437**	**599**
Television, radios, sound equipment	**416**	**141**	**357**	**246**	**390**	**524**	**634**
Pets, toys, and playground equipment	**230**	**70**	**122**	**128**	**259**	**331**	**289**
Other entertainment supplies, equipment, services	**330**	**27**	**262**	**187**	**261**	**496**	**467**
PERSONAL CARE PRODUCTS AND SERVICES	**$334**	**$148**	**$228**	**$250**	**$315**	**$405**	**$549**
READING	**$150**	**$82**	**$128**	**$122**	**$144**	**$179**	**$198**
EDUCATION	**$342**	**$107**	**$323**	**$94**	**$208**	**$365**	**$988**
TOBACCO PRODUCTS AND SMOKING SUPPLIES	**$242**	**$98**	**$162**	**$188**	**$242**	**$303**	**$376**
MISCELLANEOUS	**$578**	**$198**	**$451**	**$459**	**$496**	**$736**	**$911**
CASH CONTRIBUTIONS	**$693**	**$296**	**$566**	**$855**	**$749**	**$667**	**$1,107**
PERSONAL INSURANCE AND PENSIONS	**$2,249**	**$110**	**$1,723**	**$350**	**$1,898**	**$3,379**	**$4,061**
GIFTS OF PRODUCTS AND SERVICES	**$841**	**$456**	**$762**	**$534**	**$675**	**$1,045**	**$1,224**

Note: Average annual expenditures are based on the total number of consumer units, not just those that make purchases in the category. Numbers may not add to totals due to rounding and unlisted items in the subcategories. Expenditures for gifts of products and services are also included in the product or service category. Some items in "miscellaneous" are moved to the category "other financial products and services" in chapters 2 through 10.

Number of earners

	all cu's	SINGLE PERSONS		CONSUMER UNITS WITH TWO OR MORE PERSONS			
Indexed average annual expenditures in 1988 for all household products and services, by number of earners in consumer unit.		no earner	1 earner	no earner	1 earner	2 earners	3+ earners
Number of consumer units (in thousands)	94,862	9,297	17,274	9,443	17,872	30,868	10,108
Average age of reference person	47.0	68.9	37.8	62.8	47.7	40.6	46.2
Average number of persons per cu	2.6	1.0	1.0	2.5	3.0	3.1	4.4
AVERAGE TOTAL BEFORE-TAX INCOME	$28,540	$8,825	$19,757	$15,876	$26,511	$38,742	$46,963
AVERAGE ANNUAL EXPENDITURES	100	40	72	65	96	128	156
FOOD	100	44	62	75	103	121	162
Food at home	100	51	44	96	116	118	158
Cereals and bakery products	100	51	43	100	114	117	163
Meat, poultry, fish, and eggs	100	48	39	103	120	116	163
Dairy products	100	51	44	91	117	119	156
Fruits and vegetables	100	62	45	104	115	115	150
Other foods at home	100	45	48	85	113	122	157
Food away from home	100	35	85	47	86	125	168
ALCOHOLIC BEVERAGES	100	39	136	45	76	118	116
HOUSING	100	50	75	70	102	127	132
Shelter	100	48	89	62	98	126	124
Owned dwellings	100	34	51	49	101	146	150
Mortgage interest	100	12	51	14	94	166	154
Property taxes	100	59	48	102	111	119	146
Maintenance, repairs, insurance, other expenses	100	78	53	106	114	111	139
Rented dwellings	100	81	159	70	96	95	67
Other lodging	100	23	80	111	89	117	163
Utilities, fuels, and public services	100	64	61	92	109	115	144
Household services	100	69	32	58	102	156	108
Personal services	100	43	8	15	96	206	73
Housekeeping supplies	100	54	54	93	111	119	145
Household furnishings and equipment	100	26	59	63	103	138	148
Household textiles	100	37	53	95	104	121	165
Furniture	100	16	69	48	112	141	133
Floor coverings	100	17	37	58	86	151	186
Major appliances	100	43	50	85	114	131	130
Small appliances, misc. housewares, equipment	100	25	60	61	94	139	156
APPAREL AND APPAREL SERVICES	100	38	72	51	90	128	173
Men and boys	100	21	71	45	83	133	187
Men, aged 16 or older	100	24	84	44	67	133	186
Boys, aged 2 to 15	100	6	17	47	147	131	188
Women and girls	100	52	62	52	96	122	179
Women, aged 16 or older	100	61	71	54	84	117	188
Girls, aged 2 to 15	100	6	15	43	159	147	129

(continued from previous page)

	all cu's	SINGLE PERSONS		CONSUMER UNITS WITH TWO OR MORE PERSONS			
		no earner	1 earner	no earner	1 earner	2 earners	3+ earners
Babies, under age 2	100	11	21	58	147	160	94
Footwear	100	47	82	70	81	117	175
Other apparel products and services	100	31	98	41	83	132	153
TRANSPORTATION	100	27	68	51	91	134	181
Vehicle purchases (net outlay)	100	22	60	41	89	142	187
Cars and trucks (new)	100	26	71	45	92	145	145
Cars and trucks (used)	100	16	43	37	85	139	240
Gasoline and motor oil	100	31	69	60	95	127	179
Other vehicle expenses	100	29	74	56	89	130	178
Public transportation	100	51	102	68	104	104	153
HEALTH CARE	100	95	48	151	104	108	115
ENTERTAINMENT	100	25	81	55	93	135	150
Fees and admissions	100	27	93	50	91	124	170
Television, radios, sound equipment	100	34	86	59	94	126	152
Pets, toys, and playground equipment	100	30	53	56	113	144	126
Other entertainment supplies, equipment, services	100	8	79	57	79	150	142
PERSONAL CARE PRODUCTS AND SERVICES	100	44	68	75	94	121	164
READING	100	55	85	81	96	119	132
EDUCATION	100	31	94	27	61	107	289
TOBACCO PRODUCTS AND SMOKING SUPPLIES	100	40	67	78	100	125	155
MISCELLANEOUS	100	34	78	79	86	127	158
CASH CONTRIBUTIONS	100	43	82	123	108	96	160
PERSONAL INSURANCE AND PENSIONS	100	5	77	16	84	150	181
GIFTS OF PRODUCTS AND SERVICES	100	54	91	63	80	124	146

Note: Expenditures for gifts of products and services are also included in the product or service category. Some items in "miscellaneous" are moved to the category "other financial products and services" in chapters 2 through 10. An index of 100 represents the average for all consumer units. An index of 132 means that the average for the subgroup is 32 percent above the average for all consumer units. An index of 68 indicates spending that is 32 percent below the overall average.

Household type

AVERAGE
EXPENDITURES

When it comes to spending by type of household, the world splits neatly into two parts—married couples and everyone else. Married couples spend more than average on every major category of household products and services except alcohol. And couples with children outspend those without children in every spending category except health care, cash contributions, and gifts. People who live alone and "other" households spend above average on just one product category—alcohol. Single parents spend less than average on all major product and service categories. The profile of American households is shifting in the direction of small spenders. Although the number of married couples will increase during the 1990s, the number of people who live alone will grow three times as fast. The number of empty nesters and childless couples will increase by 21 percent, while the number of married couples with children will fall by nearly 13 percent.

Average annual expenditures in 1988 for all household products and services, by type of consumer unit.				
	all cu's	married couples	single parents	single persons and other cu's
Number of consumer units (in thousands)	94,862	52,010	5,716	37,136
Average number of persons per cu	2.6	3.3	2.9	1.5
Average number of earners per cu	1.4	1.7	1.0	0.9
AVERAGE TOTAL BEFORE-TAX INCOME	$28,540	$37,299	$16,276	$18,509
AVERAGE ANNUAL EXPENDITURES	$25,892	$32,314	$18,616	$17,951
FOOD	$3,748	$4,727	$3,005	$2,452
Food at home	2,136	2,761	1,931	1,265
Cereals and bakery products	312	407	291	179
Meat, poultry, fish, and eggs	551	710	511	328
Dairy products	274	353	256	163
Fruits and vegetables	373	475	314	235
Other foods at home	625	816	559	361
Food away from home	1,612	1,967	1,074	1,187
ALCOHOLIC BEVERAGES	$269	$263	$167	$292
HOUSING	$8,079	$9,731	$7,113	$5,903
Shelter	4,493	5,174	4,249	3,576
Owned dwellings	2,569	3,538	1,397	1,392
Mortgage interest	1,569	2,242	951	721
Property taxes	504	665	227	320
Maintenance, repairs, insurance, other expenses	496	630	218	351
Rented dwellings	1,468	1,050	2,344	1,919
Other lodging	456	587	508	265
Utilities, fuels, and public services	1,747	2,100	1,482	1,295
Household services	394	523	467	203
Personal services	171	236	333	55
Housekeeping supplies	361	463	271	227
Household furnishings and equipment	1,083	1,471	645	602
Household textiles	94	121	67	59
Furniture	326	441	178	188
Floor coverings	65	100	33	21

(continued from previous page)

	all cu's	married couples	single parents	single persons and other cu's
Major appliances	169	222	138	99
Small appliances, misc. housewares, equipment	429	587	228	235
APPAREL AND APPAREL SERVICES	**$1,489**	**$1,829**	**$1,383**	**$1,019**
Men and boys	**388**	**510**	**258**	**231**
Men, aged 16 or older	311	405	95	209
Boys, aged 2 to 15	77	106	164	22
Women and girls	**587**	**707**	**684**	**399**
Women, aged 16 or older	492	582	393	377
Girls, aged 2 to 15	95	125	291	22
Babies, under age 2	**62**	**92**	**64**	**20**
Footwear	**196**	**223**	**191**	**156**
Other apparel products and services	**257**	**296**	**186**	**213**
TRANSPORTATION	**$5,093**	**$6,523**	**$2,864**	**$3,431**
Vehicle purchases (net outlay)	**2,361**	**3,109**	**1,174**	**1,495**
Cars and trucks (new)	1,355	1,746	453	946
Cars and trucks (used)	982	1,332	714	534
Gasoline and motor oil	**932**	**1,188**	**558**	**631**
Other vehicle expenses	**1,521**	**1,912**	**952**	**1,060**
Public transportation	**279**	**314**	**180**	**245**
HEALTH CARE	**$1,298**	**$1,658**	**$578**	**$903**
ENTERTAINMENT	**$1,329**	**$1,700**	**$920**	**$870**
Fees and admissions	**353**	**448**	**189**	**245**
Television, radios, sound equipment	**416**	**500**	**330**	**310**
Pets, toys, and playground equipment	**230**	**307**	**196**	**127**
Other entertainment supplies, equipment, services	**330**	**445**	**206**	**188**
PERSONAL CARE PRODUCTS AND SERVICES	**$334**	**$413**	**$259**	**$232**
READING	**$150**	**$180**	**$90**	**$117**
EDUCATION	**$342**	**$416**	**$224**	**$257**
TOBACCO PRODUCTS AND SMOKING SUPPLIES	**$242**	**$280**	**$209**	**$194**
MISCELLANEOUS	**$578**	**$677**	**$462**	**$456**
CASH CONTRIBUTIONS	**$693**	**$875**	**$207**	**$513**
PERSONAL INSURANCE AND PENSIONS	**$2,249**	**$3,041**	**$1,135**	**$1,312**
GIFTS OF PRODUCTS AND SERVICES	**$841**	**$1,010**	**$493**	**$650**

Note: Average annual expenditures are based on the total number of consumer units, not just those that make purchases in the category. Numbers may not add to totals due to rounding and unlisted items in the subcategories. Expenditures for gifts of products and services are also included in the product or service category. "Single parents" is one-parent consumer units with a child or children under age 18 living at home. "Other cu's" includes persons living with unrelated persons and families other than married-couple and single-parent families. Some items in "miscellaneous" are moved to the category "other financial products and services" in chapters 2 through 10.

Household type

INDEXED
EXPENDITURES

Indexed average annual expenditures in 1988 for all household products and services, by type of consumer unit.

	all cu's	married couples	single parents	single persons and other cu's
Number of consumer units (in thousands)	94,862	52,010	5,716	37,136
Average number of persons per cu	2.6	3.3	2.9	1.5
Average number of earners per cu	1.4	1.7	1.0	0.9
AVERAGE TOTAL BEFORE-TAX INCOME	$28,540	$37,299	$16,276	$18,509
AVERAGE ANNUAL EXPENDITURES	100	125	72	69
FOOD	100	126	80	65
Food at home	100	129	90	59
Cereals and bakery products	100	130	93	57
Meat, poultry, fish, and eggs	100	129	93	60
Dairy products	100	129	93	59
Fruits and vegetables	100	127	84	63
Other foods at home	100	131	89	58
Food away from home	100	122	67	74
ALCOHOLIC BEVERAGES	100	98	62	109
HOUSING	100	120	88	73
Shelter	100	115	95	80
Owned dwellings	100	138	54	54
Mortgage interest	100	143	61	46
Property taxes	100	132	45	63
Maintenance, repairs, insurance, other expenses	100	127	44	71
Rented dwellings	100	72	160	131
Other lodging	100	129	111	58
Utilities, fuels, and public services	100	120	85	74
Household services	100	133	119	52
Personal services	100	138	195	32
Housekeeping supplies	100	128	75	63
Household furnishings and equipment	100	136	60	56
Household textiles	100	129	71	63
Furniture	100	135	55	58
Floor coverings	100	154	51	32
Major appliances	100	131	82	59
Small appliances, misc. housewares, equipment	100	137	53	55
APPAREL AND APPAREL SERVICES	100	123	93	68
Men and boys	100	131	66	60
Men, aged 16 or older	100	130	31	67
Boys, aged 2 to 15	100	138	213	29
Women and girls	100	120	117	68
Women, aged 16 or older	100	118	80	77
Girls, aged 2 to 15	100	132	306	23

(continued from previous page)

	all cu's	married couples	single parents	single persons and other cu's
Babies, under age 2	100	148	103	32
Footwear	100	114	97	80
Other apparel products and services	100	115	72	83
TRANSPORTATION	100	128	56	67
Vehicle purchases (net outlay)	100	132	50	63
Cars and trucks (new)	100	129	33	70
Cars and trucks (used)	100	136	73	54
Gasoline and motor oil	100	127	60	68
Other vehicle expenses	100	126	63	70
Public transportation	100	113	65	88
HEALTH CARE	100	128	45	70
ENTERTAINMENT	100	128	69	65
Fees and admissions	100	127	54	69
Television, radios, sound equipment	100	120	79	75
Pets, toys, and playground equipment	100	133	85	55
Other entertainment supplies, equipment, services	100	135	62	57
PERSONAL CARE PRODUCTS AND SERVICES	100	124	78	69
READING	100	120	60	78
EDUCATION	100	122	65	75
TOBACCO PRODUCTS AND SMOKING SUPPLIES	100	116	86	80
MISCELLANEOUS	100	117	80	79
CASH CONTRIBUTIONS	100	126	30	74
PERSONAL INSURANCE AND PENSIONS	100	135	50	58
GIFTS OF PRODUCTS AND SERVICES	100	120	59	77

Note: Expenditures for gifts of products and services are also included in the product or service category. Some items in "miscellaneous" are moved to the category "other financial products and services" in chapters 2 through 10. "Single parents" is one-parent consumer units with a child or children under age 18 living at home. "Other cu's" includes persons living with unrelated persons and families other than married-couple and single-parent families. An index of 100 represents the average for all consumer units. An index of 132 means that the average for the subgroup is 32 percent above the average for all consumer units. An index of 68 indicates spending that is 32 percent below the overall average.

Married couples

In the 1990s, businesses need to keep a close watch on the changing American household. The biggest spenders, married couples with children under age 18 at home, are a shrinking share of the market. Married couples with children outspend those without children in every major spending category except health care, cash contributions, and gifts.

Couples without dependent children at home will continue to be the largest share of households through the 1990s. But by mid-decade, couples with children at home will fall from second to third place while people who live alone will advance into second place. The typical household of the 1990s will not be Mom, Dad and the kids—or even just Mom and Dad.

Average annual expenditures in 1988 for all household products and services, by married couples with and without children.

	all cu's	all married couples	married couple only	all married couples with children	AGE OF OLDEST CHILD			other married couples
					under 6	6 to 17	18 or older	
Number of consumer units (in thousands)	94,862	52,010	20,227	28,100	5,858	14,194	8,047	3,684
Average number of persons per cu	2.6	3.3	2.0	3.9	3.5	4.1	3.9	5.1
Average number of earners per cu	1.4	1.7	1.2	2.1	1.7	1.9	2.7	2.4
AVERAGE TOTAL BEFORE-TAX INCOME	$28,540	$37,299	$33,825	$39,354	$34,318	$38,039	$45,596	$40,846
AVERAGE ANNUAL EXPENDITURES	$25,892	$32,314	$27,955	$35,015	$30,943	$35,248	$37,764	$35,740
FOOD	$3,748	$4,727	$3,815	$5,289	$4,077	$5,473	$5,966	$5,513
Food at home	2,136	2,761	2,148	3,104	2,516	3,268	3,313	3,564
Cereals and bakery products	312	407	302	467	346	515	484	529
Meat, poultry, fish, and eggs	551	710	558	792	595	813	929	932
Dairy products	274	353	266	404	340	431	408	457
Fruits and vegetables	373	475	413	500	427	509	546	633
Other foods at home	625	816	609	941	806	999	946	1,012
Food away from home	1,612	1,967	1,667	2,185	1,561	2,205	2,653	1,949
ALCOHOLIC BEVERAGES	$269	$263	$259	$265	$273	$244	$299	$272
HOUSING	$8,079	$9,731	$8,453	$10,542	$10,808	$10,850	$9,819	$10,567
Shelter	4,493	5,174	4,433	5,639	5,772	6,003	4,901	5,698
Owned dwellings	2,569	3,538	2,952	3,946	3,588	4,357	3,483	3,637
Mortgage interest	1,569	2,242	1,497	2,758	2,765	3,216	1,945	2,402
Property taxes	504	665	732	622	390	623	790	628
Maintenance, repairs, insurance, other expenses	496	630	723	566	433	518	749	607
Rented dwellings	1,468	1,050	904	1,110	1,891	1,104	553	1,387
Other lodging	456	587	577	583	294	542	865	675
Utilities, fuels, and public services	1,747	2,100	1,873	2,219	1,841	2,197	2,533	2,439
Household services	394	523	319	667	1,221	644	303	542
Personal services	171	236	9	400	982	365	39	232
Housekeeping supplies	361	463	409	499	477	491	533	488
Household furnishings and equipment	1,083	1,471	1,419	1,519	1,498	1,515	1,549	1,399
Household textiles	94	121	119	120	125	102	152	147
Furniture	326	441	405	476	532	495	403	373
Floor coverings	65	100	100	99	86	77	151	111

(continued from previous page)

	all cu's	all married couples	married couple only	all married couples with children	AGE OF OLDEST CHILD			other married couples
					under 6	6 to 17	18 or older	
Major appliances	169	222	210	231	232	232	227	222
Small appliances, misc. housewares, equipment	429	587	586	593	523	609	616	547
APPAREL AND APPAREL SERVICES	**$1,489**	**$1,829**	**$1,395**	**$2,083**	**$1,764**	**$2,182**	**$2,171**	**$2,301**
Men and boys	**388**	**510**	**402**	**579**	**428**	**608**	**653**	**586**
Men, aged 16 or older	311	405	373	425	318	396	570	429
Boys, aged 2 to 15	77	106	29	155	111	212	82	157
Women and girls	**587**	**707**	**509**	**830**	**564**	**941**	**854**	**866**
Women, aged 16 or older	492	582	486	637	481	636	780	702
Girls, aged 2 to 15	95	125	23	193	83	305	74	164
Babies, under age 2	**62**	**92**	**34**	**128**	**357**	**70**	**42**	**144**
Footwear	**196**	**223**	**166**	**247**	**159**	**274**	**275**	**364**
Other apparel products and services	**257**	**296**	**284**	**299**	**256**	**289**	**347**	**341**
TRANSPORTATION	**$5,093**	**$6,523**	**$5,695**	**$7,028**	**$6,248**	**$6,569**	**$8,412**	**$7,220**
Vehicle purchases (net outlay)	**2,361**	**3,109**	**2,743**	**3,330**	**3,224**	**3,054**	**3,894**	**3,424**
Cars and trucks (new)	1,355	1,746	1,872	1,673	1,961	1,471	1,819	1,619
Cars and trucks (used)	982	1,332	855	1,614	1,215	1,572	1,980	1,790
Gasoline and motor oil	**932**	**1,188**	**964**	**1,331**	**1,054**	**1,279**	**1,624**	**1,329**
Other vehicle expenses	**1,521**	**1,912**	**1,632**	**2,092**	**1,768**	**1,970**	**2,551**	**2,083**
Public transportation	**279**	**314**	**356**	**275**	**203**	**266**	**344**	**385**
HEALTH CARE	**$1,298**	**$1,658**	**$1,837**	**$1,473**	**$1,206**	**$1,479**	**$1,659**	**$2,086**
ENTERTAINMENT	**$1,329**	**$1,700**	**$1,366**	**$1,961**	**$1,734**	**$2,175**	**$1,748**	**$1,549**
Fees and admissions	**353**	**448**	**384**	**495**	**311**	**541**	**548**	**444**
Television, radios, sound equipment	**416**	**500**	**376**	**586**	**536**	**625**	**554**	**532**
Pets, toys, and playground equipment	**230**	**307**	**232**	**359**	**399**	**405**	**248**	**322**
Other entertainment supplies, equipment, services	**330**	**445**	**374**	**521**	**489**	**604**	**399**	**251**
PERSONAL CARE PRODUCTS/SERVICES	**$334**	**$413**	**$347**	**$456**	**$332**	**$474**	**$529**	**$443**
READING	**$150**	**$180**	**$178**	**$182**	**$150**	**$186**	**$198**	**$173**
EDUCATION	**$342**	**$416**	**$192**	**$571**	**$142**	**$521**	**$969**	**$470**
TOBACCO PDTS./SMOKING SUPPLIES	**$242**	**$280**	**$229**	**$300**	**$251**	**$293**	**$349**	**$405**
MISCELLANEOUS	**$578**	**$677**	**$588**	**$733**	**$601**	**$711**	**$871**	**$746**
CASH CONTRIBUTIONS	**$693**	**$875**	**$1,014**	**$760**	**$498**	**$731**	**$1,002**	**$994**
PERSONAL INSURANCE/PENSIONS	**$2,249**	**$3,041**	**$2,587**	**$3,373**	**$2,858**	**$3,359**	**$3,771**	**$3,001**
GIFTS OF PRODUCTS AND SERVICES	**$841**	**$1,010**	**$1,056**	**$930**	**$843**	**$810**	**$1,211**	**$1,364**

Note: Average annual expenditures are based on the total number of consumer units, not just those that make purchases in the category. Numbers may not add to totals due to rounding and unlisted items in the subcategories. Expenditures for gifts of products and services are also included in the product or service category. Other married couples include extended family members or unrelated persons in addition to the married couple. Some items in "miscellaneous" are moved to the category "other financial products and services" in chapters 2 through 10.

Married couples

Indexed average annual expenditures in 1988 for all household products and services, by married couples with and without children.

	all cu's	all married couples	married couple only	all married couples with children	AGE OF OLDEST CHILD			other married couples
					under 6	6 to 17	18 or older	
Number of consumer units (in thousands)	94,862	52,010	20,227	28,100	5,858	14,194	8,047	3,684
Average number of persons per cu	2.6	3.3	2.0	3.9	3.5	4.1	3.9	5.1
Average number of earners per cu	1.4	1.7	1.2	2.1	1.7	1.9	2.7	2.4
AVERAGE TOTAL BEFORE-TAX INCOME	$28,540	$37,299	$33,825	$39,354	$34,318	$38,039	$45,596	$40,846
AVERAGE ANNUAL EXPENDITURES	100	125	108	135	120	136	146	138
FOOD	100	126	102	141	109	146	159	147
Food at home	100	129	101	145	118	153	155	167
Cereals and bakery products	100	130	97	150	111	165	155	170
Meat, poultry, fish, and eggs	100	129	101	144	108	148	169	169
Dairy products	100	129	97	147	124	157	149	167
Fruits and vegetables	100	127	111	134	114	136	146	170
Other foods at home	100	131	97	151	129	160	151	162
Food away from home	100	122	103	136	97	137	165	121
ALCOHOLIC BEVERAGES	100	98	96	99	101	91	111	101
HOUSING	100	120	105	130	134	134	122	131
Shelter	100	115	99	126	128	134	109	127
Owned dwellings	100	138	115	154	140	170	136	142
Mortgage interest	100	143	95	176	176	205	124	153
Property taxes	100	132	145	123	77	124	157	125
Maintenance, repairs, insurance, other expenses	100	127	146	114	87	104	151	122
Rented dwellings	100	72	62	76	129	75	38	94
Other lodging	100	129	127	128	64	119	190	148
Utilities, fuels, and public services	100	120	107	127	105	126	145	140
Household services	100	133	81	169	310	163	77	138
Personal services	100	138	5	234	574	213	23	136
Housekeeping supplies	100	128	113	138	132	136	148	135
Household furnishings and equipment	100	136	131	140	138	140	143	129
Household textiles	100	129	127	128	133	109	162	156
Furniture	100	135	124	146	163	152	124	114
Floor coverings	100	154	154	152	132	118	232	171
Major appliances	100	131	124	137	137	137	134	131
Small appliances, misc. housewares, equipment	100	137	137	138	122	142	144	128
APPAREL AND APPAREL SERVICES	100	123	94	140	118	147	146	155
Men and boys	100	131	104	149	110	157	168	151
Men, aged 16 or older	100	130	120	137	102	127	183	138
Boys, aged 2 to 15	100	138	38	201	144	275	106	204
Women and girls	100	120	87	141	96	160	145	148
Women, aged 16 or older	100	118	99	129	98	129	159	143
Girls, aged 2 to 15	100	132	24	203	87	321	78	173

(continued from previous page)

	all cu's	all married couples	married couple only	all married couples with children	AGE OF OLDEST CHILD			other married couples
					under 6	6 to 17	18 or older	
Babies, under age 2	100	148	55	206	576	113	68	232
Footwear	100	114	85	126	81	140	140	186
Other apparel products and services	100	115	111	116	100	112	135	133
TRANSPORTATION	100	128	112	138	123	129	165	142
Vehicle purchases (net outlay)	100	132	116	141	137	129	165	145
Cars and trucks (new)	100	129	138	123	145	109	134	119
Cars and trucks (used)	100	136	87	164	124	160	202	182
Gasoline and motor oil	100	127	103	143	113	137	174	143
Other vehicle expenses	100	126	107	138	116	130	168	137
Public transportation	100	113	128	99	73	95	123	138
HEALTH CARE	100	128	142	113	93	114	128	161
ENTERTAINMENT	100	128	103	148	130	164	132	117
Fees and admissions	100	127	109	140	88	153	155	126
Television, radios, sound equipment	100	120	90	141	129	150	133	128
Pets, toys, and playground equipment	100	133	101	156	173	176	108	140
Other entertainment supplies, equipment, services	100	135	113	158	148	183	121	76
PERSONAL CARE PRODUCTS/SERVICES	100	124	104	137	99	142	158	133
READING	100	120	119	121	100	124	132	115
EDUCATION	100	122	56	167	42	152	283	137
TOBACCO PDTS./SMOKING SUPPLIES	100	116	95	124	104	121	144	167
MISCELLANEOUS	100	117	102	127	104	123	151	129
CASH CONTRIBUTIONS	100	126	146	110	72	105	145	143
PERSONAL INSURANCE/PENSIONS	100	135	115	150	127	149	168	133
GIFTS OF PRODUCTS AND SERVICES	100	120	126	111	100	96	144	162

Note: Expenditures for gifts of products and services are also included in the product or service category. Other married couples includes extended family members or unrelated persons in addition to the married couple. Some items in "miscellaneous" are moved to the category "other financial products and services" in chapters 2 through 10. An index of 100 represents the average for all consumer units. An index of 132 means that the average for the subgroup is 32 percent above the average for all consumer units. An index of 68 indicates spending that is 32 percent below the overall average.

Household size

AVERAGE EXPENDITURES

Spending on household products and services is generally higher for households with three or more people than for single-person or two-person households. People who live alone spend more than the average household on only rent and alcohol. Households with two people, many of which are older empty-nesters, spend above average on many items. They are the peak spenders on maintenance, repairs, and insurance for owned homes; health care; public transportation; and cash contributions.

The big spenders on most products and services are families with children. Spending on food, clothing, utilities, education, and tobacco products is highest in households with five or more people. Those with four people outspend others on owned dwellings, household services, transportation, entertainment, reading, personal insurance, and pensions. Three-person households are the most generous gift givers.

Average annual expenditures in 1988 for all household products and services, by size of consumer unit.

	all cu's	1 person	2 persons	2+ persons	3 persons	4 persons	5+ persons
Number of consumer units (in thousands)	94,865	26,571	28,750	68,291	15,612	13,998	9,931
Average age of reference person	47.0	48.7	53.2	46.3	43.1	39.7	40.9
Average number of earners per cu	1.4	0.7	1.2	1.7	1.8	2.0	2.3
AVERAGE TOTAL BEFORE-TAX INCOME	$28,540	$16,090	$30,444	$33,540	$33,862	$38,944	$34,417
AVERAGE ANNUAL EXPENDITURES	$25,892	$15,671	$26,350	$29,875	$30,446	$34,455	$32,706
FOOD	$3,748	$2,087	$3,600	$4,398	$4,402	$5,207	$5,550
Food at home	2,136	989	2,022	2,585	2,522	3,071	3,621
Cereals and bakery products	312	143	282	378	368	466	550
Meat, poultry, fish, and eggs	551	233	534	676	650	792	960
Dairy products	274	128	252	332	321	402	480
Fruits and vegetables	373	190	384	445	433	506	554
Other foods at home	625	296	570	754	750	906	1,078
Food away from home	1,612	1,099	1,578	1,813	1,880	2,137	1,928
ALCOHOLIC BEVERAGES	$269	$278	$278	$265	$268	$261	$229
HOUSING	$8,079	$5,335	$8,148	$9,147	$9,503	$10,462	$9,627
Shelter	4,493	3,363	4,420	4,932	5,105	5,632	5,157
Owned dwellings	2,569	1,154	2,624	3,119	3,218	3,894	3,304
Mortgage interest	1,569	586	1,362	1,952	2,156	2,686	2,303
Property taxes	504	262	629	598	543	654	514
Maintenance, repairs, insurance, other expenses	496	306	633	570	520	555	487
Rented dwellings	1,468	1,937	1,245	1,285	1,375	1,195	1,389
Other lodging	456	273	551	528	512	543	464
Utilities, fuels, and public services	1,747	1,084	1,794	2,005	2,013	2,213	2,315
Household services	394	178	320	478	511	739	517
Personal services	171	35	46	224	283	451	327
Housekeeping supplies	361	195	378	426	456	462	466
Household furnishings and equipment	1,083	515	1,235	1,305	1,418	1,416	1,172
Household textiles	94	45	110	113	136	102	102
Furniture	326	163	351	389	430	447	356
Floor coverings	65	19	80	83	115	76	53

Average annual expenditures in 1988 for all household products and services, by size of consumer unit.

(continued from previous page)

	all cu's	1 person	2 persons	2+ persons	3 persons	4 persons	5+ persons
Major appliances	169	81	190	203	211	245	168
Small appliances, misc. housewares, equipment	429	207	504	516	527	547	493
APPAREL AND APPAREL SERVICES	**$1,489**	**$893**	**$1,325**	**$1,722**	**$1,859**	**$2,010**	**$2,246**
Men and boys..	**388**	**208**	**350**	**458**	**461**	**564**	**614**
Men, aged 16 or older	311	198	322	355	361	395	382
Boys, aged 2 to 15	77	10	28	103	99	169	232
Women and girls	**587**	**345**	**508**	**681**	**757**	**790**	**907**
Women, aged 16 or older	492	333	473	554	636	578	624
Girls, aged 2 to 15	95	11	35	127	121	212	283
Babies, under age 2	**62**	**11**	**32**	**82**	**113**	**120**	**128**
Footwear	**196**	**137**	**163**	**219**	**237**	**239**	**321**
Other apparel products and services	**257**	**191**	**272**	**282**	**291**	**297**	**276**
TRANSPORTATION	**$5,093**	**$2,739**	**$5,403**	**$6,009**	**$6,061**	**$6,818**	**$6,540**
Vehicle purchases (net outlay)	**2,361**	**1,099**	**2,581**	**2,852**	**2,851**	**3,241**	**3,088**
Cars and trucks (new)	1,355	753	1,734	1,589	1,454	1,528	1,470
Cars and trucks (used)	982	332	831	1,235	1,375	1,653	1,597
Gasoline and motor oil...	**932**	**518**	**916**	**1,093**	**1,112**	**1,279**	**1,313**
Other vehicle expenses..	**1,521**	**888**	**1,573**	**1,768**	**1,822**	**2,027**	**1,883**
Public transportation	**279**	**234**	**333**	**296**	**276**	**272**	**257**
HEALTH CARE	**$1,298**	**$834**	**$1,607**	**$1,478**	**$1,409**	**$1,425**	**$1,287**
ENTERTAINMENT	**$1,329**	**$813**	**$1,254**	**$1,530**	**$1,575**	**$2,062**	**$1,505**
Fees and admissions	**353**	**247**	**345**	**394**	**384**	**478**	**435**
Television, radios, sound equipment	**416**	**282**	**366**	**468**	**515**	**590**	**512**
Pets, toys, and playground equipment	**230**	**104**	**219**	**280**	**285**	**392**	**287**
Other entertainment supplies, equipment, services	**330**	**180**	**323**	**388**	**390**	**602**	**270**
PERSONAL CARE PRODUCTS AND SERVICES	**$334**	**$201**	**$331**	**$385**	**$407**	**$436**	**$438**
READING	**$150**	**$112**	**$165**	**$165**	**$162**	**$182**	**$144**
EDUCATION	**$342**	**$247**	**$202**	**$379**	**$389**	**$542**	**$645**
TOBACCO PRODUCTS AND SMOKING SUPPLIES	**$242**	**$140**	**$238**	**$282**	**$302**	**$309**	**$338**
MISCELLANEOUS	**$578**	**$363**	**$614**	**$662**	**$602**	**$819**	**$674**
CASH CONTRIBUTIONS	**$693**	**$472**	**$888**	**$780**	**$746**	**$669**	**$675**
PERSONAL INSURANCE AND PENSIONS	**$2,249**	**$1,158**	**$2,298**	**$2,673**	**$2,759**	**$3,252**	**$2,809**
GIFTS OF PRODUCTS AND SERVICES	**$841**	**$658**	**$947**	**$910**	**$1,058**	**$880**	**$617**

Note: Average annual expenditures are based on the total number of consumer units, not just those that make purchases in the category. Numbers may not add to totals due to rounding and unlisted items in the subcategories. Expenditures for gifts of products and services are also included in the product or service category. Some items in "miscellaneous" are moved to the category "other financial products and services" in chapters 2 through 10.

Household size

Indexed average annual expenditures in 1988 for all household products and services, by size of consumer unit.

	all cu's	1 person	2 persons	2+ persons	3 persons	4 persons	5+ persons
Number of consumer units (in thousands)	94,865	26,571	28,750	68,291	15,612	13,998	9,931
Average age of reference person	47.0	48.7	53.2	46.3	43.1	39.7	40.9
Average number of earners per cu	1.4	0.7	1.2	1.7	1.8	2.0	2.3
AVERAGE TOTAL BEFORE-TAX INCOME	$28,540	$16,090	$30,444	$33,540	$33,862	$38,944	$34,417
AVERAGE ANNUAL EXPENDITURES	100	61	102	115	118	133	126
FOOD	100	56	96	117	117	139	148
Food at home	100	46	95	121	118	144	170
Cereals and bakery products	100	46	90	121	118	149	176
Meat, poultry, fish, and eggs	100	42	97	123	118	144	174
Dairy products	100	47	92	121	117	147	175
Fruits and vegetables	100	51	103	119	116	136	149
Other foods at home	100	47	91	121	120	145	172
Food away from home	100	68	98	112	117	133	120
ALCOHOLIC BEVERAGES	100	103	103	99	100	97	85
HOUSING	100	66	101	113	118	129	119
Shelter	100	75	98	110	114	125	115
Owned dwellings	100	45	102	121	125	152	129
Mortgage interest	100	37	87	124	137	171	147
Property taxes	100	52	125	119	108	130	102
Maintenance, repairs, insurance, other expenses	100	62	128	115	105	112	98
Rented dwellings	100	132	85	88	94	81	95
Other lodging	100	60	121	116	112	119	102
Utilities, fuels, and public services	100	62	103	115	115	127	133
Household services	100	45	81	121	130	188	131
Personal services	100	20	27	131	165	264	191
Housekeeping supplies	100	54	105	118	126	128	129
Household furnishings and equipment	100	48	114	120	131	131	108
Household textiles	100	48	117	120	145	109	109
Furniture	100	50	108	119	132	137	109
Floor coverings	100	29	123	128	177	117	82
Major appliances	100	48	112	120	125	145	99
Small appliances, misc. housewares, equipment	100	48	117	120	123	128	115
APPAREL AND APPAREL SERVICES	100	60	89	116	125	135	151
Men and boys	100	54	90	118	119	145	158
Men, aged 16 or older	100	64	104	114	116	127	123
Boys, aged 2 to 15	100	13	36	134	129	219	301
Women and girls	100	59	87	116	129	135	155
Women, aged 16 or older	100	68	96	113	129	117	127
Girls, aged 2 to 15	100	12	37	134	127	223	298

(continued from previous page)	all cu's	1 person	2 persons	2+ persons	3 persons	4 persons	5+ persons
Babies, under age 2	100	18	52	132	182	194	206
Footwear	100	70	83	112	121	122	164
Other apparel products and services	100	74	106	110	113	116	107
TRANSPORTATION	100	54	106	118	119	134	128
Vehicle purchases (net outlay)	100	47	109	121	121	137	131
Cars and trucks (new)	100	56	128	117	107	113	108
Cars and trucks (used)	100	34	85	126	140	168	163
Gasoline and motor oil	100	56	98	117	119	137	141
Other vehicle expenses	100	58	103	116	120	133	124
Public transportation	100	84	119	106	99	97	92
HEALTH CARE	100	64	124	114	109	110	99
ENTERTAINMENT	100	61	94	115	119	155	113
Fees and admissions	100	70	98	112	109	135	123
Television, radios, sound equipment	100	68	88	113	124	142	123
Pets, toys, and playground equipment	100	45	95	122	124	170	125
Other entertainment supplies, equipment, services	100	55	98	118	118	182	82
PERSONAL CARE PRODUCTS AND SERVICES	100	60	99	115	122	131	131
READING	100	75	110	110	108	121	96
EDUCATION	100	72	59	111	114	158	189
TOBACCO PRODUCTS AND SMOKING SUPPLIES	100	58	98	117	125	128	140
MISCELLANEOUS	100	63	106	115	104	142	117
CASH CONTRIBUTIONS	100	68	128	113	108	97	97
PERSONAL INSURANCE AND PENSIONS	100	51	102	119	123	145	125
GIFTS OF PRODUCTS AND SERVICES	100	78	113	108	126	105	73

Note: Expenditures for gifts of products and services are also included in the product or service category. Some items in "miscellaneous" are moved to the category "other financial products and services" in chapters 2 through 10. An index of 100 represents the average for all consumer units. An index of 132 means that the average for the subgroup is 32 percent above the average for all consumer units. An index of 68 indicates spending that is 32 percent below the overall average.

Race

Black householders spend less than average on all major categories of household products and services, while white and other householders spend above-average amounts. The annual expenditures of households headed by whites and others is 4 percent above average. For black households, it is 36 percent below average

Black households spend more than average on just a few items—meat, poultry, fish, and eggs; rent; boys' clothes; and girls' clothes. Although black households are 11 percent of all households, they account for 11 percent of the market only in those categories in which their spending is above average. In all other markets, they account for a smaller share of spending.

Average annual expenditures in 1988 for all household products and services, by race of reference person.

	all cu's	white and other	black
Number of consumer units (in thousands)	94,862	84,684	10,178
Average number of persons per cu	2.6	2.5	2.9
Average number of earners per cu	1.4	1.4	1.2
AVERAGE TOTAL BEFORE-TAX INCOME	$28,540	$29,807	$17,819
AVERAGE ANNUAL EXPENDITURES	$25,892	$27,004	$16,670
FOOD	$3,748	$3,872	$2,731
Food at home	2,136	2,176	1,807
Cereals and bakery products	312	321	237
Meat, poultry, fish, and eggs	551	545	602
Fruits and vegetables	373	377	343
Dairy products	274	285	190
Other foods at home	625	649	435
Food away from home	1,612	1,696	923
ALCOHOLIC BEVERAGES	$269	$283	$152
HOUSING	$8,079	$8,379	$5,586
Shelter	4,493	4,668	3,035
Owned dwellings	2,569	2,744	1,110
Mortgage interest	1,569	1,670	726
Property taxes	504	549	130
Maintenance, repairs, insurance, other expenses	496	525	254
Rented dwellings	1,468	1,428	1,803
Other lodging	456	496	123
Utilities, fuels, and public services	1,747	1,761	1,634
Household services	394	416	213
Personal services	171	176	135
Housekeeping supplies	361	380	202
Household furnishings and equipment	1,083	1,154	501
Household textiles	94	98	58
Furniture	326	343	181
Floor coverings	65	72	14

(continued from previous page)

	all cu's	white and other	black
Major appliances	169	176	110
Small appliances, miscellaneous housewares	429	465	138
APPAREL AND APPAREL SERVICES	**$1,489**	**$1,524**	**$1,201**
Men and boys	**388**	**404**	**254**
Men, aged 16 or older	311	329	157
Boys, aged 2 to 15	77	75	97
Women and girls	**587**	**600**	**478**
Women, aged 16 or older	492	506	379
Girls, aged 2 to 15	95	94	98
Babies, under age 2	**62**	**63**	**60**
Footwear	**196**	**197**	**185**
Other apparel products and services	**257**	**261**	**224**
TRANSPORTATION	**$5,093**	**$5,332**	**$3,101**
Vehicle purchases (net outlay)	**2,361**	**2,481**	**1,356**
Cars and trucks (new)	1,355	1,434	696
Cars and trucks (used)	982	1,021	654
Gasoline and motor oil	**932**	**970**	**613**
Other vehicle expenses	**1,521**	**1,596**	**899**
Public transportation	**279**	**285**	**232**
HEALTH CARE	**$1,298**	**$1,375**	**$653**
ENTERTAINMENT	**$1,329**	**$1,424**	**$539**
Fees and admissions	**353**	**384**	**100**
Television, radios, sound equipment	**416**	**429**	**307**
Pets, toys, and playground equipment	**230**	**248**	**83**
Other entertainment supplies, equipment, services	**330**	**364**	**49**
PERSONAL CARE PRODUCTS AND SERVICES	**$334**	**$344**	**$249**
READING	**$150**	**$161**	**$62**
EDUCATION	**$342**	**$363**	**$170**
TOBACCO PRODUCTS AND SMOKING SUPPLIES	**$242**	**$247**	**$202**
MISCELLANEOUS	**$578**	**$605**	**$352**
CASH CONTRIBUTIONS	**$693**	**$727**	**$415**
PERSONAL INSURANCE AND PENSIONS	**$2,249**	**$2,368**	**$1,257**
GIFTS OF PRODUCTS AND SERVICES	**$841**	**$906**	**$291**

Note: Average annual expenditures are based on the total number of consumer units, not just those that make purchases in the category. Numbers may not add to totals due to rounding and unlisted items in the subcategories. Expenditures for gifts of products and services are also included in the product or service category. Some items in "miscellaneous" are moved to the category "other financial products and services" in chapters 2 through 10.

Race

Indexed average annual expenditures in 1988 for all household products and services, by race of reference person.

	all cu's	white and other	black
Number of consumer units (in thousands)	94,862	84,684	10,178
Average number of persons per cu	2.6	2.5	2.9
Average number of earners per cu	1.4	1.4	1.2
AVERAGE TOTAL BEFORE-TAX INCOME	$28,540	$29,807	$17,819
AVERAGE ANNUAL EXPENDITURES	100	104	64
FOOD	100	103	73
Food at home	100	102	85
Cereals and bakery products	100	103	76
Meat, poultry, fish, and eggs	100	99	109
Dairy products	100	104	69
Fruits and vegetables	100	101	92
Other foods at home	100	104	70
Food away from home	100	105	57
ALCOHOLIC BEVERAGES	100	105	57
HOUSING	100	104	69
Shelter	100	104	68
Owned dwellings	100	107	43
Mortgage interest	100	106	46
Property taxes	100	109	26
Maintenance, repairs, insurance, other expenses	100	106	51
Rented dwellings	100	97	123
Other lodging	100	109	27
Utilities, fuels, and public services	100	101	94
Household services	100	106	54
Personal services	100	103	79
Housekeeping supplies	100	105	56
Household furnishings and equipment	100	107	46
Household textiles	100	104	62
Furniture	100	105	56
Floor coverings	100	111	22
Major appliances	100	104	65
Small appliances, miscellaneous housewares	100	108	32
APPAREL AND APPAREL SERVICES	100	102	81
Men and boys	100	104	65
Men, aged 16 or older	100	106	50
Boys, aged 2 to 15	100	97	126
Women and girls	100	102	81
Women, aged 16 or older	100	103	77
Girls, aged 2 to 15	100	99	103

	all cu's	white and other	black
Babies, under age 2	100	102	97
Footwear	100	101	94
Other apparel products and services	100	102	87
TRANSPORTATION	100	105	61
Vehicle purchases (net outlay)	100	105	57
Cars and trucks (new)	100	106	51
Cars and trucks (used)	100	104	67
Gasoline and motor oil	100	104	66
Other vehicle expenses	100	105	59
Public transportation	100	102	83
HEALTH CARE	100	106	50
ENTERTAINMENT	100	107	41
Fees and admissions	100	109	28
Television, radios, sound equipment	100	103	74
Pets, toys, and playground equipment	100	108	36
Other entertainment supplies, equipment, services	100	110	15
PERSONAL CARE PRODUCTS AND SERVICES	100	103	75
READING	100	107	41
EDUCATION	100	106	50
TOBACCO PRODUCTS AND SMOKING SUPPLIES	100	102	83
MISCELLANEOUS	100	105	61
CASH CONTRIBUTIONS	100	105	60
PERSONAL INSURANCE AND PENSIONS	100	105	56
GIFTS OF PRODUCTS AND SERVICES	100	108	35

Note: Expenditures for gifts of products and services are also included in the product or service category. Some items in "miscellaneous" are moved to the category "other financial products and services" in chapters 2 through 10. An index of 100 represents the average for all consumer units. An index of 132 means that the average for the subgroup is 32 percent above the average for all consumer units. An index of 68 indicates spending that is 32 percent below the overall average.

Region

Overall spending is higher in the Northeast and West, where average incomes are also higher. By category, however, those two regions are not always at the top. For food, housing, clothing, reading materials, education, and gifts, the Northeast and West are home to peak spenders. But western and southern households outspend others on transportation and health care, while households in the Midwest and South spend the most on tobacco products. People who live in the Midwest and West spend the most on personal care products and services. Westerners spend 25 percent more than the average household on entertainment, while households in the other regions spend less than average on this category. Northeasterners are the only ones who spend more than average on education. They spend 27 percent more than the average household on tuition, books, supplies, and other educational expenses.

Average annual expenditures in 1988 for all household products and services, by region of residence.

	all cu's	Northeast	Midwest	South	West
Number of consumer units (in thousands)	94,862	20,029	23,931	31,653	19,248
Average age of reference person	47.0	48.6	46.9	47.1	45.2
Average number of persons per cu	1.4	1.3	1.4	1.4	1.4
AVERAGE TOTAL BEFORE-TAX INCOME	$28,540	$29,774	$27,436	$27,329	$30,624
AVERAGE ANNUAL EXPENDITURES	$25,892	$26,348	$24,763	$24,671	$28,830
FOOD	$3,748	$3,993	$3,660	$3,553	$3,924
Food at home	2,136	2,212	2,084	2,039	2,282
Cereals and bakery products	312	341	304	287	334
Meat, poultry, fish, and eggs	551	606	529	539	541
Dairy products	274	277	268	264	296
Fruits and vegetables	373	398	355	351	406
Other foods at home	625	590	627	598	705
Food away from home	1,612	1,781	1,577	1,514	1,643
ALCOHOLIC BEVERAGES	$269	$272	$273	$229	$326
HOUSING	$8,079	$8,591	$7,499	$7,352	$9,461
Shelter	4,493	4,993	3,897	3,834	5,797
Owned dwellings	2,569	2,669	2,446	2,237	3,162
Mortgage interest	1,569	1,447	1,311	1,495	2,138
Property taxes	504	669	656	272	522
Maintenance, repairs, insurance, other expenses	496	552	480	470	502
Rented dwellings	1,468	1,659	1,085	1,200	2,185
Other lodging	456	665	365	397	450
Utilities, fuels, and public services	1,747	1,797	1,761	1,827	1,548
Household services	394	379	340	372	512
Personal services	171	138	168	165	221
Housekeeping supplies	361	340	406	331	375
Household furnishings and equipment	1,083	1,082	1,095	987	1,229
Household textiles	94	101	86	74	129
Furniture	326	340	320	291	375
Floor coverings	65	64	83	54	63

(continued from previous page)	all cu's	Northeast	Midwest	South	West
Major appliances	169	162	166	177	166
Small appliances, misc. housewares, equipment	429	414	440	391	496
APPAREL AND APPAREL SERVICES	**$1,489**	**$1,619**	**$1,465**	**$1,406**	**$1,521**
Men and boys	**388**	**422**	**396**	**353**	**397**
Men, aged 16 or older	311	348	318	264	339
Boys, aged 2 to 15	77	74	78	90	58
Women and girls	**587**	**658**	**591**	**554**	**562**
Women, aged 16 or older	492	552	487	468	476
Girls, aged 2 to 15	95	107	103	86	87
Babies, under age 2	**62**	**64**	**63**	**52**	**77**
Footwear	**196**	**192**	**201**	**189**	**203**
Other apparel products and services	**257**	**282**	**215**	**258**	**281**
TRANSPORTATION	**$5,093**	**$4,832**	**$4,950**	**$5,144**	**$5,458**
Vehicle purchases (net outlay)	**2,361**	**2,111**	**2,403**	**2,487**	**2,359**
Cars and trucks (new)	1,355	1,409	1,249	1,407	1,346
Cars and trucks (used)	982	691	1,131	1,064	966
Gasoline and motor oil	**932**	**812**	**893**	**1,025**	**952**
Other vehicle expenses	**1,521**	**1,516**	**1,443**	**1,422**	**1,786**
Public transportation	**279**	**394**	**210**	**209**	**361**
HEALTH CARE	**$1,298**	**$1,238**	**$1,257**	**$1,372**	**$1,289**
ENTERTAINMENT	**$1,329**	**$1,232**	**$1,255**	**$1,246**	**$1,657**
Fees and admissions	**353**	**385**	**348**	**290**	**431**
Television, radios, sound equipment	**416**	**414**	**412**	**398**	**450**
Pets, toys, and playground equipment	**230**	**236**	**215**	**213**	**272**
Other entertainment supplies, equipment, services	**330**	**196**	**280**	**345**	**505**
PERSONAL CARE PRODUCTS AND SERVICES	**$334**	**$323**	**$343**	**$309**	**$373**
READING	**$150**	**$181**	**$152**	**$121**	**$162**
EDUCATION	**$342**	**$433**	**$337**	**$316**	**$297**
TOBACCO PRODUCTS AND SMOKING SUPPLIES	**$242**	**$242**	**$257**	**$260**	**$193**
MISCELLANEOUS	**$578**	**$619**	**$515**	**$515**	**$718**
CASH CONTRIBUTIONS	**$693**	**$531**	**$617**	**$706**	**$937**
PERSONAL INSURANCE AND PENSIONS	**$2,249**	**$2,242**	**$2,182**	**$2,143**	**$2,515**
GIFTS OF PRODUCTS AND SERVICES	**$841**	**$1,013**	**$802**	**$748**	**$853**

Note: Average annual expenditures are based on the total number of consumer units, not just those that make purchases in the category. Numbers may not add to totals due to rounding and unlisted items in the subcategories. Expenditures for gifts of products and services are also included in the product or service category. Some items in "miscellaneous" are moved to the category "other financial products and services" in chapters 2 through 10.

Region

Indexed average annual expenditures in 1988 for all household products and services, by region of residence.

	all cu's	Northeast	Midwest	South	West
Number of consumer units (in thousands)	94,862	20,029	23,931	31,653	19,248
Average age of reference person	47.0	48.6	46.9	47.1	45.2
Average number of persons per cu	1.4	1.3	1.4	1.4	1.4
AVERAGE TOTAL BEFORE-TAX INCOME	$28,540	$29,774	$27,436	$27,329	$30,624
AVERAGE ANNUAL EXPENDITURES	100	102	96	95	111
FOOD	100	107	98	95	105
Food at home	100	104	98	95	107
Cereals and bakery products	100	109	97	92	107
Meat, poultry, fish, and eggs	100	110	96	98	98
Dairy products	100	101	98	96	108
Fruits and vegetables	100	107	95	94	109
Other foods at home	100	94	100	96	113
Food away from home	100	110	98	94	102
ALCOHOLIC BEVERAGES	100	101	101	85	121
HOUSING	100	106	93	91	117
Shelter	100	111	87	85	129
Owned dwellings	100	104	95	87	123
Mortgage interest	100	92	84	95	136
Property taxes	100	133	130	54	104
Maintenance, repairs, insurance, other expenses	100	111	97	95	101
Rented dwellings	100	113	74	82	149
Other lodging	100	146	80	87	99
Utilities, fuels, and public services	100	103	101	105	89
Household services	100	96	86	94	130
Personal services	100	81	98	96	129
Housekeeping supplies	100	94	112	92	104
Household furnishings and equipment	100	100	101	91	113
Household textiles	100	107	91	79	137
Furniture	100	104	98	89	115
Floor coverings	100	98	128	83	97
Major appliances	100	96	98	105	98
Small appliances, misc. housewares, equipment	100	97	103	91	116
APPAREL AND APPAREL SERVICES	100	109	98	94	102
Men and boys	100	109	102	91	102
Men, aged 16 or older	100	112	102	85	109
Boys, aged 2 to 15	100	96	101	117	75
Women and girls	100	112	101	94	96
Women, aged 16 or older	100	112	99	95	97
Girls, aged 2 to 15	100	113	108	91	92

(continued from previous page)	all cu's	Northeast	Midwest	South	West
Babies, under age 2	100	103	102	84	124
Footwear	100	98	103	96	104
Other apparel products and services	100	110	84	100	109
TRANSPORTATION	100	95	97	101	107
Vehicle purchases (net outlay)	100	89	102	105	100
Cars and trucks (new)	100	104	92	104	99
Cars and trucks (used)	100	70	115	108	98
Gasoline and motor oil	100	87	96	110	102
Other vehicle expenses	100	100	95	93	117
Public transportation	100	141	75	75	129
HEALTH CARE	100	95	97	106	99
ENTERTAINMENT	100	93	94	94	125
Fees and admissions	100	109	99	82	122
Television, radios, sound equipment	100	100	99	96	108
Pets, toys, and playground equipment	100	103	93	93	118
Other entertainment supplies, equipment, services ...	100	59	85	105	153
PERSONAL CARE PRODUCTS AND SERVICES ...	100	97	103	93	112
READING	100	121	101	81	108
EDUCATION	100	127	99	92	87
TOBACCO PRODUCTS AND SMOKING SUPPLIES	100	100	106	107	80
MISCELLANEOUS..................................	100	107	89	89	124
CASH CONTRIBUTIONS	100	77	89	102	135
PERSONAL INSURANCE AND PENSIONS	100	100	97	95	112
GIFTS OF PRODUCTS AND SERVICES	100	120	95	89	101

Note: Expenditures for gifts of products and services are also included in the product or service category. Some items in "miscellaneous" are moved to the category "other financial products and services" in chapters 2 through 10. An index of 100 represents the average for all consumer units. An index of 132 means that the average for the subgroup is 32 percent above the average for all consumer units. An index of 68 indicates spending that is 32 percent below the overall average.

Homeownership status

Homeowners spend an average of $11,100 a year more than renters. They outspend renters on all household products and services except alcohol, tobacco products, and, of course, rent. Homeowners' annual spending is 16 percent above average while renters spend 27 percent less than the average U.S. household.

Homeowners have slightly larger households than renters, averaging 2.8 people versus 2.3 for renters. The average number of earners in homeowning households is 1.5. Renters average 1.3 earners per household.

Average annual expenditures in 1988 for all household products and services, by homeownership status.			
	all cu's	homeowner	renter
Number of consumer units (in thousands)	94,862	58,639	36,224
Average number of persons per cu	2.6	2.8	2.3
Average number of earners per cu	1.4	1.5	1.2
AVERAGE TOTAL BEFORE-TAX INCOME	$28,540	$34,757	$18,714
AVERAGE ANNUAL EXPENDITURES	$25,892	$30,091	$18,994
FOOD	$3,748	$4,257	$2,874
Food at home	2,136	2,436	1,616
Cereals and bakery products	312	359	231
Meat, poultry, fish, and eggs	551	622	428
Dairy products	274	313	208
Fruits and vegetables	373	425	284
Other foods at home	625	718	465
Food away from home	1,612	1,821	1,258
ALCOHOLIC BEVERAGES	$269	$264	$277
HOUSING	$8,079	$9,161	$6,307
Shelter	4,493	4,718	4,128
Owned dwellings	2,569	4,129	43
Mortgage interest	1,569	2,517	34
Property taxes	504	813	3
Maintenance, repairs, insurance, other expenses	496	799	5
Rented dwellings	1,468	30	3,795
Other lodging	456	558	291
Utilities, fuels, and public services	1,747	2,123	1,139
Household services	394	499	224
Personal services	171	194	135
Housekeeping supplies	361	440	223
Household furnishings and equipment	1,083	1,380	593
Household textiles	94	117	55
Furniture	326	405	198
Floor coverings	65	98	11

(continued from previous page)	*all cu's*	*homeowner*	*renter*
Major appliances	169	214	94
Small appliances, miscellaneous housewares	429	546	234
APPAREL AND APPAREL SERVICES	**$1,489**	**$1,710**	**$1,113**
Men and boys..	**388**	**459**	**266**
Men, aged 16 or older	311	368	214
Boys, aged 2 to 15	77	92	52
Women and girls	**587**	**688**	**413**
Women, aged 16 or older	492	577	345
Girls, aged 2 to 15	95	111	67
Babies, under age 2	**62**	**64**	**59**
Footwear	**196**	**221**	**151**
Other apparel products and services	**257**	**277**	**224**
TRANSPORTATION	**$5,093**	**$5,887**	**$3,804**
Vehicle purchases (net outlay)	**2,361**	**2,707**	**1,799**
Cars and trucks (new)	1,355	1,556	1,030
Cars and trucks (used)	982	1,130	743
Gasoline and motor oil	**932**	**1,090**	**676**
Other vehicle expenses	**1,521**	**1,779**	**1,101**
Public transportation	**279**	**311**	**227**
HEALTH CARE	**$1,298**	**$1,639**	**$744**
ENTERTAINMENT	**$1,329**	**$1,606**	**$878**
Fees and admissions	**353**	**435**	**221**
Television, radios, sound equipment	**416**	**468**	**331**
Pets, toys, and playground equipment	**230**	**276**	**154**
Other entertainment supplies, equipment, services	**330**	**427**	**171**
PERSONAL CARE PRODUCTS AND SERVICES	**$334**	**$382**	**$251**
READING	**$150**	**$177**	**$106**
EDUCATION	**$342**	**$379**	**$283**
TOBACCO PRODUCTS AND SMOKING SUPPLIES	**$242**	**$240**	**$245**
MISCELLANEOUS..	**$578**	**$696**	**$386**
CASH CONTRIBUTIONS	**$693**	**$878**	**$394**
PERSONAL INSURANCE AND PENSIONS	**$2,249**	**$2,815**	**$1,333**
GIFTS OF PRODUCTS AND SERVICES	**$841**	**$999**	**$574**

Note: Average annual expenditures are based on the total number of consumer units, not just those that make purchases in the category. Numbers may not add to totals due to rounding and unlisted items in the subcategories. Expenditures for gifts of products and services are also included in the product or service category. Some items in "miscellaneous" are moved to the category "other financial products and services" in chapters 2 through 10. Some items in "miscellaneous" are moved to the cateogry "other financial products and services" in chapters 2 through 10.

Homeownership status

Indexed average annual expenditures in 1988 for all household products and services, by homeownership status.

	all cu's	homeowner	renter
Number of consumer units (in thousands)	**94,862**	**58,639**	**36,224**
Average number of persons per cu	**2.6**	**2.8**	**2.3**
Average number of earners per cu	**1.4**	**1.5**	**1.2**
AVERAGE TOTAL BEFORE-TAX INCOME	**$28,540**	**$34,757**	**$18,714**
AVERAGE ANNUAL EXPENDITURES	**100**	**116**	**73**
FOOD	**100**	**114**	**77**
Food at home	**100**	**114**	**76**
Cereals and bakery products	100	115	74
Meat, poultry, fish, and eggs	100	113	78
Dairy products	100	114	76
Fruits and vegetables	100	114	76
Other foods at home	100	115	74
Food away from home	**100**	**113**	**78**
ALCOHOLIC BEVERAGES	**100**	**98**	**103**
HOUSING	**100**	**113**	**78**
Shelter	**100**	**105**	**92**
Owned dwellings	100	161	2
Mortgage interest	100	160	2
Property taxes	100	161	1
Maintenance, repairs, insurance, other expenses	100	161	1
Rented dwellings	100	2	259
Other lodging	100	122	64
Utilities, fuels, and public services	**100**	**122**	**65**
Household services	**100**	**127**	**57**
Personal services	100	113	79
Housekeeping supplies	**100**	**122**	**62**
Household furnishings and equipment	**100**	**127**	**55**
Household textiles	100	124	59
Furniture	100	124	61
Floor coverings	100	151	17
Major appliances	100	127	56
Small appliances, miscellaneous housewares	100	127	55
APPAREL AND APPAREL SERVICES	**100**	**115**	**75**
Men and boys	**100**	**118**	**69**
Men, aged 16 or older	100	118	69
Boys, aged 2 to 15	100	119	68
Women and girls	**100**	**117**	**70**
Women, aged 16 or older	100	117	70
Girls, aged 2 to 15	100	117	71

(continued from previous page)	all cu's	homeowner	renter
Babies, under age 2	100	103	95
Footwear	100	113	77
Other apparel products and services	100	108	87
TRANSPORTATION	100	116	75
Vehicle purchases (net outlay)	100	115	76
Cars and trucks (new)	100	115	76
Cars and trucks (used)	100	115	76
Gasoline and motor oil	100	117	73
Other vehicle expenses	100	117	72
Public transportation	100	111	81
HEALTH CARE	100	126	57
ENTERTAINMENT	100	121	66
Fees and admissions	100	123	63
Television, radios, sound equipment	100	113	80
Pets, toys, and playground equipment	100	120	67
Other entertainment supplies, equipment, services	100	129	52
PERSONAL CARE PRODUCTS AND SERVICES	100	114	75
READING	100	118	71
EDUCATION	100	111	83
TOBACCO PRODUCTS AND SMOKING SUPPLIES	100	99	101
MISCELLANEOUS..	100	120	67
CASH CONTRIBUTIONS	100	127	57
PERSONAL INSURANCE AND PENSIONS	100	125	59
GIFTS OF PRODUCTS AND SERVICES	100	119	68

Note: Expenditures for gifts of products and services are also included in the product or service category. Some items in "miscellaneous" are moved to the category "other financial products and services" in chapters 2 through 10. An index of 100 represents the average for all consumer units. An index of 132 means that the average for the subgroup is 32 percent above the average for all consumer units. An index of 68 indicates spending that is 32 percent below the overall average.

Householders under age 25

This age group's low incomes depress spending. Fully 49 percent of the youngest householders have incomes under $10,000. They spend an average of just $9,204 a year. For all householders under age 25, average yearly expenditures amount to $15,600. Only householders aged 75 or older spend less.

Young householders with incomes of $20,000 or more spend more than the average young householder on all major categories of products and services except education. Householders under age 25 with either very high ($40,000 or more) or very low (under $10,000) incomes spend more than the average on tuition, books, supplies, and other educational expenses.

Average annual expenditures in 1987–1988 for all household products and services, by consumer units with reference person under age 25 and before-tax income of consumer unit.

(consumer units include complete income reporters only)	all cu's	under $10,000	$10,000 to $19,999	$20,000 to $29,999	$30,000 to $39,999	$40,000 and over
Number of consumer units (in thousands)	6,668	3,291	1,794	944	403	237
Average number of persons per cu	1.8	1.4	1.9	2.2	2.4	2.6
Average number of earners per cu	1.2	0.9	1.4	1.6	1.9	2.0
AVERAGE TOTAL BEFORE-TAX INCOME	$13,676	$4,689	$14,411	$23,892	$33,917	$57,883
AVERAGE ANNUAL EXPENDITURES	$15,600	$9,204	$17,185	$23,729	$28,184	$38,306
FOOD	$2,382	$1,684	$2,506	$3,338	$3,843	$4,569
Food at home	1,108	745	1,165	1,670	1,683	2,214
Cereals and bakery products	159	107	168	251	223	285
Meat, poultry, fish, and eggs	254	167	273	365	412	570
Dairy products	156	104	173	229	219	306
Fruits and vegetables	175	115	174	284	320	302
Other foods at home	364	252	378	539	509	751
Food away from home	1,274	938	1,341	1,668	2,161	2,355
ALCOHOLIC BEVERAGES	$317	$243	$353	$379	$398	$645
HOUSING	$4,529	$2,674	$5,054	$6,624	$8,184	$11,782
Shelter	2,827	1,738	3,150	4,047	5,034	6,903
Owned dwellings	389	31	256	623	1,368	3,785
Mortgage interest	286	19	158	438	1,067	3,030
Property taxes	34	8	28	59	80	267
Maintenance, repairs, insurance, other expenses	70	4	71	126	220	488
Rented dwellings	2,278	1,544	2,802	3,257	3,433	2,646
Other lodging	160	163	92	168	233	473
Utilities, fuels, and public services	854	536	977	1,200	1,476	1,901
Household services	135	45	153	261	302	481
Personal services	95	25	102	210	209	375
Housekeeping supplies	162	106	178	220	248	419
Household furnishings and equipment	551	249	596	897	1,124	2,078
Household textiles	46	35	36	48	56	287
Furniture	191	70	228	336	319	790
Floor coverings	22	8	23	44	6	130

(continued from previous page)	all cu's	under $10,000	$10,000 to $19,999	$20,000 to $29,999	$30,000 to $39,999	$40,000 and over
Major appliances	72	21	105	138	103	230
Small appliances, misc. housewares, equipment	220	115	204	331	641	640
APPAREL AND APPAREL SERVICES	**$971**	**$704**	**$970**	**$1,264**	**$1,720**	**$2,201**
Men and boys..	**194**	**151**	**203**	**218**	**323**	**414**
Men, aged 16 or older	181	139	190	200	317	408
Boys, aged 2 to 15	12	13	13	18	6	6
Women and girls	**372**	**311**	**339**	**399**	**683**	**820**
Women, aged 16 or older	354	298	319	372	666	787
Girls, aged 2 to 15	18	13	18	27	17	33
Babies, under age 2	**68**	**37**	**82**	**124**	**119**	**93**
Footwear	**112**	**83**	**73**	**184**	**248**	**234**
Other apparel products and services	**226**	**123**	**275**	**340**	**347**	**640**
TRANSPORTATION	**$3,703**	**$1,607**	**$4,437**	**$7,017**	**$7,020**	**$8,414**
Vehicle purchases (net outlay)	**1,862**	**607**	**2,388**	**4,137**	**3,309**	**3,782**
Cars and trucks (new)	1,040	244	1,260	2,622	1,643	3,101
Cars and trucks (used)	810	357	1,112	1,499	1,626	680
Gasoline and motor oil.................................	**643**	**400**	**733**	**944**	**1,202**	**1,201**
Other vehicle expenses	**1,002**	**439**	**1,135**	**1,700**	**2,227**	**2,968**
Public transportation	**195**	**161**	**181**	**236**	**283**	**463**
HEALTH CARE	**$425**	**$191**	**$548**	**$637**	**$981**	**$979**
ENTERTAINMENT	**864**	**540**	**967**	**1,127**	**1,352**	**2,681**
Fees and admissions	**245**	**196**	**210**	**297**	**422**	**683**
Television, radios, sound equipment	**336**	**225**	**382**	**467**	**481**	**736**
Pets, toys, and playground equipment	**105**	**50**	**113**	**199**	**217**	**233**
Other entertainment supplies, equipment, services	**178**	**70**	**261**	**164**	**231**	**1,029**
PERSONAL CARE PRODUCTS AND SERVICES	**$194**	**$131**	**$234**	**$211**	**$270**	**$550**
READING	**$74**	**$48**	**$83**	**$98**	**$133**	**$174**
EDUCATION	**$627**	**$861**	**$417**	**$274**	**$269**	**$1,017**
TOBACCO PRODUCTS AND SMOKING SUPPLIES	**$171**	**$122**	**$214**	**$212**	**$197**	**$304**
MISCELLANEOUS	**$232**	**$88**	**$249**	**$372**	**$516**	**$1,066**
CASH CONTRIBUTIONS	**$103**	**$49**	**$114**	**$168**	**$297**	**$188**
PERSONAL INSURANCE AND PENSIONS	**$1,007**	**$262**	**$1,039**	**$2,008**	**$3,004**	**$3,736**
GIFTS OF PRODUCTS AND SERVICES	**$397**	**$275**	**$457**	**$565**	**$466**	**$824**

Note: Average annual expenditures are based on the total number of consumer units, not just those that make purchases in the category. Numbers may not add to totals due to rounding and unlisted items in the subcategories. Expenditures for gifts of products and services are also included in the product or service category. Some items in "miscellaneous" are moved to the cateogry "other financial products and services" in chapters 2 through 10. Total expenditure exceeds total income in some income categories due to a number of factors including the underreporting of income, borrowing, and the use of savings. The "all cu's" data in this table will differ from those in age tables in other chapters because combined data from 1987 and 1988 were used for this crosstabulation. The crosstabulation required a larger sample than that available in one survey year.

Householders under age 25

Indexed average annual expenditures in 1987–1988, for all household products and services, by consumer units with reference person under age 25 and before-tax income of consumer unit.

(consumer units include complete income reporters only)	all cu's	under $10,000	$10,000 to $19,999	$20,000 to $29,999	$30,000 to $39,999	$40,000 and over
Number of consumer units (in thousands)	6,668	3,291	1,794	944	403	237
Average number of persons per cu	1.8	1.4	1.9	2.2	2.4	2.6
Average number of earners per cu	1.2	0.9	1.4	1.6	1.9	2.0
AVERAGE TOTAL BEFORE-TAX INCOME	$13,676	$4,689	$14,411	$23,892	$33,917	$57,883
AVERAGE ANNUAL EXPENDITURES	100	59	110	152	181	246
FOOD	100	71	105	140	161	192
Food at home	100	67	105	151	152	200
Cereals and bakery products	100	67	105	158	140	179
Meat, poultry, fish, and eggs	100	66	107	144	162	224
Dairy products	100	67	111	147	140	196
Fruits and vegetables	100	66	99	162	183	173
Other foods at home	100	69	104	148	140	206
Food away from home	100	74	105	131	170	185
ALCOHOLIC BEVERAGES	100	77	111	120	126	203
HOUSING	100	59	112	146	181	260
Shelter	100	61	111	143	178	244
Owned dwellings	100	8	66	160	352	973
Mortgage interest	100	7	55	153	373	1059
Property taxes	100	25	81	174	235	785
Maintenance, repairs, insurance, other expenses	100	6	101	180	314	697
Rented dwellings	100	68	123	143	151	116
Other lodging	100	102	58	105	146	296
Utilities, fuels, and public services	100	63	114	141	173	223
Household services	100	33	113	193	224	356
Personal services	100	27	107	221	220	395
Housekeeping supplies	100	66	110	136	153	259
Household furnishings and equipment	100	45	108	163	204	377
Household textiles	100	75	78	104	122	624
Furniture	100	37	119	176	167	414
Floor coverings	100	38	103	200	27	591
Major appliances	100	28	146	192	143	319
Small appliances, misc. housewares, equipment	100	52	93	150	291	291
APPAREL AND APPAREL SERVICES	100	73	100	130	177	227
Men and boys	100	78	104	112	166	213
Men, aged 16 or older	100	77	105	110	175	225
Boys, aged 2 to 15	100	105	105	150	50	50
Women and girls	100	84	91	107	184	220
Women, aged 16 or older	100	84	90	105	188	222
Girls, aged 2 to 15	100	72	102	150	94	183

(continued from previous page)

	all cu's	under $10,000	$10,000 to $19,999	$20,000 to $29,999	$30,000 to $39,999	$40,000 and over
Babies, under age 2	100	55	120	182	175	137
Footwear	100	74	65	164	221	209
Other apparel products and services	100	54	121	150	154	283
TRANSPORTATION	100	43	120	189	190	227
Vehicle purchases (net outlay)	100	33	128	222	178	203
Cars and trucks (new)	100	24	121	252	158	298
Cars and trucks (used)	100	44	137	185	201	84
Gasoline and motor oil	100	62	114	147	187	187
Other vehicle expenses	100	44	113	170	222	296
Public transportation	100	83	93	121	145	237
HEALTH CARE	100	45	129	150	231	230
ENTERTAINMENT	100	62	112	130	156	310
Fees and admissions	100	80	86	121	172	279
Television, radios, sound equipment	100	67	114	139	143	219
Pets, toys, and playground equipment	100	47	108	190	207	222
Other entertainment supplies, equipment, services	100	39	147	92	130	578
PERSONAL CARE PRODUCTS AND SERVICES	100	68	121	109	139	284
READING	100	65	112	132	180	235
EDUCATION	100	137	66	44	43	162
TOBACCO PRODUCTS AND SMOKING SUPPLIES	100	71	125	124	115	178
MISCELLANEOUS	100	38	107	160	222	459
CASH CONTRIBUTIONS	100	48	111	163	288	183
PERSONAL INSURANCE AND PENSIONS	100	26	103	199	298	371
GIFTS OF PRODUCTS AND SERVICES	100	69	115	142	117	208

Note: Expenditures for gifts of products and services are also included in the product or service category. Some items in "miscellaneous" are moved to the category "other financial products and services" in chapters 2 through 10. An index of 100 represents the average for all consumer units. An index of 132 means that the average for the subgroup is 32 percent above the average for all consumer units. An index of 68 indicates spending that is 32 percent below the overall average.

Householders aged 25 to 34

AVERAGE
EXPENDITURES

The above-average spenders in this age group have incomes of $30,000 or more. Those high-income households spend less than the average household in their age group on only rent, alcohol, and public transportation. The average household expenditures of 25-to-34-year-olds is $25,613. Since this is slightly more than the average income of 25 to 34 year old householders, this group is likely to be in debt.

Households in this age group with incomes below $30,000 spend more than average on some items such as rent, used vehicles, floor coverings, health care, education, and tobacco products.

Average annual expenditures in 1987–1988 for all household products and services, by consumer units with reference person aged 25 to 34 and before-tax income of consumer unit.

(consumer units include complete income reporters only)	all cu's	under $10,000	$10,000 to $19,999	$20,000 to $29,999	$30,000 to $39,999	$40,000 and over
Number of consumer units (in thousands)	18,952	2,747	4,495	4,430	3,036	4,244
Average number of persons per cu	2.8	2.6	2.6	2.8	3.0	2.9
Average number of earners per cu	1.5	0.9	1.3	1.6	1.7	1.8
AVERAGE TOTAL BEFORE-TAX INCOME	$28,079	$5,349	$14,823	$24,514	$34,247	$56,136
AVERAGE ANNUAL EXPENDITURES	$25,613	$11,563	$17,465	$24,048	$29,939	$41,517
FOOD	$3,687	$2,197	$2,858	$3,553	$4,076	$5,225
Food at home	2,049	1,557	1,738	1,933	2,242	2,620
Cereals and bakery products	292	210	246	283	337	360
Meat, poultry, fish, and eggs	519	450	451	491	531	645
Dairy products	276	191	253	261	296	350
Fruits and vegetables	319	244	268	279	366	418
Other foods at home	643	463	521	620	711	845
Food away from home	1,638	639	1,120	1,620	1,835	2,606
ALCOHOLIC BEVERAGES	$360	$186	$280	$379	$336	$532
HOUSING	$8,319	$4,233	$5,764	$7,640	$9,675	$13,363
Shelter	4,833	2,541	3,250	4,475	5,563	7,844
Owned dwellings	2,401	405	755	1,828	3,026	5,585
Mortgage interest	1,860	280	530	1,392	2,356	4,424
Property taxes	271	69	107	167	372	613
Maintenance, repairs, insurance, other expenses	270	57	119	268	299	548
Rented dwellings	2,155	2,061	2,404	2,425	2,226	1,619
Other lodging	277	75	91	222	311	640
Utilities, fuels, and public services	1,529	1,057	1,267	1,503	1,767	1,970
Household services	489	132	306	385	636	915
Personal services	372	90	248	305	529	644
Housekeeping supplies	342	196	231	321	409	506
Household furnishings and equipment	1,127	308	711	955	1,299	2,128
Household textiles	97	31	64	58	118	195
Furniture	352	98	191	296	380	728
Floor coverings	56	15	23	79	72	79

(continued from previous page)

	all cu's	under $10,000	$10,000 to $19,999	$20,000 to $29,999	$30,000 to $39,999	$40,000 and over
Major appliances	170	65	124	156	200	279
Small appliances, misc. housewares, equipment	452	100	308	366	529	849
APPAREL AND APPAREL SERVICES	$1,513	$713	$997	$1,414	$1,774	$2,418
Men and boys	391	156	219	346	457	700
Men, aged 16 or older	314	102	169	273	334	614
Boys, aged 2 to 15	77	53	50	73	123	86
Women and girls	529	225	383	518	647	775
Women, aged 16 or older	432	161	293	432	538	645
Girls, aged 2 to 15	97	64	89	86	109	129
Babies, under age 2	119	69	78	113	158	169
Footwear	193	142	135	190	200	273
Other apparel products and services	281	121	182	248	312	502
TRANSPORTATION	$5,095	$1,999	$3,625	$4,996	$5,964	$8,130
Vehicle purchases (net outlay)	2,455	897	1,719	2,365	2,828	4,069
Cars and trucks (new)	1,475	375	732	1,322	1,854	2,865
Cars and trucks (used)	950	508	963	974	950	1,198
Gasoline and motor oil	916	473	758	949	1,108	1,198
Other vehicle expenses	1,510	520	988	1,492	1,850	2,473
Public transportation	214	109	159	190	179	390
HEALTH CARE	$783	$309	$542	$821	$919	$1,204
ENTERTAINMENT	$1,393	$501	$902	$1,190	$1,644	$2,514
Fees and admissions	303	103	172	249	358	588
Television, radios, sound equipment	441	207	327	404	510	700
Pets, toys, and playground equipment	282	134	204	244	369	432
Other entertainment supplies, equipment, services	368	58	200	293	407	794
PERSONAL CARE PRODUCTS AND SERVICES	$325	$154	$219	$307	$356	$526
READING	$135	$60	$85	$123	$156	$235
EDUCATION	$232	$312	$188	$190	$259	$249
TOBACCO PRODUCTS AND SMOKING SUPPLIES	$244	$236	$243	$257	$268	$219
MISCELLANEOUS	$571	$217	$322	$635	$771	$852
CASH CONTRIBUTIONS	$402	$128	$210	$325	$535	$769
PERSONAL INSURANCE AND PENSIONS	$2,552	$319	$1,229	$2,218	$3,206	$5,280
GIFTS OF PRODUCTS AND SERVICES	$546	$310	$342	$457	$589	$954

Note: Average annual expenditures are based on the total number of consumer units, not just those that make purchases in the category. Numbers may not add to totals due to rounding and unlisted items in the subcategories. Expenditures for gifts of products and services are also included in the product or service category. Some items in "miscellaneous" are moved to the category "other financial products and services" in chapters 2 through 10. Total expenditure exceeds total income in some income categories due to a number of factors including the underreporting of income, borrowing, and the use of savings. The "all cu's" data in this table will differ from those in age tables in other chapters because combined data from 1987 and 1988 were used for this crosstabulation. The crosstabulation required a larger sample than that available in one survey year.

Householders aged 25 to 34

INDEXED
EXPENDITURES

Indexed average annual expenditures in 1987–1988 for all household products and services, by consumer units with reference person aged 25 to 34 and before-tax income of consumer unit.

(consumer units include complete income reporters only)	all cu's	under $10,000	$10,000 to $19,999	$20,000 to $29,999	$30,000 to $39,999	$40,000 and over
Number of consumer units (in thousands)	18,952	2,747	4,495	4,430	3,036	4,244
Average number of persons per cu	2.8	2.6	2.6	2.8	3.0	2.9
Average number of earners per cu	1.5	0.9	1.3	1.6	1.7	1.8
AVERAGE TOTAL BEFORE-TAX INCOME	$28,079	$5,349	$14,823	$24,514	$34,247	$56,136
AVERAGE ANNUAL EXPENDITURES	100	45	68	94	117	162
FOOD	**100**	**60**	**78**	**96**	**111**	**142**
Food at home	**100**	**76**	**85**	**94**	**109**	**128**
Cereals and bakery products	100	72	84	97	115	123
Meat, poultry, fish, and eggs	100	87	87	95	102	124
Dairy products	100	69	91	95	107	127
Fruits and vegetables	100	76	84	87	115	131
Other foods at home	100	72	81	96	111	131
Food away from home	**100**	**39**	**68**	**99**	**112**	**159**
ALCOHOLIC BEVERAGES	**100**	**52**	**78**	**105**	**93**	**148**
HOUSING	**100**	**51**	**69**	**92**	**116**	**161**
Shelter	**100**	**53**	**67**	**93**	**115**	**162**
Owned dwellings	100	17	31	76	126	233
Mortgage interest	100	15	28	75	127	238
Property taxes	100	26	39	62	137	226
Maintenance, repairs, insurance, other expenses	100	21	44	99	111	203
Rented dwellings	100	96	112	113	103	75
Other lodging	100	27	33	80	112	231
Utilities, fuels, and public services	**100**	**69**	**83**	**98**	**116**	**129**
Household services	**100**	**27**	**63**	**79**	**130**	**187**
Personal services	100	24	67	82	142	173
Housekeeping supplies	**100**	**57**	**67**	**94**	**120**	**148**
Household furnishings and equipment	**100**	**27**	**63**	**85**	**115**	**189**
Household textiles	100	32	66	60	122	201
Furniture	100	28	54	84	108	207
Floor coverings	100	27	41	141	129	141
Major appliances	100	38	73	92	118	164
Small appliances, misc. housewares, equipment	100	22	68	81	117	188
APPAREL AND APPAREL SERVICES	**100**	**47**	**66**	**93**	**117**	**160**
Men and boys	**100**	**40**	**56**	**88**	**117**	**179**
Men, aged 16 or older	100	32	54	87	106	196
Boys, aged 2 to 15	100	69	65	95	160	112
Women and girls	**100**	**42**	**72**	**98**	**122**	**147**
Women, aged 16 or older	100	37	68	100	125	149
Girls, aged 2 to 15	100	66	92	89	112	133

(continued from previous page)

	all cu's	under $10,000	$10,000 to $19,999	$20,000 to $29,999	$30,000 to $39,999	$40,000 and over
Babies, under age 2	100	58	66	95	133	142
Footwear	100	73	70	98	104	141
Other apparel products and services	100	43	65	88	111	179
TRANSPORTATION	100	39	71	98	117	160
Vehicle purchases (net outlay)	100	37	70	96	115	166
Cars and trucks (new)	100	25	50	90	126	194
Cars and trucks (used)	100	53	101	103	100	126
Gasoline and motor oil	100	52	83	104	121	131
Other vehicle expenses	100	34	65	99	123	164
Public transportation	100	51	74	89	84	182
HEALTH CARE	100	40	69	105	117	154
ENTERTAINMENT	100	36	65	85	118	180
Fees and admissions	100	34	57	82	118	194
Television, radios, sound equipment	100	47	74	92	116	159
Pets, toys, and playground equipment	100	48	72	87	131	153
Other entertainment supplies, equipment, services	100	16	54	80	111	216
PERSONAL CARE PRODUCTS AND SERVICES	100	47	67	94	110	162
READING	100	44	63	91	116	174
EDUCATION	100	134	81	82	112	107
TOBACCO PRODUCTS AND SMOKING SUPPLIES	100	97	100	105	110	90
MISCELLANEOUS	100	38	56	111	135	149
CASH CONTRIBUTIONS	100	32	52	81	133	191
PERSONAL INSURANCE AND PENSIONS	100	12	48	87	126	207
GIFTS OF PRODUCTS AND SERVICES	100	57	63	84	108	175

Note: Expenditures for gifts of products and services are also included in the product or service category. Some items in "miscellaneous" are moved to the category "other financial products and services" in chapters 2 through 10. An index of 100 represents the average for all consumer units. An index of 132 means that the average for the subgroup is 32 percent above the average for all consumer units. An index of 68 indicates spending that is 32 percent below the overall average.

Householders aged 35 to 44

Over one-third of all householders aged 35 to 44 have household incomes of $40,000 or more. This boosts the average expenditures of households in this age group to $32,851. The total spending of households headed by 35-to-44-year-olds with incomes of $40,000 or more is 47 percent higher than the average household in this age group. They spend less than average on only rent and tobacco products.

Households in this age group with incomes under $30,000 spend less than average on almost every product and service category. Those with incomes between $30,000 and $40,000 spend more than average on food, clothing, transportation, health care, personal care products and services, reading materials, tobacco products, insurance, and pensions.

Average annual expenditures in 1987–1988 for all household products and services, by consumer units with reference person aged 35 to 44 and before-tax income of consumer unit.

(consumer units include complete income reporters only)	all cu's	under $10,000	$10,000 to $19,999	$20,000 to $29,999	$30,000 to $39,999	$40,000 and over
Number of consumer units (in thousands)	16,588	1,932	2,641	2,878	3,223	5,912
Average number of persons per cu	3.4	3.0	3.2	3.4	3.4	3.6
Average number of earners per cu	1.8	1.1	1.5	1.7	2.0	2.1
AVERAGE TOTAL BEFORE-TAX INCOME	$36,337	$4,643	$14,877	$24,814	$34,742	$62,762
AVERAGE ANNUAL EXPENDITURES	$32,851	$14,148	$19,367	$25,838	$32,247	$48,307
FOOD	$4,721	$2,540	$3,213	$3,999	$4,846	$6,195
Food at home	2,598	1,728	2,099	2,253	2,728	3,115
Cereals and bakery products	383	247	298	341	407	460
Meat, poultry, fish, and eggs	679	491	603	584	693	794
Dairy products	336	217	276	301	356	398
Fruits and vegetables	420	309	345	361	437	498
Other foods at home	780	465	578	666	835	967
Food away from home	2,123	811	1,114	1,746	2,117	3,080
ALCOHOLIC BEVERAGES	$343	$166	$198	$304	$308	$483
HOUSING	$10,069	$5,225	$6,412	$7,814	$9,056	$14,880
Shelter	5,783	2,953	3,914	4,478	5,090	8,555
Owned dwellings	3,720	1,040	1,091	2,266	3,403	6,652
Mortgage interest	2,701	686	725	1,538	2,500	4,917
Property taxes	506	207	146	349	490	850
Maintenance, repairs, insurance, other expenses	514	147	220	379	413	885
Rented dwellings	1,442	1,795	2,308	1,822	1,205	884
Other lodging	621	119	515	391	482	1,019
Utilities, fuels, and public services	1,964	1,442	1,561	1,822	1,931	2,403
Household services	522	106	162	313	393	990
Personal services	282	36	88	196	263	500
Housekeeping supplies	430	211	243	368	441	585
Household furnishings and equipment	1,370	512	533	832	1,201	2,347
Household textiles	107	51	31	78	105	170
Furniture	443	160	159	195	364	828
Floor coverings	71	21	29	40	57	127

(continued from previous page)

	all cu's	under $10,000	$10,000 to $19,999	$20,000 to $29,999	$30,000 to $39,999	$40,000 and over
Major appliances	205	124	99	173	209	293
Small appliances, misc. housewares, equipment	542	156	215	347	466	929
APPAREL AND APPAREL SERVICES	**$2,049**	**$765**	**$1,046**	**$1,603**	**$2,067**	**$3,030**
Men and boys	**558**	**192**	**241**	**386**	**553**	**877**
Men, aged 16 or older	390	108	151	259	408	622
Boys, aged 2 to 15	168	84	90	127	145	256
Women and girls	**834**	**294**	**398**	**690**	**863**	**1,210**
Women, aged 16 or older	622	203	276	510	658	905
Girls, aged 2 to 15	212	91	122	179	205	305
Babies, under age 2	**64**	**32**	**49**	**47**	**73**	**83**
Footwear	**269**	**101**	**181**	**236**	**286**	**355**
Other apparel products and services	**324**	**146**	**177**	**244**	**292**	**504**
TRANSPORTATION	**$6,182**	**$2,441**	**$3,764**	**$4,860**	**$6,617**	**$8,878**
Vehicle purchases (net outlay)	**2,812**	**1,048**	**1,761**	**1,940**	**3,122**	**4,114**
Cars and trucks (new)	1,469	480	819	632	1,417	2,519
Cars and trucks (used)	1,314	567	915	1,280	1,667	1,561
Gasoline and motor oil	**1,138**	**629**	**811**	**1,050**	**1,241**	**1,438**
Other vehicle expenses	**1,934**	**636**	**1,023**	**1,674**	**1,982**	**2,851**
Public transportation	**298**	**128**	**169**	**197**	**272**	**475**
HEALTH CARE	**$1,167**	**$573**	**$882**	**$1,036**	**$1,228**	**$1,514**
ENTERTAINMENT	**$1,842**	**$577**	**$894**	**$1,380**	**$1,770**	**$2,931**
Fees and admissions	**500**	**126**	**196**	**322**	**487**	**851**
Television, radios, sound equipment	**539**	**231**	**345**	**484**	**536**	**751**
Pets, toys, and playground equipment	**331**	**117**	**190**	**267**	**367**	**468**
Other entertainment supplies, equipment, services	**473**	**104**	**162**	**306**	**380**	**862**
PERSONAL CARE PRODUCTS AND SERVICES	**$435**	**$216**	**$228**	**$369**	**$445**	**$605**
READING	**$181**	**$65**	**$101**	**$150**	**$182**	**$269**
EDUCATION	**$439**	**$191**	**$200**	**$318**	**$325**	**$745**
TOBACCO PRODUCTS AND SMOKING SUPPLIES	**$277**	**$274**	**$260**	**$294**	**$310**	**$259**
MISCELLANEOUS	**$791**	**$382**	**$478**	**$653**	**$814**	**$1,114**
CASH CONTRIBUTIONS	**$837**	**$285**	**$385**	**$646**	**$625**	**$1,427**
PERSONAL INSURANCE AND PENSIONS	**$3,519**	**$448**	**$1,307**	**$2,412**	**$3,655**	**$5,976**
GIFTS OF PRODUCTS AND SERVICES	**$837**	**$246**	**$382**	**$569**	**$816**	**$1,349**

Note: Average annual expenditures are based on the total number of consumer units, not just those that make purchases in the category. Numbers may not add to totals due to rounding and unlisted items in the subcategories. Expenditures for gifts of products and services are also included in the product or service category. Some items in "miscellaneous" are moved to the category "other financial products and services" in chapters 2 through 10. Total expenditure exceeds total income in some income categories due to a number of factors including the underreporting of income, borrowing, and the use of savings. The "all cu's" data in this table will differ from those in age tables in other chapters because combined data from 1987 and 1988 were used for this crosstabulation. The crosstabulation required a larger sample than that available in one survey year.

Householders aged 35 to 44

INDEXED
EXPENDITURES

(consumer units include complete income reporters only)	all cu's	under $10,000	$10,000 to $19,999	$20,000 to $29,999	$30,000 to $39,999	$40,000 and over
Number of consumer units (in thousands)	16,588	1,932	2,641	2,878	3,223	5,912
Average number of persons per cu	3.4	3.0	3.2	3.4	3.4	3.6
Average number of earners per cu	1.8	1.1	1.5	1.7	2.0	2.1
AVERAGE TOTAL BEFORE-TAX INCOME	$36,337	$4,643	$14,877	$24,814	$34,742	$62,762
AVERAGE ANNUAL EXPENDITURES	100	43	59	79	98	147
FOOD	100	54	68	85	103	131
Food at home	100	67	81	87	105	120
Cereals and bakery products	100	64	78	89	106	120
Meat, poultry, fish, and eggs	100	72	89	86	102	117
Dairy products	100	64	82	90	106	118
Fruits and vegetables	100	73	82	86	104	119
Other foods at home	100	60	74	85	107	124
Food away from home	100	38	52	82	100	145
ALCOHOLIC BEVERAGES	100	48	58	89	90	141
HOUSING	100	52	64	78	90	148
Shelter	100	51	68	77	88	148
Owned dwellings	100	28	29	61	91	179
Mortgage interest	100	25	27	57	93	182
Property taxes	100	41	29	69	97	168
Maintenance, repairs, insurance, other expenses	100	29	43	74	80	172
Rented dwellings	100	124	160	126	84	61
Other lodging	100	19	83	63	78	164
Utilities, fuels, and public services	100	73	79	93	98	122
Household services	100	20	31	60	75	190
Personal services	100	13	31	70	93	177
Housekeeping supplies	100	49	57	86	103	136
Household furnishings and equipment	100	37	39	61	88	171
Household textiles	100	48	29	73	98	159
Furniture	100	36	36	44	82	187
Floor coverings	100	30	41	56	80	179
Major appliances	100	61	48	84	102	143
Small appliances, misc. housewares, equipment	100	29	40	64	86	171
APPAREL AND APPAREL SERVICES	100	37	51	78	101	148
Men and boys	100	34	43	69	99	157
Men, aged 16 or older	100	28	39	66	105	159
Boys, aged 2 to 15	100	50	54	76	86	152
Women and girls	100	35	48	83	103	145
Women, aged 16 or older	100	33	44	82	106	145
Girls, aged 2 to 15	100	43	57	84	97	144

(continued from previous page)

	all cu's	under $10,000	$10,000 to $19,999	$20,000 to $29,999	$30,000 to $39,999	$40,000 and over
Babies, under age 2	100	50	77	73	114	130
Footwear	100	38	67	88	106	132
Other apparel products and services	100	45	54	75	90	156
TRANSPORTATION	100	39	61	79	107	144
Vehicle purchases (net outlay)	100	37	63	69	111	146
Cars and trucks (new)	100	33	56	43	96	171
Cars and trucks (used)	100	43	70	97	127	119
Gasoline and motor oil	100	55	71	92	109	126
Other vehicle expenses	100	33	53	87	102	147
Public transportation	100	43	57	66	91	159
HEALTH CARE	100	49	76	89	105	130
ENTERTAINMENT	100	31	49	75	96	159
Fees and admissions	100	25	39	64	97	170
Television, radios, sound equipment	100	43	64	90	99	139
Pets, toys, and playground equipment	100	35	58	81	111	141
Other entertainment supplies, equipment, services	100	22	34	65	80	182
PERSONAL CARE PRODUCTS AND SERVICES	100	50	53	85	102	139
READING	100	36	56	83	101	149
EDUCATION	100	44	45	72	74	170
TOBACCO PRODUCTS AND SMOKING SUPPLIES	100	99	94	106	112	94
MISCELLANEOUS	100	48	60	83	103	141
CASH CONTRIBUTIONS	100	34	46	77	75	170
PERSONAL INSURANCE AND PENSIONS	100	13	37	69	104	170
GIFTS OF PRODUCTS AND SERVICES	100	29	46	68	97	161

Note: Expenditures for gifts of products and services are also included in the product or service category. Some items in "miscellaneous" are moved to the category "other financial products and services" in chapters 2 through 10. An index of 100 represents the average for all consumer units. An index of 132 means that the average for the subgroup is 32 percent above the average for all consumer units. An index of 68 indicates spending that is 32 percent below the overall average.

Householders aged 45 to 54

AVERAGE
EXPENDITURES

Householders aged 45 to 54 with incomes of $40,000 or more spend nearly 50 percent more than the average household in this age group. They spend more than average on everything except rent and tobacco products.

Fully 39 percent of householders aged 45 to 54 have household incomes of $40,000 or more, and another 15 percent have incomes between $30,000 and $40,000. The average household in this age group spends $33,574 and brings in $38,464, making them net savers.

Average annual expenditures in 1987–1988 for all household products and services, by consumer units with reference person aged 45 to 54 and before-tax income of consumer unit.

(consumer units include complete income reporters only)	all cu's	under $10,000	$10,000 to $19,999	$20,000 to $29,999	$30,000 to $39,999	$40,000 and over
Number of consumer units (in thousands)	10,985	1,473	1,630	1,885	1,672	4,326
Average number of persons per cu	2.9	2.4	2.7	2.8	2.9	3.2
Average number of earners per cu	2.0	1.2	1.5	1.9	2.1	2.5
AVERAGE TOTAL BEFORE-TAX INCOME	$38,464	$4,795	$14,711	$24,816	$34,303	$66,433
AVERAGE ANNUAL EXPENDITURES	$33,574	$15,117	$18,081	$25,988	$31,699	$49,513
FOOD	$4,885	$2,648	$3,153	$4,152	$4,622	$6,634
Food at home	2,709	1,939	2,031	2,413	2,627	3,352
Cereals and bakery products	385	286	305	339	358	475
Meat, poultry, fish, and eggs	750	527	542	699	792	899
Dairy products	341	232	269	326	329	415
Fruits and vegetables	448	360	333	396	407	555
Other foods at home	784	534	583	652	742	1,009
Food away from home	2,176	709	1,122	1,740	1,995	3,282
ALCOHOLIC BEVERAGES	$345	$174	$178	$350	$367	$454
HOUSING	$9,373	$5,274	$5,981	$7,108	$8,546	$13,312
Shelter	4,994	2,904	3,271	3,660	4,526	7,117
Owned dwellings	3,238	1,233	1,207	2,134	2,865	5,311
Mortgage interest	2,055	686	704	1,282	1,748	3,486
Property taxes	624	220	215	434	695	971
Maintenance, repairs, insurance, other expenses	559	328	287	417	421	854
Rented dwellings	1,077	1,478	1,850	1,208	1,003	621
Other lodging	678	192	214	317	658	1,184
Utilities, fuels, and public services	2,100	1,546	1,578	1,922	2,001	2,601
Household services	300	112	94	157	227	531
Personal services	48	13	15	36	55	75
Housekeeping supplies	501	255	428	390	442	658
Household furnishings and equipment	1,479	457	610	980	1,352	2,405
Household textiles	137	45	97	110	95	212
Furniture	426	79	188	292	439	688
Floor coverings	111	6	15	39	101	214

(continued from previous page)

	all cu's	under $10,000	$10,000 to $19,999	$20,000 to $29,999	$30,000 to $39,999	$40,000 and over
Major appliances	202	102	80	165	190	302
Small appliances, misc. housewares, equipment	603	227	230	373	527	989
APPAREL AND APPAREL SERVICES	**$2,081**	**$980**	**$1,124**	**$1,513**	**$1,972**	**$3,058**
Men and boys	**538**	**200**	**279**	**329**	**501**	**844**
Men, aged 16 or older	454	139	184	284	441	727
Boys, aged 2 to 15	84	61	95	45	60	117
Women and girls	**892**	**469**	**403**	**705**	**817**	**1,303**
Women, aged 16 or older	794	406	354	630	725	1,163
Girls, aged 2 to 15	98	63	48	76	92	141
Babies, under age 2	**47**	**17**	**32**	**37**	**53**	**64**
Footwear	**265**	**159**	**278**	**220**	**247**	**315**
Other apparel products and services	**339**	**134**	**133**	**222**	**354**	**532**
TRANSPORTATION	**$6,535**	**$2,855**	**$2,908**	**$5,283**	**$6,464**	**$9,720**
Vehicle purchases (net outlay)	**2,946**	**1,236**	**944**	**2,399**	**2,987**	**4,506**
Cars and trucks (new)	1,586	540	299	1,061	1,591	2,654
Cars and trucks (used)	1,303	691	636	1,299	1,356	1,745
Gasoline and motor oil	**1,221**	**713**	**804**	**1,080**	**1,265**	**1,596**
Other vehicle expenses	**2,029**	**779**	**998**	**1,539**	**1,946**	**3,082**
Public transportation	**338**	**127**	**163**	**265**	**267**	**536**
HEALTH CARE	**$1,251**	**$665**	**$911**	**$1,223**	**$1,267**	**$1,583**
ENTERTAINMENT	**$1,594**	**$593**	**$685**	**$1,088**	**$1,338**	**$2,594**
Fees and admissions	**464**	**159**	**173**	**328**	**361**	**777**
Television, radios, sound equipment	**474**	**237**	**260**	**355**	**463**	**690**
Pets, toys, and playground equipment	**267**	**130**	**150**	**223**	**253**	**381**
Other entertainment supplies, equipment, services	**390**	**67**	**102**	**181**	**261**	**746**
PERSONAL CARE PRODUCTS AND SERVICES	**$459**	**$188**	**$315**	**$350**	**$388**	**$665**
READING	**$183**	**$85**	**$106**	**$136**	**$179**	**$267**
EDUCATION	**$642**	**$171**	**$169**	**$381**	**$618**	**$1,103**
TOBACCO PRODUCTS AND SMOKING SUPPLIES	**$335**	**$323**	**$328**	**$346**	**$352**	**$331**
MISCELLANEOUS	**$844**	**$397**	**$418**	**$867**	**$831**	**$1,145**
CASH CONTRIBUTIONS	**$1,123**	**$289**	**$494**	**$687**	**$971**	**$1,892**
PERSONAL INSURANCE AND PENSIONS	**$3,924**	**$476**	**$1,311**	**$2,503**	**$3,782**	**$6,756**
GIFTS OF PRODUCTS AND SERVICES	**$1,368**	**$410**	**$712**	**$976**	**$1,249**	**$2,130**

Note: Average annual expenditures are based on the total number of consumer units, not just those that make purchases in the category. Numbers may not add to totals due to rounding and unlisted items in the subcategories. Expenditures for gifts of products and services are also included in the product or service category. Some items in "miscellaneous" are moved to the category "other financial products and services" in chapters 2 through 10. Total expenditure exceeds total income in some income categories due to a number of factors including the underreporting of income, borrowing, and the use of savings. The "all cu's" data in this table will differ from those in age tables in other chapters because combined data from 1987 and 1988 were used for this crosstabulation. The crosstabulation required a larger sample than that available in one survey year.

Householders aged 45 to 54

Indexed average annual expenditures in 1987–1988 for all household products and services, by consumer units with reference person aged 45 to 54 and before-tax income of consumer unit.

(consumer units include complete income reporters only)	all cu's	under $10,000	$10,000 to $19,999	$20,000 to $29,999	$30,000 to $39,999	$40,000 and over
Number of consumer units (in thousands)	10,985	1,473	1,630	1,885	1,672	4,326
Average number of persons per cu	2.9	2.4	2.7	2.8	2.9	3.2
Average number of earners per cu	2.0	1.2	1.5	1.9	2.1	2.5
AVERAGE TOTAL BEFORE-TAX INCOME	$38,464	$4,795	$14,711	$24,816	$34,303	$66,433
AVERAGE ANNUAL EXPENDITURES	100	45	54	77	94	147
FOOD	100	54	65	85	95	136
Food at home	100	72	75	89	97	124
Cereals and bakery products	100	74	79	88	93	123
Meat, poultry, fish, and eggs	100	70	72	93	106	120
Dairy products	100	68	79	96	96	122
Fruits and vegetables	100	80	74	88	91	124
Other foods at home	100	68	74	83	95	129
Food away from home	100	33	52	80	92	151
ALCOHOLIC BEVERAGES	100	50	52	101	106	132
HOUSING	100	56	64	76	91	142
Shelter	100	58	65	73	91	143
Owned dwellings	100	38	37	66	88	164
Mortgage interest	100	33	34	62	85	170
Property taxes	100	35	34	70	111	156
Maintenance, repairs, insurance, other expenses	100	59	51	75	75	153
Rented dwellings	100	137	172	112	93	58
Other lodging	100	28	32	47	97	175
Utilities, fuels, and public services	100	74	75	92	95	124
Household services	100	37	31	52	76	177
Personal services	100	28	31	75	115	156
Housekeeping supplies	100	51	86	78	88	131
Household furnishings and equipment	100	31	41	66	91	163
Household textiles	100	33	71	80	69	155
Furniture	100	18	44	69	103	162
Floor coverings	100	5	14	35	91	193
Major appliances	100	50	40	82	94	150
Small appliances, misc. housewares, equipment	100	38	38	62	87	164
APPAREL AND APPAREL SERVICES	100	47	54	73	95	147
Men and boys	100	37	52	61	93	157
Men, aged 16 or older	100	31	41	63	97	160
Boys, aged 2 to 15	100	73	113	54	71	139
Women and girls	100	53	45	79	92	146
Women, aged 16 or older	100	51	45	79	91	146
Girls, aged 2 to 15	100	64	49	78	94	144

(continued from previous page)

	all cu's	under $10,000	$10,000 to $19,999	$20,000 to $29,999	$30,000 to $39,999	$40,000 and over
Babies, under age 2	100	37	69	79	113	136
Footwear	100	60	105	83	93	119
Other apparel products and services	100	40	39	65	104	157
TRANSPORTATION	100	44	44	81	99	149
Vehicle purchases (net outlay)	100	42	32	81	101	153
Cars and trucks (new)	100	34	19	67	100	167
Cars and trucks (used)	100	53	49	100	104	134
Gasoline and motor oil	100	58	66	88	104	131
Other vehicle expenses	100	38	49	76	96	152
Public transportation	100	38	48	78	79	159
HEALTH CARE	100	53	73	98	101	127
ENTERTAINMENT	100	37	43	68	84	163
Fees and admissions	100	34	37	71	78	167
Television, radios, sound equipment	100	50	55	75	98	146
Pets, toys, and playground equipment	100	49	56	84	95	143
Other entertainment supplies, equipment, services	100	17	26	46	67	191
PERSONAL CARE PRODUCTS AND SERVICES	100	41	69	76	85	145
READING	100	46	58	74	98	146
EDUCATION	100	27	26	59	96	172
TOBACCO PRODUCTS AND SMOKING SUPPLIES	100	96	98	103	105	99
MISCELLANEOUS	100	47	50	103	98	136
CASH CONTRIBUTIONS	100	26	44	61	86	168
PERSONAL INSURANCE AND PENSIONS	100	12	33	64	96	172
GIFTS OF PRODUCTS AND SERVICES	100	30	52	71	91	156

Note: Expenditures for gifts of products and services are also included in the product or service category. Some items in "miscellaneous" are moved to the category "other financial products and services" in chapters 2 through 10. An index of 100 represents the average for all consumer units. An index of 132 means that the average for the subgroup is 32 percent above the average for all consumer units. An index of 68 indicates spending that is 32 percent below the overall average.

Householders aged 55 to 64

AVERAGE
EXPENDITURES

The average household in this age group spends less than it makes. Along with 45-to-54-year-olds, these householders are savers. They spend an average of $26,202 a year on products and services.

Households in this age group with incomes under $30,000 are below-average spenders, and they account for fuly 63 percent of the total. Householders aged 55 to 64 with incomes of $30,000 to $40,000 spend 12 percent more than the average household in this age group, while those with incomes of $40,000 or more spend 77 percent more than others their age.

Average annual expenditures in 1987–1988 for all household products and services, by consumer units with reference person aged 55 to 64 and before-tax income of consumer unit.

(consumer units include complete income reporters only)	all cu's	under $10,000	$10,000 to $19,999	$20,000 to $29,999	$30,000 to $39,999	$40,000 and over
Number of consumer units (in thousands)	10,639	2,348	2,324	2,067	1,329	2,570
Average number of persons per cu	2.3	1.8	2.0	2.2	2.4	2.8
Average number of earners per cu	1.4	0.7	1.0	1.4	1.6	2.2
AVERAGE TOTAL BEFORE-TAX INCOME	$30,524	$5,492	$14,864	$24,567	$34,279	$70,410
AVERAGE ANNUAL EXPENDITURES	$26,202	$12,555	$18,028	$24,113	$29,370	$46,291
FOOD	$3,983	$2,374	$3,131	$3,953	$4,623	$6,025
Food at home	2,397	1,717	2,148	2,474	2,587	3,146
Cereals and bakery products	332	244	311	331	362	426
Meat, poultry, fish, and eggs	679	495	628	645	733	899
Dairy products	298	209	253	319	346	389
Fruits and vegetables	433	297	398	462	444	576
Other foods at home	655	473	559	716	702	856
Food away from home	1,586	657	983	1,480	2,035	2,879
ALCOHOLIC BEVERAGES	$264	$119	$177	$275	$346	$437
HOUSING	$7,461	$4,539	$5,293	$6,874	$7,770	$12,428
Shelter	3,724	2,401	2,466	3,384	3,585	6,415
Owned dwellings	2,451	1,228	1,384	2,270	2,277	4,771
Mortgage interest	1,082	489	463	742	900	2,552
Property taxes	700	339	477	733	691	1,211
Maintenance, repairs, insurance, other expenses	669	400	443	795	686	1,008
Rented dwellings	706	925	862	736	820	281
Other lodging	567	248	221	379	488	1,363
Utilities, fuels, and public services	1,878	1,405	1,656	1,824	1,958	2,511
Household services	274	75	101	207	260	673
Personal services	39	1	8	39	61	92
Housekeeping supplies	423	243	381	430	480	607
Household furnishings and equipment	1,163	414	689	1,028	1,487	2,223
Household textiles	104	55	69	82	106	197
Furniture	316	80	159	298	365	664
Floor coverings	105	23	55	100	293	113

(continued from previous page)

	all cu's	under $10,000	$10,000 to $19,999	$20,000 to $29,999	$30,000 to $39,999	$40,000 and over
Major appliances	182	83	161	138	234	301
Small appliances, misc. housewares, equipment	456	174	245	410	488	948
APPAREL AND APPAREL SERVICES	**$1,415**	**$520**	**$1,051**	**$1,116**	**$1,486**	**$2,787**
Men and boys	**395**	**133**	**253**	**335**	**363**	**843**
Men, aged 16 or older	351	128	197	291	281	798
Boys, aged 2 to 15	44	6	55	44	82	46
Women and girls	**594**	**243**	**492**	**403**	**703**	**1,104**
Women, aged 16 or older	556	231	456	367	643	1,052
Girls, aged 2 to 15	38	12	36	36	59	52
Babies, under age 2	**34**	**10**	**28**	**32**	**46**	**57**
Footwear	**172**	**61**	**168**	**153**	**179**	**293**
Other apparel products and services	**220**	**72**	**111**	**192**	**196**	**489**
TRANSPORTATION	**$4,744**	**$2,128**	**$3,122**	**$4,753**	**$5,711**	**$8,070**
Vehicle purchases (net outlay)	**1,946**	**833**	**994**	**2,072**	**2,506**	**3,432**
Cars and trucks (new)	1,245	469	354	1,198	1,522	2,655
Cars and trucks (used)	693	363	637	857	961	774
Gasoline and motor oil	**961**	**518**	**798**	**978**	**1,137**	**1,408**
Other vehicle expenses	**1,532**	**682**	**1,210**	**1,480**	**1,778**	**2,493**
Public transportation	**305**	**94**	**120**	**223**	**290**	**737**
HEALTH CARE	**$1,390**	**$1,023**	**$1,383**	**$1,484**	**$1,593**	**$1,550**
ENTERTAINMENT	**$1,178**	**$411**	**$904**	**$992**	**$1,224**	**$2,254**
Fees and admissions	**327**	**83**	**152**	**238**	**345**	**770**
Television, radios, sound equipment	**389**	**186**	**257**	**400**	**352**	**710**
Pets, toys, and playground equipment	**230**	**108**	**187**	**216**	**264**	**373**
Other entertainment supplies, equipment, services	**232**	**34**	**308**	**139**	**264**	**402**
PERSONAL CARE PRODUCTS AND SERVICES	**$371**	**$159**	**$299**	**$362**	**$417**	**$627**
READING	**$161**	**$79**	**$117**	**$141**	**$189**	**$278**
EDUCATION	**$239**	**$93**	**$96**	**$94**	**$198**	**$641**
TOBACCO PRODUCTS AND SMOKING SUPPLIES	**$268**	**$240**	**$265**	**$263**	**$299**	**$282**
MISCELLANEOUS	**$639**	**$288**	**$543**	**$523**	**$698**	**$1,132**
CASH CONTRIBUTIONS	**$1,103**	**$165**	**$488**	**$731**	**$1,405**	**$2,660**
PERSONAL INSURANCE AND PENSIONS	**$2,987**	**$418**	**$1,160**	**$2,552**	**$3,413**	**$7,118**
GIFTS OF PRODUCTS AND SERVICES	**$1,081**	**$381**	**$553**	**$911**	**$1,099**	**$2,364**

Note: Average annual expenditures are based on the total number of consumer units, not just those that make purchases in the category. Numbers may not add to totals due to rounding and unlisted items in the subcategories. Expenditures for gifts of products and services are also included in the product or service category. Some items in "miscellaneous" are moved to the category "other financial products and services" in chapters 2 through 10. Total expenditure exceeds total income in some income categories due to a number of factors including the underreporting of income, borrowing, and the use of savings. The "all cu's" data in this table will differ from those in age tables in other chapters because combined data from 1987 and 1988 were used for this crosstabulation. The crosstabulation required a larger sample than that available in one survey year.

Householders aged 55 to 64

INDEXED
EXPENDITURES

Indexed average annual expenditures in 1987–1988 for all household products and services, by consumer units with reference person aged 55 to 64 and before-tax income of consumer unit.

(consumer units include complete income reporters only)	all cu's	under $10,000	$10,000 to $19,999	$20,000 to $29,999	$30,000 to $39,999	$40,000 and over
Number of consumer units (in thousands)	10,639	2,348	2,324	2,067	1,329	2,570
Average number of persons per cu	2.3	1.8	2.0	2.2	2.4	2.8
Average number of earners per cu	1.4	0.7	1.0	1.4	1.6	2.2
AVERAGE TOTAL BEFORE-TAX INCOME	$30,524	$5,492	$14,864	$24,567	$34,279	$70,410
AVERAGE ANNUAL EXPENDITURES	100	48	69	92	112	177
FOOD	100	60	79	99	116	151
Food at home	100	72	90	103	108	131
Cereals and bakery products	100	74	94	100	109	128
Meat, poultry, fish, and eggs	100	73	93	95	108	132
Dairy products	100	70	85	107	116	131
Fruits and vegetables	100	69	92	107	103	133
Other foods at home	100	72	85	109	107	131
Food away from home	100	41	62	93	128	182
ALCOHOLIC BEVERAGES	100	45	67	104	131	166
HOUSING	100	61	71	92	104	167
Shelter	100	64	66	91	96	172
Owned dwellings	100	50	56	93	93	195
Mortgage interest	100	45	43	69	83	236
Property taxes	100	48	68	105	99	173
Maintenance, repairs, insurance, other expenses	100	60	66	119	103	151
Rented dwellings	100	131	122	104	116	40
Other lodging	100	44	39	67	86	240
Utilities, fuels, and public services	100	75	88	97	104	134
Household services	100	27	37	76	95	246
Personal services	100	2	19	100	156	236
Housekeeping supplies	100	58	90	102	113	143
Household furnishings and equipment	100	36	59	88	128	191
Household textiles	100	53	66	79	102	189
Furniture	100	25	50	94	116	210
Floor coverings	100	22	52	95	279	108
Major appliances	100	46	88	76	129	165
Small appliances, misc. housewares, equipment	100	38	54	90	107	208
APPAREL AND APPAREL SERVICES	100	37	74	79	105	197
Men and boys	100	34	64	85	92	213
Men, aged 16 or older	100	36	56	83	80	227
Boys, aged 2 to 15	100	13	126	100	186	105
Women and girls	100	41	83	68	118	186
Women, aged 16 or older	100	42	82	66	116	189
Girls, aged 2 to 15	100	32	95	95	155	137

(continued from previous page)

	all cu's	under $10,000	$10,000 to $19,999	$20,000 to $29,999	$30,000 to $39,999	$40,000 and over
Babies, under age 2	100	30	81	94	135	168
Footwear	100	36	98	89	104	170
Other apparel products and services	100	33	51	87	89	222
TRANSPORTATION	100	45	66	100	120	170
Vehicle purchases (net outlay)	100	43	51	106	129	176
Cars and trucks (new)	100	38	28	96	122	213
Cars and trucks (used)	100	52	92	124	139	112
Gasoline and motor oil	100	54	83	102	118	147
Other vehicle expenses	100	44	79	97	116	163
Public transportation	100	31	39	73	95	242
HEALTH CARE	100	74	99	107	115	112
ENTERTAINMENT	100	35	77	84	104	191
Fees and admissions	100	25	47	73	106	235
Television, radios, sound equipment	100	48	66	103	90	183
Pets, toys, and playground equipment	100	47	81	94	115	162
Other entertainment supplies, equipment, services	100	15	133	60	114	173
PERSONAL CARE PRODUCTS AND SERVICES	100	43	81	98	112	169
READING	100	49	73	88	117	173
EDUCATION	100	39	40	39	83	268
TOBACCO PRODUCTS AND SMOKING SUPPLIES	100	89	99	98	112	105
MISCELLANEOUS	100	45	85	82	109	177
CASH CONTRIBUTIONS	100	15	44	66	127	241
PERSONAL INSURANCE AND PENSIONS	100	14	39	85	114	238
GIFTS OF PRODUCTS AND SERVICES	100	35	51	84	102	219

Note: Expenditures for gifts of products and services are also included in the product or service category. Some items in "miscellaneous" are moved to the category "other financial products and services" in chapters 2 through 10. An index of 100 represents the average for all consumer units. An index of 132 means that the average for the subgroup is 32 percent above the average for all consumer units. An index of 68 indicates spending that is 32 percent below the overall average.

Householders aged 65 to 74

Fifteen percent of retirees have incomes of $20,000 to $30,000, and they spend 17 percent more than others their age. Another 8 percent have incomes between $30,000 and $40,000, and their spending is 57 percent above the average for their age group. The 9 percent of householders aged 65 to 74 with incomes of $40,000 or more spend more than twice as much as their peers. For some items, like mortgage interest, lodging other than dwellings, new cars and trucks, household services, and entertainment fees and admissions, they spend many times more than the average.

The average expenditures of householders aged 65 to 74 is $19,893, but only about one in three have incomes that high. Those with incomes under $20,000 spend more than average on some items, including entertainment, rent, used vehicles, clothing for men and boys, and health care.

Average annual expenditures in 1987–1988 for all household products and services, by consumer units with reference person aged 65 to 74 and before-tax income of consumer unit.

(consumer units include complete income reporters only)	all cu's	under $10,000	$10,000 to $19,999	$20,000 to $29,999	$30,000 to $39,999	$40,000 and over
Number of consumer units (in thousands)	10,099	3,538	3,329	1,496	809	927
Average number of persons per cu	1.9	1.5	2.0	2.2	2.4	2.5
Average number of earners per cu	0.6	0.3	0.5	0.8	1.0	1.4
AVERAGE TOTAL BEFORE-TAX INCOME	$19,635	$6,219	$14,463	$24,445	$34,358	$68,788
AVERAGE ANNUAL EXPENDITURES	$19,893	$11,418	$18,121	$23,370	$31,284	$43,967
FOOD	$3,109	$1,975	$3,050	$3,879	$4,366	$5,779
Food at home	1,998	1,436	2,064	2,336	2,575	3,106
Cereals and bakery products	291	207	306	363	361	415
Meat, poultry, fish, and eggs	545	391	563	588	710	911
Dairy products	244	187	241	302	328	344
Fruits and vegetables	390	289	400	443	498	606
Other foods at home	528	361	553	639	678	829
Food away from home	1,111	539	987	1,543	1,792	2,673
ALCOHOLIC BEVERAGES	$176	$69	$172	$198	$328	$473
HOUSING	$6,058	$4,201	$5,461	$6,786	$8,625	$12,027
Shelter	2,940	2,073	2,598	2,950	4,178	6,381
Owned dwellings	1,758	995	1,520	1,969	2,837	4,241
Mortgage interest	413	216	300	372	807	1,295
Property taxes	640	323	583	798	1,086	1,415
Maintenance, repairs, insurance, other expenses	705	457	638	799	944	1,531
Rented dwellings	794	931	783	616	649	720
Other lodging	389	147	295	366	691	1,421
Utilities, fuels, and public services	1,652	1,283	1,622	1,886	1,995	2,491
Household services	311	201	196	320	393	1,050
Personal services	41	42	16	28	84	116
Housekeeping supplies	391	274	410	469	572	550
Household furnishings and equipment	765	370	635	1,160	1,488	1,554
Household textiles	77	39	71	134	104	138
Furniture	171	69	129	216	410	422
Floor coverings	42	15	37	86	62	72

(continued from previous page)

	all cu's	under $10,000	$10,000 to $19,999	$20,000 to $29,999	$30,000 to $39,999	$40,000 and over
Major appliances	140	77	129	213	223	228
Small appliances, misc. housewares, equipment	336	171	268	510	687	694
APPAREL AND APPAREL SERVICES	**$1,060**	**$556**	**$1,002**	**$1,342**	**$1,886**	**$2,160**
Men and boys	**219**	**92**	**255**	**246**	**332**	**448**
Men, aged 16 or older	195	81	215	220	315	435
Boys, aged 2 to 15	24	11	40	26	17	13
Women and girls	**475**	**308**	**461**	**649**	**619**	**841**
Women, aged 16 or older	452	295	436	615	591	802
Girls, aged 2 to 15	23	12	25	33	29	39
Babies, under age 2	**20**	**7**	**21**	**21**	**39**	**45**
Footwear	**162**	**84**	**144**	**191**	**304**	**393**
Other apparel products and services	**185**	**66**	**122**	**234**	**592**	**433**
TRANSPORTATION	**$3,680**	**$1,595**	**$3,411**	**$4,761**	**$6,744**	**$8,185**
Vehicle purchases (net outlay)	**1,594**	**514**	**1,427**	**2,240**	**3,361**	**3,728**
Cars and trucks (new)	982	362	648	1,160	2,215	3,187
Cars and trucks (used)	611	152	779	1,079	1,145	532
Gasoline and motor oil	**696**	**401**	**692**	**907**	**1,003**	**1,228**
Other vehicle expenses	**1,102**	**529**	**1,069**	**1,332**	**1,861**	**2,374**
Public transportation	**289**	**150**	**224**	**282**	**520**	**856**
HEALTH CARE	**$1,869**	**$1,412**	**$2,052**	**$2,085**	**$2,136**	**$2,385**
ENTERTAINMENT	**$859**	**$396**	**$764**	**$990**	**$1,614**	**$2,108**
Fees and admissions	**255**	**98**	**181**	**309**	**556**	**766**
Television, radios, sound equipment	**272**	**143**	**230**	**362**	**579**	**508**
Pets, toys, and playground equipment	**154**	**93**	**119**	**182**	**336**	**317**
Other entertainment supplies, equipment, services	**178**	**62**	**234**	**137**	**143**	**517**
PERSONAL CARE PRODUCTS AND SERVICES	**$292**	**$152**	**$299**	**$393**	**$499**	**$522**
READING	**$154**	**$90**	**$135**	**$194**	**$236**	**$324**
EDUCATION	**$79**	**$29**	**$65**	**$111**	**$159**	**$189**
TOBACCO PRODUCTS AND SMOKING SUPPLIES	**$190**	**$152**	**$200**	**$240**	**$190**	**$219**
MISCELLANEOUS	**$516**	**$349**	**$467**	**$422**	**$1,101**	**$987**
CASH CONTRIBUTIONS	**$856**	**$229**	**$519**	**$890**	**$1,233**	**$4,069**
PERSONAL INSURANCE AND PENSIONS	**$997**	**$212**	**$522**	**$1,079**	**$2,166**	**$4,540**
GIFTS OF PRODUCTS AND SERVICES	**$784**	**$443**	**$667**	**$978**	**$1,527**	**$1,587**

Note: Average annual expenditures are based on the total number of consumer units, not just those that make purchases in the category. Numbers may not add to totals due to rounding and unlisted items in the subcategories. Expenditures for gifts of products and services are also included in the product or service category. Some items in "miscellaneous" are moved to the category "other financial products and services" in chapters 2 through 10. Total expenditure exceeds total income in some income categories due to a number of factors including the underreporting of income, borrowing, and the use of savings. The "all cu's" data in this table will differ from those in age tables in other chapters because combined data from 1987 and 1988 were used for this crosstabulation. The crosstabulation required a larger sample than that available in one survey year.

Householders aged 65 to 74

Indexed average annual expenditures in 1987–1988 for all household products and services, by consumer units with reference person aged 65 to 74 and before-tax income of consumer unit.

(consumer units include complete income reporters only)	all cu's	under $10,000	$10,000 to $19,999	$20,000 to $29,999	$30,000 to $39,999	$40,000 and over
Number of consumer units (in thousands)	10,099	3,538	3,329	1,496	809	927
Average number of persons per cu	1.9	1.5	2.0	2.2	2.4	2.5
Average number of earners per cu	0.6	0.3	0.5	0.8	1.0	1.4
AVERAGE TOTAL BEFORE-TAX INCOME	$19,635	$6,219	$14,463	$24,445	$34,358	$68,788
AVERAGE ANNUAL EXPENDITURES	100	57	91	117	157	221
FOOD	100	64	98	125	140	186
Food at home	100	72	103	117	129	155
Cereals and bakery products	100	71	105	125	124	143
Meat, poultry, fish, and eggs	100	72	103	108	130	167
Dairy products	100	77	99	124	134	141
Fruits and vegetables	100	74	103	114	128	155
Other foods at home	100	68	105	121	128	157
Food away from home	100	48	89	139	161	241
ALCOHOLIC BEVERAGES	100	39	98	113	186	269
HOUSING	100	69	90	112	142	199
Shelter	100	71	88	100	142	217
Owned dwellings	100	57	86	112	161	241
Mortgage interest	100	52	73	90	195	314
Property taxes	100	50	91	125	170	221
Maintenance, repairs, insurance, other expenses	100	65	91	113	134	217
Rented dwellings	100	117	99	78	82	91
Other lodging	100	38	76	94	178	365
Utilities, fuels, and public services	100	78	98	114	121	151
Household services	100	65	63	103	126	338
Personal services	100	101	40	68	205	283
Housekeeping supplies	100	70	105	120	146	141
Household furnishings and equipment	100	48	83	152	195	203
Household textiles	100	50	93	174	135	179
Furniture	100	40	76	126	240	247
Floor coverings	100	35	89	205	148	171
Major appliances	100	55	92	152	159	163
Small appliances, misc. housewares, equipment	100	51	80	152	204	207
APPAREL AND APPAREL SERVICES	100	52	95	127	178	204
Men and boys	100	42	116	112	152	205
Men, aged 16 or older	100	41	110	113	162	223
Boys, aged 2 to 15	100	44	166	108	71	54
Women and girls	100	65	97	137	130	177
Women, aged 16 or older	100	65	97	136	131	177
Girls, aged 2 to 15	100	53	107	143	126	170

(continued from previous page)

	all cu's	under $10,000	$10,000 to $19,999	$20,000 to $29,999	$30,000 to $39,999	$40,000 and over
Babies, under age 2	100	37	103	105	195	225
Footwear	100	52	89	118	188	243
Other apparel products and services	100	36	66	126	320	234
TRANSPORTATION	100	43	93	129	183	222
Vehicle purchases (net outlay)	100	32	90	141	211	234
Cars and trucks (new)	100	37	66	118	226	325
Cars and trucks (used)	100	25	128	177	187	87
Gasoline and motor oil	100	58	99	130	144	176
Other vehicle expenses	100	48	97	121	169	215
Public transportation	100	52	78	98	180	296
HEALTH CARE	100	76	110	112	114	128
ENTERTAINMENT	100	46	89	115	188	245
Fees and admissions	100	38	71	121	218	300
Television, radios, sound equipment	100	53	84	133	213	187
Pets, toys, and playground equipment	100	60	77	118	218	206
Other entertainment supplies, equipment, services	100	35	131	77	80	290
PERSONAL CARE PRODUCTS AND SERVICES	100	52	102	135	171	179
READING	100	58	88	126	153	210
EDUCATION	100	37	82	141	201	239
TOBACCO PRODUCTS AND SMOKING SUPPLIES	100	80	105	126	100	115
MISCELLANEOUS	100	68	91	82	213	191
CASH CONTRIBUTIONS	100	27	61	104	144	475
PERSONAL INSURANCE AND PENSIONS	100	21	52	108	217	455
GIFTS OF PRODUCTS AND SERVICES	100	56	85	125	195	202

Note: Expenditures for gifts of products and services are also included in the product or service category. Some items in "miscellaneous" are moved to the category "other financial products and services" in chapters 2 through 10. An index of 100 represents the average for all consumer units. An index of 132 means that the average for the subgroup is 32 percent above the average for all consumer units. An index of 68 indicates spending that is 32 percent below the overall average.

Householders aged 75 or older

AVERAGE
EXPENDITURES

The oldest householders spend less than all other households—$13,025 a year, on average. More than half of these households have incomes under $10,000. Their spending is 36 percent below average for the age group. But the lowest-income households spend more than average on rent and personal services.

In this relatively flat market, households with incomes greater than $10,000 spend more than the average for their age group on most major categories of household products and services.

Average annual expenditures in 1987–1988 for all household products and services, by consumer units with reference person aged 75 or older and before-tax income of consumer unit.

(consumer units include complete income reporters only)	all cu's	under $10,000	$10,000 to $19,999	$20,000 to $29,999	$30,000 to $39,999	$40,000 and over
Number of consumer units (in thousands)	7,282	4,069	2,011	680	197	324
Average number of persons per cu	1.5	1.3	1.8	2.0	2.1	2.2
Average number of earners per cu	0.2	0.1	0.2	0.4	0.4	0.7
AVERAGE TOTAL BEFORE-TAX INCOME	$13,308	$6,272	$13,763	$24,082	$34,142	$63,550
AVERAGE ANNUAL EXPENDITURES	$13,025	$8,338	$15,191	$19,860	$25,408	$36,825
FOOD	$2,125	$1,525	$2,650	$2,916	$3,356	$3,970
Food at home	1,516	1,211	1,816	1,985	1,979	2,161
Cereals and bakery products	239	195	279	309	379	323
Meat, poultry, fish, and eggs	399	309	506	485	482	617
Dairy products	190	162	222	229	219	242
Fruits and vegetables	318	253	375	444	410	444
Other foods at home	370	294	435	519	489	534
Food away from home	609	314	834	931	1,377	1,810
ALCOHOLIC BEVERAGES	$82	$27	$105	$173	$157	$406
HOUSING	$4,605	$3,547	$5,186	$6,002	$7,365	$9,678
Shelter	2,254	1,745	2,614	2,748	3,473	4,641
Owned dwellings	1,130	728	1,392	1,614	2,046	2,986
Mortgage interest	119	87	109	115	341	466
Property taxes	486	303	647	722	816	1,103
Maintenance, repairs, insurance, other expenses	524	338	636	776	889	1,417
Rented dwellings	937	963	952	816	996	736
Other lodging	187	54	269	318	431	918
Utilities, fuels, and public services	1,365	1,146	1,461	1,712	1,943	2,438
Household services	339	249	302	446	821	1,193
Personal services	69	82	37	41	46	176
Housekeeping supplies	269	169	385	404	533	360
Household furnishings and equipment	377	238	425	691	594	1,046
Household textiles	66	45	81	130	27	94
Furniture	70	48	65	111	181	211
Floor coverings	18	2	32	37	26	94

(continued from previous page)

	all cu's	under $10,000	$10,000 to $19,999	$20,000 to $29,999	$30,000 to $39,999	$40,000 and over
Major appliances	98	69	119	143	124	236
Small appliances, misc. housewares, equipment	125	74	128	269	237	411
APPAREL AND APPAREL SERVICES	**$512**	**$269**	**$660**	**$747**	**$2,331**	**$1,256**
Men and boys	**107**	**44**	**144**	**268**	**207**	**259**
Men, aged 16 or older	94	38	129	222	183	259
Boys, aged 2 to 15	13	7	15	45	24	0
Women and girls	**238**	**126**	**301**	**251**	**1,580**	**592**
Women, aged 16 or older	230	122	290	243	1,562	553
Girls, aged 2 to 15	8	4	11	8	17	38
Babies, under age 2	**8**	**5**	**12**	**6**	**8**	**14**
Footwear	**94**	**60**	**139**	**87**	**282**	**189**
Other apparel products and services	**65**	**33**	**63**	**135**	**255**	**202**
TRANSPORTATION	**$1,623**	**$658**	**$2,030**	**$3,807**	**$3,650**	**$5,428**
Vehicle purchases (net outlay)	**568**	**108**	**717**	**1,834**	**1,494**	**2,201**
Cars and trucks (new)	381	51	534	1,387	599	1,329
Cars and trucks (used)	187	56	184	447	895	872
Gasoline and motor oil	**347**	**216**	**436**	**543**	**591**	**862**
Other vehicle expenses	**554**	**261**	**723**	**1,089**	**1,207**	**1,684**
Public transportation	**155**	**73**	**153**	**342**	**359**	**680**
HEALTH CARE	**$1,892**	**$1,315**	**$2,404**	**$2,949**	**$2,793**	**$3,189**
ENTERTAINMENT	**$341**	**$185**	**$400**	**$621**	**$866**	**$1,027**
Fees and admissions	**94**	**30**	**114**	**193**	**314**	**447**
Television, radios, sound equipment	**131**	**91**	**151**	**213**	**226**	**276**
Pets, toys, and playground equipment	**81**	**60**	**71**	**137**	**253**	**192**
Other entertainment supplies, equipment, services	**34**	**5**	**64**	**78**	**73**	**112**
PERSONAL CARE PRODUCTS AND SERVICES	**$203**	**$121**	**$283**	**$288**	**$503**	**$381**
READING	**$98**	**$65**	**$111**	**$167**	**$215**	**$219**
EDUCATION	**$15**	**$5**	**$8**	**$67**	**$20**	**$77**
TOBACCO PRODUCTS AND SMOKING SUPPLIES	**$80**	**$68**	**$96**	**$85**	**$106**	**$107**
MISCELLANEOUS	**$249**	**$203**	**$210**	**$349**	**$445**	**$735**
CASH CONTRIBUTIONS	**$858**	**$243**	**$706**	**$1,087**	**$3,104**	**$7,674**
PERSONAL INSURANCE AND PENSIONS	**$342**	**$105**	**$345**	**$602**	**$496**	**$2,678**
GIFTS OF PRODUCTS AND SERVICES	**$567**	**$314**	**$591**	**$1,781**	**$559**	**$1,060**

Note: Average annual expenditures are based on the total number of consumer units, not just those that make purchases in the category. Numbers may not add to totals due to rounding and unlisted items in the subcategories. Expenditures for gifts of products and services are also included in the product or service category. Some items in "miscellaneous" are moved to the category "other financial products and services" in chapters 2 through 10. Total expenditure exceeds total income in some income categories due to a number of factors including the underreporting of income, borrowing, and the use of savings. The "all cu's" data in this table will differ from those in age tables in other chapters because combined data from 1987 and 1988 were used for this crosstabulation. The crosstabulation required a larger sample than that available in one survey year.

Householders aged 75 or older

Indexed average annual expenditures in 1987–1988 for all household products and services, by consumer units with reference person aged 75 or older and before-tax income of consumer unit.

(consumer units include complete income reporters only)	all cu's	under $10,000	$10,000 to $19,999	$20,000 to $29,999	$30,000 to $39,999	$40,000 and over
Number of consumer units (in thousands)	7,282	4,069	2,011	680	197	324
Average number of persons per cu	1.5	1.3	1.8	2.0	2.1	2.2
Average number of earners per cu	0.2	0.1	0.2	0.4	0.4	0.7
AVERAGE TOTAL BEFORE-TAX INCOME	$13,308	$6,272	$13,763	$24,082	$34,142	$63,550
AVERAGE ANNUAL EXPENDITURES	100	64	117	152	195	283
FOOD	100	72	125	137	158	187
Food at home	100	80	120	131	131	143
Cereals and bakery products	100	82	117	129	159	135
Meat, poultry, fish, and eggs	100	77	127	122	121	155
Dairy products	100	85	117	121	115	127
Fruits and vegetables	100	80	118	140	129	140
Other foods at home	100	79	117	140	132	144
Food away from home	100	52	137	153	226	297
ALCOHOLIC BEVERAGES	100	33	128	211	191	495
HOUSING	100	77	113	130	160	210
Shelter	100	77	116	122	154	206
Owned dwellings	100	64	123	143	181	264
Mortgage interest	100	73	91	97	287	392
Property taxes	100	62	133	149	168	227
Maintenance, repairs, insurance, other expenses	100	65	121	148	170	270
Rented dwellings	100	103	102	87	106	79
Other lodging	100	29	144	170	230	491
Utilities, fuels, and public services	100	84	107	125	142	179
Household services	100	74	89	132	242	352
Personal services	100	118	53	59	67	255
Housekeeping supplies	100	63	143	150	198	134
Household furnishings and equipment	100	63	113	183	158	277
Household textiles	100	68	123	197	41	142
Furniture	100	69	93	159	259	301
Floor coverings	100	10	176	206	144	522
Major appliances	100	70	121	146	127	241
Small appliances, misc. housewares, equipment	100	59	103	215	190	329
APPAREL AND APPAREL SERVICES	100	52	129	146	455	245
Men and boys	100	41	135	250	193	242
Men, aged 16 or older	100	40	137	236	195	276
Boys, aged 2 to 15	100	52	119	346	185	0
Women and girls	100	53	126	105	664	249
Women, aged 16 or older	100	53	126	106	679	240
Girls, aged 2 to 15	100	49	140	100	213	475

(continued from previous page)

	all cu's	under $10,000	$10,000 to $19,999	$20,000 to $29,999	$30,000 to $39,999	$40,000 and over
Babies, under age 2	100	67	151	75	100	175
Footwear	100	64	148	93	300	201
Other apparel products and services	100	51	97	208	392	311
TRANSPORTATION	100	41	125	235	225	334
Vehicle purchases (net outlay)	100	19	126	323	263	388
Cars and trucks (new)	100	13	140	364	157	349
Cars and trucks (used)	100	30	98	239	479	466
Gasoline and motor oil	100	62	126	156	170	248
Other vehicle expenses	100	47	130	197	218	304
Public transportation	100	47	99	221	232	439
HEALTH CARE	100	69	127	156	148	169
ENTERTAINMENT	100	54	117	182	254	301
Fees and admissions	100	31	121	205	334	476
Television, radios, sound equipment	100	70	115	163	173	211
Pets, toys, and playground equipment	100	74	88	169	312	237
Other entertainment supplies, equipment, services	100	14	188	229	215	329
PERSONAL CARE PRODUCTS AND SERVICES	100	60	139	142	248	188
READING	100	66	113	170	219	223
EDUCATION	100	33	52	447	133	513
TOBACCO PRODUCTS AND SMOKING SUPPLIES	100	85	120	106	133	134
MISCELLANEOUS	100	81	84	140	179	295
CASH CONTRIBUTIONS	100	28	82	127	362	894
PERSONAL INSURANCE AND PENSIONS	100	31	101	176	145	783
GIFTS OF PRODUCTS AND SERVICES	100	55	104	314	99	187

Note: Expenditures for gifts of products and services are also included in the product or service category. Some items in "miscellaneous" are moved to the category "other financial products and services" in chapters 2 through 10. An index of 100 represents the average for all consumer units. An index of 132 means that the average for the subgroup is 32 percent above the average for all consumer units. An index of 68 indicates spending that is 32 percent below the overall average.

APPENDIX A
The Consumer Expenditure Survey

History

The Consumer Expenditure Survey (CEX) is an ongoing study of the day-to-day spending of American households. Expenditure data for products and services are collected as well as information concerning the amount and sources of household income, changes in savings and debts, and demographic and economic characteristics of household members. Data collection for the CEX is done by the Bureau of the Census, under contract with the Bureau of Labor Statistics (BLS). The BLS is responsible for analysis and publication of the Survey.

Expenditure surveys are not new; they have been conducted about every ten years by the BLS or its predecessor since the late 19th century. Although the results have been used for a variety of purposes, their primary application has been the tracking of consumer prices. Beginning in 1980, the CEX became a continuous survey with annual publication of the data (with a lag-time between data collection and data publication of about two years). The Survey is still used to update prices for the market basket of products and services used in calculating the Consumer Price Index. Recently, its users have expanded to include private research groups, academic researchers, data companies, and other businesses.

Description

The CEX is actually two surveys—an interview survey and a diary survey. Interviews are conducted for five consecutive quarters with respondents who are asked to report expenditures for each three-month period. These are generally big-ticket items such as houses, cars, and major appliances, or recurring expenses such as insurance premiums, utility payments, and rent. About 95 percent of all expenditures are covered by the interview component, which includes an estimate for food and trip expenses.

Expenditures on small, frequently purchased items are recorded during a two-week period for the diary survey. These detailed records include expenses for food and beverages, at home and in eating places, and other items such as tobacco, housekeeping supplies, nonprescription drugs, and personal care products and services. The diary survey is intended to capture expenditures that respondents are likely to forget or recall incorrectly over longer periods of time.

The tables in this book are based on integrated 1988 interview and diary survey data. Integrated data, a combination of the two surveys, provide a more complete accounting of consumer expenditures and income than either survey component is designed to do alone.

Data collection and processing

Two separate nationally representative samples are used for the interview and diary surveys. For the interview survey, some 5,000 consumer units are interviewed on a rotating panel basis each quarter for five consecutive quarters. Another 5,000 consumer units keep weekly diaries for two consecutive weeks. The 10,000 diaries accumulated in a survey year are the basis for the diary survey. Data collection is carried out in 101 areas of the country.

The data are reviewed, audited, and cleaned up by the BLS, and then weighted to reflect the number and characteristics of all U.S. consumer units. CEX data are available from the BLS in the form of news releases, bulletins, analytical papers, public-use tapes, and floppy disks. Technical supplements such as standard error tables are also available.

As with any sample survey, the CEX is subject to two major types of error. Non-sampling error occurs, for example, when respondents misinterpret questions or interviewers are inconsistent. Respondents may also forget items, recall expenses incorrectly, or deliberately give wrong answers. A respondent may remember what he or she spent on a big grocery shopping trip but forget the items picked up at the local convenience store. Most surveys that request information on alcohol consumption or expenditures for alcoholic beverages suffer from underreporting on this item. Non-sampling error can also be caused by mistakes during the various stages of data processing and refinement.

Sampling error is traceable to a sample that does not accurately represent the population it is supposed to represent. This kind of error is present in every sample-based survey and is minimized by using a proper sampling procedure. As previously mentioned, standard error tables that document the extent of sampling error in the CEX are available from the BLS.

Although the CEX is our best source of information about the spending behavior of American households, it should, because of the above factors, be treated as you would any other survey—with caution. Comparisons with consumption data from other sources show that CEX data tend to underestimate expenditures except those for rent, fuel, telephone service, furniture, transportation, and personal care services. So it is possible that the expenditure levels reported in the Survey are low and you will have to judge whether or not they give you a conservative estimate.

(Source for this section or for additional information: "The Consumer Expenditure Survey: Quality Control by Comparative Analysis," by Raymond Gieseman, *Monthly Labor Review*, March 1987.)

Sampling unit: the consumer unit

The CEX uses consumer units as its sampling unit instead of households. The term "household" is used here for convenience, although there may be more than one consumer unit in a household.

Consumer units are defined by the BLS as either: 1) members of a household who are related by blood, marriage, adoption, or other legal arrangements; a person living alone or sharing a household with others or living as a roomer in a private home or lodging house or in permanent living quarters in a hotel or motel, but who is financially independent; or 2) two persons or more living together who pool their income to make joint expenditure decisions. The BLS defines financial independence in terms of "the three major expenses categories—housing, food, and 'other' living expenses. To be considered financially independent, at least two of the three major expense categories have to be provided by the respondent."

The Census Bureau uses households as its sampling unit in the decennial census and annually conducted Current Population Surveys. The Census Bureau's household "consists of all persons who occupy a housing unit. A house, an apartment or other groups of rooms, or a single room is regarded as a housing unit when it is occupied or intended for occupancy as separate living quarters; that is, when the occupants do not live and eat with any other persons in the structure and there is direct access from the outside or through a common hall."

Comparison of CEX consumer units (CUs) and Census Bureau households (HHs), 1988.

(consumer units and households in thousands; consumer units for income section are complete income reporters only)

	SAMPLE ESTIMATES			PERCENT DISTRIBUTION		
	CEX CUs	Census Bureau HHs	difference	CEX CUs	Census Bureau HHs	difference
AGE OF HOUSEHOLDER/REFERENCE PERSON						
All ages	**94,862**	**91,066**	**3,796**	**100.0%**	**100.0%**	**0.0%**
under 25	7,216	5,228	1,988	7.6	5.7	1.9
25 to 34	21,985	20,583	1,402	23.2	22.6	0.6
35 to 44	19,911	19,323	588	21.0	21.2	-0.2
45 to 54	13,601	13,630	-29	14.3	15.0	-0.6
55 to 64	12,546	12,846	-300	13.2	14.1	-0.9
65 to 74	11,319	11,410	-91	11.9	12.5	-0.6
75 and older	8,284	8,045	239	8.7	8.8	-0.1
BEFORE-TAX HOUSEHOLD INCOME						
All cu's/households	**81,354**	**91,066**	**-9,712**	**100.0%**	**100.0%**	**0.0%**
under $10,000	18,809	15,444	3,365	23.1	17.0	6.2
$10,000 to $19,999	17,652	18,288	-636	21.7	20.1	1.6
$20,000 to $29,999	14,586	15,770	-1,184	17.9	17.3	0.6
$30,000 to $39,999	10,901	13,143	-2,242	13.4	14.4	-1.0
$40,000 to $49,999	7,198	9,458	-2,260	8.8	10.4	-1.5
$50,000 and over	12,209	18,965	-6,756	15.0	20.8	-5.8
TYPE OF CU/HOUSEHOLD						
All types cu's/households	**94,862**	**91,066**	**3,796**	**100.0%**	**100.0%**	**0.0%**
All married couples	**52,010**	**51,809**	**201**	**54.8**	**56.9**	**-2.1**
Married couple only	20,227	20,054	173	21.3	22.0	-0.7
Married couples with children	28,100	30,700	-2,600	29.6	33.7	-4.1
Oldest child under age 6	5,858	6,621	-763	6.2	7.3	-1.1
Oldest child aged 6 to 17	14,194	17,979	-3,785	15.0	19.7	-4.8
Oldest child aged 18 or older	8,047	6,100	1,947	8.5	6.7	1.8
Other married couples	3,684	1,055	2,629	3.9	1.2	2.7
One parent with 1 or more child	**5,716**	**7,320**	**-1,604**	**6.0**	**8.0**	**-2.0**
Single and other	**37,136**	**31,937**	**5,199**	**39.1**	**35.1**	**4.1**
Single	26,571	21,889	4,682	28.0	24.0	4.0

Source: Almanac of Consumer Markets and Bureau of the Census, Current Population Reports: Money Income of Households, Families, and Persons in the United States: 1988 *and* Household and Family Characteristics: *March 1988.*

The definition goes on to specify that "a household includes the related family members and all the unrelated persons, if any, such as lodgers, foster children, wards, or employees who share the housing unit. A person living alone in a housing unit or a group of unrelated persons sharing a housing unit as partners is also counted as a household. The count of household excludes group quarters."

Because you are probably used to using households instead of consumer units in your work, the above table compares the two sampling units. About 95 percent of consumer units correspond to Census Bureau households. Fifty-two percent of the remaining consumer units have a reference person under age 25. So a majority of consumer units not accounted for in the Census Bureau's household measure are financially independent young people. Because there are many more consumer units than households in the under-25 age group, their average expenditures will be diluted. Dilution of the average expenditure will occur with any age, income, or household-type segment for which the number of consumer units is higher than the number of households.

APPENDIX B
Reduction of mortgage principle

The Consumer Expenditure Survey does not include the dollar amount that households allocate to reduction of mortgage principle. Since the Survey treats mortgage equity as an asset, principle reduction is a contribution to an asset rather than an expenditure.

The following table gives average annual reduction of mortgage principle for the three major variables in *Consumer Power*—age of reference person, total before-tax income of the consumer unit, and type of consumer unit. Adding these amounts to the expenditures for owned dwellings will give a more complete picture of the dollar amounts allocated to these items.

Average annual reduction of mortgage principle in 1988, by age of reference person, total before-tax income of consumer unit, and type of consumer unit.

(mortgage obtained prior to interview quarter; consumer units for income section are complete income reporters only)

Age of reference person	all cu's	under 25	25 to 34	35 to 44	45 to 54	55 to 64	65 to 74	75+
Own home	$419.72	$49.09	$354.43	$674.88	$734.16	$438.68	$206.53	$48.91
Owned vacation home	23.32	0.00	3.70	62.91	35.23	24.59	8.04	0.00
Other properties	36.48	-	42.01	51.96	66.55	30.88	18.16	-

Total before-tax income of cu	all cu's	under $10,000	$10,000 to $19,999	$20,000 to $29,999	$30,000 to $39,999	$40,000 to $49,999	$50,000 and over
Own home	$406.26	$111.44	$168.03	$306.41	$446.47	$689.37	$1,121.37
Owned vacation home	24.82	3.35	30.49	16.15	20.02	12.23	71.76
Other properties	35.09	9.50	24.23	34.14	32.13	51.03	84.58

Type of consumer unit	all cu's	married couples	single parents	single persons and other cu's
Own home	$419.72	$603.94	$233.41	$190.39
Owned vacation home	23.32	29.51	100.62	2.77
Other properties	36.48	46.04	52.20	20.68

	all cu's	all married couples	married couple only	all married couples with children	AGE OF OLDEST CHILD under 6	AGE OF OLDEST CHILD 6 to 17	AGE OF OLDEST CHILD 18 or older	other married couples
Own home	$419.72	$603.94	$416.55	$725.64	$519.19	$832.91	$686.71	$704.54
Owned vacation home	23.32	29.51	24.26	33.92	5.92	42.11	39.87	24.66
Other properties	36.48	46.04	40.12	42.76	18.98	46.83	52.91	103.52

Note: Average annual reduction of mortgage principle is not given (-) when the amount is too small to be reliable.

APPENDIX C
Glossary

The following definitions are taken from the Consumer Expenditure Survey

age The age of the reference person, also called the householder or head of household.

alcoholic beverages Includes beer and ale, wine, whiskey, gin, vodka, rum, and other alcoholic beverages.

apparel and apparel services Includes the following:
—**men's and boys' apparel** Includes coats, jackets, sweaters, vests, sportcoats, tailored jackets, slacks, shorts and short sets, sportswear, shirts, underwear, nightwear, hosiery, uniforms, and other accessories.
—**women's and girls' apparel** Includes coats, jackets, furs, sportcoats, tailored jackets, sweaters, vests, blouses, shirts, dresses, dungarees, culottes, slacks, shorts, sportswear, underwear, nightwear, uniforms, hosiery, and other accessories.
—**apparel for children under 2** Includes coats, jackets, snowsuits, underwear, diapers, dresses, crawlers, sleeping garments, hosiery, footwear, and other accessories for children.
—**footwear** Includes articles such as shoes, slippers, boots, and other similar items. It excludes footwear for children under 2 and footwear used for sports such as bowling or golf shoes.
—**other apparel products and services** Includes material for making clothes, shoe repair, alterations and sewing patterns and notions, clothing rental, clothing storage, dry cleaning, sent-out laundry, watches, jewelry, and repairs to watches and jewelry.

appliances Includes the following:
—**major appliances** Includes refrigerators, freezers, dishwashers, stoves, ovens, garbage disposals, vacuum cleaners, microwaves, air-conditioners, sewing machines, washing machines and dryers, and floor cleaning equipment.
—**small appliances/miscellaneous housewares** Includes small electrical kitchen appliances, portable heating and cooling equipment, china and other dinnerware, flatware, glassware, silver and other serving pieces, nonelectric cookware, and plastic dinnerware. Excludes personal care appliances.

cash contributions Includes cash contributed to persons or organizations outside the consumer unit including alimony and child support payments, care of students away from home, and contributions to religious, educational, charitable, or political organizations.

consumer unit
—(1) All members of a household who are related by blood, marriage, adoption, or other legal arrangements.
—(2) A person living alone or sharing a household with others or living as a roomer in a private home or lodging house or in permanent living quarters in a hotel or motel, but who is financially independent.
— (3) Two persons or more living together who pool their income to make joint expenditure decisions. Financial independence is determined by the three major expense categories: housing, food, and other living expenses. To be considered financially independent, at least two of the three major expense categories have

to be provided by the respondent. Also, for convenience, called household.

E

earner A consumer unit member, aged 14 and older, who worked at least one week during the 12 months prior to the interview date.

education Includes tuition, fees, books, supplies, and equipment for public and private nursery schools, elementary and high schools, colleges and universities, and other schools.

entertainment Includes the following:
—fees and admissions; television, radio, and sound equipment (see individual definitions)
—**other entertainment equipment and services** Includes indoor exercise equipment, athletic shoes, bicycles, trailers, campers, camping equipment, rental of campers and trailers, hunting and fishing equipment, sports equipment, winter sports equipment, water sports equipment, boats, boat motors and boat trailers, rental of boat, landing and docking fees, rental and repair of sports equipment, photographic equipment, film and film processing, photographer fees, repair and rental of photo equipment, fireworks, pinball and electronic video fames, pet services, veterinary expenses, toys, games, hobbies, and playground equipment.

expenditure The transaction cost including excise and sales taxes of goods and services acquired during the survey period. The full cost of each purchase is recorded even though full payment may not have been made at the date of purchase. Expenditure estimates include gifts.

Excluded from expenditures are purchases or portions of purchases directly assignable to business purposes and periodic credit or installment payments on goods and services already acquired.

F

fees and admissions Includes fees for participant sports; admissions to sporting events, movies, concerts, plays; health, swimming, tennis and country club memberships, and other social recreational and fraternal organizations; recreational lessons or instructions; rental of movies, and recreational expenses on trips.

floor coverings Includes installation and replacement of wall-to-wall carpets, room-size rugs, and other soft floor coverings.

food Includes food at home and food away from home.
—**food at home** Refers to the total expenditures for food at grocery stores or other food stores during the interview period for consumption at home. It is calculated by multiplying the number of visits to a grocery or other food store by the average amount spent per visit. It excludes the purchase of nonfood items.
—**food away from home** Includes all meals (breakfast, lunch, brunch, and dinner) at restaurants, carryouts, and vending machines, including tips, plus meals as pay, special catered affairs such as weddings, bar mitzvahs, and confirmations, and meals away from home on trips.

furniture Includes living room, dining room, kitchen, bedroom, nursery, porch, lawn, and other outdoor furniture.

G

gasoline and motor oil Includes gasoline, diesel fuel, and motor oil.

H

health care Includes health insurance, medical services, and medical supplies

(see individual definitions).

health insurance Includes health maintenance plans (HMOs) Blue Cross/Blue Shield, commercial health insurance, Medicare, Medicare supplemental insurance, and other health insurance.

household furnishings and operations Includes the following:
—personal services, household textiles, furniture, floor coverings, appliances (see individual definitions).
—**other household services** Includes termite and pest control products, moving, storage, and freight expenses, repair of household appliances and other household equipment, reupholstering and furniture repair, rental and repair of lawn and gardening tools, and rental of other household equipment.
—**miscellaneous household equipment** Includes typewriters, luggage, lamps and other light fixtures, window coverings, clocks, lawn mowers and gardening equipment, other hand and power tools, telephone accessories, computers for home use, calculators, office equipment for home use, floral arrangements and house plants, rental of furniture, closet and storage items, household decorative items, infants' equipment, outdoor equipment, smoke alarms, other household appliances and small miscellaneous furnishing.

household textiles Includes bathroom, kitchen, dining room, and other linens, curtains and drapes, slipcovers and decorative pillows, and sewing materials.

housing Includes the following:
—owned dwellings; rented dwellings; utilities, fuels, and public services; household furnishings and operations (see individual definitions).
—**other lodging** Includes all expenses for vacation homes, school, college, hotels, motels, cottages, trailer camps, and other lodging while out of town.

I

income Includes the following:
—**complete income reporters** Respondents who provided values for major sources of income, such as wages and

salaries, self-employment income, and Social Security income. Even complete income reporters may not have given a full accounting of all income from all sources.
—**total income** The before-tax combined income of all consumer unit members aged 14 and older during the 12 months preceding the interview. Sources of income may include wages and salaries; self-employment income; Social Security, private, and government retirement benefits; interest, dividends, rental and other property income; unemployment, workers' compensation, and veterans' benefits; public assistance, supplemental security income, and food stamps; alimony, child support, and other regular contributions for support; and other income including such things as scholarships and payment for support of foster children.

insurance (life, endowment, annuities, other personal insurance) Includes premiums for whole life and term insurance; endowments; income and other life insurance; premiums for personal life liability, accident and disability, and other non-health insurance other than homes and vehicles.

M

maintenance and repairs Includes tires, batteries, tubes, lubrication, filters, coolant, additives, brake and transmission fluids, oil change, brake adjustment and repair, front-end alignment, wheel balancing, steering repair, shock absorber replacement, clutch and transmission repair, electrical system repair, repair to cooling system, drive train repair, drive shaft and rear-end repair, tire repair, other maintenance and services, and auto repair policies.

medical services Includes hospital room and services, physicians' services, service of a practitioner other than a physician, eye and dental care, lab tests, X-rays, nursing, therapy services, care in convalescent or nursing home, and other medical care.

medical supplies Includes prescription drugs, eyeglasses, rental and repair of medical equipment, medical equipment for general use such as syringes, ice bags, thermometers, vaporizers, heating pads, and supportive or convalescent medical equipment such as braces, canes, crutches, and walkers.

miscellaneous Includes safety deposit box rental, checking account fees and other bank services, legal fees, accounting fees, funerals, cemetery lots, union dues, occupational expenses, and finance charges other than mortgage and vehicles. Some miscellaneous items are moved to the category "Other financial products and services" in detailed tables.

owned dwellings Includes interest on mortgages, property taxes and insurance, refinancing and prepayment charges, ground rent, expenses for property management/security, homeowners' insurance, fire insurance and extended coverage, landscaping expenses for repairs and maintenance contracted out (including periodic maintenance and service contracts), and expenses of materials for owner-performed repairs and maintenance for dwellings used for maintained by the consumer unit, but not dwellings maintained for business or rent.

personal care Includes wigs and hairpieces; electric personal care appliances such as hair dryers, hair setters, shavers, toothbrushes, and other similar electric appliances; personal care services for males and females such as hair care services (haircuts, bleaching, tinting, coloring, conditioning treatments, permanents, press, and curls), styling and other services for wigs and hairpieces, body massages or slenderizing treatments, facials, manicures, pedicures, shaves, electrolysis, rent, and repair and maintenance of electric personal care appliances.

personal services Includes baby sitters, day care tuition, care of invalids, and domestic and other duties.

public transportation Includes fares for mass transit, buses, trains, airlines, taxis, private school buses, and fares paid on trips for trains, boats, taxis, buses, and trains.

reading Includes subscriptions for newspapers, magazines, and books through book clubs; purchase of single-copy newspapers and magazines, books, and encyclopedias and other reference books.

reference person The first member mentioned by the respondent when asked to "Start with the name of the person or one of the persons who owns or rents the home." It is with respect to this person that the relationship of other consumer unit members is determined. Also called the householder or head of household.

rented dwellings Includes rent paid for dwellings, rent received as pay, parking fees, maintenance, and other expenses.

retirement, pensions, and Social Security Includes all Social Security contributions paid by employees; employees' contributions to railroad retirement, government retirement and private pensions programs; retirement programs for self-employed.

television, radio, and sound equipment Includes television sets, video recorders, video cassettes, tapes, disks, disk players, video game hardware, video cartridges, cable TV, radios, phonographs, tape recorders and players, sound components, records and tapes, and records and tapes through record clubs, musical instruments, and rental and repair of TV and sound equipment.

tobacco and smoking supplies Includes cigarettes, cigars, pipe tobacco, chewing tobacco, and other smoking products and accessories.

transportation Includes the following:
—vehicle purchases (net outlay), gasoline and motor oil (see individual definitions).
—**transportation, other** Includes vehicle finance charges; vehicle insurance; vehicle rent, licenses, and other charges; maintenance and repairs; public transportation (see individual definitions).

U

utilities, fuels, and public services Includes natural gas, water, garbage and trash collection, sewerage maintenance, septic tank cleaning, telephone charges, and other public services.

V

vehicle
—**vehicle finance charge** Includes the dollar amount of interest paid for a loan contracted for the purchase of vehicles described below.
—**vehicle insurance** Includes the premium paid for insuring cars, trucks, and other vehicles.
—**vehicle purchases (net outlay)** The net outlay (purchase price minus trade-in value) on new and used domestic and imported cars and trucks and other vehicles, including motorcycles and private planes.
—**vehicle rent, licenses, and other charges** Includes leased and rented cars, trucks, motorcycles, and aircraft, inspection fees, state and local registration, drivers' license fees, parking fees, towing charges, and tolls on trips.

Index

WHAT OTHERS SAY ABOUT
CONSUMER POWER: HOW AMERICANS SPEND THEIR MONEY

"CONSUMER POWER takes you inside the pocketbooks of Americans. It is full of our best kept secrets—the surprising ways we spend our money. If you need to know what people do with their dollars, then this is your Bible."

—*Cheryl Russell, author,* 100 Predictions for the Baby Boom

"CONSUMER POWER breathes life into your sales figures. It turns plain numbers into customers with age, income, and other useful identities. You don't know what your salesforce is missing until you add in the customer."

—*James Crabb, National Sales Manager, S. Martinelli & Company*

Mail to NEW STRATEGIST, P.O. Box 242, Ithaca, NY 14851; **call** (607) 273-0913; **fax** to (607) 277-5009.

☐ Please send me ____ copy(ies) of *Consumer Power: How Americans Spend Their Money*, at $69.95 each, plus $3 per book for shipping and insurance (New York State deliveries please add sales tax).

☐ Send me details about how I can save on the update of *Consumer Power* and other books about Americans' spending habits and demographics.

☐ Send me information about *Market Power Reports*, New Strategist's customized analyses of the consumer trends that drive demand for products and services.

Name _____

Company _____

Street Address _____

City / State / Zip _____

Phone no. (in case we have a question about your order) _____

☐ Check enclosed made payable to New Strategist.

☐ Bill to my ☐ MasterCard ☐ Visa

Acct. no. _____ Expiration _____

Signature _____

Bill me: corporate purchase order attached, no. _____
(Tax-exempt organizations please enclose a copy of your tax-exempt certificate.)

*The more you need to stretch your research budget,
the more you need New Strategist Publishing & Consulting*

New Strategist

P.O. Box 242, Ithaca, New York 14851 • 607 / 273-0913

WHAT OTHERS SAY ABOUT
CONSUMER POWER: HOW AMERICANS SPEND THEIR MONEY

"CONSUMER POWER takes you inside the pocketbooks of Americans. It is full of our best kept secrets—the surprising ways we spend our money. If you need to know what people do with their dollars, then this is your Bible."

—*Cheryl Russell, author,* 100 Predictions for the Baby Boom

"CONSUMER POWER breathes life into your sales figures. It turns plain numbers into customers with age, income, and other useful identities. You don't know what your salesforce is missing until you add in the customer."

—*James Crabb, National Sales Manager, S. Martinelli & Company*

Mail to NEW STRATEGIST, P.O. Box 242, Ithaca, NY 14851; **call** (607) 273-0913; **fax** to (607) 277-5009.

☐ Please send me _____ copy(ies) of *Consumer Power: How Americans Spend Their Money,* at $69.95 each, plus $3 per book for shipping and insurance (New York State deliveries please add sales tax).

☐ Send me details about how I can save on the update of *Consumer Power* and other books about Americans' spending habits and demographics.

☐ Send me information about *Market Power Reports,* New Strategist's customized analyses of the consumer trends that drive demand for products and services.

Name —————————————————————————————

Company ————————————————————————————

Street Address ———————————————————————————

City / State / Zip ———————————————————————————

Phone no. (in case we have a question about your order) ——————————

☐ Check enclosed made payable to New Strategist.

☐ Bill to my   ☐ MasterCard   ☐ Visa

Acct. no.——————————————— Expiration ——————

Signature ————————————————————————————

Bill me: corporate purchase order attached, no. ————————————
(Tax-exempt organizations please enclose a copy of your tax-exempt certificate.)

The more you need to stretch your research budget,
the more you need New Strategist Publishing & Consulting

New Strategist

P.O. Box 242, Ithaca, New York 14851 • 607 / 273-0913